Emilia-Romagna
Pages 258–273

Trentino-Alto
Adige
Pages 170–179

The Veneto and
Friuli
Pages 142–169

Venice
Pages 88–141

Umbria
Pages 352-367

Le Marche
Pages 368–377

Abruzzo, Molise
and Puglia
Pages 504–517

Basilicata and
Calabria
Pages 518–525

Sicily
Pages 526–547.

Trieste

nice

Ancona

Pescara

L'Aquila

ME
LAZIO

Foggia

Bari

SOUTHERN ITALY

Napoli

Salerno   Potenza

Taranto

Catanzaro

Palermo

Messina

SICILY   Catania

Agrigento

EYEWITNESS TRAVEL

ITALY

EYEWITNESS TRAVEL

ITALY

DK

LONDON, NEW YORK,
MELBOURNE, MUNICH AND DELHI
www.dk.com

Project Editor Fiona Wild

Art Editors Vanessa Courtier, Annette Jacobs

Editors Francesca Machiavelli, Sophie Martin, Helen Townsend, Nicky Tyrrell

Designers Jo Doran, Anthea Forlee, Paul Jackson, Marisa Renzullo

Main Contributors

Ros Belford, Susie Boulton, Christopher Catling, Sam Cole, Paul Duncan,
Olivia Ercoli, Andrew Gumbel, Tim Jepson, Ferdie McDonald, Jane Shaw

Maps

Lovell Johns Ltd, Dorling Kindersley Cartography

Photographer

John Heseltine

Illustrators

Stephen Conlin, Donati Giudici Associati srl, Stephen Gyapay, Roger Hutchins,
Maltings Partnership, Simon Roulstone, Paul Weston, John Woodcock

Printed and bound by South China Printing Co. Ltd., China

First published in the UK in 1996 by Dorling Kindersley Limited
80 Strand, London WC2R 0RL

14 15 16 17 10 9 8 7 6 5 4 3 2 1

Reprinted with revisions 1997, 1999, 2000, 2001, 2002, 2003, 2004, 2005,
2006, 2007, 2008, 2009, 2010, 2011, 2012, 2013, 2014

Copyright 1996, 2014 © Dorling Kindersley Limited, London

A Penguin Random House Company

A CIP catalogue record is available from the British Library.

ISBN 978-1-40932-694-6

Floors are referred to throughout in accordance with European usage;
ie the "first floor" is the floor above ground level.

MIX
Paper from
responsible sources
FSC™ C018179
www.fsc.org

Front cover main image: Farmhouse and Cypress Trees, Pienza, Tuscany

◄ Rolling landscape of poppies and cypresses in San Quirico d'Orcia, Tuscany

Contents

David by Bernini, Rome

Introducing Italy

Northeast Italy

Northwest Italy

Gondolas weaving through the maze of canals in Venice

A traditional shop in
Volterra, Tuscany

Basilica of San Francesco in Assisi, started in 1228

HOW TO USE THIS GUIDE

This guide helps you get the most from your visit to Italy, providing expert recommendations as well as detailed practical information. *Introducing Italy* maps the whole country and sets it in its historical and cultural context. The 15 regional chapters, plus *Rome, Florence* and *Venice*, describe important sights with the help of maps and images. Each section is introduced with features on regional architecture and food specialities. *Travellers' Needs* gives details of hotels and restaurants and the *Survival Guide* contains practical information on everything from transport to personal safety.

Rome

The centre of Rome has been divided into five sightseeing areas. Each area has its own chapter, which opens with a list of the sights described. All the sights are numbered and plotted on an *Area Map*. Each sight is presented in numerical order within the chapter making it easy to locate.

Sights at a Glance lists the chapter's sights by category: Churches, Museums and Galleries, Historic Buildings, Streets and Piazzas.

All pages relating to Rome have orange thumb tabs.

1 Area Map For easy reference, the sights are numbered and located on a map. The sights are also shown on the *Street Finder* on pages 451–61.

A locator map shows where you are in relation to other areas of the city centre.

2 Street-by-Street Map This gives a bird's-eye view of the heart of each sightseeing area.

Stars indicate the sights that no visitor should miss.

A suggested route for a walk is shown in red.

3 Detailed information All the sights in Rome are described individually. Addresses and practical information are provided. The key to the symbols used in the information block is shown on the back flap.

Italy Area by Area

Apart from Rome, Florence and Venice, Italy has been divided into 15 areas, each of which has a separate chapter. The most interesting towns and places to visit have been numbered on the section's *Regional Map*.

1 Introduction
The landscape, history and character of each region is described here, showing how the area has developed over the centuries and what it offers to the visitor today.

Each area of Italy can be identified quickly by its colour coding, shown on the inside front cover.

2 Regional Map This shows the main road network and gives an overview of the whole region. All entries are numbered and there are also useful tips on getting around the region by car and train.

3 Detailed information
All the important towns and other places to visit are described individually. They are listed in order, following the numbering given on the *Regional Map*. Within each entry, information is given on the most important sights. The name of the provincial capital is given for smaller towns at the top of each entry.

Story boxes explore specific subjects further.

For all the top sights, a Visitors' Checklist provides the practical information you need to plan your visit.

4 Italy's top sights
These are given two or more full pages. Historic buildings are dissected to reveal their interiors; museums and galleries have colour-coded floorplans to help you locate the most interesting exhibits.

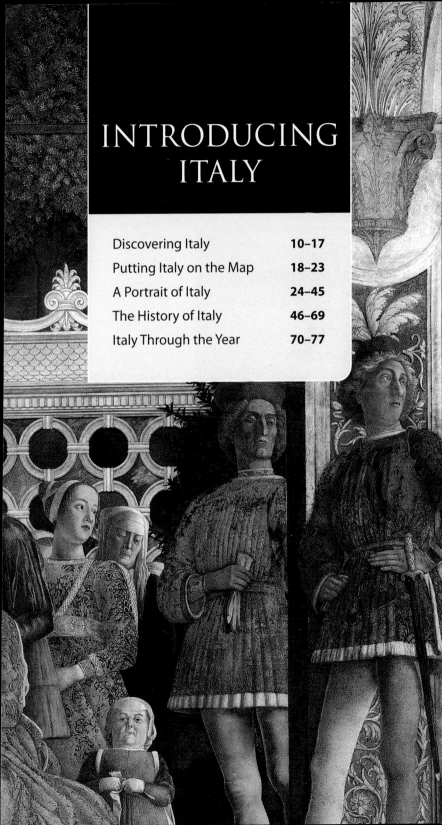

INTRODUCING ITALY

DISCOVERING ITALY

The following tours have been designed to take in as many of the country's highlights as possible, while keeping long-distance travel to a minimum. First come three 2-day tours of Italy's most glamorous cities: Rome, Florence and Venice. These itineraries can be followed individually or combined to form a week-long tour. Extra suggestions are provided for those who want to extend their stay to 10 days.

Next come two seven-day tours, covering the north and the south of Italy. These can be combined to make a superb 2-week tour of the whole country. Finally, two themed itineraries have been designed for anyone looking to tailor their trip according to a specific interest. Pick, combine and follow your favourite tours, or simply dip in and out and be inspired.

Golden fields of Tuscany
The Tuscan countryside, with its rolling hills and pencil-thin cypress trees, is a dream for artists and visitors alike.

A Week in Northern Italy

- See the artworks of the Pinoteca di Brera and shop in fashionable **Milan**.
- Take a relaxing cruise on **Lake Como** and walk in the surrounding countryside.
- Look up at Juliet's balcony in **Verona**; marvel at the architecture of **Vicenza**; admire frescoes in **Padua**.
- Enjoy a *vaporetto* ride along **Venice's** magnificent waterway, the Grand Canal.
- Take in the views of **Florence** from the Duomo and visit the city's world-famous galleries.
- Walk the dizzying pathways and hillsides of the **Cinque Terre** coastline.
- Explore the three enchanting Tuscan towns of **Lucca**, **Pisa** and **Siena**.

A Week in Southern Italy

- See treasures of the Classical World in **Rome's** museums and people-watch from the Spanish Steps.
- Marvel at sculptures and mosaics in Museo Archeologico in **Naples**; sample fantastic pizza in the city of its origin.
- Visit the evocative ruins of **Pompeii**; take a ferry to the island of **Capri**.
- Marvel at the beautiful views from the towns along the **Amalfi Coast**; enjoy the sea air at **Ravello**.
- Take a night ferry to Palermo in **Sicily** and visit the glittering Palazzo dei Normanni.
- Discover the Valley of the Temples near **Agrigento**; explore the magnificent Baroque town of **Noto**.

Key
— Northern Italy tour
— Southern Italy tour

◀ The 15th-century fresco, by Mantegna, from the Camera degli Sposi in the Palazzo Ducale

A Gourmet Tour of Central Italy

- Try fine cheeses and ham in the delightful town of **Parma**; sample vintage balsamic vinegar in **Moderna**.
- Dine in style in **Bologna** and soak up the atmosphere in the city's *entoce* (wine bars).
- Try the Tuscan speciality *Bistecca Fiorentina* in **Pisa**; enjoy *panforte* in **Siena**.
- Visit **Perugia** and stock up on the town's famous Baci chocolates; travel to **Norcia** to enjoy truffles, and pork from the region's black pigs.
- Spend a day in **Orvieto**, seeking out pecorino cheese, delicious salami and Orvieto Classico wine.

A Tour of Etruscan Italy

- Explore fabulous museums dedicated to the Etruscan civilization in **Rome**.
- Visit the vast "city of the dead" at **Cerveteri**; marvel at the frescoed tombs in **Tarquinia**.
- See remnants of Etruscan life at the Necropoli Etrusca in **Orvieto**; spend an afternoon in the hilltop town of **Todi**.
- Travel to **Chiusi** for the fine Museo Nazionale Etrusco; visit medieval **Gubbio** to see the Eugubine Tablets.
- Spend a day in **Volterra** and see Etruscan funerary urns at the Museo Guarnacci; travel to **Florence** for the fabulous Medici Etruscan collection.

Key
— Gourmet Italy tour
--- Etruscan Italy tour

Colosseum, Rome
Once the site of deadly gladiatorial combat, the Colosseum is the highlight of a trip to Rome. Tickets include access to the Forum and Palatine Museum.

Beautiful spiral staircase leading down from the Vatican Museums, Rome

2 days in Rome

The nation's capital has an overwhelming array of memorable sights, including the wonderful Vatican Museums and the Colosseum.

- **Arriving** Fiumicino (Leonardo da Vinci) is Rome's main airport, located about 30 km (18 miles) southwest of the city. The "Leonardo Express" train runs nonstop to Termini station, the city's main railway station.

- **Moving on** The journey from Rome to Florence takes 1 hour 37 minutes by Eurostar.

Day 1
Morning A couple of days in **Rome** (pp387–463) will only scrape its surface, but do devote one day to the Vatican and St Peter's. The fast route through the **Vatican Museums** (pp424–31) takes in the **Sistine Chapel** (pp428–30). Don't miss Michelangelo's *Creation of Adam* on the ceiling and his dynamic altarpiece, *The Last Judgment*. The four **Raphael Rooms** (p431) show another Renaissance master, Raphael, at the peak of his artistic powers.
Afternoon Inside the awe-inspiring **St Peter's** (pp422–25), be sure to see Michelangelo's moving *Pietà*. Climb the dome for views, then descend to the grottoes for the papal tombs. Afterwards, cross the Tiber to the *centro storico*. Look in at the **Pantheon** (p408), the only ancient Roman temple to survive intact, then spend the

evening among the exuberant Baroque fountains and cafés of **Piazza Navona** (pp402–3).

Day 2
Morning Wander through the evocative ruins of the **Roman Forum** (pp394–6), and on to the monumental **Colosseum** (p397). Nearby, the church of **San Clemente** (p439) reveals its layers of history from pagan temple to 15th-century church.
Afternoon For great city views, head up to the **Capitoline Museums** (pp390–91). The Palazzo Nuovo has a fine selection of Greek and Roman statues. For some respite, visit the pretty 17th-century pleasure gardens of **Villa Borghese** (pp442–3). Visit **Piazza di Spagna** and the **Spanish Steps** (p413) and cast a coin in the Baroque **Trevi Fountain** (pp414–5).

> **To extend your trip…**
> Take a day trip to the lovely hill-town of **Tivoli** and **Hadrian's Villa** (p472), about 5 km (3 miles) west of Tivoli.

2 days in Florence

Florence is the city for art lovers, with a wealth of breathtaking museums and galleries.

- **Arriving** Florence is served by two airports – Amerigo Vespucci airport, 4 km (2 miles) from the centre, and Pisa airport. From Amerigo Vespucci, buses run to Florence's Santa Maria Novella train station; from Pisa, catch a direct train to Santa Maria Novella.

- **Moving on** The journey from Florence to Venice is just 2 hours by train.

The dome of Florence's Duomo designed by Brunelleschi and completed in 1436,

Day 1
Morning Florence (pp274–317), the embodiment of the Renaissance, is much more compact than Rome. Feel the pull of Brunelleschi´s immense orange-tiled dome, which crowns the **Duomo** (pp284–6). Climb the dome for stunning views, then admire Ghiberti's

View of the Vatican, with St Peter's Basilica and Sant'Angelo bridge, Rome

Looking south from the upper terrace of the Boboli Gardens, Florence

famous bronze doors on the **Baptistry** (pp284–6). A few streets away, the **Bargello** (p287) holds a fantastic collection of Renaissance sculpture.
Afternoon Take a stroll around **Piazza della Signoria** (pp294–5), dominated by its towering city hall, the Palazzo Vecchio, and a copy of Michelangelo's David. Stop off at the famous Bar Vivoli Gelateria for an ice cream before tackling the **Uffizi** (pp290–93). Caravaggio, Titian, Raphael – works by all the major artists of the Renaissance and beyond are on display here.

Day 2
Morning See the real statue of David by Michelangelo in the **Galleria dell' Accademia** (p279), then visit the church of **Santa Maria Novella** (pp300–301) for Masaccio's Trinity, with its novel use of perspective.
Afternoon Visit the Gothic church of **Santa Croce** (pp288–9), the final resting place of Michelangelo, Galileo and Machiavelli. Next, cross **Ponte Vecchio** (p289) for the **Cappella Brancacci** (pp302–3) to see more frescoes by Masaccio. The fountains, grottoes and woods of the **Boboli Gardens** (p307) are perfect for a picnic, and there is plenty more art in the **Palazzo Pitti** (pp306–7).

> **To extend your trip…**
> Spend a day in the **Cinque Terre** (p245) and another exploring **Pisa** (pp328–30) and **Lucca** (pp324–7).

2 days in Venice

This unique city on the water has romantic gondolas, magnificent churches and wonderful art.

- **Arriving** Marco Polo airport is located at Tessera, 8 km (5 miles) north of the city. Alilaguna ferries, which stop at various points in the city, can be picked up a short walk from the airport. The journey time is around an hour. Water taxis are also available, but are expensive. Venice's main train station is Venezia Santa Lucia station.

Day 1
Morning Simply getting lost in Venice (pp88–141) will exceed expectations, as will the reality of the familiar sights. To make the most of a visit to this watery city, travel by vaporetto or gondola along the **Grand Canal** (pp92–5) to **Piazza San Marco** (pp112–13) and the **Basilica di San Marco** (pp114–17). The mosaics inside and out are ravishing, but so too are the Pala d'Oro (golden altarpiece), the jewels of the Treasury and the four Horses of St Mark on the balcony. Take the lift to the top of the adjacent Campanile to be rewarded with a view stretching all the way to the Alps.

Afternoon Join a pre-booked Secret Itineraries tour to get the most out of the **Palazzo Ducale** (pp118–20), where the vast Sala del Maggior Consiglio, with its magnificent Tintoretto, is the highlight. Have coffee at Caffè Florian or Grancaffè Quadri on **Piazza San Marco** (pp112–13), then cross the Grand Canal to the **Accademia** (pp110–11) for the best of the Venetian painters. If you prefer modern art, visit the **Peggy Guggenheim Collection** (pp108–9), housed in the 18th-century Palazzo Venier dei Leoni.

Day 2
Morning Make for the **Rialto** (p101) to watch boats go by from the bridge, and stock up at the city's busiest market. Nearby is the church of **Santa Maria Gloriosa dei Frari** (pp102–3) with its exquisite altarpiece, a Madonna and Child by Bellini.
Afternoon Tour the islands of **Torcello** (pp126–7) for 12th- and 13th-century mosaics, **Murano** (p125) for the glass museum and colourful **Burano** (p125) for lace. Be sure to sample some local snacks and drink an aperitivo in one of the many enticing bars back in Venice.

> **To extend your trip…**
> Take a day-trip to **Verona** (pp146–51), which has a fine Roman arena.

Smart waiters serving drinks in refined Caffè Florian, Piazza San Marco, Venice

A Week in Northern Italy

- **Airports** Arrive at Milano Malpensa airport and depart from Pisa Galileo Galilei.

- **Transport** Trains connect the cities in 2 hours or less. Use the bus to reach Siena from Florence, and hire a car for the Cinque Terre, leaving it at La Spezia for the local train. It is easy to make day trips to Lake Como from Milan, the Veneto from Venice and the Cinque Terre from Florence.

- **Booking ahead** Milan: Viewing of *Last Supper*; Venice: Basilica di San Marco; Florence: Accademia, Uffizi; Pisa: ascent of the Leaning Tower.

Day 1: Milan

If you're looking for Italian style, high fashion, art and architecture, **Milan** *(pp196–205)*, the largest city of the north, has it all. Heading up the list of sights is Leonardo da Vinci's world-famous *Last Supper (p204)*. Visit the enormous Gothic Duomo *(p197)*, which invites a climb to its roof for the best city view. For glorious paintings from the Renaissance to the present day, don't miss the Pinacoteca di Brera *(pp202– 203)*, and for those who enjoy shopping, Galleria Vittorio Emanuele II *(p198)*, with its magnificent glass dome and floor mosaics, is a must.

Day 2: Lake Como

Lake Como *(pp194–5)*, its long arms nestling between steep hillsides, is a prime example of Italy's exquisite landscapes. Cruise the lake or take short ferry hops across the water, admiring the resplendent villas along the way. Explore Bellagio, or take a funicular up into the hills.

Day 3: Venice

Pick a day from the city itinerary on p13.

Day 4: The Veneto – Verona, Vicenza and Padua

Pick from a trio of towns, all within striking distance of Venice. Lively **Verona** *(pp146– 151)* conjures up Shakespeare's *Romeo and Juliet*, and crowds still flock to see Juliet's balcony. Famous for concerts is the well-preserved Roman Arena *(p147)*, while the Romanesque church of San Zeno Maggiore *(pp150– 51)* has a lovely cloister. Admirers of Palladio will appreciate **Vicenza** *(pp154–7)*, where his elegant Classical buildings surround the Piazza dei Signori. **Padua** *(pp158–63)* is known for its Cappella dei Scrovegni *(pp160–61)*, containing some wonderful frescoes by Giotto.

Day 5: Florence

Pick a day from the city itinerary on p12.

Day 6 : Cinque Terre

The five tiny villages of the **Cinque Terre** *(p245)* – Monterosso, Vernazza, Corniglia,

Rolling fields in Tuscany

Manarola and Riomaggiore – are the jewels of Italy's northwest coast. Colourful houses cling to the rocky cliffs, making a hike along the connecting path a delight to the eye. You can do the whole trail (north to south is less steep) in five or six hours.

Day 7: Tuscany – Lucca, Pisa, Siena

These three Tuscan towns are less busy than Florence, yet they offer a cultural feast with the bonus of an enchanting landscape. If time is tight, visit two. In **Lucca** *(pp324–7)*, promenade the encircling 17th-century grassy ramparts and visit the church of San Michele in Foro, its exquisite Pisan-Romanesque façade bursting with decoration. **Pisa** *(pp328–30)* is the home of the iconic 13th-century Leaning Tower, which, together with the Duomo and Baptistry, forms the Campo dei Miracoli. **Siena** *(pp342–7)* is one of Italy's most appealing medieval towns and home to the twice-yearly Palio *(p345)*, when Piazza del Campo comes alive with spirited bareback horse racing. Within striking distance of the piazza are the Gothic Palazzo Pubblico, which contains a treasure trove of frescoes from the Middle Ages, and the magnificent Duomo *(pp346–7)*. En route from Pisa to Siena, try to catch a glimpse of the 13 medieval towers that pierce the skyline in **San Gimignano** *(pp348–9)*. The view is magical in the evening.

Pretty Bellagio, which sits on a peninsula at the top of Lake Como's two "arms"

A Week in Southern Italy

- **Airports** Arrive at Rome Fiumicino and depart from Catania airport, Sicily.

- **Transport** Train travel from Rome to Naples is fast and easy (1 hour 10 minutes is the fastest). Take the ferry for Capri and Sicily, the bus for the coastal towns of Sorrento, Positano, Amalfi and Ravenna, and for Agrigento from Palermo (2 hours). You will need a car to see inland Sicily: Piazza Armerina and Noto. Pompeii and Capri are easy to visit as day trips from Naples.

- **Booking ahead** Rome: Vatican Museums, Colosseum, Forum and Palatine; *Naples*: Museo Archeologico Nazionale, Secret Cabinet Tour.

Days 1 and 2: Rome
See the city itinerary on p12.

Day 3: Naples
Naples *(pp490–97)* is chaotic, but the rewards of visiting are manifold. The main attraction is the world-renowned Museo Archeologico Nazionale *(pp494–5)* and its vast collection of Roman and Pompeiian treasures; allow at least half a day here. Book ahead for the Secret Cabinet tour to view the erotic works from Pompeii. Tiny Cappella Sansevero *(p491)* holds intriguing works from the 18th century, notably the virtuoso alabaster and marble *Veiled Christ* by Sammartino. Santa Chiara *(p493)* is worth seeing for its charming majolica-tiled cloisters. Don't leave without eating pizza in the city of its invention.

Day 4: Pompeii and Capri
The Circumvesuviana train skirts the base of Vesuvius from Naples to Pompeii and on to Sorrento. **Pompeii** *(pp498–9)* gives you an insight into a Roman town as it was in AD 79 before it was destroyed,

The evocative ancient temple ruins at Selinunte, Sicily

most poignantly through the body casts of the people who perished here. Arrange a trip up the infamous volcano, or take a ferry from Naples or Sorrento to the idyllic island of **Capri** *(pp502–503)*, best enjoyed in the quiet of evening. Blue Grotto sea cave and Villa Jovis of Emperor Tiberius are secondary attractions to the captivating vistas you will find here.

Marina Grande on the pretty island of Capri

Day 5: Amalfi Coast
Take the hair-raising bus ride along the coast for views of a lifetime and stop off at your leisure at some of Italy's most beautiful towns. **Sorrento** *(p501)* is the most prosaic and popular, while chic **Positano** *(p501)* favours the jet set and comes with a good beach. **Amalfi** *(p501)* has a stunning 9th-century cathedral, while **Ravello** *(p501)*, set high above terraces of lemon groves, has the best of the views. Lose yourself among the bougainvillea in the lush gardens of the Villa Cimbrone or Villa Rufolo.

Days 6 and 7: Sicily
Sicily is a melting pot of Norman, Byzantine, Greek and Arab influences and deserves at least two days' exploration. Taking the night ferry from Naples to Palermo, the island's largest town, will save you time. **Palermo** *(pp530–33)* exemplifies all these influences, notably in the Palazzo dei Normanni, whose Cappella Palatina is a glittering mix of mosaics, marble and gold. The most famous Norman mosaics, however, are outside Palermo, at the highly ornamented Duomo of Monreale *(pp534–5)*. Seek out the intricate Norman cloisters here. To the south you can discover the ancient Greek legacy in the Valley of the Temples *(p540)*, near Agrigento, or at Selinunte *(p538)*, which has the benefit of a long and sandy beach. In the interior, the Villa Romana del Casale at **Piazza Armerina** *(p541)* sports some of Italy's liveliest mosaics, and beautiful **Noto** *(p547)*, aglow with golden stone, is a unique Baroque town rebuilt after the earthquake of I693.

A Gourmet Tour of Central Italy

- **Duration** 7 days – but extends to a 10-day tour with the extra suggestions.

- **Airports** Arrive at Milan Linate airport and depart from Rome Fiumicino airport. From Milan, travel by train or car to Parma for the first stop on the tour.

- **Transport** This tour can be made using Italy's rail network, but hiring a car would allow more flexibility.

This itinerary takes you to Italy's central regions – Emilia-Romagna, Tuscany and Umbria – focusing on the regional food specialities along the way. If you are travelling in summer or autumn, look out for the copious food festivals held across the region.

Day 1: Parma
Affluent **Parma** *(p263)* is synonymous with cheese and ham – *Parmigiano Reggiano* (parmesan) and *prosciutto crudo* (Parma ham). The delicatessens here are a feast for the eyes, as are the city's main sights, which include an exquisite 12th-century Baptistry and paintings by Correggio in the lovely Duomo.

Day 2: Modena
The handsome city of **Modena** *(p264)* has two main claims to fame: it is the producer of fast cars (Ferrari and Maserati) and balsamic vinegar – try the city's market for the best vintage variety. In between sampling some of the region's other specialities, such as mortadella, spicy sausage and pig's feet, be sure to visit the very fine Romanesque Duomo and the Este collection of paintings in the Palazzo dei Musei.

Day: 3 Bologna
Dress up for dinner here – **Bologna** *(pp266–9)* has some of the country's finest restaurants and atmospheric *enoteche* (wine bars). Home-made pasta comes with the famous Bolognese *(ragù)* or cream sauce, or stuffed with ricotta, pork or pumpkin. During the day, check out the medieval skyscrapers of the Due Torri and the Gothic church of San Petronio.

> **To extend your trip…**
> Cycle around the lagoons of the **Po Delta** *(p270-71)*, 97 km (60 miles) from Bologna.

Day 4: Pisa
Spend a day in **Pisa** *(pp328–30)*. The city's main draw is the Campo dei Miracoli, which contains the Duomo, Baptistry and the Leaning Tower. Pisa's culinary attractions include fish dishes, such as *cacciucco*, a hearty fish soup, and *baccalá alla Pisana*, salt cod with tomato sauce. Meat-eaters will love *Bistecca Fiorentina* (thick charcoal-grilled steak).

The iconic Leaning Tower of Pisa

Day 5: Siena
Life in **Siena** *(pp342–7)* centres on the beautiful fan-shaped piazza of Il Campo, around which *pasticcerie* sell the city's famous *panforte* cake and *ricciarelli* (almond biscuits). Admire the frescoes in the medieval Palazzo Pubblico and the treasures of the spectacular Duomo and its Museo.

> **To extend your trip…**
> Head for the coast at **Maremma Park** *(pp350–51)*, 81 km (50 miles) from Siena.

Day 6: Perugia and Norcia
Stop at **Perugia** *(pp356–7)* to stock up on Baci chocolate and see the frescoes in the Palazzo dei Priori, before travelling to the gastromic hotspot of **Norcia** *(pp366–7)*, where black truffles and salami and pork from the local black pigs are the must-try specialities.

> **To extend your trip…**
> Explore the mountains of the **Valnerina** *(p367)*, 48 km (30 miles) from Norcia.

Day 7: Orvieto
You can be assured of good-quality food here as **Orvieto** *(pp362–3)* is headquarters of the Città Slow movement and an advocate of slow food. Look out for pecorino cheese and salami, and of course, Orvieto Classico wine. Take time to visit the Romanesque-Gothic Duomo and the 16th-century Pozzo di San Patrizio.

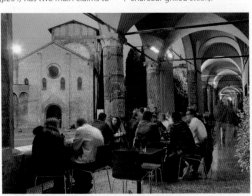
Atmospheric outdoor dining in Piazza della Mercanzia, Bologna

A Tour of Etruscan Italy

- **Duration** 7 days – but extends to a 10-day tour with the extra suggestions.
- **Airports** Arrive at Rome Fiumicino airport and depart from Pisa Galileo Galilei (trains from Florence to Pisa take 1 hour).
- **Transport** This tour is most easily done by car, though Cerveteri is accessible by bus from Rome and Tarquinia and Orvieto by train.

This tour focuses on the ancient Etruscan sights and museums of Lazio, Umbria and Tuscany, as well as other interesting sights along the way. For more on Italy's first major civilization, see pp48–9.

Day 1: Rome
Be inspired by the world's best collections of Etruscan treasures in the **Etruscan Museum of the Vatican** *(p424)* and the **Museo Nazionale Etrusco** in the **Villa Giulia** *(p444)*. The tender portrayals of people on the sarcophagi, the delicate and intricate gold jewellery and lifelike bronze sculptures display amazing craftsmanship. Leave time for the lovely gardens of the **Villa Borghese** *(pp442–3)*.

Day 2: Cerveteri
Feel the mystery of the vast necropolis at **Cerveteri** *(p470)* as you stroll its silent streets. Here, see the tombs that were built as replicas of homes, decorated with frescoes and filled with domestic furnishings. Fifty thousand Etruscans were entombed here from the 7th to the 1st century BC in what was one of the most powerful of the 12 Etruscan cities. Visit the Museo Nazionale Cerite to see displays of objects that were buried with the bodies.

> **To extend your trip…**
> Head 64 km (40 miles) from Rome to the Etruscan amphitheatre at **Sutri** *(p470)*.

Well-preserved "Street" of Etruscan tombs, Cerveteri

Day 3: Tarquinia
Spend some time in **Tarquinia** *(p470)*, the medieval centre of which was the capital of Etruria 2,500 years ago. Head uphill to the necropolis, a warren of tombs that hold lively and colourful frescoes depicting the lives of their inhabitants. For more revelations of everyday life and artistry, head for the Museo Archeologico, where, alongside the famous terracotta winged horses, are fine displays of jewellery, bronzes and ceramics.

> **To extend your trip…**
> Visit the Renaissance gardens of Villa Lante at **Viterbo** *(pp468–9)*, 64 km (40 miles) from Tarquinia.

Day 4: Orvieto and Todi
You can see more Etruscan remains in **Orvieto** *(pp362–3)*, at the Museo Archeologico Faina and Museo Civico, at the Necropoli Etrusca, and even during a tour of Orvieto Underground *(www.orvieto underground.it)*. The fine beautiful Duomo and the 16th-century Pozzo di San Patrizio add to the attractions. From here travel to nearby **Todi** *(p363)*. This dramatic hilltop town is home to the Museo Etrusco-Romano.

Day 5: Chiusi and Gubbio
Make your way northwards for **Chiusi** *(p336)* and the Museo Nazionale Etrusco for its fine display of urns and vases taken from the surrounding tombs.

Then head towards the forest-clad Appenines for charming **Gubbio** *(p356)*, where the Palazzo dei Consoli houses the famous seven bronze Eugubine Tablets inscribed with Etruscan letters, and where the strange Porte della Morte, walled up doors, were once supposedly used for the transport of coffins.

Volterra, once an important Etruscan city

Day 6: Volterra
The city of **Volterra** *(p338)* is home to the excellent Museo Guarnacci and beautiful Etruscan funerary urns, made out of alabaster, for which the region is famous. For more alabaster visit the Pinacoteca e Museo Civico and browse the craft shops.

> **To extend your trip…**
> A 32 km (20 mile) drive from Volterra takes you to **San Gimignano** *(pp348–9)* and its 13th-century towers.

Day 7: Florence
Finish your tour in Florence and visit the Medici Etruscan collection in the **Museo Archeologico** *(p281)*, which includes two outstanding sculptures – the Chimera and the Arringatore (Orator) bronze.

Putting Italy on the Map

Italy sits at the heart of the Mediterranean, shielded from the rest of Europe by the vast sweep of the Alps. The Po, its longest river, arcs across the industrial north, while the Apennine mountains split the boot-shaped peninsula down its length. With a population of 58 million, governed from Rome, Italy covers 301,268 sq km (116,320 sq miles) and includes Sicily and Sardinia.

SWITZERLAND

Lago Maggiore
Lago di Como
Lecco
Lago di Garda
Trer
S38
S42

Aosta
Arona
Bergamo
Ivrea
Milan
Brescia
Veror
Turin
Po
A4
A7
Mantova
A21
A1
Po
Tanaro
A26
S45
Parma
Modena
Cuneo
A6
Genoa
A15
A10
La Spezia
A12
Lucca
A1

Avignon
FRANCE
Nice
San Remo
Pisa
A7
A51
Monaco
Ligurian Sea
Livorno
A8
S1
Marseille
Piombino

Bastia
Elba
Orbete

Corsica

Ajaccio
Tyrrhenian Sea

Olbia
Porto Torres
Alghero

Sardinia
Arbatax

Cagliari

Key

— Motorway
— Major road
- - - Ferry service
— International boundary

Europe

North Sea
NORWAY
SWEDEN
ESTONIA
LATVIA
LITHUANIA
DENMARK
REP. OF IRELAND
UNITED KINGDOM
NETH.
BELARUS
GERMANY
POLAND
BELGIUM
CZECH REPUBLIC
SLOVAKIA
UKRAINE
Atlantic Ocean
FRANCE
AUSTRIA
HUNGARY
SWITZ.
ROMANIA
CROATIA
ITALY
SERBIA
MONTEN. KOS.
BULGARIA
MAC.
SPAIN
ALBANIA
GREECE
PORTUGAL
MOROCCO
ALGERIA
TUNISIA

Mediterranean Sea

Bizerte
Annaba
TUNISIA
Tunis

Northern Italy

Airline connections link the rest of Europe with Milan, Turin, Bologna, Pisa, Florence, Verona and Venice. Major roads and railways also provide excellent links to cities all over Europe. Transport services are very efficient, with motorways and railways along both coasts, and across the area's main east-to-west axis at the foot of the Alps. Milan, Verona and Bologna are the key transport hubs, while Florence provides the main link to the south.

Florence by Road

Good fast roads link Florence to Pisa to the west, Rome and Siena to the south, and Bologna to the north.

Florence and Environs

0 kilometres 4

0 miles 2

Key

– – International boundary

– – – Regional boundary

▬ Motorway

▬ Main road

— Railway line

For additional map symbols *see back flap*

Venice by Road
Venice is joined to the mainland by a causeway. This provides easy access to motorway links with Verona and Padua.

Venice

Marco Polo
Mestre
FS
Canale Osellino
S14
S11
Laguna Veneta
FS Santa Lucia
San Marco

0 kilometres   4
0 miles   2

AUSTRIA

Cortina d'Ampezzo
Tolmezzo
SLOVENIA
Belluno
Cividale del Friuli
Udine
Pordenone
Gorizia
Treviso
Aquileia
Trieste
VENICE
see inset above

Po Delta

Greece, Turkey, Egypt

Ravenna
Rimini
Pèsaro
SAN MARINO
Fano
Urbino
Ancona
Sansepolcro
Conero Peninsula
Jesi
Greece, Turkey, Cyprus
Grotte di Frasassi
Loreto
Sibillini
Cortona
Gubbio
Perugia
Lago Trasimeno
Assisi
Ascoli Piceno
Chiusi
Spello
Montefalco
Norcia
Todi
Spoleto
Orvieto
Pescara
Viterbo
L'Aquila
Lanciano
Isole Tremiti
Sulmona
ROME
Scanno
San Severo
Lucera
Sermoneta
Foggia
Sperlonga
Troia
Trani
Terracina
Formia
Benevento
Bari
Caserta

Key to Colour Coding

Northeast Italy
Venice
The Veneto and Friuli
Trentino-Alto Adige

Northwest Italy
Lombardy
Valle d'Aosta and Piedmont
Liguria

Central Italy
Emilia-Romagna
Florence
Tuscany
Umbria
Le Marche

0 kilometres   100
0 miles   50

Southern Italy

International airline services operate to Rome, Naples and Palermo in southern Italy. Transport links within the region are generally slower than in the north, particularly inland and on the islands of Sicily and Sardinia, where buses are often a faster option than trains. Mainland coastal road and rail links are good, however, especially those linking Rome and Naples, the region's main transport hubs, which are connected by a high-speed train service. Two trans-Apennine motorways offer the quickest cross-country routes.

Sicily and Sardinia

Ferries operate to Sicily from Naples, Villa San Giovanni and Reggio di Calabria. Onward connections include boats to Malta and Tunisia. Ferries run to Sardinia from several mainland ports, notably Civitavecchia, Genoa and Livorno.

Key

-- International boundary
-- Regional boundary
▨ Motorway
▨ Main road
— Railway line

Rome by Road
Motorway links approach Rome from Naples, Pescara and Florence. All feed into the city's ring road, the Grande Raccordo Anulare.

Rome and Environs

0 kilometres 10
0 miles 5

VATICAN CITY

Leonardo da Vinci di Fiumicino

Tevere (Tiber)

Ciampino

VIA AURELIA
S7
A12
VIA CASSIA
S2
S3
A1
VIA NOMENTANA
VIA TIBURTINA
A24
S5
VIA CASILINA
VIA APPIA NUOVA
VIA CRISTOFORO COLOMBO
A91
S7
A1
GRANDE RACCORDO ANULARE (GRA)

Isole Tremiti

Vasto
Termoli
Rodi Garganico
Vieste
Gargano Peninsula
San Severo
Manfredonia
Lucera
Foggia
Troia
Benevento
Trani
Bari
Castel del Monte
Ruvo di Puglia
Caserta
Melfi
Pompei
Salerno
Potenza
Matera
Amalfi
Sala Consilina
Taranto
Paestum
Metaponto
Cilento
Policoro
Maratea
Castrovillari
Rossano
Cosenza
Crotone
Catanzaro
Lamezia
Tropea
Vibo Valentia
Stilo
Gerace
Isole Eolie
Naples
Milazzo
Messina
Tindari
Reggio di Calabria
Taormina
Naples
Catania
Pantalica
Noto
Siracusa
Modica
Malta
Alberobello
Brindisi
Lecce
Galatina
Otranto
Greece
Croatia, Greece, Egypt

A14
S17
S90
S16
A16
S96
S407
S18
S106
S107
S280
S106
S114
S115
S117
A18
A20
A12

Key to Colour Coding

Rome and Lazio

Rome

Lazio

Southern Italy

Naples and Campania

Abruzzo, Molise and Puglia

Basilicata and Calabria

Sicily

Sardinia

0 kilometres 100
0 miles 50

A PORTRAIT OF ITALY

Italy has drawn people in search of culture and romance for many centuries. Few countries can compete with its Classical origins, its art, architecture, musical and literary traditions, its scenery or food and wine. The ambiguity of its modern image is also fascinating: since World War II Italy has climbed into the top ten world economies, yet at its heart it retains many of the customs, traditions and regional allegiances of its agricultural heritage.

Italy has no single cultural identity. From the northern snow-capped peaks of the Alps, to the rugged southern shores of Sicily, lies a plethora of distinctive regions and peoples. Politically, Italy is a young country: it did not exist as a unified nation state until 1870, and its 20 regions have maintained their cultural individuality. Visitors to Italy are often pleasantly surprised by the diversity of its dialects, cuisines and architecture. There is also a larger regional division. People speak of two distinct Italies: the rich industrial north and the poorer agricultural south,

known as *Il Mezzogiorno* or Land of the Midday Sun. The frontier separating the two is indeterminate, lying somewhere between Rome and Naples.

The north is directly responsible for Italy's place among the world's top industrial nations. It has been the powerhouse behind the Italian economic miracle, its success achieved by internationally renowned names such as FIAT, Prada, Ferragamo, Pirelli, Olivetti, Zanussi, Alessi and Armani. In contrast, the south, once a cradle of high culture and civilization, has been dogged by

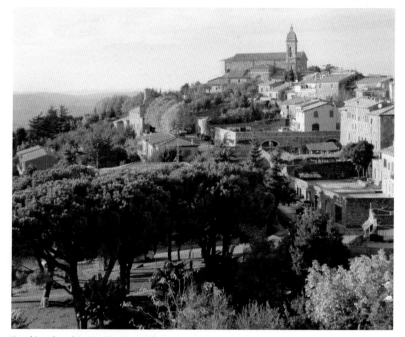

View of the rooftops of Montalcino from the town's fortress

◀ Cobbled lane in the coastal fishing town of Cefalù, Sicily unemployment and organized crime. Some of its areas rank among the most depressed in Europe, although many southern towns did benefit from an injection of funds from the Millennium Project.

The historic divide between north and south is a powerful factor in contemporary politics. The federalist party, the Northern League, owes its popularity to this split. Those in favour of separation complain that the south is a drain on resources: Milan is seen as efficient and rich, while Naples is viewed as chaotic, dirty and corrupt.

History and geography have both contributed to the division. The north is closer in both location and spirit to Germany and France while the south has suffered a succession of invasions from foreign powers: Carthaginians and Greeks in ancient times, Saracens and Normans in the Middle Ages and until the middle of the 19th century, the Bourbons from Spain held sway.

Tradition

Distinctive variations in Italy's regions have much to do with the mountainous landscape and inaccessible valleys. Tuscan and Ligurian hill-towns, for instance, have quite different silhouettes, and the farmhouses in Puglia, the famous *trulli*, are unlike those found in the landscape of Emilia-Romagna.

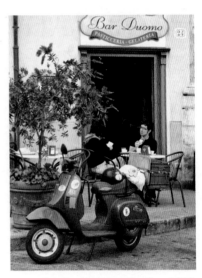

A scooter parked in front of the Bar Duomo, Piazza Duomo in Cefalù

In southern Italy the landscape, architecture, dialects, food, and even the appearance of the people have closer affinities with the Eastern Mediterranean and North Africa than with northern Europe. In the far south, study of the local dialects has revealed traces of ancient Greek and old Albanian, preserved in tightly knit communities isolated by the rugged geography. Christianity and pagan ritual are closely linked; sometimes the Virgin is portrayed as a thinly disguised Demeter, the Earth goddess.

Café-goers relaxing in Marina di Pisa, Tuscany

Medieval skyscrapers in the Tuscan landscape of San Gimignano

Throughout Italy, ancient techniques of husbandry endure and many livelihoods are closely connected to the land and the seasons. Main crops include sugar beet, maize, wheat, olives and grapes; colourful Easter celebrations *(see p70)* pay tribute to the bounty of the soil. Although some of the north's postwar economic prosperity can be attributed to industry (especially car production in and around Turin), much of it has grown from the expansion of family-owned artisan businesses and the export of hand-made goods abroad. This is recognized as a distinct sector of the economy. The internationally successful retail clothes chain Prada is a good example. The "Made in Italy" label, found on goods such as clothes, shoes and leather bags, guarantees the items have been beautifully produced.

Culture and Arts

The arts in Italy have had a long and glorious history and Italians are very proud of this. Given the fact that Italy has more than 100,000 monuments (archaeo-logical sites, cathedrals, churches, houses and statues), all of which have major historical significance, it is not surprising that there is a shortage of funds to keep them in good repair. Many museums in Italy, particularly those in the south, are closed, or partially closed. You may find churches in Venice hidden behind permanent scaffolding or those in Abruzzo shut due to earthquake damage. However, with tourism accounting for around 12 per cent of Italy's Gross Domestic Product,

Bernini's 17th-century Fontana del Tritone, Rome

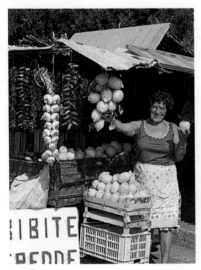
Roadside stall near Positano, Campania

reserve *ciao* (hello or goodbye) for friends your age or younger, and greet older people with *piacere* (pleased to meet you), *buon giorno* (good day) or *buona sera* (good evening) and on parting, say *arrivederci* (goodbye). Strangers are met with a handshake, but family and friends receive a kiss.

Italian chic decrees that the clothes you wear should give the impression of wealth. If Italians wear similar outfits, it is because they are conformists in fashion as in other aspects of daily life.

Italian politics, in contrast, are not so well regulated. Governments in the postwar era were characterized by short-lived coalitions, dominated by the Christian Democrats. In 1993 Italy experienced a political crisis when an organized network of corruption was exposed, disgracing a huge number of politicians and businessmen. The investigations may have failed to eradicate corruption, but they led to the formation of two large coalitions, centre-left and centre-right. Silvio Berlusconi, leader of Forza Italia, became prime minister in 1994 but lasted a short while as he, too, was accused of corruption. In 1998 Massimo D'Alema became Italy's first left-wing Prime Minister. Recent years have seen an alternation of the two coalitions, with

efforts are being made to put as many buildings and collections on show as possible. The Jubilee 2000 helped matters by allocating large amounts of money for the restoration of buildings and sites belonging to the Catholic Church.

The performing arts are also underfunded, yet there are some spectacular cultural festivals. Almost every town of any size has its own opera house and the Teatro alla Scala in Milan stages world-class productions.

Cinema is another flourishing art form in Italy and has been so since its invention. The sets at Cinecittà, on the outskirts of Rome, have been used by famous directors such as Fellini, Pasolini, de Sica, Visconti and many others. Italian films such as *La Vita è Bella* and *The Son's Room* have found critical acclaim and box-office success both in Italy and abroad. In Italy the arts belong to everyone: opera is attended by people from all backgrounds, regardless of social status, as are cinemas and galleries.

Social Customs and Politics

Italian society is still highly traditional, and Italians can be very formal. Between the generations degrees of familiarity exist:

Diners relaxing at a restaurant in Orta San Giulio, Piedmont

The solution to heavy traffic in Rome: motorbikes and scooters

Berlusconi dominating. Economist and academic Mario Monti became prime minister in November 2011. In April 2013 a coalition was sworn in made up of the Democratic Party and Berlusconi's People of Freedom Party (PDL) but the PDL has split into Berlusconi's Forza Italia and The New Centre Right (NCD).

Modern Life

Food and football are the great constants; Italians live for both. Much time is spent on preparing food and eating. The Italian diet, particularly in the south, is among the healthiest in the world. Football is a national passion and inspires massive public interest and media attention, not least as a way of expressing regional loyalties.

As far as religion is concerned, the number of practising Catholics has been in decline for some years. Although Rome lies at the centre of world Catholicism, today many Italians are uninterested in religion, but still attend mass in number on saints' days or feast days. As a result of immigration, other religions are now on the increase.

The emphasis on conformity and a commitment to the institution of the family remain key factors in Italian society despite the country's low birth rate. Grandparents, children and grandchildren often still live in family units, although this is becoming less common. Women's Liberation fought a powerful campaign in the 1970s and did much to change attitudes to women in the workplace, particularly in metropolitan areas. However, the idea that men should help with housework and the care of the children is still a fairly foreign notion among the older generation.

With the miracle of its postwar economic recovery, where industry and technology were united with design, Italy became a success story. Although the economy has been badly affected by the worldwide recessions and political upheaval including the exposure of corruption in public offices, Italy appears unchanged to foreign visitors. Its ability to keep its regional identities and traditional values seems to have allowed the country to ride out the difficulties of recent years relatively unscathed.

Medieval and Early Renaissance Art

The story of early Italian art, from the 13th century until the late 15th century, illuminates one of the richest periods in European art history. For the first time since Classical antiquity, painters and sculptors created a convincing pictorial space in which figures, modelled "in the round", were given life. Ethereal buildings were replaced by those firmly rooted in the real world, reproducing what artists actually saw. This revolution in art included the reintroduction of the fresco technique, giving artists huge surfaces for telling pictorial stories.

c.1305 Giotto di Bondone, *The Meeting at the Golden Gate* (Cappella degli Scrovegni, Padua) Giotto broke away from the ornate Byzantine style to visualize naturalness and human emotions. His way of working would later be dubbed the Florentine style.

1235 Bonaventura Berlinghieri, *St Francis Altarpiece* (San Francesco, Pescia)

1285 Duccio di Buoninsegna, *Rucellai Madonna*, panel (Uffizi, Florence). Duccio dominated the Sienese painting style which combined bold linear movements with a new human intimacy.

1339 Ambrogio Lorenzetti, *Good Government En-throned* (Sala dei Nove, Palazzo Pubblico, Siena)

1220	1240	1260	1280	1300	1320	134
Middle Ages				**Forerunners to Renaissance**		
1220	1240	1260	1280	1300	1320	134

c.1259 Nicola Pisano, Pulpit (Baptistry, Pisa cathedral)

c.1316–18 Simone Martini, *Vision of St Martin* (Lower Church of San Fran-cesco, Assisi)

c.1265 Coppo di Marcovaldo, *Madonna and Child* (Santa Monica dei Servi, Orvieto)

c.1297 Giovanni Pisano, Pulpit (Sant'Andrea, Pistoia)

c.1280 Cimabue, *Madonna Enthroned with Angels and Prophets*, also known as *Santa Trinità Madonna* (Uffizi, Florence)

c.1336 Andrea Pisano, *Baptism of St John the Baptist*, panel on the South Doors (Baptistry, Florence cathedral)

c.1291 Pietro Cavallini, *Last Judgment*, detail (Santa Cecilia, Trastevere, Rome)

c.1425–52 Lorenzo Ghiberti, *Gates of Paradise*, panel on the East Doors. (Baptistry, Florence cathedral). These elaborate doors mark a transition from the Gothic style to the Early Renaissance style, in Florence.

c.1435 Donatello, *David* (Museo del Bargello, Florence)

1357 Andrea Orcagna, *Enthroned Christ with Madonna and Saints* (Strozzi Altarpiece, Santa Maria Novella, Florence)

c.1452–65 Piero della Francesca, detail of *The Dream of Constantine* (San Francesco, Arezzo)

c.1456 Paolo Uccello, *Battle of San Romano* (Uffizi, Florence)

c.1410 Nanni di Banco, *Four Crowned Martyrs* (Orsanmichele, Florence)

1360	1380	1400	1420	1440	1460

Early Renaissance

1360	1380	1400	1420	1440	1460

1423 Gentile da Fabriano, *Adoration of the Magi* (Uffizi, Florence)

c.1440 Fra Angelico, *Annunciation* (San Marco, Florence)

c.1350 Francesco Traini, *Triumph of Death* (Campo Santo, Pisa)

c.1463 Piero della Francesca, *Resurrection* (Pinacoteca, Sansepolcro)

c.1425–8 Masaccio, *The Tribute Money* (Cappella Brancacci, Florence)

c.1465 Fra Filippo Lippi, *Madonna with Child and Angels* (Uffizi, Florence)

c.1465–74 Andrea Mantegna, *Arrival of Cardinal Francesco Gonzaga* (Palazzo Ducale, Mantova)

c.1470 Andrea del Verrocchio, *David* (Bargello, Florence)

Fresco Technique

Fresco, meaning "fresh", refers to the technique of painting on-to a thin layer of damp, freshly laid plaster. Pigments are drawn into the plaster by surface tension and the colour becomes fixed as the plaster dries. The pigments react with the lime in the plaster to produce strong, rich colours, such as those in Masaccio's *The Tribute Money*.

The Tribute Money by Masaccio (Cappella Brancacci, Florence)

High Renaissance Art

The High Renaissance in the late 15th century was marked by
an increasing sense of realism in many religious works and
the technical mastery of such renowned artists as Michelangelo,
Leonardo da Vinci and Raphael. The different schools of
Renaissance painting, while drawing on Classical models,
produced varying styles: Florentine painting was noted for its
cool clarity, while sensuous colour and warm light characterized
many Venetian works. By the mid-16th century, however, these
styles shifted to the fanciful, contorted imagery of Mannerism.

c.1480 Andrea Mantegna,
Dead Christ (Brera, Milan)

1481–2 Sistine Chapel wall
frescoes painted by various artists.

c.1481–2 Pietro Perugino,
*Christ Delivering the Keys of the Kingdom to
St Peter*, wall fresco (Sistine Chapel, Rome)

c.1483–88 Andrea del Verrocchio, completed by
Alessandro Leopardi, *Equestrian Monument of Bartolomeo
Colleoni* (Campo dei Santi Giovanni e Paolo, Venice)

c.1487 Giovanni Bellini,
San Giobbe Altarpiece
(Accademia, Venice)

**c.1495 Leonardo da
Vinci**, *Last Supper*
(Santa Maria delle
Grazie, Milan)

**c.1503–1505 Leonardo
da Vinci**, *Mona Lisa*
(Louvre, Paris)

1519–26 Titian, *Madonna of the
Pesaro Family* (Santa Maria Gloriosa
dei Frari, Venice)

1505 Raphael,
*Madonna of
the Goldfinch*
(Uffizi, Florence)

1508–12 Michelangelo,
Sistine Chapel ceiling (The Vatican,
Rome). Over 200 preliminary
drawings were made for this
incredible vision of God's power and
humanity's spiritual awakening.

1480	1500	1520
	High Renaissance	**Manneri**
1480	1500	1520

**1485
Leonardo da
Vinci**, *Virgin of
the Rocks*
(Louvre, Paris)

**1499–1504 Luca
Signorelli**, *Damned
Consigned to Hell* (Cappella
Nuova, Orvieto cathedral)

1501–1504 Michelangelo, *David*
(Galleria dell'Accademia, Florence)

1505 Giovanni Bellini, *Madonna and
Child with Four Saints* (San Zaccaria
altarpiece, Accademia, Venice)

**c.1485 Sandro
Botticelli**,
Birth of Venus
(Uffizi, Florence)

**c.1486 Leonardo
da Vinci**, *Uomo
Vitruviano* (Accademia,
Venice)

**c.1508
Giorgione**,
Tempesta
(Accademia,
Venice)

1509 Raphael, *School of Athens* (Stanza
della Segnatura, The Vatican, Rome).
The scale, magnificence and harmony
of this fresco represent the ideals of
the High Renaissance. These ideals
sought to express superhuman rather
than human values.

1517 Sodoma,
*Marriage of Alexander
and Roxana* (Villa
Farnesina, Rome)

1516 Michelangelo,
Dying Slave
(Louvre, Paris)

1512–14 Raphael, *Angel
Delivering St Peter from Prison*,
detail from the *Liberation of St
Peter from Prison* (Stanza di
Eliodoro, The Vatican, Rome)

1523 Rosso Fiorentino, *Moses Defends the Daughters of Jethro* (Uffizi, Florence)

1530–32 Giulio Romano, *Ceiling and wall frescoes* (Sala dei Giganti, Palazzo del Tè, Mantova)

c.1532 Michelangelo, *"Blockhead" Captive* (Galleria dell' Accademia, Florence)

1534–5 Paris Bordone, *Fisherman Delivering the Ring* (Accademia, Venice)

1534–41 Michelangelo, *Last Judgment*, wall fresco (Sistine Chapel, Rome)

c.1540–42 Titian, *David and Goliath* (Santa Maria della Salute, Venice)

c.1550 Moretto, *Ecce Homo with Angel* (Pinacoteca Tosio Martinengo, Brescia)

c.1562–6 Jacopo Tintoretto, *Finding of the Body of St Mark* (Brera, Milan)

1540	1560
1540	1560

1538 Titian, *Venus of Urbino* (Uffizi, Florence)

c.1546 Titian, *Portrait of Pope Paul III Farnese with his Nephews*, (Museo di Capodimonte, Naples)

c.1534–40 Parmigianino, *Madonna and Angels or Madonna with the Long Neck* (Uffizi, Florence). Attenuated proportions and contrasting colours make this a fine example of the Mannerist style.

c.1540 Agnolo Bronzino, *Portrait of Lucrezia Panciatichi* (Uffizi, Florence). Elongated features, such as Lucrezia's fingers, are typical of the exaggerated Mannerist style.

1556 Veronese, *Triumph of Mordecai* (San Sebastiano, Venice)

c.1526–30 Correggio, *Assumption of the Virgin* (Dome of Parma cathedral). Neither a Mannerist nor a High Renaissance painter, Correggio was a master of illusion, skilled at making ascending figures float convincingly, as seen in the fresco on the left.

Italian Architecture

The buildings of Italy span almost 3,000 years, drawing influences from a wide variety of sources. Etruscan and Roman buildings borrowed heavily from ancient Greece, while in later centuries Norman, Arabic and Byzantine styles coloured Italy's Romanesque and Gothic architecture. Classical ideals infused the country's Renaissance buildings, later giving way to the inspired innovations of the Baroque period.

Orvieto's Duomo displays the ornate and intricate decoration, notably sculpture, common to many Gothic cathedrals. Building stretched from the 13th to the early 17th centuries.

The Basilica di San Marco (AD 832 –1094) in Venice combines Classical, Romanesque and Gothic architecture, but its key inspiration was Byzantine *(see pp114–15)*.

The Basilica di San Marco

200	400	600	800	1000
Classical		Byzantine		Romanesque
200	400	600	800	1000

Triumphal arches such as Rome's Arch of Constantine (AD 313) were a uniquely Roman invention. Built to celebrate military victories, they were adorned with reliefs depicting episodes from successful campaigns *(see p384)*.

The round-arched Romanesque style emerged from the Dark Ages in structures such as the Duomo in Modena. The churches usually had simple interiors that derived from Roman basilicas.

The building of domes over square or rectangular spaces was a major development of the Byzantine era.

Etruscan Architecture

Virtually the only architectural memorials to the Etruscans are their necropolises (c.6th century BC), found primarily in Tuscany, Lazio and Umbria. Little else survives, probably because most day-to-day buildings were made from wood. The Etruscans' close cultural and trading ties with Greece, however, suggest their architecture would have borrowed heavily from Greek models. Rome, in turn, looked to Etruscan architecture for inspiration, and most early Roman public buildings were probably Etruscan in style.

Model of Etruscan temple with Classical Greek portico

The cathedral of Monreale in Sicily, built in the 12th century, contains Norman elements blended with exotic Arabic and Byzantine decoration *(see pp534–5)*.

Bramante's Tempietto at San Pietro in Montorio, Rome (built in 1502–10) was a Renaissance tribute to the precise, Classical temples of ancient Rome *(see p384)*.

Baroque façades, such as this one added to Syracuse's Duomo between 1728 and 1754, were often grafted onto older churches.

Industrial innovations in glass and metal were applied in new buildings, like Mengoni's imposing Galleria Vittorio Emanuele II (1865) in Milan *(see p198)*.

The Classical ideals of Rome and ancient Greece were reintroduced into Italian architecture during the Renaissance.

Papal patronage and the vigour of the Counter-Reformation fuelled the Baroque, a period of architectural splendour, invention and exuberance.

The Mole Antonelliana (1863–89), in Turin, topped by a soaring granite spire, was for a time the tallest building in the world *(p228)*.

Torre Velasca's 26-floor tower in Milan (1950s) pioneered the use of reinforced concrete.

00	1400	1600	1800	2000
	Renaissance	Baroque	19th Century	20th Century
00	1400	1600	1800	2000

Siena's Duomo (1136 –1382), an imposing Romanesque-Gothic cathedral, went through 200 years of architectural transformation *(see pp346–7)*.

Santa Maria Novella in Florence has a Renaissance façade (1456–70) by Alberti and a Gothic interior.

Gian Lorenzo Bernini (1598–1680), architect of St Peter's Square, was a dominant figure in Roman Baroque.

Andrea Palladio (1508–80) built Neo-Classical villas and palazzi. His style was imitated in Europe for over two centuries *(see p84)*.

Lantern

Inner shell

Outer skin of dome, supported by 24 ribs

Brunelleschi's dome for the Duomo in Florence, completed in 1436, was a masterpiece of Renaissance design and ingenious engineering *(see p257)*.

The Gesù in Rome was designed for the Jesuits by Vignola in 1568. With its powerful façade and lavish decoration it was the prototype for countless other Baroque churches *(see p385)*.

The Pirelli building in Milan, designed by Ponti and Nervi (late 1950s), is a great example of modern Italian architecture *(see p189)*.

Saints and Symbols in Italian Art

Saints and symbols are especially important in Italian art. They form part of an established visual language used by artists to narrate stories of the Bible and the Catholic church to church-goers. Paintings of the saints were the focus for prayer and each offered assistance in a particular aspect of daily life. Patron saints protected specific cities, or trades, and individuals who bore their name. Saints' days and religious festivals still play an important part in Italian life.

The Evangelists

The four evangelists, Matthew, Mark, Luke and John are each represented by a winged creature, standing for a divine mission

Eagle
(St John)

St John carries a book of the Gospel bearing his name.

St Thomas Aquinas is usually shown with a star, barely visible in this painting on his Dominican habit.

St Mark the Evangelist often holds his book of the Gospels.

St Dominic is usually portrayed wearing the habit of his order. The lily is another of his attributes.

St Cosmas and St Damian are always shown together, dressed in physicians' clothing.

St Lawrence carries a palm leaf as well as the gridiron on which he was roasted.

Virgin Enthroned with the Child and Saints (c.1450) was painted on dry plaster by the Dominican friar, Fra Angelico. It is on display at the Museo di San Marco, Florence *(see p280).*

The Virgin, usually shown in blue robes, is depicted as Mater Amabilis – the "Mother Worthy of Love".

St Peter Martyr, here with a palm leaf, is sometimes depicted with a head wound, carrying a sword.

Symbols

In order to identify different saints or martyrs they were given "attributes" or symbols – particular objects to carry, or clothing to wear. These were items that played a particular role in their life story. Martyrs were known by their instruments of torture or death. Symbolism also appears in the sky, animals, flowers, colours and numbers.

The lamb symbolizes Christ, the Lamb of God, or in early Christian art, the sinner.

The skull is a "memento mori" to remind us of death and impermanence.

Winged man
(St Matthew)

Winged lion
(St Mark)

Winged ox
(St Luke)

Giovanni Bellini's painting of
Madonna and Child with Four Saints
(*see p123*)

St Peter the Apostle, the "rock" on which the Christian church was founded, carries the keys to heaven.

The Madonna, with the Christ Child, is an emblem of perfect motherly love.

St Catherine of Alexandria is shown here with a piece of the wheel on which she was martyred.

St Jerome is always portrayed as an old man, often a hermit, whose life was devoted to scholarship.

Detail from Madonna and Child with Four Saints, by Giovanni Bellini. The painting was produced for an altarpiece at San Zaccaria, Venice in 1505, where it is still on display.

The angel, a messenger of God to man, is portrayed in this scene as a musician of Heaven.

St Lucy is depicted here holding her own eyes in a dish. She became the patron saint of the blind and symbolizes light.

The lily, flower of the Virgin, is the symbol of purity, resurrection, peace and chastity.

The cockle shell most often represents pilgrimage. It is a particular attribute of St Roch.

The palm represents, in Christian art, a martyr's triumph over death.

Writers, Poets and Dramatists

Italy has produced many writers (in Latin and Italian) who have won worldwide acclaim. Each of them provides an illuminating insight into the country's turbulent past: the Classical poets Virgil, Horace and Ovid give vivid accounts of the concerns and values of ancient Rome; medieval Florence and Tuscany are brought to life in the poetry of Dante and Petrarch and the salacious tales of Boccaccio. In less than a century these three great writers created a new literary language to rank with any in Europe. Italy's modern literature still commands international attention – Umberto Eco has to his credit one of the most widely read books of the 20th century.

Primo Levi (1919–87) gave an astonishing account of his survival of the Jewish Holocaust and World War II's aftermath in *The Truce* and *If This Is A Man.*

Trentin Alto Ad

Lombardy

Valle d'Aosta and Piedmont

Emilia-Romagna

Liguria

Tuscany

Dario Fo (born 1926) won the Nobel prize for Literature in 1997.

Umberto Eco (born 1932), a professor at the University of Bologna, wrote the novel *The Name of The Rose,* which explored his passion for the Middle Ages. The book was made into a film (above) in 1986.

Giovanni Boccaccio (1313–75) is notable for providing a fascinating social record of his era. *The Decameron,* his captivating collection of 100 short stories, is set in the plague-stricken Florence of 1348.

Pinocchio, written by Carlo Collodi (1826–90) in 1883, is one of the world's best known children's stories. "Collodi" was Carlo Lorenzini's pseudonym, taken after his mother's birthplace in Tuscany.

Dante's (1265–1321) *Divine Comedy* (c.1308–21), is a journey through Hell, Purgatory and Paradise. It includes horrific accounts of the torments suffered by the damned.

Venetian author Carlo Goldoni (1707–93) reacted against the satirical tradition of *La Commedia dell'Arte*, preferring to write more forgiving plays on contemporary Venice society.

The Veneto and Friuli

Classical Roman Writers

Texts in Latin by Classical Roman philosophers, poets, dramatists and politicians are part of the bedrock of Western culture. Today the names Virgil *(The Aeneid)*, Ovid *(Metamorphoses)* and Pliny *(Historia Naturalis)* are literary legends. Fascinating histories such as Livy's *Early History of Rome*, Caesar's *Gallic Wars*, Tacitus's *Annals* and Suetonius's *The Twelve Caesars*, give us an invaluable window on the distant Roman past, as do the caustic *Satires* of Juvenal. Many Latin works owe their survival to the teams of medieval monks who diligently copied and illustrated them. In the Renaissance the stories of Ovid's *Metamorphoses* were plundered by many writers and the works of Cicero had a profound influence on prose style; Seneca was seen as a master of tragedy and Plautus's *Pot of Gold* served as a model for comedies.

Detail from medieval copy of Pliny's *Historia Naturalis*

Petrarch (1304–74), one of the earliest and greatest lyric poets, produced works which showed the first indications of Humanism.

Le Marche

Umbria

Lazio

St Francis of Assisi (1182–1226) was the first author to write in Italian instead of formal Latin. As well as letters and sermons, he wrote poems and songs, including the popular *Canticle of the Sun*.

Abruzzo, Molise and Puglia

Campania

Basilicata and Calabria

Roman writer Alberto Moravia (1907–90) is usually labelled a "Neo-Realist". His novels and short stories focus on the corrupt values of contemporary society. Among his best known works are *Gli Indifferenti* and *Agostino*.

Sicily

The Sicilian Nobel Prize-winner Luigi Pirandello (1867–1936) was preoccupied with themes of illusion and reality. *Six Characters In Search Of An Author* is his most famous work.

0 kilometres 200
0 miles 100

Music and Opera in Italy

Before Italy's unification, particularly during the 17th and 18th centuries, each major city had its own traditions of music-making. Rome, as the papal city, had musical traditions less hedonistic than elsewhere, and avoided opera. Florence had its day at the turn of the 16th century, with its celebrated *camerata* (groups set on reviving the traditions of Ancient Greek spectacle). Venice fostered church music on a grand scale, and Naples, during the 18th century, was renowned for comic opera. In the 19th century, Milan became the undisputed centre of Italian opera, centred on La Scala.

The Medieval and Renaissance Periods

Through Boccaccio *(see p38)*, among others, it is known that singing, dancing and poetry often went hand in hand in medieval and Renaissance Italy. Italy concentrated on music as part of a spectacle rather than as a pure art form.

Important contributors to the music of these periods include Guido d'Arezzo (c.995–1050), a monk who perfected musical notation, and Francesco Landini (1325–97), one of the first known composers whose songs displayed a distinct concern for lyricism. The next 150 years were to be characterized by

the *Ars Perfecta* style, culminating with composer Giovanni Pierluigi da Palestrina (1525–94). His vocal style subjected dissonance to strict control, and it was employed for most church music during his lifetime. Madrigals (vocal settings of poems by Petrarch and other poets) were also popular.

The early 17th century saw Italian composers such as Carlo Gesualdo da Venosa (c.1561–1613) and Claudio Monteverdi challenge these traditions by introducing more declamation and more of the unexpected.

The Baroque Era

Claudio Monteverdi's music straddled the transition from the Renaissance period to 17th-century Baroque. The word "baroque" means highly ornamented, even bizarre, and embellishment was rife. Monteverdi's madrigals began as standard pieces for four voices but ended up as mini-operas. This was due to the popularity of an individual instrumental style and the development of the *basso continuo* (a supporting organ, harpsichord or lute that unleashed the possibility for solos

La Pietà, Venice, where Vivaldi performed

and duets). At this point, the beginnings of the string orchestra were in place.

A new fashion for declamation meant that various emotional states were being represented with sighs and sobs rather than just description. Monteverdi's *Vespers* followed others' in exploiting the stereophonic possibilities of San Marco in Venice by contrasting different

---

Major Italian Composers through the Ages

Claudio Monteverdi (1567–1643) was best known for his *Vespers* of 1610. Both his madrigals and operas are considered major landmarks in the development of music.

Antonio Vivaldi (1678–1741) wrote over 600 concertos, many of which are for the violin. *The Four Seasons*, a set of concertos, is among the best-selling classical music of all time.

Gioacchino Rossini (1792–1868) was most famous for his comic operas, like *The Barber of Seville* and *La Cenerentola*. The romantic, expressive side of his more serious works, such as *Otello*, was often overlooked.

Luciano Pavarotti performed in the most modern surroundings

forces in different parts of the building. In the 1680s, Arcangelo Corelli (1653–1713) turned to classicism. Corelli was famous for the *concerto grosso*, a style that contrasted the solo string group with the full ensemble. He was followed by Antonio Vivaldi (1678–1741), who concentrated his efforts on developing the solo form of the *concerto grosso*. He used wind and plucked instruments as well as violins.

The Emergence of Opera

Opera first emerged during the wedding celebrations of Italy's wealthy 16th-century families. Monteverdi was the first composer to establish his work

Giuseppe Verdi (1813–1901), whose first works were for the opera house La Scala *(see p197)*, was the most important opera composer of the 19th century. His most celebrated works include *Rigoletto* and *Aida*.

firmly in the opera repertoire. During the 17th century, Alessandro Scarlatti (1660–1725) formulated a model which consisted of an orchestral overture followed by a sequence of narrative, set as *recitative*, and interrupted by *da capo* (three-part) arias. Themes for the weightier *opera seria* were largely drawn from mythology, while the lighter *opera buffa* had stock scenes that sometimes owed a large debt to the traditions of *Commedia dell'Arte*. Famous for his comic operas, such as *The Barber of Seville*, was the composer Gioacchino Rossini. Among other contributors, Vincenzo Bellini (1801–35) and Gaetano Donizetti (1797–1848) developed *bel canto* singing, a style stressing fine tone and ornamentation.

Puccini's *Tosca*, first staged in 1900

The two most prominent opera composers of the latter half of the 19th century were Giuseppe Verdi and Giacomo Puccini (1858–1924). Verdi often turned to the works of Shakespeare as well as to contemporary subjects in order to form a basis for his work, while many composers, like Puccini, turned to the new trend of *verismo* (slices of realism) – *La Bohème* is one of the most refined examples of this style.

The 20th Century

In the early 20th century, Puccini's *La Fanciulla del West* (The Girl of the West) brought cowboys into opera, *Turandot* looked towards the Orient and *Tosca* brought torture and murder. Some composers have attempted to emulate French and German music, and only a few Italian pieces, such as those by Ottorino Respighi (1879–1936), have been regularly performed. The most important name in postwar Italian music was Luciano Berio (1925–2003), who developed Music Theatre, an art form lying somewhere between drama and opera. In later years, however, Berio continued the tradition of Grand Opera with his elaborate production of *Un Re in Ascolto*. But it is Luciano Pavarotti (1935–2007) who must be credited with renewing an international interest in opera. In the 1990s, his televised performances with "Three Tenors" co-stars José Carreras and Placido Domingo secured a massive world audience for opera. Another star of opera and classical music is internationally renowned conductor Riccardo Muti, former director of La Scala and now the director of Rome's Teatro dell'Opera.

The illuminated interior of Rome's Teatro dell'Opera

Italian Design

Italy has had phenomenal success evolving stylish, desirable forms for everyday objects. Its 20th-century achievements can be credited to a handful of forward-thinking industrial giants, such as Olivetti, willing to entrust important product decisions to a group of inspired designers, like Ettore Sottsass. The design genius was to rethink the function of consumer objects, apply new technology, and then make the result look seductive.

The streamlined aesthetic of Italian design extends even to pasta; this Marille version was created by car designer Giorgio Giugiaro for Voiello in 1983.

Sleek, sculptural Alessi cutlery (1988), designed by Ettore Sottsass, combines maximum utility with elegance and aesthetic integrity.

The Alessi kettle (1985), designed by Michael Graves, achieved such popularity in its first year of production that over 100,000 were sold.

One of the best known coffeemakers is Bialetti's Moka Express. Although designed in 1930, it is still enormously popular today.

Christophe Pilet's chair, designed for Giulio Cappellini's collection of contemporary furniture, is a wonderful example of the 1990s' aesthetic, and is still available for purchase.

The folding Cumano table, designed by Achille Castiglione for Zanotta in 1979, is still revered as a "designer object".

The Patty Difusa chair, with unusual wooden arms that curve into legs, was designed by William Sawaya for Sawaya & Moroni in Milan.

Pininfarina's streamlined form for the Ferrari Testarossa (1986) pushes car design almost into the realms of sculpture.

Light in weight, and compact in shape, Olivetti's Valentine typewriter revolutionized the role of the desk typewriter. Designed by Ettore Sottsass in 1969, its portability allowed the user to work anywhere.

Babc

Italian printer Giambattista Bodoni (1740–1813) designed the sophisticated typeface that bears his name and is still popular 200 years after its creation.

Milan's Giorgio Armani is best known for his updating of classic items such as the jacket, creating a flattering, smart and comfortable, "deconstructed" look.

Prada, the Milan-based fashion house headed by Miuccia Prada, features minimalist, cutting-edge designs and the use of innovative fabrics.

Florence has a long reputation as a producer of high quality crafts, particularly fashion accessories such as handbags, shoes, belts, jewellery and briefcases.

Gucci's classic items, including bags and shoes, are a revered totem for the fashion-conscious.

The Artemide company is renowned for combining metal and glass in many of their designs, especially lamps and lighting fixtures.

Piaggio's innovative Vespa scooter (1946), by Corradino d'Ascanio, provided cheap, fast and reliable transport at a time when few could afford the expense of a car. Hugely successful, the Vespa is still a common sight on Italy's streets.

The FIAT 500 (1957), like the Vespa, became a symbol of mobility and democratization, an expression of Italy's rapid postwar recovery.

Scientists, Inventors and Explorers

Italy has fostered a long tradition of important scientific thought and discovery, fuelled in the Renaissance by such men as Galileo, who searched for a new understanding of the universe. Meanwhile, explorers such as Columbus had set off to find new worlds, a move heralded in the 13th century by Marco Polo. The spirit of scientific enquiry continued up to the 20th century, with the invention of radio and pioneering work in the field of nuclear physics.

Trentino Alto Adi

Lombardy

Valle d'Aosta and Piedmont

Liguria

Emilia-Romagna

Tuscany

Genoese-born Christopher Columbus sailed west from Spain in 1492. He reached the Indies in three months, navigating with such aids as an astrolabe.

The explorer Amerigo Vespucci established that the New World was a separate land mass. A pamphlet wrongly described him as its discoverer, and so, in 1507, America acquired its name.

Guglielmo Marconi invented the first practical system for sending radio signals. In 1901, he succeeded in picking up a signal that had been sent to England from Newfoundland.

Leonardo da Vinci was the ultimate Renaissance man, accomplished in both arts and sciences. He conceived his first design for a flying machine in c.1488, more than 400 years before the first aeroplane took off. This model is based on one of his technical drawings.

The telescope enabled astronomers to produce accurate lunar maps. Domenico Cassini, astronomy professor at Bologna University, refined the instrument. In 1665 he traced the meridian line in the church of San Petronio.

```
0 kilometres          200
0 miles          100
```

The Veneto and Friuli

Padua University, founded in 1222, was a centre of scientific learning in the Renaissance. Galileo, inventor of the telescope, taught physics here, and the lectern he used is still on view.

The Venetian Marco Polo set off for the east as a youth in 1271. He stayed at the court of the Mongol emperor, Kublai Khan, for nearly two decades before returning home. He is seen here arriving at Hormuz in the Persian Gulf from India.

Galileo Galilei proved that the earth revolved around the sun, over-turning Church doctrine. He was convicted of heresy in 1633. Here he shows the rings of Saturn to Venetian senators.

Le Marche

Umbria

Winner of the Nobel Prize for Physics in 1938, Enrico Fermi directed the first controlled nuclear chain reaction. He built the world's first nuclear reactor for producing power at the University of Chicago.

Lazio

Abruzzo, Molise and Puglia

Campania

Basilicata and Calabria

Pliny the Elder wrote his catalogue of human knowledge, *Natural History*, in AD 77. He died when Vesuvius erupted two years later, but his book retained its authority for 1,500 years.

Spectacles were invented in Italy in the 13th century. They are first recorded in Venice, still an important centre for glasswork today.

Sicily

The mathematician Archimedes was born in c.287 BC in Syracuse, Sicily, then a Greek colony. Legend has it that he discovered the principle of specific gravity while in the bath.

THE HISTORY OF ITALY

The concept of Italy as a geographic entity goes back to the time of the Etruscans, but Italy's history is one of discord and division. Prior to the 19th century, the only time the peninsula was united was under the Romans, who by the 2nd century BC had subdued the other Italian tribes. Rome became the capital of a huge empire, introducing its language, laws and calendar to most of Europe before succumbing to Germanic invaders in the 5th century AD. Another important legacy of the Roman empire was Christianity and the position of the pope as head of the Catholic church. The medieval papacy summoned the Franks to drive out the Lombards and, in AD 800, crowned the Frankish king Charlemagne Holy Roman Emperor. Unfortunately, what seemed to be the dawn of a new age turned out to be anything but. For five centuries popes and emperors fought to decide which of them should be in charge of their nebulous empire.

Meanwhile, a succession of foreign invaders – Normans, Angevins and Aragonese – took advantage of the situation to conquer Sicily and the south. The north,

in contrast, saw a growth of independent city states, the most powerful being Venice, fabulously wealthy through trade with the East. Other cities, such as Genoa, Florence, Milan, Pisa and Siena, also had their days of glory. Northern Italy became the most prosperous and cultured region in western Europe and it was the artists and scholars of 15th-century Florence who inspired the Renaissance. Small, fragmented states, however, could not compete with great powers. In the 16th century Italy's petty kingdoms fell prey to a foreign invader, this time to Spain, and the north subsequently came under the control of Austria.

One small kingdom that remained independent was Piedmont, but during a war between Austria and France it fell to Napoleon in 1796. In the 19th century, however, it was Piedmont that became the focus for a movement towards a united Italy, a goal that was achieved in 1870, thanks largely to the heroic military exploits of Garibaldi. In the 1920s, the Fascists seized power and, in 1946, the monarchy was abandoned for today's republic.

16th-century map of Italy, of the kind used by Venetian and Genoese sailors

◀ *Fall of the Rebel Angels* fresco by Giacinto Brandi on the ceiling of Sant'Ambrogio e Carlo al Corso

The Age of the Etruscans

The Etruscans were Italy's first major civilization. The frescoes, jewellery and pottery found in their tombs are evidence of a highly artistic, cultured people. Their origin is a mystery, as is their language, but from the 9th century BC they spread through central Italy, their chief rivals being the Greeks in the south. Etruria was never a unified state, just a loose confederation of cities. In the 6th century Etruscan kings ruled Rome, the city that would ultimately eclipse them.

Italy in 650 BC
- Etruscan kingdoms
- Greek colonies

Terracotta Winged Horses
This beautiful relief of yoked horses (4th century BC) decorated the façade of the Ara della Regina temple at Tarquinia.

Bronze Sheep's Liver
The inscriptions served as a guide for telling the future from animals' entrails.

The double flute was a speciality of the Etruscans. The instrument was played at festivals and funerals alike.

Terracotta Cremation Urn
The lid of the urn shows the deceased holding a writing tablet. The Etruscans introduced the alphabet to Italy.

Tomb of the Leopards

Feasts and revelry are common themes in the frescoes that decorate Etruscan tombs. These musicians are from a tomb fresco (c.500 BC) at Tarquinia (see p470).

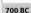

9th century BC Pre-urban communities established along river valleys in Etruria		**c.700 BC** Growth of cities in Etruria; earliest Etruscan inscriptions	**616 BC** Etruscans become rulers of Rome under Tarquino the Older
	753 BC Legendary date of foundation of Rome by Romulus		
900 BC	**800 BC**		**700 BC**
c.900 BC First traces of Iron Age in Italy; Villanovan period			
	c.800 BC Greeks settle in Sicily and south of Italy	**715–673 BC** Reign of the wise Numa Pompilius, second king of Rome	*Etruscan gold earrings*

A Boxing Match
Athletic competitions were held at funerals. This vase, which dates from about 500 BC, was made in Etruria, but imitates the Greek black-figure style of pottery.

The musicians and the dancer in the tomb painting are painted with a realism that indicates the influence of Greek art.

The lyre was made from a tortoise shell and played with a plectrum.

Apollo of Veii
This magnificent statue of Apollo (c.500 BC) shows the stylized facial features characteristic of Etruscan art.

Bronze Mirror
Wealthy Etruscans lived in great luxury. The women used polished bronze mirrors with engraved backs. This one shows Helen of Troy and the goddess Aphrodite.

Where to see Etruscan Italy

Rock tombs like these at Sovana (*p336*) are common in the volcanic tufa of central Italy.

Tuscany, Lazio and Umbria are rich in Etruscan remains, especially tombs. There are huge necropolises in Lazio at Cerveteri and Tarquinia (*p470*). The latter also has an important museum. Other museums with major collections of Etruscan art and artifacts include Villa Giulia (*p444*) and the Vatican's Museo Gregoriano (*p426*) in Rome, the Museo Archeologico in Florence (*p281*), the Museo Nazionale in Chiusi (*p336*) and the Museo Guarnacci in Volterra (*p338*).

Temple of Neptune
This fine temple at Paestum (5th century BC) is a legacy of Greek colonization of the south.

509 BC Last Etruscan king, Tarquinius Superbus, expelled from Rome; establishment of Roman Republic

Mixing bowl, imported from Greece

450 BC Roman law codified in the Twelve Tables

390 BC Gauls sack Rome; Capitol saved thanks to alarm sounded by cackling geese

600 BC	500 BC	400 BC

499 BC Battle of Lake Regillus; Romans defeat alliance of Latins and Etruscans

474 BC Etruscan fleet defeated by Greeks off Cumae; blow to Etruscan naval power

c.400 BC Gauls start to settle along valley of the Po

396 BC Veii, a major Etruscan city in present-day Lazio, falls to Rome

Relief of Capitoline geese, found in the Roman Forum

From Republic to Empire

From the scores of tribes inhabiting ancient Italy, one people, the Romans, emerged to conquer the peninsula and impose their language, customs and laws on the rest. Rome's success was due to superb skill in military and civil organization. The state was a republic ruled by two consuls, elected each year, but as the extent of Rome's conquests grew, power passed to generals such as Julius Caesar. The Republic became unworkable and Caesar's heirs became the first Roman emperors.

Cisalpine Gaul was annexed in 202–191 BC.

Etruria was in Roman hands by 265 BC.

Julius Caesar
The great general, conqueror of Gaul, returned to Italy in 49 BC to defeat Pompey. His rise to absolute power marked the end of the Republic.

Oscan Inscription
The languages of the peoples conquered by Rome lived on for centuries before being replaced by Latin. The Oscans lived in what is now Campania.

War Elephant
In 218 BC the great Carthaginian general Hannibal brought 37 elephants across the Alps – to spread alarm in the Roman ranks.

Roman Aqueduct
The Romans' talent for engineering found its most spectacular expression in huge aqueducts. These could be up to 80 km (50 miles) long, though for most of that distance the water ran underground.

High ground

Cleaning vent

Reservoir

Underground water channel

Arches carrying water across low ground

---

312 BC Building of Via Appia and Aqua Appia aqueduct

308 BC Etruscan city of Tarquinii falls to Rome

Via Appia

287–212 BC Life of Archimedes, the great Greek mathematician of Syracuse

265 BC Romans capture last Etruscan city

300 BC

275 BC Greek King Pyrrhus defeated by Romans at Beneventum

264–241 BC First Punic War (between Rome and Carthage)

237 BC Romans occupy Corsica and Sardinia

Hannibal, Carthaginian leader in the Second Punic War

250 BC

218 BC Second Punic War; Hannibal crosses the Alps

216 BC Roman defeat at Battle of Cannae

200 BC

191 BC Gaulish territory south of the Alps falls to Rome

Cicero Addresses the Senate
State business was debated in the Senate. The great orator Cicero (106–43 BC) argued for the Republic and against tyranny.

Roman Legionary
This bronze shows a legionary in standard kit of helmet, breastplate, leather kilt with iron plates, greaves on his shins, and sandals.

CORFINIUM
Via Valeria

The Via Appia
was extended from Capua to Brindisi in 190 BC.

CAPUA
Via Appia

BRUNDISIUM
Brindisi

TARENTUM
Taranto

Sicily became the first Roman province in 241 BC.

RHEGIUM
Reggio di Calabria

Where to see Republican Era Italy

Republican structures are very rare, most having been rebuilt under the Empire. In Rome itself, two notable exceptions are the 2nd-century BC Temples of the Forum Boarium (p437). However, the legacy of the age to modern Italy is not hard to appreciate. Countless roads, such as the Via Appia Antica (p445), and towns were planned originally by Roman engineers. Two striking examples of towns with original Roman street plans are Lucca (pp324–5) and Como (p195).

These huge basalt blocks at Tharros in Sardinia (p555) were part of a Roman road.

Roman Roads

After conquering other tribes, the Romans imposed their authority by building roads along which legions could march rapidly to deal with any trouble. They also built towns. Many, such as Ariminum (Rimini), were "colonies", settlements for Roman citizens – often veteran legionaries.

Aerial View of Bologna
Roman street plans are still visible in city centres today. The route of the old Via Aemilia cuts straight through the centre of Bologna.

104 BC Slave revolt in Sicily

89 BC Social War: Rome's Italian allies granted citizenship

31 BC Octavian defeats Mark Antony at Battle of Actium

146 BC End of Third Punic War; Carthage destroyed

80 BC Building starts on the first Roman amphitheatre, at Pompeii

30 BC Suicide of Mark Antony and Cleopatra in Egypt

150 BC

100 BC

50 BC

168 BC End of Third Macedonian War; Romans now masters of Greece

Milestone from the Via Aemilia

73–71 BC Slave revolt led by Spartacus

49 BC Caesar crosses the Rubicon and drives Pompey from Rome

44 BC Murder of Julius Caesar; end of Roman Republic

45 BC Introduction of 12-month Julian calendar

The Golden Age of Rome

From the age of Augustus to the reign of Trajan, Rome's power grew until her empire stretched from Britain to the Red Sea. Despite the extravagance of emperors such as Nero, taxes and booty from military campaigns continually refilled the Imperial coffers. Under the wiser rule of Trajan, Hadrian and Marcus Aurelius in the 2nd century AD, Roman citizens enjoyed wealth and comfort, with most of the work performed by slaves. Entertainment included visits to the baths, the theatre and the games. The town of Pompeii, buried when Vesuvius erupted in AD 79, preserves many fascinating details of everyday life.

Roman Empire in AD 117

Maximum extent of the Empire

Mosaic of Gladiators
Bloodthirsty gladiatorial combats were very popular. The gladiators were mostly slaves captured in war.

Frescoes of festoons and medallions

Trajan's Column
The carvings record Trajan's successful campaigns in Dacia (present-day Romania) in the first decade of the 2nd century AD.

The triclinium
(main dining room) had a beautiful frieze of cupids.

Roman Shops
Buildings in towns were lined with small shops open to the street, like this pharmacy. The front was closed with wooden panels and locked at night.

House of the Vettii
This reconstruction shows one of Pompeii's finest houses (see pp498–9). The Vettii were not aristocrats, but freedmen, former slaves, who had made a fortune through trade. The rooms were richly decorated with frescoes and sculptures.

9 BC Dedication of Ara Pacis *(see p414)* in Rome to celebrate peace after wars in Gaul and Spain

AD 17 Tiberius fixes boundary of Empire along the Rhine and Danube

Bronze cooking pots from kitchen at Pompeii

AD 79 Eruption of Vesuvius destroys Pompeii and Herculaneum

50 BC

AD 1

AD 50

27 BC Augustus takes title Princeps, in effect becoming the first Roman emperor

AD 37–41 Reign of Caligula

AD 43 Roman conquest of Britain in reign of Claudius

AD 67 Traditional date for martyrdom of St Peter and St Paul in Rome

AD 68 Deposition and suicide of Nero

AD 80 Inaugural games in Colosseum

Augustus
The adopted son of Julius Caesar became the first emperor, reducing the Roman Senate to impotence and ruling by decree.

The atrium had a skylight in the roof with a pool that collected rainwater below.

Where to see Imperial Rome

The best places to discover how people lived are Pompeii (pp498–9) and Herculaneum. Artifacts and works of art from these sites are held at the Museo Archeologico in Naples (pp494–5), while local museums all over Italy contain statues and other remains. Famous sights in Rome include the Pantheon (p408) and the Colosseum (p397). Hadrian's Villa, at Tivoli (p472), and Ostia (p471) are also fascinating to visit, but the whole country preserves traces of Rome's glory – from the Arch of Augustus in Aosta (p219) to Villa del Casale (p541) in Sicily.

The Forum (pp394–5), with its temples and law courts, was the centre of daily life in ancient Rome.

Front entrance

Reception room

Peristyle or colonnade

The internal garden was a feature borrowed by the Romans from the Greeks.

Mosaic of a Banquet
The Romans ate reclining on low couches. A popular accompaniment for many dishes was garum, a salty sauce made of dried fish.

Household Shrine
Religious rites were practised both in public and in private. This shrine from the House of the Vettii was dedicated to the lares, the household gods.

AD 97 Roman Empire reaches largest extent in reign of Trajan

AD 161–180 Reign of Marcus Aurelius

AD 193–211 Reign of Septimius Severus

AD 212 Roman citizenship extended to include people from all parts of the Empire

AD 100

AD 150

AD 200

Late 1st century AD Amphitheatre of Verona built

AD 134 Hadrian's Villa at Tivoli completed

AD 125 Pantheon rebuilt by Hadrian

Emperor Septimius Severus

AD 216 Baths of Caracalla completed in Rome

The Splitting of the Empire

A decisive turning point in the history of the Roman Empire came with Emperor Constantine's conversion to Christianity in AD 312 and his decision to build a new capital at Constantinople (Byzantium). By the 5th century the Empire was split into two. Rome and the Western Empire could not stem the tide of Germanic invaders migrating southwards and Italy fell first to the Goths and later to the Lombards. The Eastern Empire retained nominal control over parts of Italy from its stronghold at Ravenna, which became the richest, most powerful city of the age, while the great palaces and arenas of Rome were reduced to ruins.

Italy in AD 600
Byzantine territories
Lombard territories

The Donation of Constantine
A medieval legend, encouraged by the papacy, tells how Constantine granted Pope Sylvester temporal power over Rome.

Belisarius (500–565) was a general who won much of Italy back from the Goths.

Theodolinda of the Lombards
The 6th-century queen converted her people to orthodox Catholicism. Here, gold is melted for the church she built at Monza (see p205).

Justinian reigned from 527 to 565. He was a great lawgiver and one of the most powerful Byzantine emperors.

303–5 Persecution of Christians throughout the Empire in the reign of Diocletian	**404** Ravenna becomes seat of western emperor		*Gold coin of Theodoric*	**547** Church of San Vitale in Ravenna
	312 Constantine defeats rival Maxentius at Battle of the Milvian Bridge			**488** Italy invaded by the Theodoric the Ostrogoth
200	**300**	**400**	**500**	
270 Aurelian Wall built to protect Rome from Germanic invaders	**313** Edict of Milan grants freedom of worship to Christians	**324** Christianity becomes state religion	**476** End of Western Empire	**535** Belisarius lands in Sicily; reconquest of most of Italy by Byzantine Empire
		c.320 Building of first St Peter's in Rome	**410** Sack of Rome by Alaric the Visigoth	**564** Lombards invade Italy, establishing their capital at Pavia

Charlemagne
The King of the Franks was invited by the pope to crush the Lombards. In return, he was crowned Holy Roman Emperor in AD 800.

Saracens Besieging Messina *(843)*
In the 9th century Sicily was conquered by Muslims from Africa. Saracen raiders even reached Rome, where Pope Leo IV built a new wall to defend the Vatican.

The emperor holds a large gold paten, the dish in which the bread is placed for Mass.

Maximian, Archbishop of Ravenna

Where to see Early Christian and Byzantine Italy

Though the fall of the Roman Empire led to war, famine and depopulation, the continuity of the Christian religion has preserved many monuments of the late Empire and Byzantine period. Rome has the catacombs *(p446)* and great basilicas, such as Santa Maria Maggiore *(p417)*. In Ravenna, the administrative capital of the Byzantine Empire, are the churches of San Vitale and Sant'Apollinare *(pp272–3)* with their magnificent mosaics. Sicily and the south also preserve many Byzantine churches, while the finest example of late Byzantine architecture is San Marco in Venice *(pp114–15)*.

Stilo in Calabria has a beautiful Byzantine church, the Cattolica *(p524)*, dating from the 10th century.

Santa Costanza in Rome *(p445)* was built in the 4th century as the mausoleum of Constantine's daughter. Late Roman mosaics decorate the vaults.

Priests

The Court of Justinian
Byzantine churches were decorated with glorious mosaics of coloured glass and gold leaf. This one from the apse of the church of San Vitale in Ravenna (see p272), completed in 547, depicts members of the Imperial court.

c.595 Lombards control two thirds of Italy	**752** Lombard King Aistulf takes Byzantine stronghold of Ravenna	**774** Charlemagne conquers Italy and takes Lombard crown **800** Charlemagne crowned Holy Roman Emperor in St Peter's	**878** Saracens capture city of Syracuse from Byzantine Empire and gain control of Sicily
600	**700**	**800**	**900**
Gregory the Great (reigned 590–604) **599** Pope Gregory negotiates peace between the Lombards and the Byzantine Empire	**754** Pope appeals to Franks for help; King Pepin invades Italy and defeats Lombards		*6th-century Lombard gold helmet in the Bargello museum, Florence (see p287)*

The Rise of Venice

Medieval Italy saw waves of foreign invaders joining in the struggle for power between popes and emperors. In the confusion, many northern cities asserted their independence from feudal overlords. The most powerful was Venice, governed by its doge and Great Council, which grew rich through trade with the East and by shipping Crusaders to fight the Saracens in the Holy Land. Its maritime rivals on the west coast were Genoa and Pisa.

The Mediterranean (1250)
— Genoese trade routes
— Venetian trade routes

Matilda of Tuscany
Matilda, Countess of Tuscany (1046–1115) supported the radical Pope Gregory VII against the Emperor Henry IV. When she died, she left her lands to the church.

Sails – for added speed

Canopy over the half-deck

The oars, pulled by slaves, were the principal means of propulsion.

Venetian Galley
The galleys used by Venice, both as warships and for carrying cargo, were similar to ancient Greek vessels.

Basilica San Marco

Doge's Palace

The columns of San Marco and San Teodoro had been erected in the 12th century.

Marco Polo's Departure for China

Venice traded in Chinese silks and spices imported via the Middle East, but no Venetian had been to China before Marco Polo's father Nicolò. Marco Polo set off with his father in 1271, returning 25 years later with fantastic tales of his time at the court of Kublai Khan.

1000 Doge of Venice, Pietro Orseolo II, defeats Dalmatian pirates in Adriatic

11th century School of Law at Bologna develops into Europe's first university

Medieval students

1139 Naples incorporated into Kingdom of Sicily

1000

1050

1100

1030 Norman knight Rainulf granted county of Aversa by Duke of Naples

1061 Normans Robert Guiscard and Roger de Hauteville capture Messina from the Arabs

1063 San Marco in Venice rebuilt

1084 Normans sack Rome

1076 Salerno, last Lombard city, falls to Normans

1073–85 Pope Gregory VII reforms church and papacy

1130 Roger II crowned king of Sicily

1115 Death of Countess Matilda

St Francis of Assisi
(1181–1226)
In *The Dream of Pope Innocent III* by Giotto, painted around 1290–1295, St Francis holds up the tottering edifice of the Roman church. The Franciscans' rule of poverty brought about a religious revival in reaction to the wealth of the church.

Monastery of Sant'Apollonia

Today's Riva degli Schiavoni

Where to see Early Medieval Italy

Of the many churches built in this period, especially fine examples are Venice's San Marco (p114), Sant'Antonio (p162) in Padua and the Duomo in Pisa (p328).

Castello dell' Imperatore, Prato, was built about 1240.

The Leaning Tower (p330) also dates back to the 12th century. Medieval castles include Frederick II's Castel del Monte in Puglia (p513) and Castello dell'Imperatore in Prato.

Nicolò Polo, his brother Maffeo and son Marco prepare to embark. They sailed first to Acre in the Levant.

Fourth Crusade
Discord between the leaders of the crusade and Pope Innocent III culminated in the sacking of Constantinople in 1204.

Frederick II
(1194 –1250) The emperor kept a court of poets and scholars in Sicily. He won Jerusalem from the Arabs by diplomacy, but was constantly at war with the pope and the cities of Lombardy.

1155 Frederick Barbarossa crowned Holy Roman Emperor

1198 Frederick II becomes king of Sicily

1204 Sacking of Constantinople

1209 Franciscan Order founded

1216 Dominican Order founded

1250 Death of Frederick II

1260 Urban IV invites Charles of Anjou to rule Naples and Sicily

1265 Birth of Dante

1150	1200	1250

Frederick Barbarossa dressed as a Crusader

1220 Frederick II crowned Holy Roman Emperor

1228 Gregory IX excommunicates Frederick II; struggle between Guelphs (the papal party) and Ghibellines (supporters of the emperor)

1237 Lombard League defeat Frederick at Battle of Cortenuova

1271 Marco Polo sets off on journey to China

The Late Middle Ages

Old feuds between pope and emperor thrived throughout the 14th century, kept alive by two warring factions – the Guelphs, who backed the papacy, and the Ghibellines, who favoured Imperial power. The cities of Lombardy and Tuscany used the political confusion to grow in strength. It was against this turbulent backdrop that a great new age in painting was inspired by artists such as Duccio and Giotto. Also at this time the Florentine poets Dante and Petrarch laid the foundations of Italian literature.

Italy in 1350
- Papal States
- Holy Roman Empire
- Angevin Kingdom of Naples

The campanile or bell tower

A griffin, symbol of Perugia

Medieval Town Square

Throughout central Italy, the town square was an expression of civic pride and independence. Towns, such as Perugia (see pp356–7), tried to overshadow their rivals in the splendour of their town halls. The centre of Perugia has changed little since the 14th century when the town's main rival was Siena.

Condottieri
Cities paid *condottieri*, leaders of bands of mercenaries, to fight their wars. Siena hired Guidoriccio da Fogliano, seen here in a fresco by Simone Martini (1330).

The main chamber of the town hall, the Sala dei Notari, is decorated with the coats of arms of Perugia's mayors.

The Fontana Maggiore was begun in 1275 and includes panels by Nicola Pisano. Prominently placed, it is an emblem of the town's wealth.

Dante's Inferno
One of the harshest punishments in Dante's vision of hell is reserved for corrupt popes, such as Boniface VIII (reigned 1294–1303), who are placed upside down in fiery pits.

1282 Sicilian Vespers; uprising against French rule in Palermo; 2,000 French soldiers killed

1296 Work begins on the Duomo in Florence

1298 Marco Polo returns from China to Venice

1309–43 Reign of Robert the Wise of Naples

1310 Work begins on Palazzo Ducale in Venice

1313 Birth of Boccaccio

1339 Simon Boccanegra becomes first doge of Genoa; Giovanna I Queen of Naples

1275

1300

1325

1282 Peter of Aragon lands at Trapani, conquers Sicily and is crowned king in Palermo

1304 Birth of Petrarch

1309 Clement V moves papacy to Avignon

1321 Dante completes *La Divina Commedia* and dies the same year

1337 Death of Giotto

The poet and scholar Petrarch

The Black Death
Bubonic plague reached Italy in 1347, carried on Genoese ships from the Black Sea. It killed over a third of the population, reducing the remainder to a state of superstitious terror.

Where to see Late Medieval Italy

Many central Italian cities and towns have public buildings from the 13th and 14th centuries; among the most impressive are Palazzo Vecchio (p295) in Florence and Siena's Palazzo Pubblico (p344). Smaller towns that preserve much of their medieval character include Volterra (p338) and the walled Monteriggioni (p338) in Tuscany, Gubbio (p356) and Todi (p363) in Umbria and Viterbo (pp468–9) in Lazio. The Duomo in Orvieto (pp362–3) is a fine example of a late 13th-century Gothic cathedral.

Piazza dei Priori in Volterra (p328) is one of the most beautiful medieval squares in Italy.

The cathedral was started in 1350 and used to include an outside pulpit in the square.

Construction of Alessandria
Almost all towns were ringed with strong walls. This fresco (1407) by Spinello Aretino is a valuable record of medieval building techniques.

Return of Pope Gregory XI to Rome (1378)
For 70 years the popes had lived in Avignon, protected by the French kings, while nobles and republicans fought for control of Rome.

Medieval doctor

1347–9 Black Death

1350

1354 Cola di Rienzo killed in Rome

1347 Cola di Rienzo tries to re-establish Roman Republic

1375

1378 Gregory XI returns from Avignon to Rome

1378–1415 Period of Schism, with rival popes and antipopes in Rome and Avignon

1380 Genoese fleet surrenders to Venetians at Chioggia

1385 Gian Galeazzo Visconti becomes ruler of Milan

1400

1406 Pisa annexed by Florence

The Renaissance

Fifteenth-century Italy saw a flowering of the arts and scholarship unmatched in Europe since the days of Greece and Rome. Architects turned from the Gothic to Classical models for inspiration, while painting, with its new understanding of perspective and anatomy, produced a generation of artists that included such giants as Leonardo da Vinci, Raphael and Michelangelo. The patronage for this cultural "rebirth" came from the wealthy families that ruled the city states of the north, led by the Medici of Florence. In spite of intense rivalry, they oversaw a period of uneasy stability out of which the Renaissance grew.

Italy in 1492

Republic of Florence

Papal States

Aragonese possessions

Handing over the Keys of St Peter
Perugino's fresco in the Sistine Chapel *(see p430)* links the authority of the pope to the New Testament and, through the Classical buildings in the background, ancient Rome.

Galeazzo Maria Sforza was the son of Milan's ruler.

Piero de' Medici, Lorenzo's father, was given the nickname "the Gouty".

Self-portrait of the artist

Execution of Savonarola *(1498)*
Having assumed the leadership of Florence in 1494, the fanatical monk was hanged, then burned for heresy in Piazza della Signoria.

1420 Martin V re-establishes papacy in Rome

1435 Publication of *On Painting* by Alberti, which contains the first system for the use of linear perspective

1436 Brunelleschi completes dome of Florence cathedral

1458–64 War between Houses of Aragon and Anjou over Kingdom of Naples

1469 Lorenzo the Magnificent becomes ruler of Florence

1400

1425

1450

1434 Cosimo de' Medici comes to power in Florence

1442 Naples captured by Alfonso of Aragon

1452 Birth of Leonardo da Vinci

1444 Federico da Montefeltro becomes Duke of Urbino

1453 Fall of Constantinople

Cosimo de' Medici

Filippo Brunelleschi

The Battle of Pavia *(1525)*
The French King Francis I was captured at this battle against the army of the Habsburg Emperor Charles V, who won control of Italy.

The Procession of the Magi

Benozzo Gozzoli's fresco (1459) in the Palazzo Medici-Riccardi, Florence, depicts members of the Medici family and other contemporary notables. It contains many references to a great church council held in Florence in 1439.

Where to see Renaissance Italy

Many cities were flourishing centres of the arts in the 15th century. None can rival Florence *(pp274–317)* with its great palazzi and the Uffizi gallery *(pp290–93)*, but Venice *(pp88–141)*, Urbino *(pp374–5)* and Mantova *(p211)* all preserve great treasures. In Rome, do not miss the Vatican's Sistine Chapel and Raphael Rooms *(pp428–31)*.

The Spedale degli Innocenti by Brunelleschi in Florence *(p281)* shows the Classical symmetry and restraint of Renaissance architecture.

Humanism
Carpaccio's painting of St Augustine is thought to show Cardinal Bessarion *(c.1395 –1472)*, one of the scholars who revived interest in Classical philosophy, especially Plato.

Lorenzo de' Medici (the Magnificent) was depicted as one of the three kings travelling to Bethlehem.

Pope Julius II
During his reign (1503–13), the worldly Julius made the papacy a major power in European politics. Raphael's portrait shows him as a shrewd old statesman.

1487 Birth of Titian

1483 Sixtus IV consecrates Sistine Chapel

1494 Italy invaded by Charles VIII of France

1503 Giuliano della Rovere elected Pope Julius II; he proves the most powerful of the Renaissance popes

1527 Rome sacked by Imperial troops

Niccolò Machiavelli

1475

Raphael

1500

1525

1475 Birth of Michelangelo

1483 Birth of Raphael

1498 Savonarola executed; Machiavelli secretary to ruling Council in Florence

1512 Michelangelo completes Sistine Chapel ceiling

1513 Giovanni de' Medici crowned Pope Leo X

1525 Francis I of France captured at Battle of Pavia

1532 Machiavelli's book *The Prince* is published, five years after his death

The Counter-Reformation

After the Sack of Rome in 1527, Italy was at the mercy of Charles V, Holy Roman Emperor and King of Spain. Pope Clement VII, who had opposed Charles, crowned him emperor in Bologna. In response to the growing threat from Protestantism, a series of reforms, known as the Counter-Reformation and backed by the Inquisition, imposed rigid orthodoxy. New religious orders, such as the Jesuits, were set up to take the battle for men's souls far overseas. The missionary spirit of the age inspired the dramatic forms of the Baroque.

Italy in 1550

Spanish possessions

States allied with Spain

Emperor Charles V and Pope Clement VII
The two former enemies settled their differences and the future destiny of Italy in the Treaty of Barcelona (1529).

The Virgin Mary intervenes on the side of the Christians.

Baroque Stucco Decoration

This stucco relief by Giacomo Serpotta (c.1690) in the Oratory of Santa Zita in Palermo is a magnificent example of Late Baroque exuberance. The subject is a favourite of the period, the Battle of Lepanto, a great naval triumph for the combined forces of Christendom against the Turks (1571).

The centre of the ingenious creation is, in effect, a framed painting in perspective.

Baroque Architecture
Guarino Guarini's decoration of the dome of the Chapel of the Holy Shroud in Turin *(see p225)* was completed in 1694.

The young boy rests his hand on a helmet, symbol of the victorious Christians.

Andrea Palladio

1530–37 Alessandro de' Medici ruler of Florence

1542 Inquisition established in Rome

1545–63 Council of Trent sets out agenda of Counter-Reformation

1580 Death of architect Palladio

1600 Philosopher Giordano Bruno burned for heresy in Rome

1589 Palestrina publishes setting of the Latin Hymnal

1525	1550	1575	1600

1540 Founding of Jesuit Order

1541 Michelangelo completes *Last Judgment* in Sistine Chapel

1529 Charles V crowned Holy Roman Emperor in San Petronio, Bologna

1564 Birth of Galileo

1560 San Carlo Borromeo appointed Bishop of Milan

1571 Victory over Turkish fleet at Battle of Lepanto

Giovanni Pierluigi da Palestrina

Trial of Galileo
The great astronomer was often in trouble with the Inquisition. He was summoned to Rome in 1633 and forced to deny that the Earth and planets moved round the sun.

Lepanto was the last major sea battle in which Venetian galleys played an important role.

St Ignatius Loyola
The Spanish saint was the founder of the Jesuits – sanctioned by the pope in Rome in 1540.

Where to see Baroque Italy

The Ecstasy of St Teresa
by Bernini (p416) has the dynamic theatricality characteristic of the best Baroque sculpture.

The Baroque is strongly associated with Rome and in particular with its great public spaces such as Piazza Navona (pp402–3) and the many churches by Borromini and Bernini. Other cities and towns with striking Baroque architecture include Lecce (pp516–17) in Puglia, Palermo (pp530–33), Noto (p547) and Syracuse (pp546–7) in Sicily, and Turin (pp224–5).

Cherubs, a favourite motif in Baroque decoration

Revolt of Masaniello (1647)
High taxes made Spanish rule in Naples unpopular. A proposed tax on fruit sparked off this failed revolt.

The turban, symbol of the defeated Turks

1626 New St Peter's consecrated in Rome

1631 Duchy of Urbino absorbed by Papal States

1625

1633 Galileo condemned by papal authorities

1642 L'Incoronazione di Poppea by Monteverdi

1647 Revolt in Naples in response to tax on fruit

1669 Major eruption of Mount Etna

1650

1669 Venice loses island of Crete to the Turks

1674 Revolt against Spanish rule in Messina

1693 Eastern Sicily ruined by earthquake that kills 5 per cent of the island's population

1675

1678 Birth of Vivaldi

1694 Andrea Pozzo completes ceiling fresco for the church of Sant'Ignazio in Rome

The Grand Tour

The treaty of Aix-la-Chapelle in 1748 marked the start of 50 years of peace. It was about this time that Italy, with its great art treasures and Classical ruins, including the newly excavated Pompeii, became Europe's first great tourist destination. Young English "milords" visited Rome, Florence and Venice as part of a new type of pilgrimage, the Grand Tour; while artists and poets sought inspiration in Rome's glorious past. In 1800, Napoleon, who conquered and briefly united Italy, threatened to destroy the old order, but in 1815 the status quo was restored.

Charles III's Fleet at Naples *(1753)* Ruler of Naples from 1734 to 1759, when he became King of Spain, Charles attempted genuine political reforms.

Goethe in the Roman Campagna
Goethe toured Italy in the 1780s. Great poets who followed his example included the Romantics Keats, Shelley and Byron.

Farnese Hercules
(see p495)

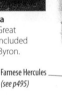

The Dying Galatian
(see p390)

Venetian Carnival
The colourful folklore of Carnival attracted many tourists, but Venice's days of greatness were over. In 1797, the proud maritime republic was ceded to Austria by Napoleon.

Gallery of Views of Ancient Rome by Pannini

Giovanni Pannini (1691–1765) painted views of Roman ruins for foreigners. This painting is a capriccio, an imaginary scene incorporating many well-known views and Classical statues.

1713 Treaty of Utrecht gives Naples and Sardinia to Austria and Sicily to Piedmont

Medici coat of arms

1725 *The Four Seasons* by Vivaldi

1735 Peace of Vienna confirms Charles III as King of the Two Sicilies (Naples and Sicily)

1748 First excavations at Pompeii

1700

1720

1740

1707 Birth of playwright Carlo Goldoni

Antonio Vivaldi, great Venetian composer

1737 End of Medici dynasty in Florence; Grand Duchy of Tuscany passes to Austrian House of Lorraine

1718 Piedmont and Sardinia united under House of Savoy; Sicily passes to Austria

View of the Roman Forum by Piranesi
The popular series of etchings *Vedute di Roma* (Views of Rome) by Giovanni Battista Piranesi (1720–78) inspired a new interest in excavating the ruins of ancient Rome.

Where to see 18th-century Italy

The 18th century produced two of Rome's best-loved tourist attractions: the Spanish Steps *(p413)* and the Trevi Fountain *(p414)*. It was also the age of the first purpose-built museums, including the Vatican's Museo Pio-Clementino *(p425)*. The Neo-Classical sculpture of Antonio Canova (1757–1822) was immensely popular during this period. His tomb is in Santa Maria Gloriosa dei Frari in Venice *(pp102–3)*. Of Neo-Classical buildings, the most imposing is a vast monument to enlightened despotism: the Palazzo Reale at Caserta *(p500)*.

Pauline Borghese, Napoleon's sister, was the model for Antonio Canova's *Venus (1805)* in the Villa Borghese collection in Rome *(p443)*.

The Colosseum was as popular a subject in the 18th century as it is on today's picture postcards.

The Laocoön *(see p421)*

View of the Pantheon *(see p408)*

Napoleon
When Napoleon conquered Italy in 1800, he was seen by many as a liberator. The enchantment wore off as he took priceless works of art back to Paris.

Congress of Vienna (1815) The conference decided that Austria should keep Lombardy and Venice, thereby sowing the seeds of the Italian unification movement.

La Scala Opera House, Milan (see p191)

1778 La Scala opened in Milan

1797 Venice given to Austria by Treaty of Campo Formio; France controls rest of northern Italy

1800–1801 Napoleon conquers Italy

1808 Murat becomes King of Naples

1809 Pope Pius VII exiled from Rome

1760

1780

1800

1773 Pope dissolves Jesuit Order

1780 Joseph II succeeds to Austrian throne; minor reforms in Lombardy

1806 Joseph Bonaparte becomes King of Naples

1768 Corsica sold by Genoa to France

1765–90 Reign of Leopold Grand Duke of Tuscany, who introduces enlightened reforms

1796–7 Napoleon's first campaign in northern Italy

1815 Congress of Vienna restores status quo in Italy, though Austria keeps Venice

The Risorgimento

The word "Risorgimento" (resurgence) describes the five decades of struggle for liberation from foreign rule, culminating in the unification of Italy in 1870. In 1848, patriots rose up against the Austrians in Milan and Venice, the Bourbons in Sicily and the pope in Rome, where a republic was declared. Garibaldi valiantly defended the republic, but all the uprisings were too localized. By 1859, the movement was better organized with Vittorio Emanuele II at its head. Two years saw the conquest of all but Venice and Rome, both of which fell within a decade.

Italy in 1861

▨ Kingdom of Italy

Giuseppe Mazzini
(1805–72)
An exile for much of his life, Mazzini fought alongside Garibaldi to unite Italy as a republic, rather than a kingdom.

The guns were rusty, old converted flintlocks.

The red shirt was the badge of the Garibaldini.

Italian Railways
The short railway line from Naples to Portici was opened in 1839. Politically fragmented, Italy was slow to create an effective rail network.

Revolt of Messina
When, in 1848, Messina revolted, Ferdinand II subjected the town to a savage bombardment, earning himself the nickname King Bomba.

1840 First major railway links established

1831 Insurrection in Romagna and Le Marche against papal rule

1852 Cavour becomes prime minister of Piedmont

1849 Accession of Vittorio Emanuele II as ruler of Piedmont

1820   **1830**   **1840**   **1850**

1820s Carbonari secret society active in Papal States

1847 Economic crisis

Daniele Manin, hero of the Venetian uprising of 1848

1831 Mazzini founds *Giovine Italia* (Young Italy) movement

1848 Revolutions throughout Italy

1849 Republic of Rome crushed by French troops

Battle of Solferino *(1859)*
With the help of a French army led by Napoleon III, the Piedmontese won Milan and Lombardy from the Austrians.

Where to see Risorgimento Italy

Almost every town in Italy honours the heroes of the Risorgimento with a Via Garibaldi, a Via Cavour, a Piazza Vittorio, a Via Mazzini and a Via XX Settembre (the date of the fall of Rome in 1870). Many cities also have Risorgimento museums. One of the best is in Turin *(p227)*.

The Victor Emmanuel Monument *(p388)* is a prominent, but largely unloved, Roman landmark.

Two old paddle steamers brought the Thousand from Quarto near Genoa.

Count Camillo di Cavour *(1810–61)* Cavour's diplomacy as prime minister of Piedmont ensured that the House of Savoy became rulers of the new Italy. He also coined the word "Risorgimento".

The skiffs were lent by other ships moored in Marsala harbour.

Garibaldi and the Thousand

Giuseppe Garibaldi (1807–82) was a leader of courage and genius. In 1860, he landed at Marsala with 1,000 volunteers. The garrison at Palermo surrendered, Sicily fell and he went on to conquer Naples, thus presenting Vittorio Emanuele with half a kingdom.

Giuseppe Verdi *(1813–1901)* Composers such as Verdi, Donizetti and Rossini made the 19th century the great era of Italian opera. Verdi's early operas inspired the Risorgimento.

1859 Battles of Magenta and Solferino; Piedmont acquires Lombardy from Austria and duchies of Parma, Modena and Tuscany

1861 Kingdom of Italy proclaimed with capital at Turin

1860

1866 Italy wins Venice from Austria

1860 Garibaldi and the Thousand capture Kingdom of the Two Sicilies

1870 Rome falls to royalist troops and is made capital of new kingdom; Vatican announces doctrine of papal infallibility

1870

Pope Pius IX, who remained a virtual prisoner in the Vatican when Rome became capital of Italy

1882 Deaths of Garibaldi and Pope Pius IX

1878 Death of Vittorio Emanuele; accession of King Umberto I

1880

1893 Troops sent to suppress insurrection in Sicily

1890

1890 Italian colony of Eritrea established by royal decree

Modern Italy

Fascism under Mussolini (1922 – 43) promised the Italians greatness, but delivered only humiliation. In spite of this, Italy has become one of Europe's leading economies with a standard of living undreamt of at the turn of the 20th century. This has been achieved in the face of great obstacles. Since 1946, the Republic has passed through many crises: a series of unstable coalitions, the terrorist outrages in the 1970s and, in the 1990s, corruption scandals involving numerous government ministers and officials.

1936 FIAT produces first "Topolino" car

1960 *La Dolce Vita*, Federico Fellini's film satire on Rome's decadent café society, is released

1922 Fascists march on Rome; Mussolini invited to form government

1940 Italy enters World War II

1918 Austrian advance halted at the river Piave, just north of Venice

1900 Assassination of King Umberto I

1911–12 Italy conquers Libya

1943 Allies land in Sicily; Italy signs armistice and new Badoglio government declares war on Germany

1900	1910	1920	1930	1940	1950	196

1900	1910	1920	1930	1940	1950	196

1908 Earthquake destroys many towns and villages in Calabria and eastern Sicily; Messina almost completely razed to the ground; over 150,000 die

1915 Italy enters World War I

1936 Italy conquers Abyssinia; pact with Germany, forming anti-Communist "Axis"

1943 Mussolini imprisoned, then freed by Germans

1946 Referendum in which Italy votes to become a republic; Christian Democrat party forms first of a long series of coalition governments

1920s Postwar years see continued emigration to the United States. Here, emigrants cheer as they reach New York aboard the *Giulio Cesare*

1957 Treaty of Rome; Italy one of the six founder members of the European Economic Community

1960 Olympic Games held in Rome

1917 Defeat at Caporetto on Italy's northeastern border; Italian troops, such as these Alpini, retreat to defensive positions

1909 In his *Futurist Manifesto*, Filippo Marinetti condemns all traditional art as too static. His idea of a new dynamic art is expressed in works such as Umberto Boccioni's bronze *Unique Forms of Continuity in Space*

1996 Fire destroys La Fenice theatre in Venice

1978 Ex-prime minister Aldo Moro kidnapped and assassinated by the Red Brigades

1994 TV magnate Silvio Berlusconi becomes prime minister after forming political party "Forza Italia". Alleged financial irregularities force him to resign later that year

1997 Earthquake in Assisi seriously damages the Basilica di San Francesco, destroying Giotto's frescoes

2000 Rome celebrates the Holy Year known as the Jubilee

2002 Euro is adopted

2006 Italy wins World Cup in Germany

2008 Silvio Berlusconi wins third term as prime minister but resigns in 2011 as the country is gripped by financial crisis

1992 Judge Giovanni Falcone killed by Mafia in Sicily

1992 Scandals expose widespread corruption in the postwar political system

2011 Mario Monti sworn in as prime minister

2013 Pope Benedict XVI resigns and Pope Francis is elected

1966 River Arno bursts its banks, flooding Florence and damaging many priceless works of art

1983 Bettino Craxi, Italy's first Socialist prime minister, forms government

1970	1980	1990	2000	2010	2020

1970	1980	1990	2000	2010	2020

1990 World Cup staged in Italy

1978 Election of Pope John Paul II

2015 Milan hosts the Universal Exposition

2013 Election results in coalition government.

2011 Italy celebrates 150 years of unification

1982 Italian football team wins World Cup in Spain

2006 Romano Prodi sworn in as prime minister

2005 Election of Pope Benedict XVI

1969 Bomb outrage in Milan at Piazza Fontana; 13 killed and many injured

1999 Roberto Benigni wins 3 Oscars for his film *La Vita è Bella*, including best actor and best foreign language film

1997 Dario Fo wins the Nobel prize for literature

Italian Cinema Since World War II

The social problems of late 1940s Italy inspired a wave of cinema known as Neo-Realism. Leading exponents included Roberto Rossellini, who made *Roma Città Aperta* (1945), Vittorio de Sica, the director of *Bicycle Thieves* (1948), Pier Paolo Pasolini and Luchino Visconti. Since that time, the major Italian directors have cultivated their own personal styles. Visconti's later films, such as *Death in Venice* (1971), show formal beauty and decadence, while Federico Fellini's *La Dolce Vita* (1960) and *Roma* (1972) depict life as a grotesque carnival. Italy has also produced some commercially successful films, such as Sergio Leone's late 1960s westerns and the Oscar-winning *Cinema Paradiso* and *La Vita è Bella*.

Vittorio de Sica (1901–74)

ITALY THROUGH THE YEAR

Throughout Italy, the variety of local character and colour is astonishing. This is mainly due to the survival of regionalism, particularly in the southern parts of the country. Old traditions, customs and lifestyles are still greatly respected and there is a deep attachment to the land, which is reflected in a healthy interest in food and produce, as well as a perseverance of seasonal religious and secular events. Annual festivals, whether in rural or urban areas, range from wine-tasting and gastronomic celebrations to elaborate commemorations of every patron saint imaginable.

Spring

The Italian spring begins early, particularly in the south. City streets and main sights are rarely overcrowded (except at Easter in Rome). The weather, however, can be unpredictable and wet in the central and northern parts of the country. Spring specialities, such as asparagus, spinach and rocket, begin to feature on restaurant menus. This is a season of great celebration; festivals and fairs abound, especially in Sicily, and the Easter papal address always draws massive crowds to St Peter's.

Tuscan asparagus

March
Dolomiti Ski Jazz Festival, *(mid-Mar)*, Val di Fiemme, Trentino-Alto Adige. Live jazz on the ski slopes.
Sa Sartiglia, Oristano, Sardinia. Three-day carnival ending on Shrove Tuesday.
Su e zo per i ponti *(Sun, varies)*,

Procession of the Grieving Madonna on the isle of Procida

Venice. A lively race through the city's streets, up and down the bridges.

April
Procession of the Grieving Madonna *(Good Friday)*, Procida, Campania. A colourful religious procession throughout the island.
Holy Week *(Easter Week)*. Numerous Easter celebrations from Palm Sunday to Easter Sunday, throughout the country.
Papal Address *(Easter Sunday)*, Rome. The pope makes his Easter address from the Vatican.
Dance of the Devils *(Easter Sunday)*, Prizzi, Sicily. Dance recital symbolizing the attempts of evil to vanquish the forces of good.
Scoppio del Carro *(Easter Sunday)*, Florence. Firework display is lit by a mechanical dove in front of the Duomo.
Festa della Madonna che Scappa in Piazza *(Easter Sunday)*, Sulmona, Abruzzo. Re-enactment of a meeting between the Virgin and the Risen Christ.
Festa degli Aquiloni *(first Sun after Easter)*, San Miniato, Tuscany. Kite lovers perform aerial acrobatics at this festival.
Festa di San Marco *(25 Apr)*, Venice. St Mark, the patron saint of Venice, is commemorated by a gondola race across St Mark's Basin.
Mostra Mercato Internazionale dell'Artigianato *(last week)*, Florence. An important European exhibition of arts and crafts.

Spring strawberries

Scoppio del Carro (Explosion of the Carriage) festival in Florence

Sagra Musicale Lucchese *(dates vary)*, Lucca, Tuscany. Festival of sacred music held in Romanesque churches.

May
Festa di Sant'Efisio *(1 May)*, Cagliari, Sardinia. Paraders in traditional Sardinian costume.
Festa di San Nicola *(7–9 May)*, Bari, Puglia. A statue of St Nicholas is taken to the sea.
Festa dei Ceri *(15 May)*, Gubbio, Umbria. Festival, including a race with four teams carrying large candles.
Festa di San Domenico Abate *(first Thu)*, Cocullo, Abruzzo. Includes a procession with a statue of St Dominic covered with live snakes.
Festa dello Speck *(late May)*, Bolzano, Trentino-Alto Adige. A celebration of the famed ham.
Greek Drama in Theatre *(May–Jun)*, Syracuse, Sicily. Festival of Greek drama.
Maggio Musicale *(May–Jun)*, Florence. This is the city's biggest arts festival, including music, drama and dance.

Street carpeted with flowers for the Infiorata in Genzano

Summer

Summer brings the crowds to Italy, particularly the cities. Italians, however, flee and head for the coast, usually in August. The queues for tourist attractions can be long and hotels are often fully booked. Festivals vary; religious events are interspersed with those of the arts and local folklore.

June

Festa della Fragola (*1 Jun*), Borgo San Martino, Piedmont. Musical and folkloric performances in celebration of the strawberry.

Biennale (*Jun –Sep*), Venice. The world's biggest exhibition of contemporary art takes place during odd-numbered years only.

Infiorata (*Corpus Christi day*), Genzano, Lazio. A procession through streets carpeted with flowers.

International Film Festival (*mid-Jun*), Taormina, Sicily.

Festa di San Giovanni (*mid-Jun–mid-Jul*), Turin, Piedmont. Festival in honour of the city's patron saint, John.

Calcio Storico (*24 Jun and two other days in Jun*), Florence. Football in 16th-century costumes; fireworks.

Festa di Sant'Andrea (*27 Jun*), Amalfi, Campania. Fireworks and processions.

Festival dei Due Mondi (*late Jun–early Jul*), Spoleto, Umbria. International festival of drama, music and dance.

Gioco del Ponte (*last Sun*), Pisa. "The Bridge Parade" of marchers in antique armour.

Estate Romana (*late Jun–mid-Sep*), Rome. Open-air cinema, performances, ballet and concerts.

July

Corsa del Palio (*2 Jul*), Siena. Tuscany's most famous event (*see p345*) presents a medieval flag-waving exhibition and horse race.

Festa della Madonna della Bruna (*first Sun*), Matera, Basilicata. A lively procession of clergymen and knights in costume.

Festa dei Noantri (*last two weeks Jul*), Rome. A colourful festival in Trastevere.

Festa della Santa Maria del Carmine (*16 Jul*), Naples. Featuring the illumination of the city's bell tower.

Umbria Jazz (*Jul*), Perugia. World-famous jazz artists perform in various settings.

Musician from Florence's Calcio

Opera Festival (*Jul–Aug*), Verona, Veneto. Renowned

The Palio of Siena in action

opera festival (*see p141*) overlapping with the **Shakespeare Festival**, providing music, drama, opera and dance.

August

Medieval Palio (*first week – end Aug*) Feltre, Veneto. Parades and archery competitions, medieval-style.

Festa del Mare (*15 Aug*), Diano Marina, Liguria. This "Festival of the Sea" boasts a spectacular firework display.

Festa dei Candelieri (*14 Aug*), Sassari, Sardinia. "Festival of the Candle", dating from the 16th century.

Corsa del Palio (*16 Aug*), Siena, Tuscany. See July entry.

Rossini Festival (*mid-Aug*), Pesaro, Le Marche. A celebration of the composer's work, in his birthplace.

Venice Film Festival (*late Aug–early Sep*). International festival on the Lido.

Settimane Musicali di Stresa (*late Aug–end Sep*), Stresa, Lombardy. Four weeks of concerts and recitals.

Sunbathers enjoying a Tuscan beach holiday

Autumn

Autumn is a slow, gentle season in Italy but that doesn't mean there are fewer festivals and fairs. In addition to the various religious events at this time of year, gastronomic festivals are especially popular, commemorating such delectables as chestnuts, local cheeses, sausages and mushrooms. Autumn is the season of the *vendemmia*, the grape harvest, which is often used as an excuse for village festivities at which the latest local wines flow freely.

The climate *(see pp76–7)* in late autumn is often cold and wet in the north. The south, however, can be quite warm right through October.

Advertisement for the September Palio in Asti, Piedmont

September

Festa di Santa Lucia *(first Sun)*, Lodè, Sardinia. Includes a contest where competitors improvise short poems.
Procession of the Macchina di Santa Rosa *(3 Sep)*, Viterbo, Lazio. Commemoration of the saint's body being transported to the Church of Santa Rosa in 1258.
Giostra del Saracino *(first Sun)*, Arezzo, Umbria. Joust of the Saracen and knights, dating from the 13th century.
Regata Storica *(first Sun)*, Venice. A procession of historic boats plus a colourful gondola race.
Human chess game *(second week)*, Marostica, near Vicenza. A popular costumed game held in the main square every even year.

The widely cultivated olive tree

Rassegna del Chianti Classico *(second week)*, Chianti, Tuscany. Celebration of the local wines.
Auditorium Parco della Musica Season *(Sep–Jul)*, Rome. The wide program includes classical, jazz and rock music, as well as a circus and a popular modern dance festival.
The Miracle of San Gennaro *(19 Sep)*, Naples. Re-enactment of the liquefaction of the saint's blood, in a lively mass at the Duomo.
Palio *(third Sun)*, Asti, Piedmont. Includes a costumed medieval procession and bareback horse racing.

October

Amici della Musica *(Oct–Apr)*, Florence, Tuscany. The popular "Friends of Music" concert season begins.
Fiera del Tartufo *(Oct–Nov)*, Alba, Piedmont. A variety of events centred around the locally grown white truffle.
Festa di San Francesco *(4 Oct)*, Assisi, Umbria. Feast in honour of one of Italy's patron saints.

Wine festivals *(first week)*, Castelli Romani, Lazio.
Sagra del Tordo *(last Sun)* Montalcino, Tuscany. Celebration of the thrush; costumed archery contests.
Festa dell'Uva *(dates vary)*, Bolzano, Trentino-Alto Adige. Grape festival with live music and a costumed procession featuring allegoric carts.
International Festival of Cinema *(dates vary)*, Rome. A week of screenings, high-profile events and celebrity spotting in the capital.

A roast chestnut stall in autumn

November

Festa dei Popoli *(Nov)*, Florence, Tuscany. Film festival showing documentary films in their original languages with Italian subtitles.
Festa della Salute *(21 Nov)*, Venice. Cherished by Venetian locals, this feast gives thanks to the Virgin Mary in memory of a 1630 plague.

The human chess game in the town square of Marostica

Winter

There are fairs, markets and religious events up and down the country at this time of year. Neapolitan Christmas cribs are famous and nearly every church has one. The Christmas holiday itself is low key; more is made of other religious events such as the liquefaction of San Gennaro's blood in Naples and the Carnevale in Venice.

December
Festa di Sant'Ambrogio
(early Dec), Milan. The official opening of La Scala Opera season *(see p197)*.
Festa della Madonna di Loreto
(10 Dec), Loreto, Le Marche. Celebration of the Virgin's Holy House.
Mercato della Befana
(mid-Dec–6 Jan), Rome. Well-known Christmas fair held in Piazza Navona.
The Miracle of San Gennaro
(16 Dec), Naples. See September. **Christmas fair** *(mid-Dec)*, Naples. Fair selling crib figures and decorations.
Fiaccole di Natale
(Christmas Eve), Abbadia di San Salvatore, Tuscany. Features carols and processions in memory of the first shepherds.
Midnight Mass *(24 Dec)*, at churches all over the country.
Christmas Day *(25 Dec)*, St Peter's Square, Rome. Public blessing by the pope.

La Befana at Piazza Navona, Rome

January
Capodanno *(1 Jan)*, all over the country. New Year's Day is celebrated with fireworks and volleys from hunters firing into the air to scare off ghosts and

Rome during one of its rare snowfalls

spirits of the old year and welcome in the new.
La Befana *(6 Jan)*, throughout Italy. Children's holiday with presents and sweets.
Pitti Immagine Uomo, Pitti Immagine Donna, Pitti Immagine Bimbo, Fortezza da Basso, Florence. Month of international fashion shows for women, men and children.
Festa di San Sebastiano *(Sun nearest 20 Jan)*, Dolceacqua, Liguria. A laurel tree covered with colourful communion hosts is carried through town.
Festa d'o'Cippo di Sant'Antonio *(17 Jan)*, Naples. A procession for St Anthony, protector of animals.
Carnevale *(a month-long event finishing Shrove Tue)*, Viareggio, Tuscany. A carnival famous for its lively, topically themed floats.
Fair of St Orsa *(30–31 Jan)*, Aosta, Valle d'Aosta. Exhibition of traditional arts and crafts.

Carnevale, Viareggio

February
Carnevale *(last ten days before Lent, finishing Shrove Tuesday)*, Venice. Pre-Lent festival meaning "farewell to meat". Events are organized, but anyone can buy a mask and watch the array of gorgeous costumes on show.

Carnevale revellers in Venice

Public Holidays
New Year's Day (1 Jan)
Epiphany (6 Jan)
Easter Sunday & Monday
Liberation Day (25 Apr)
Labour Day (1 May)
Republic Day (2 Jun)
Ferragosto (15 Aug)
All Saints' Day (1 Nov)
Immaculate Conception (8 Dec)
Christmas Day (25 Dec)
Santo Stefano (26 Dec)

Sagra delle Mandorle in Fiore
(first or second week), Agrigento, Sicily. Annual almond blossom celebration.
Bacanal del Gnoco *(dates vary)*, Verona. Traditional masked procession with both international and local allegorical floats. Masked balls are held in the town's squares.
Carnevale *(dates vary)*, Mamoiada, Sardinia. Processions include *mamuthones* wearing sinister black masks.

The Sporting Year

Football is by far the most important sport in Italy, uniting the country when the national team (*Azzurri*) plays. A range of other sporting events, including cycling, skiing and tennis, also take place throughout the year, so fans are never at a loss for something to watch. For most big matches or tournaments, tickets can be obtained for cash at club outlets such as the venue itself. Agencies provide hard-to-get tickets at often higher prices. Beware of the inevitable touts at popular events as their expensive tickets may not be valid.

Calcio Fiorentino, one of Italy's few indigenous sports, is said to be the medieval precursor of modern football.

The professional water polo season takes place from March through to July. The Canottieri Napoli team play consistently well through the championship.

Coppa Italia football final

Memorial d'Aloia rowing competition, held in Umbria

The Giro d'Italia cycling race takes place over many stages. Ivan Basso (Italian) won the race in 2006 and 2010.

January	February	March	April	May	June

Indoor Athletics Championships

Rome Marathon

International Showjumping, Rome

The Rome Masters, previously known as the Italian Open, takes place in Rome during May. The event is one of the most prestigious clay court tennis competitions in the world.

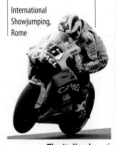

The Italian leg of the Circuito Mondiale in Mugello. Valentino Rossi has dominated the MotoGP World Championship for over a decade.

Rugby is becoming increasingly popular. Italy takes part in the Six Nations Championship in February and March, along with England, Scotland, Wales, Ireland and France.

The Italian Outdoor European Swimming Championships are held every year in July. The Olympic gold medal winner Massimiliano Rosolino, pictured here, celebrates a victory.

Italy has some of the best ski resorts in Europe, and in 2006 Turin hosted the Winter Olympics. Above is Alberto Tomba, once a champion of the slopes.

The Italian Grand Prix, held annually at Monza, is Italy's round of the international Formula One World Championship. Giancarlo Fisichella is one of Italy's most successful drivers.

Trofeo dei Templi rowing competition, Sicily

The Sanremo Car Rally, held each year in October, was made famous by driver Micky Biason and the Lancia Delta Integrale.

July	August	September	October	November	December

Siena Palio (*see p345*), held on 2 July and 16 August

Italy won the World Cup in 2006

The Italian football season runs from September through to May. It culminates with the Coppa Italia final, which is equivalent to the British FA Cup. Italy's football obsession, however, reaches fever pitch when the World Cup takes place every four years.

The Outdoor Athletics Championship has become very popular. One of Italy's foremost athletes is race walker Alex Schwazer, winner of an Olympic gold medal in 2008.

Key to Sporting Seasons

Football
Water polo
Rugby
Basketball
Volleyball
Skiing

The Climate of Italy

The Italian peninsula has a varied climate falling into three distinct geographical regions. Cold Alpine winters and warm, wet summers characterize the northern regions. In the extensive Po Valley, arid summers contrast with freezing, damp winters. The rest of Italy has a pleasant climate with long, hot summers and mild winters. Cooler weather along the backbone of the Apennines can bring snow during the winter months.

TRENTINO-ALTO ADIGE

°C	Apr	Jul	Oct	Jan
max	16	28	17	5
min	4	17	5	-5
sunshine	6 hrs	8 hrs	4 hrs	2 hrs
rainfall	67 mm	100 mm	83 mm	20 mm

- Average monthly maximum temperature
- Average monthly minimum temperature
- Average daily hours of sunshine
- Average monthly rainfall

Trento •
Aosta •
Milan •
Verona •
Turin •
Parma •
Genoa •
Bologna •
Florence •
Livorno •
Olbia •
Cagliari •

LOMBARDY

°C	Apr	Jul	Oct	Jan
max	18	28	17	6
min	8	18	10	-1
sunshine	5 hrs	9 hrs	5 hrs	3 hrs
rainfall	74 mm	78 mm	89 mm	64 mm

VALLE D'AOSTA AND PIEDMONT

°C	Apr	Jul	Oct	Jan
max	17	26	17	7
min	6	15	7	-2.5
sunshine	5 hrs	9 hrs	4 hrs	3 hrs
rainfall	95 mm	87 mm	85 mm	45 mm

LIGURIA

°C	Apr	Jul	Oct	Jan
max	18	28	21	12
min	11.5	20	14	6.5
sunshine	7 hrs	9 hrs	8 hrs	4 hrs
rainfall	66 mm	30 mm	74 mm	69 mm

SARDINIA

°C	Apr	Jul	Oct	Jan
max	19	29	22	14
min	10	20	14	7
sunshine	8 hrs	11 hrs	6 hrs	4 hrs
rainfall	31 mm	7 mm	48 mm	50 mm

TUSCANY

°C	Apr	Jul	Oct	Jan
max	17	29	20	10
min	8	16	15	2
sunshine	8 hrs	11 hrs	6 hrs	5 hrs
rainfall	72 mm	30 mm	90 mm	65 mm

EMILIA-ROMAGNA

°C	Apr	Jul	Oct	Jan
max	17	30	19	16
min	8.5	19	10	-1
sunshine	6 hrs	11 hrs	5 hrs	3 hrs
rainfall	58 mm	39 mm	81 mm	46 mm

THE VENETO AND FRIULI

°C			
17	28	18	7
7	18	9	0

☀			
7 hrs	9 hrs	4 hrs	2 hrs

☂			
112 mm	108 mm	134 mm	90 mm

| month | Apr | Jul | Oct | Jan |

LE MARCHE

°C			
16	27	19	8.5
9	20	13	3

☀			
6 hrs	10 hrs	5 hrs	3 hrs

☂			
56 mm	55 mm	77 mm	67 mm

| month | Apr | Jul | Oct | Jan |

UMBRIA

°C			
19	29	19	8
6	16	9	1

☀			
5 hrs	10 hrs	6 hrs	3 hrs

☂			
79 mm	44 mm	92 mm	75 mm

| month | Apr | Jul | Oct | Jan |

ABRUZZO, MOLISE AND PUGLIA

°C			
18	28	21	13
10	20	14	6

☀			
6 hrs	10 hrs	6 hrs	4 hrs

☂			
47 mm	27 mm	68 mm	61 mm

| month | Apr | Jul | Oct | Jan |

ROME AND LAZIO

°C			
18	29	22	12
9	19	13	4.5

☀			
6 hrs	10 hrs	7 hrs	5 hrs

☂			
51 mm	21 mm	95 mm	87 mm

| month | Apr | Jul | Oct | Jan |

NAPLES AND CAMPANIA

°C			
19	30	22	13
12	21	18	7

☀			
7 hrs	11 hrs	6 hrs	4 hrs

☂			
58 mm	12 mm	68 mm	85 mm

| month | Apr | Jul | Oct | Jan |

SICILY

°C			
19	29	24	15
12	20	16	9

☀			
8 hrs	11 hrs	7 hrs	4 hrs

☂			
29 mm	7 mm	59 mm	59 mm

| month | Apr | Jul | Oct | Jan |

BASILICATA AND CALABRIA

°C			
18	29.5	21.5	13
9.5	18.5	14	6.5

☀			
6 hrs	10 hrs	5 hrs	4 hrs

☂			
70 mm	13 mm	86 mm	90 mm

| month | Apr | Jul | Oct | Jan |

Trieste
Venice
Padova
Ferrara
Ravenna
Ancona
Perugia
Pescara
L'Aquila
Rome
Foggia
Bari
Naples
Salerno
Potenza
Taranto
Catanzaro
Reggio di Calabria
Messina
Catania
Agrigento

NORTHEAST ITALY

Northeast Italy at a Glance

The sheer variety to be found in northeast Italy makes it a fascinating area to explore. The majestic Dolomites dominate the north, straddling Trentino-Alto Adige and the Veneto, and are dotted with medieval castles and modern skiing resorts. On the plain, the cities of Verona, Vicenza and Padua are all noted for outstanding architecture and museums, while the rural hinterland boasts beautiful villas. The incomparable and spectacular city of Venice, with its magnificent monuments, rises from the lagoon. Further east, in Friuli, there are important Roman remains. This map pinpoints some of the highlights.

Malles
Venosta

Merano
(Meran)

Bressanone

Bolzano
(Bozen)

TRENTINO-ALTO-ADIGE
(See pp170–79)

Trento

Riva del
Gardo

Rovereto

Bassano
del Grappo

THE VENETO AND FRIUL
(See pp142–69)

Lake
Garda

Vicenza

Villafranca
di Verona

Verona

Padua

Montagnana

Monselic

Adige

Rovigo

Alto Adige is a dramatic region of snow-covered mountain valleys scattered with forbidding castles and onion-domed churches in the Tyrolean style *(see pp174–5)*.

The Dolomites *(see pp86–7)* form the spectacular back-drop to many towns in northeast Italy, among them Trento, the region's capital *(see pp178–9)*.

Verona is one of the loveliest cities in the Veneto, boasting the Castelvecchio and a Roman arena now used for performances of opera *(see pp146–51)*.

Vicenza, a model Renaissance city, is dominated by the buildings of Palladio, such as the Palazzo della Ragione and La Rotonda *(see pp154–7)*.

◄ Santa Maddalena with the Dolomites in the background

Udine in Friuli is an interesting city which centres on the elegant Piazza della Libertà. The piazza contains imposing statues, such as this colossal Hercules and the Porticato di San Giovanni *(see pp166–7)*.

Locator Map

0 kilometres 40
0 miles 20

Brunico

Cortina d'Ampezzo

Tarvisio

Tolmezzo

FRIULI-
VENEZIA
GIULIA

Belluno

Vittorio
Veneto

Pordenone

Udine

Gorizia

Piave

Oderzo

Monfalcone

Treviso

VENETO

Caorle

Trieste

Mestre

Venice
(see inset below)

Chioggia

Aquileia, once a splendid Roman city, is filled with ancient remains, such as this Mausoleum. Its Basilica houses early Christian mosaics *(see p168)*.

Padua boasts several major sights, among them the Basilica di Sant'Antonio and the Cappella degli Scrovegni with its frescoes by Giotto *(see pp158–63)*.

Basilica di San Marco in Venice is one of Europe's finest Byzantine buildings, with a magnificent gilded interior *(see pp114–17)*.

VENICE
(See pp88–141)

The Palazzo Ducale is a masterpiece of Venetian Gothic architecture *(see pp118–20)*.

CANNAREGIO

Canal Grande

SANTA
CROCE

SAN POLO

CASTELLO

SAN MARCO

DORSODURO

0 kilometres 1
0 miles 0.5

LA GIUDECCA

The Flavours of Northeast Italy

This diverse region is the least Italian area of Italy. Bordering on Balkan and Austro-Hungarian territory, its food reflects this rich culture and landscape. Venice's traditional trading links have given a Middle Eastern flavour to some dishes, such as sweet and sour *saor* sauce, and spices like nutmeg, saffron and cinnamon feature widely. While pasta is eaten, many dishes are accompanied with the more typical polenta, made from yellow maize flour, and risotto is also a favourite. Butter is sometimes used instead of olive oil. From hearty, rib-sticking fare to the most delicate and sophisticated of dishes, this is a region full of gastronomic surprises.

Saffron

Delicate, sweet fried pastries in a Trieste bakery

The Veneto & Venice

The Veneto is now one of Italy's main rice-growing regions. Rice was introduced from Spain by the Arabs, and is the staple ingredient for many versatile local dishes. Creamy risottos come in many guises including *di mare* (with seafood), in which cuttlefish ink gives the dish a dramatic, dark appearance. The Veneto's favourite pasta is *bigoli*, a thick, noodle-like spaghetti.

Vegetables are plentiful, including courgettes (zucchini), asparagus, red radicchio (endive) from Treviso and variegated radicchio from Castelfranco.

Venetian specialities include *cichetti* and *antipasti* – snacks and starters such as marinaded sardines, fried artichokes (*articiochi* in Venetian dialect), and seafood in bite-size portions, especially mussels (*peoci*). Venetian crab (*granceola*) is highly prized, and the local fish soup (*sopa de pesse*) is deliciously hearty. Finely sliced raw beef (*carpaccio*), had its origins here, created by Giuseppe Cipriani at Venice's Harry's Bar. Delicious, traditional *tiramisù* is also said to originate from Venice, and sorbets were common too. It was the Venetians who introduced cane sugar to Europe and their sweet tooth is still evident in the rich candied fruit, sultanas and pine nuts acquired from the Turks and Byzantines.

Caper berries | Marinated white anchovies | Olives wrapped in anchovies | Seafood cocktail

Selection of Venetian *antipasti*, the perfect appetizer

Regional Dishes and Specialities

Antipasto di frutti di mare (a mixed seafood appetizer) is a special favourite in Venice, where the ingredients come fresh from the Adriatic. From lovely Lake Garda, *anguilla del pescatore* (stewed eel), *lavarelli al vino bianco* (lake fish in white wine) and *carpione* (a type of lake trout) are all fishy delights. Another fish speciality of the region is *baccalà alla veneziana*, made with dried salt cod. Pork and salamis feature throughout the area but in Friuli goose is often used as an alternative to pork, with succulent cured meat offerings such as *salame d'oca* (goose salami). Game is also found on the menu, together with sauerkraut and filling goulash, while desserts often have an Austrian flavour too, such as *apfel strudel*. But the region is also proud of claiming as its own the decadent, classic Italian dessert *tiramisù*.

Asparagus

Sarde in Saor Venetian speciality of fried sardines in a sweet and sour onion marinade, with pine nuts.

Delivering fresh vegetables on the waterways of Venice

Staple dishes include cured meats such as *speck* (smoked ham) and salamis, as well as warming soups including the classic minestrone. Bread dumplings – *canederli* in Italian but *knödel* in Alto Adige – feature more than pasta. Trentino risottos include sweet and savoury variations. Especially good are those made with *finferli* mushrooms, highly prized and similar to Tuscan *porcini* (ceps) in flavour and quality. Alpine trout is flavoursome and game dishes, especially venison and rabbit, are popular in season, often served with polenta. The Trentino apple is crisp and delicious.

Friuli-Venezia Giulia

A culinary crossroads, this region marks the meeting point of Slavic, Germanic and Latin traditions and was once the poorest of the northern Italian regions. Varieties of Hungarian goulash and

Fresh radicchio and peppers piled high in a Treviso market

Austrian strudels often appear on local menus. The area produces fine sweet ham and prosciutto (including the fabled, succulent San Daniele). Goose is a staple dish, as is Istrian lamb, grazed in the open air on local herbs and grasses that impart a delicious flavour.

Trieste is famous for its Viennese pastries and sweet *gnocchi*, prune dumplings sprinkled with sugar and cinnamon. Friuli's dairy speciality is Montasio, a hard cheese made from cow's milk.

Trentino & Alto Adige

Strong Austrian influences from the Alto Adige combine with hearty fare from the mountainous region of Trentino as well as more southern Italian flavours.

On the Menu

Carpaccio *(Venice & the Veneto)* Wafer-thin slices of raw beef in extra virgin olive oil with rocket leaves and slivers of Parmesan cheese.

Fegato alla Veneziana Calf's liver served on a bed of onions.

Jota *(Friuli-Venezia Giulia)* A soup of barley and sauerkraut. This cheap and filling dish is often mixed with *brovada* – turnips that have been steeped in a wooden cask of grape pressings.

Strangolapreti *(Trentino-Alto Adige)* Dumplings *(gnocchi)* made with bread, spinach or potatoes, coated with butter and cheese. Literally means "priest stranglers"!

Risi e bisi Soft and moist risotto mixing rice with fresh peas, sometimes with ham and Parmesan cheese.

Polenta Cornmeal porridge served plain as a side dish, often with rabbit, or *con baccalà* (with salt cod).

Tiramisù A rich pudding of mascarpone, sponge fingers, coffee and marsala. The name means "pick me up".

Understanding Architecture in Venice and the Veneto

Trade contact with the East led medieval Venice to develop its own exotic style – known as Venetian Gothic – blending Byzantine domes and Islamic minarets with European Gothic pointed arches and quatrefoils. In the 16th century, Palladio introduced his interpretations of Classical architecture through a series of churches, public buildings and rural villas in Venice and the Veneto. The 17th century brought the Baroque style, though its exuberance was tempered by Palladio-influenced restraint.

Andrea Palladio
(1508–80)

The Architecture of Venice: Byzantine to Baroque

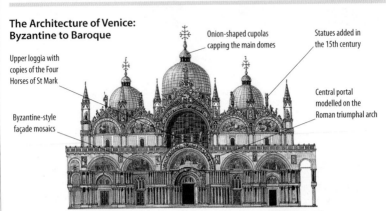

Onion-shaped cupolas capping the main domes

Statues added in the 15th century

Upper loggia with copies of the Four Horses of St Mark

Central portal modelled on the Roman triumphal arch

Byzantine-style façade mosaics

The Basilica di San Marco, western Europe's finest Byzantine church (completed 11th century), was given lavish treatment to make it a dazzling shrine for the relics of St Mark, the Evangelist, and a fitting symbol of Venetian aspirations *(see pp114–17)*.

The Genius of Palladio

Doric columns supporting the first floor, Ionic above

Shaded loggias for escaping the heat

Palazzo Chiericati is a huge mansion of 1550, its simple style borrowed from the ancient Romans. It was once surrounded by water to reflect the statues of Classical deities along its roof *(see p156)*.

Arcades linking the wings to the central block

Symmetrical façade

Villa Barbaro at Masèr was one of the villas designed by Palladio from the 1550s when it became fashionable for rich Venetians to acquire rural estates. This villa is typical, combining a working farm, housed in the side wings, with the elegant buildings of a country house *(see p153)*.

Where to see the Architecture

A vaporetto trip along the Grand Canal in Venice (*see pp92–5*) is a splendid way of getting an overview of Venetian architecture. Ca'd'Oro, Ca'Rezzonico and Ca' Pesaro may also be visited as they contain museums and a visit to

Typical Venetian Gothic window

the Basilica di San Marco and the Palazzo Ducale is a must. There are numerous examples of Palladio's architecture in the Veneto, but the star is the Villa Barbaro (*see p153*). Several of his villas line the Brenta Canal (*see p164*), and the town of Vicenza (*see pp154–7*) is full of his buildings, including La Rotonda, his famous villa.

Arcading influenced by the Palazzo Ducale

Florid tracery inlaid with azure

Finials once covered in gold leaf

Ca d'Oro, the 15th-century "House of Gold", reveals Moorish influence in its roof finials and sinuous pointed arches (*see p98*).

Deep recesses creating play of light and shade

Keystones carved as helmeted heads

Swags of fruit, ribbons and flowers

The 17th-century Ca' Pesaro typifies the Venetian Baroque style – Classical columns and rich, but subtle ornamentation (*see p93*).

Giant composite columns

Istrian marble, chosen to catch the changing light of the lagoon

Statues and memorials to patrons of the church

San Giorgio Maggiore, built in 1559–80, is marvellously sited at the entrance to the Venetian inner harbour. It broke from the prevailing Gothic style, introducing the clean simplicity and harmonious proportions of Classical architecture to Venice, and more resembles an ancient Roman temple than a Christian church (*see pp124–5*).

Pediment with coat of arms

Sundials at each end

The Dolomites

The Dolomites are the most distinctive and beautiful mountains in Italy. They were formed of mineralized coral which was laid down beneath the sea during the Triassic era, and uplifted when the European and African continental plates dramatically collided 60 million years ago. Unlike the glacier-eroded saddles and ridges of the main body of the Alps, the pale rocks here have been carved by the corrosive effects of ice, sun and rain, sculpting the cliffs, spires and "organ pipes" that we see today. The eastern and western ranges of the Dolomites have slightly different characteristics; the eastern section is the more awe-inspiring, especially the Catinaccio (or Rosengarten) range which is particularly beautiful, turning rose pink at sunset.

Onion dome, a common local feature

Strada Delle Dolomiti

One of the most spectacular routes through the Dolomites links Bolzano (see p176) with Cortina d'Ampezzo (see p165). It follows the lie of the land, passing some of the greatest peaks, and the most majestic landscape.

S49

Dobbiaco

Rienza

S51

TRE CIME DI LAVAREDO

Lago di Misurina

Cortina d'Ampezzo

SASSO LUNGO

S48

CINQUE TORRI

S51

Bolzano

Pieve di Cadore

TORRI DEL VAIOLET

Canazei

MARMOLADA

Adige

S241

S12

0 kilometres 10

0 miles 5

S51

Distinctive Peaks of the Dolomites

The peaks of the Dolomites include several with distinctive shapes and some of the highest mountains in the range. Many are easily identifiable and have been individually named.

4,000 m (13,123 ft)

3,000 m (9,842 ft)

2,000 m (6,562 ft)

1,000 m (3,281 ft)

Approximate heights

Marmolada 3,343 m (10,968 ft)

Sasso Lungo 3,179 m (10,430 ft)

Cinque Torri 2,366 m (7,762 ft)

The Cinque Torri or Five Towers rise from a single base between Passo Falzarego and Cortina d'Ampezzo.

Sasso Lungo is a tall peak easily recognized by its distinctive scar. It is joined to the Sasso Piatto.

Marmolada is the highest peak in the Dolomite chain. A cable-car ascends to 3,000 m above the glacier.

Lago di Misurina is a large and beautiful lake lying beside the resort of Misurina. The crystal clear waters reflect the surrounding mountains, mirroring various peaks such as the distinctive and dramatic Sorapiss, in shimmering colours.

Outdoor activities in this area of dramatic landscapes include skiing in winter, and walking and rambling along the footpaths, and to picnic sites, in summer. Chair-lifts from the main resorts provide easy access up into the mountains themselves, transporting you into some breathtaking scenery.

Torri del Vaiolet
2,243 m (7,375 ft)

Tre Cime di Lavaredo
2,999 m (9,839 ft)

The Torri del Vaiolet is part of the beautiful Catinaccio range, known for its colour.

Tre Cime di Lavaredo or Drei Zinnen dominate the valleys north of the Lago di Misurina.

Nature in the Dolomites

Forests and meadows support a breathtaking richness of wildlife in the region. Alpine plants, which flower between June and September, have evolved their miniature form to survive the harsh winds.

The Flora

Gentian roots are used to make a bitter local liqueur.

The orange mountain lily thrives on sun-baked slopes.

The pretty burser's saxifrage grows in clusters on rocks.

Devil's claw has distinctive pink flower heads.

The Fauna

The ptarmigan changes its plumage from mottled brown in summer to snow white in winter for effective camouflage. It feeds on mountain berries and young plant shoots.

The chamois, a shy mountain antelope prized for its soft skin, is protected in the national parks, where hunting is forbidden.

Roe deer are very common as their natural predators – wolves and lynx – are decreasing in number. An appetite for tree saplings causes problems for foresters.

VENICE

Lying in the extreme northeast of Italy, Venice, gateway to
the Orient, became an independent Byzantine province in
the 10th century. Exclusive trading links with the East and
victory in the Crusade of 1204 brought wealth and power,
which were only gradually eroded by European and Turkish
rivals. Today, Venice's ties are with the local Veneto region
which stretches from the flat river plains to the Dolomites.

Venice is one of the few cities in the
world that can be truly described as
unique. It survives against all the odds,
built on a series of low mud banks amid
the tidal waters of the Adriatic, and
regularly subject to floods. During the
Middle Ages, under the leadership of
successive doges, Venice expanded its
power and influence throughout the
Mediterranean to Constantinople
(modern Istanbul). The immense wealth
of the city was celebrated in art and
architecture throughout the city.
The riches of St Mark's alone bear
witness to Venice's position as a world
power from the 12th to 14th centuries.
After slowly losing ground to the new
states of Europe, however, it fell to
Napoleon in 1797. Finally, Venice joined
the Kingdom of Italy in 1866, so
bringing unity to the country for the
first time in its history. Today, Venice has
found a new role. Her palazzi have
become museums, shops, hotels and
apartments and her convents have been
turned into centres for art restoration. Yet
little of the essential fabric of Venice has
altered in 200 years. The city's sounds are
still those of footsteps and the cries of
boatmen. The only engines are those of
barges delivering supplies or waterbuses
ferrying passengers between stops. The
same well-worn streets are still trodden.
More than 20 million visitors a year
succumb to the magic of this improbable
place whose "streets are full of water"
and where the glories of the past are
evident at every turn.

Tourists relax at cafés along a canal in Burano, Venice

◀ Dusk settles over the peaceful Venetian Lagoon on the Adriatic Coast

Exploring Venice

Venice is divided into six ancient administrative districts or *sestieri*: Cannaregio, Castello, San Marco, Dorsoduro, San Polo and Santa Croce. You can walk to most places in Venice itself, and take a ride on a waterbus to any of the islands. The Venice Card *(see p634)* covers all transport as well as admission to most museums, such as Ca' Rezzonico, the Palazzo Ducale and Museo Correr.

Sights at a Glance

Churches

1 Madonna dell'Orto
3 San Giovanni Grisostomo
4 Santa Maria dei Miracoli
6 San Giacomo dell'Orio
7 San Polo
8 Santa Maria Gloriosa dei Frari *pp102–3*
10 San Rocco
11 San Pantalon
13 San Nicolò dei Mendicoli
14 San Sebastiano
17 Santa Maria della Salute
19 Basilica di San Marco *pp114–15*
24 Santo Stefano
25 Santi Giovanni e Paolo
27 Santa Maria Formosa
28 San Zaccaria
30 San Giovanni in Bragora

Buildings and Monuments

5 Rialto
20 Palazzo Ducale *pp118–19*
21 Torre dell'Orologio
22 Campanile

26 Statue of Colleoni
29 Scuola di San Giorgio degli Schiavoni
31 Arsenale

Museums and Galleries

2 Ca' d'Oro
9 Scuola Grande di San Rocco *pp104–5*
12 Ca' Rezzonico
15 Accademia *pp110–11*
16 Peggy Guggenheim Collection
18 Punta della Dogana
23 Museo Correr

Lagoon

33 Murano
34 Burano
35 Torcello *pp126–7*

0 metres		500
0 yards		500

Santa Maria della Salute, at the mouth of the Grand Canal

For keys to symbols *see back flap*

A gondola ride along the Grand Canal

CANNAREGIO

SANTA CROCE

SAN POLO

CASTELLO

SAN MARCO

Ponte di Rialto

Ponte dell'Accademia

PIAZZA S. MARCO

GIUDECCA

Canale della Giudecca

The Lagoon

Marco Polo

Mestre

VENICE

Getting Around

The only road into Venice is the S11 from Mestre, which carries you over the causeway to the Tronchetto and Piazzale Roma where there are car parks and bus stops. Rail travellers arrive at Santa Lucia station on the Grand Canal. In the city, public transport is by *vaporetto,* or waterbus – the No.1 is best for sightseeing as it travels the length of the Grand Canal (*see pp140–41*).

The Grand Canal: Santa Lucia to the Rialto

The best way to view the Grand Canal as it winds through the heart of the city is from a *vaporetto*, or waterbus. Two lines travel the length of the canal *(see p635)*. The palaces lining the waterway were built over a span of five centuries and present a panoramic survey of the city's history, almost all bearing the name of some once-great Venetian family.

San Marcuola
The church was rebuilt in the 18th century, but the planned new façade overlooking the canal was never completed.

San Geremia houses the relics of St Lucy, once kept in the church of Santa Lucia where the railway station now stands.

Palazzo Labia
Between 1745 and 1750, Giambattista Tiepolo decorated the ballroom with scenes from the life of Cleopatra.

Canale di Cannaregio

Palazzo Corner-Contarini

San Marcuola

Riva di Biasio

Ferrovia

FS

Ponte degli Scalzi

Fondaco dei Turchi
A warehouse for Turkish traders in the 17th–19th centuries, this is now the Natural History Museum.

San Simeone Piccolo
This 18th-century domed church is based on the Pantheon in Rome.

The Gondolas of Venice

The gondola has been a part of Venice since the 11th century. With its slim hull and flat underside, the craft is perfectly adapted to negotiating narrow, shallow canals. There is a slight leftward curve to the prow, which counteracts the force of the oar, preventing the gondola from going round in circles.

In 1562 it was decreed that all gondolas should be black to stop people making an ostentatious show of their wealth. For special occasions they are decorated with flowers. Today, gondola rides are expensive and usually taken by tourists *(see p635)*. However, *traghetti* (gondola ferries) are a cheap, convenient way of crossing the Grand Canal.

Gondolas tied up by steps

Ca' d'Oro
The delicate Gothic tracery of the façade makes this a striking landmark. Its art collection *(see p98)* includes Bernini's model for a fountain (c.1648).

Locator Map
See Venice Street Finder maps 1, 2, 3

Palazzo Vendramin Calergi
This is one of the finest early Renaissance palaces in Venice. The German composer Richard Wagner (left) died here in 1883.

The Pescheria has been the site of a busy fish market for six centuries.

Palazzo Sagredo
Graceful Veneto-Byzantine and Gothic arches are both featured on the waterfront façade.

Palazzo Michiel dalle Colonne takes its name from its distinctive colonnade.

The Rialto Bridge *(see p101)* spans the canal in the commercial heart of the city.

San Stae

Ca' d'Oro

San Stae
The façade of this Baroque church is richly adorned with statues. It is a popular concert venue.

Rialto Mercato

Ca' Pesaro
The huge, stately Baroque palace today houses a gallery of modern art and the Oriental Museum.

Rialto

The Grand Canal: the Rialto to San Marco

After passing the Rialto, the canal doubles back on itself along a stretch known as La Volta (the bend). It then widens out and the views become more spectacular approaching San Marco. Façades may have faded and foundations battered with the tides, yet the canal remains, in the words of the French ambassador in 1495, "the most beautiful street in the world".

Palazzo Mocenigo
Lord Byron stayed in this huge 18th-century palace in 1818.

Sant' Angelo

San Tomà

Palazzo Garzoni is a renovated Gothic palace, now part of the university.

Ca' Rezzonico
Now a museum of 18th-century Venice *(see p107)*, the palace was the last home of the poet Robert Browning, seen here with his son Pen.

San Samuele

Ca' Rezzonico

Palazzo Grassi
This elegant palazzo dates from the 1730s. Bought by French tycoon François-Henri Pinault in 2005, it is now used for art exhibitions.

Ponte dell'Accademia

Palazzo Capello Malipiero
The palace was rebuilt in 1622. Beside it stands the 12th-century campanile of San Samuele.

Accademia

Accademia
The world's greatest collection of Venetian paintings is housed here in the former Scuola della Carità *(see pp110–11)*, which has a Baroque façade by Giorgio Massari.

Palazzo Barbaro
Novelist Henry James wrote *The Aspern Papers* here in 1888.

The Riva del Vin is the quay where wine *(vin)* used to be unloaded. It is one of the few spots where you can sit and relax on the banks of the Grand Canal.

Locator Map
See Venice Street Finder maps 6, 7

Palazzo Barzizza, rebuilt in the 17th century, preserves its early 13th-century façade.

Peggy Guggenheim Collection
A one-storey palazzo houses Guggenheim's great modern art collection *(see pp108–9)*.

Santa Maria della Salute
The vast weight of this Baroque church is supported by over one million timber piles *(p109)*.

Palazzo Gritti-Pisani
The former home of the Gritti family is now the luxury Gritti Palace hotel *(see p563)*.

San Marco Vallaresso

Harry's Bar, founded in 1931 by Giuseppe Cipriani, is famous for its cocktails.

Salute

Santa Maria del Giglio

Palazzo Dario
Beautiful coloured marbles give the 1487 palace a highly individual façade. Legend has it the building is cursed.

The Punta della Dogana customs house, built in the 17th century, now contains the François Pinault Foundation of contemporary art. It is crowned by a golden globe topped by a weathervane *(see p109)*.

Gondolas moored along the Grand Canal at sunrise ▶

Madonna dell'Orto, with 15th-century façade statues of St Christopher and the Apostles

❶ Madonna dell'Orto

Campo Madonna dell'Orto. **Map** 2 F2. **Tel** 041 719 933. 🚊 Madonna dell'Orto. **Open** 10am–5pm Mon–Sat, noon–6pm Sun. **Closed** 1 Jan, 25 Dec. 🏛 🖂 **w** madonnadellorto.org

This lovely Gothic church, founded in the mid-14th century, was dedicated to St Christopher, patron saint of travellers, to protect the boatmen who ferried passengers to the islands in the northern lagoon. A 15th-century statue of the saint, restored by the Venice in Peril fund, stands above the main portal. The dedication was changed and the church reconstructed in the early 15th century, after the discovery, in a nearby vegetable garden (orto), of a statue of the Virgin Mary said to have miraculous powers.

The interior, faced almost entirely in brick, is large and uncluttered. On the right is a magnificent painting by Cima da Conegliano, St John the Baptist and Other Saints (c.1493). The vacant space in the chapel opposite belongs to Giovanni Bellini's Madonna with Child (c.1478), stolen in 1993 for the third time.

The church's greatest remaining treasures are the works of art by Tintoretto, who was a parishioner of the church. His tomb lies with that of his children, in the chapel to the right of the chancel. The most dramatic of his works are the

towering masterpieces that decorate the chancel (1562–4). On the right wall is the Last Judgment, whose turbulent content caused John Ruskin's wife, Effie, to flee the church in horror. In The Adoration of the Golden Calf on the left wall, the figure carrying the calf, fourth from the left, is believed to be a portrait of the artist. Inside the chapel of San Mauro, off the end of the right nave, stands a statue of the Madonna by Giovanni de' Santi. It was restored by the Venice in Peril fund, and inspired the rededication of the church.

❷ Ca' d'Oro

Calle Ca' d'Oro. **Map** 3 A4. **Tel** 041 520 03 45. 🚊 Ca' d'Oro. **Open** 8:15am–2pm Mon, 8:15am–7:15pm Tue–Sat (last adm: 6:45pm), 10am–6pm Sun. **Closed** 1 Jan, 1 May, 25 Dec; Galleria: Sun & pub hols (Jan). 🏛 🏠 🏠 ♿ 🖂 **w** cadoro.org

In 1420 Marino Contarini, a wealthy patrician, commissioned the building of what he hoped would be the city's most magnificent palace (see p85). The building's intricate carving was entrusted to a team of Venetian and Lombard craftsmen, while the façade was adorned with the most elaborate and expensive decorative finishes,

Tullio Lombardo's Double Portrait

including gold leaf, vermilion and ultramarine. Over the years the palace was extensively remodelled, and by the 18th century was in a state of semi-dereliction. In 1846 it was bought by the Russian Prince Troubetzkoy for the famous ballerina Maria Taglioni. Under her direction the palace suffered barbaric restoration, losing, among other things, its staircase and much of its original stonework. It was finally rescued by Baron Giorgio Franchetti, a wealthy patron of the arts, who bequeathed both the building and his private art collection to the state in 1915.

Pride of place on the first of the gallery's two floors goes to Andrea Mantegna's St Sebastian (1506), the artist's last work, which occupies a special alcove of its own. Elsewhere, the floor's main exhibits are ranged around the portego (gallery). This is largely dominated by the vivid 15th-century Double Portrait (c.1493) by the sculptor Tullio Lombardo; Sansovino's lunette of the Madonna and Child (c.1530); and several bronze reliefs by the Paduan Andrea Briosco, "Il Riccio" (1470–1532). Rooms leading off the portego to the right contain numerous bronzes and medallions, with some examples by Pisanello and Gentile Bellini.

Paintings here also include the famous Madonna of the Beautiful Eyes, attributed to Giovanni Bellini, a Madonna and Child, attributed to Alvise Vivarini (both late 15th century), and Carpaccio's Annunciation and Death of the Virgin (both c.1504). A room to the left of the portego contains non-Venetian paintings, notably a Flagellation by Luca Signorelli (c.1480). A lovely staircase leads to the second floor, which opens with a room hung with tapestries.

The magnificent Gothic façade of the Ca' d'Oro, or House of Gold

It has bronzes by Alessandro Vittoria and paintings by Titian and Van Dyck. The *portego* displays frescoes (c.1532) by Pordenone from the cloister of Santo Stefano, while an anteroom contains damaged frescoes by Titian taken from the Fondaco dei Tedeschi.

Giovanni Bellini's 1513 altarpiece in San Giovanni Grisostomo

❸ San Giovanni Grisostomo

Campo San Giovanni Grisostomo. **Map** 3 B5. **Tel** 041 523 52 93. Rialto. **Open** 8:15am–12:15pm, 3–7pm daily. **Closed** during mass. W sancancianovenezia.it

This terracotta-coloured church is located near to the Rialto. Built between 1479 and 1504, it is a lovely Renaissance design, the last work of Mauro Coducci.

The interior is built on a Greek-cross plan. The light meter illuminates Giovanni Bellini's *St Jerome with Saints Christopher and Augustine* (1513) above the first altar on the right. This was most probably Bellini's last painting, executed when he was in his eighties.

Over the high altar hangs Sebastiano del Piombo's *St John Chrysostom and Six Saints* (1509–11).

❹ Santa Maria dei Miracoli

Campo dei Miracoli. **Map** 3 B5. **Tel** 041 275 04 62. Rialto, Fondamenta Nuove. **Open** 10am–5pm Mon–Sat. **Closed** 1 Jan, 25 Dec. W chorusvenezia.org

An exquisite masterpiece of early Renaissance architecture, the Miracoli is the church where many Venetians like to get married. Tucked away in a maze of alleys and waterways in eastern Cannaregio, it is small and somewhat elusive.

Santa Maria dei Miracoli is decorated in various shades of marble, with some fine bas reliefs and sculpture. It was built in 1481–9 by the architect Pietro Lombardo and his sons to enshrine *The Virgin and Child* (1408), a painting believed to have miraculous powers. The picture, by Nicoló di Pietro, can still be seen above the altar.

The interior of the church is embellished by pink, white and grey marble. It is crowned by a barrel-vaulted ceiling (1528) which has 50 portraits of saints

Decorative column from inside Santa Maria dei Miracoli

and prophets. The balustrade, between the nave and the chancel, is decorated by Tullio Lombardo's carved figures of St Francis, Archangel Gabriel, the Virgin and St Clare.

The screen around the high altar and the medallions of the Evangelists in the cupola spandrels are also Lombardo's work. Above the main door, the choir gallery was used by the nuns from the neighbouring convent, who entered the church through an overhead gallery. Santa Maria dei Miracoli has undergone a major restoration programme, which was funded by the American Save Venice organization.

Santa Maria Dei Miracoli

This beautifully proportioned façade is composed of decorated panels and multicoloured polished marble.

Carving of saint

The semi-circular crowning lunette emphasizes the church's jewel-box appearance.

A false loggia is formed of Ionic arches, inset with windows. The marble used was reportedly left over from the building of San Marco.

Virgin and Child by Giorgio Lascaris

The marble panels are fixed to the bricks by metal hooks. This method prevents the build-up of damp and salt water behind the panels, and dates from the Renaissance.

Street-by-Street: San Polo

The Rialto bridge and markets make this area a magnet for visitors. Traditionally the city's commercial quarter, it was here that bankers, brokers and merchants conducted their affairs. Streets are no longer lined with stalls selling spices and fine fabrics, but the food markets and pasta shops are unmissable. Away from the bridge, streets quickly become less crowded, leading to tiny squares and quiet churches.

The Rialto Markets have existed for centuries and are renowned for their produce. The Pescheria sells fresh fish and seafood.

The 17th-century church of San Cassiano houses a carved altar (1696) and a *Crucifixion* by Tintoretto (1568).

Key

— Suggested route

0 metres 75
0 yards 75

The Frari

San Silvestro

Sant'Aponal has a façade decorated with worn Gothic reliefs. The church was founded in the 11th century, but is now deconsecrated.

For keys to map symbols see back flap

San Giovanni Elemosinario is an inconspicuous church that was rebuilt in the early 16th century, although its campanile dates from the end of the 14th century. Inside it are interesting frescoes by Pordenone.

Locator Map
*See Venice Street Finder
maps 2, 3, 6, 7*

The lively Erberia, selling fresh fruit and vegetables

San Giacomo di Rialto's
clock face (1410), which
has sadly been a poor
time-keeper over the
years, adorns one
of Venice's oldest
churches.

Market
entrance

❺ ★ Rialto
One of Venice's most famous
sights, the bridge offers fine
views of the Grand Canal, and
marks the heart of the city.

❺ Rialto

Ponte di Rialto. **Map** 7 A1. Rialto.

The Rialto takes its name from
rivo alto (high bank) and was
one of the first areas of Venice
to be inhabited. A banking and
then market district, it remains
one of the city's busiest and
most bustling areas. Locals and
visitors alike jostle among the
colourful stalls of the Erberia
(fruit and vegetable market)
and Pescheria (fish market).

Stone bridges were built
in Venice as early as the 12th
century, but it was not until
1588, after the collapse, decay
or sabotage of earlier wooden
structures, that a solid stone
bridge was designed for the
Rialto. Completed in 1591, the
new bridge remained the only
means of crossing the Grand
Canal until 1854, when the
Accademia bridge was built.

Few visitors leave Venice
without crossing the famous
bridge. It is a wonderful place
to watch and photograph the
constant activity of boats on
the Grand Canal below.

❻ San Giacomo
dell'Orio

Campo San Giacomo dell'Orio. **Map** 2
E5. **Tel** 041 275 04 62. Riva di Biasio
or San Stae. **Open** 10am–5pm Mon–
Sat. **Closed** 1 Jan, 25 Dec.
W chorusvenezia.org

This church is a focal point of
a quiet quarter of Santa Croce.
The name "dell'Orio" may derive
from a laurel tree *(alloro)* that
once stood near the church.
San Giacomo was founded
in the 9th century, rebuilt
in 1225 and thereafter

repeatedly modified, resulting
in a mixture of styles. The
campanile, basilica ground
plan vfrom the 13th century. The
ship's keel roof and the columns
are Gothic, and the apses
are Renaissance.

The sacristy contains a
beautiful ceiling by Veronese
in addition to some interesting
altar paintings.

❼ San Polo

Campo San Polo. **Map** 6 F1.
Tel 041 275 04 62. San Silvestro.
Open 10am– 5pm Mon–Sat.
Closed 1 Jan, 25 Dec.
W chorusvenezia.org

Founded in the 9th century,
rebuilt in the 15th and
revamped in the early 19th
in Neo-Classical style,
this church is worth visiting
for the lovely Gothic portal
and the Romanesque lions at
the foot of the 14th-century
campanile – one holds a
serpent between its paws,
the other a human head.

Inside, follow the signs for
the *Via Crucis del Tiepolo* – 14
pictures of the Stations of the
Cross (1749) by the painter
Giandomenico Tiepolo: many
include vivid portraits of
Venetian life. The church also
has paintings by Veronese,
Palma il Giovane (the Younger)
and a dramatic *Last Supper*
by Tintoretto.

A Romanesque lion at the base of San Polo's
14th-century campanile

❽ Santa Maria Gloriosa dei Frari

More commonly known as the Frari (a corruption of Frati, meaning brothers), this vast Gothic church dwarfs the eastern area of San Polo. The first church on the site was built by Franciscan friars in 1250–1338, but was replaced by a larger building completed in the mid-15th century. The airy interior is striking for its sheer size and for the quality of its works of art, including masterpieces by Titian and Giovanni Bellini, a statue by Donatello and several grandiose tombs.

★ **Monks' Choir**
This consists of three-tiered stalls (1468), carved with bas-reliefs of saints and Venetian city scenes.

★ **Assumption of the Virgin**
Titian's glowing and spectacular work (1518) draws the eye through the monk's choir, to the altar, and heavenwards.

Rood Screen (1475)
Pietro Lombardo and Bartolomeo Bon carved the rood screen and its decorative marble figures.

KEY

① **The campanile** is 83 m (262 ft) high, the tallest in the city after that of San Marco.

② **The former monastery**, which houses the State Archives, has two cloisters, one in the style of Sansovino, another designed by Palladio.

③ *The Madonna di Ca' Pesaro* (1526) shows Titian's mastery of light and colour.

Floorplan

The Frari's imposing cruciform interior, which is 90 m (295 ft) long, holds 12 sights that should not be missed.

VISITORS' CHECKLIST

Practical Information
Campo dei Frari. **Map** 6 D1.
Tel 041 275 04 62. **Open** 9am–6pm Mon–Sat, 1–6pm Sun & religious hols. **Closed** 1 Jan, 25 Dec. 🚫 unless attending mass. 🔔 frequent. ✉
W **basilicadeifrari.it**

Transport
🚤 San Tomà.

Key to Floorplan

1 Tomb of Canova
2 Monument to Titian
3 *Madonna di Ca' Pesaro* by Titian
4 Choir stalls
5 Corner Chapel
6 Tomb of Monteverdi
7 Tomb of Doge Nicolò Tron
8 High altar with *Assumption of the Virgin* (1518) by Titian
9 Tomb odf Doge Francesco Foscari
10 *John the Baptist* (c.1450) by Donatello
11 B Vivarini's altar painting (1474), Bernardo Chapel
12 *Madonna and Child with Saints* (1488) by Bellini

★ Madonna and Child
The sacristy's altarpiece (1488) by Bellini, with its sublime use of colour, is one of Venice's most beautiful Renaissance paintings.

Entrance

Tomb of Canova
Canova designed, but never constructed, a Neo-Classical marble pyramid like this as a monument for Titian. After Canova's death in 1822, the sculptor's pupils used a similar design for their master's tomb.

❾ Scuola Grande di San Rocco

Founded in honour of San Rocco (St Roch), a saint who dedicated his life to helping the sick, the Scuola started out as a charitable confraternity. Construction began in 1515 under Bartolomeo Bon and was continued by Scarpagnino until his death in 1549. The work was financed by donations from Venetians keen to invoke San Rocco's protection and the Scuola quickly became one of the wealthiest in Venice. In 1564 its members decided to commission Tintoretto to decorate its walls and ceilings. His earliest paintings, the first of over 50 works he eventually left in the Scuola, fill the small Sala dell'Albergo off the Upper Hall. His later paintings occupy the Ground Floor Hall, immediately within the entrance.

Restored main entrance to the Scuola di San Rocco

Tintoretto's magnificent *Crucifixion*, painted in 1565 for the Sala dell'Albergo in the Scuola di San Rocco

Ground Floor Hall

The ground floor cycle was executed in 1583–7, when Tintoretto was in his sixties, and consists of eight large paintings illustrating, among others, the life of Mary. The series starts with an *Annunciation* and ends with an *Assumption*.

The calm and tranquil scenes of *The Flight into Egypt*, *St Mary Magdalene* and *St Mary of Egypt* are remarkable for their serenity. This is portrayed most lucidly by the repentant

Detail from *The Flight into Egypt* (1582–7) by Tintoretto

hermit's isolated spiritual contemplation in *St Mary of Egypt*. In all three paintings, the landscapes are rendered with noticeably rapid strokes, and are an important part of the final composition.

Upper Hall and Sala dell'Albergo

Scarpagnino's great staircase (1544–6), with its upper flight decorated with two vast paintings commemorating the plague of 1630, leads to the Upper Hall. Here, biblical subjects decorate the ceiling and walls, painted by Tintoretto from 1575–81.

The ceiling paintings portray scenes from the Old Testament. The three large and dynamic square paintings in the centre show episodes from the Book of Exodus: *Moses Strikes Water from the Rock*, *The Miracle of the Bronze Serpent* and *The Fall of Manna in the Desert*. These all allude to the charitable aims of the Scuola

in alleviating thirst, sickness and hunger respectively. All three paintings are crowded compositions displaying much violent movement.

The vast wall paintings in the hall feature episodes from the New Testament, linking with the ceiling paintings. Two of the most striking paintings are *The Temptation of Christ*, which shows a handsome young Satan offering Christ two loaves of bread, and *The Adoration of the Shepherds*. Like *The Temptation of Christ*, *The Adoration* is composed in two halves, with a female figure, shepherds and an ox below, and the Holy Family and onlookers above.

The breathtakingly beautiful carvings below the paintings were added in the 17th century by sculptor Francesco Pianta. The figures are allegorical and include (near the altar) a caricature of Tintoretto with his palette and brushes, representing Painting.

Detail from *The Temptation of Christ* (1578–81) by Tintoretto

The easel painting *Christ Carrying the Cross* was once attributed to Giorgione, though many believe it to be by Titian.

Near the entrance to the Sala dell'Albergo, is the *Annunciation* by Titian. The Sala dell'Albergo itself holds the most breathtaking of Tintoretto's works – the *Crucifixion* (1565). Henry James

remarked of this painting: "No single picture contains more of human life; there is everything in it, including the most exquisite beauty." Tintoretto began the cycle of paintings in this room in 1564, when he won the commission with the ceiling painting *San Rocco in Glory*. On the wall opposite the *Crucifixion* are paintings of episodes from the Passion: *Christ before Pilate, The Crowning with Thorns* and *The Ascent to Calvary*.

⑩ San Rocco

Campo San Rocco. **Map** 6 D1.
Tel 041 523 48 64. 🚤 San Tomà.
Open 9:30am–5:30pm daily. ✉

On the same square as the celebrated Scuola Grande di San Rocco is the church of the same name. Designed by the sculptor and architect, Bartolomeo Bon, in 1489 and largely rebuilt in 1725, the exterior suffers from a mixture of styles. The façade was added in 1765–71. Inside, the chancel is decorated with a series of paintings by Tintoretto depicting scenes from the life of San Rocco.

⑪ San Pantalon

Campo San Pantalon. **Map** 6 D2.
Tel 041 523 58 93. 🚤 San Tomà,
Piazzale Roma. **Open** 10am–noon,
1–3pm Mon–Sat. ✉
🌐 **sanpantalon.it**

Fumiani's epic ceiling painting (1680–1740) in San Pantalon

The overwhelming feature of this late 17th-century church is its vast painted ceiling, dark, awe-inspiring and remarkable for its illusionistic effect of height. The ceiling comprises a total of 40 scenes, and admirers claim that this is the world's largest work of art on canvas.

The scenes show the martyrdom and apotheosis of the physician St Pantalon. The artist, Gian Antonio Fumiani, took 24 years (1680–1704) to achieve the masterpiece, before allegedly falling to his death from the scaffolding.

Key to Paintings

◻ Ground Floor Hall **1** The Annunciation; **2** The Adoration of the Three Kings; **3** The Flight into Egypt; **4** The Massacre of the Innocents; **5** St Mary Magdalene; **6** St Mary of Egypt; **7** The Presentation in the Temple; **8** The Assumption.

◻ Upper Hall Walls **9** San Rocco; **10** St Sebastian; **11** The Adoration of the Shepherds; **12** The Baptism of Christ; **13** The Resurrection; **14** The Agony in the Garden; **15** The Last Supper; **16** The Vision of San Rocco; **17** The Miracle of the Loaves and Fishes; **18** The Resurrection of Lazarus; **19** The Ascension; **20** Christ Heals the Paralytic; **21** The Temptation of Christ.

◻ Upper Hall Ceiling **22** Moses Saved from the Waters; **23** The Pillar of Fire; **24** Samuel and Saul; **25** Jacob's Ladder; **26** Elijah on a Chariot of Fire; **27** Elijah Fed by the Angels; **28** Daniel Saved by the Angels; **29** The Passover; **30** The Fall of Manna; **31** The Sacrifice of Isaac; **32** The Miracle of the Bronze Serpent; **33** Jonah Emerges from the Whale; **34** Moses Strikes Water from the Rock; **35** Adam and Eve; **36** Three Children in the Furnace; **37** God Appears to Moses; **38** Samson Brings out Water from the Jawbone of an Ass; **39** The Vision of the Prophet Ezekiel; **40** The Vision of Jeremiah; **41** Elisha Distributes Bread; **42** Abraham and Melchizedeck.

Ground Floor Hall　　　Upper Hall

Street-by-Street: Dorsoduro

Built on a strata of solid subsoil is the *sestiere* of Dorsoduro – the name means "hard backbone". It has as its focal point the lively Campo Santa Margherita, the largest open space in this part of Venice. The square bustles with activity, particularly in the morning when the market stalls are open, and in the evening when it is the haunt of students from nearby Ca' Foscari, now part of Venice university. The surrounding streets contain some architectural stunners, notably Ca' Rezzonico and the Scuola Grande dei Carmini, which has decorations by Tiepolo. Of the area's waterways, the delightful Rio San Barnaba is best appreciated from the Ponte dei Pugni, near the barge selling fruit and vegetables – itself a time-honoured Venetian sight. Alongside the Rio Terrà Canal there are some lively cafés and a fascinating shop selling masks for Carnevale.

Campo Santa Margherita is an ideal place for relaxing in a café.

Palazzo Zenobio, built at the end of the 17th century, has been an Armenian college since 1850. With permission, visitors can see the fine 18th-century ballroom.

Scuola Grande dei Carmini contains nine ceiling panels (1739–44) in the hall on the upper floor, painted by Tiepolo for the Carmelite confraternity.

Santa Maria dei Carmini has a Gothic side porch carved with Byzantine reliefs.

Key

— Suggested route

0 metres	50
0 yards	50

Fondamenta Gherardini runs beside the Rio San Barnaba, one of the prettiest canals in the sestiere.

★ Ca' Rezzonico
The ballroom covers the width of the palazzo once owned by Browning.

Palazzo Giustinian was home to Wagner in 1858.

Ca' Foscari was completed in 1437 for Doge Francesco Foscari.

Locator Map
See Venice Street Finder maps 5, 6

Ponte dei Pugni was a traditional scene of fist fights between rival factions. They were finally banned in 1705 for being too violent.

San Barnaba is a thriving community, with its own floating barge stall crammed with fresh fruit and vegetables. It is a focal point for tourists and locals alike.

Tiepolo's *New World* fresco, part of a series in Ca' Rezzonico

⑫ Ca' Rezzonico

Fondamenta Rezzonico 3136.
Map 6 E3. **Tel** 041 241 01 00. 🚤 Ca' Rezzonico. **Open** 10am–6pm Wed–Mon (Nov–Mar: to 5pm, last adm: 1 hr before closing). **Closed** 1 Jan, 1 May, 25 Dec. 🏛🏛🏛🏛🏛🏛🏛
Ⓦ visitmuve.it

This palazzo houses the museum of 18th-century Venice, its rooms furnished with frescoes, paintings and period pieces taken from other palaces or museums. Building began with Longhena (architect of La Salute, *see p109*) in 1667, but the funds of the Bon family, who commissioned it, ran dry before the second floor was started. In 1712 the unfinished palace was bought by the Rezzonico family of Genoa, who spent a large portion of their fortune on its completion.

The Rezzonico family sold it on, in 1888, to the famous poet Robert Browning and his son, Pen. The outstanding attraction in the palace today is Giorgio Massari's ballroom, which occupies the entire breadth of the building. It is adorned with gilded chandeliers, carved furniture by Andrea Brustolon and a ceiling with *trompe l'oeil* frescoes. Other rooms have frescoes by Giambattista Tiepolo, including his lively *Nuptial Allegory* (1758), and one by his son, Giandomenico, originally in his villa at Zianigo. There are paintings by Longhi, Guardi, and – rare in Venice – Canaletto. On the top floor is a reconstructed 18th-century apothecary's shop and the Pinacoteca Martini.

Nave of San Nicolò dei Mendicoli, one of the oldest churches in Venice

⓭ San Nicolò dei Mendicoli

Campo San Nicolò. **Map** 5 A3. **Tel** 041 275 03 82. 🚤 San Basilio. **Open** 10am–noon, 3–5:30pm Mon–Sat, 10am–noon Sun & public hols.

Contrasting with the remote and rundown area which surrounds it, this church still remains one of the most charming in Venice. Founded in the 7th century, it has been rebuilt extensively over the years. The little porch on the north flank is 15th century and once sheltered the beggars, or *mendicanti*, who gave the church its name.

Thanks to the Venice in Peril fund, in the 1970s the church underwent one of the most comprehensive restoration programmes since the floods of 1966. Flooding had become such a problem that the priest often ferried himself around the church in a small wicker boat. The floor, which was 30 cm (1 ft)

below the level of the canals, was rebuilt and raised slightly to prevent further flood damage. The roofs and lower walls were reconstructed, and paintings and statues restored.

The interior is delightfully embellished, particularly the nave with its 16th-century gilded wooden statues. These include the figure of San Nicolò himself. On the upper walls is a series of paintings of the life of Christ (c.1553) by Alvise dal Friso and other pupils of Veronese.

Outside, a small column supports a stone lion, in a humbler echo of the Column of San Marco in the Piazzetta.

⓮ San Sebastiano

Campo San Sebastiano. **Map** 5 C3. **Tel** 041 275 04 62. 🚤 San Basilio. **Open** 10am–5pm Mon–Sat. **Closed** 1 Jan, 25 Dec. 🚭 ✉
🌐 chorusvenezia.org

This church has one of the most homogeneous interiors in the whole of Venice. The splendour was created by Veronese who, from 1555 to 1560 and again in the 1570s, was commissioned to decorate the sacristy ceiling, the nave ceiling, the frieze, the east end of the choir, the high altar, the doors of the organ panels and the chancel.

The paintings feature radiant colours and rich costumes. Those on the sacristy ceiling depict the *Coronation of the Virgin* and the *Four Evangelists*.

Of the other paintings, the finest are the three that tell the story of Esther, Queen of Xerxes I of Persia, famous for securing the deliverance of the Jewish people.

Veronese is buried here. His tomb is in front of the paved chapel to the left of the chancel.

⓯ Accademia

See pp110–11.

⓰ Peggy Guggenheim Collection

Palazzo Venier dei Leoni. **Map** 6 F4. **Tel** 041 240 54 11. 🚤 Accademia. **Open** 10am–6pm Wed–Mon. **Closed** 9 Jan, 20 Feb, 25 Dec. 🚭 🚹 🚻 📷 💻 ✉
♿ 🌐 guggenheim-venice.it

Intended as a four-storey palace, the 18th-century Palazzo Venier dei Leoni in fact never rose beyond the ground floor. In 1949 the building was bought as a home by the American

The truncated palazzo housing the Peggy Guggenheim Collection

millionairess Peggy Guggenheim (1898–1979), a collector, dealer and patron of the arts who be-friended, and then furthered the careers of, many innovative abstract and Surrealist artists. One was Max Ernst, who became her second husband. The collection consists of 200 fine paintings and sculptures, each representing the 20th century's most influential modern art movements. The dining room has notable Cubist works of art, including *The Poet* by Pablo Picasso, and an entire room is devoted to Jackson Pollock, who was "discovered" by Guggenheim.

Other artists represented are Braque, Chagall, de Chirico, Dalí, Duchamp, Léger, Kandinsky, Klee, Mondrian, Miró, Malevich, Rothko, Bacon and Magritte, whose Surreal *Empire of Light* (1953–4) shows a night scene of a darkened house in a wooded setting with a bright day sky above. The sculpture collection, which includes Constantin Brancusi's elegant *Maiastra* (1912), is laid out in the house and garden.

Maiastra by Constantin Brancusi

Perhaps the most provocative piece is Marino Marini's *Angelo della Città* (Angel of the Citadel, 1948), located on the terrace overlooking the Grand Canal. This shows a prominently displayed man sitting on a horse, erect in all respects.

The Guggenheim is the best place in the city to see 20th-century art. Light-filled rooms and the large modern canvases provide a striking contrast to the Renaissance paintings in most Venetian churches and museums.

The garden has been paved and features an array of sculptures. Peggy Guggenheim's ashes are also preserved here. A shop and restaurant are located within the grounds. Check the website for information on temporary exhibits.

The large Baroque church of Santa Maria della Salute

⏱ Santa Maria della Salute

Campo della Salute. **Map** 7 A4. **Tel** 041 274 39 11. 🚤 Salute. **Open** 9am–noon, 3–5:30pm daily. Sacristy: 10am–noon, 3–5pm daily; may be closed in the morning on religious holidays. 📷 to sacristy. ♿

This great Baroque church standing at the entrance of the Grand Canal is one of the most imposing architectural landmarks of Venice. Henry James likened it to "some great lady on the threshold of her salon".

Santa Maria della Salute was built in thanksgiving for the city's deliverance from the plague epidemic of 1630, hence the name *Salute*, which means health and salvation.

Each November, in celebration, worshippers light candles and approach across a bridge of boats spanning the mouth of the Grand Canal for the occasion.

Baldassare Longhena started the church in 1630 at the age of 32, and worked on it for the rest of his life. It was completed in

1687, five years after his death. The interior consists of a large octagonal space below the cupola and six chapels radiating from the ambulatory. The large domed chancel and grandiose high altar dominate the view from the main door.

The altar's sculptural group by Giusto Le Corte represents the Virgin and Child giving protection to Venice from the plague. The best of the paintings are in the sacristy to the left of the altar: Titian's early altarpiece of *St Mark Enthroned with Saints Cosmas, Damian, Roch and Sebastian* (1511–12) and his dramatic ceiling paintings of *Cain and Abel, The Sacrifice of Abraham and Isaac* and *David and Goliath* (1540–9). *The Wedding at Cana* (1551) on the wall opposite the entrance is by Jacopo Tintoretto.

⏱ Punta della Dogana

Campo della Salute. **Map** 7 A4. **Tel** 199 139 139; 041 271 90 39 from outside Italy. 🚤 Salute. **Open** 10am–7pm Wed–Mon (ticket counter closes at 6pm). **Closed** 25 Dec. 📷 ♿ 🌐 **palazzograssi.it**

The magnificent 17th-century Punta della Dogana (formerly a customs house) was restored by Japanese architect Tadao Ando and opened in 2009 as a contemporary art gallery. Together with the Palazzo Grassi, it houses the French billionaire François Pinault's large collection of contemporary art. Many well-known artists are represented here, including Jeff Koons and Takeshi Murakami.

Punta della Dogana, a contemporary art museum

⑮ Accademia

The art collection in the Accademia offers a complete spectrum of the Venetian School, from the Byzantine era through the Renaissance to the Baroque and later. The basis of the collection was the Accademia di Belle Arti founded in 1750 by the painter Giovanni Battista Piazzetta. In 1807 Napoleon moved the collection to these premises, enriching it with artworks removed from churches and monasteries. The Accademia is currently undergoing extensive restoration, which may result in changes to the floorplan.

The Tempest
In this enigmatic landscape (c.1507), Giorgione was probably creating a fantasy rather than portraying any specific subject.

Key to Floorplan

- ▢ Byzantine and International Gothic
- ▣ Renaissance
- ▢ Baroque, Genre and Landscape
- ▢ Ceremonial Painting
- ▢ Temporary exhibitions
- ▢ Non-exhibition space

The courtyard (1561) designed by Palladio

The former church of Santa Maria della Carità

Feast in the House of Levi (1573) by Paolo Veronese

Entrance

Madonna and Child between St John the Baptist and a Saint In this beautiful painting (c.1504), Giovanni Bellini places the figures in a spacious landscape, so marking a new phase in his development.

Coronation of the Virgin
Paolo Veneziano's polyptych (1325) has a central image of the Virgin surrounded by a panoply of religious scenes. This detail shows episodes from the Life of St Francis.

Healing of the Madman (c.1496) by Vittore Carpaccio

The long corridor (12) and
the rooms that lead from it are
largely devoted to light-hearted
landscape and genre paintings
from the 18th century. Among
them are pastoral scenes by
Francesco Zuccarelli, works by
Marco Ricci, scenes of Venetian
society by Pietro Longhi and
a view of Venice by Canaletto
(1763). This is a fine example
of his sense of perspective.

Byzantine and International Gothic

Room 1 shows the influence
of Byzantine art on the early
Venetian painters. In Paolo
Veneziano's glowing *Coronation
of the Virgin* (1325), the linear
rhythms are unmistakably
Gothic, but the gold background and central panel
are distinctly Byzantine.

In contrast, *The Coronation
of the Virgin* (1448) by Michele
Giambono reveals a delicate
naturalism, typical of the
International Gothic style.

Renaissance

The Renaissance came late
to Venice, but by the second
quarter of the 15th century
it had transformed the city
into a thriving art centre
rivalling Florence and
Rome. Central to Venetian
art in the 15th century was
the *Sacra Conversazione*, in
which the Madonna is
portrayed with various
saints in a harmonious
composition. Giovanni
Bellini's altarpiece for San
Giobbe (c.1487) in room 2
is one of the finest
examples of this subject.

In contrast, the High
Renaissance exuberance
of Paolo Veronese is
exemplified in the monumental
Feast in the House of Levi (1573).
The painting occupies a whole
wall in room 10. Tintoretto's
huge masterpiece *The Miracle of
St Mark Freeing a Slave* (1548) is
also on display here.

Baroque, Genre and Landscape

Venice lacked native Baroque
painters, but a few non-
Venetians kept the Venetian
school alive in the 17th century.
The most notable was the
Genoese Bernardo Strozzi
(1581–1644). The artist was
a great admirer of the work of
Veronese, as can be seen in his
Feast at the House of Simon (1629)
in room 11. Also represented in
this room is Giambattista
Tiepolo, the greatest Venetian
painter of the 18th century.

Ceremonial Painting

Rooms 20 and 21 return to
the Renaissance, featuring two
great cycles of paintings from
the late 16th century. The detail
in these large-scale anecdotal
canvases provides a fascinating
glimpse of the life, customs
and appearance of Venice
at the time.

Room 20 houses *The
Stories of the Cross* by Venice's
leading artists. In room 21,
minutely detailed *Scenes
from the Legend of St Ursula*
(1490s) by Carpaccio mix
reality and imagination by
linking episodes from the
life of the saint to the
settings and costumes of
15th-century Venice.

Feast in the House of Levi (1573) by Paolo Veronese

Street-by-Street: Piazza San Marco

Throughout its long history Piazza San Marco has
witnessed pageants, processions, political activities and
countless Carnival festivities. Visitors flock here in their
thousands for two of the city's most important historic
sights – the Basilica and the Palazzo Ducale. These
magnificent buildings complement lesser sights, such
as the Campanile, Museo Correr and Torre dell'Orologio,
not to mention the gardens of the Giardinetti Reali,
open-air orchestras, elegant cafés – notably Quadri
and Florian's – and numerous smart shops.

㉑ Torre dell'Orologio
The clock tower, with hidden
clockwork figures, dates from
the Renaissance.

Traditionally Gondolas
have moored in the
Bacino Orseolo,
which is named after
Doge Orseolo.

The Piazza was described
by Napoleon as the "most
elegant drawing room in
Europe".

㉓ Museo Correr
Giovanni Bellini's *Pietà* (1455–60)
is one of many masterpieces
hanging in the galleries of
the Correr.

Harry's Bar has
attracted American
visitors since
Giuseppe Cipriani
and his friend Harry
set it up in 1931.
Shown here is Ernest
Hemingway, one
of the bar's many
famous patrons.

San Marco Vallaresso

MERCERIE

PROCURATIE VECCHIE

PIAZZA SAN
MARCO

PROCURATIE NUOVE

For keys to map symbols *see back flap*

⑲ ★ Basilica di San Marco
This 13th-century façade mosaic shows the body of St Mark being carried into the basilica.

Locator Map
See Venice Street Finder map 7

The Bridge of Sighs
(1600) was built as a passageway between the Palazzo Ducale and the prison. It reputedly took its name from the sighs of prisoners being led to trial.

LLE LARGA SAN MARCO

RIO DEL PALAZZO

PIAZZETTA

Ponte della Paglia

⑳ ★ Palazzo Ducale
Once home to Venice's rulers, and to the offices of State, the Doges' Palace is a triumph of Gothic architecture.

㉒ The Campanile
The present Campanile replaced one that collapsed in 1902.

MOLO SAN MARCO

San Marco Giardinetti

0 metres	75
0 yards	75

The vaulting of the stairway in the magnificent Libreria Sansoviniana (1588) is decorated with frescoes and gilded stucco. The national library of St Mark is housed here.

The Zecca, designed by Sansovino and started in 1537, was the city mint until 1870, and gave its name to the *zecchino* or Venetian ducat.

⑲ Basilica di San Marco

Venice's famous Basilica blends the architectural and decorative styles of East and West to create one of the greatest buildings in Europe. The exterior owes its almost Oriental splendour to countless treasures from the Republic's overseas empire. Among these are copies of the famous bronze horses, brought from Constantinople in 1204, and a wealth of columns, bas-reliefs and coloured marbles studded across the main façade. Mosaics from different epochs adorn the five doorways, while the main portal is framed by some of Italy's loveliest Romanesque carving (1240–65).

St Mark and Angels
The statues crowning the central arch are additions from the early 15th century.

★ Horses of St Mark
The four horses are replicas of the gilded bronze originals, now protected inside the Basilica's museum.

KEY

① **The elegant arches**, echo those of the lower floor, forming a repeat pattern.

② **The Pentecost Dome**, showing the Descent of the Holy Ghost as a dove, was probably the first dome to be decorated with mosaics.

③ **The Ascension Dome**, features a magnificent 13th-century mosaic of Christ surrounded by angels, the 12 Apostles and the Virgin Mary.

④ **St Mark's body**, believed lost in the fire of AD 976, supposedly reappeared when the new church was consecrated in 1094. The remains are housed in the altar.

⑤ **The Mosaic Pavement**, shows beautiful pictures of birds and beasts, some of which are allegorical.

⑥ **St Mark's Treasury**

⑦ **Romanesque Carvings**, adorn the arches of the main portal.

Entrance

★ Façade Mosaics
A 17th-century mosaic shows the body of St Mark being taken from Alexandria, reputedly smuggled past Muslim guards under slices of pork.

Ciborium
The fine alabaster columns of the altar canopy, or baldacchino, are adorned with scenes from the New Testament.

The Tetrarchs
This charming sculptured group in porphyry (4th-century Egyptian) is thought to represent Diocletian, Maximian, Valerian and Constantine. Collectively they were the Tetrarchs, appointed by Diocletian to help rule the Roman Empire.

The Building of St Mark's

Built on a Greek cross plan and crowned with five huge domes, this is the third church to stand on the site. The first, which enshrined the body of St Mark in the 9th century, was destroyed by fire. The second was pulled down in favour of a church reflecting Venice's growing power. The present design was inspired by the Church of the Apostles in Constantinople and was completed and decorated over the centuries. From 1075, all ships returning from abroad had, by law, to bring back a precious gift to adorn "the House of St Mark". The mosaics inside are mostly 12th–13th century and cover 4,240 sq m (45,622 sq ft). Some were later replaced by such artists as Titian and Tintoretto. Until 1807 St Mark's was the doge's private chapel, used for ceremonies of State, after which it succeeded San Pietro di Castello as the cathedral of Venice.

13th-century carving of a grape harvester on the main portal

Exploring the Basilica

St Mark's magnificent interior is clad with dazzling mosaics, which begin in the *narthex,* or atrium of the Basilica, and culminate in the glittering panels of the Pentecost and Ascension domes. The Genesis Cupola in the atrium has a stunning Creation of the World described in concentric circles. The *pavimento* or floor is also patterned with mosaics in marble and glass. Steps from the atrium lead to the Museo Marciano, home to the Basilica's famous horses. Other treasures include the jewel-encrusted Pala d'Oro, behind the high altar, the Nicopeia icon and the precious hoards of silver, gold and glassware in the Treasury.

Madonna di Nicopeia
This Byzantine icon, looted in 1204, is one of Venice's most revered images.

★ Pentecost Dome
Showing the Apostles touched by tongues of flame, the Pentecost Dome was lavishly decorated in the 12th century.

★ Ascension Dome
A mosaic of Christ in Glory decorates the enormous central dome. This masterpiece was created by 13th-century Venetian craftsmen, who were strongly influenced by the art and architecture of Byzantium.

★ Treasury
A repository for precious artifacts from both Italy and Constantinople, the treasury houses objects such as this 11th-century silver-gilt coffer.

★ Pala d'Oro
The altar-piece, created in the 10th century by medieval goldsmiths, is made up of 250 panels such as this one.

KEY

① **The columns** of the inner façade are thought to be fragments of the first basilica.

② **South side aisle**

③ **Baptistry**

④ **Cappella Zen**

⑤ **Steps to Museo Marciano**

⑥ **Atrium**

⑦ **North side aisle**

⑧ **The Porta dei Fiori**, or Gate of Flowers is decorated with 13th-century reliefs.

⑨ **Cappella dei Mascoli**

⑩ **The sacristy door** has fine bronze panels by Sansovino which include portraits of himself with Titian and Aretino.

⑪ **The Altar of the Sacrament**, is decorated with mosaics of the parables and miracles of Christ dating from the late 12th or early 13th century.

Mosaics

Clothing the domes, walls and floor of the Basilica are over 4,000 sq m (43,000 sq ft) of gleaming golden mosaics. The earliest, dating from the 12th century, were the work of mosaicists from the East. Their delicate techniques were soon adopted by Venetian craftsmen, who gradually took over the Basilica's decoration, combining Byzantine inspiration with Western influences. During the 16th century, many sketches by Tintoretto, Titian, Veronese, and other leading artists were reproduced in mosaic.

Among the most dazzling mosaics – many of which have been heavily restored – are those in the 13th-century central Ascension Dome and the 12th-century Pentecost Dome over the nave.

Pala d'Oro

Beyond the Cappella di San Clemente lies the entrance to the most valuable treasure of San Marco: the Pala d'Oro. This jewel-spangled altarpiece, situated behind the high altar, consists of 250 enamel paintings on gold foil, enclosed within a gilded silver Gothic frame. Originally commissioned in Byzantium in AD 976, the altarpiece was further embellished over the centuries.

Napoleon stole some of the precious stones in 1797, but the screen still gleams with pearls, rubies, sapphires and amethysts.

Museo Marciano

Steps from the atrium, signposted Loggia dei Cavalli, take you up to the church museum, where the gallery offers a splendid view into the basilica. The gilded bronze horses, housed in a room at the far end of the museum, were stolen from the top of the Hippodrome (ancient racecourse) in Constantinople (modern Istanbul) in 1204 but their origin, either Roman or Hellenistic, remains a mystery. Also on show are mosaics, medieval manuscripts and antique tapestries.

Baptistry and Chapels

The baptistry (closed to the public) was added by Doge Andrea Dandolo (1343–54), who is buried here, with Sansovino, who designed the font. The adjoining Cappella Zen (also closed to the public) became a funeral chapel for Cardinal Zen in 1504 in return for a bequest to the State. The left transept of the Cappella dei Mascoli is decorated with scenes from the life of Mary, while the third chapel in the same transept houses the icon of the Madonna of Nicopeia. Looted in 1204, it was once carried into battle at the head of the Byzantine army.

Noah and the Flood, atrium mosaics from the 13th century

⑳ Palazzo Ducale

The Palazzo Ducale (Doges' Palace), the official residence of Venice's rulers, was founded in the 9th century. The present palace owes its external appearance to the building work of the 14th and early 15th centuries. To create their airy Gothic masterpiece, the Venetians broke with tradition by perching the bulk of the palace (built in pink Veronese marble) on top of an apparent fretwork of loggias and arcades (built from white Istrian stone).

★ Giants' Staircase
This 15th-century staircase is crowned by Sansovino's statues of Mars and Neptune, symbols of Venice's power.

★ Porta della Carta
This 15th-century Gothic gate was once the main entrance to the palace. From it, a vaulted passageway leads to the Arco Foscari and the internal courtyard.

★ Sala del Maggior Consiglio
This vast hall was used as a meeting place for members of Venice's Great Council. Tintoretto's huge *Paradise* (1590) fills the end wall.

Sala dello Scudo
The walls of this room, once part of the doge's private apartments, are covered with maps of the world. In the centre of the room are two giant 18th-century globes.

VISITORS' CHECKLIST

Practical Information
Piazzetta. **Map** 7 C2. **Tel** 041 271 59 11. **Open** 8:30am–7pm daily (Nov–Mar: to 5:30pm, last adm: 1 hr before closing). **Closed** 1 Jan, 25 Dec. 🎧🚻♿ partial. 🖼️📷📧
W visitmuve.it

Transport
🚤 San Marco

Torture Chamber
Interrogations took place in the Torture Chamber. Suspects were hung by their wrists from a cord in the centre of the room.

Drunkenness of Noah
This early 15th-century sculpture, symbolic of the frailty of man, is set on the corner of the palace.

The Loggia
Each arch of the ground level portico supports two arches of the loggia, which commands fine views of the lagoon.

Entrance

KEY

① **Exit**

② **The Arco Foscari** has copies of Antonio Rizzo's 15th-century Adam and Eve.

③ **Courtyard**

④ **Sala del Collegio**

⑤ **Sala del Senato**

⑥ **Anticollegio**

⑦ **Sala delle Quattro Porte**

⑧ **The Bridge of Sighs**

⑨ **Sala della Bussola**

⑩ **Sala del Consiglio dei Dieci**

⑪ **The Ponte della Paglia**, built of Istrian stone, has a pretty balustrade of columns and sculpted pine cones.

Exploring the Palazzo Ducale

A tour of the Palazzo Ducale takes visitors through a succession of richly decorated chambers and halls, arranged over three floors, culminating with the Bridge of Sighs, which links the palace to the prisons. Casanova was once imprisoned here and made a daring escape from the Palazzo through a hole in the roof.

Jacopo and Domenico Tintoretto's *Paradise*, one of the world's largest paintings, in the Sala del Maggior Consiglio

Scala d'Oro and Courtyard

A passage from the Porta del Frumento opens into the palace courtyard. The ticket office and palace entrance are to the left. At the top of Antonio Rizzo's 15th-century Giants' Staircase, the new doge would be crowned with the *zogia* or dogal cap. The Scala d'Oro (golden staircase), designed by Jacopo Sansovino, leads to the palace's upper floors. It takes its name, however, from the elaborate gilt stucco vault created by Alessandro Vittoria (1554–8).

Sala delle Quattro Porte to the Sala del Senato

The second flight of the Scala d'Oro leads to the Sala delle Quattro Porte, with a ceiling designed by Palladio and frescoed by Tintoretto. The end walls of the next room, the Anticollegio, are decorated with mythological scenes by Tintoretto, while Veronese's masterly *Rape of Europa* (1580), opposite the window, is one of the palace's most dramatic works. The adjoining Sala del Collegio was where the doge

and his counsellors met to receive ambassadors and discuss matters of State. Embellishing the magnificent ceiling are 11 paintings by Veronese. In the next room, the Sala del Senato, the doge and some 200 senators discussed foreign affairs. The paintings are by Tintoretto and pupils.

A bocca di leone for denunciations

Sala del Consiglio dei Dieci to the Armeria

The Sala del Consiglio dei Dieci was the meeting room of the powerful Council of Ten, founded in 1310 to protect State security. Two fine works by Veronese adorn the ceiling: *Age and Youth* and *Juno Offering the Ducal Crown to Venice* (both 1553–4). In the Sala della Bussola, offenders awaited their fate in front of the Council of Ten. The room's *bocca di leone* (lion's mouth), was used to post secret denunciations and was just one of several in the palace. The wooden door here leads to the State Inquisitors' Room and thence to the torture chamber and prisons. The Armoury – one of the finest such collections anywhere in Europe – occupies the following rooms.

Sala del Maggior Consiglio

The Scala dei Censori leads to the second floor and past the Sala del Guariento and Antonio Rizzo's statues of Adam and Eve (1480s) to the magnificent Sala del Maggior Consiglio. A vast chamber, it was used as a meeting place for the Great Council and for grand State banquets. By the mid-16th century the Great Council had around 2,000 members. Any Venetian of high birth over 25 was entitled to a seat unless he married a commoner. Tintoretto's huge *Paradise* (1587–90) occupies the eastern wall. Measuring 7.45 by 24.65 m (25 by 81 ft), it is one of the largest paintings in the world. The itinerary then continues in more sombre vein, crossing the Bridge of Sighs to enter the dank world of the prisons.

Dialectic (c.1577) by Veronese in the Palazzo Ducale's Sala del Collegio

㉑ Torre dell'Orologio

Piazza San Marco. **Map** 7 B2. **Tel** 848 082 000 (booking). San Marco. 10 & 11am Mon–Wed, 2 & 3pm Thu–Sun (must be pre-booked). **Closed** 1 Jan, 1 May, 25 Dec. **W** visitmuve.it

This richly decorated clock tower on the north side of the piazza was built in the late 15th century. Mauro Coducci is thought to have worked on the design. With its display of the phases of the moon and the signs of the zodiac, the clock face was design-ed with seafarers in mind. According to legend, once the clock was completed, the two inventors had their eyes gouged out to prevent them from ever creating a replica.

The clock face of the Torre dell'Orologio

On the upper level, the winged lion of St Mark stands against a star-spangled blue backdrop. At the very top the two huge bronze figures, known as the *Mori*, or Moors, strike the bell on the hour.

㉒ Campanile

Piazza San Marco. **Map** 7 B2. **Tel** 041 270 83 11. San Marco. **Open** Nov–Easter: 9:30am–3:45pm daily; Easter–Jun & Oct: 9am–7pm daily; Jul–Sep: 9am–9pm daily. **W** basilicasanmarco.it

From the top of St Mark's campanile, high above the piazza, visitors can enjoy views of the city, the lagoon and, visibility permitting, the peaks of the Alps. It was from here that Galileo demonstrated his telescope to Doge Leonardo Donà in 1609. To do so he would have climbed the internal ramp. Access today is via a lift.

The first tower, completed in 1173, was built as a lighthouse to assist navigators in the lagoon. It took on a less benevolent role in the Middle Ages, when offenders were imprisoned – and in some cases left to die – in a cage hung near its summit. With the exception of several 16th-century renovations, the tower survived unharmed until July 1902 when, with little warning, it collapsed. The only casualties were the Loggetta at the foot of the tower and the custodian's cat. Donations flooded in, and in 1903 the foundation stone was laid for a new campanile *"dov'era e com'era"* ("where it was and as it was"). The new tower was opened on 25 April (the Feast of St Mark) 1912. Due to small structural shifts, the foundations have been reinforced.

㉓ Museo Correr

Procuratie Nuove. Entrance in Ala Napoleonica. **Map** 7 B2. **Tel** 041 240 52 11. San Marco. **Open** Apr–Oct: 10am–7pm; Nov–Mar: 10am–5pm (last adm: 1hr before closing). **Closed** 1 Jan, 25 Dec. (includes adm to Libreria Sansoviniana and Museo Archeologico). **W** visitmuve.it

Teodoro Correr bequeathed his extensive collection of works of art to Venice in 1830, thus forming the core of the city's fine civic museum.

Its first rooms form a suitably Neo-Classical backdrop for early statues by Antonio Canova (1757–1822). The rest of the floor covers the history of the Venetian Republic, with maps,

Young Man in a Red Hat (c.1490) by Carpaccio in the Museo Correr

coins, armour and a host of doge-related exhibits. The second floor contains a picture collection second only to that of the Accademia.

The paintings, hung chrono-logically, trace the evolution of Venetian painting, and show the influence of Ferrarese, Paduan and Flemish artists.

The gallery's most famous works are by Carpaccio: *Portrait of a Young Man in a Red Hat* (c.1490), and *Two Venetian Ladies* (c.1507). The latter is traditionally, but probably incorrectly, known as *The Courtesans* because of the ladies' low-cut dresses. The Museo del Risorgimento on the same floor looks at the history of Venice until unification with Italy in 1866.

The ceiling of Santo Stefano, built in the form of a ship's keel

㉔ Santo Stefano

Campo Santo Stefano. **Map** 6 F2. **Tel** 041 275 04 62. Accademia or Sant'Angelo. **Open** 10am–5pm Mon–Sat. **Closed** 1 Jan, 25 Dec. **W** chorusvenezia.org

Deconsecrated six times on account of the blood spilled within its walls, Santo Stefano – one of Venice's most beautiful churches – is now remarkably serene. Built in the 14th century, and altered in the 15th, the church has a carved portal by Bartolomeo Bon, and a campanile with a typical Venetian tilt. The interior has a splendid ship's keel ceiling, carved tie-beams, and the sacristy crammed with valuable paintings.

㉕ Santi Giovanni e Paolo

Known more colloquially as San Zanipolo, Santi Giovanni e Paolo vies with the Frari *(see pp102–3)* as the city's greatest Gothic church. Built by the Dominicans in the 14th century, it is striking for its vast scale and architectural austerity. Known as the Pantheon of Venice, it houses monuments to no fewer than 25 doges. Among these are several fine works of art, executed by the Lombardi family and other leading sculptors.

The Nave
The cross-vaulted interior is tied by wooden beams and supported by stone columns.

★ Tomb of Nicolò Marcello
This magnificent Renaissance monument to Doge Nicolò Marcello (died 1474) was sculpted by Pietro Lombardo.

Entrance

★ Tomb of Pietro Mocenigo
Pietro Lombardo's superb tomb (1481) commemorates the doge's military pursuits when he was Grand Captain of the Venetian forces.

★ Polyptych by Bellini
This painting (c.1465) shows St Vincent Ferrer, a Spanish cleric, flanked by St Sebastian and St Christopher.

KEY

① **The doorway**, which is decorated with Byzantine reliefs and carvings by Bartolomeo Bon, is one of Venice's earliest Renaissance architectural works.

② **The bronze statue**, is a monument to Doge Sebastiano Venier, who was Commander of the Fleet at Lepanto.

③ **Tomb of Andrea Vendramin**, Lombardo's masterpiece (1476–8) takes the form of a Roman triumphal arch.

④ **The Baroque high altar**, begun in 1619, is attributed to Baldassare Longhena.

⑤ **16th-century altar statues by Vittoria**

⑥ **16th-century frescoes attributed to Palma il Giovane**

㉖ Statue of Colleoni

Campo Santi Giovanni e Paolo.
Map 3 C5. 🚌 Ospedale Civile.

Bartolomeo Colleoni, the famous *condottiere* or commander of mercenaries, left his fortune to the Republic on condition that his statue was placed in front of San Marco. A prominent statue in the piazza would have broken with precedent, so the Senate cunningly had Colleoni raised before the Scuola di San Marco instead of the basilica. A touchstone of early Renaissance sculpture, the equestrian statue of the proud warrior (1481–8) is by the Florentine Andrea Verrocchio, but was cast in bronze after his death by Alessandro Leopardi. The statue has a strong sense of power and movement, which arguably ranks it alongside the works of Donatello.

㉗ Santa Maria Formosa

Campo Santa Maria Formosa. **Map** 7
C1. **Tel** 041 275 04 62. 🚌 Rialto.
Open 10am–5pm Mon–Sat:
Closed 1 Jan, 25 Dec. 🎨 📷
w chorusvenezia.org

Designed by Mauro Coducci in 1492, this church is most unusual in having two main façades – one overlooks the *campo,* the other the canal. The bell tower or campanile, added in 1688, is noted for the grotesque face at its base.

Two paintings stand out in the interior: a triptych (1473) by Bartolomeo Vivarini and Palma il Vecchio's *St Barbara* (c.1510).

㉘ San Zaccaria

Campo San Zaccaria. **Map** 8 D2.
Tel 041 522 12 57. 🚌 San Zaccaria.
Open 10am–noon, 4–6pm Mon–Sat,
4–6pm Sun & public hols. 🎨 chapels
and crypt. 📷

Set in a quiet square just a stone's throw from the Riva degli Schiavoni, the church of San Zaccaria is a successful blend of Flamboyant Gothic and Classical Renaissance styles.

Palma il Vecchio's *St Barbara* (c.1510) in
Santa Maria Formosa

Founded in the 9th century, its façade was later rebuilt by Antonio Gambello in Gothic style. When Gambello died in 1481, Mauro Coducci completed the upper section, adding many of its Renaissance panels.

The interior's artistic highlight is Giovanni Bellini's serene and sumptuously coloured *Madonna and Child with Saints* (1505) in the north aisle. A door off the right nave leads to the Chapel of St Athanasius, which in turn leads to the Chapel of San Tarasio. The chapel contains vault frescoes (1442) by Andrea del Castagno, and polyptychs (1443–4) by Antonio Vivarini and Giovanni d'Alemagna.

A Renaissance panel by Coducci on the
façade of San Zaccaria

❷⁹ Scuola di San Giorgio degli Schiavoni

Calle Furlani. **Map** 8 E1. **Tel** 041 522 88 28. 🚤 San Zaccaria. **Open** 9am–1pm, 2:45–6pm Tue–Sun. **Closed** 1 Jan, 1 May, 25 Dec and other religious hols. 📷 📷

Within this small gem are some of the finest paintings of Vittore Carpaccio. They were commissioned by the Schiavoni, or Dalmatian Slav community in Venice.

The Scuola was established in 1451 and rebuilt in 1551. It has changed very little since. The exquisite frieze, executed between 1502 and 1508, shows scenes from the lives of patron saints: St George, St Tryphone and St Jerome. Each episode of the narrative cycle is remarkable for its vivid colouring, minute detail and historic record of Venetian life. Outstanding among them are *St George Slaying the Dragon* and *St Jerome Leading the Tamed Lion to the Monastery.*

❸⁰ San Giovanni in Bragora

Campo Bandiera e Moro. **Map** 8 E2. **Tel** 041 520 59 06. 🚤 Arsenale. **Open** 9–11am, 3:30–5:30pm Mon–Sat, 9:30am–noon Sun. 📷

The existing church is essentially Gothic (1475–9), and the interior contains major works of art that demonstrate the transition from Gothic to early Renaissance. Bartolomeo Vivarini's altarpiece *Madonna and Child with Saints*

Lagoon entrance

Arsenale Novissimo, 15th–16th century

Old sail factory

Arsenale Vecchio, 12th–13th century

Corderia

Arsenale Novo, 14th century

18th-century engraving of the Arsenale

(1478) is unmistakably Gothic. Contrasting with this is Cima da Conegliano's *Baptism of Christ* (1492–5), on the main altar.

❸¹ Arsenale

Map 8 F1. 🚤 Arsenale. Museo Storico Navale Campo San Biagio. **Map** 8 F3. **Tel** 041 244 13 99. **Open** 8:45am–1:30pm Mon–Fri; 8:45am–1pm Sat. **Closed** public hols. 📷

The Arsenale was founded in the 12th century and by the 16th had become the greatest naval shipyard in the world, capable of constructing a whole galley in 24 hours, using an assembly-line system. Surrounded by crenellated walls, it was like a city within a city. Today the site is largely disused. Its impressive 15th-century gateway, twin towers and guardian lions can be viewed from the *campo* or bridge outside. The gateway was built by Antonio Gambello

and is often cited as Venice's first Renaissance construction.

Around the corner, in Campo San Biagio, the **Museo Storico Navale** charts Venetian naval history from the heyday of the Arsenale to the present. Exhibits include friezes from famous galleys of the past and a replica of the *Bucintoro,* the Doge's ceremonial barge.

❸² San Giorgio Maggiore

Map 8 D4. **Tel** 041 522 78 27. 🚤 San Giorgio. **Open** 9:30am–12:30pm, 2:30–5:30pm daily (to 4:30pm in winter). 📷 (Campanile). 📷 Fondazione Cini: **Tel** 041 271 04 02. **Open** 10am–4pm Sat & Sun (to 5pm Apr–Sep). 📷 📷

Appearing like a stage set across the water from the Piazzetta is the little island of San Giorgio Maggiore. The church and monastery, constructed

St George Slaying the Dragon (1502–8) by Carpaccio, in the Scuola di San Giorgio degli Schiavoni

between 1559–80, are among Andrea Palladio's greatest architectural achievements. The church's temple front and the spacious interior with its perfect proportions and cool beauty are typically Palladian *(see pp84–5)*. These qualities are echoed by the church of Il Redentore on the nearby island of Giudecca, built by Palladio in 1577–92.

On the chancel walls of San Giorgio Maggiore, are two fine paintings by Tintoretto: *The Last Supper and Gathering of the Manna* (both 1594). In the Chapel of the Dead is his last work, *The Deposition* (1592–4), finished by his son Domenico.

The top of the campanile affords superb views of the city and lagoon. You can see the monastery cloisters below, now part of the **Fondazione Cini**, a cultural centre that is used to host international exhibitions.

Palladio's San Giorgio Maggiore

③ Murano

🚤 4.1 and 4.2 from Fondamente Nuove; 3 from Ferrovia and Piazzale Roma.

Much like Venice, Murano comprises a cluster of small islands, connected by bridges. It has been the centre of the glassmaking industry since 1291, when the furnaces were moved here from the city because of the risk of fire and the disagreeable effects of smoke. Some of the houses on the water date from this period.

The colonnaded exterior of Murano's Basilica dei Santi Maria e Donato

🏛 Museo del Vetro

Palazzo Giustinian, Fondamenta Giustinian. **Tel** 041 73 95 86. **Open** 10am–6pm daily (Nov–Mar: to 5pm, last adm: 30 min before closing). **Closed** 1 Jan, 1 May, 25 Dec. 🅿 📷 🆆 visitmuve.it

In the 15th and 16th centuries Murano was the principal glass-producing centre in Europe and today, most tourists visit for glass alone. The Museo del Vetro in the Palazzo Giustinian houses a collection of antique pieces. The prize exhibit is the dark blue Barovier wedding cup (1470–80), with enamel work by Angelo Barovier.

⛪ Basilica dei Santi Maria e Donato

Fondamenta Giustinian. **Tel** 041 73 90 56. **Open** 9am–noon, 3:30–7pm Mon–Sat, 3:30–7pm Sun (Nov–Mar: to 6pm daily). 📷

With its lovely colonnaded apse, this basilica is the architectural highlight of the island. Despite major restoration, this 12th-century church still retains much of its original beauty. Note the Gothic ship's keel roof, the mosaic Madonna in the apse and the mosaic floor dating from 1140.

④ Burano

🚤 12 from Fondamenta Nuove; 14 from San Zaccaria via Lido and Punta Sabbioni.

Burano is the most colourful of the lagoon islands and can be distinguished from a distance by the tilting tower of its church. In contrast with the haunting Torcello, the island is densely populated, its waterways fringed with brightly painted houses.

The main thoroughfare is Via Baldassare Galuppi, named after the Burano-born composer. It features traditional lace and linen stalls and open-air trattorias serving fresh fish.

🏛 Museo del Merletto

Piazza Baldassare Galuppi 187. **Tel** 041 73 00 34. **Open** Apr–Oct: 10am–6pm Tue–Sun; Nov–Mar: 10am–5pm Tue–Sun (last adm: 30 min before closing). **Closed** 1 Jan, 1 May, 25 Dec. 📷 🆆 visitmuve.it

The people of Burano are fishermen and lacemakers by tradition. You can still see fishermen scraping their boats or mending nets, but today lacemakers are rare. In the 16th century the local lace was the most sought-after in Europe – it was so delicate it became known as *punto in aria* ("points in the air"). After a slump in the 18th century, the industry revived and a lace-making school was set up here in 1872. Authentic Burano lace is hard to find, but you can watch it being made at the school, now a museum, which displays fine examples of antique lace.

Venetian glass goblet

Brightly painted street in Burano

⑤ Torcello

Established between the 5th and 6th centuries, the island of Torcello boasts the oldest building in the lagoon – the cathedral of Santa Maria Assunta. Founded in AD 639, it contains some splendid ancient mosaics. The adjoining church of Santa Fosca, of pure Byzantine design, is another mark of Torcello's former glory – before being eclipsed by Venice, the island had a population of 20,000.

★ Doomsday Mosaics
The highly decorative 12th-century mosaic of the *Last Judgment* covers the west wall.

Pulpit
The present basilica dates from 1008, but includes earlier features. The pulpit contains 7th-century fragments.

KEY

① **The exquisite Byzantine marble panels** of the iconostasis, or rood screen, are carved with peacocks, lions and flowers.

② **The Roman sarcophagus**, below the altar, is said to contain the relics of St Heliodorus.

③ **The 13th-century apse mosaic** of the Madonna against a gold background, is one of the most beautiful in Venice.

④ **The central dome** and cross sections are supported by columns of Greek marble with Corinthian capitals.

⑤ **The Portico** of Santa Fosca, with its elegant stilted arches, is built on three sides of the church, and probably dates from the 12th century.

⑥ **The altar** was rebuilt in 1939 and stands below a 15th-century wood relief of *Santa Fosca Sleeping*.

Nave Columns
Two rows of slender marble columns, 18 in all, separate the three naves. Their finely carved capitals date from the 11th century.

Torcello's Last Canals
Silted canals and malaria hastened Torcello's decline. One of the remaining waterways runs from the *vaporetto* stop to the basilica.

Santa Fosca
Built in the 11th and 12th centuries on a Greek-cross plan, the church has a serene Byzantine interior with a central pentagonal apse.

Vaporetto boarding point

The Museo dell'Estuario houses many old church treasures.

Attila's Throne
It was said that the 5th-century king of the Huns used this marble seat as his throne.

Shopping in Venice

The attractive shop windows that line the narrow streets of Venice are an irresistible attraction for any visitor. Myriad fashion brands are available in gleaming ultra-modern stores, but the city also has a strong artisan tradition. Expert craftspeople in tiny workshops open to the public create delightful and highly original objects in glass, wood, leather and papier-mâché. Skilled hands transform coloured glass rods into playful miniature animals and exquisite flowers, while plaster moulds turn out shapes destined to become ornate masks. Interior-design establishments also abound, and sleek kitchenware and fabrics make unusual purchases. Beautiful boutiques offering antique furniture and accessories are concentrated in the city centre.

Where to Shop

The glittering Mercerie, which runs from Piazza San Marco to the Rialto, has been Venice's main shopping street since the Middle Ages and, along with the fashion avenue Calle Larga XXII Marzo, is still a draw for the crowds. The zigzagging Frezzeria is full of unusual shops, while across the Grand Canal, the narrow streets from the Rialto southwest towards Campo San Polo are lined with a variety of less expensive stores. The bustling Lista di Spagna, near the station, and the Strada Nova towards the Rialto cater for the everyday needs of the locals.

The islands of Murano and Burano are the places to buy traditional glass and lace.

Food and Markets

One of the delights of Venice is exploring the city's food markets and shops. Fruit and vegetable stalls sprawl to the west of the Rialto Bridge and along the Grand Canal. The Pescheria, or fish market, occupies the furthest section. The neighbouring streets are full of gourmet food shops. Wine, olive oil, vinegar and grappa in decorative bottles, as well as dried pasta in many shapes, colours and flavours are all good purchases.

Aliani's cheese shop offers a mouthwatering selection of picnic fare, while **Drogheria Mascari** has a fine range of dried fruit, coffee and alcohol. **Rizzo**, on the other side of the bridge, is a master pasta-maker.

Glass

The island of Murano is a good place to watch expert glass-blowing. However, for contemporary glass creations head back to Venice, around San Marco – try **Venini**'s showroom for stunning platters and huge vases, and **L'Isola** for Carlo Moretti's tumblers in rich colours.

The art of bead-making is alive and flourishing thanks to sisters **Marina e Susanna Sent**'s simple, irresistible necklaces. At **Perle e Dintorni**, customers can sort through an astonishing range of beautiful glass beads and create their own costume jewellery.

Clothing and Accessories

Promod, near San Marco, has reasonably priced fun gear for the young set. Nearby is **Benetton**'s megastore, with its trademark bright clothes, while, opposite, **Max Mara** has superlative womenswear. Other leading names in fashion – **Armani**, **Roberto Cavalli**, **Missoni** and **Gucci** – also have stylish shops around Piazza San Marco.

Just off San Lio, **Giovanna Zanella** can be found at her cobbler's bench crafting zany shoes and sandals. Her amazing range even includes gondola decorations.

Masks and Costumes

Mass-produced Carnival masks can be found all over the city, but a genuine one makes for a wonderful souvenir. With its striking designs, **Papier Mâché** has revived traditional mask-making. Near Campo San Polo, **Tragicomica** sells masks and costumes, as well as Commedia dell'Arte figures. You will also find these at **Leon d'Oro**, where they make string puppets too. **Ca' Macana** has a great collection of eye-catching masks. You can even participate in a mask-making workshop. Down a winding street in Cannaregio, the husband-and-wife team at **Il Pirata** make papier-mâché masks in their store. Courses are available in the decoration and history of Venetian masks.

Jewellery

Nardi, located in the arcades of Piazza San Marco, crafts an exquisite brooch with a moor's head, among other things. A short distance away are the sparkling premises of **Bulgari**, while **Cartier**, with its beautiful collection of watches, can be found along the nearby Mercerie. Shops on the Rialto Bridge sell cheaper designs; this is a good place to find bracelets and chains, the prices of which are determined by the weight of the gold. Over the bridge, under the arcades of the ancient goldsmiths' district, is **Attombri** – two brothers who design unusual jewellery from antique Murano glass beads.

Fabrics and Interior Design

Venice is famed for fine silks and velvets and sumptuous brocades, many of which are still sold at **Trois**, close to the Gritti Palace hotel. On the Grand Canal, at Sant'Angelo, **Rubelli** is fabric heaven, with a wide range of designs and rich upholstery. More down-to-earth but good-quality household linen and brilliantly coloured bath accessories are sold at **TSL**, which has several stores around town.

For original kitchen items, the choice at **Epicentro** is hard to beat; or head to **Marchiol**, hidden away in a Castello backstreet, for modern light fittings and lamps.

Books and Gifts

At the Giardinetti Reali, on the San Marco waterfront, the **Venice Pavilion Bookshop** annexe of the Tourist Board has an exhaustive collection of books dealing with many aspects of the city. The **Libreria Marco Polo** bookstore offers a decent English- language section, while **Mare di Carta** offers nautical books and magazines.

Alberto Valese-Ebru uses a distinctive marbling technique on fabrics as well as paper. Nearby, **Paolo Olbi** has a wide range of papers and artistic books for sale. On the opposite side of the Grand Canal, at San Tomà, **Daniela Porto** has lovely old printed maps and frames, perfect as gifts, and **Signor Blum** on Campo San Barnaba has charming hand-made carved and painted wooden objects and toys.

DIRECTORY

Food and Markets

Aliani (Casa del Parmigiano)
Erberia Rialto, San Polo 214/8.
Map 3 A5.
Tel 041 520 6525.

Drogheria Mascari
Calle dei Spezieri, San Polo 381.
Map 3 A5.
Tel 041 522 9762.

Rizzo
Salizzada S. Giovanni Grisostomo, Cannaregio 5778.
Map 3 B5.
Tel 041 522 2824.

Glass

L'Isola – Carlo Moretti
Campo San Moisè, San Marco 1468.
Map 7 A3.
Tel 041 523 1973.

Marina e Susanna Sent
Campo S. Vio, Dorsoduro 669.
Map 6 F4.
Tel 041 520 81 36.

Perle e Dintorni
Calle della Mandorla, San Marco 3740.
Map 7 A2.
Tel 041 346 588 16 18.

Venini
Piazzetta dei Leoncini, San Marco 314.
Map 7 B2.
Tel 041 522 4045.

Clothing and Accessories

Armani
Calle Goldoni, San Marco 4412.
Map 7 A2.
Tel 041 523 4758.

Benetton
Marzaria (Merceria) Due Aprile, San Marco 5051.
Map 7 B2.
Tel 041 296 0493.

Giovanna Zanella
Calle Carminati, Castello 5641.
Map 7 B1.
Tel 041 523 5500.

Gucci
Calle Larga XXII Marzo, San Marco 2102.
Map 7 A3.
Tel 041 241 3968.

Max Mara
Campo San Salvador, San Marco 5033.
Map 7 A1.
Tel 041 522 6688.

Missoni
Calle Vallaresso, San Marco 1312. **Map** 7 B3.
Tel 041 520 5733.

Promod
Campo S. Bartolomeo, San Marco 5377.
Map 7 B1.
Tel 041 241 0668.

Roberto Cavalli
Calle Vallaresso, San Marco 1314.
Map 7 B3.
Tel 041 520 5733.

Masks and Costumes

Ca' Macana
Calle delle Botteghe, Dorsoduro 3172.
Map 6 D3.
Tel 041 520 32 29.

Leon d'Oro
Calle Frezzeria, San Marco 1770. **Map** 7 A2.
Tel 041 520 3375.

Il Pirata
Salizzada San Canciano, Cannaregio 5559.
Map 3 B5.
Tel 041 520 6529.

Papier Mâché
Calle Lunga Santa Maria Formosa, Castello 5175.
Map 7 C1.
Tel 041 522 9995.

Tragicomica
Calle dei Nomboli, San Polo 2800. **Map** 6 F1.
Tel 041 721 102.

Jewellery

Attombri
Sottoportego degli Orefici, San Polo 65.
Map 3 A5.
Tel 041 521 2524.

Bulgari
Calle Larga XXII Marzo, San Marco 2282.
Map 7 A3.
Tel 041 241 0553.

Cartier
Mercerie San Zulian, San Marco 606.
Map 7 B2.
Tel 041 522 2071.

Nardi
Procuratie Nuove, Piazza San Marco, San Marco 69/71.
Map 7 B2.
Tel 041 522 5733.

Fabrics and Interior Design

Epicentro
Calle Frezzeria, San Marco 1728/A.
Map 7 B2.
Tel 041 523 34 92.

Marchiol
Ruga Giuffa, Castello 4920.
Map 7 C1.
Tel 041 522 5131.

Rubelli
Campiello del Teatro, San Marco 3877.
Map 6 F2.
Tel 041 523 6110.

Trois
Campo San Maurizio, San Marco 2666.
Map 6 F3.
Tel 041 522 2905.

TSL Tessile San Leonardo
Rio Terrà San Leonardo, Cannaregio 1318.
Map 2 D3.
Tel 041 718 524.

Books and Gifts

Alberto Valese-Ebru
Campiello Santo Stefano, San Marco 3471.
Map 6 F3.
Tel 041 523 8830.

Daniela Porto
Rio Terrà dei Nomboli, San Polo 2753.
Map 6 E1.
Tel 041 523 1368.

Libreria Marco Polo
Calle del Teatro Malibran, Cannaregio 5886/a.
Map 3 B5.
Tel 041 522 63 43.

Mare di Carta
Fondamenta dei Tolentini, Santa Croce 222.
Map 5 C1.
Tel 041 716 304.

Paolo Olbi
Calle della Mandola, San Marco 3653.
Map 6 F2.
Tel 041 528 5025.

Signor Blum
Campo San Barnaba, Dorsoduro 2840.
Map 6 D3.
Tel 041 522 6367.

Venice Pavilion Bookshop
Palazzetto Selva, Giardinetti Reali, San Marco 2.
Map 7 B3.
Tel 041 522 5150.

VENICE STREET FINDER

All the map references given for sights, hotels and restaurants in Venice refer to this section of the book. The key map below shows which areas of the city are covered by the Street Finder. The first figure of the map reference indicates which map to turn to, and the letter and number which follow are for the grid reference. Standard Italian spelling has been used on all the maps in this book, but when exploring Venice you will find that the names on many street signs are written in Venetian dialect. Mostly this means only a slight variation in spelling (as in the word Sottoportico/Sotoportego below), but some names look totally different. For example, the church of Santi Giovanni e Paolo *(see map 3)*, is frequently signposted as "San Zanipolo". A further map showing the vaporetto routes follows the street maps.

Recognizing Street Names

The signs for street *(calle)*, canal *(rio)* and square *(campo)* will soon become familiar, but the Venetians have a colourful vocabulary for the maze of alleys which makes up the city. When exploring, the following may help.

FONDAMENTA S.SEVERO

Fondamenta is a street that runs alongside a canal, often named after the canal it follows.

RIO TERRA GESUATI

Rio Terrà is a filled-in canal. Similar to a *rio terrà* is a *piscina*, which often forms a square.

SOTOPORTEGO E PONTE S.CRISTOFORO

Sottoportico or Sotoportego means a covered passageway.

SALIZADA PIO X

Salizzada is a main street (formerly a paved street).

RIVA DEI PARTIGIANI

Riva is a wide *fondamenta*, often facing the lagoon.

RUGAGIUFFA

Ruga is a street lined with shops.

CORTE DEI DO POZZI

Corte means a courtyard.

RIO MENUO O DE LA VERONA

Many streets and canals in Venice often have more than one name: *o* means "or".

| 0 metres | 500 |
| 0 yards | 500 |

MURANO
(Inset on maps 3–4)

Scale of Murano inset

0 metres ———————— 300

0 yards ———————— 300

Murano

3 **4**

7 **8**

Grande

Castello

San Marco

Giudecca

Key to Street Finder

- Major sight
- Place of interest
- **FS** Railway station
- Vaparetto boarding point
- Traghetto crossing
- Gondola mooring
- Bus terminus
- *i* Tourist information
- Hospital with casualty unit
- Police station
- Church
- Synagogue
- Railway line

Scale of map pages

0 metres ———————— 150

0 yards ———————— 150

1

A   B   C

1

2

Canale delle

FONDAMENTA DI SACCA SAN GIROLAMO
SACCA DI
SAN GIROLAMO

CALLE LARGA DEI PENITENTI

FONDAMENTA CASE NUOVE

FONDAMENTA CARL.
Rio di San
FONDAMENTA

CALLE FERAU

CALLE DEL FORNER

CPLO DELLE
COOPERATIVE

CALLE TINTORIA

C.D. PORPORA

Tre Archi

Canale di Cannaregio

FONDAMENTA D

FONDAMENTA DEL

Rio del

3

Canale Colombola

FONDAMENTA D SAN GIOBBE

CALLE DELLE BECCARIE

CRIO D. BECCARIE

C.D. MAGAZEN

CALLE D. CANNE

Ponte dei
Tre Archi

CALLE D. MADONNA

C.D. STP SCURO

FONDAMENTA Canal

CALLE D. TINTOR

C.D. COLORI

San
Giobbe

Crea

CALLE BUSELLO

CALLE CENDON

CALLE DELLA CERERIA

Rio di San Giobbe

CAMPO
SAN GIOBBE

FMTA SAVORGNAN

CALLE BISCOTELLA

Rio della Crea

CALLE SECONDA D. DO.CORTI

PONTE DELLA LIBERTA

Rio della Crea

Rio della Crea

CALL

CALLE PISARO

RAMO D.
MISERICORD

CALLE DELLA MISERICORD

4

CALLE PRIULI DETTA DEI CAVALLETTI

RIO TERR

Scalzi

PMTA D. SCALZI

Ponte
degli Scalzi

Stazione Ferrovie
dello Stato
Santa Lucia

FS

Ferrovia

FONDAMENTA SANTA LUCIA

CALLE SAN SIMEON PICCOLO

CRIO D.
COMARE

S Simeòn
Piccolo

CALLE TRAGHETTO CAMPRE

DI SANTA LUCIA

CALLE BERGAMASCHI

5

Can D. Santa Chiara

FONDAMENTA DI SANTA CHIARA

FONDAMENTA DI SANTA CHIARA

C.VOLTO DI SANTA CHIARA

Piazzale
Roma

Ponte
della
Costituzione

CROCE

FONDAMENTA
DEI TOLENTINI

FONDAMENTA

GIARDINO
EX PAPADOPOLI

CORTE CASE NUOVE

CAMPO DELLA LAN

5

A   B   C

MURANO

CAMPO SPORTIVO

Calle del Convento
Calle Volpi

Canale Ondello

FONDAMENTA SEBASTIANO SANTI
FMTA SAN LORENZO
FONDAMENTA LORENZO RADI

Calle dell'Artigiano
Calle Brussa
Calle San Bernardo
VIA BAROVIER
STRADA COM D. CIMITERO
FONDAMENTA SEBASTIANO VENIER
Calle San Salvador
Canale

Campo San Bernardo
Calle del Cristo
Calle del Mistro
Calle Conterie

Basilica dei Santi Maria e Donato

Venier
degli
Angeli
Canale Serenella

Calle VIVARINI
Da Mula
RAMO DA MULA
FMTA DA MULA

Campo San Bernardo

Museo Vetraria
Museo

Ponte San Donato

GIUSTINIAN
FONDAMENTA ANDREA NAVAGERO

Palazzo da Mula
FONDAMENTA CAVOUR
Canal Grande di Murano
Ponte Vivarini
FMTA ANTONIO COLLEONI
CPO STO STEFANO

San Pietro Martire

CPLO TURELLA
CPLO BIGAGLIA

Calle S GIACZMO

Serenella

STRADA VICINALE ORTI
Calle San Cipriano
Calle Bertolini

C PARADISO

Navagero

C BERTOLINI
FONDAMENTA DEGLI VETRAI
FONDAMENTA DEI VETRAI
Calle F ODELL'OLIO
Calle MIOTI
VIALE GARIBALDI
FMTA SAN GIOVANNI DEI BATTUTI

VIA BRIATI

FONDAMENTA SERENELLA

FMTA PIAVE
Faro

Faro

Colonna

Canale dei Marani

Canale delle Fondamente Nuove

Ospedale

FONDAMENTE NUOVE

Calle D. Moschette
Calle delle Cappuccine
Rio di Santa Giustina
FONDAMENTA DI SANTA GIUSTINA
Calle San Francesco

Celestia

Calle degli Orti
FMTA CASE NUOVE

C SAGREDO

Ospedaletto

BARBARIA DELLE TOLE

San Francesco della Vigna

4
1
2
3
4
5

D   **E**   **F**

8

Venice Vaporetto Routes

The ACTV network runs regular services around the city and out to most of the islands. Some services are circular; others extend their routes during the high season. There are also additional lines during the summer months. More details of the different types of *vaporetti* and how to use them are given on pages 634–5.

Key

✈ Airport	▬ City centre route 1	▬ City centre route 5.2 (clockwise)
FS Railway station	▬ City centre route 2 (part seasonal)	▬ City centre route 6
🚢 Car ferry	▬ City centre route 3	▬ City centre route 7 (seasonal)
P Car parking	▬ City centre route 4.1 (anticlockwise)	▬ City centre route 8 (seasonal)
🚌 Main bus terminal	▬ City centre route 4.2 (clockwise)	▬ City centre route 10 (part seasonal)
O Waterbus stop	▬ City centre route 5.1 (anticlockwise)	▬ ▬ ▬ Night service N

enella
Venier
Da Mula
Museo
MURANO
Colonna
Faro
Navagero
ero
Celestia
Bacini
CASTELLO
aria
Arsenale
San Pietro
Certosa
Giardini
Sant' Elena
San Servolo
San Lazzaro

Torcello
Burano
Mazzorbo
Punta Vela
Chiesa
Lazzaretto
Nuovo
Cappannone
Vignole
Forte Massimiliano

Treporti
Punta
Sabbioni
San Nicolò
Ferry-Boat
San Nicolò

LIDO
Lido Santa
Maria Elizabetta

Lido Casinò

Chioggia ↓

Lagoon route 9
Lagoon route 12 (part seasonal)
Lagoon route 13
Lagoon route 14
Lagoon route 15
Lagoon route 18 (seasonal)

Lagoon route 19 (seasonal)
Lagoon route 20 (part seasonal)
Lagoon route 22
Terminal route A
Terminal route B
Terminal route O (seasonal)

Terminal route R (part seasonal)
Terminal route 16
Terminal route 17 (car ferry)
Terminal route 21 (seasonal)

THE VENETO AND FRIULI

The Veneto is a region of tremendous contrasts, encompassing the breathtaking natural beauty of the Dolomites, Lake Garda (Italy's largest lake) and the rolling Euganean Hills, and the man-made delights of magnificent ancient cities such as Verona, Vicenza and Padua. Neighbouring Friuli-Venezia Giulia lines the border with Slovenia to the east, taking in the Carnic Hills in the north, the Roman town of Aquileia and the bustling Adriatic port of Trieste.

The Romans built frontier posts on this fertile land of silt deposits, and these survive today as the cities of Vicenza, Padua, Verona and Treviso. Strategically placed at the hub of the empire's road network, the cities prospered under Roman rule, but suffered in the wave of Germanic invasions of the 5th century AD.

The region's fortunes revived under the benign rule of the Venetian empire. The medieval cities of the Veneto lay on important trade routes such as the Serenissima, the road connecting the flourishing port cities of Venice and Genoa, and the Brenner Pass, used by commercial travellers crossing the Alps from northern Europe. Wealth from agriculture, commerce and the spoils of war paid for the beautification of these cities through the building of Renaissance palaces and public buildings, many designed by the Veneto's great architect, Andrea Palladio. His palazzi and villas are telling symbols of the leisured existence once enjoyed by the area's aristocrats.

Today the Veneto is a thriving wine exporter, textile producer and agricultural centre, and Friuli is a focus for new technology, while remaining largely agricultural. Both regions are popular tourist destinations, despite lying a little in the shadow of Venice, and boast an abundant and enchanting variety of attractions.

A leisurely *passeggiata* in one of Verona's ancient streets

◀ The Renaissance Alpini Bridge by Palladio at Bassano del Grappa in the Veneto

Exploring the Veneto and Friuli

The flat landscape of the Veneto plain is dramatically offset by the spectacular Dolomite mountains which form the northwestern border to the Veneto. Friuli, Italy's most northeasterly region, lies tucked up against Austria to the north and Slovenia to the east. Both the Veneto and Friuli are bordered to the south by the Adriatic, with its beaches and ports, which provide a contrast with the area's gently rolling countryside, the vast stretch of Lake Garda and the many attractive resorts and ancient towns.

View of Verona from the Teatro Romano

Misu

CORTINA D'AMPEZZO 13

Bolzano

Piev di Cador

Alleghe

Monte Pelmo 3168m

Monte Civetta 3220m

Forno di Zoldo

Agordo

Longarone

Monte Schiara 2563m

BELLUNO 12

Monte Pavione 2334m

Sedico

Mel

Fonzaso

Feltre

Vittorio Veneto

Primolano

Cordign

Valdobbiadene

CONEGLIANO 11

Pederobba

Suse

Asiago

BASSANO DEL GRAPPA

Masèr

Montebelluna

4

ASOLO 3

Arsiero

Riva del Garda

Bolzano Trento

Malcesine

Marostica

Fanzolo

TREVIS 10

Monte Baldo 2200m

Recoaro Terme

Schio

Thiene

Cittadella

CASTELFRANCO VENETO 5

Paese

Valdagno

VENETO

Peri

Garda 2

Volargne

Tregnago

Montecchio Maggiore

VICENZA 6

Piazzola sul Brenta

Scorzè

Mogl Venet

Lazise

Bussolengo

Grezzana

Longare

Mirano

Mest

Sirmione

Peschiera

VERONA 1

Lonigo

San Bonifacio

PADOVA (PADUA) 7

Strà

9

Malcont

Fusina

Vené (Ven)

Brescia

Villafranca di Verona

San Giovanni Lupatoto

Abano Terme

BRENTA CANAL

Isola della Scala

EUGANEAN HILLS 8

Montegrotto Terme

Arquà Petrarca

Pellestrin

Mantova

Montagnana

Este

Piove di Sacco

Chiogg

Legnano

Villa Estense

Monselice

Nogara

Stanghella

Cavarzere

Castagnaro

Lendinara

Rovigo

Loreo

Rosol

Trecenta

Adria

Castelmassa

Taglio di Po

Polesine

Polesella

Ariano nel Polesine

Occhiobello

Ferrara Bologna

Key

━━━ Motorway

= = Motorway under construction

━━━ Major road

━━━ Secondary road

┄┄┄ Minor road

━━━ Scenic route

━┄━ Main railway

─── Minor railway

▓▓▓ International border

▒▒▒ Regional border

△ Summit

0 kilometres   25

0 miles   20

For additional map symbols *see back flap*

Getting Around

An extensive rail network and good bus services make this region easy to explore by public transport, though only buses operate around Lake Garda. Motorways and main roads provide good links between the main cities. The Venice Simplon-Orient-Express train, which operates from London to Venice, offers a novel approach to the area.

The bridge at Cividale del Friuli

A mountain chalet in Cortina d'Ampezzo

Sights at a Glance

1. *Verona pp146–51*
2. Lago di Garda
3. Bassano del Grappa
4. Asolo
5. Castelfranco Veneto
6. *Vicenza pp154–7*
7. *Padua (Padova) pp158–61*
8. Euganean Hills
9. Brenta Canal
10. Treviso
11. Conegliano
12. Belluno
13. Cortina d'Ampezzo
14. Tolmezzo
15. Pordenone
16. Udine
17. Cividale del Friuli
18. Gorizia
19. Aquileia
20. Trieste

Venice pp88–141

❶ Verona

Verona is a vibrant trading centre, the second biggest city in the Veneto region (after Venice) and one of the most prosperous in northern Italy. Its ancient centre boasts many magnificent Roman ruins, second only to those of Rome itself, and fine palazzi built of *rosso di Verona*, the local pink-tinged limestone, by the city's medieval rulers. Verona has two main focal points: the massive 1st-century Arena, which is still the setting for major events including a large opera festival, and Piazza Erbe with its colourful market. One of the main attractions, however, is the church of San Zeno Maggiore *(see pp150–51)*, which boasts unusual medieval bronze door panels: they are carved with extraordinary scenes, some biblical, others on the life of San Zeno.

View of Verona from the Museo Archeologico

Verona's Rulers

In 1263 the Scaligeri began their 124-year rule of Verona. They used ruthless tactics in their rise to power, but once established, the Scaligeri family brought peace to the city. They proved to be relatively just and cultured rulers – the poet Dante was welcomed to their court in 1301, and dedicated the final part of his epic *Divine Comedy* to the ruling Cangrande I. Today their legacy remains in their ornate tombs and in Castelvecchio.

In 1387 Verona fell to the Visconti of Milan, and a succession of outsiders – Venice, France and Austria – then ruled the city until the Veneto was united with Italy in 1866.

🏠 Castelvecchio

Corso Castelvecchio 2. **Tel** 045 592 985. **Open** 8:30am–7:30pm daily (from 1:30pm Mon, last adm: 45 mins before closing). **Closed** 1 Jan, 25 & 26 Dec. 🎫 🔲 📷

This impressive castle, built by Cangrande II between 1355 and 1375, houses one of the finest art galleries in the Veneto outside Venice.

The first section contains late Roman and early Christian items. The section on medieval and early Renaissance art demonstrates the influence of northern art on local painters: the emphasis is on brutal realism as opposed to serene

Verona's enormous Roman Arena seen from Piazza Brà

Ponte Scaligero, part of the old defence system of Castelvecchio

idealism. The late Renaissance works include a fine collection of 15th-century Madonnas.

Jewellery, armour, swords and Veronese's *Deposition* (1565) are also on display.

A walkway offers views of the river Adige, the Ponte Scaligero and the 14th-century statue of Cangrande I from his tomb *(see p148)*.

🏠 Ponte Scaligero
This medieval bridge was built by Cangrande II between 1354 and 1376. Such is the Veronese affection for the bridge that it was rebuilt after the retreating Germans blew it up in 1945, an operation that involved dredging the river to salvage the masonry. The bridge leads from Castelvecchio to the Arsenal on the north bank, fronted by public gardens.

🏠 San Lorenzo
Corso Cavour. **Tel** 045 59 28 13. **Open** daily. 🏠
San Lorenzo is one of Verona's lesser known churches, but is one of the city's most beautiful. Built in 1117 on the remains of a paleo-Christian basilica, the Romanesque exterior, with alternate strips of stone and bricks, is typical of Veronese churches. The bell tower dates to the 15th century and inside there are some 13th-century frescoes. The church features two unusual cylindrical towers.

🏠 Arena
Piazza Brà. **Tel** 045 800 51 51.
Open 8:30am–7:30pm daily (from 1:30pm Mon, last adm: 1 hr before closing. **Closed** 1 Jan, 25 & 26 Dec; Jun–Aug: from mid-afternoon on performance days. 🏠 🏠 partial.

Completed in AD 30, this is the world's third-largest Roman amphitheatre, after Rome's

Colosseum and the amphitheatre at Santa Maria Capua Vetere, near Naples. It could hold almost the entire population of Roman Verona, and visitors came from across the Veneto to watch gladiatorial combats. Since then, the arena has seen executions, fairs, bull-fights and opera productions.

🏠 San Fermo Maggiore
Stradone San Fermo. **Tel** 045 59 28 13. **Open** daily. 🏠 🏠
San Fermo Maggiore is not one but two churches: this is most clearly seen from the outside, where the apse has pointed Gothic elements rising above a sturdy Romanesque base. The lower church, begun in 1065 by Benedictine monks on the site of an earlier sanctuary, has frescoes on the simple arcades.

The more impressive upper church dates from 1313 and is covered with a splendid ship's keel roof. The interior also boasts much medieval fresco work, including a 14th-century section by Stefano da Zevio. Nearby is the Brenzoni mausoleum (c.1440) by Giovanni di Bartolo, and above it a 1426 fresco of the Annunciation by Pisanello (1377–1455).

Sights at a Glance

The 11th-century apse of the lower church of San Fermo Maggiore

Exploring Verona

Since the days of the Roman Empire, Piazza Erbe – built on the site of the ancient Roman forum – has been the centre of Verona. Many of the city's fine palazzi, churches and monuments are nearly as ancient, several dating from the medieval period.

The fountain, erected in the 14th century at the centre of Piazza Erbe

🏛 Piazza Erbe

Piazza Erbe is named after the city's old herb market. Today's stalls, shaded by umbrellas, sell everything from herb-flavoured roast suckling pig in bread rolls to succulent fresh-picked fruit and delicious wild mushrooms.

At the northern end of the square is the Baroque **Palazzo Maffei** (1668), surmounted by statues. In front of it rises a column supporting the **Venetian lion** marking Verona's absorption into the Venetian empire (1405). On the west side is the **Casa dei Mercanti**, a largely 17th-century building that dates originally from 1301. Opposite, wall frescoes are still visible above the cafés.

The **fountain** in the middle of the piazza is often overshadowed by the market stalls, though the statue at its centre dates from Roman times. It serves as a reminder that this piazza has been used as a market-place for 2,000 years.

🏛 Piazza dei Signori

Torre dei Lamberti. **Tel** 045 927 30 27. **Open** 8:30am–7:30pm daily (Jun–Sep: to 8:30pm Sat–Thu, to 11pm Fri). 🅿

In the centre of the square is a 19th-century **statue of Dante**, whose gaze seems fixed on the forbidding **Palazzo del Capitano**, once the home of Verona's military

commanders. Beside it is the equally intimidating **Palazzo della Ragione**, the palace of Reason, or law court; both were built in the 14th century. The courtyard of the law court has a handsome external stone staircase, added in 1446–50. Stunning views of the Alps can be enjoyed from atop the 84-m (275-ft) **Torre dei Lamberti**, which rises from the western side of the courtyard.

Behind the statue of Dante is the **Loggia del Consiglio** (1493), the council chamber. The building is topped by statues of Roman worthies born in Verona: they include Pliny the Elder, the natural historian, and Vitruvius, the architectural theorist.

The square is linked to Piazza Erbe by the Arco della Costa, or the Arch of the Rib, named after the whale rib long ago hung beneath it.

The frescoed Renaissance façade of the Loggia del Consiglio on Piazza dei Signori

🏛 Tombs of the Scaligeri

Via Arche Scaligeri.

Beside the entrance to the tiny Romanesque church of **Santa Maria Antica**, once the parish church of the powerful Scaligeri family, lie a profusion of bizarre tombs of the onetime rulers of Verona.

Over the entrance to the church is the impressive tomb of Cangrande I (died 1329), surmounted by an equestrian statue of the ruler, a copy of the original which is now in Castelvecchio *(see p147)*.

The other Scaligeri tombs are next to the church, behind a wrought iron fence which incorporates the ladder emblem of the family's original name *(della Scala,* meaning "of the steps"). Towering above the fence are the tombs of Mastino II (died 1351) and Cansignorio (died 1375), splendidly decorated with a profusion of tiny Gothic spires. Other members of the Scaligeri family lie within a series of plainer tombs which stand nearer the church wall.

14th-century Scaligeri tomb

🏛 Sant'Anastasia

Piazza Sant'Anastasia. **Tel** 045 59 28 13. **Open** daily. 🎨 🅰 🖾

The huge and lofty church of Sant'Anastasia was begun in 1290. Faded 15th-century frescoes and carved scenes from the life of St Peter Martyr adorn its Gothic portal.

Inside, there are two holy-water stoups, supported on figures of beggars, known as *i gobbi* (the hunch-backs). These figures were carved a century apart: the earlier one (on the left) dates from 1495. The sacristy, off the north aisle, is home to a fine (but damaged) fresco by Pisanello: *St George and the Princess* (1433–8).

Romeo and Juliet

The tragic story of Romeo and Juliet, two young lovers from rival families, was written by Luigi da Porto of Vicenza in the 1520s and has inspired countless dramas, films and ballets.

At the **Casa di Giulietta** (Juliet's house), No. 23 Via Cappello, Romeo is said to have climbed to Juliet's balcony; in reality this is a restored 13th-century inn. Crowds throng to see the simple façade and stand on the small marble balcony. The run-down **Casa di Romeo** is a few streets away, in Via Arche Scaligeri.

The so-called **Tomba di Giulietta** is displayed in a crypt below the cloister of San Francesco al Corso on Via del Pontiere. The stone sarcophagus lies in an extremely atmospheric setting.

Both the Casa and the Tomba di Giulietta are open daily (on Mondays in the afternoon only). There is an admission charge.

The so-called Casa di Giulietta

⌂ Duomo
Piazza Duomo. **Tel** 045 59 28 13.
Open daily. 🅿 ♿ ⛟

Verona's cathedral was begun in 1139 and is fronted by a magnificent Romanesque portal carved by Nicolò, one of the two master masons responsible for the façade of San Zeno (see pp150–51). Here he sculpted the sword-bearing figures of Oliver and Roland, two of Charlemagne's knights, whose exploits were much celebrated in medieval poetry. Alongside them stand evangelists and saints with wide eyes and flowing beards. To the south there is a second Romanesque portal carved with Jonah and the Whale and with comically grotesque caryatids.

The highlight of the interior is Titian's lovely *Assumption* (1535–40), and outside there is a Romanesque cloister in which the excavated ruins of earlier churches are visible. The 8th-century baptistry, or San Giovanni in Fonte (St John of the Spring), was built from Roman masonry; the marble font was carved in 1200.

⌂ Teatro Romano
🏛 Museo Archeologico
Regaste Redentore 2. **Tel** 045 800 03 60. **Open** 1:30–7:30pm Mon (all day if pub hol); 8:30am–7:30pm Tue–Sun. The theatre closes early in the afternoon on performance days.
Closed 1 Jan, 25 & 26 Dec. 🅿 ♿

This Roman theatre was built in the 1st century BC; little survives of the stage area, but the semicircular seating area is largely intact. It offers great views over Verona: in the foreground is the only one of three Roman bridges to have survived, though it was rebuilt after World War II.

A lift carries visitors from the Teatro Romano up the cliffs to the monastery above, now an interesting archaeological museum. The exhibits around the tiny cloister and in the old monks' cells include mosaics, pottery and glass. There is also a fine bronze bust of the first Roman emperor, Augustus (63 BC–AD 14), who in 31 BC overcame his opponents, including Mark Antony and Cleopatra, to become the sole ruler of the Roman world.

Statuary and formal hedges in the Renaissance Giardino Giusti

🌳 Giardino Giusti
Via Giardino Giusti 2. **Tel** 045 803 40 29. **Open** 9am–8pm daily (Oct–Mar: to 7pm). **Closed** 25 Dec. 🅿 ♿

This fine Renaissance garden was laid out in 1580. As with other gardens of the period, there is a deliberate juxtaposition of nature and artifice: the formal lower garden of clipped box hedges, gravel walks and potted plants contrasts with wilder, natural woods above.

John Evelyn, the English author and diarist who visited Verona in 1661, thought this the finest garden in Europe.

⌂ San Giorgio in Braida
Lungadige San Giorgio. **Tel** 045 834 02 32. **Open** daily. **Closed** during mass.

This lovely domed Renaissance church was begun in about 1530 by Michele Sanmicheli. The altar includes the famous *Martyrdom of St George* (1566) by Veronese, and above the west door is the *Baptism of Christ*, usually attributed to Tintoretto (1518–94).

The imposing façade of Verona's Duomo, Santa Maria Matricolare

Verona: San Zeno Maggiore

San Zeno, built in 1120–38 to house the shrine of Verona's patron saint, is the most ornate Romanesque church in northern Italy. The façade is adorned with an impressive rose window, marble reliefs, and a graceful porch canopy. The highlight, however, is the fascinating 11th- and 12th-century bronze door panels. A squat tower just north of San Zeno is said to cover the tomb of King Pepin of Italy (777–810).

Nave Ceiling
The nave has a magnificent example of a ship's keel ceiling, so called because it resembles the inside of an upturned boat. This ceiling was constructed in 1386 when the apse was rebuilt.

Altarpiece by Mantegna
The Madonna's halo in Andrea Mantegna's altarpiece of the Virgin and Child with saints (1457–59) echoes the shape of the church's rose window.

VISITORS' CHECKLIST

Practical Information
P. San Zeno. **Tel** 045 59 28 13.
Open 8:30am–6pm Mon–Sat, 12:30–6pm Sun (Nov–Feb: 10am–1pm, 1:30–5pm Tue–Sat, 12:30–5pm Sun). **Closed** for mass. 🅿 🚻 times vary. 🚻
🅦 basilicasanzeno.it

★ Cloister (1293–1313)
The arches are rounded Romanesque on one side, pointed Gothic on another.

Bronze Door Panels

The 48 bronze panels of the west doors are primitive but force-ful in their depiction of biblical stories and scenes from the life of San Zeno. Those on the left date from 1030 and survive from an earlier church on the site; those on the right were made after the earthquake in 1137. The panels are the work of three separate craftsmen and are linked with masks. Huge staring eyes and Ottoman-style hats, armour and architecture feature prominently. Among the scenes, some of which are unclear, are Adam and Eve, Salome dancing for the head of John the Baptist, and a startling Descent into Limbo.

Descent into Limbo   Christ in Glory   Human head

KEY

① **Former washroom**

② **The bell tower**, started in 1045, reached its present height of 72 m (236 ft) in 1173.

③ **The rose window**, dating from the early 12th century, symbolizes the Wheel of Fortune: figures on the rim show the rise and fall of human luck.

④ **The Romanesque porch** is one of the finest examples of the style in northern Italy. Since 1138 it has shielded biblical bas-reliefs, above the west doors, from the elements.

⑤ **Marble side panels**, which were carved in 1140, depict events from the Life of Christ (to the left of the doors) and scenes from the Book of Genesis (to the right).

⑥ **Striped brickwork** is typical of Roman-esque buildings in Verona. Courses of local pink brick are alternated with ivory-coloured tufa.

⑦ **The Crypt** has a vaulted crypt contains the tomb of San Zeno, appointed eighth bishop of Verona in AD 362, who died in AD 380.

Nave and Main Altar
The plan of the church is modelled on an ancient Roman basilica, the Hall of Justice. The main altar is situated in the raised sanctuary where the judge's throne would have stood.

★ West Doors
Each of the wooden doors has 24 bronze plates nailed on to make the doors look like solid metal. A multi-coloured bas-relief above them depicts San Zeno, flanked by the people of Verona, vanquishing the devil.

❷ Lago di Garda

Garda, the largest and easternmost of the Italian lakes, borders three regions: Trentino to the north, Lombardy to the west and south, and the Veneto to the south and east. The low-lying countryside around the southern stretches becomes increasingly dramatic further north, until impressive rocky cliffs, sometimes swathed in pines, hug the shoreline of the northern tip. The numerous sporting facilities, many sights, and splendid scenery of snow-capped mountains help make the lake a favourite summer playground.

VISITORS' CHECKLIST

Practical Information
Brescia, Verona & Trento. ℹ Viale Marconi 8, Sirmione (030 91 61 14). Il Vittoriale: Gardone.
Tel 0365 29 65 11. **Open** daily.
🏰 Rocca Scaligera: Sirmione.
Tel 030 91 64 68. **Open** Tue–Sun.
🏰 ☑ 🅦 sirmionebs.it

Transport
🚇 Peschiera del Garda, Desenzano del Garda.
🚌 🚍 to all towns.

Eastern tip of Sirmione Peninsula
Beyond the town is a path which follows the rim of the peninsula, passing boiling sulphur springs.

Riva's waterfront is dominated by a 12th-century fortress. Windsurfers favour this resort because of the consistent off-shore winds.

The streets of Malcesine cluster below an imposing medieval castle. A cable car climbs to the summit of Monte Baldo (1,745 m/ 5,725 ft), offering far-reaching views.

Gardone is noted for its exotically planted park and for Il Vittoriale, the Art Deco villa of the poet Gabriele d'Annunzio, which is filled with curiosities.

The Republic of Salò was established here by Mussolini in 1943. The cathedral in this elegant town of pastel-painted houses contains a 14th-century altarpiece by Veneziano.

The lake is named after this long-established town.

Bardolino gave its name to the well-known red wine.

Peschiera's attractive enclosed harbour and fortress were built by the Austrians in the 1860s, during the Italian Wars of Independence.

The hydrofoils, catamarans and steamers which ply the lake offer glimpses of villas and gardens, which cannot be seen from the coastal road.

Sirmione
A fascinating medieval castle, the Rocca Scaligera dominates the town of Sirmione. At the tip of the peninsula lie Roman ruins.

0 kilometres 5
0 miles 5

Key

••• Steamer route

••• Car ferry

Riva del Garda
Torbole
Limone sul Garda
Tremosine
Campione del Garda
Malcesine
Assenza
Tignale
Brenzone
Castelletto
Gargnano
Bogliaco
Toscolano Maderno
Gardone Riviera
Salò
Portese
San Felice del Benaco
Torri del Benaco
Garda
Monerba Moniga
Bardolino
Lazise
Padenghe sul Garda
Sirmione
Desenzano
Peschiera del Garda

The 16th-century wooden bridge by Palladio at Bassano del Grappa

❸ Bassano del Grappa

Vicenza. 🚹 39,000. FS 🚌 ℹ️ Largo Corona d'Italia 35 (0424 52 43 51). 🏪 Thu & Sat am.

This peaceful town lies at the foot of Monte Grappa. The river Brenta is straddled by the graceful Ponte degli Alpini, which was designed in 1569 by Palladio. It is built of timber to allow it to flex when hit by the spring meltwaters. Bassano is well known for its majolica products (decorated and glazed earthenware), some of which are on display in the **Palazzo Sturm**. The town is also synonymous with the popular Italian after-dinner drink, the clear spirit known as *grappa*. It is produced from the lees *(graspa)* left over from wine production; information about the process is given in the **Museo degli Alpini**.

🏛 **Palazzo Sturm**
Via Schiavonetti. **Tel** 0424 52 49 33. **Open** Tue–Sun. 🚫

🏛 **Museo degli Alpini**
Via Angarano 2. **Tel** 0424 50 36 62. **Open** Tue–Sun. 🆆 **museibassano.it**

❹ Asolo

Treviso. 🚹 2,000. 🚌 ℹ️ Piazza Garibaldi 73 (0423 52 90 46). 🏪 Sat. 🆆 **asolo.it**

Asolo is beautifully sited among the cypress-clad foothills of the Dolomites. This tiny walled town was once ruled by Queen Caterina Cornaro (1454–1510), the Venetian wife of the King of Cyprus, who poisoned her husband so that Venice would gain Cyprus. Cardinal Pietro Bembo, a poet, coined the verb *asolare* to describe the bittersweet life of enforced idleness she endured in exile here. Among others who fell in love with the narrow streets and grand houses was poet Robert Browning, who named a volume of poems *Asolanda* (1889) after Asolo.

Environs
At Maser, 10 km (6 miles) east of the town, stands the magnificent **Villa Barbaro** *(see pp84–5)*. It was designed by Palladio in about 1555, in conjunction with the artist Veronese, and perfectly blends symmetry and light, airy rooms with sumptuous *trompe l'oeil* frescoes.

🏛 **Villa Barbaro**
Maser. **Tel** 0423 92 30 04. **Open** opening times vary; check website for details. **Closed** 1 Jan, Easter Sun, 25 Dec. 🚫 🆆 **villadimaser.it**

❺ Castelfranco Veneto

Treviso. 🚹 30,000. FS 🚌 ℹ️ Via Francesco M Preti 66 (0423 49 50 00). 🏪 Tue am & Fri am.

Fortified in 1199 by rulers of Treviso as a defence against the neighbouring Paduans, the historic core of this town lies within well-preserved walls. In the **Casa di Giorgione**, said to be the birthplace of the painter Giorgione (1478–1511), about whom little is known, there is a museum devoted to his life. Giorgione innovatively used landscape to create mood, adding figures to intensify the atmosphere – for instance in his most famous work, the broodingly mysterious but evocative *The Tempest (see p110)*. Another of his few directly attributable works hangs here in the **Duomo**: the *Madonna and Child with Saints Liberal and Francis* (1504).

Environs
About 8 km (5 miles) northeast of the town, at Fanzolo, lies the **Villa Emo** (c.1555). Designed by Palladio, it is a typical example of his work: a cube flanked by two symmetrical wings. Inside there are lavish frescoes by Zelotti.

🏛 **Casa di Giorgione**
Piazza San Liberale. **Tel** 0423 72 50 22. **Open** Tue–Sun. **Closed** pub hols. 🚫

🏛 **Villa Emo**
Via Stazione 5, Fanzolo. **Tel** 0423 47 63 34. **Open** May–Oct: daily (pm only Mon–Sat); Nov–Apr: daily. **Closed** 1 Jan, 25, 26 & 31 Dec. 🚫 🏛

Fresco (c.1561) by Veronese adorning the Villa Barbaro near Asolo

❻ Street-by-Street: Vicenza

Vicenza is known as the adoptive city of
Andrea Palladio (1508–80), who started
out as a stonemason and became the most
influential architect of his time. The evolution
of his distinctive style is visible all around the
city. In the centre is the monumental basilica
he adapted to serve as the town hall, nearby
is the Teatro Olimpico, and all around are the
palaces he built for Vicenza's wealthy citizens.

Contrà Porti is
bordered by some
of the most elegant
palazzi in Vicenza.

Loggia del Capitaniato
This covered arcade
was designed by
Palladio in 1571.

Palazzo Valmarana Braga
Palladio's impressive building of 1566 is
decorated with giant pilasters and sculpted
scenes. It was not completed until 1680,
100 years after the architect's death.

Duomo
Vicenza's cathedral
was rebuilt after bomb
damage during World
War II left only the façade
and choir entirely intact.

San Lorenzo

Piazza Stazione

Andrea Palladio
This memorial to
Vicenza's most
famous citizen is
usually surrounded
by market stalls.

CORSO ANDREA PALLADIO
CONTRA CAVOUR
PIAZZA DE SIGNC
CONTRA PALLADI
C MUSCHERIA
CONTRA GARIBALDI
CONTRA PESCHERIE VECCHIE
VIA BATTISTI
CONTRA P LAMPERTICO
PIAZZA DEL DUOMO
CONTRA SAN ANTONIO
CONTRA

0 metres		2
0 miles		1

Key

— Suggested route

A large hall is all that remains of the 15th-century Palazzo della Ragione.

Torre di Piazza, built in the 12th century, is an impressive 82 m (269 ft) high.

Santa Corona

Teatro Olimpico Museo Civico

COVNTRA S BARBARA

PIAZZA DELLE BIADE

CONTRA CATENA

CONTRA C GAZZOLE

PIAZZA DELL' ERBE

CONTRA PESCARIA

CONTRA SAN PAOLO

CONTRA PIANCOLI

CONTRA PONTE SAN MICHELE

RETRONE

VISITORS' CHECKLIST

Practical Information
116,000. Piazza Matteotti 12 (0444 32 08 54). Tue & Thu. May–Jun: concert season; Sep–Oct: theatre season; end Jun–early Jul: Concerti in Villa.
W vicenzae.org

Transport
FS Piazza Stazione.

The lion of St Mark gazing down on Piazza dei Signori

☷ Piazza dei Signori

Basilica: **Tel** 0444 32 36 81. **Open** for exhibitions only, when it is possible to walk along the balustrade and visit the loggia (call tourist office for timings).

This square at the heart of Vicenza is dominated by the Palazzo della Ragione, often referred to as the **Basilica**. Its green, copper-clad roof is shaped like an upturned boat with a balustrade bristling with the statues of Greek and Roman gods. The colonnades were designed by Palladio in 1549 as a facing to support the city's 15th-century town hall, which had begun to subside. The Basilica is now used as an exhibition space. Beside it stands the 12th-century Torre di Piazza.

The **Loggia del Capitaniato**, to the northwest, was built by Palladio in 1571: the Loggia's upper rooms contain the city's council chamber.

★ **Piazza dei Signori**
Palladio's elegant buildings flank the Piazza dei Signori, including the majestic two-tier colonnades of the 16th-century "Basilica", built around the old Palazzo della Ragione.

The Quartiere delle Barche contains numerous attractive palaces built in the 14th-century Venetian Gothic style.

☷ Contrà Porti

Contrà (an abbreviation of *contrada*, or district) is the Vicenza dialect word for street. On one side of the Contrà is a series of pretty Gothic buildings with painted windows and ornate balconies, reminiscent of Venice and a reminder that Vicenza was once part of the Venetian empire.

Several elegant Palladian palazzi stand on this street. Palazzo Porto Barbarano (No. 11), Palazzo Thiene (No. 12) and Palazzo Iseppo da Porto (No. 21) illustrate the variety of Palladio's style – all share Classical elements but each is unique. An intriguing detail is that Palazzo Thiene appears to be of stone, but it is in fact built of cheap brick, rendered to look like masonry.

Ponte San Michele
This elegant stone bridge, built in 1620, provides lovely views of the surrounding town.

La Rotonda Monte Berico Villa Valmarana ai Nani

Piazza delle Erbe, the city's market square, is overlooked by a 13th-century prison tower.

Casa Pigafetta
This striking 15th-century house was the birthplace of Antonio Pigafetta, who in 1519 set sail round the world with Magellan.

Exploring Vicenza

Vicenza, the great Palladian city and one of the wealthiest cities in the Veneto, is celebrated the world over for its splendid and varied architecture; it also offers the visitor elegant shops and cafés to visit.

Brusazorzi's ceiling fresco in the large entrance hall of the Museo Civico

🏛 Museo Civico
Piazza Matteotti 37–39.
Tel 0444 22 28 11.
Open 9am–5pm Tue–Sun.
🅿 ♿ 🌐 museicivicivicenza.it

This museum is housed in **Palazzo Chiericati** (see p84) which was built by Palladio. Inside is a fresco by Domenico Brusazorzi of a naked charioteer, representing the Sun, who seems to fly over the entrance hall. Among the Gothic altarpieces from churches in Vicenza is Hans Memling's *Crucifixion* (1468–70), the central panel from a triptych whose side panels are now in New York.

Other rooms contain works by the local artist Bartolomeo Montagna (c.1450–1523).

🏛 Santa Corona
Contrà Santa Corona.
Tel 0444 32 36 44. **Open** Tue–Sun.

This Gothic church was built in 1261 to house a thorn donated by Louis IX of France and said to be from Christ's Crown of Thorns. The Cappella Porto houses the tomb of Luigi da Porto, author of *Giulietta e Romeo*, on which Shakespeare based his famous play. Notable paintings include Giovanni Bellini's *Baptism of Christ* (c.1500) and the *Adoration of the Magi* (1573) by Paolo Veronese.

🎭 Teatro Olimpico
Piazza Matteotti 11. **Tel** 0444 22 28 00.
Open 9am–5pm Tue–Sun. **Closed** during performances, 1 Jan, 25 Dec. 🅿 ♿ 📷
🌐 teatrolimpicovicenza.it

Europe's oldest surviving indoor theatre is a remarkable structure, largely made of wood and plaster, and painted to look like marble. Palladio began work on the design in 1579, but he died the year after. His pupil Vincenzo Scamozzi took over the project, completing the theatre in time for its opening performance of Sophocles' tragic drama *Oedipus Rex* on 3 March 1585.

Odeon Frescoes
The gods of Mount Olympus, after which the theatre is named, decorate the Odeon, a room used for music recitals.

The Anteodeon contains frescoes depicting the theatre's opening performance and oil lamps from the original stage set.

Main ticket office

Stage Set
Scamozzi's scenery represents the Greek city of Thebes. The streets are cleverly painted in perspective and rise at a steep angle to give the illusion of great length.

The Auditorium was designed by Palladio to resemble the outdoor theatres of ancient Greece and Rome, such as the Arena at Verona (see p147), with a semi-circle of "stone" benches and a ceiling painted to portray the sky.

⬆ San Lorenzo

Piazza San Lorenzo. **Open** daily.

The portal of this church is a magnificent example of Gothic stone carving, richly decorated with the figures of the Virgin and Child, and St Francis and St Clare. Inside there are fine tombs and damaged frescoes. The lovely cloister, north of the church, is an attractive, flower-filled haven of calm.

⬆ Monte Berico

Basilica di Monte Berico. **Tel** 0444 55 94 11. **Open** daily (only pm Sun).

Monte Berico is the green, cypress-clad hill to the south of Vicenza to which wealthy residents once escaped, in the heat of summer, to enjoy the cooler air and pastoral charms of their country estates. Today, shady *portici*, or colonnades, adorned with shrines, line the wide avenue linking central

La Rotonda (1550–52), most famous of all Palladio's works

Vicenza to the basilica on top of the hill. The domed basilica itself, built in the 15th century and enlarged in the 18th, is dedicated to the Virgin who appeared here during the 1426–8 plague to announce that Vicenza would be spared.

The ornate interior contains a moving *Pietà* fresco (1500) by Bartolomeo Montagna, a fossil collection in the cloister, and Veronese's fine painting, *The Supper of St Gregory the Great* (1572), in the refectory.

The Baroque hilltop church, the Basilica di Monte Berico

🏛 Villa Valmarana ai Nani

Via dei Nani 8. **Tel** 0444 32 18 03. **Open** 10am–12:30pm, 3–6pm Tue–Sun. **Closed** 5 Nov–9 Mar.
W villavalmarana.com

The wall alongside the Villa Valmarana, built in 1688 by Antonio Muttoni, is topped by figures of dwarfs (*nani*) which give the building its name.

Inside, the walls are covered with frescoes by Tiepolo, in which the gods of Mount Olympus float about on clouds watching scenes

from the epics of Homer and Virgil. In the separate Foresteria (guest house), the 18th-century frescoes depicting peasant life and the seasons, painted by Tiepolo's son Giandomenico, are imbued with an earthy realism.

The villa can be reached by a 10-minute walk from the basilica on Monte Berico. Head downhill along Via Massimo d'Azeglio to the high-walled convent on the right where the road ends, then take Via San Bastiano.

🏛 La Rotonda

Via Rotonda 45. **Tel** 0444 32 17 93. Villa: **Open** 13 Mar–4 Nov: Wed & Sat. 🌳 Garden: **Open** Tue–Sun.
🌳 **W** villalarotonda.it

With its perfectly regular, symmetrical forms, this villa, also known as the Villa Capra Valmarana, is the epitome of Palladio's architecture (see pp84–5) of which there are several fine examples throughout the Veneto. The design, consisting of a dome rising above a cube, received immediate acclaim for the way it blends perfectly with its surroundings. A pleasant contrast exists between the terracotta roof tiles, the white walls and the green lawns.

The villa, built in 1550–52, has inspired many copies in cities as far away as London, St Petersburg and Delhi. Fans of *Don Giovanni* will enjoy spotting locations used in Joseph Losey's 1979 film.

La Rotonda can be reached by bus from town, or on foot, following the path alongside the Villa Valmarana ai Nani.

The façade statues of stately toga-clad figures are portraits of sponsors who paid for the theatre's construction.

The courtyard giving access to the Teatro is decorated with ancient sculptures. These were donated by members of the Olympic Academy, the learned body that built the theatre.

Main entrance

❼ Street-by-Street: Padua

Padua (Padova) is an old university town with an illustrious academic history. Rich in art and architecture, it has two particularly outstanding sights. The magnificent Cappella degli Scrovegni *(see pp160–61)*, north of the city centre, is famous for Giotto's lyrical frescoes. Close to the railway station, it forms part of the complex incorporating the Eremitani church and museums. The Basilica di Sant'Antonio, which forms the focal point in the southern part of the city, is one of the most popular pilgrimage destinations in Italy.

Palazzo del Capitanio
Built between 1599 and 1605 for the head of the city's militia, the tower incorporates an astronomical clock made in 1344.

Corte Capitaniato, a 14th-century arts faculty (open for concerts), contains frescoes which include a rare portrait of the poet Petrarch.

Ufficio di Turismo

Loggia della Gran Guardia
This fine Renaissance building dating from 1523 once housed the Council of Nobles. It is now used as a conference centre.

PIAZZA CAPITANIATO

VIA SAN CLEMENTE

PIAZZA DEI SIGNORI

VIA MANIN

V GRITT

PIAZZA DEL DUOMO

VIA SONCIN

VIA VANDELLI

★ Duomo and Baptistry
The 12th-century baptistry of the Duomo contains one of the most complete medieval fresco cycles to survive in Italy, painted by Giusto de' Menabuoi in 1378.

Piazza dei Signori is bordered by attractive arcades which house small speciality shops, cafés and old-fashioned wine bars.

The Palazzo del Monte di Pietà has 16th-century arcades and statues enclosing a medieval building.

Key
— Suggested route

0 metres　　75
0 yards　　　75

For hotels and restaurants in this region see pp562–77 and pp580–605

Caffè Pedrocchi
Built like a Classical temple, the Caffè Pedrocchi has been a famous meeting place for students and intellectuals since it opened in 1831.

A bronze statue of a woman (1973) by Emilio Greco stands at the centre of this largely pedestrianized square.

Stazione Chiesa Degli Eremitiani Cappella Degli Scrovegni Museo Civico

PIAZZA CAVOUR

VIA GORIZIA

PIAZZA DELLE FRUTTA

VIA OBERDAN

VIA VIII FEBBRAIO

PITTA GARZERIA

PIAZZA DELLE ERBE

V SAN CANZIANO

Basilica di Sant'Antonio
Orto Botanico

Palazzo della Ragione, the medieval court of justice, contains magnificent frescoes.

Padua University
Founded in 1222, this is Italy's second oldest university. Elena Piscopia was the first woman graduate, in 1678.

Piazza delle Erbe
There are some excellent views to be had over the market place from the 15th-century loggia which runs alongside the 13th-century Palazzo della Ragione.

🏛 Duomo and Baptistry
Piazza Duomo. Baptistry: **Tel** 049 65 69 14. **Open** 10am–6pm daily. **Closed** 1 Jan, Easter, 25 Dec.

The Duomo was built in 1552 to plans partly by Michelangelo, on the site of an earlier 14th-century cathedral. Beside it stands a domed baptistry (c.1200). The interior is entirely decorated with vibrant frescoes painted by Giusto de' Menabuoi, dating from around 1378. The frescoes depict episodes from the Bible, including scenes of the Creation, the Miracles, the Passion, the Crucifixion and the Resurrection of Christ.

🏛 Palazzo della Ragione
Piazza delle Erbe (entrance via the town hall). **Tel** 049 820 50 06. **Open** 9am–7pm Tue–Sun (Nov–Jan: to 6pm). **Closed** 1 Jan, 1 May, 25 & 26 Dec.

The "Palace of Reason" was built in 1218 to serve as Padua's law court and council chamber. The vast main hall was originally decorated with frescoes by Giotto, but fire destroyed his work in 1420. The Salone is breathtaking in its sheer size. It is the largest undivided medieval hall in Europe, 80 m (260 ft) long, 27 m (90 ft) wide and 27 m (90 ft) high. Frescoes painted in 1420–25 by Nicola Miretto cover its walls: the 333 panels depict the months of the year, with appropriate gods, signs of the zodiac and seasonal activities. A 1466 copy of the huge Gattamelata statue (see p162) by Donatello stands at one end of the hall.

🏛 Caffè Pedrocchi
Via VIII Febbraio 15. **Tel** 049 878 12 31. **Open** daily. **Closed** Aug. Museum: **Open** Tue–Sun.

Caffè Pedrocchi opened in 1831, and became famous as the café that never closed its doors. Today people come as much to talk, play cards or watch the world go by as to eat or drink. The upstairs rooms, decorated in Moorish, Egyptian and other styles, house a museum documenting modern Italian history.

Padua: Cappella degli Scrovegni

Enrico Scrovegni built this chapel in 1303, hoping thereby to spare his dead father, a usurer, from the eternal damnation in hell described by the poet Dante in his *Inferno*. The interior of the chapel is entirely covered with beautiful frescoes of scenes from the life of Christ, painted by Giotto between 1303 and 1305. As works of great narrative force, they exerted a powerful influence on the development of European art.

The Nativity
The naturalism of the Virgin's pose marks a departure from Byzantine stylization, as does the use of natural blue for the sky, in place of celestial gold.

Expulsion of the Merchants
Christ's physical rage, the cowering merchant and the child hiding his face show an animation that is characteristic of Giotto's style.

The Coretti
Giotto painted the two panels known as the Coretti as an exercise in perspective, creating the illusion of an arch with a room beyond.

View towards altar

West entrance   **North side**   **Altar**   **South side**   **West entrance**

Gallery Guide

Due to the Cappella degli Scrovegni's small size, the number of visitors allowed in at any one time is strictly limited. Prior to entering, visitors are required to spend 15 minutes in a decontamination chamber, where multimedia and multilingual information on the chapel is provided. The visit itself is also restricted to 15 minutes. Advance booking is compulsory, either by phone (049 201 00 20) or online (www. cappelladegliscrovegni.it), with a credit card payment.

Key

- Episodes of Joachim and Anna
- Episodes from the Life of Mary
- Episodes from the Life and Death of Christ
- The Virtues and Vices
- The Last Judgment

The Last Judgment

This scene fills the entire west wall of the chapel. Its formal composition is closer to Byzantine tradition than some of the other frescoes, with parts probably painted by assistants. A model of the chapel is shown (centre left, at the bottom) being offered to the Virgin by Scrovegni.

View towards entrance

Mary is Presented at the Temple
Giotto sets many scenes against an architectural background, using the laws of perspective to give a sense of three dimensions.

Injustice
The Vices and Virtues are painted in monochrome. Here Injustice is symbolized by scenes of war, murder and robbery.

Lament over the Dead Christ
Giotto's figures express their grief in different ways: some huddle together, another gestures wildly.

Giotto

The Florentine artist Giotto (1266–1337) is regarded as the father of the Renaissance, the great revival in the Classical traditions of Western art. His work, with its sense of pictorial space, naturalism and narrative drama, marks a decisive break with the Byzantine tradition of the preceding 1,000 years. Although he was regarded in his lifetime as a great artist, few of the works attributed to him are fully documented. Some may have been painted by others, but his authorship of the frescoes in the Scrovegni Chapel need not be doubted.

Exploring Padua

Padua is a city of many attractions, with a rich history: this is reflected in the major museum complex which occupies a group of 14th-century monastic buildings attached to the church of the Eremitani, a reclusive Augustinian order. Next door is the Cappella degli Scrovegni *(see pp160–61)*. Padua is, in addition, the setting for one of Italy's most important churches – the splendid Basilica di Sant'Antonio – and for one of the earliest universities to be founded in Italy.

🏛 Chiesa degli Eremitani and Museo Civico Eremitani

Piazza Eremitani 8. **Tel** 049 820 45 50.
Museum: **Open** Tue–Sun.

The Eremitani church, built from 1276 to 1306, contains magnificent roof and wall tombs. Among them is that of Marco Benavides (1489–1582), a professor of law at the city university, whose Renaissance tomb was the work of Florentine architect Ammannati (1511–92). Celebrated frescoes (1454–7) by Mantegna, portraying scenes from the lives of St James and St Christopher, were destroyed during a bombing raid in 1944. Two scenes from this magnificent series survive in the Cappella Ovetari, south of the sanctuary: *The Martyrdom of St James* and *The Martyrdom of St Christopher*.

A 1st-century AD tomb in the archaeological collection

The Museo Civico Eremitani comprises a coin collection (which includes rare Roman medallions and an almost complete set of Venetian coinage), an archaeological section and an impressive art gallery.

The rich archaeological collection contains interesting Roman tombs, fine mosaics and impressive life-size statues. Renaissance bronzes include the comical *Drinking Satyr* by Il Riccio (1470–1532).

The beautiful 14th-century Crucifix from the Cappella degli Scrovegni is in the Quadreria Emo Capodilista, as well as works by Giotto, and 15th- to 18th-century paintings from the Venetian and Flemish schools.

15th-century *Angels in Armour* by Guariento, Museo Civico Eremitani

⛪ Basilica di Sant'Antonio

Piazza del Santo. **Tel** 049 822 5652.
Open 7am–7:30pm daily.

This exotic church, with its minaret-like spires and Byzantine domes, is also known as Il Santo. It was built from 1232 to house the remains of St Anthony of Padua, a preacher who modelled himself on St Francis of Assisi. Although he was a simple man who rejected worldly wealth, the citizens of Padua built a lavish church to serve as his shrine.

The influence of Byzantine architecture is clearly visible in the basilica's outline: a coneshaped central dome rises above seven encircling domes; the façade combines Gothic and Romanesque elements.

Inside, the high altar features Donatello's magnificent reliefs (1444–5) on the miracles of St Anthony, and his statues of the Crucifixion, the Virgin and Paduan saints. The tomb of St Anthony, hung with offerings, lies in the north transept; large marble reliefs depicting the saint's life, carved in 1505–77 by various artists, adorn the walls around it. A lively fresco scene of the Crucifixion by Altichiero da Zevio (1380s) adorns the south transept.

🗿 Statue of Gattamelata

Beside the entrance to the basilica stands one of the great works of the Renaissance: a statue of the mercenary soldier Gattamelata. This gritty portrait was created in 1443–52, in honour of a man who during his life did great service to the Venetian Republic. The artist Donatello won fame for the monument, the first equestrian statue made on such a large scale since Roman times.

The Basilica di Sant'Antonio, and Donatello's statue of Gattamelata

🖾 Scuola del Santo and Oratorio di San Giorgio

Piazza del Santo 11. **Tel** 049 822 56 52. **Open** daily. 🖾

Five excellent frescoes, including the earliest documented paintings by Titian, are to be found in these two buildings. The Scuola del Santo contains two scenes from the life of St Anthony, which were painted by Titian in 1511. The works in the San Giorgio oratory are by Altichiero da Zevio and Jacopo Avenzo, who painted them in 1378–84.

🖸 Orto Botanico

Via Orto Botanico 15. **Tel** 049 827 21 19. **Open** daily (Nov–Mar: Mon–Sat). 🖾 🖾 **ortobotanico.unipd.it**

Padua's botanical garden, one of the oldest in Europe (1545), still retains much of its original appearance. The gardens and hothouses were used to cultivate the first lilac trees (1568), sunflowers (1568) and potatoes (1590) to be grown in Italy.

🖾 Palazzo del Bo

Via VIII Febbraio 2. **Tel** 049 827 51 11. **Open** for guided tours only. 🖾 Tue, Thu, Sat am, Mon, Wed, Fri pm. Times vary – phone to check. 🖾 🖾 **unipd.it**

The historic main university building originally housed the medical faculty, renowned throughout Europe. Among its famous teachers and students was Gabriele Fallopio (1523–62), after whom the Fallopian tubes are named.

Guided tours include the pulpit Galileo used when he taught physics here from 1592 until 1610 and the wooden anatomy theatre, built in 1594 and now the oldest surviving medical lecture theatre in the world.

The 16th-century anatomy theatre in the old medical faculty of the university's Palazzo del Bo, Padua

The Euganean Hills, formed by ancient volcanic activity

❽ Euganean Hills

🖭 🚌 to Terme Euganee, Montegrotto Terme. 🛈 Viale Stazione 60, Montegrotto Terme (049 892 83 11). 🖾 **turismopadova.it**

The conical Euganean Hills, remnants of long-extinct volcanoes, rise abruptly out of the surrounding plain. Hot water springs bubble up out of the ground at Abano Terme and Montegrotto Terme where scores of establishments offer thermal treatments, ranging from mud baths to immersion in the hot sulphurated waters. Spa cures originated in Roman times; remains of the original baths and theatre are still visible at Montegrotto Terme.

🖾 Abbazia di Praglia

Via Abbazia di Praglia 16, Bresseo di Teolo. **Tel** 049 999 93 00. **Open** Tue–Sun (pm only). **Closed** religious holidays. 🖾 Donations welcome. 🖾 **praglia.it**

The Benedictine monastery at Praglia, 6 km (4 miles) west of Abano Terme, is a peaceful haven in the hills where the monks grow herbs and restore manuscripts. They lead guided tours of parts of the abbey and the church (1490–1548), noted for its beautiful cloister. There are also richly carved stalls in both the choir and the refectory, and paintings and frescoes by Zelotti, a 16th-century painter from Verona.

🖾 Casa di Petrarca

Via Valleselle 4, Arquà Petrarca. **Tel** 0429 71 82 94. **Open** Tue–Sun (also Mon if pub hol). **Closed** pub hols. 🖾 🖾

The picturesque town of Arquà Petrarca, on the southern edge of the Euganean Hills, is named after Francesco Petrarca (1304–74). This medieval poet, known in English as Petrarch, spent the final years of his life here, in a house frescoed with scenes from his lyrical poems, overlooking a landscape of olive groves and vineyards. He lies buried in a simple sarcophagus in front of the church.

The Casa di Petrarca (part 14th-century) in Arquà Petrarca

🖾 Villa Barbarigo

Valsanzibio. **Tel** 049 805 92 24. **Open** Mar–Nov: 10am–1pm, 2pm–sunset daily. 🖾 🖾 🖾

This 18th-century villa to the north of Arquà boasts one of the finest Baroque gardens in the Veneto. These were planned by Antonio Barbarigo in 1669, and are a grandiose mix of statuary, fountains, a maze, formal parterres, lakes and avenues of cypress trees.

The 16th-century Villa Foscari at Malcontenta, beside the Brenta Canal

❾ Brenta Canal

Padua and Venice. **FS** Venezia Mestre, Dolo, Mira. 🚌 to Mira, Dolo and Strà. Canal trips on Il Burchiello: Venice. **Tel** 041 241 32 96. **Closed** 25 Jan–7 Feb. 🐾 **w** ilburchiello.it

Over the centuries, in order to prevent the Venetian lagoon silting up, the rivers flowing into it were diverted. The river Brenta was canalized in two sections: the older branch, between Padua and Fusina (just west of Venice), dates back to the 1500s and flows for 36 km (22 miles). Its potential as a transport route was quickly realized and fine villas were built along its length. Many of these elegant buildings can still be admired today – the S11 road runs alongside most of the canal's length – and several of them are open to the public.

The 18th-century **Villa Pisani** at Strà has an extravagant frescoed ceiling by Tiepolo. The **Barchessa Valmarana** at Mira (a pretty village) boasts 18th-century decorations. In the village of Malcontenta is **Villa Foscari**, or Villa Malcontenta, one of Palladio's loveliest villas (see pp84–5). It was built in 1560 and the interior decorated with magnificent frescoes by Zelotti. These villas may also

be visited as part of an indulgent 8.5-hour guided tour from Padua, travelling to Venice (or, on alternate days, from Venice to Padua) along the river in a leisurely fashion on board the *Burchiello* motor launch – the cost, however, is fairly prohibitive.

🏠 Barchessa Valmarana
Via Valmarana 11, Mira. **Tel** 041 426 63 87. **Open** Apr–Oct: 10am–6pm Tue–Sun; Nov–Feb: Sat & Sun, groups only by appt. 🐾 👍 💷

🏠 Villa Pisani
Via Pisani, Strà. **Tel** 049 50 20 74. **Open** Tue–Sun. **Closed** 1 Jan, 1 May, 25 Dec. 🐾 📷 🏠 Fri–Sun (in Italian).

🏠 Villa Foscari
Via dei Turisti 9, Malcontenta. **Tel** 041 547 00 12. **Open** Tue & Sat am. **Closed** Nov–Mar. 🐾

❿ Treviso

🏛 81,700. 🚌 **FS** ℹ️ Piazzale Duca d'Aosta 25 (0422 54 76 32). 🛒 Tue & Sat am. **w** turismo.provincia. treviso.it

Despite comparisons with Venice, the lovely fortified city of Treviso has its own very distinctive character.

A good place to start a tour of the streets, some lined with attractive balconied houses, is **Calmaggiore**. The street links the Duomo with the Palazzo dei Trecento, the rebuilt 13th-century town hall. The **Duomo** was founded in the 1100s but rebuilt several times. Inside, Titian's *Annunciation* (1570) vies for attention with the striking *Adoration of the Magi* fresco (1520) by Titian's archrival, Il Pordenone. More paintings by Titian and other artists of the Renaissance may be seen in the **Museo Civico**.

The fish market, which dates from medieval times, is held on an island in the middle of Treviso's river Sile; this allows the remains of the day's trading to be flushed away.

The Dominican church of **San Nicolò**, nestling by the 16th-century city wall, contains interesting tombs and frescoes, including, on a wall of the chapter house, the first-ever depiction of spectacles in art. A magnificent tomb (1500) by Antonio Rizzo is framed by a fresco of pageboys by Lorenzo Lotto.

🏛 Museo Civico
Chiesa di Santa Caterina, Piazzeta Mario Botter 1. **Tel** 0422 54 48 64. **Open** Tue–Sun. **Closed** public hols. 🐾 👍

The houses of the medieval town of Treviso overlooking ancient canals

The façade and entrance to the Renaissance Palazzo dei Rettori in Belluno

⓫ Conegliano

Treviso. 🚍 35,000. 🚉 🚌 ℹ️ Via XX Settembre 61 (0438 212 30). 🛒 Fri.

Conegliano lies among Prosecco-producing vineyards, and winemakers from all over Italy learn their craft at Conegliano's renowned wine school. Via XX Settembre, the arcaded main street, is lined with fine 15th- to 18th-century palazzi, many in the Venetian Gothic style or decorated with fading frescoes. The **Duomo** contains the town's one great work of art, an altarpiece painted by local artist Cima da Conegliano (1460–1518) depicting the *Virgin and Child with Saints* (1493).

Reproductions of Cima's most famous works are on show in the **Casa di Cima**, the artist's birthplace. The detailed landscapes in the background of his paintings were based on the hills around the town; the same views can still be seen from the gardens surrounding the Castelvecchio (old castle).

A mythical statue on Conegliano's theatre

🎭 Casa di Cima
Via Cima 24. **Tel** 0438 21 660. **Open** Sat & Sun, pm only and during temporary exhibitions. 🖼️

⓬ Belluno

🚍 36,000. 🚉 🚌 ℹ️ Piazza Duomo 2 (0437 94 00 83). 🛒 Sat. 🖥️ infodolomiti.it

Picturesque Belluno, capital of Belluno province, serves as a bridge between the two different parts of the Veneto, with the flat plains to the south and the Dolomite peaks to the north. Both are encapsulated in the views to be seen from the 12th-century **Porta Rugo** at the southern end of Via Mezzaterra, the main street of the old town. More spectacular still are the views from the bell tower of the 16th-century **Duomo** (subsequently rebuilt). The nearby baptistry houses a font cover with the figure of John the Baptist carved by Andrea Brustolon (1662–1732). Brustolon's works also grace the churches of San Pietro (on Via San Pietro) and Santo Stefano (Piazza Santo Stefano). North of Piazza del Duomo stands the elegant **Palazzo dei Rettori** (1491) – once home to the town's Venetian rulers – and the 12th-century **Torre Civica**, all that now survives of a medieval castle.

The **Museo Civico** contains paintings by Bartolomeo Montagna (1450–1523) and Sebastiano Ricci (1659–1734), and a notable archaeological section. North of the museum is Belluno's finest square, the **Piazza del Mercato**, with its arcaded Renaissance palaces and its fountain of 1410.

South of the town are the ski resorts of the Alpe del Nevegal; in the summer a chair lift operates from Faverghera up the flank of the mountain to a height of 1,600 m (5,250 ft), offering extensive views.

🏛️ Museo Civico
Piazza Duomo 16. **Tel** 0437 94 48 36. **Open** Tue–Sun. **Closed** Wed, Thu, Sat & Sun pm. 🖼️ 📷 🏠

⓭ Cortina d'Ampezzo

Belluno. 🚍 6,800. 🚌 ℹ️ Piazzetta San Francesco 8 (0436 32 31). 🛒 Tue am & Fri am. 🖥️ infodolomiti.it

Italy's top ski resort, much favoured by the smart set from Turin and Milan, is well supplied with restaurants and bars. Cortina is set amid the extremely dramatic scenery of the Dolomites (*see pp86–7*), which explains part of the resort's attraction: all around, crags and spires thrust their distinctive weather-beaten shapes above the trees.

Cortina benefits from better-than-average sports facilities, thanks to hosting the 1956 Winter Olympics. In addition to downhill and cross-country skiing, there is also a ski jump and a bobsleigh run for those who favour something more adventurous than usual, as well as an Olympic ice stadium, several swimming pools, tennis courts and riding facilities.

During the summer months, Cortina becomes an excellent base for walkers. Useful information on trails and guided walks is available from the tourist office or, during the summer, from the Guides' office opposite.

Corso Italia in Cortina d'Ampezzo, Italy's most important ski resort

Traditional copper pans on display in the Museo Carnico in Tolmezzo

⑭ Tolmezzo

🏔 10,000. 🚌 ℹ Via della Vittoria 4 (0433 448 98). 🏛 Mon am.
🌐 turismofvg.it

Tolmezzo is the capital of the Carnia region, named after the Celtic tribe that inhabited the area around the 4th century BC. The town is surrounded by the high peaks of the Carnic Alps, including the pyramidal Monte Amariana (1,906 m/6,253 ft) to the east. The best place to begin a tour of the region is the **Museo delle Arti Popolari**, which has displays of local costumes, crafts, textiles and agriculture.

Southwest of the town, a scenic road climbs 14 km (9 miles) to the ski resort of **Sella Chianzutan**, a good base for walking in the summer. More resorts line the road, west of Tolmezzo, to **Ampezzo**, at which point a minor road heads north through the gorge of the River Lumiei. Following this road to the Ponte di Buso bridge and the **Lago di**

Sauris is an excellent introduction to the majestic Carnic Alps.

Above this point the road is often impassable in winter, but in summer there are flower-filled meadows all along the road up to Sella di Razzo, and then back along the **Pesarina Valley**, via Comeglians and Ravascletto. Returning south, **Zuglio** was once the Roman town of Forum Iulii Carnicum, guarding the road over the pass. Today it is worth a detour for the remains of its Roman basilica, baths and forum.

🏛 Museo delle Arti Popolari
Via della Vittoria 2. **Tel** 0433 432 33.
Open Tue–Sun (Aug: daily).
Closed 1 Jan, 25 Dec. 🚫 ♿ 🖼

⑮ Pordenone

🏔 49,000. 🚆 🚌 ℹ Via Damiani 2/c (0434 52 03 81). 🏛 Wed & Sat am.
🌐 turismofvg.it

Old Pordenone consists of one long street, the **Corso Vittorio Emanuele**, lined with pretty arcaded houses of pink brick, some with the faded traces of decorative frescoes on their façades. The 13th-century **Palazzo Comunale** forms a striking conclusion to the street, with its eccentrically shaped roofline of curves and minaret-like side towers, and its 16th-century clock tower. Opposite is the **Museo d'Arte**,

housed in the 17th-century Palazzo Ricchieri, where works by the local artist Il Pordenone (1484–1539) are on display.

Around the corner stands the **Duomo**, which contains the lovely altar painting of the *Madonna della Misericordia* (1515) by Il Pordenone. The bell tower beside the Duomo is a fine example of Romanesque decorative brickwork.

🏛 Museo d'Arte
Corso Vittorio Emanuele II 51. **Tel** 0434 39 29 35. **Open** Tue–Sun (pm only Tue–Sat). 🚫 ♿ 🖼

⑯ Udine

🏔 99,000. 🚆 🚌 ℹ Piazza I Maggio 7 (0432 29 59 72). 🏛 Sat.

Udine is a city of varied and surprising architecture. In the center lies **Piazza della Libertà**, where the Loggia del Lionello (1448–56), built of pink stone in Venetian Gothic style, stands beside the Art Deco Caffè Contarena. Opposite, the Renaissance symmetry of the Porticato di San Giovanni is interrupted by the Torre dell'Orologio (Clock Tower, 1527), crowned by two bronze Moors which strike every hour. Note also the fountain of 1542, the two 18th-century statues, and the column supporting the Lion of St Mark.

Beyond the **Arco Bollani**, a gateway designed by Palladio in 1556, steps lead up to a 26-m (85-ft) hill that offers sweeping views over the city. On the hill is the 16th-century castle, now the **Musei Civici e Galleria di Storia e Arte Antica**, which houses fine art and archaeology collections.

Southeast of Piazza Matteotti, at the end of Via Savorgnana where a small market is held, stands the **Oratorio della Purità**, and the **Duomo** with its octagonal bell tower. Both contain important paintings and frescoes by Giambattista Tiepolo (1696–1770). More of Tiepolo's work can be seen in the **Museo Diocesano e Galleria Tiepolo**, formerly the Palazzo Arcivescovile, which the artist decorated with frescoes.

Lago di Sauris, an artificial lake lying in the Carnic Alps above Tolmezzo

The arcaded Porticato di San Giovanni on Piazza della Libertà, Udine

Environs

Outside Codroipo, 24 km (15 miles) west, rises the imposing **Villa Manin**. A road passes through the villa's grounds, so it can be seen even when the house – once the retreat of Ludovico Manin, the last doge of Venice (1725–1802) – and its gardens are closed to the public.

Musei Civici e Galleria di Storia e Arte Antica
Castello di Udine. **Tel** 0432 27 15 91. **Open** Tue–Sun. **Closed** 1 Jan, Easter, 1 May, 25 Dec.

Museo Diocesano e Galleria Tiepolo
Piazza Patriarcato 1. **Tel** 0432 298 056. **Open** Wed–Sun. **Closed** 1 Jan, Easter, 25 Dec.

Villa Manin
Passariano. **Tel** 0432 821 210. **Open** daily. **Closed** 1 Jan, 25 Dec. for exhibitions only.

⑰ Cividale del Friuli

🔼 11,000. 🚈 🚌 ℹ Piazza Paolo Diacono 10 (0432 71 04 60). 🔁 Sat.
🌐 cividale.net

A gate in the medieval walls of Cividale leads down the main street and straight to the dramatic ravine of the River Natisone, which is spanned by the arch of the **Ponte del Diavolo** (Devil's Bridge).

Above the river's north bank stands the **Tempietto Longobardo** (Lombardic Chapel), a very rare example of an 8th-century church decorated with reliefs of saints, modeled in stucco. The town's history is traced in the excellent **Museo**

Archeologico Nazionale, which contains the excavated remains of buildings from a Roman town, and a collection of Lombardic items including jewelry, ivory and weapons.

Next door is the **Duomo**, rebuilt in 1453 after a fire, with its beautiful silver altarpiece (13th century). The **Museo Cristiano**, off the south aisle, contains sculptures from the original church: of particular interest is the altar donated by Ratchis, the Lombardic Duke of Friuli and later King of Italy (737–44), which is finely carved with scenes from the Life of Christ. There is in addition the unusual baptismal font of Patriarch Callisto (737–56): this octagonal structure, with a roof supported by pillars, is decorated with symbols of the Evangelists.

Tempietto Longobardo
Via Monastero Maggiore 34. **Tel** 0432 70 08 67. **Open** daily.

Interior view of the Tempietto Longobardo in Cividale del Friuli

Museo Archeologico Nazionale
Palazzo dei Provveditori Veneti, P.za del Duomo 13. **Tel** 0432 70 07 00. **Open** 9am–2pm Mon, 8.30am–7.30pm Tue–Sun. **Closed** 1 Jan, 25 Dec.

Museo Cristiano
Via Condotti 1. **Tel** 0432 73 04 03. **Open** Jun–Sep: daily; Oct–May: Wed–Sun. **Closed** 1 Jan, 25 Dec.

⑱ Gorizia

🔼 37,000. 🚈 🚌 ℹ Corso Italia 9 (0481 53 57 64). 🔁 Thu, Fri.
🌐 turismofvg.it

Gorizia was at the center of fierce fighting during both world wars and was split in two by the 1947 Treaty of Paris, leaving part in Italy, part in Yugoslavia (now Slovenia).

The town's arcaded streets and pastel-painted houses have been carefully restored following substantial damage during World War II. The modern Museo Provinciale della Grande Guerra (Museum of the Great War), housed in the basement of **Museo Provinciale**, provides a fascinating introduction to the realities of war. Videos, photographs, and life-size mock-ups of trenches, latrines and gun emplacements are used to show the waste, squalor and heroism of war.

The Lion of Venice above the entrance to Gorizia's castle

Rooms on the upper floor of the museum house temporary exhibitions and items from the town's art collection, which includes works by local artists.

On a mound nearby rises the castle, encircled by 16th-century fortifications. From here there are extensive views stretching over the town.

Environs

Southwest of Gorizia, scenic country roads pass through the foothills of the **Carso**, a limestone plateau stretching down to Trieste. The plateau is dotted with fields enclosed by drystone walls and gouged with tunnels, caves and underground rivers.

Museo Provinciale
Borgo Castello 13. **Tel** 0481 53 39 26. **Open** Tue–Sun. **Closed** 25 Dec.

The attractive harbourside at Grado, along the coast south of Aquileia

⑲ Aquileia

🏛 3,300. 🚌 ℹ️ Piazza Capitolo 4 (0431 91 087). 🏛 Tue.
🌐 turismofvg.it

Aquileia, now little more than a village but encircled by the ruins of palatial villas, baths, temples and market buildings, provides a poignant reminder of the lost splendour of the Roman Empire.

It was here that Emperor Augustus received Herod the Great, King of Judea, in 10 BC, and it was here too, in AD 381, that the early Christian church held a major council attended by the learned saints Ambrose and Jerome to settle doctrinal issues. In the 5th century, however, the town was abandoned following several sackings. Fortunately, substantial parts of the early Christian basilica have survived, which contain the town's particular treasure: ornate floor mosaics.

🏛 Basilica

Piazza Capitolo. **Tel** 0431 919 719. **Open** daily. **Closed** during mass. Crypt 🎫 ♿

The basilica was founded in about AD 313 and much of the original structure still survives, including the magnificent floor mosaics of the nave and **Cripta degli Scavi** below. The designs are a mixture of geometric patterns, biblical stories and scenes from everyday life in ancient Aquileia. There is a lively portrayal of the tale of Jonah, who was swallowed by an extraordinary sea monster: the fishing boats are also surrounded by a rich array of creatures from the deep, including wide-eyed dolphins and squid.

🏛 Museo Archeologico Nazionale

Via Roma 1. **Tel** 0431 910 16.
Open 8:30am–7:30pm Tue–Sun. 🎫 ♿ 🚻 🌐 **museoarcheo-aquileia.it**

The mosaics in the basilica demonstrate a tradition of craftsmanship that flourished in the city from the 2nd century AD. Additional examples of mosaics and stone carvings from the Classical era (1st to 3rd centuries) are on display in this museum, together with glass, amber, and a collection of flies, beautifully worked in gold, that formed the adornment of a Roman matron's veil.

🏛 Museo Paleocristiano

Località Monastero. **Tel** 0431 911 31.
Open 8:30am–1:45pm Tue–Sun.
Closed 1 Jan, 1 May, 25 Dec. 🎫 ♿ 🚻

This museum, which stands not far from Aquileia's ancient harbour beside the once-navigable River Natissa, focuses on the development of art during the early Christian era.

Environs

South of Udine, **Palmanova** is worth a visit for its remarkable octagonal layout and intact walls. The town was built in 1593 by the Venetians to commemorate the Battle of Lepanto.

Grado sits on a group of low islands in the middle of the Adriatic lagoon, attached to the mainland by a narrow causeway. The town grew into a port for Aquileia in the 2nd century and was used as a haven by Aquileia's citizens during the barbarian invasions. Today, Grado is a popular seaside resort. At the centre of the old town is the **Duomo**, which contains 6th-century frescoes in the apse, similar to those on the vaults of San Marco in Venice (see pp114–17). Nearby, in the church of **Santa Maria delle Grazie**, there are more 6th-century mosaics.

Symbolism in Early Christian Art

Christians were persecuted until their religion was granted official status by Constantine the Great in AD 313. Prior to this they had developed a language of secret symbols to express their beliefs, many of which can be seen in the mosaics and marble tomb chests of Aquileia. Many of these and other symbols later found their way into popular bestiaries and folk art.

Part of the 4th-century floor mosaic in the basilica at Aquileia

The Winged figure of Victory holding a laurel wreath was a Classical symbol of triumph and holiness. Later, it came to represent Christ's resurrection, and more generally, victory over death.

㉓ Trieste

218,000. ✈ FS 🚌 𝒊 Piazza Unità d'Italia 4/b (040 347 83 12). 🚢 Tue–Sat. **w** turismofvg.it

Trieste is an atmospheric city, tucked up next to Slovenia, with a long, bustling harbour lined with handsome buildings and lapped by the waves of the Adriatic Sea.

🏛 Acquario Marino

Molo Pescheria 2, Riva Nazario Sauro 1. **Tel** 040 30 62 01. **Open** 9am–7pm Tue–Sun (Nov–Mar: to 1pm). 🚻 ♿

The aquarium, one of Trieste's most popular attractions, contains examples of the fascinating marine life in the Adriatic.

🏰 Castello di San Giusto

Pza Cattedrale 3. **Tel** 040 30 93 62. **Open** daily. Castle: 9am–6pm (Nov–Mar: to 5pm); museums: 9am–1pm. 🚻

Up above the harbour stands a hilltop castle built by Trieste's Venetian governors from 1368. It is set on a terrace that offers sweeping views over the Gulf of Trieste. The castle houses two museums containing Roman mosaics, and a collection of weapons and armour.

⛪ Basilica Paleocristiana

Via Madonna del Mare 11. **Tel** 040 4362. **Open** 10am–noon Wed; other times by appointment only.

Beside the castle lie the substantial ruins of the Roman basilica or law court built around AD 100. Note the stone magistrates' bench and throne.

⛪ Duomo

Pza Cattedrale 2. **Tel** 040 30 96 66. **Open** daily. ♿

In the church of **San Giusto**, the city's Duomo, magistrates' bench and throne of the Roman basilica were reinterpreted to become the seat of the bishop and clergy. Because the building was formed in the 14th century by linking two 5th-century churches that stood side by side, there are two thrones and benches here. The two apses are decorated with very fine 13th-century mosaics in the Venetian style.

🏛 Museo di Storia ed Arte ed Orto Lapidario

Piazza della Cattedrale 1. **Tel** 040 31 05 00. **Open** 10am–5pm Tue–Sun. **Closed** public hols. 🚻

The important archaeological collection here provides fascinating evidence of Trieste's extensive trade links with the ancient Greek world.

13th-century mosaics in the apse of San Giusto, Trieste's Duomo

Environs

From **Villa Opicina**, just north of Trieste, sweeping views may be had over the city, its bay and south down the coast of Slovenia. A little beyond, at Borgo Grotta Gigante, lies the **Grotta del Gigante**, a huge cavern filled with stunning "organ pipe" formations and tall columns of stalagmites.

At Grignano, 8 km (5 miles) northwest of the city, stands the **Castello di Miramare**, a white castle set in lush green gardens beside the sparkling blue Adriatic. It was built by the Habsburg Archduke Maximilian in 1856–60 as his summer retreat, a few years before he was assassinated in Mexico. It is still furnished in contemporary style.

🦇 Grotta del Gigante

Borgo Grotta Gigante 42a. **Tel** 040 32 73 12. **Open** Tue–Sun (Jul & Aug: daily). 🚻 📷

🏰 Castello di Miramare

Viale Miramare, Grignano. **Tel** 040 22 41 43. **Open** daily. ♿ 🚻 (castle).

The Castello di Miramare on the bay of Trieste

The Tortoise hiding in his shell represented darkness and ignorance, while the cockerel, who crows at dawn, signified light and enlightenment.

ICHTHUS, or fish, was an acronym for Iesous CHristos THeou Uios Soter – Jesus Christ, Son of God, Saviour, in ancient Greek.

Colourful birds, such as peacocks, symbolized immortality and the glorious transformation of the soul when it arrives in Heaven.

TRENTINO-ALTO ADIGE

The Italian-speaking Trentino – named after Trento, the regional capital – and the German-speaking Alto Adige or Südtirol (South Tyrol, the region bordering the upper reaches of the River Adige) differ dramatically in culture. However, they do share one feature in common: the majestic Dolomites that form the backdrop to every town and village, covered in snow for three months of every year and carpeted with exquisite Alpine plants for another three.

The region's mountains have been cut by glaciers into a series of deep, broad valleys. Many of these face south, so it remains unusu-ally warm and sunny, even in winter. Travellers have passed up and down these valleys for generations – as confirmed by the extraordinary discovery, in 1991, of a 5,000-year-old man's body found emerging from the surface of a melting glacier in Alto Adige. The frozen corpse wore leather boots, stuffed with hay for warmth, and was armed with a copper ice pick.

The paths that Neolithic man once trod became major road networks under the Romans, when many of the region's cities were founded. By the Middle Ages, Alto Adige had established its very own distinctive culture under the Counts of Tyrol, whose land (later appropriated by the Habsburgs) straddled both sides of today's Italian/Austrian border. The Tyrolean nobility built the castles that still line the valleys and the mountain passes, in order to protect travellers from brigands.

Another ancient legacy is the tradition of hospitality to be found in the numerous guesthouses along the valleys. Many of these are built in the distinctive Tyrolean style, with beautiful timber balconies for making the most of the winter sun, and overhanging roof eaves to keep snow at a distance. Cosy in winter, with log fires and warming food, and offering marvellous views, they make the ideal base for enjoying the region's mountain footpaths and ski slopes.

Skiers enjoying the slopes around Monte Spinale, near Madonna di Campiglio, in Trentino

◄ Trekkers climbing the glowing peaks of the Rosengarten mountain range in the Dolomites, South Tyrol

Exploring Trentino-Alto Adige

Trentino-Alto Adige is a region where unspoiled nature is complemented by a wealth of sporting opportunities. The tributary valleys feeding into the Adige valley contain lakes, rivers and streams, and also woodland, vineyards and Alpine pasture full of butterflies, birds and flowers. Southeast of the region rise the distinctive limestone peaks of the Dolomites, while further north the area becomes more mountainous still, enclosed finally by the splendid heights of the Alps.

Via Ponte Aquila in Bressanone

Sights at a Glance

1. Malles Venosta (Mals im Vinschgau)
2. Merano (Meran)
3. Vipiteno (Sterzing)
4. Brunico (Bruneck)
5. Bressanone (Brixen)
6. Bolzano (Bozen)
7. Ortisei (Sankt Ulrich)
8. Canazei
9. Cavalese
10. San Martino di Castrozza
11. Cembra
12. Madonna di Campiglio
13. Trento
14. Rovereto
15. Castello di Avio

Key

=== Motorway

=== Major road

— Secondary road

=== Minor road

— Scenic route

--- Main railway

---- Minor railway

▪▪▪▪ International border

▪▪▪▪ Regional border

△ Summit

For additional map symbols see back flap

↑Landeck

Passo di Resia

Resia

Melago

Moso in Pas

Lago di Resia

Curon Venosta

Abbazia di Monte Maria

Alpi Venoste

l'Altissima 3480m

Senales

MALLES VENOSTA 1

Monte Alto 3260m

Tiro

Castel Coira

MERANO

Glorenza

Silandro

Adige

Guardia Alta 2608m

Lar

Prato allo Stelvio

Laces

Passo dello Stelvio

Trafoi

Solda

Santa Gertrude

Senale

Monte degl 2656m

TRE

Bormio

Ortles 3899m

Marcena

Malos

Monte Cevedale 3757m

Bagni di Rabbi

Revo

Pejo

Dimaro

Cles

Tuenno

ALTO

Der

Voce

Vermiglio

S43

Sondrio

MADONNA DI CAMPIGLIO 12

Mezzolombardo

Sarca

Cascate di Nardis

Pinzolo

Cima Brenta 3150m

Andalo

Adamello

Cima Tosa 3159m

Lago di Molveno

Paganella 2125m

Stenico

Vezzano

TRENTO

Re di Castello 2885m

Tione di Trento

Sarche

Vason

S45b

Lardaro

Valli Giudicarie

Monte Cadria 2254m

Dro

Calliano

Tiarno

Tenno

Arco

ROVERETO 14

Riva del Garda

Torbole

Ruina Dantes

Storo

S12

Brentonico

Raoss

CASTELLO DI AVIO 15

Ala

A22

↓Verona

0 kilometres   25

0 miles   10

Vetta d'Italia
2912m

Innsbruck
Passo del Brennero
Brennero
Casere
Monte Lovello
3378m
Cadipietra
San Giacomo
Colle Isarco
Riva di Tures
Lappago
VIPITENO **3**
Campo Tures
Passo di Croce Domini
3134m
Mules
Monte Gruppo
2809m
Anterselva
San Leonardo
in Passiria
Rio di
Pusteria
Rienza
4 BRUNICO
Fortezza
Monguelfo
iobianco
Pennes
Abbazia
di Novacella
Castello
di Rodengo
Val Pusteria
Dobbiaco
San Candido
Cima San
Giacomo
2741m
Castello
di Rodengo
Sesto
Lienz
nta Cervina
2084m
5 BRESSANONE
Marebbe
Lago di
Braies
Castello di
Velturno
Plancios
S51
Sarentino
Chiusa
Santa
Maddalena
Cima Dieci
3023m
velengo
Ponte
Gardena
ORTISEI
7
Selva di Val
Gardena
Pedraces
Cortina d'Ampezzo
Belluno
Siusi
Corvara
Alpi di
Siusi
BOLZANO
6
Alpi Dolomitiche
Appiano
Nova
Levante
CANAZEI **8**
Laives
Vigo
di Fassa
Marmolada
3343m
Caldaro
S48
Ora
Moena
Avisio
A22
San
Lugano
Predazzo
S50
S12
Bellamonte
apriano
Tesero
CAVALESE **9**
Lagorai
SAN MARTINO
DI CASTROZZA **10**
Catena dei
Alpe Tognola
2163m
MBRA
Piramidi di
Segonzano
Fiera di Primiero
Monte Croce
2488m
Imer
Baselga di Pinè
S50
Pergine
Valsugana
Castello
Tesino
Val
Sugana
Borgo
Valsugana
Grigno
S47
Brenta
Levico Terme
Padova
Vincenza
Caldonazzo
Lavarone
enza

The Val di Funes, South Tyrol

Getting Around

The region's main artery is the Brenner Pass road: it runs from Austria in the north, following the River Adige from Bolzano to Trento, and southwards on to Verona. Both the motorway and the main road beside it are among the busiest in Europe, and the valley roads can also be congested during the ski season. Winter driving can be hazardous, requiring special tyres and snow chains. An excellent rail and coach network serves the whole area.

View of the Dolomites from Madonna di Campiglio

Abbazia di Monte Maria, founded in the 12th century, near Malles Venosta

❶ Malles Venosta

Mals Im Vinschgau

🏘 4,600. 🚆 🚌 ℹ️ Via San Benedetto 1 (0473 83 11 90). 🛒 Wed. 🌐 **altavenosta-vacanze.it**

Malles Venosta sits in high border country, close to Switzerland and Austria, and was a customs point during the Middle Ages. The town has several Gothic churches, whose spires and towers give an appealing skyline, mirroring the jagged peaks that rise all around. The oldest is the tiny church of **San Benedetto**, a 9th-century Carolingian building on Via San Benedetto, with frescoes of its patrons.

Environs

The medieval **Castel Coira** (Churburg) rises at Sluderno (Schluderns), 4 km (2.5 miles) southeast of Malles. It contains an excellent collection of weapons and armour.

Clinging to the mountainside above the town of Burgusio (Burgeis), 5 km (3 miles) north of Malles, is the Benedictine **Abbazia di Monte Maria** (Marienberg), founded in the 12th century but enlarged in the 18th and 19th. The church's crypt shelters an outstanding series of 12th-century frescoes.

The glorious medieval town of **Glorenza** lies just 2 km (1 mile) south of Malles.

🏰 **Castel Coira**
Churburg, Sluderno. **Tel** 0473 61 52 41. **Open** 20 Mar–Oct: Tue–Sun (& Mon if pub hol). 📷 compulsory. 🅿️

🏠 **Abbazia di Monte Maria**
Tel 0473 83 13 06. **Open** Apr–Oct: Mon–Sat; Nov–Apr: groups by appt only. **Closed** public hols. 📷 🎫

❷ Merano

Meran

🏘 35,000. 🚆 🚌 ℹ️ Corso della Libertà 45 (0473 27 20 00). 🛒 Tue, Fri. 🌐 **meran.eu**

Merano is an attractive spa town popular with Austrians, Germans and Italians. On Corso Libertà, a street of smart shops and hotels, stands the **Kurhaus** or Spa Hall built in 1914, now a concert venue. Furnished in period style, the 15th-century **Castello Principesco** was home to the Habsburg Archduke Sigismund. Inviting gardens line the River Passirio, which winds

The Art Nouveau façade of the Kurhaus in Merano

its way through the town. The Passeggiata Lungo Passirio d'Inverno (Winter Walk) follows the north bank to the Roman bridge, Ponte Romano; the Passeggiata d'Estate (Summer Walk) on the south bank leads to the medieval Ponte Passirio.

Environs

The romantic 12th- century **Castel Tirolo** lies 4 km (2.5 miles) to the north. It hosts a museum of Tyrolean history.

The grounds of **Castel Trauttmansdorff** house a fascinating botanical garden.

🏰 **Castello Principesco**
Via Galilei. **Tel** 3290 18 63 90. **Open** Tue–Sun & public hols. **Closed** Jan–Feb. 📷 🎫

🏰 **Castel Tirolo**
Via Castello 24, Tirolo. **Tel** 0473 22 02 21. **Open** mid Mar–10 Dec: Tue–Sun. **Closed** Dec–mid-Mar. 📷 ♿ 🏠 💻

🏰 **Castel Trauttmansdorff**
Via S. Valentino 51a. **Tel** 0473 27 01 72. **Open** 1 Apr–15 Nov: daily. 📷 🔍 🎫 ✏️ 🌐 **touriseum.it**

❸ Vipiteno

Sterzing

🏘 5,600. 🚆 🚌 ℹ️ Piazza Città 3 (0472 76 53 25). 🛒 daily.

Surrounded by mineral-rich valleys, Vipiteno is very Tyrolean in feel. On Via Città Nuova, lined with fine mansions, rise the Gothic **Palazzo Comunale**, containing Renaissance sculpture and paintings, and the Torre dei Dodici, the symbol of the town. Wood carvings in the **Museo Multscher** are by Hans Multscher; the Bavarian sculptor came to Vipiteno in 1456–8 to carve the altar for the parish **church**, which lies just south of the town.

To the west, the charming **Val di Racines** includes waterfalls and a natural rock bridge.

🏛 **Palazzo Comunale**
Via Città Nuova 21. **Tel** 0472 72 37 00. **Open** Mon–Fri. **Closed** Fri pm & public hols.

🏛 **Museo Multscher**
Via della Commenda 11. **Tel** 0472 76 64 64. **Open** Apr–Oct: Tue–Sat. **Closed** public hols. 📷

The medieval castle dominating the town of Brunico

❹ Brunico

Bruneck

🏔 13,000. 🚆 🚌 ℹ️ Piazza Municipio 7 (0474 55 57 22). 🛒 Wed. 🌐 bruneck.com

This attractive town, overlooked by the imposing form of its medieval **castle**, retains 14th-century fortifications and a network of narrow streets that can only be explored on foot. The church of **St Ursula**, to the northwest of St Ursula's Gate, holds a series of outstanding mid-15th-century altar reliefs of the Nativity. The **Museo Etnografico di Teodone** offers displays of traditional agricultural life and local costumes; this folklore museum also provides an ideal opportunity to visit a 16th-century farmhouse and barn.

St Ursula's Gate sundial, Brunico

🏛 **Museo Etnografico di Teodone**
Via Duca Teodone 24, Teodone. **Tel** 0474 55 20 87. **Open** Easter–Oct: Tue–Sat, Sun and public hols pm (Aug: also Mon). ♿ 🚫

❺ Bressanone

Brixen

🏔 18,000. 🚆 🚌 ℹ️ Via Ratisbona 9 (0472 83 64 01). 🛒 Mon. 🌐 brixen.org

The narrow medieval alleys of Bressanone cluster around the cathedral and the palace of the prince-bishops who ruled the town for much of its history. The **Duomo**, on Piazza del Duomo, was rebuilt in the 18th century but retains its 12th-century cloister, decorated with superb 15th-century frescoes. The lavish interiors of Palazzo Vescovile, the bishops' Renaissance palace, house the **Museo Diocesano**. It contains precious items from the Middle Ages, as well as the **Museo dei Presepi**, with its collection of wooden crib figures that are carved locally.

Environs

At Velturno (Feldthurns), just 8 km (5 miles) southwest, stands the Renaissance **Castello di Velturno**, the summer retreat of the rulers of Bressanone noted for its frescoed rooms. A little over 3 km (2 miles) north of Bressanone lies the **Abbazia di Novacella**, a picturesque group of fortified monastic buildings with an outstanding series of cloister frescoes. Further north up the valley, at **Rio di Pusteria** (Mühlbach), the remains of a 16th-century fortified barrier can be seen to the east of the town. The barrier funnelled ancient travellers through the customs post that divided Tyrol from the Görz district.

High above Rio di Pusteria, to the southeast, looms the massive outline of the **Castello di Rodengo** (Rodeneck). The castle contains wonderful 13th-century frescoes showing battle scenes, the Last Judgment and courtly episodes from the *Iwein* romance by Hartmann von Aue, the medieval poet.

🏛 **Museo Diocesano & Museo dei Presepi**
Piazza Palazzo Vescovile 2. **Tel** 0472 83 05 05. Museo Diocesano: **Open** 10am–6pm Tue–Sun (Jul–Sep: 7pm–midnight). **Closed** Nov–mid-Mar. Museo dei Presepi: **Open** mid-Mar–Oct: 10am–6pm Tue–Sun (Dec–6 Jan: to 5pm). **Closed** 24 & 25 Dec. 🚫

🏰 **Castello di Velturno**
Velturno. **Tel** 0472 85 55 25. **Open** Mar–Nov: Tue–Sun. 📷 only. 🚫

🏰 **Abbazia di Novacella**
Via Abbazia 1/2b, Varna. **Tel** 0472 83 61 89. **Open** Mon–Sat. **Closed** Mon (Jan–Mar) & pub hols. 📷 only. 🚫

🏰 **Castello di Rodengo**
Rodengo. **Tel** 0472 45 40 56. **Open** May–mid-Oct: Sun–Fri. 📷 🚫

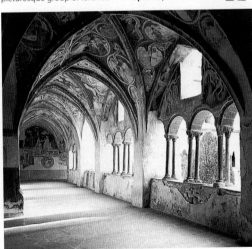

The cloisters of Bressanone Duomo with their 15th-century frescoes

The Baroque interior of the church of St Ulrich in Ortisei

❻ Bolzano
Bozen

🚹 98,000. 🚆 🚌 ℹ️ Piazza Walther 8 (0471 30 70 00). 🛒 Sat.
🌐 **bolzano-bozen.it**

Bolzano, the capital of the Alto Adige, is the gateway between the Italian-speaking Trentino region and the German-speaking Alto Adige, or Südtirol, and has a marked Tyrolean atmosphere. The old centre, **Piazza Walther**, is dominated by the 15th-century Gothic **Duomo**, with its multicoloured mosaic-patterned roof and elaborate spire. The "wine door" inside the Duomo is carved with figures at work among vines and reflects the importance of wine to the local economy. In the middle of Piazza Walther is a statue of Walther von der

The Duomo spire, Bolzano

Vogelweide, the 13th-century troubadour – born, according to legend, in this area. North of the square, the streets are lined with houses adorned with intricate gables, balconies and oriel windows. The outdoor market, starting at Piazza Grano, forms an inviting array of local produce that continues along the arcaded Via dei Portici. The modern **Museo Archeologico** houses impressive finds from the Stone Age, the Bronze Age, the Iron Age, Roman times and the time of Charlemagne. A key exhibit is

Ötzi, the famous 5,000-year-old "Iceman". The **Chiesa dei Domenicani** (Dominican church), on Piazza Domeni-cani, has 14th-century *Triumph of Death* frescoes and a frescoed cloister.

🏛️ **Museo Archeologico**
Via Museo 43. **Tel** 0471 32 01 00.
Open Tue–Sun (Jul, Aug & Dec: daily).
Closed 1 Jan, 1 May, 25 Dec. 🎥 📷
📷 🌐 **iceman.it**

❼ Ortisei
Sankt Ulrich

🚹 4,500. 🚌 ℹ️ Via Rezia 1 (0471 77 76 00). 🛒 Fri. 🌐 **valgardena.it**

Ortisei is the prosperous main resort for the pretty Val Gardena and Alpe di Siusi region, and a major centre for woodcarving; examples of local craftsmanship may be seen in local shops, in the **Museo della Val Gardena** (which also focuses on local

archaeology), and in the church of **St Ulrich**.

To the south is the **Alpe di Siusi** (Seiser Alm) region, noted for its Alpine meadows, balconied farmsteads and onion-domed churches. The best way to explore this beautiful area is by cableway from Ortisei: to the northeast another cable-car runs to 2,518-m (8,260-ft) high Monte Seceda, and walks from here lead into the Odle Dolomites.

🏛️ **Museo della Val Gardena**
Via Rezia 83. **Tel** 0471 79 75 54.
Open Jan–Mar: Tue–Fri; mid-May–Oct: Mon–Fri; Jul & Aug: Mon–Sat. 🎥
🌐 **museumgherdeina.it**

❽ Canazei

🚹 1,800. 🚌 ℹ️ Piazza Marconi 5 (0462 60 96 00). 🛒 Sat (Jul–Sep).
🌐 **fassa.com**

Located at the base of some of the highest and most awe-inspiring groups of peaks, Canazei is a good base for exploring the Dolomites. In summer, chair-lifts climb to viewpoints where the beauty of the encircling mountains can be appreciated to the full. The most popular viewpoints are Pecol and Col dei Rossi, reached by the Belvedere cableway from Via Pareda in Canazei: the cliffs of the Sella group are visible to the north, with Sasso Lungo to the west and Marmolada, the highest of the Dolomites at 3,343 m (10,965 ft), to the south.

Skiers enjoying views of the Dolomites above Canazei

Environs

At **Vigo di Fassa**, 13 km (8 miles) southwest, the **Museo Ladino** focuses on the Ladin-speaking people of some of the valleys. Ladin – a Rhaeto-Romance language – is taught in local schools and the ancient traditions still thrive.

🏛 **Museo Ladino**
Località San Giovanni, Vigo di Fassa. **Tel** 0462 76 01 82. **Open** Tue–Sat pm (late Jun–mid-Sep & 20 Dec–6 Jan: daily). 🖼 🎫 ♿ 🏪 🅦 **istladin.net**

The frescoed façade of the Palazzo della Magnifica Comunità

🟠 Cavalese

🏔 3,600. 🚌 🏻 Via Fratelli Bronzetti 60 (0462 24 11 11). 🚢 last Tue of month (not Jul). 🅦 **visitfiemme.it**

Cavalese is the chief town in the Val di Fiemme, a pretty region of flower-filled aromatic pastures, delightful wooded valleys and Tyrolean architecture. At the centre of the town stands the **Palazzo della Magnifica Comunità**. Originally built in the 13th century, this was the seat of the medieval governing council which ruled the area as a semi-autonomous region. Today the panelled interiors contain medieval paintings by local artists, and an archaeology collection. Most visitors come for the excellent summer and winter resort facilities, and to climb, by cable car, to the 2,229 m (7,311 ft) top of **Alpe Cermis**, the mountain that rises to the south of the town.

Environs

The church in **Tesero**, the next village east, bears a 15th-century fresco by an unknown painter depicting Sabbath-breakers. The church itself, dating back to 1450, has a flurry of Gothic vaulting, and a modern representation of the Crucifixion painted against a background of the village.

At **Predazzo**, about 13 km (8 miles) east, the **Museo di Geologia e Etnografia** explains the local geology.

🏛 **Palazzo della Magnifica Comunità**
Piazza Cesare Battisti 2. **Tel** 0462 34 03 65. **Open** Tue–Sun. 🖼 🎫 ♿ 🅦 **palazzomagnifica.eu**

🏛 **Museo di Geologia e Etnografia**
Via Cesare Battisti 4. **Tel** 0462 50 23 92. **Open** 10am–noon & 5–7pm Mon–Sat (mid-Sep–Feb by appt).

🟠 San Martino di Castrozza

🏔 470. 🚌 🏻 Via Passo Rolle 165 (0439 76 88 67). 🅦 **sanmartino.com**

The resort of San Martino occupies one of the most scenic and accessible valleys in the southern Dolomites, making it very popular with walkers and skiers. Cable cars rise to the peak of **Alpe Tognola** (2,163 m, 7,095 ft), southwest of the town, and up the **Cima della Rosetta** (2,609 m, 8,557 ft) to the east. Both offer fabulous views of the Pale di San Martino peaks, a stirring sight as the massive rock peaks, split by glaciers, rise above a sea of green meadows and woodland.

Piramidi di Segonzano, near Cembra

San Martino is almost entirely surrounded by forest, which once supplied the Venetian Republic with timber for ships. The forest is now protected, and as a result it is possible to see Alpine flowers, mushrooms, birds and other wildlife with relative ease.

🟠 Cembra

🏔 2,500. 🚌 🏻 Piazza San Rocco 10 (0461 68 31 10). 🚢 Wed am.

The wine-producing town of Cembra nestles on the terraced slopes of a scenic valley of flower-filled villages. Some 6 km (4 miles) east of Cembra stand the **Piramidi di Segonzano**, a rare series of erosion pillars, some over 30 m (100 ft) high, each topped by a rock. The footpath to the pillars is well signposted, with informative noticeboards along the way explaining the formation of the bizarre columns, which are similar in appearance to giant termites' nests. Their setting amid bird-filled woodland makes the steep climb up to the site well worthwhile. A further reward is the fine view, from the top of the hill, along the Cembra valley and westwards as far as the Brenta group of Dolomites.

🌲 **Piramidi di Segonzano**
Strada Statale 612 to Cavalese. **Open** daily.

Vines growing on the terraced slopes of the Cembra valley

The impressive falls of the Cascate di Nardis, Madonna di Campiglio

⑫ Madonna di Campiglio

🏔 1,300. 🚌 ℹ️ Via Pradalago 4 (0465 44 75 01). 🎪 Jul–Aug: Tue & Thu. 🌐 **campigliodolomiti.it**

Madonna di Campiglio is the chief resort in the Val Meledrio. Nestling between the Brenta and Adamello groups of peaks, it makes the perfect base for walking or skiing amid the magnificent mountain terrain. Cableways radiate out from the town in every direction, giving easy access to the peaks.

Environs

The church at **Pinzolo**, 14 km (9 miles) south, has a well-preserved fresco depicting a *Dance of Death* (1539). The inevitable march of the figures, both rich and poor, is underlined by a text written in local dialect.

North of Pinzolo, the road west from Carisolo leads to the verdant and popular, yet unspoilt, **Val Genova**. About 4 km (2 miles) along the valley is the spectacular **Cascate di Nardis**, a waterfall that plunges down 90 m (300 ft). The two masses of rock at the bottom are said to be the forms of petrified demons.

⑬ Trento

🏔 105,000. 🚊 🚌 ℹ️ Via Manci 2 (0461 21 60 00). 🎪 Thu am.

Trento, the capital of the region to which it gave its name, is also the most attractive town in Trentino: it has a fine Romanesque cathedral and a richly decorated castle, and streets lined with handsome Renaissance mansions. Trento is noted as the venue for the **Council of Trent** (1545–63), set up by the Catholic Church to consider reforms that might encourage breakaway groups, in particular the German Protestants, to return to the fold. The reforms, which ushered in the period of the Counter-Reformation, were only partly successful.

The **Duomo**, site of some of the Council meetings, was built in robust Romanesque style from the 13th century. It was three centuries before it was completed, in 1515, but the builders maintained architectural harmony by ignoring Gothic and Renaissance styles entirely. The result is a church of unusual integrity, noble and assured. The Duomo stands on **Piazza Duomo**, the city's main square, which was first laid out by the Romans as their central market place or forum. Trento's Roman name, Tridentum, is commemorated in the figure of Neptune who stands holding his trident at the top of the 18th-century fountain, which stands in the middle of the main square.

Inner courtyard of the Magno Palazzo

🏛 Museo Diocesano Tridentino

Piazza Duomo 18. **Tel** 0461 23 44 19. **Open** Wed–Mon. **Closed** 1 Jan, 25 Dec. 🅿️ ♿ 🌐 **museodiocesanotridentino.it**

This museum is housed in the **Palazzo Pretorio**, an imposing medieval building that stands on the eastern side of Piazza Duomo. Its contents include early ivory reliquaries, Flemish tapestries and paintings de-picting the Council of Trent.

🏰 Castello del Buonconsiglio

Via Bernardo Clesio 5. **Tel** 0461 23 37 70. **Open** Tue–Sun. **Closed** 1 Jan, 25 Dec. 🅿️ 📷 🌐 **buonconsiglio.it**

This large castle, built in the 13th century and later enlarged with additional buildings, is part of the defences of the town. Trento was an important frontier on the main road linking Italy to northern Europe, and thick walls still encircle the town.

The southern section of the castle consists of the magnificent **Magno Palazzo** (1530), built for the ruling prince-bishops of Trento, who were given extensive powers by the Holy Roman Emperor to foster loyalty and discourage defection to the pope. The lavish decoration (including frescoes of virile satyrs and nymphs by Gerolamo Romanino, 1531–2) speaks of huge wealth and a luxurious lifestyle. The palazzo houses the **Museo Provinciale**, with paintings, ceramics and 15th-century wood carvings, and prehistoric, Etruscan and Roman items.

Palazzo Pretorio and the Duomo in Trento's main square

The commanding form of the Ossario del Castel Dante in Rovereto

The **Torre dell' Aquila** (Eagle Tower) nearby contains frescoes painted around 1400 that depict the months of the year.

Environs
Immediately to the west of Trento a scenic round-trip along a winding road leads up the north flank of **Monte Bondone** and back, via **Vezzano**, down the western slopes. The views along the route are magnificent, in particular from Vaneze and Vason. East of Trento, Pergine marks the start of the **Val Sugana**, a broad valley with lakes. In the hills north of Lake Levico lies the spa town of **Levico Terme**, distinguished by elegant Neo-Classical buildings set amid beautifully wooded parkland.

⑭ Rovereto

🏙 33,000. � 🚌 ℹ️ Corso Rosmini 16 (0464 43 03 63). 🛒 Tue.
🌐 visitrovereto.it

Rovereto was at the centre of fierce fighting during World War I, after which the Venetian castle (built in 1416) that dominates the town was transformed into the **Museo Storico Italiano della Guerra**, a war museum. The displays include sections on wartime humour, propaganda and spying. Near the museum entrance, stairs lead out on to the castle roof for a view of the imposing **Ossario del Castel Dante.**

Some distance away is the **Campana dei Caduti** (Bell of the Fallen), which was cast from melted-down cannons at the end of World War II and mounted in an imposing building above the town; it is rung daily at sunset.

Below the war museum is the **Museo Civico**, with its collections on archaeology, art, natural history and folklore. Another branch of the museo, in Corso Bettini, houses a collection of sculpture by Carlo Fait. The Mario Botta-designed **Museo di Arte Contemporanea di Trento e Rovereto (MART)** showcases 20th-century Italian art. A second site, in Via Portici, holds Italian Futurist art.

Environs
A little over 8 km (5 miles) north of Rovereto is **Castel Beseno**, rising on a hill to the east. This enormous castle was built and rebuilt from the 12th century to the 18th to guard the junction of the three valleys.

Five kilometres (3 miles) south of Rovereto, the main road passes through a valley littered with massive boulders created by landslips: these are known as Lavini di Marco or **Ruina Dantesca**, because they are mentioned in Dante's *Inferno* (XII, 4–9). Fossilized dinosaur footprints have been discovered there.

🏛 Museo Storico Italiano della Guerra
Via Castelbarco 7. **Tel** 0464 43 81 00.

Open Tue–Sun. **Closed** 1 Jan, 24, 25, 31 Dec. 🌐

🏛 Museo Civico
Borgo Santa Caterina 41.
Tel 0464 45 28 00; Palazzo Alberti: Corso Bettini 41. **Tel** 0464 45 28 30.
Open Tue–Sun. **Closed** 1 Jan, 5 Aug, 1 Nov, 25 Dec. 🌐 🚻
🌐 museocivico.rovereto.tn.it

🏛 MART
Corso Bettini 43. **Tel** 0464 43 88 87; Casa d'Arte Futurista Depero: Via Portici 38. **Tel** 0464 43 18 13.
Open Tue–Sun. 🌐 🎬 🚻 🍴 🖥 🚫

🏰 Castel Beseno
Besenello. **Tel** 0464 83 46 00.
Open Mar–Oct: Tue–Sun (Mon if public hol); Nov–Feb: Sat & Sun. 🌐

Castello di Avio in its lush setting

⑮ Castello di Avio

Via Castello, Sabbionara d'Avio.
Tel 0464 68 44 53. 🚌 🚉 to Vo, then 3-km (2-mile) walk. **Open** Mar–Sep: 10am–6pm Wed–Sun (open Tue in Aug); Oct–Nov: 10am–5pm Tue–Sun. **Closed** Dec–Feb. 🌐 🎬 🖥 🚫

Castles line the Adige valley all the way to the Brenner Pass, but few are as accessible as the Castello di Avio. It was founded in the 11th century, extended in the 13th, and today offers visitors far-reaching views. Among the numerous frescoes is a rare series in the Casa delle Guardie (the Sentry House) depicting 13th-century battle scenes.

The extensive walls enclosing Castel Beseno above Rovereto

NORTHWEST ITALY

Northwest Italy at a Glance

The northwest of Italy is made up of three very different geological regions: the jagged Alps, the flat plain, and the undulating shoreline of the Mediterranean. This is one of the country's most prosperous areas, with much of its fortune made in the major cities of Genoa, Milan and Turin. The northwest is also known for its beautiful lakes, wild national parks and elegant historic homes. The major sights, in the regions of Valle d'Aosta and Piedmont, Liguria and Lombardy, are shown on this map.

The Parco Nazionale del Gran Paradiso is a beautiful wilderness, and the habitat of rare Alpine fauna and flora *(see pp220–21)*.

Aosta

VALLE D'AOSTA

Biella

Ivrea

Nova

Vercelli

Po

Turin

Moncalieri

Pinerolo

Asti

VALLE D'AOSTA
AND PIEDMONT
(See pp214–33)

Alessand

Alba

LIGURI
(See pp234–

Cuneo

Savona

The capital of Piedmont is Turin, an elegant and bustling city of splendid Baroque architecture. Its skyline is dramatically dominated by the Mole Antonelliana *(see p228)*.

Imperia

Sanremo

Sanremo is a typical Riviera resort, with palm trees and a casino. The onion-domed outline of the Russian church adds an exotic flavour to the town *(see p238)*.

The Basilica di Sant'Andrea in Vercelli is an important Romanesque building, one of the earliest to use Gothic elements *(see p232)*.

◀ The picturesque Isola San Giulio in the centre of Lake Orta, Valle d'Aosta

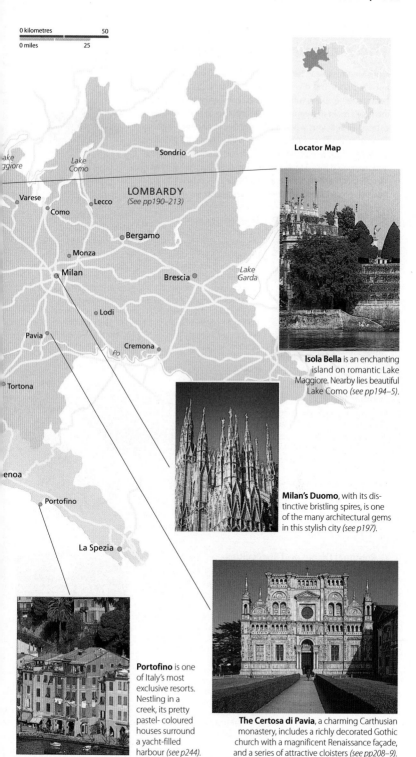

0 kilometres 50

0 miles 25

Locator Map

Sondrio

Lake Maggiore

Lake Como

LOMBARDY
(See pp190–213)

Varese

Como

Lecco

Bergamo

Monza

Milan

Brescia

Lake Garda

Lodi

Pavia

Cremona

Po

Tortona

Genoa

Portofino

La Spezia

Isola Bella is an enchanting island on romantic Lake Maggiore. Nearby lies beautiful Lake Como *(see pp194–5)*.

Milan's Duomo, with its distinctive bristling spires, is one of the many architectural gems in this stylish city *(see p197)*.

Portofino is one of Italy's most exclusive resorts. Nestling in a creek, its pretty pastel-coloured houses surround a yacht-filled harbour *(see p244)*.

The Certosa di Pavia, a charming Carthusian monastery, includes a richly decorated Gothic church with a magnificent Renaissance façade, and a series of attractive cloisters *(see pp208–9)*.

The Flavours of Northwest Italy

From Mediterranean Liguria to the Alps, the Lombardy plain and Piedmont, this diverse area is characterized by its rich, hearty cuisine. Along with the Veneto, Lombardy and Piedmont are Italy's main rice-growing areas and risotto features widely, especially delicious when made with local wild mushrooms. The white truffles of Alba are the "white gold" of Piedmont, while lush pastures produce some of the country's best meat and many of Italy's finest cheeses. The mild Ligurian climate favours olives and herbs – especially basil, used in pesto sauce. And fish teem in the sparkling Mediterranean.

Fresh basil

A precious haul of aromatic Piedmontese truffles

Lombardy

This is the home of dishes prepared *alla Milanese*, rich in butter, *ossobuco* (shin of veal), vegetable soups and boiled meats *(bollito misto)*. From veal to beef and from pork to poultry, Lombardy produces some of the country's finest meat, but it is also associated with *cucina povera* (the cuisine of the poor) in which polenta (maize porridge) still features from its days as the staple diet of impoverished countryfolk. The other staple food, the short-grained rice that is used in risotto, grows abundantly in the area around Pavia. Lombardy is one of Italy's largest cheese-making regions, the most famous including Gorgonzola, Mascarpone, Bitto and Grana Padano.

Piedmont and Valle d'Aosta

The "Slow Food" movement was born in Piedmont in 1986. Its mission is "to defend biodiversity in our food supply, spread taste education and connect producers of excellent food". The movement now has more than 100,000 members in more than 50 countries. Piedmontese flavours are robust,

Grana Padano   Gorgonzola   Fontina

Bitto

Mascarpone   Taleggio

Mouthwatering range of northwest Italy's finest cheeses

Regional Dishes and Specialities

Veal is especially popular in Lombardy and Piedmont, and a great favourite with the Milanese is *ossobuco*. Another classic Piedmontese dish, *vitello tonnato* is a surprisingly delicious blend of cold roast veal served with a sauce made with mayonnaise, tuna, gherkins and capers. As well as pesto, a traditional dish from Genoa is *buridda alla Genovese* – a delicious fish soup or stew containing mussels, shrimps, octopus, squid and clams. Shavings of truffle in dishes such as risotto and *fagiano tartufato* (pheasant stuffed with white truffle and pork fat) give a taste of sheer luxury and, fortunately, a little of this very expensive delicacy goes a long way. And, for those with a sweet tooth, *panettone* is a soft Christmas cake studded with dried and candied fruit, another Milanese speciality.

Gianduiotti

Bagna Caôda From Piedmont; a warm mix of olive oil, anchovies and garlic into which raw vegetables are dipped.

Boxes of fresh fish are unloaded onto a Ligurian quayside

Liguria

The Mediterranean climate is perfect for growing herbs, fruit and vegetables, nuts and olives. Ligurian olive oil is of the highest quality and is used in the preparation of many dishes. To accompany pasta, pesto is the signature sauce, made from basil, pine nuts, garlic and olive oil, as well as a mix of Pecorino and Parmesan. This use of aromatic herbs is typical of Ligurian cuisine in general.

Not surprisingly, fish and seafood are as common as meat and dairy in this region, where the vast majority of people live on the coast.

rich and earthy, laced with French flair, reflecting a history of French rule and influence.

The paddy fields of Vercelli are the rice capital of Europe and truffle risotto, especially when flavoured using the prized white variety from Alba, is truly memorable fare.

The mountains are famous for cow's milk cheese, especially the semi-soft Fontina from the Valle d'Aosta, cured meats, salamis, terrines and game. Piedmont also produces Italy's greatest red wines, and the prized Barolo and Barbaresco often feature as a marinade in beef dishes.

The Turinese are passionate about chocolate, echoing Turin's tradition of chocolate-making originating in the 17th century. Most famous are the sublime ingot-shaped *gianduiotti*, filled with a rich chocolate-hazelnut cream. The city is also the birthplace of *grissini*, crisp breadsticks that grace every restaurant table. The tradition of the *aperitivo* also originates in Turin. The spread that accompanies a glass of Prosecco or a cocktail in bars throughout the city between 6pm and 8pm is substantial.

Delicious foccacia bread made with Ligurian olive oil

ON THE MENU

Agnolotti Piedmont pasta speciality – crescent-shaped ravioli stuffed with meat or vegetables. Served with *ragù* or a creamy sauce.

Brasato al Barolo Braised beef cooked gently with vegetables in Barolo wine.

Lumache Piedmontese snails, the best of which come from Cherasco, served either in garlic and butter or in a sauce of olive oil, tomatoes and garlic.

Oca alla Piemontese Goose preserved in fat.

Risotto alla Milanese Rich, saffron-scented dish of rice with white wine, onion and Parmesan cheese.

Trenette con pesto A Ligurian dish of flat noodles with a sauce of basil, garlic, pine nuts and olive oil.

Ossobuco Milanese shin of veal, braised slowly in white wine. The bone marrow is considered a delicacy.

Zabaione A frothy dessert of egg yolks, sugar and Marsala, zabaione is a speciality of the Piedmont region.

The Wines of Northwest Italy

Grapes are grown throughout the northwest – from the cliffs of Liguria to the steep mountainsides of Valle d'Aosta. The best wines, however, come from Piedmont, in particular the Langhe hills southwest of Turin, source of two of Italy's finest reds: the rich, powerful, long-lived Barolo and Barbaresco. Both of these are now showing the benefits of modern techniques and a renewed interest in high-quality wine making. Lighter, everyday red wines that go well with the local cuisine include Dolcetto and the popular Barbera. Another Piedmont speciality is sparkling *spumante,* Italians' instinctive choice whenever there is something around to celebrate.

Castiglione Falletto in the heart of Piedmont

Barbera d'Alba comes from the adaptable Barbera grape, which can grow on almost any slope. Its ubiquitous nature means that the wines it yields can be light and full of fruit, as well as dense, strong and full-flavoured. Good producers include Aldo Conterno, Voerzio, Pio Cesare, Altare, Gaja, Vaira and Vietti.

Dolcetto is grown in seven different areas. Dolcetto d'Alba has a delicious perfume and deep purple colour. Best drunk within one or two years, it ranges in flavour from fresh and fruity to the rich, concentrated plumminess of some of the top wines, such as those produced by Giuseppe Mascarello.

Turin
Chieri
Piedmont
MONFERRATO
Canale
Barbaresc
Alba
Bra
Saluzzo
Barolo • Castigli
Falletto
Dogliani
Mondovi • LANGH
Cuneo

Key

- ▢ Barolo
- ▢ Barbaresco
- ▨ Other vineyard areas

| 0 kilometres | 25 |
| 0 miles | 15 |

Barolo, prized the world over for its complex array of flavours and firm tannins, is made from the Nebbiolo grape and may take up to 20 years to mature. Vigna Colonnello is a top Barolo from Aldo Conterno, made only in the best years, like 2006, 2005, 2004 and 1993.

The white truffle of Alba is an autumn speciality from the Langhe hills. Highly prized for its earthy scent, it is excellent with Barolo.

Moscato d'Asti is an excellent *aperitivo* or light dessert wine made from the aromatic, fruity Moscato grape. It is light in alcohol with a gently sweet finish and may have a slight sparkle. Ideal for refreshing the palate after a hearty Piedmontese meal, Araldica's versatile Moscato is delicious when served well chilled.

Grapes of the Northwest

The Nebbiolo grape is used to produce two of Italy's finest red wines, Barolo and Barbaresco, as well as other regional wines in the Valtellina and north of Turin. It is a difficult grape to cultivate and requires a long growing season to soften its high acidity. However, the final results are worth it: in the Langhe region the Nebbiolo offers complex perfumes and a range of flavours, often encased within strong tannins. Easier to handle and lighter, the Dolcetto and Barbera both came from the Monferrato region originally. These reds yield lighter, fruitier wines but, when at their best, no less distinctive than those of the Nebbiolo. Of the white grapes, the Moscato is Piedmont's oldest known variety. Famous for the successful sparkling Asti Spumante, the best grapes are reserved for Moscato d'Asti.

Nebbiolo grapes

How to Read the Label

The name of the wine is shown in the centre of the label: *bricco* is local dialect for a good hilltop vineyard.

The producer's name

Producer's emblem

Year of production

ROCCHE DEI MANZONI®

BRICCO
MANZONI
1985

IMBOTTIGLIATO DA
PODERE ROCCHE DEI MANZONI
IN VALENTINO
MONFORTE D'ALBA (ITALIA)

VINO DA TAVOLA DELLE LANGHE

13,5% vol.   75 cl. e

Alcoholic strength

Size of bottle

The official category; in this case a table wine from the Langhe region.

The bottler's name and address

Good Vintages
Barolo and Barbaresco had good years in *2006, 2005, 2004, 2003, 2000, 1998, 1997.*

Barolo is aged in wooden casks for at least two years before being put in bottles. This may be done in either the traditional, large *botte* or the smaller *barrique*, which imparts a strong oaky flavour to the wine.

Casale Monferrato

LOMBARDY

alvo

Voghera

sti

Alessandria

Tortona

Canelli

Nizza Monferrato

Novi Ligure

no

Acqui Terme

Ovada

Gavi

LIGURIA

ssello

Genoa

Savona

Understanding Architecture in Northwest Italy

Although the buildings of the northwest tend to be solid and imposing – a result partly of the more severe climate – there is no distinctive architectural stamp as there is around Venice, Florence or even in Rome. Instead, a variety of buildings in different styles, many borrowed or reinterpreted from elsewhere, are dotted across the area: enchanting medieval castles, outstanding Romanesque and Gothic buildings, unusual Baroque structures. The northwest is also rich in modern architecture – in terms of both design and materials – influenced by the region's industrial developments and its strong flair for innovative design, which also often draws its inspiration from earlier architectural styles.

Castello Sforzesco, 1451–66 *(see p192)*

Characteristics of Northwest Italian Architecture

Double row of defensive walls

Wooden balcony

Few windows

Massive square tower

Pointed turret

Battlements

Castello di Fénis, one of the finest castles in the Valle d'Aosta, is a 14th-century fortress with asymmetrical towers, turrets and crenellated walls. Frescoes adorn the interior *(see p215)*.

Alternating bands of marble

Rose window

Lions support columns and porch above

Elaborate carving

Rose window

Octagonal drum influenced by the Duomo in Florence

Cappella Colleoni, Bergamo (1476), mixes rich, decorative elements in this early Renaissance masterpiece *(see p201)*.

Highly ornate façade

Patterned marble design

Monza's Duomo (1390s) typifies the Lombard style of Romanesque architecture with its marble stripes and ornate carving *(see p201)*.

Massive scale

Ornate window surrounds

Rotunda

Balcony

Curved brickwork

Palazzo Carignano is perhaps the finest product of Turin's idiosyncratic Baroque school. Guarini's masterpiece (1679) boasts an extraordinary undulating brick façade and a fine rotunda *(see p223)*.

Where to see the Architecture

The road to Aosta is flanked by numerous medieval castles *(see p214)* while inspirational Romanesque and Gothic churches are found in Lombardy – at Monza *(p201)*, Pavia *(p203)*, Milan *(pp192–201)*, and Como *(pp190–91)*. The 15th-century Certosa di Pavia *(pp204–5)* is a must, as well as the charming city of Mantua *(p207)*. Turin *(pp220–24)* is famous for its unique Baroque school, and Bergamo for its exuberance. Architecture from the last two centuries is best represented in Milan and Turin, and in Genoa some exciting redevelopment projects are taking place.

Renzo Piano's mast structure (1992) in Genoa's redeveloped port

19th–20th Century Architecture

Galleria Vittorio Emanuele II in Milan, designed by Mengoni in 1865, was the first Italian building to use glass and iron structurally *(see p194)*.

Central dome

Mosaics

Top reaches 167 m (550 ft)

Aluminium replaces original granite top

Square-sided dome

Glass balcony

Overhanging upper storeys

Struts support the top

The Mole Antonelliana (1863–97), designed by Antonelli, was the tallest building in the world when it was built *(see p224)*.

Torre Velasca, Milan is a 26-floor tower south of the Duomo. The design, from the 1950s, was influenced by medieval castles such as the Castello Sforzesco.

Elliptical shape

Taller windows

Tapering struts

Spiral ramps up to roof

Roof served as test track

Reinforced concrete

The Lingotto building, Turin, was built in 1915–18 as FIAT's car factory. Made of advanced materials, it was the first large-scale modern building in Italy. The structure of the ramps up to the roof is similar to the interior of Guarini's Baroque dome for San Lorenzo in Turin.

Milan's Pirelli building, by Ponti and Nervi, is an elegant and innovative skyscraper built in 1959.

LOMBARDY

The region of Lombardy stretches from the Alps, on the border with Switzerland, down through the romantic lakes of Como and Maggiore to the broad, flat plain of the River Po. It is an area of lakeside villas with azalea-filled gardens, of wealthy towns with imposing palazzi and highly decorated churches, and of efficient, modern industry and large-scale agriculture, the financial heart of Italy. At its centre stands Milan, the style-conscious capital of Lombardy.

The region was named after the Lombards or Longobards, a Germanic tribe that invaded Italy in the 6th century AD. During the Middle Ages, Lombardy was part of the Holy Roman Empire, but not always loyal to its German emperors. The Lombards, who had a talent for banking and commerce, resented any outside interference with their prosperity.

The 12th century saw the rise of the Lega Lombarda, or Lombard League, a band of forceful separatists founded to counter the brutal imperialism of Frederick Barbarossa (their most modern incarnation being the Lega Nord political party). Power was seized by the region's great families, most notably the Visconti and the Sforza of Milan, from the 14th to the early 16th century. These dynasties also became great patrons of the arts, commissioning exquisite palaces, churches and artworks, many of which can still be seen. Bergamo, Mantua and Cremona – not to mention Milan itself – contain a remarkably rich array of art treasures. Here are such pinnacles of European civilization as the charterhouse at Pavia, Leonardo da Vinci's *Last Supper* and the magnificent paintings of the Pinacoteca di Brera in Milan.

Lombardy – famous as the birthplace of Virgil, Monteverdi, Stradivarius and Donizetti – today offers visitors the contrasting pleasures of lyrical lakeside landscapes (resorts on lakes Como and Maggiore have attracted poets, aristocrats and gamblers for centuries) and beautiful, bustling cities.

Strolling through Milan's enormous Galleria Vittorio Emanuele II

◀ The village of Corenno Plinio on the peaceful eastern shores of the beautiful Lake Como

Exploring Lombardy

The enormous plain of the River Po runs through much of Lombardy, providing a landscape that is flat and perfectly suited to the consequent expansion of industry in the region. This is, however, also a region of great contrasts. To the north, in a still unspoilt setting in the foothills of the mountains, lie the lakes Como and Maggiore, as well as the dramatic valleys and peaks of the Parco Nazionale dello Stelvio around Bormio, Sondrio and Val Camonica. Further south, busy industrialized areas give way to huge tracts of agriculture dotted with towns of great beauty such as Cremona, Mantua and Pavia, which offer a splendid array of artistic treasures.

A view of Isola Bella on Lake Maggiore

Sights at a Glance

1. Lago di Como
2. Lago Maggiore
3. *Milan (Milano) pp196–205*
4. Monza
5. Bergamo
6. Parco Nazionale dello Stelvio
7. Val Camonica
8. Lago d'Iseo
9. Brescia
10. Lodi
11. Pavia
12. *Certosa di Pavia pp208–9*
13. Cremona
14. Sabbioneta
15. Mantua

For additional map symbols *see back flap*

The colourful façade of the Cappella Colleoni in Bergamo

Coira
Montespluga
Madesimo
Chiavenna
Pizzo Badile 3308m
Bagni del Masino
Gravedona
Adda
Monte Legnone 2609m
Bellinzona
Cannobio
Maccagno
LAGO DI COMO
Porlezza
Bellano
Premana
Luino
Tremezzo
Bellagio
Pizzo dei Tre Signori 2554m
LAGO MAGGIORE
Lago di Lugano
Argegno
Magreglio
Mogg
Stresa
Laglio
Lecco
Gavirate
Varese
Como
Erba
Calolziocor
Lago di Varese
Arona
Sesto Calende
Giussano
Merate
BERGAMO
Tradate
Seregno
Dalmine
Gallarate
Saronno
MONZA
Vimercate
Busto Arsizio
Legnano
Tre
Nerviano
Sesto San Giovanni
Turbigo
Rho
Novara
MILAN
Magenta
Paullo
Pan
Abbiategrasso
Melegnano
Cre
Palestro
Vigevano
Binasco
Siziano
LODI
Mortara
CERTOSA DI PAVIA
Sant'Angelo Lodigiano
Candia Lomellina
Garlasco
PAVIA
Belgioioso
Mede
Lomello
Stradella
Po
Casei Gerola
Broni
Casteggio
Genova
Voghera
Godiasco
Zavattarello
Varzi

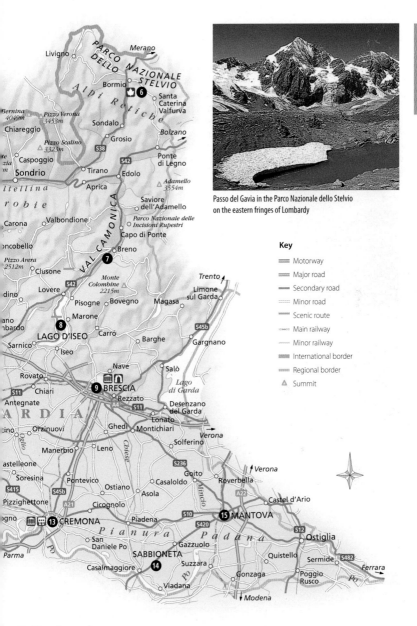

Passo del Gavia in the Parco Nazionale dello Stelvio
on the eastern fringes of Lombardy

Key

═══ Motorway

═══ Major road

─── Secondary road

┈┈┈ Minor road

─── Scenic route

━━━ Main railway

─── Minor railway

▬▬▬ International border

▬▬▬ Regional border

△ Summit

Getting Around

Milan has three international airports, which are
obvious gateways into northern Italy, and the vast and
flat Lombard plain has its advantages when it comes
to transport: roads and railway lines criss-cross it and
make trips between the larger towns very easy. The
lakes, however, are better visited by car, as only two
main towns are served by trains, though there are bus
and boat services around the shores. The Parco Nazionale
dello Stelvio and the mountains are more remote still,
but offer good tourist facilities.

0 kilometres   25

0 miles   20

❶ Lago di Como

Set in an idyllic landscape of mountains and rugged hillsides, Lake Como has for centuries attracted visitors who come here to go boating, for walks in the hills, or for relaxation and inspiration. The northern stretches, in particular, are shrouded in an almost eerie calm. The long and narrow lake, shaped into a wishbone by glacial erosion, offers fine views up to the Alps and down to the towns of Como and Lecco.

View of the lake near Como

The northern stretches are wilder and less populated than the southern part, offering visitors great tranquillity.

Menaggio is one of a string of popular resorts lining the west bank.

Varenna, a ferry port, is overlooked by a ruined 11th-century castle. At Fiumelatte, just south, there is a foaming stream, the "river of milk".

Villa Carlotta nestles among lush gardens with lovely views.

Bellagio
This delightful resort on the cusp of the lake's two arms has elegant lakeside promenades and cafés.

Cernobbio was a favourite resort aof the exiled Queen Caroline of England in the early 19th century.

The southeastern arm of the lake is also called the Lago di Lecco.

The scenic route just south of Bellagio climbs a hill to offer far-reaching lake views.

Lecco, home to the 19th-century novelist Manzoni.

Domaso
Gravedona
Còlico
S36
S38
Dèrvio
Bellano
Menaggio
Varenna
Fiumelatte
Griante
Tremezzo
Bellagio
Mezzegra
Argegno
Onno
S340
S36
S583
S583
Cernobbio
Como
Lecco
A9-E35

0 metres   10
0 miles   10

Como
The town, which gave its name to the lake, boasts a fine Duomo in mixed Gothic and Renaissance styles, with carvings on its façade.

Key

••• Car ferry route
••• Ferry route
▬▬ Motorway
▬▬ Major road
══ Minor road

VISITORS' CHECKLIST

Practical Information
ℹ️ Pza Cavour 17, Como (031 26 97 12); Via Sauro 6, Lecco (0341 29 57 20). 🆆 lakecomo.org.uk

Transport
🚆 Como, Lecco.
🚌 🛥️ all towns.

Tadoline's copy (1834) of Canova's *Cupid and Psyche* in Villa Carlotta

Exploring Lago di Como

In the heart of **Como** lies the elegant Piazza Cavour. Nearby rises the beautiful 14th-century **Duomo**, with its 15th- and 16th-century reliefs and paintings, and fine tombs. The 18th-century dome is by Turin's famous Baroque architect, Juvarra. Next to the Duomo stand the 13th-century Broletto (town hall), charmingly striped in white, pink and grey, and the tall Torre del Comune. At Tremezzo, **Villa Carlotta** is an elegant 18th-century summer-house known for its gardens. In springtime, all sorts of flowers burst into colour in this pretty setting. The villa houses a collection of sculptures.

Lecco, a small industrial town lying to the south of the lake's eastern arm, was home to Alessandro Manzoni (1785–1873). The writer's childhood home, the **Villa Manzoni**, is devoted to memorabilia of his life and works. A monument in Piazza Manzoni depicts scenes from his most famous novel, *I Promessi Sposi (The Betrothed)* – set in 17th-century Lecco and Milan.

🏛️ Villa Carlotta
Via Regina 2b, Tremezzo. **Tel** 0344 404 05. **Open** Apr–mid-Oct: 9am–6pm daily (mid-Mar–end Mar & mid-Oct–early-Nov: 10am–5pm daily). 🅿️

🏛️ Villa Manzoni
Via Guanella 1, Lecco. **Tel** 0341 48 12 47. **Open** 9.30am–5:30pm Tue–Sun. **Closed** 1 Jan, Easter, 1 May, 15 Aug, 25 Dec. 🅿️

❷ Lago Maggiore

Verbania. 🚆 🚌 🛥️ Stresa, Verbania, Baveno & the islands. ℹ️ Piazza Marconi 16, Stresa (0323 301 50).
🆆 distrettolaghi.it

Lake Maggiore, the second largest Italian lake after Lake Garda, is a long expanse of water nestling right against the mountains and stretching into Alpine Switzerland; it is warmer in atmosphere and more romantic than Lake Como. The gently sloping shores are dotted with camellias, azaleas and verbena vegetation – from which the ancient lake derived its Roman name, Verbanus.

A huge copper statue of Cardinal San Carlo Borromeo, the chief patron of the lake, stands in **Arona**, the town where he was born in 1538. It is possible to climb up and look out over the lake through his eyes and ears. Arona also boasts a ruined castle and a chapel, Santa Maria, dedicated to the Borromeo family.

Further up the western coast of the lake is **Stresa**, the chief resort and main jumping-off point for visits to the islands; the town boasts many grand hotels, handsome villas and pleasant gardens. Behind Stresa, a cable car ride away, rises Monte Mottarone, a snow-capped peak offering spectacular panoramic views of the surrounding mountains, including Monte Rosa.

The statue of Carlo Borromeo in Arona

The **Borromean islands**, at the centre of the lake near Stresa, are small jewels of natural beauty augmented by artificial grottoes, architectural follies and landscaped gardens. The **Isola Bella** is home to the 17th-century **Palazzo Borromeo** and its splendid gardens, while Isola Madre is largely given over to a botanical garden. The only island inhabited all year round is Isola dei Pescatori, with a population of 50. The private Isola di San Giovanni is the smallest of the isles, with a villa that once belonged to the great conductor Arturo Toscanini (1867–1957).

The lake becomes quieter towards the Swiss border, but continues to be lined with attractive villas. The **Villa Taranto**, located on the outskirts of Verbania, houses a fine exotic botanical collection.

About 3 km (2 miles) west of **Cannobio**, a market town near Switzerland, is the dramatic gorge and tumbling waterfall of Orrido di Sant'Anna, which can be reached by boat.

🏛️ Palazzo Borromeo
Isola Bella. 🛥️ from Stresa. **Tel** 0323 305 56. **Open** mid-Mar–mid-Nov: daily. 🅿️ 🆆 borromeoturismo.it

🏛️ Villa Taranto
Via Vittorio Veneto 111, Verbania, Pallanza. **Tel** 0323 55 66 67. **Open** mid-Mar–Oct: daily. 🅿️ ♿

Isola Bella's 17th-century Palazzo Borromeo and garden on Lago Maggiore

❸ Milan

Centre of fashion, business and finance, Milan has a bustling, businesslike feel about it. It is smart rather than attractive – a city of wealth as opposed to imagination and the heartland of the Italian economy. Its name is thought to come from a composite of the Latin words *medio* and *planum*, meaning "middle of the plain". It has long been an important trading centre at the junction of transalpine routes, and a prize for powerful dynasties. Today, it is the best place to see Italy at its most cosmopolitan and stylish.

Portrait of a Young Woman by Pollaiuolo, Museo Poldi-Pezzoli

🏰 Castello Sforzesco
Piazza Castello. **Tel** 02 88 46 37 00.
Castello: **Open** daily. Musei del
Castello: **Open** 9am–5:30pm Tue–Sun.
Closed public hols. 🎨 ♿
w milanocastello.it

The first castle on this site was built by the Visconti family, but demolished when their reign ended in the mid-15th century. Milan's new ruler, Francesco Sforza, built in its place this Renaissance palace. The castle is based on a series of courtyards, the most beautiful of which, the Cortile della Rocchetta, is a graceful arcaded square designed by Bramante and Filarete. The palace now contains, together with sections on Applied Arts, Archaeology and Coins, the **Musei del Castello**. This fine collection of furniture, antiquities and paintings includes Michelangelo's unfinished sculpture known as the *Rondanini Pietà*. The canvases

in the picture collection, dating from the Renaissance to the 18th century, are particularly impressive.

🏛 Museo Poldi-Pezzoli
Via Alessandro Manzoni 12. **Tel** 02 79 48 89. **Open** 10am–6pm Wed–Mon.
🎨 **w** museopoldipezzoli.it

Giacomo Poldi-Pezzoli was a wealthy nobleman who, on his death in 1879, bequeathed his magnificent art collection to the state. Its most famous painting is the 15th-century Renaissance *Portrait of a Young Woman* by Antonio Pollaiuolo, though there are also works by Piero della Francesca, Botticelli and Mantegna, among others. The applied arts section is richly endowed with fascinating items ranging from rugs and lace to glass, enamels and porcelain, as well as sculpture, jewellery and sundials.

Michelangelo's *Rondanini Pietà* (c.1564) in the Castello Sforzesco

Sights at a Glance

Stazione Porta Garibaldi 1.5 km (1 mile)

Parco Sempione ⑬

Castello Sforzesco ①

Milan Malpensa 50 km (31 miles) ✈

Cadorna FS M
PIAZZALE CADORNA

Cairoli M 🛈 LARGO CAIROLI

Santa Maria delle Grazie NOVARA

Palazzo Litta

Civico Museo Archeologico ⑫

PIAZZA SANT'AMBROGIO

Sant'Ambrogio ⑩

Sant'Ambrogio M

Stazione Porta Genova 800 m (880 yds) FS

San Lorenzo Maggiore ⑪

PAVIA

0 metres 500
0 yards 500

▥ Teatro alla Scala

P.za della Scala. **Tel** 02 887 91. Box
Office **Tel** 02 72 00 37 44. ♿ Museo
Teatrale: Largo Ghiringhelli 1 (Piazza
Scala). **Tel** 02 88 79 24 73. **Open** 9am–
noon, 1:30–5pm daily. ♿ ♿ ▥
w teatroallascala.org

This Neo-Classical theatre opened
in 1778 and is one of the world's
most prestigious opera houses.
It has one of the largest stages
in Europe and hosts sumptuous
productions. Two hours before
each performance the box office

The façade of the world-famous
Teatro alla Scala

opens to sell tickets at discount
prices. The **Museo Teatrale**
houses sets and costumes of
past productions and theatrical
items dating back to Roman
times. There is also a good view
of the auditorium, with its
gilded box galleries, *trompe-l'oeil*
effects and huge chandelier.

The Gothic Duomo, crowned with spires

For keys to map symbols *see back flap*

VISITORS' CHECKLIST

Practical Information
🅜 1,325,000. 🛈 P. del Duomo
19 (02 77 40 43 43); Stazione
Centrale (02 77 40 43 19).
🗓 daily. 🎉 7 Dec: Sant'Ambrogio. 🅦 visitamilano.it

Transport
✈ Malpensa 50 km (31 miles)
NW; Linate 8 km (5 miles) E.
🚉 Stazione Centrale, P.za Duca
d'Aosta. 🚌 P.za Freud.

🏛 Duomo

Piazza del Duomo. **Tel** 02 72 02 26 56.
Open 7am–6:45pm daily. Baptistry
digs: **Open** 10am–5.30pm. Treasury:
Open 9:30am–5.30pm Mon–Fri (to
5pm Sat); 1:30–3.30pm Sun & public
hols. Roof: **Open** 9am–6:10pm (to
7pm Nov–Feb). ♿ for roof. ♿
w duomomilano.it

Milan's cathedral is one of the
largest Gothic churches in the
world. It was begun in the 14th
century under Prince Gian
Galeazzo Visconti but not
completed until more than
500 years later. The building's
most startling feature is the
extraordinary roof, with its
135 spires, innumerable
statues and gargoyles, and
from which, on a clear day, there
are views of the Alps. Below, the
façade boasts an assortment of
styles from Gothic through to
Renaissance and Neo-Classical.
The bronze doors are faced with
bas-reliefs recounting episodes
from the life of the Virgin and of
Sant'Ambrogio, and scenes
retelling the history of Milan.

The aisles are divided by 52
giant pillars and well lit
by stained-glass
windows. Look out for
the Visconti family
symbol – a serpent
swallowing a man – in
the fine tracery of the
apse windows. Among
the many statues is a
depiction of the flayed
San Bartolomeo
carrying his own skin.
The treasury, beneath
the main altar, contains
much medieval gold
and silverwork, and
the remains of a
4th-century baptistry.

Exploring Milan

In addition to the great monuments in Milan, such as the cathedral and the castle, there is a host of varied and interesting museums, churches and civic buildings which provide an enthralling mix of old and new. This chic and busy metropolis offers plenty of opportunities for cultural activities, gastronomic adventures, designer-fashion shopping or just strolling about, Milan-style.

The glass ceiling and dome covering the Galleria Vittorio Emanuele II

🏛 Galleria Vittorio Emanuele II

Main entrances on Piazza del Duomo and Piazza della Scala.

This ornate shopping arcade, known as *il Salotto di Milano* (Milan's drawing room), was designed by the architect Giuseppe Mengoni in 1865. The galleria had a tragic start, however, as Mengoni fell to his death from the scaffolding not long before its inauguration in 1877 (a year before the arcade was actually finished). Tourists are nevertheless attracted to its stylish shops and cafés, as well as Savini, one of Milan's historic restaurants.

The galleria itself has a floor plan in the shape of a Latin cross, with an octagonal centre adorned with mosaics representing four continents (Europe, America, Africa and Asia), together with others representing Art, Agriculture, Science and Industry. Its finest feature is its metal and glass roof, crowned with a magnificent central dome. The roof was the first structure in Italy to use metal and glass in a structural way, rather than ust decoratively. The floors are decorated with mosaics of the signs of the zodiac; tourists may be seen stepping on the genitals of Taurus the Bull, which is said to bring good luck.

🏛 Palazzo Reale

Piazza del Duomo. **Tel** 02 88 46 52 36.
Open Museo della Reggia. ♿
The former royal palace, for centuries home to the Visconti and other rulers of Milan, houses the Museo della Reggia. It displays the sumptuous interiors of the building and showcases the four historic phases of the palace including the Neo-Classical era and the Restoration. Palazzo Reale is also a prestigious venue for temporary art exhibitions. The building abutting it to the west (the Arengario) has been transformed into a Modern Art museum, the Museo del Novecento, and many Italian art works from the 20th century are displayed here.

🏛 Villa Belgiojoso Bonaparte and Galleria d'Arte Moderna

Villa Belgiojoso Bonaparte, Via Palestro 16. **Tel** 02 88 44 59 47.
Open 9am–1pm, 2–5:30pm Tue–Sun.
♿ 🅦 gam-milano.com

Milan's 19th-century and Modern Art collections are housed in a Neo-Classical villa built by Leopold Pollack in 1790 for Count Ludovico Barbiano di Belgiojoso. It was lived in by Napoleon in 1802 and later by Marshal Radetzky. The villa houses 19th-century Italian art, showing all the major art movements, as well as the Grassi and Vismara collections of 19th- and 20th-century Italian and foreign artists and the Marino Marini Museum. Of particular note are works by Giorgio Morandi (1890–1964), Carlo Carrà (1881–1966), as well as by Modigliani (1884–1920) and De Chirico (1888–1978). Non-Italian artists include Van Gogh, Cézanne, Gauguin, Picasso, Matisse, Klee, Mondrian and Kandinsky.

Still Life (1920) by Giorgio Morandi in the Galleria d'Arte Moderna

Fruit Basket (c. 1596) by Caravaggio in the Pinacoteca Ambrosiana

🏛 Pinacoteca Ambrosiana

Piazza Pio XI 2. **Tel** 02 80 69 21.
Open 10am–6pm Tue–Sun. 🖼
w ambrosiana.eu

The Ambrosiana is home to Cardinal Federico Borromeo's magnificent library of 36,000 manuscripts. These include a 5th-century illustrated *Iliad*, early manuscripts of Dante's *Divine Comedy* (1353) and the *Atlantic Codex* (1478–1519) by Leonardo da Vinci. In order to exhibit as much of the *Atlantic Codex* as possible, the pages on show are changed every three months.

The building also houses an art gallery, bequeathed by Borromeo in 1618. The collection ranges from 14th-century pieces to works of the early 19th century. Among the canvases are *Portrait of a Musician* by Leonardo, the *Madonna of the Canopy* by Botticelli (15th century), a cartoon version of Raphael's Vatican fresco, *The School of Athens* (16th century), and Caravaggio's *Fruit Basket*. There is also a strong collection of Venetian art, with paintings by Giorgione, Titian, Bassano and Tiepolo, and panel paintings by the late 15th-century Lombard painter Bergognone.

⛪ San Satiro

Via Speronari 3. **Tel** 02 87 46 83.
Open 7:30am–noon, 3–6:30pm Mon–Fri; 3:30–7pm Sat; 8:30am–12:30pm, 3:30–7pm Sun.

Santa Maria presso San Satiro church is one of the most beautiful Renaissance buildings in Milan. It was built on the site of a 9th-century sanctuary, little of which remains apart from the Cappella della Pietà, beside an 11th-century bell tower.

The interior seems to be in the shape of a Greek cross, but this is an illusion created by *trompe-l'oeil* effects, since space restrictions led Bramante to choose a T-shaped plan. Above the altar is a 13th-century fresco. An octagonal baptistry lies off the right aisle. The church's façade was finished in the 19th century.

🏛 Civico Museo Archeologico

Corso Magenta 15. **Tel** 02 88 44 52 08.
Ⓜ 1, 2 Cadorna. 🚋 16, 19, 27. 🚌 50, 58, 94. **Open** 9am–5:30pm Tue–Sun.
♿ (phone ahead). 🖼 📷 ✉

At the entrance to this museum is a model of Roman Milan, which illustrates urban planning and architecture in Milan from the 1st to the 4th century AD. The exhibition begins in a hall on the right, containing clay objects and Roman sculpture. At the end of this room is a huge fragment of a torso of Hercules and 3rd-century AD floor mosaics. Also in this room are two of the most important works in the museum: the Parabiago Patera and the Diatreta Cup. The Patera is a gilded silver plate with a relief of the goddess Cybele (4th century AD). The Diatreta Cup, dating from the same period, is a single piece of coloured glass, with finely wrought, intricate decoration.

🌳 Parco Sempione

Piazza Castello–Piazza Sempione.
Ⓜ 1 Cadorna, Cairoli, 2 Lanza, Cadorna. 🚂 Ferrovie Nord, Cadorna.
🚋 1, 2, 4, 12, 14, 19, 27. 🚌 43, 57, 61, 94. **Open** May: 6:30am–10pm; Jun–Sep: 6:30am–11:30pm; Oct–Apr: 6:30am–9pm.

Although it covers an area of about 47 ha (116 acres), this park occupies only a part of the old Visconti ducal garden, enlarged by the Sforza in the 15th century to make a 300-ha (740-acre) hunting reserve.

The present-day layout was designed by Emilio Alemagna between 1890–93.

Among the trees are monuments to Napoleon III by Francesco Barzaghi, De Chirico's *Mysterious Baths*, the sulphur water fountain and the Torre Branca, a tower of steel tubes made in 1932 to a design by Gio Ponti.

🏛 Gallerie d'Italia

Via Manzoni 10. **Tel** 800 16 76 19.
Open 9:30am–7:30pm Tue–Sun (to 10:30pm Thu). 🖼
w gallerieditalia.com

Housed in the Palazzo Anguissola Antona Traversi and Palazzo Brentani, Gallerie d'Italia has around 200 works of art from the 1800s. This collection offers a fascinating journey through one century of Italian art, with pieces by such artists as Antonio Canova, Angelo Inganni and Umberto Boccioni.

View of the Parco Sempione with the Arco della Pace in the background

Shopping in Milan

In Milan, one of the most affluent cities in Italy, shopping is synonymous with buying designer apparel. High-fashion flagship stores here are invariably smart and stylish, especially in the city centre, and looking is almost as satisfying as making a purchase. However, Milan also has many independent boutiques with a range of styles to suit all tastes. If you are looking for gifts to take home, there are some excellent *pasticcerie* (pastry shops), where you can buy authentic delicacies and traditional local confectionery. Alternatively, a cutting-edge object of design will make for an impressive souvenir of your trip to the city.

Where to Shop

All leading fashion designers have shops in the area between Via Montenapoleone, Via della Spiga, Via Manzoni and Via Sant'Andrea, the so-called "fashion quadrilateral".

Those interested in interior design will enjoy Via Durini, while lovers of antiques should head to Brera or the Navigli, where antiques markets are held monthly.

If time is of the essence, call ahead to check opening hours. In Milan generally, non-food shops are closed on Monday mornings, and food shops are closed on Monday afternoons. The largest shops tend to stay open throughout the day, but sometimes a lunch break is taken. Shops are closed on Sundays, except for the run-up to Christmas and during the main fashion shows.

Designer Fashion

Milan is renowned as a world capital of fashion, and most national and international designers have a flagship store here. As well as the designers that you would expect to find in a fashion centre, such as **Dolce & Gabbana**, **Giorgio Armani**, **Gucci**, **Prada** and **Hugo Boss**, there are many smaller designer stores. For an overview of what's new, check out multibrand boutiques such as **Banner**, which features a selection of the best from a wide array of names. For the latest on what the younger set is wearing, go to **Amedeo D** or to the Corso di Porta Ticinese area.

Up-and-coming designers are gathering in the areas around Corso Garibaldi and Corso Como. As well as of-the-moment clothes and accessories, **10 Corso Como** offers a bookshop, record store, art gallery, café and restaurant, and even a top-class B&B. The **Gianfranco Ferrè** boutique, on the other hand, has a spa attached.

Most designers carry men's as well as women's apparel. Specialist men's stores include **Pal Zileri, Ermenegildo Zegna** and **Corneliani.**

Regular Clothing

Designer outlets sell samples, seconds and last season's goods at a discount. Among Milan's longest-established outlets are **Salvagente** and **DMagazine**. Many designers also have their own outlets: fans of Max Mara, for example, should head for **Diffusione Tessile**.

Milan's main department stores are **La Rinascente** and **Coin**. The former carries many leading-edge fashion designers, while the latter features smaller fashion labels, handbags, costume jewellery and housewares. There is more to Milan than upmarket, cutting-edge designer fashion, though. For good-value casualwear for the whole family, try **Oviesse**.

Many fashion shoppers also scour the stalls at the Saturday market at Viale Papiniano, at the Piazza Sant'Agostino end, which starts at 8.30am and goes on until 5pm. Corso Vercelli is also recommended.

Accessories

Handbags, shoes, hats and jewellery, real or otherwise, are also worth seeking out. Chains such as **Furla** and **Coccinelle** offer a wide array of bags, while those looking for shoes can head to **René Caovilla** for a pair of stylish heels, or purchase comfortable shoes with a twist from **Tod's** and **Hogan**. **Garlando** carries a number of classic styles in a wide array of colours and sizes, while **Ghigodonna** has elegant shoes in larger sizes. **Borsalino** is synonymous with stylish headwear.

The "fashion quadrilateral" also features many jewellers, such as **Federico Buccellati**, **Bulgari** and **Pianegonda**.

Food and Wine

Gourmands will have a great time in Milan. **Peck** consists of three floors of the best that Italy can offer, in terms of both food and wine. **Giovanni Galli Marroni e Canditi** offers a different take on chocolate-coated delicacies.

For those who like a hands-on approach to their food, **High Tech** is a goldmine for kitchen tools, including all the top names such as Alessi, as well as plates and cutlery.

Design, Books and Gifts

Milan is the cradle of designer furniture. Several top stores are around Piazza San Babila. A stroll down Via Durini will reveal, among others, **Cassina** and **B&B**. For lighting, see **Flos** and **Artemide**. Those interested in 20th-century design could visit **Spazio 900**.

If an item of furniture is not an option, the next best thing might be a book on design or architecture. Visit the bookshop of the **Triennale** or that of the art-catalogue publisher **Skira** for the best on the market.

Fabriano, the company that developed the first paper mill in the 1200s, has a store selling handsome writing paper, envelopes and gift items.

DIRECTORY

Designer Fashion

10 Corso Como
Corso Como 10.
Tel 02 2900 2674.
Tel 02 626 163 (B&B).
Tel 02 2901 3581
(bar & restaurant).
Tel 02 653 531 (gallery).
W 10corsocomo.it

Amedeo D
Corso Vercelli 23.
Tel 02 4800 4048.
W amedeod.it

Banner
Via Sant'Andrea 8.
Tel 02 7600 4609.
W biffi.com

Corneliani
Via Montenapoleone 26.
Tel 02 7631 7955.
W corneliani.com

Dolce & Gabbana
Via della Spiga 26
(women).
Tel 02 7600 1155.
Corso Venezia 15 (men).
Tel 02 7602 8485.
Via della Spiga 2
(women's accessories).
Tel 02 795 747.
Corso Venezia 7 (D&G).
Tel 02 7600 4091.
W dolcegabbana.it

Ermenegildo Zegna
Via Montenapoleone 27.
Tel 02 7600 6437.
W zegna.com

Gianfranco Ferrè
Via Sant'Andrea 15.
Tel 02 7601 7526 (spa and
beauty parlour).
W gianfrancoferre.com

Giorgio Armani
Via Sant'Andrea 9.
Tel 02 7600 3234.
Via Manzoni 31
(megastore).
Tel 02 7231 8600.
Via Montenapoleone 2
(Collezioni).
Tel 02 7639 0068.
Via Montenapoleone 10
(Armani Junior).
Tel 02 783 196. Via
Manzoni 37 (Armani Casa).
Tel 02 657 2401.
Corso di Porta Ticinese 60
(Armani Jeans).
Tel 02 8324 1924.
W armani.com

Gucci
Via Montenapoleone 5–7.
Tel 02 771 271.
Galleria Vittorio Emanuele II
11 (accessories).
Tel 02 859 7991.
W gucci.com

Hugo Boss
Corso Matteotti 11 (men).
Tel 02 7639 4667.
Corso Matteotti 8
(women).
Tel 02 7601 3266.
W hugoboss.com

Pal Zileri
Via Manzoni 20.
Tel 02 7639 4680.
W palzileri.com

Prada
Galleria Vittorio
Emanuele 63–65.
Tel 02 876 979.
Via Montenapoleone 8
(women).
Tel 02 777 1771.
Via Montenapoleone 6
(men).
Tel 02 7602 0273.
Via della Spiga 18
(accessories).
Tel 02 780 455.
W prada.com

Regular Clothing

Coin
Piazza Cinque Giornate.
Tel 02 5519 2083.
Corso Vercelli 30.
Tel 02 4399 0001.
Piazza Cantore 12.
Tel 02 5810 4385.
W coin.it

Diffusione Tessile
Galleria San Carlo 6.
Tel 02 7600 0829.

DMagazine
Via Montenapoleone 26.
Tel 02 7600 6027.

Oviesse
Galleria Passarella 2.
Tel 02 7628 1677.
Corso Garibaldi 72.
Tel 02 655 1649.
Corso Buenos Aires 35.
Tel 02 20 40 48 01.
W oviesse.it

La Rinascente
Piazza del Duomo.
Tel 02 88 521.
W rinascente.it

Salvagente
Via Fratelli
Bronzetti 16.
Tel 02 7611 0328.
W salvagentemilano.it

Accessories

Borsalino
Galleria Vittorio
Emanuele II 92.
Tel 02 8901 5436.
W borsalino.com

Bulgari
Via Montenapoleone 2.
Tel 02 777 001.
W bulgari.com

Coccinelle
Via Manzoni 26.
Tel 02 7602 8161.
Corso Buenos Aires 16.
Tel 02 2040 4755.

**Federico
Buccellati**
Via della Spiga 2.
Tel 02 7600 3867.
W federicobuccellati.it

Furla
Piazza Duomo 31.
Tel 02 8909 6794.
Corso Vercelli 11.
Tel 02 4801 4189.
W furla.com

Garlando
Via Madonnina 2.
Tel 02 874 665.
W alfonsogarlando.it

Ghigodonna
Viale Tunisia 2.
Tel 02 2940 8414.
W ghigocalzature.com

Hogan
Via Montenapoleone 23.
Tel 02 7601 1174.
W hogan.com

Pianegonda
Via Montenapoleone 6.
Tel 02 7600 3038.
W pianegonda.com

René Caovilla
Via Bagutta 28.
Tel 02 7631 9049.
W renecaovilla.com

Tod's
Via della Spiga 22.
Tel 02 7600 2423.
Galleria Vittorio
Emanuele.
Tel 02 877 997.
W todsgroup.com

Food and Wine

**Giovanni Galli
Marroni e Canditi**
Via Victor Hugo 2.
Tel 02 8646 4833.

High Tech
Piazza XXV Aprile 12.
Tel 02 624 1101.

Peck
Via Spadari 9.
Tel 02 802 3161.
W peck.it

Design, Books and Gifts

Artemide
Corso Monforte 19.
Tel 02 7600 6930.
W artemide.com

B&B
Via Durini 14.
Tel 02 764 4411.
W bebitalia.it

Cassina
Via Durini 16.
Tel 02 7602 0745.
W cassina.it

Fabriano
Via Ponte Vetero 17.
Tel 02 7631 8754.
W cartierefabriano.it

Flos
Corso Monforte 7.
Tel 02 794 559.
W flos.net

Skira
Via Torino 61.
Tel 02 724 441.
W skira.it

Spazio 900
Viale Campania 51.
Tel 02 7012 5737.
Corso Garibaldi 42.
Tel 02 7200 1775.
W spazio900.net

Triennale
Viale Alemagna 6.
Tel 02 724 341.
W triennale.it

Milan: Pinacoteca di Brera

Milan's finest art collection is held in an imposing 17th-century building, the Palazzo di Brera. This is where, in the 18th century, the Accademia di Belle Arti was founded; the picture collection developed alongside the academy. Inside the Brera hang some of the finest examples of Italian Renaissance and Baroque painting, including works by Piero della Francesca, Mantegna, Canaletto, Bellini, Raphael, Tintoretto, Veronese and Caravaggio. The collection also includes 20th-century works by some of Italy's most famous modern artists.

★ Dead Christ by Mantegna
The subtle lighting and dramatic perspective of this lamentation by Mantegna (1430–1506) make it one of his greatest masterpieces.

Gallery Guide

The collection is displayed in 38 rooms, and was first built up by paintings from churches, later from acquisitions. Not all of it is permanently on view – this is due to restoration work and research.

Twin staircases lead up to the first-floor entrance of the Pinacoteca.

The Kiss *(1859)*
Francesco Hayez's painting is one of the most reproduced works of Italian 19th-century art. Patriotic and sentimental, it became a symbol of the optimism surrounding the unification of Italy.

The bronze statue (1809) by Canova depicts Napoleon as a demi-god with Victory wings in his hand.

Key to Floorplan

- 15th- to 16th-century Italian painting
- 16th- to 17th-century Dutch and Flemish painting
- 17th-century Italian painting
- 18th- to 19th-century Italian painting
- 20th-century Italian painting and sculpture and Jesi Collection
- Non-exhibition space

Works by Rubens and Van Dyck represent some of the non-Italian artists on show.

Mother and Son
(1917)
The metaphysical paintings of Carlo Carrà show a dream world full of strange and obscure symbols.

VISITORS' CHECKLIST

Practical Information
Via Brera 28. **Tel** 02 72 26 32 64; 02 72 26 32 29. **Open** 8:30am–7:15pm Tue–Sun (last adm: 45 min before closing). **Closed** 1 Jan, 1 May, 25 Dec. 🅿 ♿
Ⓦ brera.beniculturali.it

Transport
Ⓜ Lanza, Montenapoleone & Duomo. 🚌 61, 97.

Portrait of Moisè Kisling
Modigliani's angular portrait of 1915 reflects his interest in African sculpture.

Twinned columns support the arcades in the courtyard.

The stone façade presents a regular and slightly austere appearance.

Madonna della Candeletta *(c.1490)*
This painting by Carlo Crivelli was the central part of a polyptych. It is richly detailed with much distinctive ornamentation.

Main entrance from Via Brera

★ **Marriage of the Virgin by Raphael**
This graceful altarpiece was painted in 1504. The circular temple is signed with the artist's name.

15
20
21
22
23
24
27
28

Milan: Southwest of the Centre

Some of Milan's finest treasures are to be found in its religious buildings: the ancient monasteries and churches make up some very fine architectural ensembles in themselves, as well as incorporating important ruins and relics dating back to Roman times. It is also in Milan that one of the most famous images in the world is to be found: Leonardo's evocative masterpiece, *The Last Supper*.

The entrance to Sant'Ambrogio, flanked by unequal bell towers

⬆ Sant'Ambrogio

Piazza Sant'Ambrogio 15. **Tel** 02 86 45 08 95. Basilica: **Open** 10am–noon, 2:30–6pm Mon–Sat, 3–5pm Sun. Museum: **Open** 9:30am–noon, 2:30–6pm Mon–Sat, 3–5pm Sun. ♿
Ⓦ basilicasantambrogio.it

Sant'Ambrogio, or St Ambrose, Milan's patron saint and its bishop in the 4th century, was so eloquent that bees were said to fly into his mouth, attracted by his honey tongue. This is the basilica that he began in AD 379, though today most of it is 10th-century Romanesque. A gateway leads to the bronze doors of the entrance, flanked by two bell towers. Inside, note the fine rib vaulting and pulpit, and the 9th-century altar decorated with gold, silver and gems. In a chapel off the south aisle, fine mosaics line a stunning cupola. In the crypt lies the tomb of Sant'Ambrogio himself.

Above the portico, a small museum contains architectural fragments, tapestries and paintings relating to the church.

⬆ San Lorenzo Maggiore

Corso di Porta Ticinese 39. **Tel** 02 89 40 41 29. **Open** 7:30am–6:45pm Mon–Sat, 9am–7pm Sun. Cappella Sant'Aquilino: **Open** 9am–6:30pm daily. 🔊 for the Cappella.
Ⓦ sanlorenzomaggiore.com

This church contains a vast collection of Roman and early Christian remains. The octagonal basilica was built in the 4th century, above what was probably a Roman amphitheatre, and rebuilt in the 12th and 16th centuries.

In front of the church stands a row of 16 Roman columns and a statue of Emperor Constantine. Fine 4th-century mosaics adorn the Cappella di Sant'Aquilino, a Romanesque chapel, with two early Christian sarcophagi. Other Roman architectural elements of this church are in a chamber below the chapel.

San Lorenzo Maggiore viewed from the northeast

⬆ Santa Maria delle Grazie

Piazza Santa Maria delle Grazie 2. **Tel** 02 46 76 111. Cenacolo: **Tel** 02 92 80 03 60 (booking compulsory – up to 60 days in advance). **Open** 8:15am–6:45pm Tue–Sun. **Closed** public hols. 🔊 ♿ Ⓦ cenacolovinciano.org

This beautiful 15th-century Renaissance convent, its lovely apse and calm small cloister designed by Bramante, contains one of the key images of western civilization: the *Cenacolo (The Last Supper)* by Leonardo da Vinci. The image captures the moment at which Christ tells his disciples that one of them will betray him. The Christ figure is unfinished: Leonardo did not consider himself worthy enough to complete it.

The artist also spurned the standard fresco technique of painting on wet plaster, applying tempera to the dry wall instead. The result has deteriorated badly: the paint is flaking off, and restoration has proved difficult. The painting is now protected by a filtering system.

Leonardo da Vinci's *Last Supper* (1494–7) adorning the refectory wall of Santa Maria delle Grazie

❹ Monza

Monza. 🚇 120,000. 🚈 🚌 ℹ️ P.za
Carducci 2 (039 32 32 22). **Open** 9am–
noon, 3–6pm daily. 🛍️ Thu & Sat.

These days Monza is mostly
famous for its international
Formula One **Autodromo**,
which lies inside a vast park
that also has an elegant Rococo
hunting lodge, the Villa Reale,
and a golf course. At one time,
however, Monza was one of
the most important towns in
Lombardy. Theodolinda, the
6th-century Lombard queen,
built its first cathedral and
bequeathed her treasure to
the town.

In the town centre is the
Duomo, with its notable green
and white 14th-century façade
and beautiful 15th-century
frescoes portraying Theodolinda's life. Behind the high altar
is the small Iron Crown,
believed to have belonged to
Emperor Constantine: it is
prized for the iron strip, said to
have been one of the nails from
the cross of Christ. More local
treasures may be found in the
Duomo's **Museo e Tesoro del
Duomo**, including a silver hen
standing over seven tiny chicks
– which symbolize Lombardy
and the seven provinces it ruled
– and a relic said to be John the
Baptist's tooth.

🚇 Autodromo
Parco di Monza. **Tel** 039 248 21.
Open daily. **Closed** public hols. 🅿️ ♿

🏛️ Duomo
Piazza Duomo. **Tel** 039 38 94 20.
Museo e Tesoro del Duomo: **Open**
9am–1pm, 2–6pm Tue–Sun. 🅿️

Leonello d'Este (c.1440) by Pisanello in the
Accademia Carrara, Bergamo

❺ Bergamo

🚇 120,000. 🚈 🚌 ℹ️ Via Gombito
13 (035 24 22 26). **Open** 9am–5:30pm
daily. 🛍️ Mon.
🌐 **turismo.bergamo.it**

Bergamo owes much of its artistic
inspiration and architectural
splendour to the influence of
Venice, which ruled it from the
15th to the late 18th century.
The town is divided into two
distinct parts: Bergamo Alta,
crowning the hill with its cluster
of attractive medieval and
Renaissance buildings, and
the more modern Bergamo
Bassa below.

The jewel of the upper town
is **Piazza Vecchia**, containing
one of the most appealing
architectural ensembles in the
region. Its buildings include the
12th-century Torre del Comune
with its fine clock and curfew
bell that rings daily at 10pm, the
late 16th-century Biblioteca
Civica and the attractive
12th-century Palazzo della

Ragione, or law courts, adorned
with a bass-relief of the Lion
of Venice.

The arcades of the Palazzo
della Ragione lead to Piazza del
Duomo, the square of the Neo-
Classical Duomo. The square is
dominated by the **Cappella
Colleoni** (see p184), a chapel
built in 1476 to house the tomb
of Bergamo's famous political
leader, Bartolomeo Colleoni. It is
flanked by two 14th-century
buildings: an octagonal
baptistry and the porch leading
to the Romanesque basilica of
Santa Maria Maggiore. The
basilica's austere exterior
contrasts with its Baroque
interior, which contains the
tomb of Bergamoborn
composer Gaetano Donizetti
(1797–1848).

The collection from the
**Galleria dell' Accademia
Carrara**, a major picture gallery
with works by Venetian masters
and local artists, as well as
masterpieces from the rest of
Italy, is housed temporarily in
Palazzo della Ragione while
the building is being restored. It
includes 15th- and 16th-century
works by Pisanello, Crivelli,
Mantegna, Giovanni Bellini,
Botticelli, Titian, Raphael and
Perugino, 18th-century
canvases by Tiepolo, Guardi and
Canaletto, as well as paintings
by Holbein, Dürer, Brueghel
and Velázquez.

🏛️ Palazzo della Ragione
Città Alta. **Tel** 035 39 96 77.
Open Jun–Sep: 10am–9pm
Tue–Sun (to 11pm Sat); Oct–May:
9:30am–5:30pm Tue–Fri,
10am–6pm Sat–Sun. 🅿️ ♿

The Edict of Milan

Emperor
Constantine

Milan was colonized by the Romans in 222 BC,
and quickly grew to be an important city at the
junction of various trading routes. As the Roman
Empire grew and then split into two, the
emperors began to neglect Rome for the better-
placed Mediolanum (literally, city in the middle of
the plain). It was here that Emperor Constantine
declared his edict of AD 313, in which Christianity
was recognized as one of the permitted religions
of the empire, ending centuries of persecution.
The emperor is said to have converted following a
vision, but by the 4th century adopting Christianity
was also one way to unite the disparate empire.

Detail from the Cappella Colleoni

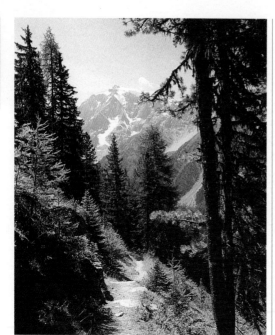

A leafy pathway through the Parco Nazionale dello Stelvio

❻ Parco Nazionale dello Stelvio

Trento, Bolzano, Sondrio & Brescia. 🚌 from Bormio to Santa Caterina Valfurva & Madonna dei Monti. 🛈 Via de Simoni 42, Bormio (0342 90 08 11). 🆆 stelviopark.it

The Stelvio, Italy's largest national park, is the gateway from Lombardy to the glacier-strewn Dolomite mountains stretching into Trentino-Alto Adige. The glaciers are dotted with more than 50 lakes, and dominated by craggy peaks such as Gran Zebrù, Cevedale and Ortles – the tallest mountain here at 3,905 m (12,811 ft).

For walkers, the area offers excellent hiking, and access to remote areas populated by ibexes, marmots, chamois and eagles. The only real population centre in the Lombardy part of the park is at **Bormio**, which boasts plenty of winter and summer sports facilities, and is a good base from which to explore the area. The town's **Giardino Botanico**, a 1 km (0.6 mile) walk from the centre, displays some of the species of mountain plants found in the region.

🌳 Giardino Botanico Alpino Rezia

Via Sertorelli, Loc. Rovinaccia, Bormio. **Tel** 0342 90 08 55. **Open** May–mid-Sep: daily. 🆆 stelviopark.it

❼ Val Camonica

Brescia. 🇫🇸 🚌 Capo di Ponte. 🛈 Via Briscioli 42, Capo di Ponte (0364 420 80). 🆆 proloco.capo-di-ponte.bs.it

This attractive broad valley formed by a glacier is the setting for an extraordinary series of prehistoric rock carvings. These form an astonishing outdoor mural from the Lago d'Iseo to Capo di Ponte and beyond, and

the valley is an UNESCO cultural protection zone. More than 180,000 engravings from the Neolithic era until early Roman times have been discovered; the best are in the **Parco Nazionale delle Incisioni Rupestri**. Do not miss the Naquane rock, carved with nearly 1,000 figures from the Ice Age. The **Centro Camuno** focuses on the Roman settlement in the valley.

🏛 Centro Camuno di Studi Preistorici
Via Marconi 7, Capo di Ponte. **Tel** 0364 420 91. **Closed** to tourists. ♿

🏛 Parco Nazionale delle Incisioni Rupestri
Capo di Ponte. **Tel** 0364 421 40. **Open** 8:30am–7:30pm Tue–Sun (mid-Oct–Feb to 4:30pm). **Closed** 1 Jan, 1 May, 25 Dec.

❽ Lago d'Iseo

Bergamo & Brescia. 🇫🇸 🚌 🚢 Iseo. 🛈 Lungolago Marconi 2, Iseo (030 98 02 09). 🆆 lagodiseo.org

This glaciated lake is surrounded by tall mountains and waterfalls and boasts a mini-mountain of its own, in the form of the island of Monte Isola. Along the shores of the lake are a clutch of fishing villages such as Sale Marasino and Iseo itself. From Marone, on the east bank of the lake, a road leads to the village of **Cislano**, about 5 km (3 miles) away. Here, extraordinary spire-like rock formations rise from the ground, each spire topped by a boulder. These distinctive erosion pillars, one of the strangest natural wonders in Lombardy, are known as the "Fairies of the Forest".

Prehistoric engraving of a mounted hunter and stag in the Val Camonica

The partly Renaissance Ponte Coperto, straddling the River Ticino at Pavia

🟑 Brescia

🏙 195,000. 🚉 🚍 ℹ️ Via Musei 32 (030 374 96 16). 🗓 Sat.

Lombardy's second city after Milan boasts a rich artistic heritage, ranging from Roman temples to the triumphalist Mussolini-era architecture of Piazza Vittoriale. The major sights include the Roman ruins around Piazza del Foro, consisting of the **Tempio Capitolino** – a three-part temple incorporating the **Museo di Santa Giulia**, Brescia's main gallery – and a theatre. The **Pinacoteca Civica Tosio Martinengo** has masterpieces by Raphael, Lorenzo Lotto and Tintoretto; it is currently closed for restoration but important paintings are on display at the Museo di Santa Giulia. The **Duomo** on Piazza Paolo VI, with its 11th-century core and 17th-century exterior, is another main attraction. One of the relics in the Duomo is the banner from the *Carroccio*, or sacred ox cart, which served as a symbol for the medieval Lega Lombarda. **Piazza della Loggia**, where the market is held, is named after the Renaissance loggia, built in Palladian style. The 18th-century church of San Nazaro e San Celso on Via Bronzoni contains an altarpiece by Titian.

🏛 **Tempio Capitolino**
Via Musei 57a. **Open** 11am–4pm Tue–Sun. 🖼

🏛 **Museo di Santa Giulia**
Via Musei 81b. **Tel** 030 297 78 34. **Open** Tue–Sun. 🖼 ♿

🏛 **Pinacoteca Civica Tosio Martinengo**
Via Martinengo da Barcol. **Tel** 030 377 49 99. **Closed** for restoration.

🟑 Lodi

Lodi. 🏙 44,000. 🚉 🚍 ℹ️ Via Fanfulla 14 (0371 44 27 11). 🗓 Tue, Thu, Sat & Sun. 🖥 turismo.provincia.lodi.it

This is a charming medieval town of pastel-coloured houses, pretty courtyards and gardens. Just off Piazza della Vittoria, the arcaded square on which the 12th-century Duomo stands, is the fine Renaissance church of the **Incoronata**. The magnificent octagonal interior is entirely decorated with wall paintings and gilding, and crowned with a dome. One of the chapels has 15th-century works by Bergognone.

🟑 Pavia

🏙 71,000. 🚉 🚍 ℹ️ Palazzo del Broletto, Piazza della Vittoria (0382 07 99 43). 🗓 Wed & Sat. 🖥 turismo.provincia.pv.it

During Pavia's golden age, the city was the Lombards' capital, and later witnessed coronations of Charlemagne and Frederick Barbarossa.

The Roman Tempio Capitolino in Brescia

Even after it lost its status to Milan in 1359, Pavia remained an important city, and great Romanesque churches, tall towers and other monuments still reflect this.

As well as the Charterhouse (Certosa) *(see pp204–5)*, there is the sandstone **Basilica di San Michele** off Corso Garibaldi. The building was founded in the 7th century but largely rebuilt in the 12th. Its façade is decorated with symbols and friezes of fantastic animals, and inside there are intricate carvings on the columns; a chapel to the right of the main altar contains a 7th-century silver crucifix.

In the town centre, around Piazza della Vittoria, are several ancient monuments, such as the medieval **Broletto** (town hall), with its 16th-century façade, and the **Duomo**, originally begun in 1488 and worked on in turn by Amadeo, Leonardo and Bramante. The dome was added in the 1880s. The 11th-century tower that stood next to it collapsed suddenly in 1989. Crossing the river is the **Ponte Coperto**, a Renaissance covered bridge with a consecrated chapel halfway along it. The bridge was rebuilt after World War II.

Pavia is also the site of one of Europe's oldest (1361) and most respected universities, now residing around a series of Neo-Classical courtyards off Strada Nuova. This road continues northwards to the 14th-century castle, now home to the **Museo Civico**.

Northwest of Piazza Castello is the 12th-century church, **San Pietro in Ciel d'Oro**. It no longer boasts the fine gilded ceiling after which it is named, but does still contain a magnificent shrine to St Augustine, whose bones were allegedly brought to Pavia in the 8th century. The body of the philosopher Boëthius (c.480–524) is buried down in the crypt.

🏛 **Museo Civico**
Castello Visconteo, Viale XI Febbraio 35. **Tel** 0382 338 53. **Open** 10am– 5:50pm. Tue–Sun (Jan, Jul, Aug & Dec: 9am– 1:30pm). **Closed** public hols. 🖼 ♿

⓰ Certosa di Pavia

The Charterhouse 8 km (5 miles) north of Pavia is the pinnacle of Renaissance architecture in Lombardy, a gloriously decorated Carthusian monastery built over 200 years. Conceived as a monument to Gian Galeazzo Visconti, the Milanese ruler who founded the complex in 1396, this shrine was created by the great 15th-century craftsman Giovanni Antonio Amadeo, among others, who used innovative techniques of relief work and multicoloured decoration. The Certosa is still home to Carthusian monks, who are under a strict vow of silence.

Pietra Dura Altar
Several of the 17th-century altars in the chapels have lavish designs worked in semi-precious stones ("pietra dura").

KEY

① **The side chapels** are richly decorated with marble, *trompe l'oeil* frescoes and ornate altars and altarpieces.

② **The interior** of the church is largely Gothic.

③ **The grilles** date from c.1660.

④ **The choir stalls** (15th century) are deeply carved and inlaid with intricate marquetry.

⑤ **The tomb** of Gian Galeazzo Visconti (1351–1402) is in the south transept.

⑥ **The New Sacristy** is painted with colourful ceiling frescoes.

⑦ **Monk's cell**

⑧ **This delightful**, arcaded Small Cloister, with fine terracotta ornamentation, contains a small garden, planted in formal designs.

⑨ **Main entrance** to the Certosa.

Tomb of Ludovico il Moro and Beatrice d'Este
This realistic marble portrait of Ludovico and his child bride was begun by Cristoforo Solari in 1497, some 11 years before Ludovico's death.

★ **Frescoes by Bergognone** (c.1488–93)
This striking portrait of Christ is one of several frescoes by Bergognone in the transept and chapels, together with an altar painting of Sant'Ambrogio.

Great Cloister
This huge cloister is reached through the Small Cloister. It is framed on three sides by the two-storey monks' cells, each backed by a small garden. A hatch beside the door permits food to be delivered without any communication.

VISITORS' CHECKLIST

Practical Information
Viale del Monumento 4, Pavia.
Tel 0382 92 56 13. from Pavia & Milan.
Open 9–11:30am, 2:30–4:30pm Tue–Sun & pub hols (Mar, Oct: to 5pm; Apr, Sep: to 5:30pm; May–Aug: to 6pm). (Last adm: 30 mins before closing.) Donation to guide.

Transport
FS Certosa. Followed by 1 km (0.5 mile) walk

★ Altarpiece by Perugino
The six-panel altarpiece was painted in 1499 but now only one panel – that depicting God the Father – is original; it is flanked by two paintings by Bergognone.

★ Renaissance Façade
The 15th-century lower part of the façade is profusely decorated with statues and carvings of Roman emperors, saints (here St Peter), apostles and prophets. The upper part dates from 1500.

The Duomo on Piazza del Comune, Cremona

⓫ Cremona

🏙 72,000. 🚆 🚌 ℹ️ Piazza del Comune 5 (0372 40 63 91). 🚩 Wed & Sat. 🌐 **turismocremona.it**

Cremona, a major agricultural market, is most famous for music, thanks to native sons such as the composer Claudio Monteverdi (1567–1643) and the violin-maker Stradivarius (1644–1737). The town itself is dominated by the beautiful Piazza del Comune.

The main attraction is the exuberant part-Romanesque **Duomo**, and its bell tower – said to be the tallest medieval tower in Italy – known as the **Torrazzo**; the two are linked by a Renaissance loggia. The wonderful façade is dominated by the large 13th-century rose window and by a number of intricate touches, including a small portico with statues of the Virgin and saints. Inside, the Duomo is sumptuously decorated with magnificent early 16th-century frescoes and Flemish tapestries, as well as paintings in the side chapels. The top of the Torrazzo offers sweeping views. Outside the Duomo, note the pulpit where itinerant preachers, including San Bernardino of Siena, spoke.

Next to the Duomo stands an octagonal 12th-century baptistry, while on the other side of the piazza rise the arcades of the late 13th-century **Loggia dei Militi**

where the town's lords once met, now a war memorial.

The **Palazzo del Comune** is the other major building on the square. It was rebuilt in the 1200s and houses the Stradivari family collection of violins and masterpieces by Amati and Guarnieri.

The **Museo Civico**, in a 16th-century palazzo, houses the Pinacoteca, containing paintings, wood carvings, the cathedral's treasure and ceramics. The **Museo di Violino** has a large display of important historic instruments. It also tells in detail the history of the violin and the importance of Cremona in the history of violin making.

On the eastern outskirts of the town, on the road to Casalmaggiore, lies the Renaissance church of **San Sigismondo** (closed at lunchtime). It was here in a small chapel that Francesco Sforza married Bianca Visconti in 1441. The interior is richly decorated with 16th-century paintings, altar-pieces and frescoes by artists of the Cremona school (Campi family, Gatti and Boccaccino).

🕍 **Torrazzo**
Piazza del Comune. **Tel** 0372 49 50 29.
Open 10am–1pm, 2:30–6pm
Tue–Sun. 🚫

🏛 **Palazzo del Comune**
Piazza del Comune. **Tel** 0372 80 36 18.
Open 9am–6pm Tue–Sat; 10am–6pm
Sun. **Closed** public hols. 🚫 ♿

🏛 **Museo Civico**
Via Ugolani Dati 4. **Tel** 0372 80 36 22.
Open 10am–5pm Tue–Sun.
Closed public hols. 🚫 ♿

🏛 **Museo di Violino**
Piazza Marconi 5. **Tel** 0372 80 18 01.
Open 10am–6pm Tue–Sun.
Closed public hols. 🚫

⓮ Sabbioneta

Mantua. 🏙 4,400. 🚌 from Mantua.
ℹ️ Piazza d'Armi 1 (0375 520 39).
🚩 Wed am. 🎫 apply at tourist office.
🚫 🌐 **iatsabbioneta.org**

Sabbioneta is the result of a delightful experiment in the theory of Renaissance architecture. It was built by Vespasiano Gonzaga Colonna (1531–91) as an ideal city, and within its hexagonal walls is a perfect gridwork arrangement of streets and buildings designed on a human scale. The finest buildings include the splendid Teatro All'Antica designed by Scamozzi, the Palazzo Ducale and the frescoed Palazzo del Giardino, which may be visited as part of a tour of the town.

Antonio Stradivari and his Violins

The city of Cremona has been synonymous with violin-making since the 1530s, when Andrea Amati's instruments became sought after at the royal courts throughout Europe because of their superior tone to the medieval fiddle.

However, it was Antonio Stradivari, known as Stradivarius (1644–1737) – the pupil of Andrea Amati's grandson Niccolò – who

19th-century engraving of
Antonio Stradivari

raised the level of violin craftsmanship to genius. He went walking in the forests of the Dolomites in search of the perfect wood for his instruments. Stradivarius produced more than 1,100 violins in his workshop, of which more than 400 exist today. The main stopping-off points on a Stradivarius tour of Cremona are the Museo di Violino, the string collection in the Palazzo del Comune and the great man's tombstone in the public gardens in Piazza Roma.

The ceiling of the Camera degli Sposi, by Mantegna, in the Palazzo Ducale

⓯ Mantua

🏛 49,000.. 🚂 🚌 ℹ️ Piazza Andrea Mantegna 6 (0376 43 24 32). 🗓 Thu.
🌐 turismo.mantova.it

Mantua (Mantova in Italian) is a striking place of fine squares and aristocratic architecture, bordered on three sides by lakes formed by the River Mincio. The climate can be humid as a result, but the city makes up for it with its cultural history: it was the birthplace of the poet Virgil and the playground of the Gonzaga dukes for three centuries. It was also the refuge where Shakespeare sent Romeo into exile from Verona, and the setting for Verdi's opera *Rigoletto*. These links are all celebrated in street names, signposts and monuments around the town. The theatrical connections are enhanced by the 18th-century **Teatro Accademico Bibiena**, on Via Accademia, which Mozart's father claimed was the finest he had ever seen.

Mantua is focused on three attractive main squares: Piazza delle Erbe, Piazza Broletto, named after the 13th-century building adorned with a statue of the poet Virgil, and the cobbled Piazza Sordello. On one side of Piazza Sordello is the **Duomo**, with an 18th-century façade and fine interior stuccoes by Giulio Romano (c.1492–1546); on another side, the forbidding façade of the Palazzo Bonacolsi, with its tall prison tower. Piazza delle Erbe is dominated by the **Basilica di Sant'Andrea**

(15th century), designed largely by Leon Battista Alberti, the early Renaissance architect and theorist, and now flanked by an arcade of shops. The square is also notable for the appealing 11th-century Rotonda di San Lorenzo, and the part-13th-century Palazzo della Ragione with its 15th-century clock tower.

Detail from the 15th-century clock tower on Piazza delle Erbe

🏛 Palazzo Ducale
Piazza Sordello 40. **Tel** 0412 41 18 97. **Open** 8:15am–7:15pm (last adm: 6pm) Tue–Sun. **Closed** 1 Jan, 1 May, 25 Dec. 🎫 🚫 Camera degli Sposi: Book ahead on **Tel** 041 241 18 97 or 🌐 ducalemantova.org

The vast, 500-room home of the Gonzaga family covers the northeastern corner of the town and incorporates Castello San Giorgio (a 14th-century fortress), a basilica, and the palace proper.

The many works of art include an unfinished series of 15th-century frescoes by Pisanello, retelling episodes from the Arthurian legends; a large portrait by Rubens (17th century) of the ducal family in the Salone degli Arcieri; and – most absorbing of all – the frescoes by Mantegna in the **Camera degli Sposi** (1465–74). These portray Lodovico Gonzaga and members of his family and court in all their magnificence *(pp208–9)*. The entire room is decorated with images of people, animals and fantastic landscapes, and completed by a light-hearted *trompe l'oeil* ceiling of figures, *putti* and a blue sky.

🏛 Palazzo Tè
Viale Tè. **Tel** 0376 32 32 66. **Open** 1–6pm Mon, 9am–6pm Tue–Sun. **Closed** 1 Jan, 1 May, 25 Dec. 🚫 🚫
🌐 palazzote.it

At the other end of town stands the early 16th-century Palazzo Tè, built by Giulio Romano for the Gonzaga family as a base from which they could go horse riding. Here the artworks conspire with the architecture to produce striking effects: in the **Sala dei Giganti**, for instance, the frescoed Titans seem to be tearing down the very pillars of the room. Also remarkable is the **Sala di Amore e Psiche**, decorated with erotic scenes from Apuleius' *Golden Ass* and said to celebrate Federico II's love for his mistress. Other rooms are lavishly painted with horses and signs of the Zodiac.

The 13th-century façade of Palazzo Ducale overlooking Piazza Sordello

Late Renaissance fresco, by Romano, in the Duomo di Mantua, Mantua ▶

VALLE D'AOSTA AND PIEDMONT

Piedmont and the neighbouring Valle d'Aosta are – apart from Turin and its cultural splendours – essentially countryside. To the north lie the Alps, with ski resorts such as Courmayeur, and the wild stretches of the Parco Nazionale del Gran Paradiso. To the south lie the vineyard-clad hills around Barolo, and seemingly endless fields of grain and rice, used in the local dish, risotto.

The northwest is also rich in culture. From the 11th century to the 18th, both the verdant Valle d'Aosta and Piedmont were part of the French-speaking principality of Savoy and enjoyed the influences of both sides of the Alpine divide. Even today, French and dialectal variants are still spoken in the remote valleys of Piedmont and in much of the Valle d'Aosta. It was only under Duke Emanuele Filiberto in the 16th century that the region was brought definitively into the Italian sphere of influence; and later it was to play the key role in the Risorgimento *(see pp66–7)*, the ambitious movement that united Italy under a king from Piedmont. The vestiges of this history are to be found in the medieval castles of the Valle d'Aosta and the clusters of

chapels known as *sacri monti* (sacred mountains) built into the foothills of the Alps. Piedmont also spawned a school of painting, which is in evidence in the small parish churches and excellent fine art collections in the region. The most impressive architecture in the northwest, however, is undoubtedly to be found in Turin, a much underrated and surprisingly elegant Baroque city which boasts, among other things, one of the best Egyptian museums in the world. Piedmont is also known for its industry – FIAT in Turin, Olivetti in Ivrea, Ferrero in Alba – but it has not forgotten its agricultural roots, and food and drink play an important role in the life of the region: the hills of southern Piedmont produce many of the great Italian red wines.

Traditional pavement café in the heart of Turin

◄ Banners hanging outside of the Gothic Duomo in Asti, Piedmont

Exploring Valle d'Aosta and Piedmont

The vast flat plain of the Po, covered with the watery expanse of rice fields around Vercelli and Novara, eventually gives way, in the west, to the majestic heights of the Alps. Turin, the largest city in the area and the capital of Piedmont, stands at the edge of the plain, nestling almost in the shadow of the mountains. Further northwest, attractive Alpine valleys headed by dramatic peaks provide the setting for the traditional villages, ancient towns and castles around Aosta. The Parco Nazionale del Gran Paradiso is an unspoilt tract of breathtaking scenery.

Rice fields around Vercelli

Sights at a Glance

1. Monte Bianco
2. Colle del Gran San Bernardo
3. Monte Cervino
4. Monte Rosa
5. Aosta
6. *Parco Nazionale del Gran Paradiso pp220–21*
7. Ceresole Reale
8. Via Lattea
9. Susa
10. Sacra di San Michele
11. Avigliana
12. Pinerolo
13. *Turin (Torino) pp224–9*
14. Palazzina di Caccia Stupinigi
15. Basilica di Superga
16. Venaria Reale
17. Santuario d'Oropa
18. Domodossola
19. Varallo
20. Lago d'Orta
21. Novara
22. Vercelli
23. Asti
24. Cuneo
25. Bossea Caves
26. Garessio

For additional map symbols *see back flap*

Turin, the capital of Piedmont, in the valley of the Po

Getting Around

The Fréjus Pass and the Mont Blanc Tunnel link France with northwest Italy, while the tunnel under the Simplon or Sempione Pass provides a direct rail route from Switzerland. From the rest of Italy there are excellent motorway connections across the plain to Turin and up to Aosta. The region is well served with rail links, and buses connect the main towns and outlying resorts. Getting around the mountains is more difficult, making the car the best method of transport.

St Pierre castle in the Valle d'Aosta

0 kilometres   25

0 miles   20

Key

- ━━━ Motorway
- ━━━ Major road
- ━━━ Secondary road
- ┄┄┄ Minor road
- ━━━ Scenic route
- ┅┅┅ Main railway
- ──── Minor railway
- ▮▮▮ International border
- ▪▪▪ Regional border
- △ Summit

❶ Monte Bianco

Aosta. **FS** Pré-St-Didier. 🚌 Courmayeur. **ℹ** Piazzale Monte Bianco 13, Courmayeur (0165 84 20 60).

Monte Bianco (Mont Blanc), the tallest mountain in the Alps at 4,810 m (15,780 ft), dominates the western Aosta valley and its attractive all-year resort, **Courmayeur**. A series of cable car rides from Entrèves, 5 km (3 miles) further north, leads to Chamonix. Passing its highest point (3,842 m, 12,606 ft) at Aiguille du Midi, it offers a spectacular view. From Pré- St-Didier, below Courmayeur, the **Little St Bernard Pass**, with its small glaciers, forests and ravines, can be explored.

❷ Colle del Gran San Bernardo

Aosta. **FS** 🚌 Aosta. **ℹ** Strada Nazionale Gran San Bernardo 13, Etroubles (0165 785 59). **Open** daily.

The Great St Bernard pass is synonymous with the hardy mountain rescue dogs that have been trained locally by Catholic monks since the 11th century.

The **Monks' Hospice,** founded around 1050 by St Bernard of Aosta, lies just over the Swiss border (bring your passport), on the shores of a lovely lake; the dogs are still being trained here. The pretty Great St Bernard valley itself includes the town of Etroubles, set in a forest of conifers, the hamlet of St-Oyen with its pretty parish church, and the resort of St-Rhémy-en-Bosses.

A St Bernard dog

🏠 **Monks' Hospice**
Colle San Bernardo, Switzerland.
Tel 00 41 277 87 12 36. **Open** daily.

❸ Monte Cervino

Aosta. **FS** 🚌 Breuil-Cervinia. **ℹ** Piazza Rey Guido, Breuil-Cervinia (0166 94 91 36).

The distinctive triangular peak of Monte Cervino (the Matterhorn) rises to 4,478 m (14,691 ft) and is easily recognizable. Below the mountain lies a scattering of attractive villages like Antey-St-André, Valtournanche (which gave its name to the valley) and

the resort of **Breuil-Cervinia**. From Breuil a cable car rises to the Plateau Rosa (3,480 m, 11,418 ft) offering dramatic views of the surrounding mountains. This entire area is a paradise for both skiers and walkers.

❹ Monte Rosa

Aosta. **FS** Verrès. 🚌 St-Jacques. **ℹ** Route Varasc, Champoluc/Ayas (0125 30 71 13).

Monte Rosa, Italy's second-highest mountain, overlooks the picturesque Ayas and Gressoney valleys. The rolling lower Ayas valley is dominated by the ruins of the 11th-century **Castello di Graines**. Higher up, the resort of Champoluc has a cable car connection with the striking **Testa Grigia** (3,315 m/10,877 ft). The Gressoney valley is home to the Walser people, who speak a German dialect. At the bottom of the valley, north of Pont- St-Martin, lies **Issime:** the 16th-century church here has a fresco of the Last Judgment on its façade.

🏠 **Castello di Graines**
Graines, Strada Statale 506.

Medieval Castles and Forts in the Valle d'Aosta

The mountains alone provided insufficient protection to the fragmented fiefs that covered the Valle d'Aosta in the Middle Ages. The medieval lords, who ruled ruthlessly over their small domains, built castles to enforce their often fragile power. Of the many built, 70 castles survive in some form to this day. You will pass a number of them if you drive into Italy by the Mont Blanc tunnel; they stretch from Aosta to Pont-St-Martin.

Originally Aosta castles were designed to be defensive and threatening, such as the looming tower of **Montmayer**, perched high on a huge rock by the Valgrisenche valley. Nearby, the equally forbidding dark tower of **Ussel** throws a melancholy, brooding watchfulness over the valley.

Fénis and **Verrès** represent an important shift in the function of the feudal castle. Both Fénis, a splendid 14th-century showpiece *(see p184)*, and Verrès were not just important military outposts but also examples of palatial opulence and good living. **Issogne** too furthered this luxurious trend with its elaborate frescoes, loggias and fountains. Decoration

was also important to Vittorio Emanuele II, owner of **Sarre**, who turned the halls of his fortress into a plush hunting lodge. The owners of **Châtelard**, set in some of the highest vineyards in Europe, placed fine wine production alongside military aims.

The strategically sited 14th-century castle at Verrès

The 12th-century cloister, with 40 carved columns of darkened marble, in Sant'Orso

❺ Aosta

🏘 35,000. FS 🚌 ℹ️ Porta Pretoria 3 (0165 23 66 27). 🛍 Tue. 🌐 lovevda.it

Lying on a plain surrounded by dramatic mountains, the town of Aosta provides a remarkable mixture of ancient culture and spectacular scenery. The Romans captured it from the Salassian Gauls in 25 BC, and Aosta is still dotted with fine Roman architecture built in honour of Emperor Augustus – indeed the town was once called *Augusta Praetoria*, its name only evolving into Aosta over the centuries. The medieval town was later fortified by the Challant family and then by the Dukes of Aosta, who added towers to the old Roman walls.

Modern Aosta is a bustling crossroads for local industries and tourists on their way to the mountains. The centre, however, still consists of a delightful grid of large squares and surprising architectural treasures, which justify Aosta's nickname of "Rome of the Alps".

🏛 Roman Ruins
Roman Theatre: Via Baillage. **Open** 9am–8pm daily (to 7pm Sep–Mar, to 6:30pm Oct & Feb, to 5pm Nov–Jan). Roman Forum: Piazza Giovanni XXIII. **Open** daily.

In Roman times, entry to Aosta was over the **bridge** to the east of the town (beyond the modern bridge) and through the **Arch of Augustus**. This triumphal arch is today marred by a roof added in the 18th century. Ahead stands the **Porta Pretoria**, its double row of stone arches flanked by a medieval tower; the gateway

originally stood about 2.5 m (8 ft) higher than at present. Also worth a look is the 20-m (65-ft) high façade of the **Roman Theatre**. A little to the north is the elliptical amphitheatre, although this is almost completely buried apart from three columns which form part of the convent of San Giuseppe. In the old town, next to the cathedral, lies the **Roman Forum**, or market place, with its huge cryptoporticus: the function of this impressive underground gallery remains the subject of speculation.

Detail of a medieval mosaic on the floor of Aosta's Cattedrale

🏛 Cattedrale
Piazza Giovanni XXIII. **Open** 6:30am–12:30pm, 2–7:30pm Mon–Fri, 7am–noon, 2–6pm Sat & Sun (early Sep–Easter: 6:30am–noon, 3–7pm). Museo del Tesoro: **Tel** 0165 404 13. **Open** 3–5:30pm Sat & Sun. **Closed** during religious services. 📷

This relatively modest shrine to St John the Baptist was first built in the 12th century, but has been

altered many times since. The interior is Gothic, with finely carved 15th-century choir stalls, and floor mosaics. Next door, the **Museo del Tesoro** contains a rich collection of statuettes and reliquaries, and a number of impressive medieval tombs.

🏛 Sant'Orso
Via Sant'Orso. **Open** daily. ♿
East of the town walls is the architectural highlight of Aosta: a medieval complex of church buildings. Sant'Orso itself has an unusual Gothic façade with a narrow, tall portal. The interior has 11th-century frescoes, a crypt holding the tomb of St Orso, patron saint of Aosta, and a beautiful **cloister** with carved columns and capitals.

Environs
The castle at **Fénis** (*see p218*), 12 km (8 miles) east, is one of the few castles in the Aosta valley with a well-preserved interior, including beautiful frescoes and wooden galleries. **Issogne**, 38 km (23 miles) southeast, is the setting for another highly decorated castle, remodelled around 1490. It has many frescoes and decorative motifs, including an octagonal fountain with a centrepiece in the shape of a pomegranate tree.

🏰 Castello di Fénis
Fénis. **Tel** 0165 76 42 63. **Open** daily. **Closed** Tue (Nov–Feb); 1 Jan, 25 Dec. 📷

🏰 Castello di Issogne
Issogne. **Tel** 0125 92 93 73. **Open** daily. **Closed** Wed (Nov–Feb); 1 Jan, 25 Dec. 📷

Some of the impressive ruins standing in the Roman Forum in Aosta

❻ Parco Nazionale del Gran Paradiso

A breathtaking wilderness of dramatic mountains and lush meadows, the Gran Paradiso is Italy's foremost national park, created in 1922 from part of a former royal hunting reserve of the House of Savoy. It is mainly a summer resort for walkers due to its unspoiled scenery, rare wildlife and unusual Alpine flowers, though there is also cross-country skiing during the winter months. The king of the park is the ibex, a relative of the goat family all but extinct in the rest of Europe. The park is also prized by naturalists for its chamois, ptarmigan, golden eagles, rare butterflies and marmots.

Castello di Aymavilles
The 18th-century core of this castle is framed by medieval corner towers.

Val di Rhêmes-Notre-Dame
This peaceful and broad valley offers magnificent scenery with waterfalls and fast-flowing streams running from the glacier at its head.

KEY

① **Goletta Waterfall** is an impressive cascade near the Lago di Goletta.

② **Cogne** is the main resort and a good base from which to explore the park. Maps of the park's routes and footpaths are available here.

③ **Lillaz** is sedate and off the beaten track, while Valnontey and Cogne are two of the busiest resorts.

0 kilometres   5

0 miles   5

★ Paradisia Alpine Garden

The botanic garden contains a collection of Alpine plants, including the delicate "twinflower".

Cascata di Lillaz

This tall, dramatic waterfall, situated a little to the east of the rustic village of Lillaz, is best observed after the spring snow melt.

VISITORS' CHECKLIST

Practical Information
Piemonte and Valle d'Aosta.
🛈 Segreteria Turistica, Cheriettes Aymavilles (0165 90 26 93); Centro Visitatori Parco Nazionale del Gran Paradiso, Ceresole Reale, (0124 95 31 66).
🗝 Paradisia Alpine Garden: Valnontey, Cogne. **Tel** 0165 741 47. **Open** mid-Jun–mid-Sep: daily. ♿ ♿ 🅦 pngp.it 🅦 parks.it

Transport
🚆 Aosta & Pont Canavese.
🚌 from Aosta or Pont Canavese to the different valleys.

★ Valnontey

This lovely valley, after which the resort is named, provides dramatic views of glaciers and easy access to various footpaths.

Épinel
Cogne
Lillaz
Valnontey
Pont Canavese Cuorgne
Pont Canavese Cuorgne
Pont Canavese Cuorgne
S460

Key
= Main road

Male Ibex

The ibex lives largely above the tree line. Groups are often seen around Col Lauson at dawn and dusk, and also around Pont in June.

The small resort of Ceresole Reale under winter snow

❼ Ceresole Reale

Turin. 🚌 to Ceresole Reale.
ℹ️ Palazzo Comunale, Ceresole Reale (0124 95 32 00).
🆆 turismotorino.org

On the southern, Piedmont side of the extensive Parco Nazionale del Gran Paradiso *(see pp216–17)* lies the small resort of Ceresole Reale. The route from Cuorgnè traverses rolling countryside and follows the S460 along a narrow gorge with a cascading stream. At **Noasca**, a spectacular waterfall may be seen high above the houses.

Ceresole Reale lies in a basin surrounded by meadows and forests of larch, and framed by mountains – the Gran Paradiso range to the north, Levanna to the southwest – which are reflected in the clear waters of a spectacular artificial mountain lake, which is actually a dammed reservoir, providing energy to supply Turin with electricity. This nevertheless unspoiled corner of the country is a good base for walking, climbing and hiking, and also offers facilities for skiing during the winter.

❽ Alta Val Susa

Turin. 🄵🅂 Oulx. 🚌 to Sauze d'Oulx.
ℹ️ Via Louset, Sestriere (0122 75 54 44). 🆆 vialattea.it

The closest ring of mountain resorts to Turin, and as a consequence popular for weekend excursions, is also known colloquially as the Via Lattea or "milky way". Villages such as **Bardonecchia** and **Sauze d'Oulx** preserve traditional old stone and wood buildings that have been a feature of the region for centuries. The small church in Bardonecchia has, in addition, a fine 15th-century carved choir. In contrast, the super-modern complex at **Sestriere** was purpose-built to accommodate skiers in winter and hikers in summer.

From Bardonecchia a chair-lift operates some of the way up **Punta Colomion**, which rises immediately to the south of the resort. The summit, at 2,054 m (6,738 ft), offers fine views, and numerous hiking and walking possibilities.

❾ Susa

Turin. 🄼 6,500. 🄵🅂 🚌 ℹ️ Corso Inghilterra 39 (0122 62 24 47). 🗓 Tue.
🆆 turismotorino.org

This attractive mountain town flourished in Roman times: the **Arch of Augustus**, built in 8 BC, commemorates the alliance between the local Gaulish

The impressive part-Roman gateway, Porta Savoia, in Susa

chieftain and the Emperor Augustus. Other relics from the Roman period include two arches of an aqueduct, sections of an amphitheatre and traces of the old town walls. **Porta Savoia**, an imposing Roman gateway dating from the 4th century, was remodelled in the Middle Ages.

Most of the historic centre of the town is medieval, including the castle of Countess Adelaide and the **Duomo**, both originally 11th century. The Duomo, much altered since then, houses a polyptych (c.1500) attributed to Bergognone, and a copy of a precious 14th-century Flemish triptych portraying the *Virgin and Saints*. South of the town lies the Gothic church of **San Francesco**, surrounded by an area of early medieval houses.

A street in the traditional village of Bardonecchia, in Alta Val Susa

Carved capitals on the Porta dello Zodiaco at the Sacra di San Michele

❿ Sacra di San Michele

Strada Sacra San Michele. **Tel** 011 93 91 30. 🚌 May–Sep: Sun pm from Avigliana & Turin. **Open** 9:30am–noon, 2:30–6pm Tue–Sun (mid-Oct–mid-Mar: to 5pm). Phone to arrange group visits. 🅿 🅦 **sacradisanmichele.com**

This somewhat forbidding abbey complex is perched on a ridge halfway up Monte Pirchiriano, at 962 m (3,156 ft). Its monastic community was founded around the year 1000, possibly on the site of a previous sanctuary, though the exterior looks every bit as much a fortress as the spiritual refuge that it was for 600 years.

During its prime, the abbey attracted pilgrims on their way to Rome, and as a result it grew enormously wealthy and powerful, controlling over 100 other abbeys in Italy, France and Spain. It was subsequently looted several times, despite being fortified, before falling into decline and eventually being suppressed in 1662.

The sanctuary is reached by climbing 154 steep steps hewn out of the rock, which offer wonderful views over the surrounding countryside and up to the Alps. At the very top of this stairway, known as the Scalone dei Morti (Stairway of the Dead), is the Romanesque Porta dello Zodiaco, a doorway carved with creatures and symbols relating to the signs of the Zodiac. Beyond the doorway a few more steps lead into the church itself, which dates from the 12th–13th centuries and incorporates traces of an earlier building. The interior houses 15th- and

16th-century paintings and frescoes, and a 16th-century triptych by the Piedmontese artist Defendente Ferrari. The crypt holds the tombs of the early dukes and princes of the House of Savoy-Carignano.

⓫ Avigliana

Turin. 🚗 12,000. 🚆 🚌 *i* Piazza Conte Rosso 17 (011 97 69 111). 🛒 Thu. 🅦 **comune.avigliana.to.it**

On a fine day, this small town perched beside two glacier-fed lakes and encircled by tall mountains looks breath-takingly beautiful. Avigliana is overlooked by a castle, first erected in the mid-10th century but now in ruins, which was once the home of the Counts of Savoy. Until the early 15th century the town was one of their favourite bases.

The medieval houses here are largely unspoiled, particularly in the two main *piazzas*, Santa Maria and Conte Rosso. Other buildings of note are the Casa della Porta Ferrata and the 15th-century Casa dei Savoia, both on Via XX Settembre. The church of San Giovanni

(13th–14th century) contains early 16th-century paintings by Defendente Ferrari.

⓬ Pinerolo

Turin. 🚗 36,000. 🚆 🚌 *i* Viale Giolitti 7/9 (0121 79 55 89). 🛒 Wed & Sat. 🅦 **turismotorino.org**

Pinerolo lies in an attractive setting beside hills at the confluence of the Lemina and Chisone valleys. The town was the capital of the Acaia family, a branch of the House of Savoy, and in the 14th and 15th centuries it was known for the cultural atmosphere that prevailed here under the family's patronage. However, the town enjoyed none of the stability of Turin: it was occupied by the French five times between the 15th and 18th centuries. During the 17th century the French demolished many of the town's ancient buildings in order to make Pinerolo a defensive stronghold; among the political prisoners allegedly held here was the notorious "Man in the Iron Mask". Today the town is a busy centre of commerce.

A number of monumental buildings do remain, however. The **Duomo**, at the centre of the town, was remodelled in Gothic style in the 15th–16th centuries and has a fine portal and an impressive bell tower. Via Principi d'Acaia climbs up to the 14th-century palace of the Princes of Acaia, and to the 15th-century church of **San Maurizio**, where the Acaia princes are buried; beside it rises a 14th-century bell tower.

The medieval arcades surrounding Piazza Conte Rosso in Avigliana

⑬ Turin

Mention Turin (Torino) and most people will think of industry and prosperity. It is certainly an economic powerhouse but it is also a town of grace and charm, with superb Baroque architecture, elegant arcades of shops and excellent museums, set against the dramatic scenery of the foothills of the Alps. Turin is also, of course, home to the famous Turin Shroud, the FIAT car company and the Juventus football team.

Statue of Emperor Augustus in front of the Roman Porta Palatina

Exploring Turin

Though settled by the Romans (**Porta Palatina** is an impressive 1st-century AD relic), and the seat of a university since the Middle Ages, Turin came into its own only after 1563, when Emanuele Filiberto of Savoy moved his capital here. Three centuries of prosperity ensued. Turin then became the base for Italy's unification movement and, from 1861 to 1865, the first capital of the newly united country. Subsequently its main power was

The FIAT car factory logo

economic. In 1899 the Agnelli family created the car company **FIAT** (Fabbrica Italiana Automobili Torino), which grew to be one of the biggest in Europe. After World War II, Turin attracted thousands of poor Italians from the south who came to work in its factories. Though there have been social conflicts and labour disputes as a result, managers and workers unite over football: the Juventus team is owned by the Agnelli family.

🛈 Duomo

Piazza San Giovanni. **Tel** 011 436 15 40.
Open daily. ♿

The cathedral, which was built in 1491–8 and dedicated to St John the Baptist, is the only

Turin Town Centre

① Porta Palatina
② Duomo
③ San Lorenzo
④ Palazzo Reale
⑤ Armeria Reale
⑥ Palazzo Madama
⑦ Museo Egizio and Galleria Sabauda
⑧ Palazzo Carignano
⑨ Mole Antonelliana

0 metres   500
0 yards   500

For keys to map symbols see back flap

The 15th-century Duomo, with the Cappella della Sacra Sindone beyond

example of Renaissance architecture in Turin. The sober square bell tower, which pre-dates the rest of the church by 30 years, stands in refreshing contrast to Turin's sumptuous Baroque buildings; its top was designed by Filippo Juvarra in 1720. Inside, the Duomo is heavy with statuary and paintings. On the right side of the church is the **Cappella della Sacra Sindone** (Chapel of the Holy Shroud), which is incorporated into the Palazzo Reale (*see p224*). The chapel is a remarkable feat, designed by Guarino Guarini (1624–83), with an extraordinary mesh-like cupola; the exterior view is equally eccentric.

🏛 Palazzo Madama
Piazza Castello. **Tel** 011.443.3501. **Open** 10am–6pm Tue–Sat, 10am–7pm Sun (last adm: 1 hour before closing). 🅿 🌐 palazzomadamatorino.it

Turin's main square once contained a medieval castle which incorporated elements of the original Roman city walls. The castle was later enlarged and remodelled, and a new façade by Juvarra was added, at the request of a royal widow, in the 18th century. The Palazzo Madama – as it was renamed – sits in the centre of the square with a stately façade. The interior, with its grand staircase and first floor,

both designed by Juvarra, houses the **Museo Civico d'Arte Antica**. This collection contains treasures ranging from the Graeco-Roman era to the 19th century. The display includes *Portrait of an Unknown Man* by Antonello da Messina (15th century) among the paintings and sculptures, and reproductions of the Duc de Berry's *Book of Hours* from c.1420. Glass, jewellery, textiles and furniture are also on display.

The façade of the Palazzo Madama, designed by Filippo Juvarra in 1718–21

Detail of the mysterious 12th-century Holy Shroud

The Holy Shroud

The most famous – and most dubious – holy relic of them all is kept in Turin's Duomo. The Shroud, said to be the winding-sheet in which the body of Christ was wrapped after His crucifixion, owes its fame to the fact that the Shroud bears the imprint of a crucified man with a wound in his side, and bruises from what might have been a crown of thorns.

The Shroud is one of the most famous medieval relics. Its early history is unclear, but the House of Savoy was in possession of it around 1450, and had it displayed in Guarini's chapel from 1694. The "original" Shroud – which sits in a silver casket inside an iron box within a marble coffer – is not on view, though a replica is, together with a welter of scientific explanations as to the Shroud's possible origins. In 1988, however, the myth of the Shroud was exploded: a carbon-dating test showed that it dates back no further than the 12th century. The Shroud nevertheless remains an object of religious veneration.

The 17th-century Basilica dell'Assunta dominating Sacro Monte, Varallo

⑯ Venaria Reale

Pza della Repubblica 4. **Tel** 011 499 23 33. **FS** 🚌 **Open** 9am–6pm Tue–Sun (to 8pm Sat & Sun). 🚗
W lavenaria.it

This grandiose complex dates from the mid-17th century, when Charles Emanuel II of Savoy decided to build a royal hunting lodge on the site of the existing town of Altessano Superiore. Venaria Reale incorporates the **Reggia di Diana**, a formal palace and garden built between 1660 and 1671, as well as **La Mandria**, the 3,000-hectare park surrounding it.

Venaria's historical centre was designed by Amadeo di Castellamonte between 1667 and 1690; its focal point is the Piazza dell'Annunziata, with statues depicting the Angel Gabriel and the Virgin Mary.

⑰ Santuario d'Oropa

Via Santuario d'Oropa 480, Comune di Biella. **Tel** 015 255 512 00. **FS** Biella. 🚌 from Biella. 🦽 Basilica Antica: **Open** 7:30am–7pm daily. Basilica Superiore: **Open** 8:30am–4:30pm daily. **W** santuariodioropa.it

Perched above the wool town of Biella stands the tranquil church and hospice complex of Oropa, comprised of a series of three squares surrounded by pale buildings with stone-shingled roofs, cut into the hillside. The sanctuary was founded in the

4th century by Sant'Eusebio, Bishop of Vercelli. It was intended as a hospice for the poor, and to honour the "Black Madonna" which he had brought back from the Holy Land. The Madonna, said to be the work of St Luke himself, is the object of some of the most important pilgrimages in the region.

The statue of the Madonna is kept in the restored **Basilica Antica** (Old Church). Beyond it, at the top of the complex, is the imposing Neo-Classical **Basilica Superiore** (Upper Church), which was begun in 1885 but completed only in 1960.

⑱ Domodossola

Verbania. 🚶 19,000. **FS** 🚌 **i** Stazione entrance, Pza Matteotti 24 (0324 24 82 65). 🛒 Sat. **W** prodomodossola.it

At the centre of this pretty mountain town of Roman origin lies the **Piazza Mercato**, or market square, framed by attractive arcades and houses from the 15th and 16th centuries. The Ossola valley, where the town lies, sits in an Alpine landscape of pasture and forest sliced by rivers and streams. Pretty villages north of the town include **Crodo**, with its cold-water mineral spas, and **Baceno**, where the 14th–16th – century church contains fine frescoes and wood carvings.

⑲ Varallo

Vercelli. 🚶 7,500. **FS** 🚌 **i** Corso Roma 38 (0163 56 44 04). 🛒 Tue. **W** atlvalsesiavercelli.it

The small town and tourist resort of Varallo lies halfway up the attractive Sesia valley, and boasts a remarkable church, **Santa Maria delle Grazie**. The late 15th-century church is notable for its beautiful frescoed wall depicting the Life of Christ and trompe l'oeil architectural elements; the paintings are the work of Gaudenzio Ferrari (1484–1546).

A long stairway behind the church (and also a cableway) climbs up to the extraordinary **Sacro Monte**, a religious community built at an altitude of about 610 m (2,000 ft). This "Sacred Mount" was founded as a sanctuary of the New Jerusalem in 1486 under the patronage of the Archbishop of Milan, San Carlo Borromeo.

The Basilica dell'Assunta, with a 19th-century façade, is set in a tranquil courtyard with palm trees and a fountain; the interior is a riot of ornate Baroque architecture. Dotted around it are over 40 chapels representing the sacred sites of Jerusalem, with statues and painted figures positioned in front of frescoed backdrops painted by Gaudenzio Ferrari, Tanzio da Varallo and others.

Christ Condemned (16th century) in a chapel at Varallo's Sacro Monte

The interior of the church of San Giulio in the centre of Lago d'Orta

⑳ Lago d'Orta

Novara. ⬛ ⬛ ⬛ Orta. ℹ️ Via Panoramica, Orta San Giulio (0322 90 56 14). 🅦 **distrettolaghi.it**

Lago d'Orta is one of Italy's least visited lakes – unjustly, as it is delightfully set among the foothills of the Alps.

The lake's main resort is **Orta San Giulio**, a small town containing handsome palazzi, and houses decorated with wrought-iron balconies. In the lakeside **Piazza Principale** stands the Palazzo della Comunità, a frescoed building of 1582 resting on arcades. A cobbled pathway leads up to the 15th-century church of **Santa Maria Assunta** (rebuilt in the 17th century), with a Romanesque doorway and an interior that is richly decorated with 17th-century frescoes and paintings.

Above Orta San Giulio is the sanctuary of **Sacro Monte**, a UNESCO World Heritage site built from 1591 to 1770 and dedicated to St Francis of Assisi. A winding path, offering lovely

views of the lake, climbs to the church. The path is lined by 21 chapels, most of them Baroque, in which frescoes and life-size figure groups by various artists depict scenes from the life of St Francis.

In the centre of the lake rises the picturesque **Isola San Giulio**. The island was said to have been liberated from snakes and monsters by the 4th-century Christian preacher Julius, from whom the island's name derives. The basilica here is notable for its 12th-century black marble pulpit and for the 15th-century frescoes – including one attributed to Gaudenzio Ferrari, of the *Virgin and Child Enthroned*.

Fresco detail of a horseman (17th century) by Morazzone in San Gaudenzio, Novara

㉑ Novara

🏙️ 105,000. ⬛ ⬛ ℹ️ Baluardo Quintino Sella 40 (0321 39 40 59). 🅗 Mon, Thu & Sat. 🅦 **turismonovara.it**

Novara has distant origins as the Roman city of Nubliaria – meaning "surrounded in mist". Nowadays its delightful arcaded streets and squares, and historic buildings, exude a quiet affluence. Many of the most

important buildings stand around Piazza della Repubblica. They include the beautiful Renaissance courtyard of the **Broletto** (town hall), with its graceful 15th-century red-brick arcades and covered stairway.

Across the piazza rises the **Duomo**, rebuilt by the architect Alessandro Antonelli in around 1865 in Neo-Classical style, with a huge central doorway. The interior contains dramatic Renaissance paintings of the Vercelli school and Flemish tapestries, as well as the remains of an earlier sanctuary on this site: these include the frescoed 12th – century chapel of San Siro and the 15th-century cloisters. The octagonal **Baptistry** next door dates in part from the 5th century and is painted with medieval scenes of the Apocalypse. The **Museo della Canonica del Duomo** beside the Duomo has tombstones and inscriptions from the Roman and early Christian eras.

A few streets away stands the **Basilica di San Gaudenzio**. It is strikingly crowned by an elongated fourtiered dome and spire. Designed by Antonelli, it is reminiscent of his Mole Antonelliana in Turin *(224)*. At the top of the spire, which is 121 m (400 ft) high, is a statue of San Gaudenzio himself. Inside, the late 16th-century church contains a fine collection of Renaissance and Baroque paintings by artists from Piedmont: these include a notable 17th-century battle scene by Tanzio da Varallo, a 16th-century altarpiece by Gaudenzio Ferrari, and a fresco painting by Pier Francesco Morazzone (c.1572–1626).

🏛️ **Baptistry**
Piazza della Repubblica. **Tel** 0321 66 16 35. **Open** to book visit the Curia Arcivescovile.

🏛️ **Museo della Canonica del Duomo**
Vicolo della Canonica 9. **Tel** 0321 66 16 35. **Open** 3–6pm Sat–Sun.

View across Lago d'Orta to the Isola San Giulio

㉒ Vercelli

47,000. FS i Viale Garibaldi 90 (0161 58 002). Tue & Fri.
W atlvalsesiavercelli.it

Vercelli is the rice capital of Europe, set in a vast plain of paddy fields that provide a sight of shimmering sheets of water stretching far into the distance. Vercelli itself also developed its own school of painting in the 16th century, and has one major architectural treasure, the 13th-century **Basilica di Sant'Andrea**.

The Basilica, standing just across from the railway station, is famous as the first example of Italian architecture to be influenced by the Gothic style of northern France – note the beautiful vaulted nave and the flying buttresses, typical Gothic elements. Overall, however, the Basilica remains a stunning achievement in Romanesque architecture, built from 1219 to 1227 as part of an abbey for the papal legate Cardinal Guala Bicheri. The façade, curiously, changes colour half-way up, the blue-grey of the lower part turning to red and white in the twin towers; these are linked by a double arcade. A carving attributed to Antelami (12th century) adorns the central lunette.

The three-aisled interior is gently illuminated through rose windows. The muted decoration is largely focused on the vaulting, which is supported by tall, slender shafts. Off the north side is the simple 13th-century cloister, beautifully framed by arcades rising from clustered columns.

Vercelli's other important historic buildings are not far away, including the imposing 16th-century **Duomo**, the church of **San Cristoforo**, with frescoes and a particularly fine Madonna degli Aranci (both c.1529) painted by Gaudenzio Ferrari, and the **Piazza Cavour** with its medieval arcades. The **Museo Borgogna** is the best place to admire the masterpieces of the Vercelli school. The main shopping street, Corso Libertà, has a handful of attractive 15th-century houses and courtyards.

🏛 **Museo Borgogna**
Via A Borgogna 4/6. **Tel** 0161 25 27 76. **Open** Tue–Fri pm, Sat am, Sun am & pm. **Closed** 1 Jan, 15 Aug, 1 Nov, 25 Dec. W **museoborgogna.it**

The 13th-century cloisters of the Basilica di Sant'Andrea in Vercelli

㉓ Asti

77,000. FS i Piazza Alfieri 29 (0141 53 03 57). Wed & Sat.
W astiturismo.it

Renowned for its *spumante* (sparkling) wine, Asti is at the centre of Italy's most prestigious wine region (*see p186–7*) and

Detail of the carving on the 15th-century porch at the entrance to the Duomo in Asti

also a tranquil and noble city of medieval towers, elegant churches and warm red roofs.

Just north of the main railway station lies the Piazza del Campo del Palio, the largest square in Asti and formerly the site of its annual horse race, now in Piazza Alfieri. The race, held on the third Sunday of September to coincide with the local wine fair, rivals the Palio in Siena (*see p345*) for outrageous horsemanship and medieval pageantry.

Beyond this square lies the triangular-shaped **Piazza Alfieri**. A statue here commemorates the local poet and dramatist Vittorio Alfieri (1749–1803), in whose honour both this square and the main street were renamed.

Corso Alfieri runs the entire length of the old city centre. At its eastern end stands the 15th-century church of **San Pietro in Consavia**, with its terracotta decoration, 17th-century frescoes, and attractive cloister. Beside it is the circular Romanesque **baptistry** which dates from the 10th–12th centuries; it was once the church of the knights of the Order of St John of Jerusalem, who had their headquarters here.

West of Piazza Alfieri is the **Collegiata di San Secondo** (13th–15th century), named after Asti's patron saint, which houses a Renaissance polyptych by Gandolfino d'Asti and 15th-century frescoes. The area around the western section of Corso Alfieri contains a few of the medieval towers for which the town was once famous; they include the Torre dei Comentini, the very elegant

The watery expanses of the rice fields around Vercelli

Torre Troyana and, at the far end, the Torre Ropa. This was built on the ruins of a tower in which San Secondo, a Roman soldier, was held. The nearby 14th-century Gothic **Duomo** has a 15th-century porch and, inside, 18th-century frescoes, and two 12th- to 13th-century carvings on the west corner of the transept.

㉔ Cuneo

🗺 55,000. 🚆 🚌 ℹ Via Amedeo II 8a (0171 69 02 17). 🏪 Tue, Fri.
🌐 cuneoholiday.com

"Cuneo" in Italian means wedge-shaped, and this perfectly describes the sliver of land that the town occupies at the confluence of two rivers, the Gesso and the Stura di Demonte. In early November the town hosts the regional cheese fair, with unusual local cheese varieties.

The town centres on a large square, **Piazza Galimberti**, with its old arcades, where the traders come to hawk their wares every Tuesday. Much of the town was rebuilt in the 18th and 19th centuries, providing Cuneo with wide, treelined boulevards, though the impressive viaduct that takes the railway line into town dates from the 1930s. The deconsecrated 13th-century church of **San Francesco** has a fine 15th-century portal. The

The Castello di Casotto in the hills above the resort of Garessio

18th-century church of **Santa Croce** has a concave façade by Francesco Gallo.

Cuneo is a good base for exploring the pretty local valleys, such as the Valle Stura, where rare flowers grow.

㉕ Bossea Caves

Località Bossea, Comune Frabosa Soprana. **Tel** 0174 34 92 40.
🚆 Mondovì. 🚌 from Mondovì.
Open daily for guided tours only. 🎫
🌐 grottadibossea.com

Some 25 km (16 miles) south of Mondovì, near the end of a scenic route that follows the valley of the Torrente Corsaglia up into the Maritime Alps, are the caves of Bossea, some of the finest in Italy. The series of caves contains remarkable stalactite columns and shapes that have formed over many hundreds of thousands of years. Guided tours lead through different chambers – some of them surprisingly vast – following the underground rivers and lakes. The skeleton of a prehistoric bear, *Ursus spelaeus*, which was discovered here, is also on display.

Bring a sweater – the temperature rarely rises above 9°C (50°F).

㉖ Garessio

Cuneo. 🗺 3,400. 🚆 🚌 ℹ Corso Statuto 1 (0174 80 31 45). 🏪 Fri.
🌐 garessio.net

One of the prettier resorts of the Maritime Alps, Garessio is no more than a sprinkling of houses spread out over the hills, surrounded by woods of chestnut trees. It is also a popular spa.

According to legend, the waters here have miraculous powers: in about AD 980 an octogenarian nobleman found instant relief from his kidney and circulatory problems by drinking the mineral rich water. Since then, the waters have been drunk for their remedial properties – linked in particular with the relief of diuretic and digestive problems – and for their refreshing taste.

Environs
About 10 km (4 miles) west of Garessio stands the **Castello di Casotto**, the dramatically sited summer palace used by the House of Savoy. The royal family used to come here to enjoy the local mineral water, the attractive scenery and the exceptionally pure air of the hills.

The town of **Ormea**, 12 km (7 miles) southwest, is interesting for its ruined 11th-century castle, its church with late 14th-century Gothic frescoes, and its attractive houses.

🏛 **Castello di Casotto**
Garessio. **Tel** 0174 80 31 45. **Open** call ahead for opening times. 🎫

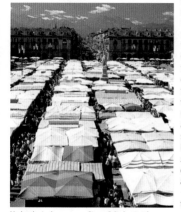
Market day in the enormous Piazza Galimberti at the centre of Cuneo

LIGURIA

Liguria is a long, thin coastal strip nestling at the foot of vine-covered mountains. Here pastel-coloured houses bask in the Mediterranean sun, while their gardens, flourishing in the mild climate, are a riot of colourful plants. In contrast with resorts like Portofino and even Sanremo, the bustling city of Genoa, for centuries a trading port of immense power, is the only major population centre.

Genoa has a long history as a seafaring power, achieving greatness first as a trading post with ancient Greece and Phoenicia, and later, as the capital of a small commercial empire that at one stage eclipsed even Venice. The great sea admiral Andrea Doria came from Genoa, as did the 15th-century explorer of the Americas, Christopher Columbus.

Genoa's rise began in the 12th century, when it succeeded in beating the Saracen pirates that plagued the Ligurian coast. Thereafter, the maritime republic prospered, profiting from the Crusades to set up trading posts in the Middle East and marshalling its naval might to humble its rivals. The golden age lasted from the 16th to the mid-17th century, and included the glorious reign of Andrea Doria who enriched the city by financing the wars of Genoa's European allies through the offices of the city's bank. Factionalism among the ruling aristocracy, however, and foreign conquest, by the French in 1668 and the Austrians in 1734, led to the region's decline. It was only in the early 19th century, with unification fervour spreading thanks to native son Giuseppe Mazzini and the revolutionary Garibaldi, that Liguria ever recaptured a glimpse of its former prominence. Today, sheltered by the steep slopes that rise from the sea, faded, elegant mansions lie along the coast, particularly in Sanremo, where aristocrats came to spend the winter at the end of the 19th century.

Green shutters and rich ochre walls characterize the houses of Portofino

◄ The sunlight harbour of Riomaggiore, one of the Cinque Terre

Exploring Liguria

Liguria divides neatly into two parts. The western coastline, known as the Riviera Ponente, is a thin strip of coastal plain stretching across to the French border, while the eastern coastline, or Riviera Levante, is more rugged and picturesque, descending directly into the sea. Between the two lengths of coast lies the region's capital and biggest port, Genoa (Genova). The faded elegance of the tranquil coastal villages contrasts with this cramped and busy port which snakes along the coast, hemmed in between the sea and the mountains rising steeply behind it.

Stag motif of the city of Cervo, above the cathedral doors

Genoese street market selling fruit and vegetables

Sights at a Glance

1 Balzi Rossi
2 Villa Hanbury
3 Dolceacqua
4 Sanremo
5 Bussana Vecchia
6 Cervo
7 Albenga
8 Grotte di Toirano
9 *Genoa (Genova) pp240–41*
10 Camogli
11 Portofino Peninsula
12 Rapallo
13 Cinque Terre
14 Portovenere
15 Lerici

Key

═══ Motorway
═══ Major road
─── Secondary road
═══ Minor road
─── Scenic route
─··─ Main railway
─── Minor railway
▥▥▥ International border
▦▦▦ Regional border
△ Summit

For additional map symbols *see back flap*

The smart resort of Sanremo on the Riviera Ponente, west of Genoa

Milano

Vobbia

Monte Antola
1597m

Santo Stefano d'Aveto

Monte Maggiorasca
1799m

Casella

Montebruno

Rezzoaglio

Pontedecimo

Torriglia

S45

Monte Còllere
1288m

LIGURIA

Doria

Cicagna

Taro

9 GENOA

Uscio

Borzonasca

Varese Ligure

Nervi

A12

RAPALLO

San Pietro Vara

CAMOGLI **10**

12

Chiavari

Sesta Godano

Genova

S. Margherita Ligure

S523

PORTOFINO PENINSULA **11**

Lavagna

S1

Castiglione Chiavarese

Parma

Sestri Levante

Moneglia

Riviera di Levante

Deiva Marina

A12

Borghetto di Vara

Bonassola

13

CINQUE TERRE

Monterosso al Mare

La Spezia

Sarzana

IGURE

Corniglia

Riomaggiore

15 LERICI

PORTOVENERE **14**

Isola Palmaria

Bocca di Magra

Pisa

0 kilometres 25
0 miles 10

Getting Around

If you keep to the coast, transport in Liguria is straightforward. The A10–E80 motorway, becoming the A12–E80 at Genoa, and a mainline railway hug the shore from the French border to Tuscany. The main stations along the route are at Ventimiglia, Sanremo, Imperia, Savona, Genoa and La Spezia. There are good road and rail links between Genoa and Milan and Turin. Access to inland Liguria is harder because of the mountains. Bus services link many of the coastal towns with the prettiest hill villages. You can explore some of the countryside by car by following the smaller routes, such as the S28 from Imperia towards Garessio in Piedmont, the S334 from Albisola or the S456 from Voltri towards Milan.

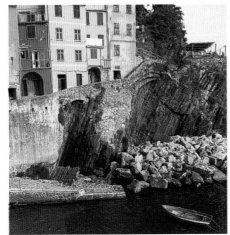

Houses wedged into the cliffs in Riomaggiore, Cinque Terre

The spectacular gardens of the Villa Hanbury near Ventimiglia

❶ Balzi Rossi

Imperia. 🚆 Ventimiglia & Menton. 🚌 from Ventimiglia to Ponte San Luigi & then a 10-minute walk. 🌐 archeoge.arti.beniculturali.it

An unassuming promontory is the setting for some of the most important caves in northern Italy. Guided tours lead through the traces of the cave-dwelling civilization of pre-Iron Age Liguria. The caves contain excavated burial sites where the dead were adorned with sea-shells. The **Museo Nazionale dei Balzi Rossi** contains tools, weapons and stone-etched female figures dating from 100,000 years ago. There is also a reproduction of an etching of a horse.

🏛 Museo Nazionale dei Balzi Rossi

Via Balzi Rossi 9. **Tel** 0184 381 13. **Open** Tue–Sun. **Closed** 1 Jan, 1 May, 25 Dec. 📷

❷ Villa Hanbury

Corso Monte Carlo 43, Località La Mortola. **Tel** 0184 22 95 07. 🚆 Ventimiglia. 🚌 from Ventimiglia. **Open** 9:30am–5pm (Mar–mid-Jun & mid-Sep–mid-Oct: to 5pm; mid-Jun–mid-Sep: to 6pm; mid-Oct–Feb: to 4pm) daily. **Closed** Mon Nov–Feb. 📷 🌐 giardinihanbury.com

In 1867 the English botanist Sir Thomas Hanbury and his brother bought this villa on the Mortola promontory. They took full advantage of the exceptionally mild Ligurian climate to establish a garden of exotic plants along the sloping pathways of the seaside villa.

The collection, gathered by Hanbury on trips to Africa and Asia, has grown to number more than 3,000 varieties of tropical flora including rubber trees, palms and wild cacti.

The garden is now run by the state and is one of the most impressive botanical gardens in Italy, even during the winter.

❸ Dolceacqua

Imperia. 🚹 2,000. 🚆 🚌 ℹ Via Barberis Colomba 3 (0184 20 66 66). 🛒 Thu. 🌐 dolceacqua.it

This pretty village, 8 km (5 miles) north of Ventimiglia, is built on either side of the churning River Nervia, its two halves joined by an arching 33 m (108 ft) medieval stone bridge. The highlight is the ruined 12th- to 15th-century **castle**, inhabited for a while in the 16th century by the powerful Doria family from Genoa. The two square towers at the front dominate

the village. The terraced vineyards in the surrounding hills produce grapes for general consumption as well as for a robust red wine known as Rossese or vino di Dolceacqua.

The Casinò Municipale in Sanremo, completed in 1906

❹ Sanremo

Imperia. 🚹 57,000. 🚆 🚌 ℹ Largo Nuvoloni 1 (0184 590 59). 🛒 Tue & Sat am. 🌐 visitrivieradeifiori.it

Sanremo is a pleasant resort of faded elegance. The composer Tchaikovsky, Alfred Nobel (the father of modern explosives) and the nonsense poet Edward Lear all stayed in the stuccoed mansions of the palm-lined seafront avenue, the Corso Imperatrice. The focus of the town, then as now, is the Casino. A little further down the Corso stands the ornate Russian Orthodox church of San Borilio.

The old town, La Pigna (fir cone), is a huddle of narrow lanes with medieval houses and pastel-coloured shutters. A coach service goes from Sanremo to San Romolo, a small village 786 m (2,579 ft) above sea level that offers beautiful views of the area.

A delightful flower market is held in Valle Armea (5–7am, Jun–Oct, by appt, 0184 517 11), while the Italian Song Festival takes place here in February.

❺ Bussana Vecchia

Imperia. Off Sanremo–Arma di Taggia road.

Bussana Vecchia is a marvellously atmospheric ghost town. In February 1887 an earthquake shook the village, reducing its Baroque church and

The village of Dolceacqua with its medieval bridge and ruined castle

surrounding houses to ruins. (One survivor, Giovanni Torre del Merlo, went on to invent the ice-cream cone.)

The town was rebuilt closer to the sea and since then the original village has been taken over by artists, who have restored some interiors, providing a venue for summer concerts and exhibitions.

❻ Cervo

Imperia. 🚆 1,200. 🚉 🚌 ℹ️ Piazza Santa Caterina 2 (0183 40 81 97). 🏛️ Thu. 🌐 **cervo.com**

Cervo is the prettiest of the many old seafront villages just east of Imperia, with a narrow complex of streets and houses rising dramatically up from the shingle beach. At the top of the village stands the concave Baroque façade of **San Giovanni Battista**. Charming chamber orchestra performances are held in front of the church in July and August. The church is also known as the *"dei corallini"*, after the coral fishing which once brought prosperity to the local people. Now Cervo is an unassuming but characteristic Ligurian holiday resort, with unspoilt hotels near the beach.

Spectacular rock formations in the grottoes of Toirano

❼ Albenga

Savona. 🚆 24,000. 🚉 🚌 ℹ️ Piazza del Popolo (0182 55 84 44). 🏛️ Wed. 🌐 **inforiviera.it**

Until the Middle Ages, the Roman port of Albium Ingaunum played an important maritime role. The sea, however, gradually moved further out, leaving the town, now called Albenga, stranded on the Centa River. Most striking now is its Romanesque brick architecture, in particular the three 13th-century towers clustered around the cathedral of **San Michele**. The cathedral's interior was restored to its medieval form in the late 1960s. To the south is an intriguing 5th-century **Baptistry** with a ten-sided exterior and octagonal interior. Inside, the original 5th-century blue and white mosaics of doves represent the 12 apostles. To the north of the cathedral is the small Piazza dei Leoni, named after its three stone lions imported from Rome.

In a 14th-century palace on Piazza San Michele is the **Museo Navale Romano**, founded in 1950 following the salvage of a Roman ship that had sunk in the 1st century BC. The museum contains ancient amphorae as well as exhibits salvaged from more recent shipwrecks.

The 5th-century Baptistry at Albenga

🏛️ **Baptistry**
Piazza San Michele. **Tel** 0182 502 88. **Open** 10am–noon, 3–6pm Tue–Sun. **Closed** 1 Jan, Easter, 25 Dec. 📷

🏛️ **Museo Navale Romano**
Piazza San Michele 12. **Tel** 0182 512 15. **Open** 10am–12:30pm, 2:30–6pm Tue–Sun. **Closed** 1 Jan, Easter, 25 Dec. 📷

❽ Grotte di Toirano

Piazzale delle Grotte, Toirano. **Tel** 0182 980 62. 🚌 from Albenga to Borghetto Santo Spirito. 🚉 to Borghetto Santo Spirito or Loano. **Open** 9:30am–12:30pm, 2–5pm daily. **Closed** 25 Dec–1 Jan. 📷 times vary (book ahead). 🌐 **toiranogrotte.it**

Beneath the delightful medieval town of Toirano lies a series of caves containing relics of Paleolithic life dating from 100,000 years ago.

The **Grotta della Basura** (Witch's Cave) has remarkable prehistoric human and animal footprints, and a collection of ancient bear bones and teeth in the "bear cemetery".
The **Grotta di Santa Lucia** reveals the full beauty of the yellow and grey stalactites and stalagmites that have formed here over hundreds of thousands of years.

The **Museo Etnografico della Val Varatella**, housed in the 16th century stables of the Palazzo del Marchese, has a collection of agricultural and domestic tools from the 17th to the early 20th century.

🏛️ **Museo Etnografico della Val Varatella**
Via Giuseppe Polla, Toirano. **Tel** 0182 98 99 68. **Open** 10am–1pm, 3–8pm daily. 📷

San Giovanni Battista at Cervo

❾ Street-by-Street: Genoa

There is something refreshingly rough-edged about Genoa (Genova in Italian), Italy's most important commercial port. In contrast to the genteel resorts along the neighbouring coast, the narrow streets of the old town are the haunts of sailors and streetwalkers.

With its natural harbour and the mountains to protect it, Genoa rose to prominence as a sea-based power. During the 16th century Andrea Doria cemented Genoa's importance, and also proved an astute patron of the arts.

Musei di Strada Nuova

Piazza San Matteo
The houses and church of San Matteo were built by the Doria family in 1278. Palazzo Quartara has a bas relief of St George above the doorway.

The port and Palazzo Reale

San Lorenzo
The black and white striped Gothic façade of the Duomo dates from the early 13th century.

Palazzo Ducale
Once the seat of the doges of Genoa, this elegant building with its two fine 16th-century courtyards and arcades now contains a major arts and cultural centre.

San Donato has a splendid 12th-century octagonal bell tower.

Sant'Agostino
The 13th-century church and convent were bombed during World War II, but the bell tower remains. The cloisters now house sculpture like this fragment from the tomb of Margaret of Brabant by Pisano (1312).

Key
— Suggested route

0 metres 100
0 yards 100

Church of Gesù
This Baroque church, built between 1589 and 1606, is also known as the church of Santi Ambrogio e Andrea.

VIA XXV APRILE

PIAZZA

VIA XX SETTEMBRE

DE FERRARI

VIA DANTE

PORTA SOPRANA

SALITA DEL PRIONE

VIA RAVECCA

VISITORS' CHECKLIST

Practical Information
🏛 610,000. ℹ Aeroporto Cristoforo Colombo (010 601 52 47); Stazione Principe (010 246 26 33). 🍴 Mon, Wed & Thu. 🎉 24 Jun: San Giovanni Battista; Jul: Ballet Festival; Oct: Fiera Nautica. 🌐 turismoinliguria.it

Transport
✈ Cristoforo Colombo 6 km (4 miles) W. 🚉 Stazione Principe, Piazza Acquaverde. ⛴ Stazione Marittima, Ponte dei Mille.

Piazza De Ferrari is the site of the Neo-Classical Banco di Roma and the Accademia, as well as the restored Teatro Carlo Felice.

The bronze fountain in Piazza De Ferrari was constructed in 1936.

Porta Soprana
The eastern gateway to the city has curved outer walls and stands close to the site of Christopher Columbus's house.

Sant'Andrea
The 12th-century cloisters standing in a small garden are all that remain of the convent that once stood here.

🏛 San Lorenzo (Duomo)
Piazza San Lorenzo. **Tel** 010 254 12 50. **Open** daily. Museo del Tesoro: **Tel** 010 254 12 50. **Open** 9am–noon, 3–6pm Mon–Sat. 🏛

The Duomo, with its black and white striped exterior, blends many architectural styles, from the 12th-century Romanesque side portal of San Giovanni to the Baroque touches of some of its side chapels. The three portals at the west end are in French Gothic style.

The most sumptuous of the chapels is dedicated to St John the Baptist, patron saint of the city; it includes a 13th-century sarcophagus that once held the venerated saint's relics.

Steps lead down from the sacristy to the **Museo del Tesoro di San Lorenzo**. It houses such treasures as the Roman green glass dish said to have been used at the Last Supper, and a blue chalcedony plate on which the head of John the Baptist was allegedly served up to Salome.

🏛 The Port
Aquarium Ponte Spinola. **Tel** 010 234 56 78. **Open** 9:30am–7:30pm daily (to 8:30pm Sat, Sun & hols); Jul & Aug: 8:30am–10pm daily. Last adm: 90 mins before closing. 🅿🅿🅿🅿 🌐 acquariodigenova.it

The port is the heart of Genoa and the origin of its power as a seafaring city state in the 11th and 12th centuries. A workaday place, it is ringed by busy roads and 1960s buildings.

Among the vestiges of its medieval glory is the **Lanterna** lighthouse (restored in 1543) near the Stazione Marittima. In the old days fires would be lit at the top of the Lanterna to guide ships into port. Today, regeneration of the port is in part due to the Renzo Piano-designed conference centre (*see p189*) and the **Aquarium**, one of the largest in Europe and an ideal place to sample the richness of marine life.

Exploring Genoa

Visitors are well rewarded when they explore Genoa – a city proud of its history and legends. The palazzi of Via Balbi and Via Garibaldi, and the paintings and sculptures dotted around the city in churches and museums, are among the finest in northwestern Italy. The environs, too, provide scenic and relaxing locations for excursions along the coast or in the steep hills behind.

The courtyard of the University on Via Balbi

⬆ Sant'Agostino

Piazza Sarzano 35. **Tel** 010 251 12 63.
Museo di Architettura e Scultura Ligure: **Tel** 010 251 12 63. **Open** 9am–7pm Tue–Fri, 10am–7pm Sat & Sun. **Closed** public hols. 🅿 👌

This Gothic church was begun in 1260, but it was bombed to pieces in World War II. It is now deconsecrated and all that remains of the original building is the fine Gothic bell tower, decorated with coloured tiles. The monastery, of which the church of Sant'Agostino was once a part, was also bombed. What remained were two ruined cloisters – one of which forms the only triangular building in Genoa.

The cloisters have been reconstructed and converted into the **Museo di Architettura e Scultura Ligure**. The museum contains the city's collection of architectural pieces, some dating back to the Roman era, along with fragments of sculpture and frescoes – all salvaged from Genoa's other destroyed churches. The finest piece is a magnificent fragment from the tomb of Margaret of Brabant, who died in 1311. She was the wife of Emperor Henry VII who invaded Italy in 1310. Carved by Giovanni Pisano around 1313, the sculptures from her tomb were restored and repositioned in 1987. The figures, whose garments are arranged in simple folds, seem to be helping Margaret to lie down to rest.

⊞ Palazzo Reale

Via Balbi 10. **Tel** 010 271 02 36.
Open 9am–1:30pm Tue & Wed, 9am–7pm Thu–Sun (last adm: 30 mins before closing). **Closed** 1 Jan, 1 May, 25 Dec. 🅿 👌

This austere-looking residence, used by the Kings of Savoy from the 17th century onwards, has a highly ornate Rococo interior – notably its ballroom and its Hall of Mirrors. Among the paintings is a *Crucifixion* by Van Dyck. The garden, which slopes down towards the old port, includes an intriguing cobblestone mosaic around the central fountain, depicting houses and animals.

Opposite the palace is the old **University** (1634) designed by the architect Bartolomeo Bianco, as was much of Via Balbi. The large building brilliantly overcomes Genoa's hilly topography, and is constructed on four levels.

⊞ Palazzo Bianco

Via Garibaldi 11. **Tel** 010 557 21 93.
Open 9am–7pm Tue–Fri (from 10am Sat & Sun). 🅿 Palazzo Rosso: **Tel** 010 557 49 72. **Open** as for Palazzo Bianco. 🅿 Palazzo Tursi: **Tel** 010 557 21 93. **Open** as for Palazzo Bianco. 🅿 👌

The Palazzo Bianco is situated on Genoa's most beautiful street, **Via Garibaldi**, where there are numerous fine 16th-century mansions and palazzi. The Palazzo Bianco contains the city's prime collection of paintings, including the works of many Genoese artists such as Luca Cambiaso, Bernardo Strozzi,

---

Christopher Columbus in Genoa

The house where Columbus
may have lived

The name of Cristoforo Colombo, or Christopher Columbus, as English speakers know him, is in evidence all over Genoa. A statue of the explorer of the New World greets you as soon as you emerge in Piazza Acquaverde from Porta Principe railway station; various public buildings bear his name; even the airport is named after him. In the 17th-century Palazzo Belimbau, built on top of the old city walls, is a series of frescoes by the local artist Tavarone celebrating the explorer's life, and you can see three of his letters in the Sala del Sindaco in Palazzo Tursi (the city hall) on Via Garibaldi. It is not certain whether Columbus (c.1451–1506) was born in Genoa, in Savona 15 km (9 miles) to the west, or even outside Italy. However, city registers mention his father, a weaver, and various family homes within the city. The small ivy-clad house adjacent to Porta Soprana may have been Columbus's childhood home, where he first discovered his passion for the sea.

A portrait of Columbus, Villa
Doria at Pegli

The romantic gardens at Villa Durazzo-Pallavicini in Pegli

Domenico Piola and Giovanni Benedetto Castiglione. Better-known artists include Filippino Lippi Van Dyck, Veronese and Rubens. At number 9 Via Garibaldi, **Palazzo Tursi** hosts the Lord Mayor's boardrooms, as well as an extension of the Palazzo Bianco Gallery. Across the street in the **Palazzo Rosso** are more paintings, including works by Dürer and Caravaggio, as well as ceramics and furniture.

Fine tomb architecture from the huge Staglieno Cemetery

🪦 Staglieno Cemetery
Piazzale Resasco, Staglieno. **Tel** 010 87 01 84. **Open** daily. **Closed** pub hols. ♿

This grandiose cemetery, just over the hills northeast of Genoa along the Bisagno River, is so big (33 ha, 81.5 acres) that it has its own internal bus system. Founded in 1844, its tombs and monuments make up an eerie city of miniature cathedrals, Egyptian temples and Art Nouveau palaces. Its most famous resident is Giuseppe Mazzini, the Genoese revolutionary who died near Pisa in 1872.

Environs
Until World War II, **Pegli**, 6 km (4 miles) west of the city centre, was a popular weekend retreat for rich Genoese. Now it forms part of the city, but maintains an air of tranquillity thanks to its parks and two villas, the 19th-century **Villa Durazzo-Pallavicini** and the 16th-century **Villa Doria, Museo Navale**. The latter is a naval history museum celebrating Genoa's glorious past: you can see compasses, astrolabes, globes, model ships and a portrait of Columbus, ascribed to Ghirlandaio, probably dating from 1525. An archaeological museum in the Villa Durazzo-Pallavicini relates the pre-Roman history of the Ligurian coast. The villa's garden is landscaped with romantic grottoes, pavilions and fountains.

Nervi, 8 km (5 miles) to the east of the city, is another former resort town, famous for its seafront promenade, the **Passeggiata Anita Garibaldi** (named after Garibaldi's wife). The walk follows a route that has been cut into the rock face, giving panoramic views of the coast. The lush **Parco Municipale** is another feature of Nervi. It once formed the grounds of two aristocratic villas – the Villa Serra and the Villa Gropallo. The former, on Via Capolungo, now houses the **Galleria d'Arte Moderna** featuring modern Italian painting. The **Villa Luxoro** on Via Aurelia is notable for its collection of clocks, fabrics, furniture and lace. The area is also famous as Garibaldi's departure point when he set off for Sicily with his *Mille* (the famous "Thousand" men) to help bring about the unification of Italy. A large monument at Quarto dei Mille, about 3 km (2 miles) back towards the city, marks the place where the volunteers met in May 1860 to follow the intrepid revolutionary (*see p66–7*). **Villa Grimaldi** houses an art and sculpture collection showing late 18th- and early 19th-century works by Fattori, Boldi and Messina.

🏛 Galleria d'Arte Moderna
Villa Serra, Via Capolungo 3, Nervi. **Tel** 010 372 60 25. **Open** Tue–Sun. ♿

🏛 Villa Doria, Museo Navale
Piazza Bonavino 7, Pegli. **Tel** 010 696 98 85. **Open** Tue–Sun. **Closed** public hols. ♿♿

🏛 Villa Durazzo-Pallavicini
Via Pallavicini 11, Pegli. **Tel** 010 698 10 48. **Open** 9am–7pm Tue–Fri (from 10am Sat–Sun). **Closed** pub hols. ♿♿

🏛 Villa Grimaldi
Via Capolungo 9, Nervi. **Tel** 010 32 23 96. **Open** Tue–Sun.

🏛 Villa Luxoro
Via Mafalda di Savoia 3, Nervi. **Tel** 010 32 26 73. **Open** Tue–Sat. **Closed** public hols. ♿

Pini (c.1920) by Rubaldo Merello in the Galleria d'Arte Moderna at Nervi

Pastel-coloured houses near the pebbly beach at Camogli

⑩ Camogli

Genoa. 🚗 5,500. 🚆 🚌 ⛴ 🛈 Via XX Settembre 33 (0185 77 10 66). 🛒 Wed. 🌐 **camogli.it**

Built on a pine-wooded slope, Camogli is a fishing village where sea-shells adorn the pastel-painted house walls, and the smell of frying fish wafts out from the small restaurants into the streets. Near the pebble beach and fishing port is the medieval Castello della Dragonara.

Camogli celebrates its famous festival of the Blessing of the Fish on the second Sunday of May when sardines are fried in a huge pan 4 m (13 ft) in diameter. The fish is distributed free to all-comers.

⑪ Portofino Peninsula

Genoa. 🚌 ⛴ Portofino. 🛈 Via Roma 35 (0185 26 90 24). 🌐 **turismoinliguria.it**

Portofino is the most exclusive harbour and resort town in Italy, crammed with the yachts of the wealthy. You can reach Portofino by road (although cars are not allowed into the village), or by boat, from the resort of Santa Margherita Ligure. Above the town are the church of **San Giorgio**, containing relics said to be those of the dragon-slayer, and a castle.

On the other side of the peninsula, which you have to reach on foot (a two-hour walk) or by boat, is the **Abbazia di San Fruttuoso**, named after a 3rd-century saint whose followers were ship-wrecked here and, according to legend, protected by three lions. The white abbey buildings, set among pines and olive trees, date mostly from the 11th century, although the imposing Torre dei Doria was added 500 years later. You can take a boat to try to locate the **Cristo degli Abissi**, a bronze statue of Christ that sits on the sea bed near San Fruttuoso, protecting sailors. Further west along the coast is

The 16th-century castle jutting into Rapallo harbour

Punta Chiappa, a rocky promontory famous for the changing colours of the surrounding sea.

🏛 **Abbazia di San Fruttuoso**
San Fruttuoso. **Tel** 0185 77 27 03. **Open** Mar–Oct: daily; Nov–Jan: Tue–Sun. **Closed** Feb. 🎟

⑫ Rapallo

Genoa. 🚗 31,000. 🚆 🚌 ⛴ 🛈 Lungomare Vittorio Veneto 7 (0185 23 03 46). 🛒 Thu. Cable car **Tel** 0185 523 41. 🌐 **turismoinliguria.it**

Historians know Rapallo as the place where two post-World War I treaties were signed, while film buffs might recognize it from the 1954 movie *The Barefoot Contessa*, which was shot here. Rapallo was also a haven for writers such as DH Lawrence and Ezra Pound. Its villas still have a patrician feel to them, as do the riding stables, golf course and tennis courts. The palm-lined esplanade ends in a small 16th-century **castle**, in which art exhibitions are occasionally held. A cable car from the centre of the town leads to the 16th-century **Santuario di Montallegro**, which houses a Byzantine icon said to possess miraculous powers.

🏛 **Santuario di Montallegro**
Montallegro. Tel 0185 23 90 00. **Open** daily (**closed** noon–2:30pm).

Large yachts moored in Portofino's famous harbour

The dramatic coastline near Corniglia in the Cinque Terre

⓭ Cinque Terre

La Spezia. 🚆 to all towns.
🚢 Monterosso, Vernazza.
ℹ️ Via Fegina 40, Monterosso
(0187 81 70 59) (summer only);
Piazza Rio Finale 26, Riomaggiore
(0187 92 06 33).
🌐 parconazionale5terre.it

The Cinque Terre are five self-contained villages – Monterosso al Mare, Vernazza, Corniglia, Manarola and Riomaggiore – located on the rocky coastline of the Riviera di Levante. Clinging dramatically to the steep cliffs, these villages are linked only by an ancient footpath known as the Sentiero Azzurro (Blue Path), which offers spectacular views of the rocky coastlines and terraced vineyards that produce the local dry white Cinque Terre wines. The footpath also provides access to secluded beaches.

These days the five villages suffer from some depopulation. The largest, **Monterosso al Mare**, on the northwestern edge of the Cinque Terre, overlooks a wide bay with its own sandy beach. **Vernazza**, further down the coast, has streets linked by steep steps or *arpaie*. **Corniglia**, perched at the pinnacle of rocky terraces, seems untouched by the passage of time, as does **Manarola**, which is linked by the famous Via dell'Amore, or

Lovers' Lane, to **Riomaggiore**, a 15-minute walk away.

The best way to visit the villages is by boat (from La Spezia, Lerici or Porto Venere) or by train (La Spezia–Genoa railway line).

⓮ Portovenere

La Spezia. 🚆 3,900. 🚌 🚢 ℹ️ Piazza
Bastreri 1 (0187 79 06 91). 🛒 Mon.
🌐 portovenere.it

Named after the goddess Venus, Portovenere is one of the most romantic villages on the Ligurian coast with its cluster of narrow streets lined with pastel-coloured houses. In the upper part of the village is the 12th – century church of **San Lorenzo**. A sculpture over the doorway here depicts the martyrdom of the saint who was roasted alive on a grill. On the stone promontory that curls out into the sea is the small, black-

Above the doorway of San Lorenzo in Portovenere

and-white 13th-century church of **San Pietro**. From here, or from the 16th-century castle on top of the cliffs on the northwestern side of the village, there are superb views of the Cinque Terre and the small island of Palmaria, about 400 m (435 yds) offshore.

⓯ Lerici

La Spezia. 🚆 10,500. 🚌 🚢 ℹ️ Via
Biagini 6, Località Venere Azzurra
(0187 96 73 46). 🛒 Sat am.
🌐 parconazionale5terre.it

This stretch of coast, along the Gulf of La Spezia or Poets' Gulf, was once popular with such literati as Yeats and DH Lawrence. The village of San Terenzo, across the bay from Lerici, was where the poet Shelley spent the last four years of his life. It was from his home, the Casa Magni, that he set out in 1822 on a voyage to meet Leigh Hunt in Livorno. Tragically, he was shipwrecked near Viareggio and drowned.

The popular resort of Lerici sits on the edge of a beautiful bay overlooked by pastel-coloured houses. The forbidding mediéval **Castello di Lerici** (13th century), built by the Pisans and later passed to the Genoese, dominates the holiday villas below. Today it houses a museum of geopaleontology and hosts art exhibitions and concerts.

🏛️ **Castello di Lerici**
Piazza San Giorgio. **Tel** 0187 96 90 42.
Open Tue–Sun. **Closed** 9–26 Dec. 🎫
🌐 castellodilerici.it

The harbour of Vernazza in the Cinque Terre

Brightly painted buildings in Manarola, one of the villages that make up the Cinque Terre ▶

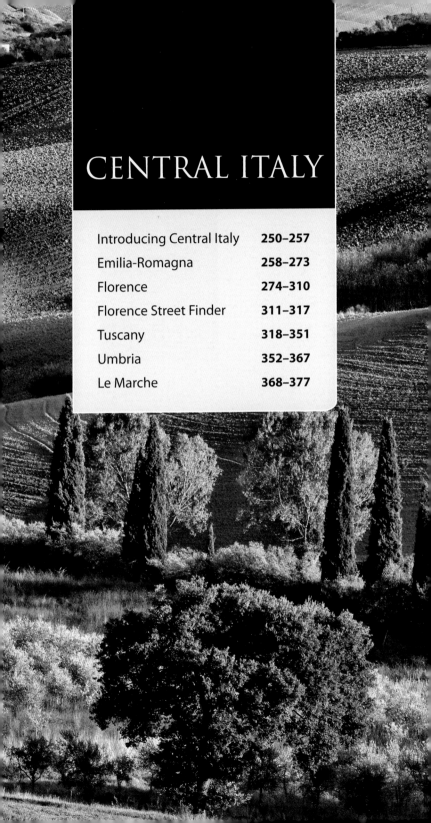

CENTRAL ITALY

Central Italy at a Glance

The central regions of Italy offer a range of beautiful landscapes, towns rich in culture and history and outstanding churches, towers and palaces. Emilia-Romagna is home to the impressive Po Delta, which provides a haven for wildlife. Tuscany is dominated by Florence, one of Italy's most celebrated cities. Umbria and Le Marche offer gentle pastoral countryside and picturesque hilltowns. The major sights of this popular area are shown here.

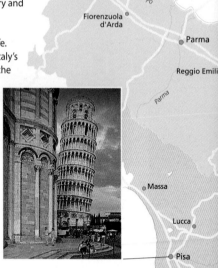

The Leaning Tower of Pisa and the Duomo *(see pp328–30)*, splendid examples of 12th- and 13th-century architecture, are decorated with Arabic-inspired, complex geometric patterns.

Florence
(See pp274–317)

SAN LORENZO

S. MARIA NOVELLA

CENTRO STORICO

Arno

OLTRARNO

SANTA CROCE

Giardino di Boboli

The Duomo and the Baptistry, set in the heart of Florence, dominate the city *(see pp284–6)*. The dome dwarfs many surrounding buildings.

The Uffizi contains a superb collection of Florentine art from Gothic to High Renaissance and beyond *(see pp290–93)*.

The Palazzo Pitti, begun in 1457 for the banker Luca Pitti, became the main residence of the Medici. It now houses their treasures *(see pp306–7)*.

0 kilometres 1
0 miles 0.5

0 kilometres 50
0 miles 25

Piacenza

Fiorenzuola d'Arda

Po

Parma

Reggio Emili

Parma

Massa

Lucca

Pisa

Livorno

Volterr

Campiglia Marittima

Piombino

◄ Sun setting over a tranquil vineyard in Tuscany

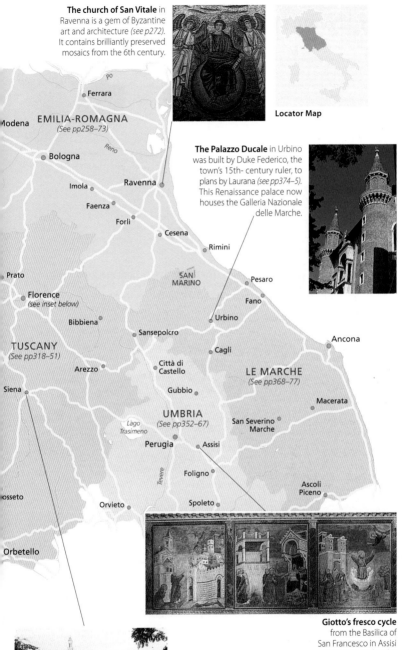

The church of San Vitale in Ravenna is a gem of Byzantine art and architecture *(see p272)*. It contains brilliantly preserved mosaics from the 6th century.

Locator Map

The Palazzo Ducale in Urbino was built by Duke Federico, the town's 15th- century ruler, to plans by Laurana *(see pp374–5)*. This Renaissance palace now houses the Galleria Nazionale delle Marche.

EMILIA-ROMAGNA
(See pp258–73)

Modena

Po

Ferrara

Bologna

Reno

Imola

Ravenna

Faenza

Forlì

Cesena

Rimini

Prato

SAN MARINO

Pesaro

Florence
(see inset below)

Fano

Bibbiena

Sansepolcro

Urbino

TUSCANY
(See pp318–51)

Ancona

Cagli

Arezzo

Città di Castello

LE MARCHE
(See pp368–77)

Siena

Gubbio

Macerata

UMBRIA
(See pp352–67)

Lago Trasimeno

San Severino Marche

Perugia

Assisi

Tevere

Foligno

Ascoli Piceno

osseto

Orvieto

Spoleto

Orbetello

Giotto's fresco cycle from the Basilica of San Francesco in Assisi was executed in the 13th century *(see pp358–61)*. The church is visited by thousands of pilgrims each year.

Siena, a medieval town steeped in tradition, centres around the Campo, the large piazza shaped like a scallop shell *(see pp342–7)*. The lively horse race, the Corsa del Palio, is held here in July and August.

The Flavours of Central Italy

Emilia-Romagna is Italy's gourmet capital, and home to Parmesan, Parma ham and balsamic vinegar. Bologna has earned the epithet *La Grassa* ("the fat") for rich dishes in which butter, cheese and velvety sauces feature strongly. The lush lands and rolling hills of Tuscany, Umbria and Le Marche tend to offer simpler flavours and more rustic, peasant cuisine. Top-quality pork from the Cinta Senese pig, beef from the Chianina cattle of Tuscany, fabulous *fungi* and Umbrian truffles, superb wild boar, and saffron-scented fish soups from the coast of Le Marche are all gastronomic delights of Central Italy.

Italian tomatoes

Tray of perfect, freshly made tortellini pasta

Emilia-Romagna

Not only is this rich, fertile land the home of many of Italy's most classic ingredients, but it has also given the world *bolognese* sauce (*ragù*). The authentic sauce contains some 20 ingredients and is usually served with tagliatelle – never spaghetti. Pasta is an art form here. Legend has it that tagliatelle was invented in honour of Lucrezia Borgia's golden hair, while tortellini pasta is said to be modelled on the shape of Venus's navel.

The region's pork butchers are the most famous in Italy, making excellent sausages, *salumi* and mortadella, and using every part of the animal including the trotters, which are stuffed to form the local speciality *zamponi*. Emilia and coastal Romagna were once two provinces, and there is still a culinary distinction between them. While Emilia's gastronomy is liberally laced with butter, cheese and mushrooms, Romagna's keynotes tend to be olive oil, garlic and onions – and fish. The Adriatic in this region teems with life and is an especially good catching ground for turbot (*rombo*) – the "pheasant of the sea".

Nostrano   Milano   Finocchiona   Bococcini

Porchetta
Spianatta romana   Mortadella

Selection of the finest Italian salumi and other cooked meats

Regional Dishes and Specialities

Tuscan olive oil is outstanding in quality. It has many uses and is an integral part of *crostini*, slices of toasted bread smeared with olive oil on which different toppings are spread, such as chicken livers in *crostini alla Toscana*. *Salumi* producers are a great feature of the region and *prosciutto di cinghiale* (wild boar ham) is a rich, gamey delicacy. As well as *tagliatelle al ragù* in Bologna, other very popular pastas include tortellini and tortelloni (the latter being larger than the former), often filled with cheese, butter and herbs. *Panforte* is the Italian Christmas speciality – a delicious confection of fruits, nuts, honey, sugar and spices originating in Siena. Try also *ricciarelli*, diamond-shaped almond biscuits, and *torta di riso* – a rich, golden cake made with rice.

Crostini alla Toscana

Cacciucco A fish and seafood soup from Livorno, flavoured with herbs and tomatoes and ladled over garlicky toast.

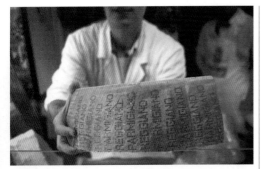

Just part of a gigantic wheel of Parmigiano-Reggiano, or Parmesan

Tuscany

Tuscany is the orchard and vegetable garden of Italy. It is also famous for red meat, especially from the prized Valdichiana cattle, from south of Arezzo. Pork is also excellent, and the Tuscan passion for hunting ensures that hare, pheasant and wild boar, often served with local chestnuts, feature prominently on menus.

If there is one staple Tuscan ingredient it is fruity olive oil, liberally used in cooking and for seasoning everything from bread to salads, vegetables, stews and soups.

Broths and soups are very popular, often made with beans, especially white cannellini beans. Not for nothing are Tuscans known as *toscani mangiafagioli* (Tuscan bean-eaters).

Umbria & Le Marche

Umbria, "the green heart of Italy", is the only area outside Piedmont where truffles are found in such high concentration. Norcia is the capital of the black truffle and shops everywhere

Tuscan market stall piled high with fresh, ripe vegetables

sell truffle paste and truffle oils. Norcia is also famous for its pigs, and a favourite dish is *porchetta* – whole roast suckling pig stuffed with herbs. Wild mushrooms are plentiful in season, in particular *porcini* (ceps). Game features too, usually in the form of pheasant, guinea fowl or pigeon, with the odd songbird thrown in, although it is now illegal to catch wild songbirds. The rural interior of Le Marche also features *porchetta*; lamb and rabbit are popular, too. The long coastline yields a bounty of fish, often made into fish broths and, a speciality of Ancona, *zuppa di pesce*, fish soup with saffron.

ON THE MENU

Baci From Perugia, these are chocolate-coated hazelnuts, their name literally meaning "kisses" in Italian.

Bistecca alla Fiorentina Steak, marinated in herbs, garlic and finest extra virgin olive oil, rapidly grilled over wood coals. The best meat for this is Chianina beef.

Cinghiale in Umido Traditional Tuscan wild boar stew with red wine, tomatoes, garlic and vegetables. Usually served with polenta.

Vincisgrassi A baked, layered dish from Le Marche of ham, pasta and béchamel sauce, sprinkled with truffle shavings.

Tagliatelle al ragù Flat strips of pasta are tossed with the quintessential Italian meat sauce from Bologna.

Arista alla Fiorentina Pork loin is roasted in the oven with garlic and rosemary, a speciality of Florence.

Zuccotto A Tuscan speciality, light sponge cake filled with hazelnuts, almonds, chocolate and cream.

The Wines of Central Italy

Vineyards are seen everywhere in Central Italy, from the rolling cypress-fringed hills of Tuscany to the flatter, Lambrusco-producing plains of Emilia-Romagna. The finest red wines are made in the hills of southeastern Tuscany: Chianti Classico, Brunello di Montalcino and Vino Nobile di Montepulciano. Today's innovative mix of modern and traditional techniques is steadily improving the quality of much of the region's wine.

Chianti Classico is the heart of the Chianti zone. Chianti may be light and fruity or dense and long-lived – price is the usual guide. Rocca delle Macie is very reasonably priced.

Vernaccia di San Gimignano is a Tuscan white wine with a long, distinguished history. Traditionally a golden, often oxidized wine, it is now also produced in a fresher style, for early drinking. Teruzzi e Puthod make consistently good Vernaccia.

Vino Nobile di Montepulciano is made from the same grapes as Chianti. It can be of superior quality, hence its claim to be a "noble wine". The vineyards are set around the delightful hilltop village of Montepulciano.

Brunello di Montalcino is made from Sangiovese, Brunello being its local name. Its firm tannins may need up to ten years to soften before the rich, spicy flavours are revealed. Rosso di Montalcino, on the other hand, can be enjoyed much younger.

Super-Tuscans

During the 1970s innovative wine makers set out to create new, individual wines even though under the existing rules they would be labelled as simple table wine. A trend which started with Antinori's Tignanello (a Sangiovese-Cabernet Sauvignon blend), this approach has reinvigorated Tuscan wine, to produce some exciting variations.

Sassicaia, a red wine made from the Cabernet Sauvignon grape

0 kilometres 50

0 miles 25

Chianti estate at Badia a Passignano in Tuscany

Key

- ☐ Chianti
- ▨ Chianti Classico
- ☐ Vernaccia di San Gimignano
- ▨ Brunello di Montalcino
- ■ Vino Nobile di Montepulciano
- ☐ Orvieto Classico
- ☐ Orvieto
- ▨ Verdicchio dei Castelli di Jesi
- ☐ Lambrusco

Verdicchio is a dry white wine from Le Marche with a crisp, slightly salty taste. The single-vineyard Verdicchio, such as Umani Ronchi's CaSal di Serra, is winning much acclaim.

Orvieto Classico is a popular Umbrian white wine. This fresh, dry *(Secco)* version from the Antinori estate is a good example of a modern-style Orvieto. The wine also comes in a sweeter form, known as *Abboccato*.

Grapes of Central Italy

The versatile Sangiovese grape dominates wine making in Central Italy. It is the main grape in Chianti, in Vino Nobile di Montepulciano, in Brunello di Montalcino, and in many of the Super-Tuscan wines. Of the established whites, Trebbiano and Malvasia head the list. Imported varieties such as Chardonnay and Cabernet Sauvignon play a role, often being used to complement and enhance native varieties, of which there has been a resurgence.

Sangiovese grapes

How to Read the Label

The DOCG name guarantees the origin of the wine.

Producer's name

Year of production

The bottler's name and address are given so the region of production is clear.

Alcoholic content

Good Wine Producers

Chianti: Antinori, Badia a Coltibuono, Brolio, Castello di Ama, Castello di Rampolla, Fattoria Selvapiana, Felsina Berardenga, Il Palazzino, Isole e Olena, Monte Vertine, Riecine, Rocca delle Macìe, Ruffino, Tenuta Fontodi. **Brunello di Montalcino**: Argiano, Altesino, Caparzo, Castelgiocondo, Costanti, Il Poggione, Villa Banfi. **Vino Nobile di Montepulciano**: Avignonesi, Le Casalte, Poliziano. In **Umbria**: Adanti, Lungarotti.

Good Chianti Vintages
2008, 2007, 2004, 2003, 2001, 2000, 1999, 1997, 1995, 1993, 1990, 1988.

Understanding Architecture in Central Italy

Central Italy has countless fine Renaissance buildings, many of them concentrated in and around Florence. Their clear lines, elegant simplicity and harmonious proportions came out of a re-evaluation of the past. Turning their backs on the Gothic style, the architects of the Renaissance returned to Classical Rome for inspiration. Most of the large buildings had been started by the late 15th century, paid for by the Catholic Church or by powerful noble families, such as the Medici of Florence.

The Palazzo Ducale in Urbino (begun 1465)

Religious Buildings

Arched bays trisect the façade.

Pope Pius II's coat of arms

One of 12 roundels by Luca della Robbia

Small circular windows

Square plan topped by small dome

Harmonious proportions

Symmetrical floorplan is based on a Greek cross.

Pienza's Duomo was built by Bernardo Rossellino in 1459 for Pope Pius II as part of his vision of the ideal Renaissance city (see p337).

The Pazzi Chapel of Santa Croce in Florence (1433) is one of Brunelleschi's most famous works, decorated with terracotta roundels by Luca della Robbia (see pp288–9).

Santa Maria della Consolazione in Todi, begun in 1508, owes much to the ideas of the architect Bramante (see p363).

Town and Country Houses

The cornice was designed to cast a shadow over the face of the palace around midday.

Square windows are found only on the ground floor.

Wedge-shaped masonry

Strong horizontal line

The Palazzo Strozzi in Florence (1489–1536) is typical of many Tuscan city palaces (see p332). The three storeys are given equal importance, and the massive rusticated stonework conveys the impression of strength and power (see p297).

Where to see the Architecture

The simple canons of the Renaissance were interpreted differently away from the hotbed of artistic thought and cultural endeavour of Florence, which has the greatest number of churches and palaces. Alberti's Tempio Malatestiano at Rimini (see p270) evokes the sobriety of ancient Roman architecture yet

Vista in the Boboli Gardens, Florence

seeks to reinterpret it in his own unique fashion. Urbino's Palazzo Ducale (pp374–5) perfects the grace and polish of the era and is a truly noble period residence. On a smaller scale are the planned Renaissance centres of elegant towns such as Ferrara (p265), Pienza (p337) and Urbania (p373). All three centres are examples of enlightened patronage, and pay homage to the art of antiquity.

The weight of the lantern prevents the dome from springing apart.

Timber ribs provide the main support.

Outer shell

Inner shell

Classical triangular pediment

The top edge of the frieze divides the façade in two.

Volute connects the lower and upper parts.

The Duomo in Florence is crowned by the revolutionary dome (1436) by Brunelleschi, which had to be built without scaffolding due to its size. The timber structure is covered by an inner and outer shell (see pp284–5).

The façade of Santa Maria Novella in Florence (1458–70) was designed by Leon Battista Alberti. He incorporated some of the existing Gothic features into an overall design typical of the Renaissance (see pp300–1).

The villa at Poggio a Caiano (1480) was redesigned in the Renaissance by Giuliano da Sangallo (see p332). The graceful, curved staircase was added around 1802.

Clock, a later addition

Classical frieze

Colonnade derived from a Classical temple

Classical portico

EMILIA-ROMAGNA

Emilia-Romagna is the heartland of central Italy, a broad corridor through the hills and plains of the Po Valley that marks the watershed between the cold north of the Alps and the hot Mediterranean south. With its rich agricultural land, historic cities and thriving industry, it is one of the most prosperous areas in Italy.

Most of the major towns in Emilia-Romagna lie near the Via Aemilia, a Roman road built in 187 BC, which linked Rimini on the Adriatic coast with the garrison town of Piacenza. Prior to the Romans, the Etruscans had ruled from their capital, Felsina, located on the site of present-day Bologna. After the fall of Rome, the region's focus moved to Ravenna, which became a principal part of the Byzantine Empire administered from Constantinople.

During the Middle Ages pilgrims heading for Rome continued to use the Via Aemilia. Political power, however, passed to influential noble families – the Malatesta in Rimini, the Bentivoglio in Bologna, the d'Este in Ferrara and Modena, and the Farnese in Parma and Piacenza. Great courts grew up around the families, attracting poets such as Dante and Ariosto, as well as painters, sculptors and architects whose works still grace the medieval centres of these towns. Cobbled together from separate Papal States in 1860, modern Emilia-Romagna was given its present borders in 1947. Emilia, the western part of the region, is traditionally associated with a more northern outlook and a tendency towards the left in politics. Romagna, on the other hand, has witnessed an increase in the support for right-wing parties calling for political independence from Rome.

The entire region has a reputation as a great gastronomic centre. Agriculture has long thrived on the Po's alluvial fringes, earning the Pianura Padana (Po Plain) epithets such as the "bread basket" and "fruit bowl" of Italy. Pigs still outnumber humans in many areas, and some of the country's most famous staples – Parma ham and Parmesan cheese – originate here.

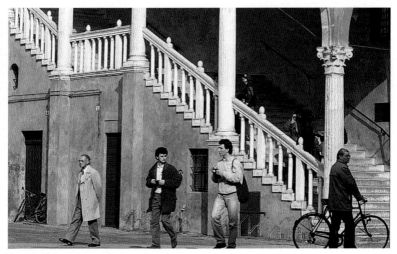

The medieval Palazzo del Comune in Ferrara

◀ The statue of Garibaldi that stands in front of the Palazzo del Governatore, Parma

Exploring Emilia-Romagna

Emilia-Romagna is a chequerboard of fields and plains between the Po river to the north and the forest-covered Apennine mountain slopes to the south. The best place to begin a tour of the region is centrally situated Bologna. Modena, its long-time rival, boasts one of the country's loveliest Romanesque cathedrals. Parma has a more provincial feel and Ferrara, too, has an easy-going air. Castell'Arquato offers a taste of the smaller villages that dot the hills south of the Po.

Piazza Cavalli, Piacenza's central square

0 kilometres 25

0 miles 20

Reed-lined shores along the Po Delta

Sights at a Glance

1. Piacenza
2. Castell'Arquato
3. Fidenza
4. Parma
5. Modena
6. Ferrara
7. *Bologna pp266–9*
8. Faenza
9. Rimini
10. Po Delta
11. *Ravenna pp271–3*

For additional map symbols *see back flap*

Getting Around

Excellent road and rail links, aided by mostly flat terrain, make this region quick and easy to get around. Bologna is connected by the A1–E35 to Florence and by the A13 to Ferrara and Venice. The busy A1–E35 links Bologna to Milan via Piacenza, Fidenza and Parma. The A15–E31 connects Parma with La Spezia, and the A21–E70 joins Piacenza and Cremona. Fast, frequent train services run along almost parallel routes.

The beach at Cesenatico, north of Rimini on the Adriatic coast

Key

▬▬ Motorway

▬▬ Major road

▬▬ Secondary road

▭▭ Minor road

▬▬ Scenic route

▬▬ Main railway

▬▬ Minor railway

▬▬ International border

▬▬ Regional border

△ Summit

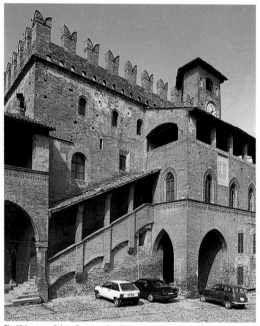

The 13th-century Palazzo Pretorio in Castell'Arquato

❶ Piacenza

🚂 105,000. **FS** 🚌 **i** Piazza Cavalli 7 (0523 32 93 24). 🛒 Wed & Sat.

Piacenza traces its history back to Roman times. Located near the Po, it served as a fortified camp protecting the Emilian plain from invasion. The centre is still based on the Roman plan.

Piacenza has a pleasantly understated old centre full of fine medieval and Renaissance buildings. Pride of place goes to two bronze equestrian **statues** in the central Piazza Cavalli, the work of the 17th-century sculptor Francesco Mochi, a pupil of Giambologna. Lauded as masterpieces of Baroque sculpture, the statues represent Alessandro Farnese, a soldier of fortune, and his son, Ranuccio: both were rulers of 16th-century Piacenza.

Behind the statues is the redbrick **Palazzo del Comune**, also known as "Il Gotico", an evocatively battlemented Lombard-Gothic palace begun at the end of the 13th century. It is one of Italy's most beautiful medieval buildings. The **Duomo**, at the end of Via XX Settembre,

has a rather leaden Lombard-Romanesque exterior (begun in 1122), and a 14th-century campanile. The interior features Guercino's painted cupola and medieval frescoes. There are also frescoed saints near the main door, painted to resemble members of the congregation.

The **Museo Civico** offers an eclectic mixture of sculpture and paintings – the star among these is the *Madonna and Child with John the Baptist* by Botticelli (1444–1510). There is also an armoury and archaeology section. The highlight here is the so-called *Fegato di Piacenza*, an Etruscan bronze representation of the sheep livers once used by priests for divination, inscribed with deities' names.

🏛 **Museo Civico**
Palazzo Farnese, Piazza Cittadella. **Tel** 0523 49 26 61. **Open** Tue –Sun (Tue–Thu am only). **Closed** public hols. 🐾

❷ Castell'Arquato

Piacenza. 🚂 4,500. 🚌 **i** Piazza Municipio 1 (0523 80 32 15). 🛒 Mon.

Tucked into the folded hills between Fidenza and Piacenza, Castell'Arquato is one of the prettiest villages in the countryside south of the Po. Day visitors come at the weekends to escape Emilia's larger cities, thronging the restaurants and bars around the beautiful **Piazza Matteotti**. The best medieval building on the piazza is the 13th-century **Palazzo Pretorio**, a Romanesque basilica. The impressive **Rocca Viscontea** (14th century), a former fortress, is on Piazza del Municipio. The village's hilltop site offers good views, particularly over the verdant Arda valley to the east.

❸ Fidenza

Parma. 🚂 25,000. **FS** 🚌 **i** Piazza Duomo 16 (0524 833 77). 🛒 Wed & Sat.

Like many towns hugging the line of the Po, Fidenza owed its early prominence to the Via Aemilia (the old Roman road). The town assumed greater importance as a medieval way station for pilgrims en route to Rome. Today Fidenza is visited for its superb **Duomo** on Piazza Duomo (13th century), a composite piece of architecture that embraces Lombard, Gothic and transitional Romanesque elements. The most immediately eye-catching feature is the opulent façade, most probably created by the craftsmen who worked with Benedetto Antelami on Parma's Duomo. Inside, the walls are dotted with fragments of medieval frescoes, while the crypt contains the relics of San Donnino, the Duomo's patron.

Detail from façade of Duomo in Fidenza

Interior of Parma Baptistry

❹ Parma

🏛 190,000. 🚊 🚌 ℹ Via Melloni 1a (0521 21 88 89). 🛒 Wed & Sat; Thu (flea market). 🌐 **turismo.comune.parma.it**

Few Italian towns are as prosperous as Parma, not only a byword for fine food and good living but also a treasure trove of excellent paintings, superlative sculpture and fine medieval buildings. It boasts one of Italy's top opera houses and a panoply of elegant shops and first-rate bars and restaurants.

The Lombard-Romanesque **Duomo** on Piazza Duomo, among the greatest in northern Italy, is renowned for the painting that fills its main cupola, the *Assumption* (1526–30) by Antonio da Correggio. The nave is adorned with the work of Correggio's pupils. The south transept features a carved frieze of *The Deposition* (1178) by Benedetto Antelami, who was also responsible for much of the exquisite **Baptistry** (1196) just south of the cathedral. The reliefs inside and outside the latter – particularly those describing the months of the year – are among the most important of their age in Italy.

East of the Duomo is the church of **San Giovanni Evangelista** (rebuilt 1498–1510) whose dome features a fresco (c.1520) of the *Vision of St John at Patmos* by Correggio. Frescoes by Parmigianino can be seen here and in the 16th-century church of **Madonna della Steccata** on Via Dante.

🏛 Palazzo Pilotta
Piazzale della Pilotta 15. Galleria: **Tel** 0521 23 36 17. **Open** Tue–Sun am. 🎨 ♿ Museo: **Tel** 0521 23 37 18. **Open** Tue–Sat am, Sun pm. 🎨 ♿

This vast palace was built for the Farnese family during the 1500s and rebuilt after bomb damage from World War II. It comprises several parts, including the **Teatro Farnese** (1628), a copy of Palladio's ravishing theatre in Vicenza, built entirely of wood.

Both Correggio and Parmigianino are represented in the palace's **Galleria Nazionale**, which also houses works by Fra Angelico, El Greco and Bronzino, and two paintings by Ludovico Carracci: the *Apostles at the Sepulchre* and the *Funeral of the Virgin* (both late 16th century).

The **Museo Archeologico Nazionale**, on the lower floor, has exhibits from Velleia, an Etruscan necropolis, and from prehistoric sites in the hills around Parma.

🏛 Camera di Correggio
Via Melloni. **Tel** 0521 23 33 09. **Open** Tue–Sun (am only). 🎨 ♿

Originally the refectory of the Benedictine convent of San Paolo, this room was frescoed by Correggio in 1518 with mythological scenes.

Campanile and Baptistry in Parma

The Making of Parmesan Cheese and Parma Ham

No cheese is as famous or as vital to Italy's cuisine as Parmesan *(Parmigiano)*. There are two types: the superior Parmigiano-Reggiano and the lower-quality Grana. The cheese is made using techniques that have barely altered in centuries. Partially skimmed milk is added to whey, to promote fermentation, and rennet is used to curdle the milk. The cheese is then salted and shaped. Parmesan is not only used in cooking but is delicious eaten on its own, or with pears – an Italian speciality. Parma

Shop selling Parmesan cheese and Parma ham

ham owes its excellence to techniques perfected over many years and to the special conditions in which it is cured. It is made from pigs fattened on whey left over from the making of Parmesan cheese. The meat has a character that requires little more than salt and pepper to produce the famous *prosciutto crudo*. The breezy hills of Langhirino, south of Parma, are ideal for curing the hams, which are aged for up to ten months. Each ham is branded with the five-pointed crown of the old Duchy of Parma.

Flora by Carlo Cignani (1628–1719) in the Galleria Estense in Modena

❺ Modena

🏠 185,000. 🚉 🚌 ℹ️ Piazza Grande 14 (059 203 26 60). 🛒 Mon.
🌐 turismo.comune.modena.it

To most Italians Modena means fast cars, for both Ferrari and Maserati have factories in its industrial outskirts, and opera, since this is the birthplace of Luciano Pavarotti. Monuments to an earlier age, however, make this one of Emilia's most enticing historic destinations. A thriving colony since Roman times, the city rose to medieval prominence on the back of its broad agricultural hinterland and the arrival in 1598 of the d'Este nobles from Ferrara. This family continued to rule the city until the 18th century.

🏛 Duomo
Corso Duomo. **Tel** 059 21 60 78.
Open daily. Torre Ghirlandina:
Open Apr–Oct: 9:30am–12:30pm, 3–7pm Sun. **Closed** Aug. 🚶

Modena's superlative **Duomo** rises alongside the old Roman Via Emilia. One of the region's greatest Romanesque buildings, it was founded by Countess Matilda of Tuscany, ruler of Modena in the 11th century. It was designed by Lanfranco and dedicated to San Geminiano, the city's patron saint, whose stone coffin lies under the

choir. Its most noticeable feature is the **Torre Ghirlandina**, a perilous- ly leaning tower begun at the same time as the Duomo and completed two centuries later. It once housed the *Secchia*, a wooden bucket whose 1325 theft from Bologna allegedly sparked a war between the two cities. It also inspired Tassoni's 17th-century mock epic poem *La Secchia Rapita* (The Stolen Bucket), and became the symbol of a rivalry between the cities.

The large reliefs on the Duomo's main (west) façade are the work of the 12th-century sculptor Wiligelmus. The highlight of the rather severe interior is a large carved *tribuna* (rood screen) decorated with 12th-century scenes from the Passion.

🏛 Palazzo dei Musei
Largo di Porta Sant'Agostino 337.
Galleria Estense: **Tel** 059 439 57 11.
Open Call for opening times. 🅿️ ♿
Biblioteca Estense: **Tel** 059 22 22 48.
Open Tue–Thu (Mon, Fri & Sat am).
Closed pub hols. 📷

Northwest of the Duomo, and reached through an attractive warren of old streets, is the Palazzo dei Musei. Formerly an arsenal and workhouse, it is now home to the city's best museums and galleries. Its finest section is the **Galleria Estense**, given over to the d'Este private art collection, which was transferred here when the city of Ferrara, the family's former dominion, became part of the Papal States. Most of the paintings are by Emilian and Ferrarese artists (notably Reni and the Carracci) but there are also works by Velázquez, Tintoretto, Bernini and Veronese.

Among the permanent displays in the **Biblioteca Estense**, the d'Este Library, are a 1481 edition

of Dante's *Divine Comedy*, and dozens of fascinating maps and diplomatic letters, many dating back centuries. A map dated 1501 was among the first to show the 1492 voyage by Columbus to the New World. The jewel of the collection is the magnificent illuminated Borso d'Este Bible, with gloriously decorated pages containing over 1,200 miniatures by 15th-century artists of the Ferrara school, most notably Taddeo Crivelli and Franco Russi. Certain sections of the museum are closed due to damage caused by an earthquake, but are due to reopen in late 2013.

Environs
The **Ferrari** factory, 20 km (12 miles) to the south, was founded by Enzo Ferrari in 1945. The FIAT-owned manufacturer now produces around 2,500 cars annually. The **Galleria Ferrari** has an excellent exhibition featuring memorabilia, classic engines and many vintage cars.

🏛 Galleria Ferrari
Via Dino Ferrari 43, Maranello. **Tel** 0536 94 97 13. **Open** 9:30am–6pm daily (to 7pm summer). **Closed** 1 Jan, 25 Dec. 📷 ♿

❻ Ferrara

🏠 135,000. 🚉 🚌 ℹ️ Castello Estense, Largo Castello (0532 20 93 70). 🛒 Mon & Fri.

The d'Este Dynasty has left an indelible mark on Ferrara, one of the region's greatest walled towns. The noble family took control of the town under Nicolò II in the late 13th century, holding power until 1598, when the family was forced by the papacy to move to Modena.

Ferrari 250 SWB, produced between 1959 and 1962

For hotels and restaurants in this region see p562–77 and pp580–605

⊞ Castello Estense

Largo Castello. **Tel** 0532 29 92 33.
Open Tue–Sun (Mar–May: daily).
Closed public hols.

With its towers and battlements, the Este family's dynastic seat (begun 1385) looms over the town centre. Ferrante and Giulio d'Este were incarcerated in its dungeons for plotting to overthrow Alfonso I d'Este. Parisina d'Este, wife of Nicolò III, was executed here for having an affair with Ugo, her illegitimate stepson.

⊞ Palazzo del comune

Piazza Municipale.
Bronze statues of Nicolò III and Borso d'Este, one of Nicolò's reputed 27 children, adorn this medieval palace (begun 1243). Both are copies of the 15th-century originals by Leon Battista Alberti.

The impressive medieval Castello Estense in Ferrara

Façade of the Duomo in Ferrara

⊞ Museo della Cattedrale

Via San Romano. **Tel** 0532 76 12 99.
Open Tue–Sun. **Closed** 1 & 6 Jan, Easter, 25 & 26 Dec.

Ferrara's 12th-century Duomo is a Romanesque-Gothic hybrid designed by Wiligelmus, who is widely regarded as the first great Italian sculptor. Fine reliefs on the façade depict scenes from the Last Judgment. The excellent **museum** (in a deconsecrated church opposite the cathedral) contains a fine set of marble reliefs of the *Labours of the Months* (late 1100s), two painted organ shutters (1469) of *St George* and the *Annunciation* by Cosmè Tura, and the *Madonna of the Pomegranate* (1408) by Jacopo della Quercia.

⊞ Palazzo Schifanoia

Via Scandiana 23. **Tel** 0532 24 49 49.
Open Tue–Sun. **Closed** public hols.

Building work in the d'Este summer retreat begun in 1385. The estate is famous for its Salone dei Mesi (Room of the Months), decorated with beautiful 15th-century murals by Tura and other Ferrarese painters with detailed scenes depicting the different months of the year.

⊞ Museo Archeologico Nazionale

Palazzo di Ludovico il Moro, Via XX Settembre 122. **Tel** 0532 66 29 9.
Open 9:30am–5pm Tue–Sun.
Closed 1 May, 25 Dec.

The most interesting exhibits in the Museo Archeologico Nazionale are artifacts that were excavated from Spina, a Greco-Etruscan trading post near Comacchio on the Po Delta.

⊞ Palazzo dei Diamanti

Corso Ercole d'Este 21.
Tel 0532 24 49 49. **Open** 9am–7pm daily.

Named after the diamond motifs on its façade, the Palazzo dei Diamanti houses a modern art gallery, an interesting museum devoted to the Risorgimento, and the Pinacoteca Nazionale, which contains works from leading exponents of the local Renaissance school.

The d'Este Family Dynasty

During their medieval heyday, the d'Este family presided over one of Europe's leading courts, combining the roles of blood-crazed despots with enlightened Renaissance patrons. Nicolò III, for example, had his wife and her lover brutally murdered. Alfonso I (1503–34) married Lucrezia Borgia, descendant of one of Italy's most notorious families, while Ercole I (1407–1505) attempted to poison a nephew who tried to usurp him (and eventually had him executed). At the same time the d'Este court attracted writers like Petrarch, Tasso and Ariosto, and painters such as Mantegna, Titian and Bellini. Ercole I also rebuilt Ferrara, creating one of Europe's finest Renaissance cities.

Portrait of Alfonso I d'Este by Titian (c.1485–1576)

🄻 Street-by-Street: Bologna

The historic city centre of Bologna is a handsome ensemble of brick buildings and charming porticoed streets. Medieval palaces are clustered around the two central squares, Piazza Maggiore and Piazza del Nettuno, flanked to the south by the churches of San Petronio and San Domenico. The university of Bologna is the oldest in Europe and the venerable Archiginnasio was its first official building. Further afield, the skyline is dominated by the Asinelli and Garisenda towers, and by the campanile of Santo Stefano.

Fontana di Nettuno
The famous Neptune fountain (1566) was designed by Tommaso Laureti and decorated with magnificent bronze figures by Giambologna.

★ San Petronio
The Martyrdom of St Sebastian (15th century) in the Cappella di San Sebastiano is by Lorenzo Costa of the Ferrarese School.

The Palazzo del Podestà (13th century) was remodelled in 1484.

Railway station

VIA UGO BASSI

Modena ←

VIA RIZZOLI

VIA OREFICI

PIAZZA MAGGIORE

VIA IV NOVEMBRE

Archiginnasio

VIA DELL ARCHIGINNASIO

VIA FARINI

Piazza Cavour
The flagged medieval streets and shady porticoed buildings found in this pleasant piazza are typical of Bologna's elegant city centre.

PIAZZA CAVOUR

VIA GARIBALDI

Key

— Suggested route

0 metres	150
0 yards	150

San Domenico
(1251) is dedicated to St Dominic, who is buried here in a magnificent tomb.

San Giacomo Maggiore
The *Triumph of Death* fresco by Costa (1483–6) adorns the Cappella Bentivoglio.

↗ Pinacoteca Nazionale
Museo di Anatomia
Umana Normale

VIA ZAMBONI

VIA SAN VITALE → Ravenna

STRADA MAGGIORE

PIAZZA DI PORTA VEGNANA

VIA CASTIGLIONE

VIA SANTO STEFANO

Firenze ↙

Torri degli Asinelli e Garisenda
The colossal towers are two of the few remaining towers begun by Bologna's important families in the 12th century.

San Giacomo Maggiore
Piazza Rossini. **Open** daily.
This Romanesque-Gothic church, begun in 1267 but altered substantially since, is visited mainly for the Cappella Bentivoglio, a superb family chapel founded by Annibale Bentivoglio in 1445 and consecrated in 1486. Pride of place naturally goes to a portrait with subtle characterization of the patrons by Lorenzo Costa (1460–1535), who was also responsible for the frescoes of the *Apocalypse*, the *Madonna Enthroned* and the *Triumph of Death*. The chapel's altarpiece, depicting the *Virgin and Saints with Two Angel Musicians* (1488), is the work of Francesco Francia. The Bentivoglio family is further glorified in the tomb of Anton Galeazzo Bentivoglio (1435) opposite the chapel. It was among the last works of the noted Sienese sculptor, Jacopo della Quercia. The Oratory of Santa Cecilia features frescoes on the lives of Santa Cecilia and San Valeriano by Costa and Francesco Francia (1504–6).

The Bentivoglio tomb (1435) by Jacopo della Quercia

Abbazia di Santo Stefano
The Fontana di Pilato, or Pilate's fountain, in the courtyard features a basin with Lombard inscriptions from the 8th century.

Exploring Bologna

Monuments to Bologna's rich cultural heritage are scattered across the city, from the leaning towers and the church of San Petronio in the old centre to the Pinacoteca Nazionale in the university district.

▦ Torri degli Asinelli e Garisenda

Piazza di Porta Ravegnana. Torre degli Asinelli: **Open** daily.

The famous leaning towers – Torre degli Asinelli and Torre Garisenda – are among the few survivors of the original 200 that once formed the skyline of Bologna. Both were begun in the 12th century, though there were probably earlier towers on the site – Dante mentioned a pair of towers here in his *Inferno*. Torre Garisenda was shortened as a safety measure within only a few years of its construction, and still leans some 3 m (10 ft) from the vertical. At 97 m (318 ft) tall, Torre Asinelli is the fourth highest tower in Italy after those in Cremona, Siena and Venice. Its 500-step ascent offers fine views over the city's rooftops to the hills beyond.

🏛 Abbazia di Santo Stefano

Via Santo Stefano 24. **Tel** 051 22 32 56. **Open** 9am–noon, 3:30–6:30pm daily.

Santo Stefano is a curious collection of four medieval churches (originally seven) jumbled together under one roof. The 11th-century church of the Crocifisso provides little more than a corridor to

Exterior of the Abbazia di Santo Stefano

🏛 San Petronio

Piazza Maggiore. **Tel** 051 23 14 15. **Open** daily.

Dedicated to the city's 5th-century bishop, this church ranks among the greatest of Italy's brick-built medieval buildings. Founded in 1390, it was originally intended to be larger than St Peter's in Rome, but its size was scaled down when the church authorities diverted funds to the nearby Palazzo Archiginnasio. The resulting financial shortfall left the church decidedly lopsided, with a row of columns on its eastern flank that were intended to support an additional internal aisle. The project's financial profligacy, nonetheless, was said to have been instrumental in turning Martin Luther against Catholicism.

The altarpiece of the *Martyrdom of St Sebastian* is from the late Ferrarese School.

The pink and white interior adds to the overall light and airy effect.

The canopied main portal features beautiful biblical reliefs (1425–38) by Jacopo della Quercia.

Gothic Interior
The interior is airy, with graceful pillars supporting the roof. Twenty-two chapels, shielded by screens, open off the nave. In 1547 the Council of Trent (174) was temporarily moved here due to the plague.

Entrance

Unfinished upper façade

The meridian line was traced in 1655 by the astronomer Gian Domenico Cassini. It is 67 m (219 ft) long.

The stained-glass windows (1464–6) in this chapel are by Jacob of Ulm.

polygonal San Sepolcro, the most appealing of the quartet. Also dating from the 11th century, its centrepiece is the tomb of St Petronius, a marvellously overstated affair modelled on the Holy Sepulchre of Jerusalem. The courtyard contains the so-called Fontana di Pilato, an 8th-century basin.

The 5th-century Santi Vitale e Agricola is the oldest church in the city. It was rebuilt in the 8th and 11th centuries. Inside are the sarcophagi of Saints Vitalis and Agricola, martyred in the 4th century. Santa Trinità features a small museum of minor paintings and religious artifacts, including wooden statues of the *Adoration of the Magi* painted by Simone dei Crocifissi (c.1370).

Bell tower

Choir Stalls The exquisite inlaid choir stalls of the Chapel of the Holy Sacrament were made by Raffaello da Brescia in 1521.

🏛 Pinacoteca Nazionale

Via delle Belle Arti 56. **Tel** 051 420 94 11. **Open** Tue–Sat. **Closed** 1 Jan, 1 May, 15 Aug, 25 Dec. 🎫 ♿

Bologna's principal art gallery, and one of northern Italy's most important collections, stands on the edge of the city's university district, a bustling area of bars, bookshops and cheap restaurants. The gallery is mainly dedicated to work by Bolognese painters, notably Vitale da Bologna, Guido Reni, Guercino and the Carracci family. Members of the Ferrarese School are also represented, in particular Francesco del Cossa and Ercole de' Roberti. The two highlights are Perugino's *Madonna in Glory* (c.1491) and Raphael's famous *Ecstasy of St Cecilia*, painted around 1515, both artists having worked in Bologna.

The Ecstasy of St Cecilia (c.1515) by Raphael in Bologna's Pinacoteca Nazionale

🏛 Museo delle Cere Anatomiche

Via Irnerio 48. **Tel** 051 209 15 33/ 209 15 56. **Open** 9am–1pm, 2–4pm Mon–Fri. **Closed** 1 Jan, Easter, 1 May, 25 Dec, pub hols. 🎫

The Museum of Anatomical Waxworks is one of the more memorable of Bologna's smaller museums, featuring occasionally gruesome visceral waxworks and numerous models of organs, limbs and flayed bodies. Sculpted rather than made from casts, they have an artistic as well as scientific appeal. The models were used as medical teaching aids until the 19th century. Exhibits from the 18th century are in Palazzo Poggi, which also contains the Museo Cartageographica.

🏛 San Domenico

Piazza di San Domenico 13. **Tel** 051 640 04 11. **Open** daily. ♿

Bologna's San Domenico can lay claim to being the most impor-tant of Italy's many Dominican churches. Begun in 1221, after St Dominic's death, it was built to house the body of the saint, who died here and lies buried in a tomb known as the Arca di San Domenico. A magnificent composite work, the tomb's statues were executed by Nicola Pisano; the reliefs of scenes from the *Life of St Dominic* were the work of Nicola Pisano and his assistants; the canopy (1473) is attributed to Nicola di Bari; while the figures of the angels and Saints Proculus and Petronius are early works by Michelangelo. The reliquary (1383) behind the sarcophagus contains St Dominic's head.

Arca di San Domenico in the Basilica di San Domenico

Fresco of Malatesta and St Sigismund (1451) by Piero della Francesca in the Tempio Malatestiano, Rimini

❽ Faenza

Ravenna. 🚗 54,000. 🚆 🚌
ℹ️ Voltone Molinella 2 (0546 252 31).
🏪 Tue, Thu & Sat.

Faenza is synonymous with the *faïence* ceramic-ware to which it gave its name. Renowned across Europe for over 500 years, the pottery, with its distinctive blue and ochre colouring, is still made in countless small factories around the town.

The highlight of Faenza is the **Museo Internazionale delle Ceramiche**, one of the largest ceramic collections in Italy. Its exhibits feature not only examples of local ware, but also pottery from other countries and other periods, including Roman ceramics and medieval majolica. There is also a section devoted to the modern ceramic art of Picasso, Matisse and Chagall.

🏛 Museo Internazionale delle Ceramiche
Viale Baccarini 19. **Tel** 0546 69 73 11.
Open Apr–Oct: Tue–Sun; Nov–Mar: Tue–Sun (Tue–Thu am only). **Closed** 1 Jan, 1 May, 15 Aug, 25 Dec. ♿ 📷

❾ Rimini

🚗 140,000. 🚆 🚌 ℹ️ Piazzale Fellini 3 (0541 70 45 87). 🏪 Wed & Sat.
🌐 riminiturismo.it

Rimini was once a quaint sea side resort, whose charms were celebrated in the early films of Federico Fellini (1920–93), the director born and raised here. Today it is the largest beach resort in Europe. The seafront, which stretches unbroken for almost 15 km (9 miles), is lined with clubs, bars and restaurants. The crowded beaches are clean and well groomed, though entrance fees are charged at private beaches.

The town's old quarter, by contrast, is pleasantly quiet. Its charming cobbled streets gather around **Piazza Cavour**, dominated by the 14th-century **Palazzo del Podestà**. Rimini's finest building is the **Tempio Malatestiano**, built as a Franciscan church but converted in 1450 by Leon Battista Alberti, the great Florentine architect, into one of Italy's great Renaissance monuments. The work was commissioned by Sigismondo Malatesta (1417–68), a descendant of Rimini's ruling medieval family, and reputedly one of the most evil and debauched men of his time. Ostensibly designed as a chapel, the Tempio became little more than a monument to Malatesta. Inside are sculptures by Agostino di Duccio and a fresco (1451) by Piero della Francesca of Malatesta kneeling before St Sigismund (1451).

The entwined initials of Malatesta and his fourth wife, Isotta degli Atti, provide a recurring decorative motif, and there are reliefs depicting scenes of bacchanalian excess and oddities such as strangely posed elephants (a Malatesta family emblem). All this led Pope Pius II to condemn the building as "a temple of devil-worshippers", and to burn Malatesta's effigy for acts of "murder, violation, adultery, incest, sacrilege and perjury".

Environs
Further along the coast, the resorts become relatively quieter. **Cesenatico**, 18 km (11 miles) north, offers all the usual facilities yet the beaches are less crowded.

🏛 Tempio Malatestiano
Via IV Novembre. **Tel** 0541 511 30.
Open 8:30am–12:30pm, 3:30–7pm daily (9am–1pm, 3:30–7pm Sun). ♿

❿ Po Delta

Ferrara. 🚆 Ferrara Ostellata. 🚌 to Goro or Gorino. ⛴ from Porto Garibaldi, Goro & Gorino. ℹ️ Via Mazzini 4, Comacchio (0533 31 41 54). Parco Delta del Po: **Tel** 0533 31 40 03.
🌐 parcodeltapo.it

The Po is Italy's longest river. Its vast basin covers some 15 per cent of the country and

Façade of the Renaissance Tempio Malatestiano in Rimini

supports around a third of the nation's population. Although ravaged in many places by industrial pollution, at its finest it offers beautifully subtle landscapes – rows of poplar trees across misty fields and vistas over the shifting sands of its vast delta, an estuary of marshes, dunes and islands.

The immense **Parco Delta del Po** is a national park stretching for 600 sq km (234 sq miles), all the way to the Veneto. Wetland areas such as the **Valli di Comacchio** north of Ravenna have long been nature reserves, a winter home to thousands of breeding and migrating birds. Ornithologists gather here to see gulls, coots, bean geese and black terns, and far rarer species such as the white egret, hen harrier and pygmy cormorant. **Comacchio**, the nearest settlement, comprises 13 tiny islands connected by bridges. It is one of several fishing villages in the area, and its most famous catch is eels, often caught using methods, like water gates, that date back as far as Roman times.

Other nature reserves include the **Bosco della Mesola**, a tract of ancient woodland planted by the Etruscans and cared for by generations of monks. You can either walk or cycle through it, with excellent opportunities for seeing large herds of deer.

For a good look at the entire region, follow the S309 – part of the old Via Romea pilgrimage trail to Rome – that runs north to south through some 100 km (62 miles) of the park. A number of smaller lanes branch off into the wilderness. There are also boat trips to some of the delta's more remote corners; key departure points include the villages of Ca'Tie-polo, Ca'Vernier and Taglio di Po. Most areas also offer the possibility of hiring bicycles. The 125-km (78-mile) ride along the right bank of the Po is very popular with cyclists.

Piazza del Popolo, Ravenna's central square

Hen harrier, found in the Po Delta

⓫ Ravenna

🏙 160,000. 🚆 🚌 🛈 Via Salara 8–12 (0544 357 55/354 04). 🗓 Wed & Sat; antiques on 3rd weekend of each month. 🆆 turismo.ravenna.it

Most people visit Ravenna for its superb mosaics from the Byzantine period *(see p22–3)*, but the town itself is a surprisingly pleasant medley of old streets, fine shops and peaceful piazzas. The **Museo Nazionale** has a wide range of icons, paintings and archaeological displays. The best place to take a break from sightseeing is Piazza del Popolo, a lovely ensemble of medieval buildings.

🏛 **Museo Nazionale**
Via Fiandrini. **Tel** 0544 21 56 18. **Open** Tue–Sun. **Closed** 1 Jan, 1 May, 25 Dec. 🅿 ♿

The peaceful landscape along the banks of the river in the Po Delta

A Tour of Ravenna

Ravenna rose to power in the 1st century BC under the Emperor Augustus, who built a port and naval base at nearby Classe, currently the site of a major excavation project. As Rome's power declined, Ravenna was made the capital of the Western Empire (AD 402), a role it retained during the Ostrogoth and Byzantine rule in the 5th and 6th centuries. Ravenna is renowned for its early Christian mosaics – the town had converted to Christianity in the 2nd century AD. The mosaics span the years of Roman and Byzantine rule, offering comparisons between Classically inspired designs and later Byzantine motifs.

② **The Good Shepherd**
This mosaic adorns the tiny Mausoleo di Galla Placidia. Begun in 430, this exquisite building probably never received the remains of Placidia, wife of a barbarian emperor.

① **San Vitale**
San Vitale's apse mosaics (526–547) show Christ, San Vitale (being handed a martyr's crown), two angels and Bishop Ecclesius, who began the church *(see pp54–5)*.

③ **Baptism of Jesus**
The 5th-century Battistero Neoniano (Neonian Baptistry) is named after the bishop who may have commissioned its decoration, including this beautiful mosaic. It was built near the remains of a Roman bathhouse and is Ravenna's oldest monument.

⑤ Battistero degli Ariani
The cupola of this late 5th-century baptistry has a mosaic showing the Apostles ringed around a centrepiece depicting the Baptism of Christ.

VISITORS' CHECKLIST

Practical Information
San Vitale & Mausoleo di Galla Placidia: Via Fiandrini. **Tel** 0544 54 16 88. **Open** Apr–Sep: 9am–7pm daily; Nov–Feb: 9:30am–5pm; Mar & Oct: 9am–5:30pm (last adm: 15 mins before closing). **Closed** 1 Jan, 25 Dec. Battistero Neoniano: Via Battistero. **Tel** 0544 54 16 88. **Open & Closed** as above, except Nov–Feb: 10am–5pm.
Sant'Apollinare Nuovo: Via di Roma. **Tel** 0544 54 16 88. **Open** & **Closed** as above.
Tomba di Dante: Via Dante Alighieri. **Tel** 0544 336 62. **Open** Apr–Sep: 9:30am–6:30pm daily; Oct–Mar: 10am–4pm daily. **Closed** 1 Jan, 25 Dec.
Battistero degli Ariani: Via degli Ariani. **Tel** 0544 54 37 11. **Open** 8:30am–7:30pm daily (last adm: 15 mins before closing). **Closed** 1 Jan, 1 May.
A combined ticket is available. For reservations (mandatory for Mausoleo di Galla Placidia): **Tel** 800 303 999, 0544 54 16 88.
W turismo.ravenna.it

⑥ Sant'Apollinare Nuovo
This glorious 6th-century church, named after Ravenna's first bishop, is dominated by two rows of mosaics. Both show processions of martyrs and virgins bearing gifts for Christ and the Virgin.

④ Tomba di Dante
Dante's wanderings around Italy after his exile from Florence eventually brought him to Ravenna, where he died in 1321. A lamp in his sepulchre (1780) is fed by oil given by the city of Florence.

Key
— Suggested route

0 metres 200
0 yards 200

FLORENCE

Florence is a vast and beautiful monument to the Renaissance, the artistic and cultural reawakening of the 15th century. Writers such as Dante, Petrarch and Machiavelli contributed to its proud literary heritage, though it was the paintings and sculptures of artists such as Botticelli, Michelangelo and Donatello that turned the city into one of the world's greatest artistic capitals.

While the Etruscans had long settled the hills around Fiesole, Florence first sprang to life as a Roman colony in 59 BC. Captured by the Lombards in the 6th century, the city later emerged from the Dark Ages as an independent city state. By the 13th century a burgeoning trade in wool and textiles, backed by a powerful banking sector, had turned the city into one of Italy's leading powers. Political control was wielded first by the guilds, and later by the Florentine Republic. In time, power passed to leading noble families, of which the most influential were the Medici, a hugely wealthy banking dynasty. Florence, and later Tuscany, remained under the family's almost unbroken sway for three centuries. During this time the city was at the cultural and intellectual heart of Europe, its cosmopolitan atmosphere and wealthy patrons providing the impetus for a period of unparalleled artistic growth. Artists, sculptors and architects flocked to the city, filling its streets, churches and palaces with some of the world's greatest Renaissance works. By 1737 the Medici had died out, leaving the city under Austrian (and briefly Napoleonic) control until Italian Unification in 1860. Between 1865 and 1871 Florence was the capital of the new Kingdom of Italy. The historic streets and artistic heritage were ravaged by the Arno floods of November 1966.

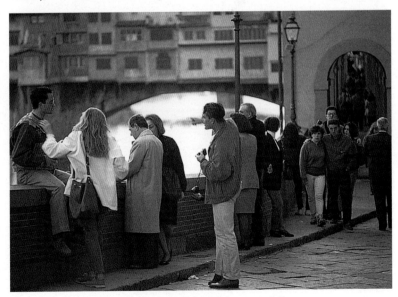

Florentines strolling in front of Ponte Vecchio (1345), the old bridge lined with shops spanning the Arno

◀ A replica of Michelangelo's *David* in Piazza della Signoria

Exploring Florence

Historic Florence is a surprisingly compact area, and the majority of the sights described on the following pages can be reached easily on foot. Most visitors head for the Duomo, the city's geographical and historical focus, to explore the Campanile, Baptistry and Museo dell'Opera del Duomo. To the south is Piazza della Signoria, long the city's political heart, flanked by the Palazzo Vecchio, Florence's town hall, and the Uffizi, one of Italy's leading art galleries. To the east lies the church of Santa Croce, home to frescoes by Giotto and the tombs of some of Florence's greatest men. To the west stands Santa Maria Novella, the city's other great church, also adorned with fresco-filled chapels. Across the Ponte Vecchio and the Arno – the river that bisects the city – is the district of Oltrarno, dominated by Santo Spirito and the vast Pitti Palace, containing galleries with works by great Renaissance artists including Raphael and Titian.

Getting Around

Florence has an excellent bus service. Three tram lines operate in the city; one links the city centre to the outskirts. The compact city centre, a restricted traffic area, is best negotiated on foot.

Key

- Major Sight
- Place of interest
- Pedestrian street
- City Walls

Ponte Vecchio with Ponte Santa Trinità in the foreground

For additional map symbols *see back flap*

Sights at a Glance

Churches

❷ Convento di San Marco
❸ Santissima Annunziata
❼ *Duomo and Baptistry pp280–82*
❽ Orsanmichele
❿ Santa Croceg Ognissanti
⓲ San Lorenzo
⓳ Cappelle Medicee
㉑ Santa Maria Novella
㉕ Ognissanti
㉖ *Cappella Brancacci pp298–9*
㉗ Santo Spirito
㉙ Santa Felicita
㉛ San Miniato al Monte

Buildings, Monuments and Squares

❺ Spedale degli Innocenti
⓬ Ponte Vecchio
⓮ Piazza della Signoria
⓯ Palazzo Vecchio
⓰ Palazzo Davanzati
⓱ Palazzo Strozzi
⓴ Mercato Centrale
㉒ Palazzo Antinori
㉓ Palazzo Rucellai
㉚ Piazzale Michelangelo

Museums and Galleries

❶ Galleria dell'Accademia
❹ Museo Archeologico
❻ Museo dell'Opera del Duomo
❾ Bargello
⓫ Museo Galileo
⓭ *Uffizi pp286–9*
㉔ Museo Nazionale Alinari della Fotografia
㉘ *Palazzo Pitti pp302–3*

Bell tower, Palazzo Vecchio

0 metres		500
0 yards		500

Street-by-Street: Around San Marco

The buildings in this part of Florence once
stood on the fringes of the city, serving as
stables and barracks. The Medici menagerie of
lions, elephants and giraffes was housed here.
Today it is a student quarter and the streets
are often busy with young people attending
the university or the Accademia di Belle Arti,
the world's oldest art school, founded in 1563.

❸ **Santissima Annunziata**
This fine Renaissance
church has an opulent
Baroque interior.

**Palazzo
Pandolfini** was
designed by
Raphael in
1516.

❷ ★ **Convento di San Marco**
The Annunciation (c.1445) is an example of
Fra Angelico's exquisite fresco decoration.

Sant'Apollonia features a
fresco of the *Cenacolo* (Last
Supper) by Andrea del
Castagno (1450).

VIA DELLA DOGANA

VIA CAVOUR

VIA GIORGIO LA PIRA

VIA DEGLI ARAZZIERI

VIA SAN GALLO

PIAZZA DI SAN MARCO

VIA CESARE BATTISTI

VIA RICASOLI

PIAZZA DELLA
SANTISSIMA
ANNUNZIATA

Luigi Cherubini
(1760–1842), the
Florentine composer,
trained at the
Conservatorio.

❶ ★ **Galleria
dell'Accademia**
This detail is from a
14th-century altarpiece, the
Madonna and Saints, by an
unnamed master.

Giambologna's statue
of Duke Ferdinando I was
cast by Tacca in 1608.

Locator Map
See Florence Street Finder map 2

0 metres 50

0 yards 50

Key

— Suggested route

The Giardino dei Semplici was opened in 1543.

④ Museo Archeologico
Many of the Etruscan objects in the museum were originally in the Medici collections.

⑤ Spedale degli Innocenti
Opened in 1444, the city orphanage by Brunelleschi was decorated with cameos by Andrea della Robbia.

Part of the 15th-century *Cassone Adimari* by Lo Scheggia in the Accademia

❶ Galleria dell'Accademia

Via Ricasoli 60. **Map** 2 D4. **Tel** 055 238 86 12 (information); 055 29 48 83 (reservations). **Open** 8:15am– 6:50pm Tue–Sun (occasional extended hours in the summer). **Closed** public hols.

The Academy of Fine Arts, founded in 1563, was the first school established in Europe specifically to teach the techniques of drawing, painting and sculpture. The art collection displayed here was formed in 1784 to provide material for students to study and copy.

The most famous work is Michelangelo's *David* (1504), a colossal (5.2 m/ 17 ft) nude of the biblical hero who killed the giant Goliath. The sculpture was commissioned by the city for Piazza della Signoria, but it was moved to the Accademia for safe-keeping in 1873. One copy now stands in its original position *(see pp294–5)* and a second is on Piazzale Michelangelo. The *David* established Michelangelo, at the age of 29, as the foremos sculptor of his time.

Michelangelo's other masterpieces in the Accademia include the *Quattro Prigionieri* (the Four Prisoners), sculpted between 1521 and 1523 and intended to adorn the tomb of Pope Julius II. The muscular figures struggling to free themselves from the stone

Michelangelo's *David*

are among the most dramatic of Michelangelo's works. The statues were presented to the Medici family in 1564 by the artist's nephew, Leonardo. They were then moved to the Grotta Grande in the Boboli Gardens, where casts of the originals can now be seen.

The Accademia also contains an important collection of paintings by 15th- and 16th-century Florentine artists, among them Filippino Lippi, Fra Bartolomeo, Bronzino and Ridolfo del Ghirlandaio. The major works include the *Madonna del Mare* (Madonna of the Sea), attributed to Botticelli (1445–1510), and *Venus and Cupid* by Jacopo Pontormo (1494–1556), based on a preparatory drawing by Michelangelo. Also here is an elaborately painted wooden chest, the *Cassone Adimari* (1440– 45) by Lo Scheggia, the step-brother of Masaccio. Originally part of a wealthy bride's trousseau, it is decorated with details of Florentine life, clothing and architecture. A scene of the bridal party appears on the chest in front of the Baptistry.

The Salone della Toscana (Tuscany Room) features modest paintings and sculptures by 19th-century members of the Accademia and plaster models by sculptor, Lorenzo Bartolini.

The light and airy former library, designed by Michelozzo

❷ Convento di San Marco

Piazza di San Marco. **Map** 2 D4.
Tel 055 28 76 28 (information). **Open**
7am–noon, 4–8pm. 🏛 Museo di San
Marco: **Tel** 055 238 86 08 (reservations).
Open 8:15am–1:50pm (to 4:50pm Sat,
Sun). **Closed** 1 Jan, 1 May, 25 Dec, 2nd
& 4th Mon and 1st, 3rd & 5th Sun of
each month. 🅿 ♿ 🚾

The Convent of San Marco was
founded in the 13th century
and enlarged in 1437 when
Dominican monks from nearby
Fiesole moved there at
the invitation of
Cosimo il
Vecchio.

He paid a considerable sum to
have the convent rebuilt by his
favourite architect, Michelozzo,
whose simple cloisters and
cells provide the setting for a
remarkable series of devotional
frescoes (c.1438–45) by
Florentine painter and
Dominican friar Fra Angelico.
The convent and art collections
form the **Museo di San Marco**.

Michelozzo's magnificent
Chiostro di Sant'Antonino was
named after the convent's first
prior, Antonino Pierozzi (1389–
1459), who later
became the
Archbishop of
Florence. Most of the
faded frescoes in
this cloister
describe scenes
from the saint's
life by
Bernardino
Poccetti. The
panels in the
corner are by Fra
Angelico. A door
in the right side of the cloister
leads to the **Ospizio dei
Pellegrini** (Pilgrims' Hospice).
Today it houses the museum's
free-standing paintings,
including two famous
masterpieces: Fra
Angelico's

A detail from Fra Angelico's poignant
Deposition (c. 1440)

moving *Deposition* (c.1435–40),
an altarpiece painted for the
church of Santa Trinità, and the
Madonna dei Linaiuoli,
commissioned by the Linaiuoli
(flaxworkers' guild) in 1433.

In the courtyard, right of the
convent's former bell, is the
vaulted **Sala Capitolare**
(Chapter House), decorated
with a noted but over-restored
Crucifixion and Saints (1440)
painted by Fra Angelico.

Covering one wall of the small
Refettorio (refectory) is a fresco
of the *Last Supper* (c.1480) by
Domenico Ghirlandaio. Stairs
from the courtyard lead to
the first floor, where
you suddenly see Fra
Angelico's
Annunciation
(c.1440), thought
by many to be
among the city's
most beautiful
Renaissance
paintings. Beyond,
ranged around
three sides of the cloister, are
the **Dormitory Cells**. These 44
tiny monastic cells are frescoed
with scenes from *The Life of
Christ* by Fra Angelico and
assistants (1439– 45). The cells
numbered 1 to 11 are generally
attributed to Fra Angelico
personally, as is the lovely fresco
of the *Madonna and Saints* on
the right of the corridor (*see p36*).

Cells 12–14 were once
occupied by Savonarola, the
zealous Dominican monk who
became Prior of San Marco in
1491. Among other deeds,
Savonarola incited Florentines
to rebel against the Medici and
was responsible for the burning
of many works of art.
Denounced as a heretic, he was
burned at the stake in Piazza
della Signoria in 1498.

Along the third corridor lies
an airy colonnaded hall,
formerly a public **library**
designed by Michelozzo in 1441
for Cosimo il Vecchio. Beyond it
lie two cells (38 and 39) which
were used by Cosimo when he
went on retreat here. Each is
decorated with two frescoes
(the other cells have only one),
and they are both larger than
any of the neighbouring rooms.

Fra Angelico's allegorical fresco, the *Mocking of Christ* (c. 1442), showing Jesus blindfolded
and being struck by a Roman guard

The Birth of the Virgin (1514) by del Sarto in Santissima Annunziata

❸ Santissima Annunziata

Piazza della Santissima Annunziata. **Map** 2 E4. **Tel** 055 26 61 81. **Open** 7:30am–12:30pm, 4pm–6:30pm daily.

Founded by the Servite order in 1250, the church of the Holy Annunciation was later rebuilt by Michelozzo between 1444 and 1481. Its atrium contains frescoes by the Mannerist artists Rosso Fiorentino, Andrea del Sarto and Jacopo Pontormo. Perhaps the finest of its panels are *The Journey of the Magi* (1511) and *The Birth of the Virgin* (1514) by Andrea del Sarto.

The heavily decorated, dark interior has a frescoed ceiling completed by Pietro Giambelli in 1669. Here is one of the city's most revered shrines, a painting of the Virgin Mary begun by a monk in 1252 but miraculously completed by an angel, according to devout Florentines. Newly-wed couples traditionally visit the shrine (on the left as you enter the church) to present a bouquet of flowers to the Virgin and to pray for a long, fruitful and fecund marriage.

A door from the north transept leads to the **Chiostrino dei Morti** (Cloister of the Dead), so called because it was originally used as a burial ground. Today it is best known for del Sarto's beautiful fresco, *The Madonna del Sacco* (1525). The church is situated on the northern flank of **Piazza della**

Santissima Annunziata, one of the finest Renaissance squares in Florence. Designed by Brunelleschi, the delicate nine-bay arcade fronts the Spedale degli Innocenti to its right, while at the centre of the square stands a bronze equestrian statue of Duke Ferdinando I. Started by Giambologna, it was finished in 1608 by his assistant Pietro Tacca (who designed the square's bronze fountains).

❹ Museo Archeologico

Via della Colonna 36. **Map** 2 E4. **Tel** 055 235 75. **Open** 8:30am–7pm Tue–Fri, 8:30am–2pm Sat & Sun. **Closed** 1 Jan, 1 May, 25 Dec.

The Archaeological Museum in Florence is in a palazzo built by Giulio Parigi for the Princess Maria Maddalena de' Medici in 1620. It now exhibits an outstanding col- lection of Etruscan, Greek, Roman and Egyptian artifacts, although parts of the collection are being restored following the flood in 1966.

The first floor contains a splendid series of Etruscan bronzes as well as the famous *Chimera* (4th century BC), a mythical lion with a goat's head imposed on its body and a serpent for a tail. Equally impressive is the 1st-century *Arringatore* bronze found near Lake Trasimeno in Umbria. It is inscribed with the name of

Etruscan warrior, Museo Archeologico

Aulus Metellus. A large section on the second floor is dedicated to Greek vases, notably the famed François Vase, found in an Etruscan tomb near Chiusi.

❺ Spedale degli Innocenti

Piazza della Santissima Annunziata 12. **Map** 2 E4. **Tel** 055 203 73 08. **Open** 8:30am–7pm daily. **Closed** 1 Jan, Easter, 25 Dec.

Named after Herod's biblical Massacre of the Innocents, the "Hospital" opened in 1444 as Europe's first orphanage. Part of the building is still used for this purpose. Brunelleschi's arcaded loggia is decorated with glazed terracotta roundels, added by Andrea della Robbia around 1498, showing babies wrapped in swaddling bands. At the left end of the portico you can see the *rota*, a rotating stone cylinder on which anonymous mothers could place their unwanted children and ring the bell for them to be admitted to the orphanage.

Within the building lie two elegant cloisters: the **Chiostro degli Uomini** (Men's Cloister), built between 1422 and 1445 and decorated with *sgraffito* roosters and cherubs, and the smaller Women's Cloister (1438). A small upstairs gallery contains a handful of fine works, including terracottas by della Robbia and pictures by Botticelli, Piero di Cosimo and Domenico Ghirlandaio.

Part of Brunelleschi's arcaded loggia, Spedale degli Innocenti

Street-by-Street: Around the Duomo

While much of Florence was rebuilt during the Renaissance, the eastern part of the city retains a distinctly medieval feel. With its maze of tiny alleys, it is an area that would still be familiar to Dante (1265–1321), whose birthplace allegedly lay somewhere among these lanes. The poet would recognize the church of Santa Maria de' Cerchi where he first glimpsed Beatrice, as well as the gaunt outlines of the Bargello. He would also be familiar with the Baptistry, one of the city's oldest buildings, though he would not know the Campanile nor the Duomo, whose foundations were laid in the poet's old age.

❼ ★ Duomo and Baptistry
The exteriors of the Duomo and Baptistry are richly decorated with marbles and reliefs, such as this detail from the Duomo's façade.

Key

— Suggested route

The Loggia del Bigallo (1358) is where abandoned children were once left. They were then sent to foster homes if they remained unclaimed.

```
0 metres        100
0 yards         100
```

❽ Orsanmichele
The church's niche carvings depict patron saints of trade guilds, such as this copy of Donatello's *St George*.

Via dei Calzaiuoli, lined with smart shops, is the city's liveliest street.

PIAZZA DI SAN GIOVANNI

PIAZZA DEL DUOMO

VIA DELL'OCHE

VIA D. STUDIO

VIA DE' MEDICI

VIA ROMA

VIA D. SPEZIALI

VIA DEI CALZAIUOLI

VIA DE' CERCHI

V.D. TAVOLINI

V.D. CIMATORI

V. DE' LAMBERTI

CALIMALA

VIA PORTA ROSSA

Piazza della Signoria →

6 Museo dell'Opera del Duomo
Works from the Duomo, Campanile and Baptistry are displayed in this museum.

Pegna sells a range of fine wines, oil and honey

Locator Map
See Florence Street Finder map 6

VIA FOLCO PORTINARI

VIA DELL'ORIVOLO

Badia Fiorentina, the abbey church founded in 978, is home to *The Virgin Appearing to St Bernard* (1485) by Filippino Lippi.

BORGO DEGLI ALBIZI

VIA DE'GIRALDI

VIA DEL PROCONSOLO

VIA DE'PANDOLFINI

VIA DEL PRESTO

VIA DELL'ACQUA

ALIGHIERI

DOTTA   PIAZZA DI S. FIRENZE

Casa di Dante, a restored medieval house, is reputedly Dante's birthplace.

9 ★ Bargello
The city's old prison is home to a rich collection of applied arts and sculpture, including this figure of *Mercury* by Giambologna (1564).

Carving from Luca della Robbia's choir loft in the Museo dell'Opera

6 Museo dell'Opera del Duomo

Piazza del Duomo **Map** 2 D5 (6 E2). **Tel** 055 230 28 85. **Open** 9am–7:30pm daily (to 1:40pm Sun & public hols) (last adm: 40 mins before closing). **Closed** 1 Jan, Easter, 25 Dec.

The Cathedral Works Museum has reopened after extensive remodelling and now a series of rooms is dedicated to the history of the Duomo. The main ground-floor room holds statues from Arnolfo di Cambio's workshop which were once placed in the cathedral's niches. Nearby is Donatello's *St John*. Another room contains 14th- and 15th-century religious paintings and reliquaries.

Michelangelo's *Pietà* has pride of place on the staircase. The hooded figure of Nicodemus is widely believed to be a self-portrait.

The first room on the upper floor contains two choir lofts, dating to the 1430s, by Luca della Robbia and Donatello. Carved in crisp white marble and decorated with coloured glass and mosaic, both depict children playing musical instruments and dancing.

Other works by Donatello in this room are his statue of *La Maddalena* (1455) and several Old Testament figures.

The room to the left contains an exhibition of the tablets that used to decorate the bell tower. A lower level houses examples of the tools used by Brunelleschi's workmen and a copy of di Cambio's original cathedral façade.

❼ Duomo and Baptistry

Rising above the heart of the city, the richly-decorated Duomo – Santa Maria del Fiore – and its orange-tiled dome have become Florence's most famous symbols. Typical of the Florentine determination to lead in all things, the cathedral is Europe's fourth largest church, and to this day it still remains the city's tallest building. The Baptistry, with its celebrated bronze doors, may date back to the 4th century, making it one of Florence's oldest buildings. The Campanile, designed by Giotto in 1334, was completed in 1359, 22 years after his death.

Campanile
At 85 m (276 ft), the Campanile is 6 m (20 ft) shorter than the dome. It is clad in white, green and pink Tuscan marble.

★ Baptistry
Colourful 13th- century mosaics illustrating the *Last Judgment* decorate the ceiling above the octagonal font, where many famous Florentines, including Dante, were baptized. The doors are by Andrea Pisano (south) and Lorenzo Ghiberti (north, east).

Campanile Reliefs
Copies of reliefs by Andrea Pisano on the Campanile's first storey depict the Creation of Man, and the Arts and the Industries. The originals are kept in the Museo dell'Opera del Duomo (see p283).

Main entrance

North Doors

East Doors
(See p286)

South Doors

KEY

① **The Neo-Gothic marble facade** echoes the style of Giotto's Campanile, but was only added in 1871–87.

② **Gothic windows**

③ **The top of the dome** offers spectacular views over the city.

④ **The *Last Judgment* frescoes** (1572–4) by Vasari were completed by Zuccari.

⑤ **Bricks were set** between marble ribs in a self-supporting herringbone pattern – a technique

Brunelleschi copied from the Pantheon in Rome.

⑥ **The marble sanctuary** around the High Altar was created by Baccio Bandinelli in 1555.

★ **Dome by Brunelleschi**
Brunelleschi's dome, finished in 1463, was the largest of its time to be built without scaffolding. The outer shell is supported by a thicker inner shell that acts as a platform for it.

Entrance leading to the dome

VISITORS' CHECKLIST

Practical Information
Piazza del Duomo.
Map 2 D5 (6 E2).
Tel 055 230 28 85.
Cathedral: **Open** 10am–5pm Mon–Sat (4:30pm Thu, 4:45pm Sat), 1:30–4:45pm Sun. 🕇 &
Crypt: **Open** 10am–5pm Mon–Sat (4:45pm Sat). 🎟 Baptistry: **Open** 12:15–7pm Mon–Sat, 8:30am–2pm Sun. 🎟 🕇 Dome: **Open** 8:30am–7pm Mon–Sat (5:40pm Sat). 🎟 Campanile: **Open** 8:30am– 7:30pm daily. 🎟 All buildings: **Closed** 1 Jan, Easter, 15 Aug, 8 Sep, 25 Dec.
Ⓦ operaduomo.firenze.it

Transport
🚌 1, 6, 14, 17, 23

Chapels at the East End
The three apses, crowned by smaller copies of the dome, have five chapels each. The 15th-century stained glass is by Ghiberti.

Marble Pavement
The colourful, intricately inlaid pavement (16th century) was designed in part by Baccio d'Agnolo and Francesco da Sangallo.

Dante Explaining the Divine Comedy *(1465)*
This painting by Michelino shows the poet outside Florence against a backdrop of Purgatory, Hell and Paradise.

The East Doors of the Baptistry

Lorenzo Ghiberti's famous bronze Baptistry doors were commissioned in 1401 to mark the city's deliverance from the plague. Ghiberti was chosen to make a set of new doors after a competition that involved seven leading artists, including Donatello, Jacopo della

Ghiberti's winning panel

Quercia and Brunelleschi. The trial panels by Ghiberti and Brunelleschi are so different from Florentine Gothic art of the time, notably in the use of perspective and individuality of figures, that they are often regarded as the first works of the Renaissance.

"Gate of Paradise"
Having spent 21 years working on the North Doors, Ghiberti was commissioned to make the East Doors (1424–1452). Michelangelo enthusiastically dubbed them the "Gate of Paradise". The original ten relief panels showing scriptural subjects are now exhibited in the Museo dell'Opera del Duomo (see p283); those on the Baptistry are copies.

Abraham and the Sacrifice of Isaac
The jagged modelled rocks symbolizing Abraham's pain are carefully arranged to emphasize the sacrificial act.

Joseph Sold into Slavery
Ghiberti, a master of perspective, formed the architectural elements in shallower relief behind the figures to create the illusion of depth in the scene.

Key to the East Doors

1	2
3	4
5	6
7	8
9	10

1 Adam and Eve are Expelled from Eden
2 Cain Murders his Brother, Abel
3 The Drunkenness of Noah and his Sacrifice
4 Abraham and the Sacrifice of Isaac
5 Esau and Jacob
6 Joseph Sold into Slavery
7 Moses Receives the Ten Commandments
8 The Fall of Jericho
9 The Battle with the Philistines
10 Solomon and the Queen of Sheba

Detail of carvings by Donatello on the wall of Orsanmichele

❽ Orsanmichele

Via dell'Arte della Lana. **Map** 3 C1 (6 D3). **Tel** 055 28 49 44. **Open** 10am–5pm daily. **Closed** 1 Jan, 1 May, Mon in Aug, 25 Dec.

Built in 1337 as a grain market, Orsanmichele was later converted into a church which took its name from *Orto di San Michele*, a monastic garden long since vanished. The arcades of the market became windows, which are today bricked in, but the original Gothic tracery can still be seen. The decoration was entrusted to Florence's major *Arti* (guilds). Over 60 years they commissioned sculptures of their patron saints to adorn the 14 exterior niches; however today many of the figures are copies. Among the sculptors were Lorenzo Ghiberti, Donatello and Verrocchio.

The beautifully tranquil interior contains an opulent 14th-century altar by Andrea Orcagna, a *Virgin and Child* by Bernardo Daddi (1348) and a statue of the *Madonna and Child with St Anne* by Francesco da Sangallo (1522).

❾ Bargello

Via del Proconsolo 4. **Map** 4 D1 (6 E3). **Tel** 055 29 48 83. 14, A. **Open** 8:15am–5pm daily. **Closed** 2nd & 4th Mon of each month; 1 Jan, 1 May, 25 Dec.

Florence's second-ranking museum after the Uffizi, the Bargello contains a wonderful medley of applied arts and Italy's finest collection of Renaissance sculpture. Begun in 1255, the fortress-like building was initially the town hall (making it the oldest seat of government in the city), but later became a prison and home to the chief of police (the *Bargello*). It also became known for its executions, which took place in the main courtyard until 1786, when the death sentence was abolished by Grand Duke Pietro Leopoldo. Following extensive renovation, the building opened as one of Italy's first national museums in 1865.

The key exhibits range over three floors, beginning with the Michelangelo Room, superbly redesigned after extensive damage during the 1966 flood. Three contrasting works by Michelangelo lie dotted around the room, the most famous a tipsy-looking *Bacchus* (1497), the sculptor's first large free-standing work. Close by is a powerful bust of *Brutus* (1539–40), the only known portrait bust by Michelangelo, and a beautifully delicate circular relief depicting the *Madonna and Child* (1503–5). Countless works by other sculptors occupy the same room. Among them is an exquisite *Mercury* (1564) by the Mannerist genius, Giambologna, as well as several virtuoso bronzes by the sculptor and goldsmith Benvenuto Cellini (1500–71).

Donatello's *David* (c.1430) in the Bargello

Brunelleschi's *Sacrifice of Isaac* (1402) in the Bargello

Across the courtyard, full of fragments and the coats of arms of the Bargello's various incumbents, two more rooms contain exterior sculptures removed from sites around the city. The courtyard's external staircase leads to the first floor, which opens with a wonderfully eccentric bronze menagerie by Giambologna. To the right is the Salone del Consiglio Generale, a cavernous former courtroom that contains the cream of the museum's Early Renaissance sculpture. Foremost among its highlights is Donatello's heroic *St George* (1416) – the epitome of "youth, courage and valour of arms" in the words of Vasari.

Commissioned by the Armourers' Guild, the statue was brought here from Orsanmichele in 1892. At the centre of the room, in direct contrast, is Donatello's androgynous *David* (c.1430), famous as the first free-standing nude by a Western artist since antiquity. Among the room's more easily missed works, tucked away on the right wall, are two reliefs depicting *The Sacrifice of Isaac* (1402). Created by Brunelleschi and Lorenzo Ghiberti respectively, both were entries in the competition to design the Baptistry doors.

Beyond the Salone, the Bargello's emphasis shifts to the applied arts, with room after room devoted to rugs, ceramics, silverware and a host of other beautiful *objets d'art*. The most celebrated of these rooms is the Salone del Camino on the second floor, which features the finest collection of small bronzes in Italy. Some are reproductions of antique models, others are copies of Renaissance statues. Giambologna, Cellini and Antonio del Pollaiuolo are represented.

Bacchus (1497) by Michelangelo

⑩ Santa Croce

Work began around 1294 on the Gothic church of Santa Croce, which contains tombs and monuments of famous Florentines, such as Michelangelo, Galileo and Machiavelli, as well as radiant early 14th-century frescoes by Giotto and his pupil Taddeo Gaddi. In the cloister alongside the church stands the Cappella de' Pazzi (Pazzi Chapel), a Renaissance masterpiece designed by Filippo Brunelleschi.

★ **Cappella de' Pazzi**
Brunelleschi's domed chapel with Classical proportions was begun in 1443. The roundels (c.1442–52) are by Luca della Robbia.

Tomb of Leonardo Bruni (1447)
Rossellino's effigy of this great humanist was unusual in its sensitive realism and lack of monumental pomp.

Ticket booth and entrance

Cimabue's Crucifixion
Badly damaged in the flood of 1966, this 13th-century masterpiece is among the highlights of the collection, as is Taddeo Gaddi's magnificent *Last Supper* (c.1355–60).

KEY

① **Refectory**

② *Tree of Life* **by Taddeo Gaddi**

③ **Vasari's Tomb of Michelangio** is decorated with figures representing sculpture and architecture.

④ **The Neo-Gothic façade** by Niccolò Matas was added in 1863.

⑤ **Tomb of Galileo**

⑥ **Tomb of Machiavelli**

⑦ *Annunciation* **by Donatello (15th century)**

⑧ **The Cappella Baroncelli**, frescoed by Taddeo Gaddi between 1332 and 1338, contains the first true night scene in Western art.

⑨ **Sacristy**

⑩ **The Neo-Gothic campanile**, was added in 1842, after the original was destroyed in 1512 by lightning.

Exit

VISITORS' CHECKLIST

Practical Information
Piazza di Santa Croce. **Map** 4 E1
(6 F4). **Tel** 055 246 61 05. Basilica:
Open 9:30am–5:30pm daily (from
2pm Sun). Ticket office closes at
5pm. **Closed** during mass. ⛪ &
📷 (includes visit to the Museo.)
📸 📷 Museo, Cloister &
Cappella de' Pazzi: **Open** as
above. **Closed** 1 Jan, Easter,
13 Jun, 4 Oct, 25 & 26 Dec. & 📷
(includes visit to the Basilica.)

Transport
🚌 C2, C3.

★ **Cappella Bardi Frescoes**
Giotto frescoed the Bardi
and Peruzzi chapels to the
right of the high altar between
1315 and 1330. This touching
scene from the left-hand
wall of the hapel shows
The Death of St Francis (1317).

⓫ Museo Galileo

Piazza de' Giudici 1. **Map** 4 D1 (6 E4).
Tel 055 26 53 11. **Open** 9:30am–6pm
daily (to 1pm Tue). **Closed** 1 & 6 Jan,
1 May, Easter, 24 Jun, 13 Aug, 1 Nov,
8, 25 & 26 Dec. 📷 📸

This lively and superbly
presented museum devotes
two floors to various scientific
themes, illustrating each with
countless fine displays and a
panoply of old and beautifully
made scientific instruments. It is
also something of a shrine to
the Pisa-born scientist Galileo
Galilei (1564–1642), and
houses the only
surviving
instruments he
designed and
built, including
two telescopes
and the
objective lens
from the
telescope with
which he discovered
Jupiter's moons.
A number of rooms
are devoted to
astronomical, mathematical and

Astrolabe, Museo Galileo

navigational instruments, with
galleries concentrating on
Galileo, telescopes and optical
games. The museum also
houses the scientific collections
of the two dynasties that once
ruled Florence: the Medici and
the House of Lorraine.
Some of the best exhibits on
display are early maps, globes
and astrolabes, antique
microscopes, thermometers and
barometers. There are also some
fine old clocks, mathematical
instruments, calculators, a horri-
fying collection of 19th-century
surgical instruments, and some

graphic anatomical models.
The museum has installed a
large bronze sundial outside
the entrance that can be used
to read the hour and the date.

⓬ Ponte Vecchio

Map 4 D1 (6 E4).

Ponte Vecchio, the oldest
surviving bridge in the city, was
built in 1345, the last in a
succession of bridges and fords
on the site that dated back to
Roman times. Designed by
Giotto's pupil Taddeo
Gaddi, it was originally
the domain of
blacksmiths,
butchers and
tanners (who
used the river
for disposing
of waste). They
were reviled for
their noise and
stench and were
evicted in 1593 by
Duke Ferdinando I –
replaced by jewellers
and goldsmiths. The elevated
Corridoio Vasariano runs along
the eastern side of the bridge,
above the shops. Giorgio Vasari
designed the corridor in 1565 to
allow the Medici family to move
about their residences without
having to mix with the public.
This was the city's only bridge to
escape destruction during
World War II and visitors today
come as much to admire the
views as to browse among the
antique shops and specialized
jewellery shops. A bust of the
famous goldsmith Benvenuto
Cellini stands in the middle
of the bridge.

Ponte Vecchio viewed from the Ponte Santa Trinità

⑬ Uffizi

The Uffizi, Italy's greatest art gallery, was built in 1560–80 to house offices *(uffici)* for Duke Cosimo I. The architect Vasari used iron as reinforcement, enabling his successor, Buontalenti, to create an almost continuous wall of glass on the upper storey. This was used as a gallery for Francesco I to display the Medici art treasures. In the 19th century the collection's ancient objects were moved to the archaeological museum and sculpture to the Bargello, leaving a priceless collection of paintings. Continuing renovations may mean some room closures; check the website for details.

Main staircase

Entrance hall

Entrance

45
44 43
42
41
38
31 32
29 30

Corridor ceilings are frescoed with 1580s "grotesques" inspired by Roman grottoes.

Buontalenti staircase

Bacchus *(c.1589)*
Caravaggio's early work depicting the god of wine can be found in the first floor exhibition rooms. The mood of dissipation is echoed in the foreground in the decaying fruit.

Annunciation *(1333)*
The Sienese painter Simone Martini was strongly influenced by French Gothic art, and this is one of his masterpieces. The two saints are by Martini's pupil and brother-in-law, Lippo Memmi.

Gallery Guide

Ancient Greek and Roman sculptures are in the second floor corridor around the inner side of the horseshoe-shaped building. The paintings are hung in a series of rooms off the main corridor, in chronological order, to show the development of Florentine art from Gothic to Renaissance and beyond. Many well-known paintings are in rooms 7–18. The restoration work may result in some exhibits being moved around the gallery and some being loaned to other galleries.

Ognissanti Madonna *(c.1310)*
Giotto's grasp of spatial depth and substance in this altar-piece was a milestone in the mastery of perspective.

Key to Floorplan

☐ East Corridor
☐ West Corridor
☐ Arno Corridor
☐ Gallery rooms 1–45
☐ Non-exhibition space

The Duke and Duchess of Urbino *(c.1465–70)*
Piero della Francesca's portraits of Federico da Montefeltro
and his wife Battista Sforza were painted after Battista died
aged 26. Her portrait was probably based on her death mask.

The Tribune, decorated in red and gold, contains the works most valued by the Medici.

The Birth of Venus *(c.1485)*
Botticelli shows the goddess of love flanked by Zephyrus, god of the
west wind, who blows the risen Venus to shore on a half-shell.
The myth may symbolize the birth of beauty through
the divine fertilization of matter.

The Holy Family
(1507)
Michelangelo's painting, the first to break with the convention of showing Christ on the Virgin's lap, inspired Mannerist artists through its expressive handling of colour and posture.

Vasari's Classical Arno façade
(begun 1560)

The Venus of Urbino *(1538)*
Titian's sensuous nude, inspired by Giorgione's Sleeping Venus, may in fact be a portrait of a courtesan deemed sufficiently beautiful to represent a goddess.

The Vasari Corridor is a passageway across the Arno to the Pitti Palace.

Exploring the Uffizi

The Uffizi offers not only the chance to see the world's greatest collection of Italian Renaissance paintings, but also the opportunity to enjoy other European masterpieces from Holland, Spain and Germany. Accumulated over the centuries by the Medici, the collection was first housed in the Uffizi in 1581, and eventually bequeathed to the Florentine people by Anna Maria Lodovica, the last of the Medici.

Madonna and Child with Angels (1455–66) by Fra Filippo Lippi

Gothic Art

Past the statues and antiquities of room 1, the Uffizi proper opens in style with three altarpieces of the *Maestà*, or Madonna Enthroned, by Giotto, Duccio and Cimabue, some of Italy's greatest 13th-century painters. Each work marks a stage in the development of Italian painting away from the stilted conventions of Byzantium to the livelier traditions of Gothic and Renaissance art. The shift is best expressed in Giotto's version of the subject (known as the *Ognissanti Madonna*), where new feeling for depth and naturalistic detail is shown in the range of emotion displayed by the saints and angels, and by the carefully evoked three-dimensionality of the Virgin's throne.

Giotto's naturalistic influence can also be seen among the paintings of room 4, which is devoted to the 14th-century Florentine School, an interesting counterpoint to the Sienese paintings of Duccio and his followers in room 3. Among the many fine paintings here are works by Ambrogio and Pietro Lorenzetti, and Simone Martini's *Annunciation*.

Room 6 is devoted to International Gothic, a highly decorative style that represented the height of Gothic expression. It is exemplified by Gentile da Fabriano's exquisite, glittering *Adoration of the Magi* painted in 1423.

Early Renaissance

A new understanding of geometry and perspective during the 15th century increasingly allowed artists to explore the complexities of space and depth. None became more obsessed with these new compositional possibilities than Paolo Uccello (1397–1475), whose picture of *The Battle of San Romano* (1456) in room 7 is one of the gallery's most fevered creations.

Room 7 also contains two panels from 1460 by Piero della Francesca, another artist preoccupied with the art of perspective. The panels, which are among the earliest Renaissance portraits, depict the Duke and Duchess of Urbino on one side and representations of their virtues on the other.

While such works can seem coldly experimental, Fra Filippo Lippi's *Madonna and Child with Angels* (1455–66), in room 8, is a masterpiece of warmth and humanity. Like many Renaissance artists, Lippi uses

Sandro Botticelli's allegorical painting, *Primavera* (1480)

a religious subject to celebrate earthly delights such as landscape and feminine beauty. A similar approach is apparent in the works of Botticelli, whose famous paintings in rooms 10–14 are for many the highlight of the gallery. In *The Birth of Venus*, for example, Venus takes the place of the Virgin, expressing a fascination with Classical mythology common to many Renaissance artists. The same is true of the *Primavera* (1480), which breaks with Christian religious painting by illustrating a pagan rite of spring.

Detail from *The Annunciation* (1472–5) by Leonardo da Vinci

High Renaissance and Mannerism

Room 15 features works attributed to the young Leonardo da Vinci, notably a sublime *Annunciation* (1472–5), which reveals hints of his still emerging style, and the *Adoration of the Magi* (1481), which remained unfinished when he left Florence for Milan to paint *The Last Supper* (1495–8).

Room 18, better known as the Tribune, was designed in 1584 by Buontalenti in order to accommodate the best-loved pieces of the Medici collection. Its most famous work is the so-called Medici Venus (1st century BC), a Roman copy of a Greek statue deemed to be the most erotic in the ancient world. The copy proved equally salacious and was removed from Rome's Villa Medici by Cosimo III to keep it from corrupting the city's art students. Other highlights in room 18 include

Agnolo Bronzino's portraits of *Cosimo I and Eleonora di Toledo*, both painted around 1545, and Pontormo's *Charity* (1530) and the portrait of *Cosimo il Vecchio* (1517).

Rooms 19 to 23 depart from the gallery's Florentine bias, demonstrating how rapidly Renaissance ideas and techniques spread beyond Tuscany. Painters from the German and Flemish schools are well represented, together with painters from Umbria like Perugino, but perhaps the most captivating works are the paintings by Venetian and northern Italian artists such as Mantegna, Carpaccio, Correggio and Bellini.

Room 25, which returns to the Tuscan mainstream, is dominated by Michelangelo's *Holy Family* or Doni Tondo (1456), notable for its vibrant colours and the Virgin's unusually twisted pose. The gallery's only work by Michelangelo, it was to prove immensely influential with the next generation of painters, especially Bronzino (1503–72), Pontormo (1494–1556) and Parmigianino (1503–40). The last of these was responsible for the *Madonna of the Long Neck* (c.1534) in room 29. With its contorted anatomy, unnatural colours and strange composition, this painting is a masterpiece of the style that came to be called Mannerism. Earlier, but no less remarkable masterpieces in rooms 26 and

Madonna of the Goldfinch (1506) by Raphael

Madonna of the Long Neck (c.1534) by Parmigianino

28 include Raphael's sublime *Madonna of the Goldfinch* (1506) and Titian's notorious *Venus of Urbino* (1538), censured by Mark Twain as the "foulest, the vilest, the obscenest picture the world possesses". Others hold it to be one of the most beautiful nudes ever painted.

Later Paintings

Visitors, already sated by a surfeit of outstanding paintings, are often tempted to skim through the Uffizi's final rooms. The paintings in rooms 30 to 35 – which are mainly from the Veneto and Emilia-Romagna – are mostly un-exceptional, but the gallery's last rooms (41–45) contain important paintings. Rooms 41 and 42 have works by Rubens and Van Dyck. Room 44, dedicated to Rembrandt and northern European painting, features Rembrandt's *Portrait of an Old Man* (1665) and two self-portraits of the artist as a young and old man (painted in 1634 and 1664, respectively). Rooms on the first floor hold works by Caravaggio. These include *Medusa* (1596–8), painted for a Roman cardinal; *Bacchus* (c.1589), one of the artist's earliest works; and the *Sacrifice of Isaac* (c.1590), whose violent subject is belied by the painting's gentle background landscape. These rooms also hold works by Guido Reni.

⓮ Piazza della Signoria

Piazza della Signoria and Palazzo Vecchio have been at the heart of Florence's political and social life for centuries. The great bell once used to summon citizens to *parlamento* (public meetings) here, and the square has long been a popular promenade for both visitors and Florentines. The piazza's statues (some are copies) commemorate the city's major historical events, though its most famous episode is celebrated by a simple pavement plaque near the loggia: the execution of the religious leader Girolamo Savonarola who was burnt at the stake.

David
This copy of the famous Michelangelo statue symbolizes triumph over tyranny. The original *(see p279)* stood in the piazza until 1873.

Heraldic Frieze
The crossed keys on this shield represent Medici papal rule.

KEY

① **The Fontana di Nettuno**, created by Ammannati (1575), is of the Roman sea god surrounded by water nymphs and commemorates Tuscan naval victories.

② **Sala dei Gigli**

③ **The Uffizi**

④ **The Loggia dei Lanzi**, designed by Orcagna (1382), is named after the Lancers, the bodyguards of Cosimo I who were billeted here.

⑤ **Roman statues**, possibly of emperors, line the Loggia.

⑥ **The Marzocco** is a copy of the heraldic lion of Florence carved by Donatello in 1420. The original is in the Bargello *(see p287)*.

Salone dei Cinquecento (1495)
This vast chamber contains a statue of Victory by Michelangelo and frescoes by Vasari describing Florentine triumphs over Pisa and Siena.

★ **Palazzo Vecchio** (completed 1332)
This Republican frieze over the palace entrance is inscribed with the words, "Christ is King", implying that no mortal ruler has absolute power.

★ **The Rape of the Sabine Women by Giambologna** (1583)
The writhing figures in Giambologna's famous statue were carved from a single block of flawed marble.

★ **Perseus by Cellini**
This bronze statue (1554) of Perseus beheading Medusa was intended to warn Cosimo I's enemies of their probable fate.

⓲ Palazzo Vecchio

Piazza della Signoria (entrance on via della Ninna). **Map** 4 D1 (6 D3). **Tel** 055 276 83 25. A, B. **Open** Apr–Sep: 9am–midnight (to 2pm Thu); Oct–Mar: 9am–7pm (to 2pm Thu). **Closed** 1 Jan, Easter, 1 May, 15 Aug, 25 Dec. Secret Itineraries & Children's Museum (by reservation only). **Tel** 055 276 83 25.

The "Old Palace" still fulfils its original role as town hall. It was completed in 1322 when a huge bell, used to call citizens to meetings or warn of fire, flood or enemy attack, was hauled to the top of the imposing bell tower. While retaining much of its medieval appearance, the interior was remodelled for Duke Cosimo I in 1540. The redecoration was undertaken by Vasari, who incorporated bombastic frescoes (1563–5) of Florentine achievements. Michelangelo's *Victory* statue (1525) graces the Salone dei Cinquecento, which also has a tiny study decorated by Florence's leading Mannerist painters in 1569–1573. Other highlights include the Cappella di Eleonora, painted by Bronzino (1540–45); the loggia, with its views over the city; the Sala dei Gigli (Room of Lilies) with Donatello's *Judith and Holofernes* (c.1455) and frescoes of Roman heroes by Ghirlandaio (1485); as well as the excellent museum for children and the secret rooms and passageways.

A copy of Verrocchio's Putto fountain in Vasari's courtyard

Street-by-Street: Around Piazza della Repubblica

Underlying the street plan of modern Florence is the far older pattern of the ancient Roman city. Nowhere is this more evident than in the grid of narrow streets around Piazza della Repubblica, site of the old Roman forum. This pivotal square housed the city's main food market until the 1860s, when redevelopment tidied up the area, and added the triumphal arch that now stands in today's café-filled square.

VIA DEL CAMPIDOGLIO
VIA DE' BRUNELLESCHI
VIA DE' PESCIONI
VIA DE' VECCHIETTI
VIA DEGLI STROZZI
PIAZZA
REPUBB
VIA DE' TORNABUONI
VIA DE' SASSETTI
ANSELMI
PELLICCERIA
PIAZZA DEGLI STROZZ
VIA DEGLI ANSELMI
VIA MONALDA
PIAZZA DE' DAVANZATI
PIAZZA DAVANZATI
VIA PORTA ROSSA
VIA PARIONE
PIAZZA DI S. TRINITA
VIA DELLE TERME
V. D FIORDALISO
SO CORNINO
BORGO SS. APOSTOLI
LUNGARNO DEGLI ACCIAIUOLI

Santa Trìnita has frescoes by Ghirlandaio on the Life of St Francis (1486), depicting events that took place in this area. Here, a child is revived after falling from the Palazzo Spini-Ferroni.

Palazzo Spini-Ferroni

Ponte Santa Trìnita was built in wood in 1290 and then rebuilt by Ammannati in 1567 to celebrate the defeat of Siena.

Key

— Suggested route

0 metres	200
0 yards	200

⑰ Palazzo Strozzi
This monumental palazzo dominates the square.

Santi Apostoli was reputedly founded by Charlemagne.

⑯ Palazzo Davanzati
Frescoes with exotic birds decorate the Sala dei Pappagalli, which was once the dining room of this 14th-century palazzo.

Locator Map
See Florence Street Finder maps 5, 6

Piazza della Repubblica, which dates from the 19th century, is lined by some of Florence's oldest and best known cafés.

Mercato Nuovo, the "New Market" (1547), now deals mainly in souvenirs.

Palazzo di Parte Guelfa was the headquarters of the Guelphs, the dominant political party of medieval Florence.

Ponte Vecchio
(See p289)

Detail of a frieze illustrating a medieval romance in Palazzo Davanzati

⓰ Palazzo Davanzati

Via Porta Rossa 13. **Map** 3 C1 (5 C3). **Tel** 055 238 86 10. **Open** 8:15am–1:50pm daily. **Closed** 1st, 3rd & 5th Mon and 2nd and 4th Sun of the month, 1 Jan, 1 May, 25 Dec. 10am, 11am, noon (2nd floor only).

This wonderful museum, also known as the Museo dell'Antica Casa Fiorentina, uses original fittings and furniture to recreate a typical well-to-do 14th-century town house. Among the highlights are the Salone Madornale, where large gatherings would have been held, and the Sala dei Pappagalli (Parrots Room), with its frescoes and rich tapestries.

Pelting holes in the vaulted ceiling of the entrance courtyard were for dropping missiles on unwanted visitors. In one corner of the inner courtyard is a well and a pulley system to raise pails of water to each floor – a real luxury since most medieval households had to fetch water from a public fountain.

⓱ Palazzo Strozzi

Piazza degli Strozzi. **Map** 3 C1 (5 C3). **Tel** 055 264 51 55. **Open** 9am–8pm daily (to 11pm Thu). 🚻 🎟 for exhibitions. 🔲 **palazzostrozzi.org**

Sheer size accounts for the impact of the Palazzo Strozzi, and although it is only three storeys high, each floor exceeds the height of a normal palazzo. It was commissioned by the wealthy banker Filippo Strozzi, who had 15 buildings demolished to make way for the palazzo. He hoped it would rival the Medici palaces elsewhere in the city. Strozzi died in 1491, just two years after the first stone was laid.

Work on the building continued until 1536, with three major architects contributing to its design – Giuliano da Sangallo, Benedetto da Maiano and Simone del Pollaiuolo (also known as Cronaca). The exterior, built of huge rusticated masonry blocks, remains unspoiled. Look out for the original Renaissance torch-holders, lamps and the rings for tethering horses that still adorn the corners and façades. The palace is now primarily used as an exhibition venue, when visitors can also access "La Strozzina", a vaulted gallery space in the basement, where small temporary exhibitions are held.

Exterior of Palazzo Strozzi, with masonry block rustication

⑱ San Lorenzo

San Lorenzo was the parish church of the Medici family, and in 1419 Brunelleschi was commissioned to rebuild it in the Classical style of the Renaissance. Almost a century later Michelangelo submitted some plans for the façade, and began work on the Medici tombs in the Sagrestia Nuova (the Old Sacristy). He also designed a library, the Biblioteca Mediceo-Laurenziana, to house the family's collection of manuscripts. The lavish family mausoleum, the Cappella dei Principi, was started in 1604.

Cappella dei Principi
The Medici mausoleum, behind the high altar, was begun in 1604 by Matteo Nigetti, and forms part of the Cappelle Medicee.

Biblioteca Staircase
Michelangelo's Mannerist staircase, one of the artist's most innovative designs, was built by Ammannati in 1559.

KEY

① **St Joseph and Christ in the Workshop**, a striking work showing the young Christ with his father, is by Pietro Annigoni (1910–88), one of the few modern artists whose work is seen in Florence.

② **The cloister garden** is planted with box hedges, pomegranate and orange trees.

③ **Michelangelo** designed the desks and ceiling of the Biblioteca, where exhibitions of Medici manuscripts are often held.

④ **The Old Sacristy** was designed by Brunelleschi and decorated by Donatello.

⑤ **The huge dome** by Buontalenti echoes that of the Duomo (see pp284–6).

⑥ **Campanile**

⑦ **The Cappelle Medicee** complex comprises the Cappella dei Principi and its crypt, the Sagrestia Nuova (see p299).

⑧ **A simple stone** slab marks the unostentatious grave of Cosimo il Vecchio (1389–1464), founder of the Medici dynasty.

⑨ **Michelangelo** submitted several designs for the façade of San Lorenzo, but it remains unfinished.

The Martyrdom of St Lawrence

Entrance to church

The Tomb of the Duke of Nemours (1520–34)
by Michelangelo in the Cappelle Medicee's
New Sacristy

Pulpits by Donatello
The bronze pulpits in the
nave were Donatello's last
works. Completed by his
pupils in 1460, the reliefs
capture the flinching pain of
Christ's Passion and the glory
of the Resurrection.

**The Martyrdom of
St Lawrence**
Bronzino's vast Mannerist
fresco of 1569 is a
bravura, choreographed
study of the human
form, rather than a
reverential response to
the agony of the saint.

⑲ Cappelle Medicee

Piazza di Madonna degli Aldobrandini.
Map 1 C5 (6 D1). **Tel** 055 29 48 83.
(reservations). 🚌 many routes.
Open 8:15am–5pm daily (Nov & Dec:
8:15am–1:50pm daily). Last adm:
30 mins before closing. **Closed** 1st,
3rd, & 5th Mon of each month, 2nd &
4th Sun, 1 Jan, 1 May, 25 Dec. 🅿 ♿

The Medici Chapels divide into
three distinct areas. Beyond the
entrance hall lies a low-vaulted
crypt, a suitably subdued space
for the brass-railed tombs of
many lesser members of the
Medici family. From here steps
lead to the octagonal **Cappella
dei Principi** (Chapel of Princes),
a vast family mausoleum begun
by Cosimo I in 1604. The ceiling
is garishly frescoed and the
walls are smothered in huge
swathes of semi- precious *pietre
dure* (inlaid stone). Spaced
around the walls are the tombs

of six Medici Grand Dukes.
A corridor leads to
Michelangelo's **New Sacristy**,
designed as a counterpoint to
Brunelleschi's Old Sacristy in San
Lorenzo. Three groups of
statues, all carved by
Michelangelo between 1520
and 1534, stand around the
walls: that on the near left-hand
wall is *The Tomb of the Duke of
Urbino* (grandson of Lorenzo the
Magnificent). Opposite is *The
Tomb of the Duke of Nemours*
(Lorenzo's third son). Close to
the unfinished *Madonna and
Child* (1521) is the simple tomb
containing Lorenzo the
Magnificent and his murdered
brother, Giuliano (died 1478).

⑳ Mercato Centrale

Piazza del Mercato Centrale. **Map** 1 C4
(5 C1). **Open** 7am–2pm Mon–Sat.

At the heart of the San Lorenzo
street market is the bustling
Mercato Centrale, Florence's
busiest food market. It is housed
in a vast two-storey building of
cast-iron and glass, built in 1874
by Giuseppe Mengoni.
The ground floor stalls sell
meat, poultry, fish, hams,
cheeses and olive oils. There are
also Tuscan takeaway foods
such as *porchetta* (roast suckling
pig), *lampredotto* (pig's
intestines) and *trippa* (tripe).
Fresh fruit, vegetables and
flowers are sold on the top floor:
look out for wild mushrooms
and truffles in the autumn,
and broad beans and baby
artichokes in early spring.

Yellow courgette flowers and other vegetables in the Mercato Centrale

㉑ Santa Maria Novella

The Church of Santa Maria Novella was built by the Dominicans between 1279 and 1357. The lower Romanesque part of its façade was incorporated into one based on Classical proportions by the pioneering Renaissance architect Leon Battista Alberti in 1456–70. The Gothic interior contains superb frescoes, including Masaccio's powerful Trinity. The famous Green Cloister, frescoed with perspective scenes by Paolo Uccello, and the dramatically decorated Spanish Chapel now form a museum.

The Nave
The piers of the nave are spaced closer together at the altar end. This trick of perspective creates the illusion of an exceptionally long church.

Trinity by Masaccio
This pioneering fresco (c.1428) is renowned as a masterpiece of perspective and portraiture. The kneeling figures flanking the arch are the painting's sponsors, judge Lorenzo Lenzi and his wife.

KEY

① **Chiostro Verde** takes its name from the green base used in Uccello's frescoes, which were sadly damaged by the 1966 floods.

② **Cappellone degli Spagnuoli**, the chapel used by the Spanish courtiers of Eleonora of Toledo, has frescoes of salvation and damnation.

③ **Monastic buildings**

④ **The arcade arches** are emphasized by grey and white banding.

⑤ **The Strozzi Tomb** is by Benedetto da Maiano (1493).

⑥ **Cappella di Filippo Strozzi** features Filippino Lippi's frescoes of St John raising Drusiana from the dead and St Philip slaying a dragon.

Main door

Entrance to museum

Entrance (via courtyard)

Cappella Strozzi
The 14th-century frescoes by Nardo di Cione and his brother Andrea Orcagna were inspired by Dante's epic poem, *The Divine Comedy*.

Ghirlandaio's *Madonna della Misericordia* (1472) in Ognissanti

Cappella Tornabuoni
Ghirlandaio's famous fresco cycle, *The Life of John the Baptist* (1485), peoples the biblical episodes with Florentine aristocrats in contemporary dress.

㉒ Palazzo Antinori

Piazza Antinori 3. **Map** 1 C5 (5 C2). **Closed** to the public. Cantinetta Antinori: **Tel** 055 29 22 34. **Open** 12:30–2:30pm, 7–10:30pm Mon–Fri.

Palazzo Antinori was built in 1461–6 and is one of the finest small Renaissance palazzi in Florence. It was acquired by the Antinoris in 1506 and has remained with the family ever since. The dynasty produces a range of wines, oils and liqueurs that can be sampled – along with fine Tuscan dishes – in the Cantinetta Antinori, the wine bar off the main courtyard.

㉓ Palazzo Rucellai

Via della Vigna Nuova 16. **Map** 1 C5 (5 B2). **Closed** to the public.

Built in 1446–51, this is one of the most ornate Renaissance palaces in the city. It was commissioned by Giovanni Rucellai, whose enormous wealth derived from the import of a rare and costly red dye made from lichen found only on the Spanish island of Majorca. The precious dye was called *oricello*, from which the name Rucellai is derived. Giovanni commissioned several buildings from the architect Leon Battista Alberti, who designed this palace as a virtual textbook illustration of the major Classical orders. The palazzo used to house the Museo Alinari but the collection has now moved to Piazza Santa Maria Novella.

㉔ Museo Nazionale Alinari della Fotografia

Piazza Santa Maria Novella 14ar. **Map** 1 B5 (5 B2). **Tel** 055 21 63 10. **Open** 10am–6:30pm Thu–Tue. mnaf.it

The Alinari brothers began taking pictures of Florence in the 1840s. They supplied high-quality postcards and prints to visitors to Florence in the 19th century. The exhibits offer a vivid insight into the social history of Florence at that time. The museum also houses a collection of cameras, documents and objects that illustrate the history of photography.

㉕ Ognissanti

Borgo Ognissanti 42. **Map** 1 B5 (5 A2). **Tel** 055 239 87 00. Church: **Open** 7am–12:30pm, 4–8pm daily. Ghirlandaio's The Last Supper **Open** 9am–noon Mon, Tue, Sat.

Ognissanti, or All Saints, was the parish church of the Vespucci, one of whose members, the 15th-century navigator Amerigo, gave his name to the New World. The young Amerigo is depicted in Ghirlandaio's fresco of the *Madonna della Misericordia* (1472) in the second chapel on the right; Ghirlandaio's *The Last Supper* (1480) can be seen in the convent next door.

In a chapel to the left of the transept hangs the 14th-century, 5 m- (16 ft-) high Ognissanti Crucifix by Giotto di Bondone.

㉖ Cappella Brancacci

The Church of Santa Maria del Carmine is famous for the Brancacci Chapel, which contains frescoes on *The Life of St Peter* commissioned by the Florentine merchant Felice Brancacci around 1424. Although the paintings were begun by Masolino in 1425, many of the scenes are by his pupil, Masaccio (who died before completing the cycle) and by Filippino Lippi, who completed the work in 1480. Masaccio's revolutionary use of perspective, his narrative drama and the tragic realism of his figures placed him in the vanguard of Renaissance painting. Many great artists, including Michelangelo, later visited the chapel to study his pioneering work.

St Peter Healing the Sick
Masaccio's realistic portrayal of cripples and beggars was revolutionary in his time.

KEY

① **Masaccio's simple style** allows us to focus on the figures central to the frescoes without distracting detail.

② **The grouping** of stylized figures in Masaccio's frescoes reflects his interest in the sculpture of Donatello.

③ **In every scene**, St Peter is distinguished from the crowds as the figure in the orange cloak.

④ **St Peter** is depicted against a background of Florentine buildings.

⑤ **Masolino's Temptation of Adam and Eve** is gentle and decorous, in contrast with the emotional force of Masaccio's painting on the opposite wall.

Expulsion of Adam and Eve
Masaccio's ability to express emotion is well illustrated by his harrowing portrait of Adam and Eve being driven out of the Garden of Eden, their faces wracked by misery, shame and the burden of self-knowledge.

Key to the Frescoes: Artists and Subjects

- ☐ Masolino
- ☐ Masaccio
- ☐ Lippi

1 Expulsion of Adam and Eve
2 The Tribute Money
3 St Peter Preaching
4 St Peter Visited by St Paul
5 Raising the Emperor's Son;
St Peter Enthroned
6 St Peter Healing the Sick

7 St Peter Baptizing the Converts
8 St Peter Healing the Cripple;
Raising Tabitha
9 Temptation of Adam and Eve
10 St Peter and St John Giving Alms
11 Crucifixion; Before the Proconsul
12 The Release of St Peter

VISITORS' CHECKLIST

Practical Information
Piazza del Carmine.
Map 3 A1 (5 A4).
Tel 055 238 21 95
(reservation required).
Open 10am–5pm Mon,
Wed–Sat; 1–5pm Sun.
Closed pub hols. ⬛

Transport
🚌 D.

Woman in a Turban
The freshness of Masaccio's original colours is seen in this rediscovered roundel, hidden behind the altar for 500 years.

Two Figures
Masolino's work tends to be more formal, less naturalistic and less animated than that of Masaccio.

Before the Proconsul
Filippino Lippi was called in to complete the cycle of frescoes in 1480. He added this emotional scene showing the Proconsul sentencing St Peter to death.

Street-by-Street: Oltrarno

For the most part, the Oltrarno is a homely area of small houses, quiet squares and shops selling antiques, bric-a-brac and foodstuffs. The Via Maggio, a busy thoroughfare, breaks this pattern, but step into the side streets and you escape the bustle to discover a corner of old world Florence. The restaurants serve authentic, reasonably priced food, and the area is full of studios and workshops restoring antique furniture. Among the things to see are Santo Spirito and Palazzo Pitti, one of the city's largest palaces, whose medley of museums contains an art collection second only to that of the Uffizi.

㉗ Santo Spirito
Brunelleschi's simple church was completed after the architect's death.

Ponte Santa Trinità

Cenacolo di Santo Spirito, the old refectory of a monastery that once stood here, contains a dramatic fresco attributed to Orcagna (c.1360).

★ Palazzo Guadagni
(1500) was the first in the city to be built with a roof-top loggia, setting a trend among the aristocracy.

★ Palazzo di Bianca Cappello
(1579) is covered in ornate *sgraffito* work and was the home of the mistress of Grand Duke Francesco I.

Masks and murals are handmade at this shop, Frieze of Papier Mâché.

The **16th-century fountain** and gargoyle in Piazza de' Frescobaldi were designed by Buontalenti, as was the façade (1593–4) of the nearby church of Santa Trinità.

Locator Map
See Florence Street Finder maps 3, 5

Ponte Vecchio
(see p289)

Palazzo Guicciardini was the birthplace of historian Francesco Guicciardini.

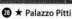

㉘ ★ Palazzo Pitti

Several museums are contained in this massive palazzo, including an outstanding collection of paintings. This painting of Palazzo Pitti was made by Giusto Utens in 1599.

Key

— Suggested route

0 metres   100
0 yards   100

㉗ Santo Spirito

Piazza di Santo Spirito 30. **Map** 3 B2 (5 B4). D. **Tel** 055 21 00 30. **Open** 9:30am–12:30pm, 4–5:30pm Mon–Sat; 11:30am–12:30pm & 4–5:30pm Sun. **Closed** Wed.

The Augustinian foundation of this church dates from 1250. The present building, dominating the northern end of the pretty Piazza di Santo Spirito, was designed by the architect Brunelleschi in 1435, but not completed until the late 15th century. The unfinished, modest façade was added in the 18th century.

Inside, the harmony of the proportions has been somewhat spoiled by the elaborate Baroque baldacchino and the High Altar, which was finished in 1607 by Giovanni Caccini. The church has 38 side altars, decorated with 15th- and 16th-century Renaissance paintings and sculpture, among them works by Cosimo Rosselli, Domenico Ghirlandaio and Filippino Lippi. The latter painted a magnificent *Madonna and Child* (1466) for the Nerli Chapel in the south transept.

In the north aisle, a door beneath the organ leads to a vestibule with an ornate coffered ceiling. It was designed by Simone del Pollaiuolo, more commonly known as Cronaca, in 1491. The sacristy adjoining the vestibule, in which 12 huge columns are crammed into a tiny space, was designed by Giuliano da Sangallo in 1489.

Interior of Santo Spirito with colonnaded aisle

㉘ Palazzo Pitti

The Palazzo Pitti was originally built for the banker Luca Pitti. The huge scale of the building, begun in 1457 and attributed to Brunelleschi, illustrated Pitti's determination to outdo the Medici family through its display of wealth and power. Ironically, the Medici later purchased the palazzo when building costs bankrupted Pitti's heirs. In 1550 it became the main residence of the Medici, and subsequently all the rulers of the city lived here. Today the richly decorated rooms exhibit countless treasures from the Medici collections.

Judith (1620–30) by Artemisia Gentileschi

The Three Ages of Man (c.1510), attributed to Giorgione

Galleria Palatina

The Palatine Gallery, which forms the heart of the Pitti museum complex, contains countless masterpieces by artists such as Botticelli, Titian, Perugino, Andrea del Sarto, Tintoretto, Veronese, Giorgione and Gentileschi. The works of art, accumulated by the Medici family and the house of Habsburg-Lorraine, are still hung much as the grand dukes wished, regardless of subject or chronology. The gallery consists of 11 main salons, the first 5 of which are painted with allegorical ceiling frescoes glorifying the Medici. Begun by Pietro da Cortona in 1641, they were completed in 1665 by his pupil Ciro Ferri. Room 1 (Sala di Venere) contains Antonio Canova's statue of the *Venus Italica* (1810), commissioned by Napoleon to replace the *Venus de' Medici* (which was to be taken to Paris). Room 2 (Sala di Apollo) features Titian's *Portrait of a Gentleman* (1540), perhaps the finest of several paintings by the artist in the gallery. Still finer pictures adorn rooms 4 and 5, including some by Perugino, Andrea del Sarto and a host of paintings by Raphael. The most beautiful of the last group are Raphael's High Renaissance *Madonna della Seggiola* or Madonna of the Chair (c.1514–15), and the *Donna Velata* or Veiled Woman (c.1516), whose model was reputedly the artist's mistress. Other paintings in the remaining gallery rooms include Fra Filippo Lippi's lovely *Madonna and Child*, painted in the mid-15th century, and Caravaggio's *The Sleeping Cupid* (1608).

Madonna of the Chair (c.1515) by Raphael

Galleria Palatina

The Museo degli Argenti, or the silverware museum, also displays precious objets d'art.

The Boboli Gardens

Entrance to museums and galleries

Brunelleschi designed the palace façade, which was eventually extended to three times its original length.

Appartamenti Reali

The Galleria d'Arte Moderna is a 30-room gallery featuring paintings from the years 1784 to 1924.

Sl

Few
vari
thro
Itali
fam
a ce
fine
ther
othe
sou
– wi

Wh

The
with
fashi
seco
tiny j
Pont
item
gold
are n
Via d
and \
barg
the J

Clot

Most
name
Versa
– can
Torna
Stroz
its co
cloth
Gabb
Pepp
Via de
speci
linge
Vigna
afforc
be fo
Mo
sell cl
fashic
upma
desig
a grea
For
fashic
Barbe
both
from
The
hand-
dei Te

The Palmieri Rotonda by Giovanni Fattori (1825–1908)

Appartamenti Reali

The Royal Apartments on the first floor of the south wing of the palazzo were built in the 17th century. They are decorated with frescoes by various Florentine artists, a series of portraits of the Medici by the Flemish painter Justus Sustermans, who worked at the court between 1619 and 1681, and a group of 18th-century Gobelins tapestries. In the late 18th and early 19th centuries, the apartments were revamped

The Throne Room of the Appartamenti Reali

in Neo-Classical style by the Dukes of Lorraine when they succeeded the Medici dynasty as the rulers of Florence.

The apartments are lavishly appointed with ornate gold and white stuccoed ceilings and rich decoration, notably the walls of the Parrot Room, which are covered with an opulent crimson fabric detailed with a bird design. The Tapestry Rooms are hung with 17th- and 18th-century tapestries of French, Belgian and Italian manufacture. The apartments reflect the tastes of three distinct historical periods.

Other Collections

The Museo degli Argenti (Silverware Museum) is housed in rooms formerly used by the Medici as summer apartments. The family's lavish taste is reflected in the vast array of precious objects on display. These embrace beautiful examples of Roman glassware, ivory, carpets, crystal, amber, and fine works by Florentine and German goldsmiths. Pride of place goes to 16 *pietre dure* vases (decorated with hard or semi-precious inlaid stones), once owned by Lorenzo the Magnificent.

The Galleria del Costume, which opened in 1983, reflects the changing taste in the courtly fashion of the late 18th century up to the 1920s. The highlights of the Galleria d'Arte Moderna (Modern Art Gallery) are the wonderful paintings of the *Macchiaioli* (spot-makers), who were a group of Tuscan artists with a style very similar to that of the French Impressionists.

Galleria del Costume

Piazza della Signoria depicted in precious stones

A copy of Giambologna's *Oceanus Fountain* (1576)

The Boboli Gardens

The Boboli Gardens, a lovely place to escape the rigours of sightseeing, were laid out for the Medici after they bought the Palazzo Pitti in 1549. An excellent example of stylized Renaissance gardening, they were opened to the public in 1766. The more formal parts of the garden, nearest the palazzo, consist of box hedges clipped into symmetrical geometric patterns. These lead to wilder groves of ilex and cypress trees, planted to create a contrast between artifice and nature. Countless statues adorn the gardens, particularly along the Viottolone, an avenue of cypress trees planted in 1637. High above the gardens stands the Forte di Belvedere, designed by Buontalenti in 1590 for the Medici Grand Dukes.

3

A
B
C

SEE PAGES 5-6 FOR ENLARGEMENT OF THIS AREA

1

LUNGARNO SODERINI

LUNGARNO CORSINI

PIAZZA DELLA REPUBBLICA

PIAZZA CARLO GOLDONI

V.D. VIGNA NUOVA

V.D. INFERNO

V.D. PARIONE

Palazzo Strozzi

PIAZZA DEGLI STROZZI

V.D. ANSELMI

Orsann

Palazzo Corsini

Pte alla Carraia

BORGO SAN

Palazzo Spini-Ferroni

SANTA TRINITA

DI S. TRINITA

V.D. TERME

V. P.TA ROSSA

Palazzo Davanzati

Me

CALIMALA

Palazzo di Parte Guelfa

Spez Erbor

PIAZZA DI VERZAIA

PIAZZA DEL TIRATOIO

San Frediano in Cestello

FREDIANO

LUNGARNO GUICCIARDINI

Pte S. Trinita

LUNG. D. ACCIAIUOLI

Santi Apostoli

BORGO

SAN GIOVANNI

PIAZZA DE' NERLI

BORGO DELLA STELLA

VIA DI SANTO SPIRITO

PIAZZA DI FRESCOBALDI

Pte Vecchio

San Stefa al Pont

LUNGARNO D. ARCHIBUSIE

PIAZZA DEL CARMINE

VIA SANTA MONACA

MAFFIA

Santo Spirito

VIA DE' COVERELLI

BORGO SAN JACOPO

VIA

PIAZZA

VIA

PIAZZA PIATTELLINA

Cappella Brancacci (Santa Maria del Carmine)

Cenacolo di Santo Spirito

PIAZZA DI SANTO SPIRITO

VIA DEL PRESTO DI S. MARTINO

VIA DELLO SPRONE

PIAZZA DI S. FELICITA

Santa Felicita

VIA SANT'AGOSTINO

MAGGIO

SDRUCCIOLO DE' PITTI

COSTA

2

GIARDINO TORRIGIANI

VIA DELLE CALDAIE

BORGO

V.D. VELLUTI

PIAZZA DE' PITTI

Palazzo Pitti

VICOLO D.

3

4

5

VIALE FRANCESCO PETRARCA

VIA DEL RONCO

GIARDINO DI BOBOLI

Forte di Belvedere

Museo La Specola

PIAZZA DELLA CALZA

PIAZZALE DELLA PORTA ROMANA

VIALE NICCOLÒ MACHIAVELLI

VIALE NICCOLÒ MACHIAVELLI

VIALE DEL POGGIO IMPERIALE

VIA SENESE

V.LE EVANGELISTICA TORRICELLI

PIAZZALE GALILEO

VIA DI SAN LEONARDO

VIAL

TUSCANY

Renowned for its art, history and evocative landscapes, Tuscany is thought to offer the quintessential Italian experience, and is understandably popular as a result. Hill-towns gaze across the countryside, many encircled by Etruscan walls and slender cypress trees. Handsome palaces testify to the region's wealth while medieval town halls indicate a long-standing tradition of democracy and self-government.

In the countryside, among the vineyards and olive groves, there are hamlets and farmhouses, as well as fortified villas and castles – reminders of the violence and intercommunal strife that tore Tuscany apart during the Middle Ages. Several imposing castles and villas were built for the Medici family, the great patrons of the Renaissance who supported eminent scientists, such as Galileo.

Northern Tuscany, and the heavily populated plain between Florence and Lucca, is dominated by industry, with intensively cultivated land between the cities and the wild mountainous areas.

The area centred around Livorno and Pisa is now the region's economic hub. Pisa, at the height of its powers, dominated the western Mediterranean from the 11th to the 13th centuries.

Its navy opened up extensive trading routes with North Africa, and brought to Italy the benefits of Arabic scientific and artistic achievement. During the 16th century the Arno estuary began to silt up, ending Pisan power.

At the heart of central Tuscany lies Siena, which was involved in a long feud with Florence. Its finest hour came with its victory in the Battle of Montaperti in 1260, but it was devastated by the Black Death in the 14th century and finally suffered a crushing defeat by Florence in the siege of 1554–5.

Northeastern Tuscany, with its mountain peaks and woodland, provided refuge for hermits and saints, while the east was home to Piero della Francesca, the early Renaissance painter whose timeless and serene works are imbued with an almost religious perfection.

A timeless view and way of life in Casole d'Elsa, near San Gimignano in central Tuscany

◀ The picturesque farmlands of Pienza in Tuscany

Exploring Tuscany

The Tuscan cities of Florence, Siena and Pisa, together with smaller towns like Lucca, Cortona and Arezzo, contain some of Italy's most famous artistic treasures. Medieval villages such as San Gimignano, with its famous towers, or Pienza, a tiny Renaissance jewel, sit at the heart of the glorious countryside for which the region is equally renowned. Elsewhere landscapes range from the spectacular mountains of the Alpi Apuane to the gentle hills of Chianti.

Sights at a Glance

View of Cortona in eastern Tuscany

For additional map symbols see back flap

0 kilometres 25
0 miles 20

Cypress trees, a classic feature of the Tuscan landscape

Bologna
Piancaldoli
Firenzuola
S325
Marradi
Marcello
oiese S564
Vernio
Scarperia
iastre
Barberino
di Mugello
A1
Borgo San Lorenzo
S65
San Godenzo
9 PISTOIA
Dicomano
S67
uarrata
10 PRATO
S310
Monte Falterona
1654m
Eremo di Camaldoli
Campi
Bisenzio
13 FIESOLE
Rufina
Badia
Prataglia
Sestino
8
11 ARTIMINO
Florence
Pontassieve
cecchio
Bibbiena
Pieve Santo Stefano
Empoli
Imprunteta
Poppi
SAN MINIATO
San Casciano in
Val di Pesa
Figline
Valdarno
S3b
Castelfiorentino
S429
Certaldo
Elsa
RA3
Gréve
S69
Loro Ciuffenna
15 SANSEPOLCRO
T O S C A N A
Montevarchi
Subbiano
Anghiari
S73
abassi
24
Poggibonsi
Radda
in Chianti
Capannole
Monterchi
14 AREZZO
IGNANO
Colle di Val d'Elsa
23 MONTERIGGIONI
Castiglion Fiorentino
5 VOLTERRA
Monte San
Savino
S71
asole d'Elsa
SIENA
22
21 CRETE SENESI
Foiano
della Chiana
16 CORTONA
Pomarance
Rosia
Larderello
Monteroni
d'Arbia
Asciano
Sinalunga
Terontola
rrazzano
RA6
Cornate
1060m
26 SAN GALGANO
Torrita
di Siena
Perugia
Montieri
Buonconvento
PIENZA
S73
18 MONTEPULCIANO
S223
20
19
MASSA
27 MARITTIMA
Roccastrada
MONTALCINO
Chianciano
Terme
17 CHIUSI
Valpiana
Civitella Marittima
S2
Gavorrano
Paganico
Roma
Montepescali
Cinigiano
Piazze
Vetulonia
Monte Amiata
1738m
Radicofani
Santa Fiora
M A R E M M A
Roccalbegna
Monte Civitella
1107m
Castell'Azzara
arina di
rosseto
Grosseto
SOVANA
Alberese
Scansano
Saturnia
Sorano
29
Marina di
Alberese
31
Magliano in
Toscana
30 PITIGLIANO
Talamone
Manciano
Albegna
S74
miche di
rosseto
Albinia
Capalbio
orto Santo Stefano
S1
Roma
iglio
npese
Orbetello
Porto Ercole
32
sola del
Giglio
MONTE
ARGENTÁRIO

Key

≡ Motorway
≡ Major road
— Secondary road
⋯ Minor road
— Scenic route
↭ Main railway
— Minor railway
— Regional border
△ Summit

Getting Around

Motorways or fast dual carriageways link Florence, the hub of Tuscany's road and rail network, to Siena, Pisa, Lucca and the south. The Via Aurelia and A12–E80 motorway serve the Tuscan coast. Rural roads, however, can be slow and winding. Rail links are good, and connect most major towns.

❶ Carrara

Massa Carrara. 🚗 200,000. 🚉 🚌
ℹ️ Lungomare Vespucci 24 (0585 24
00 63). 🛒 Mon.

Internationally renowned for its
marble quarries, Carrara's almost
flawless white stone has been
prized for centuries by famous
sculptors from Michelangelo to
Henry Moore (the stone for
Michelangelo's *David* came
from Carrara). The region's 300
or more quarries date back to
Roman times, making this one
of the oldest industrial sites in
continuous use in the world.
Many of the town's marble-
sawing mills and workshops
welcome visitors, offering them
the chance to see the ways in
which marble and quartz are
worked. These techniques –
along with marble artifacts old
and new – can be seen at the
Museo Civico del Marmo.

Local marble is put to good
use in the town's **Duomo** in
Piazza del Duomo, particularly
in the fine Pisan-Romanesque
façade with its delicate rose
window. The cathedral square
also contains Michelangelo's
house, used by the sculptor

A quarry in the marble-bearing hills around Carrara

during his visits to select blocks
of marble. The town has some
lovely corners to explore, in
particular the elegant Piazza
Alberica. Most visitors head for
the stone quarries that are open
to the public at nearby
Colonnata and at **Fantiscritti**
(take one of the regular town
buses or follow the signs to the
"Cave di Marmo"). The latter
features a small museum with
displays of various marble
quarrying techniques.

🏛️ **Museo Civico del Marmo**
Viale XX Settembre. **Tel** 0585 84 57 46.
Open Mon–Sat.

❷ Garfagnana

Lucca. 🚉 🚌 Castelnuovo di
Garfagnana. ℹ️ Piazza delle
Erbe, Castel-nuovo di Garfagnana
(0583 651 69).

A verdant, silent valley wedged
between the Orecchiella mountains and the Alpi Apuane, the
Garfagnana region can be
explored from **Seravezza**, **Barga**
or **Castelnuovo di Garfagnana**.
While the town of Barga makes
the prettiest base, thanks to its
tawny stone cathedral and
charming streets, Castelnuovo is
more convenient for drives and
walks in the surrounding
mountains. **San Pellegrino in
Alpe** in the Orecchiella has a
fascinating folklore museum,
the **Museo Etnografico**. It is
easily seen in conjunction
with the **Orto Botanico
Pania di Corfino** at the
headquarters of the **Parco
dell'Orecchiella** at Pania di
Corfino, with its collection of
local Alpine trees.

To the west is the Parco
Naturale delle Alpi Apuane,
an area whose spectacular
jagged peaks and wooded
valleys are criss-crossed by
hiking trails and scenic
mountain roads.

🏛️ **Museo Etnografico**
Via del Voltone 15, San Pellegrino in
Alpe. **Tel** 0583 64 90 72. **Open** Tue–
Sun (Jul–Aug: daily). 🖼️

🌳 **Parco dell'Orecchiella**
Centro Visitatori, Orecchiella. **Tel** 0583
61 90 02. **Open** Jun & Sep: 10am–5pm
daily; Jul & Aug: 9am–7pm daily. ♿

🌳 **Orto Botanico Pania di Corfino**
Parco dell'Orecchiella. **Tel** 0583 64 49
11. **Open** May–Sep: daily.

The Parco Naturale delle Alpi Apuane on the edge of the Garfagnana

One of many seaside cafés lining the waterfront in the popular beach resort of Viareggio

❸ Bagni di Lucca

Lucca. 🚗 7,400. 🚌 ℹ️ Via E. Wipple c/o Chiesa Inglese (0583 80 57 45). 🛍️ Sat.

All over Tuscany there are hot springs of volcanic origin, like Bagni di Lucca. The Romans first exploited the springs and built bath complexes where army veterans who settled in the area could relax. More spas came into prominence wwin the Middle Ages and the Renaissance, and they have continued to be recommended for relieving a variety of ailments, such as arthritis.

Tuscan spas really came into their own in the early 19th century when Bagni di Lucca reached its heyday as one of Europe's most fashionable spas, frequented by emperors, kings and aristocrats. Visitors came not only for thermal cures, but also for the **Casino** (1837), one of Europe's first licensed gambling houses. These days the town is rather sleepy, and its main sights are the19th-century monuments, including the Neo-Gothic **English Church** (1839) on Via Crawford and the **Cimitero Anglicano** (Protestant Cemetery) on Via Letizia.

Environs

Southeast of Bagni di Lucca lies another popular spa town, **Montecatini Terme**. Developed in the 18th century, this town is one of the most interesting with a wide range of spa architecture, from Neo-Classical to Art Nouveau spa establishments.

❹ Viareggio

Lucca. 🚗 65,000. 🚆 🚌 ℹ️ Viale Carducci 10 (0584 96 22 33). 🛍️ Thu.

Known for its carnival, held in January and early February, this is also the most popular of the resorts on the Versilia coast. Its famous "Liberty" (Art Nouveau) style of architecture can be seen in the grand hotels, villas and cafés built in the 1920s after the resort's original boardwalk and timber chalets went up in flames in 1917. The finest example of the architecture is the **Gran Caffè Margherita** at the end of Passeggiata Margherita, designed by the prolific father of Italian Art Nouveau, Galileo Chini.

❺ Torre del Lago Puccini

Lucca. 🚗 11,000. 🚆 🚌 ℹ️ Viale Kennedy 2 (0584 35 98 93). 🛍️ Fri.

A glorious avenue of lime trees, the Via dei Tigli, connects Viareggio with Torre del Lago Puccini, once the home of the opera composer Giacomo Puccini (1858–1924). He and his wife are buried in their former home, now the **Museo Villa Puccini**, a small museum that features the piano on which the maestro composed many of his works. Equal prominence is given to the villa's original fittings, including the gun room that housed Puccini's hunting rifle. **Lago Massaciuccoli**, a nature reserve for rare and migrant birds, provides a pretty backdrop for open-air performances of Puccini's works.

🏛️ **Museo Villa Puccini**
Piazzale Belvedere Puccini 226.
Tel 0584 34 14 45. **Open** Tue–Sun. **Closed** Nov, 25 Dec. ♿ ♿

Near Puccini's lakeside home at Torre del Lago Puccini

❻ Street-by-Street: Lucca

Lucca's regular grid of streets still follows the pattern of the Roman colony founded in 180 BC. Great, solid ramparts, built in the 16th to 17th centuries, help to shut out traffic, making the city a pleasant place to explore on foot. San Michele in Foro – one of the town's many fine Pisan-Romanesque churches – stands on the site of the Roman forum *(foro)*, the city's main square laid out in ancient times. It is still Lucca's main square today.

San Frediano
Palazzo Pfanner

In Via Fillungo, Lucca's main shopping street, several shop fronts are decorated with Art Nouveau details.

Casa Natale di Puccini
Giacomo Puccini (1858–1924), composer of hugely popular operas, including La Bohème, was born in this house.

Piazza Napoleone
This sprawling square is named after Napoleon, whose sister, Elisa Baciocchi, ruled Lucca from 1805 to 1815.

Railway station

★ San Michele in Foro
The extraordinary Pisan-Romanesque façade (11th to 14th century) has three tiers of twisted or carved columns, each one different from the rest.

San Giovanni

The Museo dell'Opera del Duomo features treasures removed from San Martino.

Key

— Suggested route

0 metres 300
0 yards 300

Anfiteatro Romano and tourist information

Torre dei Guinigi

Villa Bottoni Pinacoteca Nazionale

Giardino Botanico

★ San Martino
Lucca's beautiful 11th-century Duomo is one of the outstanding examples of the exuberant Pisan-Romanesque style.

Apostles from the mosaic on the façade of San Frediano in Lucca

🏛 San Frediano
Piazza San Frediano. **Open** daily.
San Frediano's striking façade features a colourful 13th-century mosaic, The Ascension, a fine prelude to the church's wonderfully atmospheric interior. Pride of place goes to a splendid Romanesque font on the right, its sides carved with scenes from the Life of Christ and the story of Moses. Note the scene of Moses and his followers (dressed as medieval knights) as they pass through the divided Red Sea. In the second chapel in the north aisle, Aspertini's frescoes (1508–9) tell the story of Lucca's precious relic, the Volto Santo – a carving said to date from the time of the Crucifixion. The fine altarpiece (1422) in the fourth chapel of San Frediano's north aisle is by Jacopo della Quercia.

🏛 San Michele in Foro
Piazza San Michele. **Open** daily.
Built on the site of the old Roman forum (foro), San Michele's rich mixture of twisted marble columns and Cosmati work (inlaid marble) adorns one of the most exuberant Pisan-Romanesque façades in Tuscany. Built between the 11th and 14th centuries, its decoration is overwhelmingly pagan. Only the huge winged figure of St Michael on the pediment marks this out as a church. The interior has little of interest except for the beautiful

painting of Saints Helena, Jerome, Sebastian and Roch by Filippino Lippi (1457–1504).

🏠 Casa Natale di Puccini
Corte San Lorenzo 9. **Tel** 0583 58 40 28. **Open** Apr–Oct: 10am–6pm daily; Nov–Mar: 11am–5pm. **Closed** Tue, 1 Jan, 25 Dec.

The fine 15th-century house in which Giacomo Puccini (1858–1924) was born is now a shrine to the great opera composer. It contains portraits of Puccini, costume designs for his operas and the piano he used when composing his last opera, Turandot.

🏠 Via Fillungo
Lucca's principal shopping street winds its way through the heart of the city towards the Anfiteatro Romano. Its northern end has several shops with Art Nouveau ironwork; halfway down lies the deconsecrated church of San Cristoforo, built in the 13th century, with a lovely interior.

One of the many bars and shops along Via Fillungo

Exploring Lucca

Lucca's peaceful narrow lanes wind among the medieval buildings, opening suddenly to reveal churches, tiny piazzas, and many other reminders of the city's long history, including a Roman amphitheatre.

Medieval buildings mark the outline of Lucca's old Roman amphitheatre

🏛 Anfiteatro Romano

Piazza del Mercato.

Roman *Luca* was founded in 180 BC, and stones from the ancient Roman amphitheatre have been ransacked over the centuries to build churches and palaces, leaving only a handful of original fragments studded into today's arena-shaped Piazza del Mercato. Slum housing clogged the piazza until 1830, when it was cleared on the orders of Marie Louise, the city's Bourbon ruler of that time. It was then that the amphitheatre's original shape was revealed, a graphic and evocative reminder of Lucca's rich Roman heritage. Low archways at the piazza's cardinal points mark the gates through which beasts and gladiators would once have entered the arena.

🏛 Museo dell'Opera del Duomo

Piazza Antelminelli 5. **Tel** 0583 49 05 30. **Open** daily. **Closed** 1 Jan, Easter (am), 25 Dec. 🔲 🔥

The museum, housed in the former Archbishop's Palace (14th century), displays the treasures of the Duomo of San Martino. These include the 11th-century carved stone head of a king and a rare

🏛 San Martino

Piazza San Martino. **Tel** 0583 95 70 68. **Open** daily. 🔲 for sacristy.

Lucca's cathedral was built after the campanile, hence the façade's cramped and asymmetric appearance. The main portals contain remarkable 13th-century carvings by Nicola Pisano and Guidetto da Como. The Tempietto inside houses a painting by Tintoretto and the Volto Santo, a revered 13th-century effigy once believed to have been carved at the time of the Crucifixion.

Domed chapels encircling the apse

Romanesque blind arcades and carved capitals

Façade
The cathedral façade is decorated with Romanesque sculptures and colonnading (1204).

The campanile was begun in 1060 as a defensive tower.

Ghirlandaio's painting of The Madonna and Saints (1449–94) is in the Sacristy.

Tomb of Ilaria del Carretto
This beautiful portrait in marble by Jacopo della Quercia (1405–6) is of the youthful bride of Paolo Guinigi.

Matteo Civitali's marble Tempietto (1184)

Circular clerestory windows, in the nave and above the aisle roof, illuminate the church's unusually tall nave.

Nicola Pisano
(1200 –78) carved the Journey of the Magi and Deposition on the left portal.

Baroque gods and goddesses in the garden of the Palazzo Pfanner

12th-century Limoges casket, possibly created for a relic of St Thomas à Becket. The Croce dei Pisani, made by Vincenzo di Michele in 1411, is a sublime masterpiece of the goldsmith's art. It shows Christ on the Tree of Redemption, surrounded by angels, the Virgin, St John and the other Evangelists.

Palazzo Pfanner
Via degli Asili 33. **Tel** 0583 954 029.
Open Apr–Oct: 10am–6pm; 1–15 Nov: 11am–4pm; rest of year: by appt.

This elegant, imposing house (1667) has a beautiful outside staircase. It also boasts one of Tuscany's most delightful formal gardens. Laid out in the 18th century, the garden's central avenue is lined with Baroque statues of the gods and goddesses of ancient Roman mythology. The garden can also be viewed while walking along the ramparts.

The house itself contains an interesting collection of furniture, antiques and medical instruments.

Ramparts
One of the pleasures of visiting Lucca is strolling along the ramparts – the magnificent city walls, whose tree-lined promenade offers some entrancing views of the city. Work on the ramparts began

around 1500, when advances in military technology made the old medieval defences ineffective. On their completion in 1645, the walls were some of the most advanced of their time. One of their most curious features was the open space that lay beyond them, and which survives to this day, cleared to prevent the enemy taking cover in trees and undergrowth. Ironically, the walls never actually had to be defended, and they were eventually converted into a public park in the early 19th century.

Romanesque lion in the Museo Nazionale Guinigi

Part of the imposing 17th-century ramparts that encircle Lucca

Santa Maria Forisportam
Piazza di Santa Maria Forisportam.
Open daily.

This church was built at the end of the 12th century, beyond the Roman walls of Lucca. Its name, Forisportam, means "outside the gate". The unfinished marble façade, in Pisan-Romanesque style, has blind arcading. Above the central portal is a relief of the *Coronation of the Virgin* (17th century). The interior was redesigned in the early 16th century, resulting in the nave and transepts being raised. The fourth altar of the south aisle contains a painting of *St Lucy*, and the north transept has an *Assumption*, both by Guercino (1591–1666).

Museo Nazionale di Villa Guinigi
Via della Quarquonia. **Tel** 0583 49 60 33.
Open 8:30am–7pm Tue–Sat.
Closed 1 Jan, 1 May, 25 Dec.

This massive Renaissance villa was built in 1418 for Paolo Guinigi, leading light of the noble family who ruled Lucca in the early 15th century. A familiar landmark of the city is the battlemented tower, the Torre dei Guinigi, with oak trees growing at the top. It offers good views over the city and the Apuan Alps. The garden features traces of a Roman mosaic, together with a pride of Romanesque lions removed from the city's walls.

Inside, the museum's first floor is devoted to sculptures and archaeological displays. The highlights are works by Matteo Civitali, Jacopo della Quercia and fine Romanesque reliefs removed from several of Lucca's churches. Most of the paintings in the gallery on the floor above are by minor local artists, with the exception of two by Fra Bartolomeo (c.1472–1517): *God the Father with Saints Catherine and Mary Magdalene* and the *Madonna della Misericordia*. The floor also has furnishings, church vestments and choir stalls from Lucca's cathedral, inlaid with marquetry views of the city carved in 1529.

➐ Pisa

For much of the Middle Ages, Pisa's powerful navy ensured its dominance of the western Mediterranean. Trading links with Spain and North Africa in the 12th century brought vast mercantile wealth and formed the basis of a cultural revolution that is still reflected in Pisa's splendid buildings – especially the Duomo, Baptistry and Campanile (the eponymous leaning tower). Pisa's decline began in 1284, with its defeat by Genoa, and was hastened by the silting up of the harbour. The city fell to the Florentines in 1406, but suffered its worst crisis in 1944 when it fell victim to Allied bombing.

A detail from the Duomo pulpit

da Camaino, and a mosaic of *Christ in Majesty* in the apse, completed by Cimabue in 1302.

The circular Baptistry was begun in 1152 along Roman-esque lines, and finished a century later (the delay caused by a shortage of money) in a more ornate Gothic style by Nicola and Giovanni Pisano. The former was responsible for the marble pulpit (1260) in the interior, carved with reliefs of the *Nativity*, the *Adoration of the Magi*, the *Presentation*, the *Crucifixion* and the *Last Judgment*. The pillars that support the pulpit feature statues of the Virtues. The inlaid marble font (1246) is by Guido da Como.

The Baptistry, Duomo and Leaning Tower in Pisa's Campo dei Miracoli

🏛 Leaning Tower
See p330. **Tel** 050 83 50 11/12.
Open daily. 🕐 Visits last 30 mins.
No children under 8 allowed. 🅿
🌐 opapisa.it (reservations).

🏛 Duomo and Baptistry
Piazza Duomo. **Tel** 050 83 50 11.
Open daily (Duomo: pm only on Sun).
🌐 opapisa.it

Pisa's famous Leaning Tower is now the best-known building in the Campo dei Miracoli (Field of Miracles). Originally, however, it was intended as a campanile to complement the Duomo, which was begun by Buscheto in 1064. Today the Duomo stands as one of the finest Pisan-Romanesque buildings in Tuscany, its wonderful four-tiered façade a medley of creamy colonnades and intricate blind arcades. Buscheto's tomb is in the left arch of the façade. Other important features of the exterior include the Portale di San Ranieri (leading to the south transept) and the bronze doors (1180), decorated with reliefs cast by Bonanno Pisano, the first architect of the Leaning Tower. Inside, the highlights are the carved pulpit (1302–11) by Giovanni Pisano, the *Tomb of Emperor Henry VII* (1315) by Tino

🏛 Camposanto
Piazza dei Miracoli. **Tel** 050 83 50 11.
Open daily. **Closed** 1 Jan, 25 Dec.

The Camposanto (cemetery) is the fourth element in the Campo dei Miracoli's lovely ensemble. Begun in 1278 by Giovanni di Simone, the vast marble arcades of this long, rectangular building are said to enclose soil from the Holy Land. Bombs in World War II all but destroyed its once famous frescoes, leaving only traces of *The Triumph of Death* (1360–80). Nearby is the Orto Botanico, one of Europe's oldest botanical gardens.

A fresco from the *Triumph of Death* cycle in the Camposanto

Santa Maria della Spina alongside the River Arno in Pisa

🏛 Museo dell'Opera del Duomo

Piazza del Duomo 6. **Tel** 050 83 10 11. **Open** daily.

Housed in the cathedral's 13th-century former Chapter House, this excellent modern museum displays exhibits removed over the years from the Duomo, Baptistry and Camposanto. Among the highlights is an imposing 10th-century hippogriff (half horse, half griffin). Cast in bronze by Moorish craftsmen, this statue was looted by Pisan adventurers during the wars against the Saracens. There are also works by both Nicola and Giovani Pisano, notably Giovanni's ivory *Virgin and Child* (1300), carved for the Duomo's high altar. Other exhibits include paintings, Roman and Etruscan remains, and ecclesiastical treasures.

10th-century bronze hippogriff

🏛 Museo Nazionale di San Matteo

Lungarno Mediceo, Piazza San Matteo 1. **Tel** 050 54 18 65. **Open** 9am–7pm Tue–Sun (only am Sun).

This museum is located on the banks of the Arno in San Matteo, an elegantly fronted medieval convent that in the 1800s also served as a prison. Much of the building has been closed for years – several of the rooms have no numbers and some of the exhibits are poorly labelled. Nevertheless, the museum presents a unique opportunity to examine the complete sweep of Pisan and Florentine art from the 12th to the 17th centuries.

The first rooms are devoted to sculpture and early Tuscan paintings. The best exhibits include a 14th-century polyptych by Francesco Traini of *Scenes from the Life of St Dominic*, Simone Martini's fine polyptych of *The Madonna and Saints* (1321), and a 14th-century statue of the *Madonna del Latte*, attributed to Andrea Pisano, another member of Pisa's talented school of medieval sculptors. The half-length statue, in gilded marble, shows Christ feeding at his mother's breast. In room 6 are some of the highlights of the museum, including Masaccio's *St Paul* (1426), Gentile da Fabriano's radiant 15th-century *Madonna of Humility*, and Donatello's reliquary bust of *San Rossore* (1424–7). Additional rooms contain paintings by Guido Reni, Benozzo Gozzoli, Rosso Fiorentino, and an important picture of *Christ* attributed to Fra Angelico (c.1395–1455).

🏛 Santa Maria della Spina

Lungarno Gambacorti. **Tel** 055 12 19 19. **Open** Tue–Sun.

The roofline of this tiny church, located just beyond the Ponte Solferino, bristles with spiky Gothic pinnacles, spires and niches sheltering statues of saints and apostles. The decoration reflects the history of the church, which was built between 1230 and 1323 to house a thorn *(spina)* from Christ's Crown of Thorns, the gift of a Pisan merchant. The church was once even closer to the Arno, but was rebuilt on the present site in 1871 to protect it from flooding.

🏛 Piazza dei Cavalieri

The huge building on the north side of this square is the Palazzo dei Cavalieri, home to one of Pisa University's most prestigious colleges: the Scuola Normale Superiore. Designed by Vasari in 1562, the building, which is covered in black and white *sgraffito* decoration (designs scratched into wet plaster), served as the headquarters of the Cavalieri di Santo Stefano, an order of knights created by Cosimo I in 1561.

The Virgin and Child (1321) by Simone Martini in the Museo Nazionale

The Leaning Tower of Pisa

Begun in 1173 on sandy silt subsoil, the Leaning Tower (Torre Pendente) started to tilt even before the third storey was finished in 1274. Despite the shallow foundations, construction continued and the structure was completed in 1350. The tower's apparent flouting of the laws of gravity has attracted many visitors over the centuries, including the Pisan scientist Galileo, who climbed to the top to conduct his experiments on the velocity of falling objects. After several engineering interventions that decreased its leaning angle by 38 cm (14 in), the tower is once again safe and open to the public.

Galileo Galilei
(1564–1642)

1995: 5.4 m (17 ft 6 in) from vertical

1817: 3.8 m (12 ft 10 in) from vertical

1350: tower leaning 1.4 m (4 ft 6 in) from vertical

True vertical axis

1301: tower completed as far as belfry

Marble columns

Staircase

Empty core

Central Staircase
This cross section of the third level shows how the staircase rises around the tower's empty core.

1274: third storey added; tower first starts to lean

Entrance

The bells add to the pressure on the tower.

Six of the tower's eight storeys consist of galleries with delicate marble arcading wrapped around the central core.

Doorway linking staircases to galleries

Naval Supremacy
Pisa's powerful navy consisted partly of small ships like the one carved in relief alongside the entrance to the tower.

The tower is supported on a shallow stone raft only 3 m (10 ft) deep.

Sand and clay soil with stone and rubble

Grey-blue clay

Sandy subsoil composed of various minerals

❽ Vinci

Florence. 🚗 15,000. 🚌 🚊 Wed.

Famous as the birthplace of Leonardo da Vinci (1452–1519), this hilltop town celebrates the genius in the **Museo Leonardiano**, housed in the 13th-century castle. Among the displays are wooden models of Leonardo's machines and inventions, most are based on drawings from his notebooks, copies of which are shown alongside. These include a bicycle, his conception of a car, an armoured tank and even a machine-gun.

🏛 Museo Leonardiano
Castello dei Conti Guidi. **Tel** 0571 93 32 51. **Open** daily. 📷

Model bicycle based on designs by Leonardo, Museo Leonardiano

❾ Pistoia

🚗 93,000. 🚆 🚌 ℹ️ Palazzo dei Vescovi, Piazza del Duomo (0573 216 22). 🚊 Wed & Sat.

Pistoia's citizens were once known for violence and intrigue, a reputation grounded in the medieval disputes between the city's rival factions, the Bianchi and Neri (Whites and Blacks). Their favoured weapon was a tiny, locally made dagger known as a *pistola*. Long a centre of metalwork, everything from buses to mattress springs are now made here. In the centre, several fine historic buildings are preserved.

🔵 Duomo
Piazza del Duomo. **Open** daily.
Piazza del Duomo, Pistoia's main square, is dominated by the Duomo (San Zeno) and its bulky 12th-century campanile, originally built as a watchtower in the city walls. The interior of the Duomo is rich in funerary

Detail of frieze (1514–25) by Giovanni della Robbia, Ospedale del Ceppo

monuments. The finest of these, in the south aisle, is the tomb of Cino da Pistoia. He was a friend of Dante and fellow poet, and is depicted in a relief (1337) lecturing to a class of young boys.

Nearby is the chapel of St James and its extraordinary silver altar decorated with more than 600 statues and reliefs. Although the earliest of these dates from 1287, the altar was not completed until 1456. One of the craftsmen involved was Brunelleschi, who began his career as a silversmith before turning to architecture. Also in the Piazza del Duomo is the octagonal Baptistry, completed in 1359.

🔵 Ospedale del Ceppo
Piazza Giovanni XXIII.
This hospital and orphanage, founded in 1277, was named after the *ceppo* (hollowed-out tree trunk) that was used to collect donations for its work. The main façade features coloured terracotta panels (1514–25) by Giovanni della Robbia illustrating the *Seven Works of Mercy*. The portico is by Michelozzo.

The Pisan-Romanesque façade of Pistoia's Duomo (San Zeno)

🔵 Cappella del Tau
Corso Silvano Fedi 70. **Tel** 0573 322 04. **Open** 8:30am–1:30pm Mon–Sat.
The Cappella del Tau (1360) is so called because the monks who built it wore on their cloaks the letter T (*tau* in Greek), symbolizing a crutch and their work with the sick and disabled. Inside there are frescoes by Niccolò di Tommaso on *The Creation* and the *Life of St Anthony Abbot* (1370). Two doors down, the **Palazzo Tau** has work by Marino Marini, Pistoia's best-known 20th-century artist.

The Fall (1372) by Niccolò di Tommaso in the Cappella del Tau

🔵 San Giovanni Fuorcivitas
Via Cavour. **Open** daily.
Built in the 12th to 14th centuries, the striking church of San Giovanni Fuorcivitas (literally "St John Outside the City") once stood beyond the city walls. Its north flank is clad in banded marble and there is a Romanesque relief of the Last Supper over the portal. Inside, the holy water stoup, carved in marble with figures of the Virtues, is by Giovanni Pisano (1245–1320). A masterly pulpit, carved in 1270 with scenes from the New Testament, is by Guglielmo da Pisa. Both are among the finest works of this period, when artists were reviving the art of carving.

⑩ Prato

🏛 190,000. 🚇 ℹ️ Piazza Buonamici 7 (0574 241 12). 🛍 Mon.

While textile factories gird Prato's outskirts, the city centre retains several important churches and museums. The **Duomo** (begun 1211) is flanked by the Pulpit of the Holy Girdle (1434–8), designed by Donatello and Michelozzo, used once a year to display a girdle, reputedly given to Thomas the Apostle before the Assumption of the Virgin. Inside the Duomo is *The Life of John the Baptist* (1452–66) by Fra Filippo Lippi, and a fresco cycle (1392–5) by Agnolo Gaddi.

Other sights include the **Museo Civico**, **Santa Maria delle Carceri**, a Renaissance church in Piazza delle Carceri; the **Castello dell'Imperatore**, a fortress built by Emperor Frederick II in 1237; the **Centro per l'Arte Contemporanea Pecci**; and the **Museo del Tessuto**, which traces the history of Prato's textile industry.

🏛 **Museo Civico**
Palazzo Pretorio, Piazza del Comune. **Tel** 0574 183 61.
Closed for restoration.

🏰 **Castello dell'Imperatore**
Piazza delle Carceri. **Open** Wed–Mon.

🏛 **Centro per l'Arte Contemporanea Pecci**
Viale della Repubblica 277. **Tel** 0574 53 17. **Open** Wed–Mon. 🚻

🏛 **Museo del Tessuto**
Via Puccetti 3. **Tel** 0574 61 15 03.
Open Tue–Sun. 🚻 free Sun.

Madonna del Ceppo by Fra Filippo Lippi in Prato's Museo Civico

Buontalenti's Villa di Artimino, or "Villa of a Hundred Chimneys"

⑪ Artimino

Prato. 🏛 400. 🚇

A small fortified hamlet, Artimino is remarkable for the unspoiled Romanesque church of **San Leonardo**. Outside the walls lies the **Villa di Artimino**, designed by Buontalenti in 1594 for Grand Duke Ferdinando I. Also known as the "Villa of a Hundred Chimneys" – after the chimney pots crowding the roofline – it houses the **Museo Archeologico Etrusco**, a collection of beautiful archaeogical exhibits.

Environs
Lovers of Pontormo's paintings, should visit the church of **San Michele** in Carmignano, 5 km (3 miles) north of Artimino, because it contains *The Visitation* (1530). East of here lies the villa of **Poggio a Caiano**. Built in 1480 by Giuliano da Sangallo for Lorenzo de' Medici *(see p257)*, it was the first Italian villa to be designed in the Renaissance style.

🏠 **Villa di Artimino**
Viale Papa Giovanni 23. Villa: **Tel** 055 875 14 27. **Open** Tue am by appt. Museum: **Tel** 055 871 81 24. **Open** 9:30am–1:30pm daily. **Closed** Wed. 🚻

🏠 **Poggio a Caiano**
Piazza Medici. **Tel** 055 87 70 12. **Open** Tue–Sun; also 1st & 4th Mon of month. 🚻 ♿

⑫ San Miniato

Pisa. 🏛 3,900. 🚇 ℹ️ Piazza del Popolo (0571 427 45). 🛍 Tue.

This hilltop town manages to remain aloof from the vast industrial sprawl of the Arno

valley. Its key building is the semi-derelict Rocca (castle), built for Frederick II, German Holy Roman Emperor, in the 13th century. Close by stands the **Museo Diocesano**, which is home to a *Crucifixion* (c.1430) attributed to Filippo Lippi, a terracotta bust of Christ attributed to Verrocchio (1435–88), and the *Virgin of the Holy Girdle* by Andrea del Castagno (c.1417–57). Next door, the red-brick Romanesque façade of the **Duomo** dates from the 12th century. Its strange inset majolica plates, evidence of trade with Spain or North Africa, probably represent the North Star and the constellations of Ursa Major and Minor (all three were key points of reference for early navigators).

🏛 **Museo Diocesano**
Piazza Duomo. **Tel** 0571 41 80 71.
Open 10am–1pm, 2–5pm Thu–Sun (Apr–Sep: 10am–6pm). 🚻

Façade of the Duomo in San Miniato

⑬ Fiesole

Florence. 🏛 15,000. 🚇 ℹ️ Via Portigiani 3 (055 596 13 23). 🛍 Sat.

Fiesole stands in rolling hilly countryside 8 km (5 miles) north of Florence. Idyllically situated among olive groves, it is a popular retreat from the city thanks to its hilltop position which attracts cool breezes. Founded in the 7th century BC, the original Etruscan colony was a powerful force in central Italy,

A view over the hills and rooftops of Fiesole from Via di San Francesco

only surrendering its supremacy after the foundation of Florence (1st century BC).

The restored **Duomo** of San Romolo in Piazza Mino da Fiesole was begun in 1028. It has a massive bell tower and a bare Romanesque interior. Behind the Duomo, an archaeological area contains the remains of a 1st-century BC **Roman theatre**, traces of **Etruscan walls** from the 4th century BC, and the **Museo Faesulanum**, with a collection of bronzes, ceramics and jewellery dating from the Bronze Age.

Via di San Francesco, a steep lane offering lovely views, leads to the Franciscan friary of **San Francesco** (14th century) and the interesting 9th-century church of **Sant'Alessandro**, with a Neo-Classical façade.

Via Vecchia Fiesolana leads to the hamlet of **San Domenico**, where the 15th-century church of the same name contains a painting of the *Madonna with Angels and Saints* (c.1430) by Fra Angelico and the Chapter House contains a fresco of *The Crucifixion* (c.1430), also by him. Close by, on the Via della Badia dei Roccettini, is the **Badia Fiesolana**, a pretty Romanesque church with a striped marble façade and interior of local grey sandstone, *pietra serena*.

Museo Faesulanum
Via Portigiani 1. **Tel** 055 596 12 93. **Open** daily (Oct–Mar: Wed–Mon).

Arezzo

100,000. Piazza della Repubblica 28 (0575 268 50). Sat.

Arezzo is one of Tuscany's wealthiest cities, its prosperity based on a thriving jewellery industry. Although much of its medieval centre was destroyed during World War II, resulting in extensive rebuilding and many medieval alleys being replaced by broad avenues, the city preserves some outstanding sights: foremost are Piero della Francesca's famous frescoes in the church of **San Francesco** *(see pp334–5)*. Close to the church on Corso Italia, the main street, stands the **Pieve di Santa Maria**, which boasts one of the most ornate Romanesque façades in the region. To its rear stretches the steeply sloping **Piazza Grande**, flanked by an arcade (1573) designed by Vasari, and by the **Palazzo della**

Fraternità dei Laici (1377–1552). The latter features a *Madonna* relief by Bernardo Rossellino. The huge **Duomo** to the north is best known for its 16th-century stained glass and a small fresco of *Mary Magdalene* by Piero della Francesca (1416–92). The **Museo Diocesano (Mudas)** features three wooden crucifixes, dating from the 12th and 13th centuries, a bas relief of *The Annunciation* (1434) by Rossellino and paintings by Vasari. More works by Vasari can be seen in the **Casa di Vasari**, a house built by the artist in 1540. Still more frescoes by him are displayed in the **Museo d'Arte Medioevale e Moderna**, a museum that is famed for its excellent collection of majolica pottery.

The **Fortezza Medicea**, a ruined Medici castle built by Antonio da Sangallo during the 16th century, has fine views.

Museo Diocesano (Mudas)
Piazzetta Dietro il Duomo 12. **Tel** 0575 402 72 68. **Open** daily.

Casa di Vasari
Via XX Settembre 55. **Tel** 0575 40 90 40. **Open** Wed–Mon.

Museo d'Arte Medioevale e Moderna
Via di San Lorentino 8. **Tel** 0575 40 90 50. **Open** Tue–Sun.

Fortezza Medicea
Parco il Prato. **Tel** 0575 37 76 78. **Open** daily.

The monthly antiques market held in Arezzo's Piazza Grande

Arezzo: San Francesco

The 13th-century Church of San Francesco houses one of Italy's greatest fresco cycles, the *Legend of the True Cross* (1452–66), Piero della Francesca's masterpiece. The scenes, on the walls of the choir, are now visible again after a long restoration. They describe the history of the Cross used to crucify Christ, from sprig to Tree of Knowledge, to its use as a bridge during the reign of Solomon, and ultimately its discovery by Helena, mother of Constantine, the first Christian emperor.

A Group of Onlookers
These figures kneel in wonder while Heraclius returns the True Cross to Jerusalem.

Excavation of the Cross
The town, meant to be Jerusalem, gives a fair representation of 15th-century Arezzo.

KEY

① **The Defeat of Chosroes** depicts the defeat of a Persian king who had stolen the Cross.

② **The Cross** returns to Jerusalem.

③ **Judas reveals** where the Cross is hidden.

④ **The 13th-century Crucifix** forms the focal point of the fresco cycle. The figure at the foot of the Cross represents St Francis, to whom the church is dedicated.

⑤ **The prophets** appear to play no part in the narrative cycle; their presence may be for purely decorative reasons.

⑥ **The wood** of the Cross is buried in a pit.

⑦ **The Queen of Sheba** recognizes the wood of the Cross.

⑧ **The buildings** in the fresco reflect the newly fashionable styles of Renaissance architecture.

⑨ **Constantine dreams** of the Cross on the eve of battle against rival emperor Maxentius.

⑩ **Constantine leads** his cavalry into battle.

Key to Frescoes

1 The Death of Adam; a sprig from the Tree of Knowledge is planted over his grave.

2 The Queen of Sheba visits Solomon and foresees that a bridge made from the Tree will be used to crucify the greatest king in the world.

3 Solomon, assuming he is the greatest king in the world, orders the bridge to be buried.

4 The Annunciation: Christ's death is foreshadowed in the panel's cruciform structure.

The Death of Adam
Piero's vivid portrayal of Adam and Eve in old age shows an adept treatment of anatomy. He was one of the first Renaissance artists to paint nude figures.

VISITORS' CHECKLIST

Practical Information
P. San Francesco. **Tel** 0575 35 27 27 (booking mandatory).
Open 9am–6:30pm Mon–Fri, 9am–5:30pm Sat, 1–5:30pm Sun.
Closed 1 Jan, 25 Dec.

5 Constantine has a vision of the Cross and hears a voice saying "In this sign you shall conquer".

6 Constantine defeats his rival Maxentius.

7 The Levite Judas is tortured and reveals the location of the True Cross.

8 Three crosses are dug up; Constantine's mother Helena recognizes the True Cross.

9 The Persian king Chosroes is defeated after stealing the Cross.

10 The True Cross is returned to Jerusalem.

Solomon's Handshake
The handshake between the Queen of Sheba and Solomon, King of Israel, portrays 15th-century hopes for a union between the Orthodox and Western churches.

Piero's *The Resurrection* (1463) in Sansepolcro

⓯ Sansepolcro

Arezzo. 🔼 16,000. 🚌 ℹ️ Via Matteotti 8 (0575 74 05 36). 🔄 Tue, Sat.

Sansepolcro is the birthplace of Piero della Francesca (1410–92). The town's **Museo Civico** contains two of his masterpieces: *The Resurrection* (1463) and the *Madonna della Misericordia* (1462). It also has a 15th-century *Crucifixion* by Luca Signorelli. In the church of **San Lorenzo** on Via Santa Croce there is a *Deposition* in the Mannerist style by Rosso Fiorentino (1494–1541).

Another renowned painting by Piero della Francesca, the *Madonna del Parto* (1460), can be seen at Via Reglia 1 in Monterchi, 13 km (8 miles) southwest of Sansepolcro.

🏛️ **Museo Civico**
Via Aggiunti 65. **Tel** 0575 73 22 18. **Open** daily. **Closed** public hols. 🔲 🔳

⓰ Cortona

Arezzo. 🔼 23,000. 🚆 🚌 ℹ️ Piazza Signorelli 9 (0575 63 72 23). 🔄 Sat.

Cortona was founded by the Etruscans and apart from being one of the oldest hill-towns in Tuscany, it is also one of the most scenic. A major power in the Middle Ages, it was able to hold its own against Siena and Arezzo. Today it is a charming maze of old streets and medieval buildings, like the **Palazzo**

Comunale on Piazza della Repubblica. The town's early history is traced in the **Museo dell'Accademia Etrusca**, which contains Etruscan artifacts and a wide variety of Egyptian and Roman remains. The small **Museo Diocesano** features several fine paintings, in particular a *Crucifixion* by the Renaissance artist Pietro Lorenzetti, a *Deposition* (1502) by Luca Signorelli, and a sublime *Annunciation* (c.1434) by Fra Angelico. Signorelli, born in Cortona, is buried in the church of **San Francesco** (built in 1245), which contains an *Annunciation* painted in Baroque style by Pietro da Cortona, another native artist. The **Madonna del Calcinaio** (1485), a gem of Renaissance architecture, is located on the southern outskirts of town.

The 13th-century Palazzo Comunale in Cortona

🏛️ **Museo dell'Accademia Etrusca**
Palazzo Casali, Piazza Signorelli 9. **Tel** 0575 63 72 35. **Open** daily (except Mon in winter). 🔲

🏛️ **Museo Diocesano**
Piazza del Duomo 1. **Tel** 0575 628 30. **Open** daily (Tue–Sun in winter). 🔲

⓱ Chiusi

Siena. 🔼 10,000. 🚆 🚌 ℹ️ Via Porsenna 79 (0578 22 76 67). 🔄 Tue.

Chiusi is now a largely modern town, but in the past it was one of the most powerful cities in the Etruscan league, reaching the height of its influence in the 7th and 6th centuries BC (*see p48–9*). Numerous Etruscan tombs lie dotted in the surrounding countryside, the source of the exhibits in the town's **Museo Nazionale Etrusco**. Founded in 1871, the museum is packed with cremation urns, vases decorated with black figures and Bucchero ware, burnished to resemble bronze.

The Romanesque **Duomo** in Piazza del Duomo incorporates recycled Roman pillars and capitals. The wall decorations in the nave, resembling frescoes, were painted by Arturo Viligiardi in 1887. There is a Roman mosaic underneath the high altar. Visits can be made to several Etruscan tombs under the town from the **Museo della Cattedrale**, a museum in the cloister of the Duomo that has displays of Roman, Lombardic and medieval sculpture.

🏛️ **Museo Nazionale Etrusco**
Via Porsenna 93. **Tel** 0578 201 77. **Open** 9am–8pm daily (to 2pm Sun & public hols). 🔲 🔳

🏛️ **Museo della Cattedrale**
P. del Duomo. **Tel** 0578 22 64 90. **Open** daily (Jan–Mar: Tue, Thu, Sat, Sun). 🔲

Etruscan frieze in the Museo Nazionale Etrusco in Chiusi

Pienza's Piazza Pio II, designed by Bernardo Rossellino (1459)

⑱ Montepulciano

Siena. 🔼 14,000. 🚌 ℹ️ Piazza Don Minzoni 1 (0578 75 73 41). 🚢 Thu.
🌐 prolocomontepulciano.it

This is one of Tuscany's highest hill-towns, its walls and fortifications offering broad views over Umbria and southern Tuscany, and the vineyards providing the Vino Nobile wine that has made its name famous. The streets are brimming with Renaissance palazzi. The main street, the Corso, climbs to the **Duomo** (1592–1630), the setting for one of the masterpieces of the Sienese School, the *Assumption* (1401) by Taddeo di Bartolo. The High Renaissance church, **Tempio di San Biagio** (1518–34), lies off the road to Pienza.

⑲ Pienza

Siena. 🔼 2,300. ℹ️ Piazza Dante Alighieri 18 (0578 74 83 59). 🚢 Fri.

Pienza is a delightful village whose intimate little centre was almost completely re-designed in the 15th century by Pope Pius II. Born as Aeneas Sylvius Piccolomini in 1405, when the village was known as Corsignano, he became a leading Humanist scholar and philosopher. Elected pope in 1458, he decided to rebuild his birthplace, renaming it Pienza in his own honour. The Florentine architect and sculptor, Bernardo Rossellino, was commissioned to build a cathedral, papal palace and town hall (all completed in the three years from 1459 to 1462), but the grander scheme for a planned model Renaissance town was never realized. Some idea of what might have been, however, can still be gained from the **Palazzo Piccolomini**, the former papal palace, which continued to be inhabited by Pius's descendants until 1968. The rooms open to the public include Pius's bedroom and library, though the highlight of a visit is the superb panorama from the loggia and arcaded courtyard at the palace's rear.

Pleasant walks and more great views can be had from the village walls. The airy **Duomo** *(see p256)* next door contains six altarpieces of the *Madonna and Child*, each commissioned from the leading Sienese painters of the day. Rossellino was forced to build the Duomo on a cramped site with poor foundations, and cracks appeared in the building before it was even completed. Today the church's eastern end suffers from severe subsidence.

🏛️ **Palazzo Piccolomini**
Piazza Pio II. **Tel** 0577 28 63 00.
Open 10am–6:30pm Tue–Sun (to 4:30pm mid-Oct–mid-Mar). **Closed** Jan–mid-Feb, mid–end Nov. 🚫 📷

⑳ Montalcino

Siena. 🔼 5,100. 🚌 ℹ️ Costa del Municipio 1 (0577 84 93 31). 🚢 Fri.

Hilltop Montalcino sits at the heart of vineyards that produce Brunello, one of Italy's finest red wines. It can be sampled in the Enoteca (wine shop) situated in the 14th-century **Fortezza** with its impressive ramparts. The town's timeless streets are a pleasure to wander, and there are some buildings of interest. On the way from the fortress into town is the monastery of Sant' Agostino and its 14th-century church and, just beyond, the Palazzo Vescovile. On Piazza del Popolo the slim tower of the Palazzo Communale, constructed in the 13th and 14th centuries, stands tall above the town.

🏰 **Fortezza**
Piazzale della Fortezza. **Tel** 0577 84 92 11. 🚫 for ramparts. Enoteca:
Open 9am–8pm daily (Nov–Mar: 9am–6pm Tue–Sun).

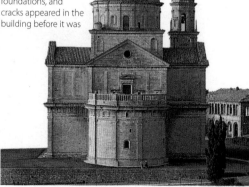

The Tempio di San Biagio on the outskirts of Montepulciano

The landscape of the Crete Senesi

㉑ Crete Senesi

Asciano. 🚉 🚌 ℹ️ Via delle Fonti (0577 71 88 11).

To the south of Siena and central Tuscany is the area known as the Crete Senesi, which is characterized by round clay hillocks eroded by heavy rain over the centuries. Dubbed the "Tuscan desert", it is almost completely barren. Cypress and pine trees, planted to provide windbreaks along roads and around isolated farm houses, are an important feature in this empty, primeval landscape. Shepherds tend flocks of sheep here; the milk is used to produce the strongly flavoured *pecorino* cheese that is popular throughout Tuscany.

㉒ Siena

See pp342–7.

㉓ Monteriggioni

Siena. 🚗 99,000. 🚌 ℹ️ Piazza Roma (0577 30 48 34).
🌐 monteriggioniturismo.it

Monteriggioni is a gem of a medieval hilltop town. It was built in 1203 and ten years later became a garrison town. It is completely encircled by high walls with 14 heavily fortified towers, built to guard the northern borders of Siena's territory against invasion by Florentine armies.

Dante used Monteriggioni as a simile for the deepest abyss at the heart of his *Inferno*, which compares the town's "ring-shaped citadel... crowned with

towers" with giants standing in a moat. The perfectly preserved walls are best viewed from the Colle di Val d'Elsa road. Within the walls, the sleepy town consists of a large piazza, a pretty Romanesque church (on the piazza), a few houses, a couple of craft shops, restaurants, and shops selling many of the locally produced Castello di Monteriggioni wines.

Environs

West of Monteriggioni by 3 km (2 miles) lies the former Cistercian Abbey of **Abbadia dell' Isola** (12th century). This Romanesque church was largely rebuilt in the 18th century, after the cupola fell apart. It contains frescoes by Taddeo di Bartolo and Vincenzo Tamagni.

Detail from the pulpit in Volterra's Duomo

㉔ San Gimignano

See pp348–9.

㉕ Volterra

Pisa. 🚗 13,000. 🚌 ℹ️ Piazza dei Priori 20 (0588 872 57). 🛒 Sat.
🌐 volterratur.it

Like many Etruscan cities, Volterra is situated on a high plateau, offering fine views over the surrounding hills. In many places the ancient Etruscan

walls still survive. The **Museo Guarnacci** contains one of the best collections of Etruscan artifacts in Italy. Of special interest is the group of over 600 cinerary urns, made from alabaster or terracotta, many of which were gathered from local tombs.

The **Palazzo dei Priori**, the medieval seat of government on Piazza dei Priori, is the oldest of its kind in Tuscany. It was begun in 1208 and there are 14th-century frescoes inside. The Pisan-Romanesque **Duomo**, located on Piazza San Giovanni, has a fine 13th-century pulpit with sculptured panels. Volterra's excellent art gallery and museum, the **Pinacoteca e Museo Civico**, features works by Florentine artists. *Christ in Majesty* (1492) by Ghirlandaio shows Christ hovering above an idealized Tuscan landscape. Luca Signorelli's *Virgin and Child with Saints* (1491) states his debt to Roman art through the reliefs on the base of the Virgin's throne. Painted in the same year, his *Annunciation* is a beautifully balanced composition. Another highlight is Rosso Fiorentino's Mannerist painting, *The Deposition* (1521).

The city is famous for its craftsmen who have been

The beautifully preserved walls of Monteriggioni in central Tuscany

The ruined abbey at San Galgano, surrounded by dense woodland

carving elaborate statues and *objets d'art* from locally mined alabaster for 2,500 years.

🏛 Museo Guarnacci
Via Don Minzoni 15. **Tel** 0588 863 47. **Open** daily. **Closed** 1 Jan, 25 Dec. 🗞

🏛 Pinacoteca e Museo Civico
Via dei Sarti 1. **Tel** 0588 875 80. **Open** daily. **Closed** 1 Jan, 25 Dec. 🗞

🟤 San Galgano

Siena. 🚌 from Siena. Abbey & oratory: **Open** daily.
W sangalgano.org

The remote Cistercian abbey at San Galgano lies in a superb setting. San Galgano (1148–81) was a brave but dissolute knight who turned to God, renouncing the material world. When he tried to break his sword against a rock as a symbol of his rejection of war, it was swallowed by the stone. This he interpreted as a sign of God's approval. He built a hut on a hill above the abbey (the site of today's beehive-shaped chapel at **Montesiepi**, built c.1185). Here he later died a hermit. Pope Urban III declared him a saint.

The abbey, begun in 1218, is Gothic in style, reflecting the French origins of the Cistercian monks who designed it. They avoided contact with the outside world and divided their lives between prayer and labour. Despite an emphasis on poverty, the monks became wealthy from the sale of wood, and by the middle of the 14th century the abbey was corruptly administered and gradually fell into decline.

In the late 14th century, the English mercenary Sir John Hawkwood sacked the abbey and by 1397 the abbot was its sole occupant. It was eventually dissolved in 1652.

St Galgano's sword stands embedded in a stone just inside the door of the circular **oratory**. The 14th-century stone walls of the side chapel are covered with worn frescoes showing scenes from Galgano's life by Ambrogio Lorenzetti (1344).

🟤 Massa Marittima

Grosseto. 🗺 9,500. 🚌 🛈 Amatur, Via Todini 3–5 (0566 90 27 56). 🖪 Wed.

Set in the Colline Metallifere (metal-bearing hills) where lead, copper and silver ores were mined as early as Etruscan times, Massa Marittima is far from being a grimy industrial town. Examples of Romanesque architecture survive from the time when the town became an independent republic (1225–1335). The Romanesque-Gothic **Duomo** in Piazza Garibaldi is dedicated to St Cerbone, a 6th-century saint whose story is sculpted in stone above the main portal. Inside the building, the *Maestà* is attributed to Duccio (c.1316).

The **Museo della Miniera** (museum of mining) is located partially inside a former mine shaft and has exhibits that explain mining techniques, tools and minerals.

The **Museo Archeologico e Museo d'Arte Sacra** has material from Paleolithic to Roman times. Other attractions are the Fortezza Senese and the Torre della Candeliera.

🏛 Museo della Miniera
Via Corridoni. **Tel** 0566 90 22 89. **Open** Tue–Sun. 🎥 compulsory. 🗞

🏛 Museo Archeologico e Museo d'Arte Sacra
Palazzo del Podestà, Pza Garibaldi. **Tel** 0566 90 22 89. **Open** Tue–Sun. 🗞

View across the rooftops of Massa Marittima

The Gothic Palazzo Pubblico (town hall) in Siena ▶

㉒ Street-by-Street: Siena

Siena's principal sights cluster in the maze of narrow streets and alleys around the fan-shaped Piazza del Campo. One of Europe's greatest medieval squares, the piazza sits at the heart of the city's 17 *contrade*, a series of parishes whose ancient rivalries are still acted out in the twice-yearly Palio *(see p345)*. Loyalty to the *contrada* of one's birth is fierce, and as you wander the streets you will see the parishes' animal symbols repeated on flags, plaques and carvings. Siena's hilly position also means that city walks offer delightful hidden corners and countless sudden views.

The Duomo dominating Siena's skyline

Via della Galluzza leads to the house of St Catherine.

The Baptistry has fine frescoes and a font with reliefs by Donatello, Jacopo della Quercia and Ghiberti.

★ Duomo
Striped black and white marble pillars, surmounted by a carved frieze of the popes, support the Duomo's vaulted ceiling, painted blue with gold stars to resemble the night sky.

Each tier of the Duomo's bell tower has one more window than the floor below.

Museo dell'Opera del Duomo
Duccio's *Maestà*, one of the greatest Sienese paintings, was paraded around Siena's streets on its completion in 1311, and influenced the city's painters for decades to come.

Key

— Suggested route

0 metres   300
0 yards   300

Loggia della Mercanzia
Built in 1417, the arcade is where Siena's medieval merchants and money dealers carried out their business.

VISITORS' CHECKLIST

Practical Information
60,000 ℹ Piazza del Campo 56 (0577 28 05 51). Wed. 2 Jul, 16 Aug: Palio; Jul: Settimana Musicale Chigiana (classical music).
🌐 terresiena.it

Transport
FS Piazzale Rosselli.
Piazza S. Domenico.

The Logge del Papa, or Pope's colonnade, was built in honour of Pius II in 1462.

Tourist information

Drummer in Siena's Palio

🏛 Piazza del Campo
Italy's loveliest piazza occupies the site of the old Roman forum, and for much of Siena's early history was the city's principal marketplace. It began to assume its present shape in 1293, when the Council of Nine, Siena's ruling body at the time, began to acquire land with a view to creating a grand civic piazza. The red brick paving was begun in 1327 and completed in 1349, its distinctive nine segments designed to reflect the authority of the Council of Nine and to symbolize the protective folds of the Madonna's cloak. The piazza has been the focus of city life ever since, a setting for executions, bullfights and the twice-yearly drama of the Palio *(see p341),* a festival centred around a bareback horse race. Cafés, restaurants and fine medieval palazzi now line the Campo's fringes, dominated by the **Palazzo Pubblico** (1297–1342) and **Torre del Mangia**, built in 1348 *(see p340).* This imposing ensemble tends to overshadow the little **Fonte Gaia** on the piazza's northern edge. The fountain is a 19th-century copy of an original carved by Jacopo della Quercia in 1409–19. Its reliefs depict the *Virtues, Adam and Eve,* and the *Madonna and Child* (the originals are on the rear loggia of the Palazzo Pubblico). The fountain's water is still supplied by a 500-year-old aqueduct.

Fonte Gaia
These reliefs are 19th-century copies of originals by Jacopo della Quercia.

★ **Palazzo Pubblico**
The graceful Gothic town hall was completed in 1342. At 102 m (330 ft), the bell tower, Torre del Mangia, is the second highest medieval tower ever built in Italy.

The Piazza del Campo and Fonte Gaia from the Torre del Mangia

Exploring Siena

Once a capital to rival Florence, Siena is Italy's prettiest medieval town, still endowed with the grandeur of the age in which it was at its peak (1260–1348). Begin an exploration of its historic centre in Piazza del Campo and the surrounding maze of medieval alleys.

Lorenzetti's *Allegory of Good Government* (1338), Palazzo Pubblico

🏛 Palazzo Pubblico
Piazza del Campo 1. **Tel** 0577 29 22 26/ 29 22 23. Museo Civico & Torre del Mangia: **Open** Mid-Mar–end Oct: 10am–7pm daily; Nov–mid-Mar: to 6pm daily. 📷

Although it continues in its ancient role as Siena's town hall, the Palazzo Pubblico's medieval rooms, some decor-ated with paintings of the Sienese School, are open to the public. The **Museo Civico** is housed here. The main council chamber, or Sala del Mappamondo, is named after a map of the world painted by Ambrogio Lorenzetti in the early 14th century. One wall is covered by Simone Martini's fresco of the *Maestà* (1315), which depicts the Virgin in Majesty as the Queen of Heaven, attended by the Apostles, saints and angels. Opposite is a fresco (attributed to Simone Martini, but possibly later) of the mercenary *Guidoriccio da Fogliano* (1330). The walls of the chapel are covered with frescoes of the *Life of the Virgin* (1407) by Taddeo di Bartolo, and the choir stalls (1428)

are decorated with wooden panels inlaid with biblical scenes. The Sala della Pace contains the famous *Allegory of Good and Bad Government* (1338–40), a pair of frescoes by Ambrogio Lorenzetti. They form one of the most important series of secular paintings from the Middle Ages. In the *Good Government* fresco civic life flourishes, while the *Bad Government*, presided over by a demon, reveals rubbish-strewn streets and ruins.

The Sala del Risorgi-mento is covered with late 19th-century frescoes illustrating the events leading up to the unification of Italy under King Vittorio Emanuele II.

In the palace courtyard is the entrance to the magnificent **Torre del Mangia**, the palace's huge bell tower. Rising 102 m (330 ft), it is a prominent feature of Siena's skyline. Built by the brothers Muccio and Francesco di Rinaldo between 1338 and 1348, it was named after the first bell-ringer, whose idleness led to the nickname *Mangiaguadagni* (literally "eat the profits"). There are 505 steps to the top, which has wonderful views.

🏛 Santuario e Casa di Santa Caterina
Costa di Sant'Antonio. **Tel** 0577 28 81 75. **Open** daily.

Siena's patron saint, Catherine Benincasa (1347–80), was the daughter of a tradesman. At the age of eight she devoted herself to God and had many visions, as well as later receiving the stigmata (wounds of Christ). Like her namesake, St Catherine of Alexandria, she was believed to have been betrothed to the Christ child in a vision – a scene which inspired many artists. Her eloquence persuaded Pope Gregory XI to return the seat of the papacy to Rome in 1376, after 67 years of exile in Avig-non. St Catherine died in Rome and was canonized in 1461.

Today Catherine's house is surrounded by chapels and cloisters. Among them is the Church of the Crucifixion, which was built in 1623 in her orchard to house the late 12th-century Crucifixion, in front of which she received the stigmata in 1375. The house is decorated with paintings of events from her life by artists including her contemporaries Francesco Vanni and Pietro Sorri.

Cloister of Santuario e Casa di Santa Caterina, birthplace of Siena's patron saint

▦ Palazzo Piccolomini

Piazza Pio II. **Tel** 0577 28 63 00.
Open 10am–6:30pm Tue–Sun (to 4:30pm Oct–Mar). **Closed** 7 Jan– 14 Feb, 16–30 Nov.

Siena's most imposing private palazzo was built for the wealthy Piccolomini family in the 1460s by the Florentine architect and sculptor Bernardo Rossellino. It now contains the Sienese state archives, account books and taxation documents dating back to the 13th century. Some of the leading artists of their day were employed to paint the wooden bindings used to enclose the tax and account records. The paintings, now on display in the Sala di Congresso, often show scenes of Siena itself or episodes from the city's past.

Other records include a will attributed to Boccaccio and the council's contract with Jacopo della Quercia for the Fonte Gaia *(see p343)*.

A detail from Martini's *Blessed Agostino Novello* (c.1330)

▥ Pinacoteca Nazionale

Via San Pietro 29. **Tel** 0577 28 61 43.
Open daily (Sun & Mon am only).
Closed 1 Jan, 1 May, 25 Dec. ▨ ♿

This fine gallery, which is housed in the 14th-century Palazzo Buonsignori, contains an unsurpassed collection of paintings by artists of the Sienese School. Arranged in chronological order, from the 13th century through to the Mannerist period (1520– 1600), highlights include Duccio's *Madonna dei Francescani* (1285) and Simone Martini's masterpiece *The Blessed Agostino Novello and Four of His Miracles* (c.1330). Pietro Lorenzetti's *Two Views,* from the 14th century, are early examples of landscape painting, and Pietro da Domenico's *Adoration of the Shepherds* (1510) shows

The austere exterior of the church of San Domenico (begun 1226).

how the art of Siena remained visibly influenced by its Byzantine roots long after the naturalism of the Renaissance had reached across the rest of Europe.

⛪ San Domenico

Piazza San Domenico. **Open** daily.
The preserved head of the city's patroness, St Catherine of Siena (1347–80), can be seen in a gilded tabernacle on the altar of a chapel dedicated to her in the huge, barn-like Gothic church of San Domenico (begun 1226). The chapel itself was built in 1460 for this purpose and is dominated by Sodoma's frescoes (1526), to the right and left of the altar, which show Catherine in states of religious fervour and her early life. The church has the only portrait of St Catherine considered authentic, painted by her friend Andrea Vanni. The fresco by Vanni can be found in the Chapel of the Vaults.

The Palio of Siena

The Palio is Tuscany's most celebrated festival and it occurs in the Campo each year on 2 July and 16 August at 7pm. This special event is a bareback horse race first recorded in 1283, but it may have had its origins in Roman military training. The jockeys represent 10 of Siena's 17 *contrade* (districts); the horses are chosen by the drawing of lots and are blessed

A *contrada* symbol

at the local *contrada* churches. Preceded by days of colourful pageantry, costume processions and heavy betting, the races themselves last only 90 seconds each. Thousands of spectators crowd into the piazza to watch the race, and rivalry between competitors is intense. The winner is rewarded with a silk *palio* (banner). Festivities for the winners can last for weeks.

The Sienese displaying their flag-throwing skills before the Palio

Siena: Duomo

Siena's Duomo (1136–1382) is one of Italy's greatest
cathedrals, a spectacular mixture of sculpture, paintings
and Pisan-influenced Romanesque-Gothic architecture.
Had 14th-century plans to create a new nave come to
fruition, the building would have become the largest
church in Christendom. In the event the plan came to
nothing, abandoned when the plague of 1348 virtually
halved the city's population. Among the Duomo's treasures
are sculptural masterpieces by Nicola Pisano, Donatello and
Michelangelo, a fine inlaid pavement and a magnificent
fresco cycle by Pinturicchio.

Baptismal Font
This Renaissance font by della
Quercia, Ghiberti and Donatello
stands in the Baptistry.

Pulpit Panels
Carved in 1265–8 by Nicola Pisano,
with help from Arnolfo di Cambio and
his son Giovanni, the panels on the
octagonal pulpit depict scenes from
the *Life of Christ*.

KEY

① **In the nave** black and white
marble pillars support the vault.

② **The Campanile** was added
in 1313.

③ **Archway** leading to the Baptistry.

④ **The Museo dell'Opera del
Duomo** occupies the side aisle of
the unfinished nave, which was
roofed over to house the museum.

⑤ **The façade** gives indication of
planned size of nave.

⑥ **The unfinished nave**, if
completed, would have measured
50 m (162 ft) in length and 30 m
(97 ft) in breadth.

⑦ **The doors** were built in 1284–97,
the rest of the façade a century later.

⑧ **The north aisle** contains
sculptures by Michelangelo of
Saints Peter, Pius, Gregory and
Paul (1501–4).

⑨ **Chapel of St John the Baptist**

Inlaid Marble Floor

**Piccolomini
Library**
Pinturicchio's
frescoes (1509)
portray the life of
the Piccolomini
pope, Pius II. Here
he presides at the
betrothal of
Frederick III
to Eleonora
of Portugal.

Inlaid Marble Floor
The Massacre of the Innocents is one of a series of scenes in the inlaid marble floor. The marble is usually uncovered during September each year.

Façade Statues
Many façade statues have been replaced by copies; the originals are in the Museo dell'Opera del Duomo.

Entrance to Duomo

VISITORS' CHECKLIST

Practical Information
Piazza del Duomo. **Tel** 0577 28 63 00. Duomo & Library: **Open** Mar–Nov: 10:30am–7pm (Duomo: 1:30–6pm Sun); Nov–Feb: 10:30am–5:30pm (Duomo: 1:30–5:30pm Sun).
w operaduomo.siena.it

Transport
Pollicino.

🏛 Museo dell'Opera del Duomo

Piazza del Duomo 8. **Tel** 0577 28 63 00. **Open** daily; call for opening times.

Part of this museum is devoted to items removed from the Duomo, including a tondo of a *Madonna and Child*, probably by Donatello, as well as several badly eroded Gothic statues by Giovanni Pisano and Jacopo della Quercia. The highlight is Duccio's huge *Maestà* (1308–11), one of the Sienese School's finest works. It depicts the Madonna and Child on one side, and scenes from the Life of Christ on the other. It was originally placed on the Duomo's high altar, where it replaced the striking *Madonna of the Large Eyes* (1220–30) by an anonymous Sienese painter, also in the museum.

Statues from the Duomo now on show in the Museo dell'Opera

🏰 Fortezza Medicea

Piazza Libertà 1 **Open** daily. Enoteca: **Tel** 0577 22 88 43. **Open** noon–1am Mon–Sat.

This huge red-brick fortress was built for Cosimo I by Baldassarre Lanci in 1560, following Siena's defeat by the Florentines in the 1554–5 war. After an 18-month siege, during which more than 8,000 Sienese died, the town's banking and wool industries were suppressed by the Florentine masters and all major building work ended.

The fortress now houses the Enoteca Italica, offering visitors the chance both to taste and to buy quality wines from all over Italy. There is also a restaurant on the site.

㉔ Street-by-Street: San Gimignano

The 13 towers that dominate San Gimignano's skyline were built by noble families in the 12th and 13th centuries, when the town's position – on the main pilgrim route from northern Europe to Rome – brought it great prosperity. The plague of 1348, and the diversion of the pilgrim route, led to its decline as well as its preservation. Today only one of the towers, the Torre Grossa, is open. San Gimignano is rich in works of art, as well as good shops and restaurants, although many close from November to March.

San Gimignano's famous skyline, almost unchanged since the Middle Ages

The Museo Civico provides access to the tallest of the town's 13 remaining towers.

Collegiata
This 11th-century church's interior is full of frescoes, including *The Creation* (1367) by Bartolo di Fredi.

Palazzo del Popolo
The council chamber of the town hall (1288–1323) features a large *Maestà* (1317) by Lippo Memmi.

The Annunciation by Ghirlandaio
This painting, completed in 1482, is located in a courtyard loggia alongside the Collegiata.

Bus station
Museo San Gimignano 1300

Via San Giovanni is lined with shops selling local goods.

VISITORS' CHECKLIST

Practical Information
Siena. 7,000. Piazza del
Duomo 1 (0577 94 00 08).
Thu. Patron saints' festivals:
31 Jan San Gimignano & 12 Mar
Santa Fina; varying dates in Feb:
Carnival; 1st Sun in Aug: Fiera
di Santa Fina; 29 Aug: Fiera di
Sant'Agostino; 8 Sep: Festa della
Madonna di Panacole.
w sangimignano.com

Transport
Porta San Giovanni.

Among the Piazza del Duomo's
historic buildings is the Palazzo
Vecchio del Podestà (1239),
whose tower is probably the
town's oldest.

Piazza della Cisterna
This square
is named after
the well at
its centre and is
the heart of the
old town.

Key

— Suggested route

0 metres   250
0 yards   250

🏛 Museo Civico
Palazzo del Popolo, Piazza del Duomo.
Tel 0577 99 03 12. Museum & tower:
Open 1 Apr–30 Sep: 9:30am–7pm
daily; 1 Oct–31 Mar: 11am–5:30pm
daily. **Closed** 25 Dec.

Frescoes in the courtyard of
this museum feature the coats
of arms of city mayors, as well as
a 14th-century *Virgin and Child*
by Taddeo di Bartolo.

The first room is the Sala di
Dante, where an inscription
recalls a visit by the poet in
1300. The floor above has an art
collection, which includes
excellent works by Pinturicchio,
Bartolo di Fredi, Benozzo Gozzoli
and Filippino Lippi. The famous
Wedding Scene frescoes by
Memmo di Filippucci (early
14th century) show a couple
sharing a bath and going to bed
– an unusual record of life in
14th-century Tuscany.

🏛 Collegiata
Piazza del Duomo. **Open** daily.
This 12th-century Romanesque
church contains a feast of
frescoes. In the north
aisle the frescoes
comprise 26 episodes
from the Old
Testament (1367) by
Bartolo di Fredi.
The opposite wall
features scenes from
the *Life of Christ* (1333–
41) by Lippo Memmi,
while at the back of the church
there are scenes from the
Last Judgment painted by
Taddeo di Bartolo.

The ceiling of the Collegiata, painted
with gold stars

🏛 Sant'Agostino
Piazza Sant'Agostino. **Open** daily.
Consecrated in 1298, this
church has a simple façade,
contrasting markedly with the
heavily decorated Rococo
interior (c.1740) by Vanvitelli.
Above the main altar is the
Coronation of the Virgin by
Piero del Pollaiuolo, dated
1483. The choir is covered in
a cycle of frescoes of *The Life
of St Augustine* (1465) executed
by the Florentine artist
Benozzo Gozzoli.

Bartolo di Fredi's *Christ*,
Sant'Agostino

🏛 Museo San Gimignano 1300
Via San Giovanni 50.
Tel 327 439 5165. **Open**
10am–7pm daily.
This museum houses
a reconstruction of
San Gimignano as
it was during the 13th
and 14th centuries. The
exhibits have been made entirely
by hand and include 72 "tower
houses", a symbol of the city's
power during the middle ages.

Fresco from the early 14th-century *Wedding Scene* cycle by Memmo di Filippucci
in the Museo Civico

㉘ Elba

Livorno. 🚂 30,000. 🚢 Portoferraio.
🚌 ℹ️ Calata Italia 26 (0565 91 46 71).
🛥️ Portoferraio: Fri.

Elba's most famous resident was
Napoleon, who spent nine
months here after the fall of
Paris in 1814. Today Italy's
third largest island is mainly
populated by holiday-makers,
who come by ferry from
Piombino, 10 km (6 miles) away
on the mainland. The main
town is Portoferraio, with an old
port and a modern seafront of
hotels and fish restaurants.

The landscape of the island is
varied. On the west coast, which
tends to be a little quieter, there
are sandy beaches suitable for
all water sports. The east coast,
centred on the town of Porto
Azzurro, the island's second
port, is more rugged, with high
cliffs and stony beaches. Inland,
olive groves and vineyards line
hillsides, and vegetation covers
the mountains. A good way to
see the interior is to take the road
from Marciana Marina to the old
medieval village of Marciana
Alta. Close by, a minor road leads
to a cable car that runs to Monte
Capanne (1,018 m/3,300 ft), a
magnificent viewpoint.

Marciana Marina on Elba

㉙ Sovana

Grosseto. 🚂 100. ℹ️ Piazza Busatti 8
(0564 63 30 99).

Sovana is one of southern
Tuscany's prettiest villages.
Its single little street ends in
Piazza del Pretorio, home to the
ancient church of Santa Maria,

View over Pitigliano and the town's dramatic cliffs and caves

which contains frescoes and
a 9th-century altar canopy.
A lane beyond leads through
olive groves to the Romanesque
Duomo, filled with reliefs and
carvings from an earlier church
on the site. Some fine Etruscan
tombs lie in the surrounding
countryside, many of them
clearly signed and easily visited
from the village.

㉛ Maremma

Grosseto. ℹ️ Viale Monterosa 206,
Grosetto (0564 46 26 11). 🚌 to
entrances from Alberese. **Open** daily.
🎫 🅿️ Inner Park Areas: 🚌 from
Alberese to tour departure point.
Open 8:30am–2pm daily. 🅿️
🌐 **parcomaremma.it**

The Etruscans, followed by
the Romans, were the first
to cultivate the marshes
and low hills of the
Maremma. Following the
collapse of the Roman
Empire, however, the area fell
prey to flooding and malaria,
twin scourges that left it
virtually uninhabited until the
18th century. The land has since
been reclaimed, the irrigation
canals unblocked and
farming developed on the
fertile soil. The stunning Parco
Naturale della Maremma was
set up in 1975 to preserve the
area's native flora and fauna,
and to prevent development
on one of Italy's few pristine
stretches of coastline. Entrance
to much of the park is restricted
to access on foot or by a
park bus from Alberese.
Other more marginal areas,
however, such as the excellent
beach at Marina di Alberese
and the countryside around
Talamone in the south, are
easier to see.

㉚ Pitigliano

Grosseto. 🚂 4,400. 🚌 ℹ️ Piazza
Garibaldi 51 (0564 61 71 11). 🛥️ Wed.

Pitigliano is spectacularly situated
high above the cave-riddled
cliffs of the Lente valley. Its maze
of tiny medieval streets includes
a small Jewish ghetto, formed in
the 17th century by Jews fleeing
from Catholic persecution.

Trappola

Irrigated salt
marsh

Fiume Ombrone

Ma
di Albe

Beaches

The Ombrone estuary is a mixture of
pines, marsh and dunes and is home
to birds such as the flamingo, sea
eagle, roller and bee-eater.

Key

— Roads

▭ Paths

▭ Canals and rivers

— Itineraries

0 kilometres   2
0 miles   1

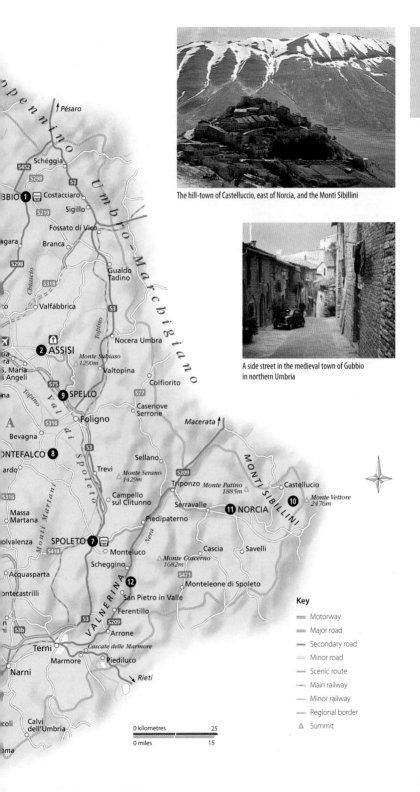

The hill-town of Castelluccio, east of Norcia, and the Monti Sibillini

A side street in the medieval town of Gubbio in northern Umbria

↑ Pésaro

S452
Schéggia
S298
S3
GUBBIO ❶ 🏛 Costacciaro
S219
Sigillo
Fossato di Vico
agara
Branca
S298
Gualdo
S318
Tadino
Chiascio
Valfábbrica
to
Topino
Nocera Umbra
✈
ASSISI ❷
ra
Monte Subiaso
△1290m
S. Maria
i Angeli
Valtopina
S575
Topino
Colfiorito
na
SPELLO ❾
Val di Spoleto
A
S316
Foligno
Casenove
S77
Serrone
Bevagna
Macerata ↑
MONTEFALCO ❽
S3
Trevi
Sellano
ardo
Monte Serano
△1429m
S209
Triponzo
Monte Patino
1885m △
Castelluccio
S316
MONTI SIBILLINI
❿
Monte Vettore
Campello
Serravalle
△2476m
Massa
sul Clitunno
Martana
NORCIA
Piedipaterno
❶❶
olvalenza
SPOLETO ❼ 🏛
Monti Martani
Nera
Monteluco
S418
Cascia
Savelli
Acquasparta
Scheggino
△Monte Coscerno
1682m
ontecastrilli
❶❷
S471
San Pietro in Valle
Monteleone di Spoleto
VALNERINA
Ferentillo
n
S3
ni
S3b
S209
Arrone
Terni
Cascate delle Marmore
Marmore
Piediluco
Narni
↗ Rieti
coli
Calvi
dell'Umbria
oma

Key

━━ Motorway
━━ Major road
━━ Secondary road
═══ Minor road
━━ Scenic route
▬▬ Main railway
── Minor railway
▬▬ Regional border
△ Summit

0 kilometres   25
0 miles   15

❶ Gubbio

Perugia. 🏔 33,000. 🚆 Fossato di Vico-Gubbio. 🚌 *i* Via della Repubblica 15 (075 922 06 93). 🛒 Tue.

Gubbio vies with Assisi for the title of Umbria's most medieval town. The beauty of its twisting streets and terracotta-tiled houses is enhanced by the forest-swathed Apennines. Founded by the Umbrians in the 3rd century BC as Tota Ikuvina, it assumed greater prominence in the 1st century AD as a Roman colony (Eugubium). It emerged as an independent commune in the 11th century having spread up the slopes of Monte Ingino. From 1387 to 1508 Gubbio was ruled from Urbino by the Dukes of Montefeltro.

The 13th-century **Duomo** is distinguished by a wagon-vaulted ceiling whose curved arches symbolize hands in prayer. Medieval Via dei Consoli leads to the 13th-century **Palazzo del Bargello** – a stone-faced building formerly the headquarters of the chief of police. Also here is the **Fontana dei Matti** (Fountain of the Mad), named after the tradition that anyone who walks around it three times will go insane.

Macabre legends surround the walled-up **Porte della Morte** (Doors of Death) that can be seen in Via dei Consoli and elsewhere in the town. Reputedly used for the passage of coffins from houses, the doors, once tainted, were sealed and never used again. Their purpose was probably defensive. In the lower town, the church of **San Francesco** (1259–82) is known for 17 faded frescoes showing scenes

The interior of Perugia's San Pietro, rebuilt in the 15th century

from the *Life of the Virgin* (1408–13) by Ottaviano Nelli. Opposite is the **Tiratoio** (Weavers' Loggia). Wool was stretched out to dry in its shady arcade. West of here are the ruins of a 1st-century AD Roman amphitheatre.

🏛 Palazzo dei Consoli

Piazza Grande. **Tel** 075 927 42 98. **Open** 10am–1pm, 3–6pm daily (Nov–Mar: 10am–1pm, 2:30–5:30pm). **Closed** 1 Jan, 13–15 May, 25 Dec. 🖼

Dominating the skyline of Gubbio is this mighty civic palace, begun in 1332 by Gattapone. Its Salone dell'Arengo houses the Museo Civico, best known for the Eugubine Tablets (250–150 BC). Discovered in 1444, the seven bronze slabs are in-scribed with Etruscan and Roman characters, probably a phonetic translation of prayers and rituals from the ancient Umbrian and Etruscan languages. Upstairs a small art gallery contains works by local painters.

One of the Eugubine Tablets in Gubbio

🏛 Palazzo Ducale

Via Federico da Montefeltro. **Tel** 075 927 58 72. **Open** 8:30am–7pm Tue–Sun. **Closed** 1 Jan, 25 Dec. 🖼 ♿

Attributed to Francesco di Giorgio Martini, this palace was built in 1470 for the Montefeltro as a copy of the family home in Urbino (*see pp374–5*). It also has a pretty Renaissance courtyard.

Façade of the Palazzo dei Consoli in Gubbio

❷ Assisi

See pp358–9.

❸ Perugia

🏔 160,000. 🚆 🚌 Piazza Vittorio Veneto. *i* Piazza Matteotti 18 (075 573 64 58). 🛒 Tue, Sat. 🌐 turismo. comune.perugia.it

Perugia's old centre hinges around the pedestrianized Corso Vannucci, named after the local painter Pietro Vannucci (Perugino). At its northern end is Piazza IV Novembre, dominated by the **Fontana Maggiore**, a 13th-century fountain by Nicola and Giovanni Pisano. To the rear rises the 15th-century **Duomo**, its entrance flanked by a statue of Pope Julius II (1555) and a pulpit built for Siena's San Bernardino (1425). Its Cappella del Santo Anello contains the Virgin's "wedding ring", a weighty piece of agate said to change colour according to the character of the person wearing it. The third pillar in the south nave holds a Renaissance painting of the *Madonna delle Grazie* by Gian Nicola di Paolo. The figure is credited with miraculous powers, and mothers bring newly baptized children to kneel before it. Buried in the transepts are Popes Urban IV and Martin IV.

Away from the Corso is the **Oratorio di San Bernardino** (1457–61) on Piazza San Francesco, with a colourful façade by Agostino di Duccio.

For hotels and restaurants in this region see pp562–77 and pp580–605

Beyond the old city walls on Borgo XX Giugno stands **San Pietro**. Founded in the 10th century and rebuilt in 1463, the best feature of the fine interior is the wooden choir (1526).

Piazza Giordano Bruno is home to **San Domenico** (1305–1632), Umbria's largest church, which is known for the Gothic tomb of Benedict XI (c.1304) and decoration by Agostino di Duccio.

Museo Archeologico Nazionale dell'Umbria
San Domenico, Piazza Giordano Bruno 10. **Tel** 075 572 71 41. **Open** daily. **Closed** 1 Jan, 1 May, 25 Dec.

Housed in the cloisters of San Domenico, this museum exhibits prehistoric, Etruscan and Roman artifacts.

Palazzo dei Priori
Corso Vannucci 19. **Tel** 075 573 64 58. **Open** daily (Sun: am only). **Closed** 1 Jan, 1 May, 25 Dec & 1st Mon each month. Collegio del Cambio: **Open** daily.

The monumental walls and bristling crenellations of this palace mark it as Umbria's finest public building (see pp58–9). Among its fine rooms is the Sala dei Notari (c.1295), the former lawyers' hall, vividly frescoed with scenes from the Old Testament – the work of a follower of Pietro Cavallini. The doorway is guarded by a pair of large bronzes made in 1274: a Guelph lion and a griffin, the medieval emblem of

Medieval street in Perugia

Perugia. The Sala di Udienza del Collegio della Mercanzia, built around 1390, was formerly used by the Merchants' Guild. This room is late Gothic in style, with exquisite panelling and 15th-century inlaid wood.

Also in the palace is the **Collegio del Cambio**, Perugia's former money ex-change, which was begun in 1452. This room was used by the Bankers' Guild. Its walls are covered with superlative frescoes (1498–1500) by Perugino, works devoted to Classical and religious scenes. A glum self-portrait scowls down from the centre of the left wall, while the hand of Perugino's pupil Raphael may be evident in some panels on the right wall.

Entrance of Palazzo dei Priori, Perugia

Galleria Nazionale dell'Umbria
Palazzo dei Priori, Corso Vannucci 19. **Tel** 075 58 66 84 10. **Open** Tue–Sun. **Closed** 1 Jan, 1 May, 25 Dec.

Umbria's greatest collection of paintings is displayed here on the third floor of the palace. Most of the works are 13th- to 18th- century paintings by local artists, but the highlights are altarpieces by Piero della Francesca and Fra Angelico.

Lake Trasimeno
Perugia. Castiglione del Lago. Piazza Mazzini 10, Castiglione del Lago (075 965 24 84). **W** regioneumbria.eu

Edged with low hills, this is Italy's fourth-largest lake. Its miles of placid water and reed-lined shores have a tranquil, melancholy beauty.

Drainage of the lake began under the Romans, but today the lake is gently drying up of its own accord. The town of **Castiglione del Lago**, jutting out on a fortified promontory, has an easy-going atmosphere and small sandy beaches. The 16th-century **castle** is used for summer concerts. The church of **Santa Maria Maddalena**, begun in 1836, has a fine Madonna and Child (c.1500) by Eusebio di San Giorgio.

Like Castiglione, **Passignano sul Trasimeno** offers boat trips to **Isola Maggiore**. The island's charming village is known for lace-making.

The battle of Lake Trasimeno
In 217 BC the Romans suffered one of their worst ever military defeats on the shores of Lake Trasimeno. The Carthaginian general, Hannibal, lured the Romans (who were led by the consul Flaminius) into a masterful ambush close to present-day Ossaia (Place of Bones) and Sanguineto (Place of Blood). Some 16,000 legionaries perished, hacked down on the lake's marshy fringes. Hannibal, by contrast, lost only 1,500 men. Today you can explore the battlefield, which includes over 100 mass graves found near Tuoro sul Trasimeno.

19th-century engraving of General Hannibal

Colourful façade of Perugia's Oratorio di San Bernardino

Assisi: Basilica di San Francesco

The burial place of St Francis, this basilica was begun in 1228, two years after the saint's death. Over the next century its Upper and Lower Churches were decorated by the foremost artists of their day, among them Cimabue, Simone Martini, Pietro Lorenzetti and Giotto, whose frescoes on the *Life of St Francis* are some of the most renowned in Italy. The basilica, which dominates Assisi, is one of the great Christian shrines and receives vast numbers of pilgrims throughout the year.

Lower Church
Side chapels were created here in the 13th century to accommodate the growing number of pilgrims.

St Francis
Cimabue's simple painting (c.1280) captures the humility of the revered saint, who stood for poverty, chastity and obedience.

KEY

① **The crypt** contains the tomb of St Francis.

② **Steps to the Treasury**

③ **The choir**, (1501) features a 13th-century stone papal throne.

④ **The campanile** was built in 1239.

⑤ **Faded paintings**, by Roman artists line the walls above Giotto's Life of St Francis.

⑥ **The façade** and its rose window are early examples of Italian Gothic.

★ **Frescoes by Lorenzetti**
The bold composition of Pietro Lorenzetti's fresco, entitled *The Deposition* (1323), is based around the truncated Cross, focusing attention on the twisted figure of Christ.

Upper Church
The soaring Gothic lines of the 13th-century Upper Church symbolized the heavenly glory of St Francis. This style also influenced later Franciscan churches.

Entrance to Upper Church

Entrance to Lower Church

★ **Frescoes by Giotto**
The Ecstasy of St Francis is one of 28 panels that make up Giotto's cycle on the *Life of St Francis* (c.1290–95).

★ **Cappella di San Martino**
The frescoes in this chapel on the *Life of St Martin* (1315) are by the Sienese painter Simone Martini. This panel shows the *Death of the Saint*. Martini was also responsible for the fine stained glass in the chapel.

❷ Assisi

Perugia. 🚶 25,000. ⓕⓢ 🚌 🛈 Piazza del Comune 22 (075 81 25 34). 🗓 Sat. **w** conoscerelumbria. regioneumbria.eu

This beautiful medieval town, with its geranium-hung streets, lovely views and fountain-splashed piazzas, is heir to the legacy of St Francis (c.1181–1226), who is buried in the **Basilica di San Francesco**. Sadly the town suffered serious damage during the earthquake of September 1997, but restoration was relatively swift – completed in approximately two years. The tourist office can give information on which sights are open to visitors.

Piazza del Comune, Assisi's main square, is dominated by the columns of the **Tempio di Minerva**, a Roman temple-front from the Augustan age. The Palazzo Comunale, opposite, is home to the **Pinacoteca Comunale**, an art gallery with works by local medieval artists.

Down Corso Mazzini lies the **Basilica di Santa Chiara**, the burial place of St Clare – Francis's companion and the founder of the Poor Clares (an order of nuns). One of its chapels contains the crucifix that is said to have bowed its head and ordered Francis to "Repair God's church". It came from **San Damiano**, a sublime church set amid olive groves south of the Porta Nuova.

The **Duomo (San Rufino)**, built during the 12th and 13th centuries, has a superb Romanesque façade. Inside is a small museum of paintings, and there are archaeological items in the crypt. From the Duomo, Via Maria delle Rose leads to the **Rocca Maggiore** (rebuilt in 1367), an evocative if much-restored castle.

Thirteenth-century **San Pietro**, on Piazza San Pietro, is a simple and carefully restored Romanesque church. The nearby **Oratorio dei Pellegrini**, a 15th-century pilgrims' hospice, contains well-preserved frescoes by Matteo da Gualdo.

Giotto's fresco, *St Francis Appearing to the Friars at Arles* (c.1295), in the Basilica di San Francesco, Assisi ▶

❺ Orvieto

Terni. 🏔 22,000. 🚉 🚌 ℹ️ Piazza Duomo 24 (0763 34 17 72). 🛍 Thu & Sat. 🌐 orvietoonline.com

Perched on a a 300-m (984-ft) plateau, Orvieto looks down over a vineyard-spotted plain. Visitors flood into the town to admire the **Duomo**, among the greatest of Italy's Romanesque-Gothic cathedrals.

The tiny 14th-century church of **San Lorenzo in Arari** is at the end of Via Scalza. Its walls feature frescoes describing the martyrdom of St Lawrence, who was grilled to death. The altar Is made from an Etruscan sacrificial slab. Via Malabranca leads to **San Giovenale** at Orvieto's western tip, a church that is beautifully and almost completely covered in detailed frescoes from the 15th and 16th centuries. It offers broad views over the surrounding countryside. **Sant'Andrea**, in Piazza della Repubblica, is distinguished by a curious 12-sided campanile, part of the original 12th-century building.

🏛 **Museo dell' Opera del Duomo & Museo d'Arte Moderna "Emilio Greco"**

Piazza Duomo. **Tel** 0763 34 35 92. **Open** Apr–Sep: 9:30am–7pm daily; Nov–Feb: 9:30am–1pm, 2:30–5pm daily; Mar & Oct: 9:30am–6pm daily. ♿ 🌐 opsm.it

The Museo dell'Opera del Duomo is an interesting little museum containing an eclectic collection of treasures given to the Duomo. Among the highlights are paintings by Lorenzo Maitani (died 1330) and sculptures by Andrea Pisano (c.1270–1348).

The "Emilio Greco" museum is devoted to the modern Sicilian sculptor, Emilio Greco, who made the bronze doors (1964–70) of the Duomo in Orvieto.

View into the Pozzo di San Patrizio in Orvieto

🏛 **Museo Archeologico Faina & Museo Civico**

Piazza Duomo 29. **Tel** 0763 34 10 39. **Open** 8:30am–7:30pm daily. **Closed** 1 Jan, 1 May, 25 Dec. ♿ 🎟 ⬆️

The first of these two museums has a well-known, low-key collection of Etruscan remains including many Greek vases that were found in Etruscan tombs in the surrounding area. The Museo Civico contains ancient Greek artifacts and Etruscan copies of Greek works.

🏛 **Duomo of Orvieto**

Piazza Duomo. **Tel** 0763 34 11 67. **Open** daily. ♿

Some 300 years in the building, Orvieto's Duomo (begun 1290), with its breathtaking façade, is one of Italy's greatest cathedrals. It was inspired by the Miracle of Bolsena in which real blood from a consecrated host supposedly fell on the altar cloth of a church in nearby Bolsena.

Carved choir stalls

The exterior is characterized by horizontal bands of white travertine and blue-grey basalt.

Cappella Nuova

14th-century rose window by Orcagna

The reliquary of the Corporal contains the altar cloth from Bolsena.

Cappella del Corporale
This chapel contains Lippo Memmi's *Madonna dei Raccomandati* (1320). There are also frescoes (1357–64) by Ugolino di Prete Ilario of the *Miracle of Bolsena* and *Miracles of the Sacrament*.

Bronze doors by Emilio Greco (1964–70)

⛲ Pozzo di San Patrizio

Viale San Gallo. **Tel** 0763 34 37 68.
Open daily. 🎫 allows entry at Museo d'Arte Moderna.

This well was commissioned in 1527 by Pope Clement VII and designed by the Florentine architect Antonio da Sangallo to provide the town with a water supply in case of attack. Two 248-step staircases drop into its dank interior, cleverly arranged as a double helix (spiral) so as not to intersect. The 62-m (203-ft) shaft took ten years to complete.

🏛 Necropoli Etrusca – Crocefisso del Tufo

Strada Statale 71 to Orvieto Scalo, km 1,600. **Tel** 0763 34 36 11. **Open** 8:30am–7pm (Oct–Mar: to 5pm) daily. **Closed** 1 Jan, 1 May, 25 Dec. 🎫 ♿

This Etruscan necropolis from the 6th century BC has burial chambers built of blocks of tufa. Etruscan letters, thought to be the names of the deceased, are inscribed on the tombs.

Cappella Nuova
Luca Signorelli's great fresco cycle of the *Last Judgment* (1499 –1504) features prominently in this chapel. Fra Angelico and Benozzo Gozzoli worked here before Signorelli.

The Façade
There are detailed carvings (c.1320–30) at the base of its four main pilasters. By Lorenzo Maitani, they depict scenes from the Old and New Testaments, including hell and damnation.

View of the hill-town of Todi in southern Umbria

❻ Todi

Perugia. 🚶 17,000. 🚆 🚌 ℹ️ Piazza del Popolo 38 (075 894 54 16). 🚩 Sat.

Looking down over the Tiber valley from its hilltop eyrie, Todi is one of the most strikingly situated of Umbria's famous hill-towns. An ancient Etruscan, and then Roman settlement, it still preserves an uncorrupted medieval air, with several tiny churches, three austere public palaces and many sleepy corners.

Most people are drawn here by the **Piazza del Popolo**, the main square, flanked by the lovely plain-faced **Duomo**. Built in the 13th century on the site of a Roman temple to Apollo, it has a dusky interior and one of Umbria's finest choirs (1521–30). Note Ferraù da Faenza's huge painting (1596) on the rear wall, a less than totally successful copy of Michelangelo's *Last Judgment*, and the altarpiece at the end of the right aisle by Giannicola di Paolo (a follower of Perugino).

Also flanking the piazza are the **Palazzo dei Priori** (1293–1337) and the linked **Palazzo del Capitano** (1290) and **Palazzo del Popolo** (1213). In the Palazzo del Capitano, distinguished by its redoubtable medieval interior, lies the **Museo Etrusco-Romano**. The museum contains a collection of local Etruscan and Roman artifacts. There are altarpieces and sacred objects in the **Pinacoteca Comunale**, also housed in the palace.

A few steps from the piazza rises **San Fortunato** (1292–1462), named after Todi's first bishop, with a florid Gothic doorway (1415–58). The high vaulted plan is based on German Gothic "hall" churches and the "barn" churches of Tuscany, characterized by a low-pitched vault, polygonal apse and naves and aisles of equal height. The choir (1590) is superb, but the church's most famous work is a *Madonna and Child* (1432) by Masolino da Panicale (fourth chapel on the right). The crypt contains the tomb of Jacopone da Todi (c.1228–1306), a noted medieval poet and mystic.

To the right of the church are some shady gardens, from which a path (past the tiny castle) drops through the trees to emerge in front of **Santa Maria della Consolazione** (1508–1607), near the N79. One of central Italy's finest Renaissance churches, and based on a Greek cross, it may have been built to a plan by Bramante. The stark, chill interior is overshadowed by the harmonious exterior.

🏛 Museo Etrusco-Romano and Pinacoteca Comunale

Piazza del Popolo 29/30. **Tel** 075 894 41 48. **Open** Tue–Sun. 🎫 ♿

Santa Maria della Consolazione in Todi

❼ Spoleto

Perugia. 🏔 38,000. 🚉 🚌 ℹ️ Piazza della Libertà 7 (0743 21 86 20 or 21 86 21). 🗓 Fri. 🌐 **regioneumbria.eu**

Founded by the Umbrians, Spoleto was one of central Italy's most important Roman colonies, a prominence maintained by the Lombards, who in the 7th century made it the capital of one of their three Italian dukedoms. After a spell as an independent city state, in 1354 Spoleto fell to the papacy.

Spoleto, within its wooded setting, is the loveliest of the Umbrian hill-towns. Its urbane atmosphere is enhanced by its superb monuments and by the Festival dei Due Mondi, one of Europe's leading arts festivals held annually in June and July.

At the southern end of Piazza del Mercato is the **Arco di**

Ponte delle Torri, Spoleto

Druso, a 1st-century AD Roman arch. It is flanked by the church of **Sant'Ansano**, whose crypt is covered in frescoes that may date from the 6th century. Via Aurelio Saffi, at the piazza's northern end, leads to **Sant'Eufemia**. This utterly simple 10th- century Romanesque church is known for its matroneum (women's gallery), once used to segregate the congregation.

A short way beyond, the fan-shaped Piazza del Duomo opens out to reveal Spoleto's 12th-century **Duomo**, graced with an elegant Romanesque façade. Filling the apse of the Baroque interior is a great fresco cycle. The final work of Fra Lippo Lippi, from 1467–9, it describes episodes from the *Life of the Virgin*. The Cappella Erioli is adorned with Pinturicchio's unfinished *Madonna and Child* (1497).

The best of the exceptional churches in the lower town is 4th-century **San Salvatore**, located in the main cemetery, a spot suited to the church's eerie sense of antiquity. Nearby stands **San Ponziano**, fronted by a captivating three-tiered Romanesque façade typical of Umbria.

Façade of San Pietro in Spoleto

It has a 10th-century crypt, supported by odd little columns and decorated with Byzantine frescoes.

Romanesque **San Gregorio** in Piazza Garibaldi dates from 1069, but its cramped façade and stolid campanile incorporate fragments of Roman buildings. Inside is a raised presbytery and a lovely multi-columned crypt. Well-preserved patches of fresco dot the walls. Some 10,000 Christian martyrs are supposedly buried near the church. They were reputedly slaughtered in the town's Roman **amphitheatre**, traces of which can be seen in the barracks on Via del Anfiteatro.

🌉 Ponte delle Torri

This magnificent 14th-century aqueduct, the "bridge of towers", is 80 m (262 ft) high. Designed by Gattapone (from Gubbio), it is the town's single most famous monument.

12th-century campanile

Renaissance portico

Romanesque churches in Umbria

Umbria's church-building tradition had its roots in ancient Roman basilicas and in the chapels built over the shrines of its many saints and martyrs. The region's Romanesque façades are usually divided into three tiers, often with three rose windows arranged above a trio of arched portals. The three doors usually correspond to the interior's nave and two aisles, which derive from the simple barn-like plan of Roman basilicas. Inside, the presbytery is often raised in order to allow for the building of a crypt, which usually contained the relics of a saint or martyr. Many of the churches took centuries to build, or were repeatedly modified over time, often acquiring elements of Gothic, Baroque or Renaissance styles.

San Lorenzo di Arari in Orvieto takes its name from an Etruscan altar *(arari)*. This 14th-century church has a very simple façade *(see p362)*.

Spoleto's Duomo (1198) has eight rose windows, a mosaic (1207) and a Renaissance portico (1491). The tower was built from old Roman remains.

From the bridge, there are views of the bastions of the **Rocca Albornoz**, a huge papal fortress built in 1359–64, also by Gattapone. Across the bridge a path leads to the Strada di Monteluco and the church of **San Pietro**, famous for the fascinating 12th-century carvings on its façade.

Rocca Albornoz
Piazza Campello 1. **Tel** 0743 22 49 52. **Open** daily. compulsory.

Museo del Tessile e del Costume
Via delle Terme. **Tel** 0743 459 40. **Open** 3:30–7:30pm Sat & Sun. **Closed** 1 Jan, 25 Dec.
Among the exhibits in this exquisite collection are sacred vestments complete with headgear, ties and gold chains, and a series of 17th-century tapestries that once belonged to Queen Christina of Sweden.

❾ Montefalco

Perugia. 4,900. Mon.

Montefalco, whose name (Falcon's Mount) draws inspiration from its lofty position and sweeping views, is the best of the fascinating villages in the Vale of Spoleto. Criss-crossed by streets almost too narrow for cars, it takes less than five minutes to walk through the village. Yet you might happily spend a morning here, most of it in the polished **Museo Civico** housed

A panel from Gozzoli's fresco cycle (1452) in Montefalco's Museo Civico

in the former church of San Francesco. Its highlight is Benozzo Gozzoli's *Life of St Francis* (1452), a radiant fresco cycle that borrows heavily from Giotto's cycle in Assisi *(see pp358–61)*. Other painters represented here are Perugino, Tiberio d'Assisi and Nicolò Alunno, all leading medieval Umbrian artists.

The simple Gothic church of **Sant'Agostino** (begun 1279) on Corso Mameli is dotted with frescoes from the 14th–16th centuries. The church also contains three mummies.

In the main square local wines on sale include the rich, red Sagrantino di Montefalco. Just outside the town walls, the church of **Sant'Illuminata** is covered with charming frescoes, the work of the local 16th-century artist

Francesco Melanzio. About 2 km (1 mile) beyond, the prettily situated church of **San Fortunato** is decorated with frescoes by Gozzoli and Tiberio d'Assisi.

Environs
The village in the Vale of Spoleto with the most spectacular setting is **Trevi**. The churches of **San Martino** (16th century), on Passeggiata di San Martino, and **Madonna delle Lacrime** (1487–1522), south of Trevi on the road into the village, contain paintings by Perugino and Tiberio d'Assisi, among others.

Museo Civico di San Francesco
Via Ringhiera Umbra 9. **Tel** 0742 37 95 98. **Open** daily (Nov–Feb: Tue–Sun). **Closed** 1 Jan, 25 Dec.

The Duomo (1253) in Assisi is a fine example of the three-tiered façades found across central Italy *(see p359)*. It has a pointed arch and a row of arcading.

11th-century campanile / Carved figures

Rose window / Rounded portal
Todi's Duomo was begun in the 12th century, but work on its windows and portals continued until the 17th century *(see p363)*.

18th-century rose window
San Michele (c.1195) in Bevagna has a beautiful portal that combines both Romanesque and old Roman fragments *(see p366)*.

9 Spello

Perugia. 8,000. FS i Piazza Matteotti 3 (0742 30 10 09). Wed.

Spello is one of the better known villages in the Vale of Spoleto. It is renowned for a fresco cycle by Pinturicchio in the Cappella Baglioni of the church of **Santa Maria Maggiore** (12th–13th century) on Via Consolare. Executed around 1500, the frescoes depict scenes from the New Testament. Towards the centre of the village is the Gothic church of **Sant'Andrea** (13th century) on Via Cavour. This road becomes Via Garibaldi, which leads to **San Lorenzo**, a Baroque gem of a church dating from the 12th century.

Spello also boasts Roman ruins from the age of Augustus: the **Porta Consolare** at the end of Via Consolare, and the twin-towered **Porta Venere** by Via Torri di Properzio.

The road to Assisi over **Monte Subasio** offers stunning views from the top of the mountain above Spello.

Environs
The least known village in the Vale of Spoleto is **Bevagna**. Like Spello, it sprang to life as a way-station on the Via Flaminia (the Roman road that ran through this part of Umbria). The medieval Piazza Silvestri is the setting for two Romanesque churches.

The lofty peaks of the Monti Sibillini in eastern Umbria

San Silvestro (1195) is the more atmospheric of the pair, thanks to its shadowy interior and ancient crypt, but **San Michele** (late 12th century) has an elegant portal, famed for the little gargoyles on either side. Both churches are the work of Maestro Binello.

10 Monti Sibillini

Macerata. FS Spoleto. Visso. i Piazza del Forno 1, Visso (0737 97 27 11). W sibillini.net

The national park of the Monti Sibillini in eastern Umbria provides the region's wildest and most spectacular scenery. A range 40 km (25 miles) long, the mountains form part of the Apennines, a chain that runs the length of the Italian peninsula. **Monte Vettore** is the loftiest point, and the peninsula's third highest; it stands at

2,476 m (8,123 ft), a great whale-backed peak close to the cave of the mythical sibyl that gave the region its name.

Good maps and trails make this a superb walking area, while drivers can follow hairpin roads to some of Italy's most magical landscapes. Chief of these is the **Piano Grande**, a huge upland plain surrounded by a vast amphitheatre of mountains. Bare but for flocks of sheep and bedraggled haystacks, the plain blazes with wild flowers in spring and with lentils later in the year. The only habitation is **Castelluccio**, a beautiful, neglected mountain village now being restored. It can be reached by road from Norcia and Arquata del Tronto.

Shop front in Norcia displaying the town's varied meats

11 Norcia

Perugia. 4,700. i Piazza San Benedetto (0743 82 49 11). Thu.

The birthplace of St Benedict, Norcia is a robust mountain town and an excellent base for exploring Valnerina and Monti Sibillini. One of Italy's culinary capitals, it is renowned for truffles and for some of Italy's best hams, sausages and salamis. Indeed, the Italian word for a pork butcher's (*norcineria*) derives from the name of the town.

Norcia's main sights are in **Piazza San Benedetto**. On the eastern flank, the church of **San Benedetto** has a 14th-century portal adorned with statues of Benedict and his sister (Santa Scolastica). Legend claims that the church marks the site of Benedict's birth – indeed there are the remains of a 5th-century building in the crypt. However,

Pinturicchio's *Annunciation* (c.1500) in Spello's Santa Maria Maggiore

The 8th-century monastery of San Pietro in Valle, set in the beautiful Valnerina

the church was more likely to have been built over the site of an old Roman temple, since the forum of the Roman colony of Nursia once occupied this spot.

Left of the church stands the **Palazzo Comunale**, a monument to the town's period as a free commune during the 13th and 14th centuries. On the opposite side of the square rises the **Castellina** (1554), a blunt papal fortress designed by Vignola to help impose order on an unruly mountain district. The **Duomo** (1560), to the left of the Castellina, has been ravaged by earthquakes over the centuries. Indeed, Norcia has been the victim of successive earthquakes and its houses are low and heavily buttressed with thick walls to protect them from further

damage. **Sant'Agostino** on Via Anicia features a range of good 16th-century frescoes. A little way beyond, the **Oratorio di Sant'Agostinaccio** in Piazza Palatina contains a superb 17th-century ceiling. Via Umberto shelters the **Edicola** (1354), a strange tabernacle believed to have been carved for a Holy Week procession.

⓬ Valnerina

Perugia. 🚆 Spoleto, then bus. 🛈 Piazza Garibaldi 1, Cascia (0743 711 47).

The Valnerina (Little Valley of the River Nera) curves through a broad swathe of eastern Umbria, draining the mountains around Norcia and the Sibillini before emptying into the Tiber.

It is edged with craggy, tree-covered slopes and dotted with upland villages and fortified hamlets.

The high spot is **San Pietro in Valle**, an idyllically situated monastery in the hills above the village of Colleponte. Founded in the 8th century, it is one of the few surviving memorials to the Lombards, whose central Italian duchy had its capital in Spoleto. The main body of the monastery church dates from this period, as does the high altar. The nave walls are covered in a wealth of 12th-century frescoes. Some of the best Romanesque carvings in Umbria can be found here.

More popular than the monastery are the **Cascate delle Marmore** near Terni, among Europe's highest waterfalls at 165 m (541 ft). Created by the Romans during drainage work, their waters are now diverted to produce hydroelectric power on all but a few special days. You can view the falls from Marmore village or the S209.

🏠 **San Pietro in Valle**
Località Ferentillo, Terni. **Tel** 0744 78 01 29. **Open** daily (Sat & Sun in winter).

🏞 **Cascate delle Marmore**
7 km (4 miles) along S209 Valnerina, Terni. **Open** daily. Visit the website for opening hours. 🌐 **marmorefalls.it**

Piazza San Benedetto and the church of San Benedetto in Norcia

LE MARCHE

Tucked away in a remote corner between the Adriatic Sea and the Apennine mountains, Le Marche (the Marches) is an enchanting rural patchwork of old towns, hill country and long, sandy beaches. In pre-Christian times the area was settled by the Piceni, a tribe eventually assimilated by the Romans.

In the 4th century BC, exiles from Magna Graecia colonized much of the region. The most notable town was Ancona, also the northernmost point of Greek influence on the Italian peninsula. During the early Middle Ages the region marked the edge of the Holy Roman Empire, giving rise to its present name (*march* meant border area).

The region's historical peak was reached in the 15th century under Federico da Montefeltro, whose court at Urbino became one of Europe's leading cultural centres. Much of Urbino's former grandeur survives, particularly in Federico's magnificent Renaissance Palazzo Ducale, now home to a regional art collection. Ascoli Piceno is almost as enchanting as Urbino, its central Piazza del Popolo among the most evocative

old squares in Italy. Smaller towns like San Leo and Urbania and the republic of San Marino also boast fine medieval monuments.

Today probably as many people come to Le Marche for its beaches and towns as for its hilly, unspoilt interior. Especially beautiful are the snowcapped peaks of the Monti Sibillini, situated in magnificent walking and skiing country.

Regional cuisine encompasses the truffles and robust cheeses of the mountains, tender hams and salamis, *olive ascolane* (olives stuffed with meat and herbs) and *brodetto*, fish soup made in several versions up and down the coast. Dry, white Verdicchio is the best known wine, although more unusual names, such as Bianchello del Metauro, are gaining in popularity.

A field of poppies and olive trees in the heart of Le Marche's countryside

◀ A view of the Piazza del Popolo, built in traventine marble, in the town of Ascoli Piceno

Exploring Le Marche

The medieval towns of Urbino and Ascoli Piceno are the highlights of the region, but the rolling hills of the interior contain an abundance of smaller towns and all but undiscovered villages. San Leo, with its dramatic fortress, is one of the best. Most of the countryside is a pretty mixture of woods and remote hills, rising in the west to the majestic Monti Sibillini. Ancona and the attractive town of Pèsaro are the pivotal points of the vast coastline.

Rolling countryside between Loreto and Ascoli Piceno

Rimini

Gabicce Mare

SAN MARINO ❷
San Marino

Cesena

PÈSAR ❸

Novafeltria

❶ SAN LEO

Mercatino Conca

Montecchio

FANC

Sant'Agata Feltria

Montefeltro

Macerata Feltria

Carpegna

Sassocorvaro

Foglia

Mombaroc

Casteldelci

Belforte all' Isauro

Lunano

S423

Calcinelli

S73b

❺ URBINO

S73b

Fossombrone

Mercatello sul Metauro

URBANIA ❻

Fermignano

Mondavio

S73b

Acqualagna

San Lorenzo in Campo

Piobbico

Pergola

Apecchio

Monte Nerone
△1525m

Cagli

Arezzo

Monte Petrano
1162m △

S3

Cantiano

Monte Catria
1701m △

Ar

Key

━━ Motorway

━━ Major road

━━ Secondary road

━━ Minor road

━━ Scenic route

━━ Main railway

━━ Minor railway

━━ International border

━━ Regional border

△ Summit

Sassoferra

Appennino

GROTTE DI FRASASSI ❼

Sar Vittore

Fabriano

S76

Matelic

Umbro - Marchigian

S361

Pioracc

Foligno ↓

Mu

S77

View of Ascoli Piceno, one of the prettiest towns in Le Marche

For additional map symbols *see back flap*

Sights at a Glance

1. San Leo
2. San Marino
3. Pèsaro
4. Fano
5. *Urbino pp374–5*
6. Urbania
7. Grotte di Frasassi
8. Jesi
9. Ancona
10. Conero Peninsula
11. Loreto
12. Ascoli Piceno

The rocky reef near Portonovo on the Conero Peninsula

Getting Around

The A14–E55 provides easy access to the coastal resorts. Dual-carriageway spurs from the A14–E55 lead to Jesi, Urbino and Ascoli Piceno, but north-south roads in the interior can be slow. Bus services are generally good, but in the interior can be infrequent. The railway service along the coast is excellent, with a good service through the heart of the region, though it can be slow.

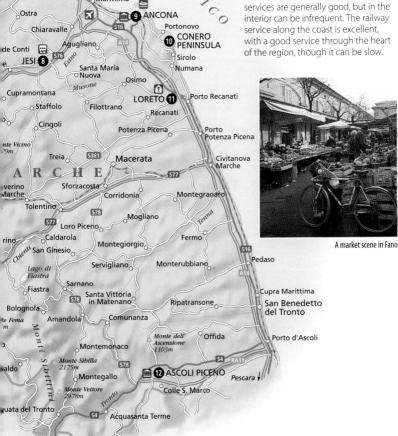

A market scene in Fano

The bell tower of the Duomo rising above the village of San Leo

❶ San Leo

Pèsaro. 🏠 3,000. 🛈 Piazza Dante
Alighieri 14 (0541 91 63 06).
🚌 from Rimini, change at Villanova.
🌐 san-leo.it

Few castles are as impressive as
the great **fortress** that towers
over the village of San Leo.
Dante used this crag-top site
as a model for the landscapes
of *Purgatorio*, while Machiavelli
considered the citadel to be
the finest piece of military
architecture in Italy. Its rocky
ramparts once contained the
Mons Feretrius, a Roman temple
dedicated to Jupiter.

An earlier Roman fortress on
the site became a papal prison
in the 18th century. Its most
famous inmate was the larger-
than-life Conte di Cagliostro.
A swindler, womanizer, necro-
mancer, quack and alchemist,
Cagliostro was imprisoned
for heresy in the 1790s. His cell
was specially built so that its
window faced the village's two
churches. It is still visible, together
with a small picture gallery,
state rooms, and the majestic
Renaissance ramparts, built by
Francesco di Giorgio Martini for

the dukes of Montefeltro in the
15th century.

The captivating village has a
quaint cobbled square with a
superb 9th-century **Pieve** (parish
church). Built partly with stone
from the ruined Mons Feretrius,
the church was raised over the
site of a 6th-century chapel.

Just behind is the 12th-century
Duomo, a fine Romanesque
building with Corinthian capitals
and Roman columns from the
Mons Feretrius. The lid of St Leo's
sarcophagus is in the crypt.
Ancient pagan carvings can be
seen on the wall behind the altar.

🏰 **Fortress**
Via Leopardi. **Tel** 0541 91 63 06.
Open daily. **Closed** lunch Oct–Mar. 🅿️

❷ San Marino

🏠 26,000. 🚌 San Marino
Città (fr Rimini). 🛈 Contrada
Omagnano (0549 88 29 14).
🌐 visitsanmarino.com

Europe's oldest republic, tiny
San Marino was reputedly
founded by St Marinus, a
4th-century monk and stonemason forced to flee the
religious persecution of
the Emperor Diocletian.
With him was St Leo,
founder of the nearby
town of San Leo. Situated
on the slopes of Monte
Titano, the country has
its own mint, stamps,
football team – even its
own 1,000-strong army.
It is also famous for
Formula One racing.
There are no customs

formalities in this country, whose
borders are just 12 km (7 miles)
apart at the widest point. Sadly,
the capital, **San Marino**, is
overrun with visitors and
souvenir stalls through the year.
Garibaldi sought shelter here
after fleeing Venice in 1849 and
is honoured by a monument in
Piazza Garibaldi. The town of
Borgomaggiore lies at the foot
of Monte Titano, with a cable
car to the capital above.

❸ Pèsaro

🏠 110,000. FS 🚌 🛈 Viale Trieste
164 (0721 693 41). 🛒 Tue & 1st Thu
of month.

One of the Adriatic's larger seaside resorts, Pèsaro has managed
to retain a stylish air. Behind the
promenade and the wall of white
stucco hotels is a lively, attractive
medieval area.

The art gallery of the **Musei
Civici** contains Giovanni Bellini's
sumptuous polyptych, the
Coronation of the Virgin (c.1470).
The museum also features
Renaissance ceramics.

The **Museo Archeologico
Oliveriano** presents historical
displays from Roman remains
to Iron Age artifacts from the
necropolis of nearby Novilara.

The best of the town's
churches is **Sant'Agostino** on
Corso XI Settembre, remarkable
for its choir stalls, each a
patchwork of inlaid landscapes
and narrative scenes.

Pèsaro is also a point of musical
pilgrimage because the
composer Gioacchino Rossini
was born here in 1792. His home,
Casa Rossini, contains memorabilia, while his piano and some

Duty-free shop in San Marino

Detail of the *Coronation of the Virgin* by
Bellini (c.1470) in the Musei Civici

original manuscripts lie in the **Conservatorio Rossini**. His operas are performed in **Teatro Rossini** in Piazza Lazzarini during the annual August music festival.

🏛 Musei Civici
Pza Mosca 29. **Tel** 0721 38 72 95.
Open Tue–Sun. **Closed** 1 Jan, 25 Dec. 🖼

🏛 Museo Archeologico Oliveriano
Via Mazza 97. **Tel** 0721 333 44.
Open Mon–Sat. ♿

🏠 Casa Rossini
Via Rossini 34. **Tel** 0721 38 73 57.
Open Tue & Wed am, Thu–Sun. 🖼

🏠 Conservatorio Rossini
Piazza Olivieri 5. **Tel** 0721 336 71.
Open Mon–Sat, but phone first to arrange. **Closed** public hols.

❹ Fano

Pèsaro. 🔼 65,000. 🚉 🚌 🚌 ℹ️ Via Cesare Battisti 10 (0721 80 35 34). 🚍 Wed & Sat.

Ancient Fano stands out from the string of beach resorts south of Pèsaro, thanks to its fine old centre and historic monuments. Named after Fanum Fortunae, a pagan temple to the goddess Fortuna, it became the terminus of the Via Flaminia (an important consular road from Rome) and the largest Roman colony on the Adriatic coast. The **Arco d'Augusto** (AD 2), on Via Arco d'Augusto, is Fano's most significant ancient monument, having narrowly escaped destruction at the hands of Federico da Montefeltro in 1463. He destroyed its upper section while besieging the town as a papal *condottiere*.

The 16th-century **Fontana della Fortuna**, in Piazza XX Settembre, is dedicated to the goddess Fortuna. The large **Palazzo Malatesta** that rises up to its rear was built around 1420 and enlarged in 1544 for Fano's rulers, the Rimini-based Malatesta family. Inside is the small **Museo Civico** and the **Pinacoteca Malatestiana**, with works by Guercino, Guido Reni and the Venetian artist, Michele Giambono.

🏛 Museo Civico and Pinacoteca Malatestiana
Piazza XX Settembre. **Tel** 0721 82 83 62. **Open** Tue–Sun. **Closed** 1 Jan, 25 & 26 Dec. 🖼

Entrance to the Palazzo Ducale in Urbania

❺ Urbino

See pp374–5.

❻ Urbania

Pèsaro. 🔼 7,200. 🚌 ℹ️ Corso Vittorio Emanuele 21 (0722 31 31 40). 🚍 Thu.

Urbania, with its elegant arcaded centre, takes its name from Pope Urban VIII (1623–44), who entertained the notion of converting the old medieval village known as Castel Durante into a model Renaissance town.

Its chief attraction is a monument from an earlier age, the huge **Palazzo Ducale**, built by the dukes of Montefeltro as one of several residential alternatives to the Palazzo Ducale in nearby Urbino. It was begun in the 13th century, and then rebuilt in the 15th and 16th centuries. Beautifully situated alongside the Metauro river, it houses a small art gallery, a modest museum, old maps and globes, and the remnants of Duke Federico's famous library.

🏛 Palazzo Ducale
Palazzo Ducale. **Tel** 0722 31 31 51.
Open Tue–Sun. **Closed** public hols. 🖼

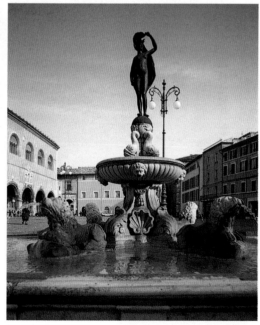
Fontana della Fortuna in Fano

Fresh seafood and fishing boats in the harbour at Ancona

❼ Grotte di Frasassi

Ancona. **Tel** 0732 97 21 66. 🚉 Genga San Vittore Terme. **Open** daily. Guided tours only (70 mins). **Closed** 1 Jan, 10–30 Jan, 4 Dec, 25 Dec. 🚫 📷
W **frasassi.com**

Some of Europe's largest publicly accessible caverns lie in the cave network gouged out by the River Sentino southwest of Jesi. Of the vast network of 18 km (11 miles), an area of about 1,000 m (3,281 ft) is open to the public. The colossal **Grotta del Vento** is large enough to contain Milan cathedral – its ceiling extends to a height of 240 m (787 ft). This cavern has been used for a range of experiments, from sensory deprivation to an exploration of the social consequences of leaving a group of people alone in its depths for long periods.

❽ Jesi

Ancona. 🗺 41,000. 🚉 🚌 🛈 Piazza della Repubblica 11 (0731 53 84 20). 🚢 Wed & Sat. W **comune.jesi.an.it**

Perched on a long, rocky ridge, Jesi lies in the heart of the verdant hill country where Verdicchio is produced. A crisp, white wine, Verdicchio is bottled in unique containers – glass models of the terracotta amphorae once used to export the wine to ancient Greece. There are many vineyards in the surrounding countryside.

Housed in the town's 18th-century Palazzo Pianetti is the **Pinacoteca e Musei Civici**, which contains fine late-period

paintings by Lorenzo Lotto. Almost as alluring as the gallery's paintings, however, is the great central salon – an orgy of Rococo decoration that once formed the centrepiece of the Palazzo Pianetti. The nearby **Palazzo della Signoria** features an interesting collection of archaeological finds, while beyond the old town's Renaissance walls stands the 14th-century church of **San Marco**, known for its collection of well-preserved Giottesque frescoes.

🏛 **Pinacoteca e Musei Civici**
Via XV Settembre. **Tel** 0731 53 83 42.
Open Tue–Sun. 📷

🏛 **Palazzo della Signoria**
Piazza Colocci. **Tel** 0731 53 83 45.
Open Mon–Sat. **Closed** Mon am & Sat pm.

❾ Ancona

🗺 98,000. ✈ 🚉 🚌 ⛴ 🛈 Via della Loggia 50 (071 35 89 91). 🚢 Tue & Fri.
W **turismo.marche.it**

The capital of Le Marche and its largest port (with ferries to and from Greece and Croatia), Ancona dates back to at least the 5th century BC, when it was settled by Greek exiles from Siracusa. Its name derives from *ankon* (Greek for elbow), a reference to the rocky spur that juts into the sea to form the town's fine natural harbour.

Heavy bombing during World War II destroyed much of the medieval town. The 15th-century **Loggia dei Mercanti** (merchants' exchange) on Via della Loggia survives as a monument to the town's medieval heyday.

Just north of the loggia is the Romanesque church of **Santa Maria della Piazza**, with a lovely façade. The nearby **Pinacoteca Comunale F Podesti e Galleria d'Arte Moderna** includes canvases by Titian and Lorenzo Lotto. In the **Museo Archeologico Nazionale delle Marche** there are displays of Greek, Gallic and Roman art. The **Arco di Traiano**, by the harbour, was erected in AD 115 and is one of Italy's better preserved Roman arches.

An impressive cavern in the cave system of the Grotte di Frasassi

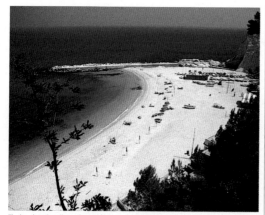

The beach at the village of Sirolo on the Conero Peninsula

🏛 Pinacoteca Comunale F
Podesti e Galleria d'Arte Moderna
Via Pizzecolli 17. **Tel** 071 222 50 41.
Open Tue–Sat daily (Sun pm).
Closed public hols. 🖼 ♿

🏛 Museo Archeologico
Nazionale delle Marche
Via Ferretti 1. **Tel** 071 20 26 02. **Open**
8:30am–7pm Tue–Sun. **Closed**
1 Jan, 1 May, 15 Aug, 25 Dec. 🖼 ♿

⓾ Conero Peninsula

Ancona. 🚉 🚢 Ancona. 🚌 from
Ancona to Sirolo or Numana. 🛈 Via
della Loggia 50, Ancona (071 35 89 91).
🌐 parcodelconero.eu

The beautiful cliff-edged Conero
Peninsula is the only natural
feature to disturb the almost
unbroken line of beaches along
the coast of Le Marche. Easily
accessible from Ancona to the
north, it is a semi-wild area
known for its scenery, its wines
(notably Rosso del Conero) and
for a collection of coves,
beaches and little resorts.

The best of these resorts is
Portonovo, above whose
beach stands **Santa Maria
di Portonovo**, a pretty
11th-century Romanesque
church mentioned by Dante in
Canto XXI of *Paradiso*. **Sirolo** and
Numana are busier and more
commercialized, but you can
escape the crowds by hiking the
flower-swathed slopes of Monte
Conero, which stands at 572 m
(1,877 ft), or by taking a boat trip
to the smaller beaches beyond
the resorts.

⓫ Loreto

Ancona. 🚶 11,000. 🚉 🚌 🛈 Via
Solari 3 (071 97 02 76). 🛒 Fri.

Legend has it that in 1294
the house of the Virgin
Mary (**Santa Casa**)
miraculously
up-rooted itself from
the Holy Land and
was brought by
angels to a laurel
grove *(loreto)* south
of Ancona. Each year
several million
pilgrims visit the **Santa
Casa** in Loreto and its **Basilica**.
Begun in 1468, the latter was
designed and built in part by
Renaissance architects Bramante,
Sansovino and Giuliano da
Sangallo. Its paintings include
works by Luca Signorelli.
The **Museo-Pinacoteca** has
16th-century paintings by
Lorenzo Lotto.

Santa Casa in Loreto

⓵ Basilica and Santa Casa
Piazza Santuario. **Tel** 071 97 01 04.
Open daily. ♿

🏛 Museo-Pinacoteca
Palazzo Apostolico. **Tel** 071 974 71 98.
Open Apr–Oct: Tue–Sun; Nov–Mar:
Fri–Sun. 🖼

⓬ Ascoli Piceno

🚶 54,000. 🚌 🛈 Palazzo Comunale,
Piazza Arringo (0736 25 30 45).
🛒 Wed & Sat.

This alluring town takes its name
from the Piceni, a tribe eventually
conquered by the Romans in

89 BC. The gridiron plan of
Roman Asculum Picenum is
visible in the streets today, but it
is the town's medieval heritage
that attracts most visitors.

The enchanting **Piazza del
Popolo** is dominated by the
13th-century **Palazzo dei
Capitani del Popolo**, whose
façade was designed by Cola
dell'Amatrice, and the church of
San Francesco, a large and
faintly austere Gothic ensemble
built between 1262 and 1549.

Via del Trivio leads north to a
medieval district overlooking the
River Tronto. Along Via Cairoli lies
the 13th-century church of **San
Pietro Martire**. Opposite is the
church of **Santi Vincenzo e
Anastasio** (11th century), with
an ancient crypt built over a
spring said to cure leprosy.

Around Piazza dell'Arringo is
the 12th-century **Duomo**,
spoiled by a Baroque overlay.
Its Cappella del
Sacramento contains
a polyptych by the
15th-century artist
Carlo Crivelli. The
Pinacoteca Civica has
more works by Crivelli
and by Guido Reni,
Titian and Alemanno.
The **Museo
Archeologico** contains Roman,
Piceni and Lombard artifacts.

🏛 Pinacoteca Civica
Palazzo Comunale, Piazza Arringo.
Tel 0736 29 82 13. **Open** Tue–Sun.
🖼 ♿

🏛 Museo Archeologico
Palazzo Panighi, Piazza Arringo.
Tel 0736 25 35 62. **Open** Tue–Sun.
Closed 1 Jan, 1 May, 25 Dec. 🖼 ♿

A view of the medieval town of Ascoli Piceno

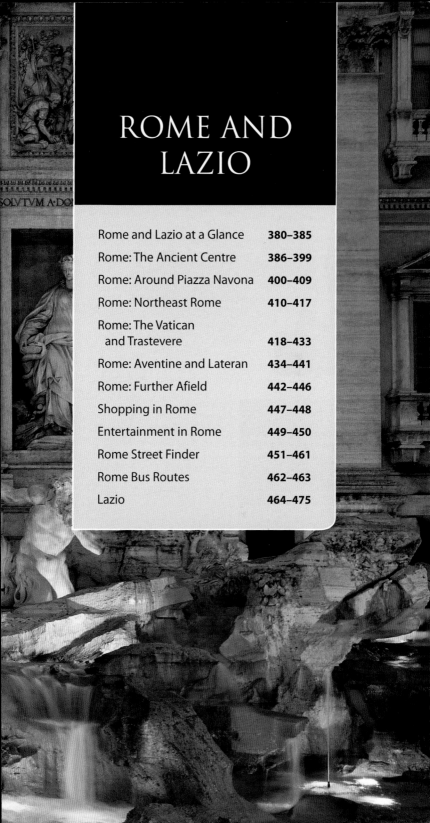

ROME AND LAZIO

Rome and Lazio at a Glance

The first settlements in the region can be traced back to the early Etruscan civilization in northern Lazio. Rome grew to rule a vast empire and, as the empire began to divide, the region became the centre of the Christian world. Artists and architects flocked to work for the popes and their families, notably in the Renaissance and Baroque periods when some magnificent architectural works were created. The legacy of this uninterrupted history can be seen all over the city and the surrounding area.

St Peter's, with its majestic dome by Michelangelo, is a magnificent and sumptuous 16th-century basilica (see pp422–3).

Piazza Navona, flanked by cafés, contains three Baroque fountains, including the colossal Fontana dei Quattro Fiumi, one of Bernini's finest works (see p403).

Santa Maria in Trastevere, probably the first Christian church in Rome, holds some remarkable mosaics such as this detail from Cavallini's *Life of the Virgin* which dates from 1291 (see p432).

PIAZZA NAVONA (See pp40●)

THE VATICAN AND TRASTEVERE (See pp418–33)

Lazio
(See pp464–75)

Viterbo
Rieti
Tarquinia
Magliano Sabina
Civitavecchia
Tivoli
ROME (See main map)
Velletri
Anagni
Sermoneta
Anzio
Terracina
Sperlonga

0 kilometres 15
0 miles 10

Cerveteri is one of the many necropolises left by the Etruscan civilization in northern Lazio. The larger tumulus tombs often contained frescoes and utensils useful for the afterlife (see p470).

◀ The famous Trevi Fountain, designed by Nicola Salvi

The Pantheon, built between AD 118 and 125, is a marvel of Roman engineering with its huge dome hidden behind the Classical portico *(see p408)*.

Locator Map

Santa Maria Maggiore's richly decorated interior blends different architectural styles, such as this baldacchino from the 18th century *(see p417)*.

NORTHEAST ROME
(See pp410–17)

THE ANCIENT CENTRE
(See pp386–99)

San Giovanni in Laterano, the Cathedral of Rome, incorporates the elaborate Corsini Chapel built in the 1730s *(see p440)*.

AVENTINE AND LATERAN
(See pp434–41)

| 0 metres | | 750 |
| 0 yards | | 750 |

The Capitoline Museums have held treasures of the Classical world since the Renaissance, including this colossal 4th-century head of Constantine *(see pp390–91)*.

The Colosseum was constructed in AD 80 by Emperor Vespasian. His aim was to gain popularity by staging deadly gladiatorial combats and wild animal fights for public viewing *(see p397)*.

The Flavours of Rome and Lazio

The countryside of Lazio varies from gently rolling hills to mountains to shimmering coast. Olive groves and vineyards cloak this fertile area, where wild boar roam and many other kinds of game find their way on to the table. But authentic Roman cuisine takes its origins from offal and slow, inventive cooking transforms these traditionally "poor" cuts into flavoursome dishes. Pasta is still the vital ingredient in any meal, and several well-known dishes originate from Rome. Many of the capital's top restaurants are dedicated to fish and seafood and, as home of *la dolce vita*, there is a long tradition of delicious pastries, cakes and ice cream.

Globe artichokes

A stall of Lazio vegetables, fresh from field to market

Traditional Roman cuisine originated in the Testaccio area, near the old slaughterhouse whose butchers (*vaccinari*) were paid partly in meat, generally offal. The "fifth quarter" (*quinto quarto*) included head, trotters, tail, intestines, brain and other bits of the beast not for the squeamish, but which, when cooked slowly and richly flavoured with herbs and spices, became a culinary delight.

These robust dishes, such as the signature dish *coda alla vaccinara* (literally, oxtail in the style of the slaughterhouse butcher) still feature on many menus.

Cucina Romana

Authentic *cucina romana* also has its roots in Jewish cuisine of the atmospheric Ghetto area, whose origins date back over 400 years. Plump,

locally grown globe artichokes are fried whole in olive oil (*carciofi alla giudia*) or served *alla romana*, with oil, garlic and Roman mint. Just as popular are salt cod fillets (*filetti di baccalà*) deep fried, Jewish-style.

Seafood and fish restaurants are among the best in Rome and, while not cheap, many are temples of gastronomy. It was in response to the launch of

Fusilli | Tagliatelle | Spaghettini | Lumaconi | Ravioli | Tortellini | Orecchiette

Just a few of the hundreds of types of pasta available in Italy

Regional Dishes and Specialities

Crispy fried vegetables, especially artichokes and courgette (zucchini) flowers, are often served as an *antipasto*. For the *primo* course, pasta dishes include *bucatini all'amatriciana* – long, thin pasta tubes in a delicious spicy tomato and bacon sauce, sprinkled with grated Pecorino cheese made from tangy ewe's milk. Veal is a great favourite and features on many restaurant menus, look out for *rigatoni alla pajata* (pasta with milk-fed veal intestines). Lamb is also very popular, with dishes such as *abbacchio al forno* (roasted milk-fed lamb) or *alla cacciatore* ("huntsman's style" with anchovy sauce). Offal is very common in traditional *trattorie*, and delicacies include *cervelle* (calves' brains), *ossobuco* (beef shins with marrow jelly), *pajata* (veal intestines) and *trippa* (tripe).

Bruschetta

Gnocchi alla romana Little dumplings, made with semolina flour, are usually served with a tomato or meat *ragù*.

Sumptuous Roman pizzas, sizzling hot from the wood-fired oven

the first McDonald's in Rome in 1986 that the Slow Food Movement started in Piedmont (see p178), but more typical Roman fast food includes bruschetta ("lightly burnt bread" in Roman dialect) rubbed with garlic, sea salt and olive oil and topped with a selection of intense flavours. There's also authentic thin and crispy pizza romana from wood-fired ovens, often served al taglio – by the slice.

Pasta, Pasta

Pasta is still the mainstay of the Roman meal, especially spaghetti. Spaghetti alla carbonara, made with pancetta (cured bacon) or guanciale (pig's cheek), egg yolks and cheese, is a classic Roman dish, as is spaghetti alle vongole, with garlic and clams. At a

conservative estimate, there is one type of pasta for every day of the year, many of which have wonderfully descriptive or poetic names, such as capelli d'angelo (angel's hair) or ziti (bridegrooms) whose shape is best left to the imagination.

An array of mouthwatering gelati in a Roman ice-cream parlour

La Dolce Vita

For those with a taste for "the sweet life", nuts, fruits and versatile ricotta cheese are often combined in mouth-wateringly delicious sweets.

Ice cream is an art form in Rome, where some parlours offer over 100 flavours of homemade gelati. Types vary from the classic crema and frutta to grattachecca (water ice), from semifreddo (a half-frozen sponge pudding, similar to tiramisù in consistency) to granità (ice shavings flavoured with fruit syrups). Glorious gelato is one of the great pleasures here, to be enjoyed at any time of the day – or night.

ON THE MENU

Abbacchio alla cacciatore Lamb cooked with anchovies, garlic, Castelli Romani wine, rosemary and olive oil.

Coda alla vaccinara Oxtail braised in herbs, tomato and celery.

Fave al guanciale Young spring broad (fava) beans simmered in olive oil with pig's cheek and onion.

Filetti di baccalà Salt cod fillets in batter – once a Jewish speciality, now a feature of Roman cuisine.

Spigola alla romana Sea bass with porcini mushrooms (ceps), Roman-style.

Spaghetti alle vongole The classic Italian pasta is here served with a sauce made of baby clams and tomatoes.

Saltimbocca alla romana Veal slices are rolled with prosciutto and sage. Saltimbocca means "jump in the mouth".

Torta di ricotta Ricotta cheese is baked in a tart with sugar, lemon, brandy, eggs and cinnamon.

Understanding Architecture in Rome and Lazio

The architecture of Imperial Rome, a combination of Etruscan and Classical Greek styles, gradually developed new and uniquely Roman forms based on the arch, the vault and the dome. During the early Christian period simple, rectangular basilicas were built, forms which by the 12th century had been incorporated into the stark Romanesque style. The Renaissance, inspired by the example of Florence, saw a return to Classical ideals of simplicity and harmonious proportions, though it was to be in the flamboyance of the 17th-century Baroque that Rome once again found great architectural expression.

The extravagant Baroque style of the Fontana di Trevi, Rome

From Etruscan to Classical Rome

The Podium made the temple more prominent.

A portico was a porch with columns.

The arch became a feature of Roman architecture.

Reliefs were scavenged from earlier monuments.

Three naves divided the interior of the basilica.

Etruscan temples, based on Greek models, inspired early Roman architecture. A front portico was the only entrance.

The Arch of Constantine (AD 315) is typical of triumphant Imperial Roman architecture *(see p393)*. It stands at a colossal 25 m (82 ft).

Early Christian basilicas (4th century) were based on a rectangular floorplan.

From Renaissance to Baroque

Doric columns recall Classical architecture.

Bramante adopted the circular form of ancient temples.

Rustication, massive blocks divided by deep joints, was used for palazzi.

Ionic pilasters lend an air of elegance to the imposing upper storeys.

The elliptical staircase was a typical feature of Mannerist houses.

The Tempietto at San Pietro in Montorio, Rome (1502) is a model of Renaissance architecture: simple and perfectly proportioned *(see p433)*.

Palazzo Farnese at Caprarola, a pentagonal building completed in 1575 *(see p469)*, combines some Mannerist tricks of architecture with the strict geometric proportions characteristic of the Renaissance.

Where to see the Architecture

A walk through the back streets of the centre of Rome will reveal masterpieces of virtually every architectural age. The most ancient treasures are seven obelisks stolen from Egypt. One stands on the back of Bernini's elephant (see p408). Highlights from Ancient Rome include triumphal arches and temples such as the Pantheon (see p408). Romanesque elements survive in the church of San Clemente (see p439), while the Renaissance finds expression in the dome of St Peter's (see pp422–3). Magnificent Baroque treasures dot the entire city, in particular flamboyant fountains that adorn the squares. Outside the city the outstanding sights are the late Renaissance villas such as Caprarola (see p469).

Part of Bernini's elephant supporting an ancient Egyptian obelisk

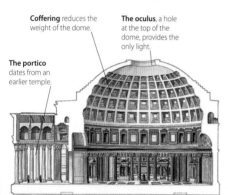

Coffering reduces the weight of the dome.

The oculus, a hole at the top of the dome, provides the only light.

The portico dates from an earlier temple.

The Pantheon (see p408) is one of the cardinal buildings of late Roman architecture. Completed in AD 125, it reveals how the form of the Greek temple was elaborated upon to create a masterpiece of perfect proportions.

Corinthian capitals were decorated with acanthus leaves.

Doric columns had straight capitals.

Ionic columns had scrolled capitals.

The orders of Classical architecture were building styles based on ancient Greek models, identified by the column capitals.

Columns around the altar draw attention away from the prominent lateral axis.

A concave portico reflects the oval body of the church.

The oval floorplan of the Baroque Sant'Andrea al Quirinale (see p415) makes ingenious use of restricted space.

Engaged pillars replace the flat pilasters of the Renaissance.

Deep recesses create complex effects of light and shade.

The Gesù façade (1584) epitomizes Counter-Reformation architecture and has been imitated throughout the Catholic world (see p407).

Two superimposed equilateral triangles form the complex hexagonal floorplan.

Sant'Ivo alla Sapienza's floorplan (1642) favoured grandiose design over Classical form (see p404).

THE ANCIENT CENTRE

The Capitol, the southern summit of the Capitoline Hill, was the symbolic centre of the Roman world and home to the city's three most important temples. These were dedicated to the god Jupiter Optimus Maximus, protector of Rome, Minerva, goddess of wisdom and war, and Juno Moneta, a guardian goddess. Below the Capitol lies the Forum, once the focus of political, social, legal and commercial life; the Imperial Fora, built when Rome's population grew; and the Colosseum, the centre of entertainment. Overlooking the Forum is the Palatine Hill, where Romulus is said to have founded Rome in the 8th century BC, and emperors made their home for over 400 years.

Sights at a Glance

Churches
❸ Santa Maria in Aracoeli

Museums and Galleries
❶ Capitoline Museums pp390–91

Historic Piazzas
❷ Piazza del Campidoglio

Ancient Sites and Buildings
❹ Trajan's Forum and Markets
❺ Forum of Augustus

❼ Forum of Caesar
❽ Roman Forum pp394–5
❾ Colosseum p397
❿ Arch of Constantine
⓫ Palatine pp398–9

0 metres 250
0 yards 250

See also Rome Street Finder maps 3, 6, 7, 10

◀ View of the Colosseum's Ionic and Corinthian tiers

For keys to symbols see back flap

Street-by-Street: The Capitoline Hill

The Capitol, citadel of ancient Rome, was redesigned by Michelangelo in the 16th century. He was responsible for the trapezoid Piazza del Campidoglio as well as the Cordonata, the broad flight of steps leading up to it. The piazza is flanked by Palazzo Nuovo and Palazzo dei Conservatori, housing the Capitoline Museums, with their fine collections of sculpture and paintings. It is also well worth walking behind the museums to the Tarpeian Rock, for a superb view of the Forum lying below.

The Victor Emmanuel Monument was begun in 1885 and inaugurated in 1911 in honour of Victor Emmanuel II, the first king of unified Italy.

San Marco, dedicated to the patron saint of Venice, has splendid 9th-century mosaics in the apse.

PIAZZA VENEZIA

Palazzo Venezia, once the home of Mussolini, now holds a museum of fine and decorative arts. Exhibits include this medieval gilt and enamel angel.

The Aracoeli Steps were completed in 1348 to commemorate the end of the plague.

The Cordonata is presided over by the colossal statues of Castor and Pollux.

VIA DEL TEATRO DI MARCELLO

① ★ Capitoline Museums
The collections of art and ancient sculpture include this statue of the Emperor Marcus Aurelius, a replica of which stands in the centre of the piazza.

Key

— Suggested route

0 metres   75
0 yards   75

❸ **Santa Maria in Aracoeli**
The brick façade hides treasures such as this 15th-century fresco of *The Funeral of San Bernardino* by Pinturicchio.

Locator Map
See Rome Street Finder map 3

❶ Capitoline Museums

See pp390–91.

❷ Piazza del Campidoglio

Map 3 A5. 🚌 40, 63, 70, 81.

When Emperor Charles V announced he was to visit Rome in 1536, Pope Paul III Farnese asked Michelangelo to give the Capitoline a facelift. He redesigned the piazza, renovated the façades of its palaces and built a new flight of steps, the Cordonata. This gently rising ramp is now crowned with the massive statues of Castor and Pollux.

❸ Santa Maria in Aracoeli

Piazza d'Aracoeli. **Map** 3 A5. **Tel** 06 69 76 38 39. 🚌 63, 70, 81. **Open** 9am–6:30pm daily (9:30am–5:30pm in winter).

This church stands on the site of the temple of Juno on the northern summit of the Capitoline Hill, and dates back at least to the 6th century. The church is famous for its ornate gilded ceiling and a very fine series of frescoes by Pinturicchio, dating from the 1480s. They depict scenes from the life of San Bernardino of Siena. The miracle-working *Santo Bambino* figure, stolen in 1994, has been replaced by a replica.

Palazzo Nuovo was made into a public museum in 1734.

Palazzo Senatorio, the splendid Renaissance seat of the city government, is built on the ruins of the ancient Tabularium.

❷ **Piazza del Campidoglio**
Michelangelo designed the geometric paving and the façades of the buildings.

Palazzo dei Conservatori

The Temple of Jupiter, represented on this coin, was dedicated to Jupiter Optimus Maximus, the most important of the Roman gods. He was believed to have the power to protect or destroy the city.

The Tarpeian Rock is a cliff from which traitors were believed to have been thrown to their death in ancient Rome.

Steps to the Capitoline

The marble steps and austere façade of Santa Maria in Aracoeli

❶ Capitoline Museums:
Palazzo Nuovo

A collection of Classical sculptures has been kept on the Capitoline Hill since Pope Sixtus IV donated a group of bronze statues to the city in 1471. Paintings as well as sculpture are now housed in two palaces designed by Michelangelo. The Palazzo Nuovo contains a fine selection of Greek and Roman sculptures. Access is via the Palazzo dei Conservatori *(opposite)*.

Locator Map
See Rome Street Finder map 10

Discobolus
The twisted torso was part of a Greek statue of a discus thrower. An 18th-century sculptor turned him into a wounded warrior.

Mosaic of the Doves
This 1st-century AD naturalistic mosaic once decorated the floor of Hadrian's Villa at Tivoli *(see p472)*.

Alexander Severus as Hunter
In this marble of the 3rd century AD, the emperor's pose is a pastiche of the mythical hero, Perseus, holding up the head of Medusa the Gorgon after he had killed her.

Hall of the Philosophers
The hall contains Roman copies of portrait busts of Greek politicians, scientists and poets. These adorned the homes of wealthy Romans.

Stairs to ground floor

Stairs to first floor

Courtyard

Exit

Dying Galatian
Great compassion is conveyed in this Roman copy of a Greek work of the 3rd century BC.

Key to Floorplan
- Ground floor
- First floor
- Second floor
- Non-exhibition space

Palazzo dei Conservatori

The Palazzo dei Conservatori was the seat of the city's magistrates during the late Middle Ages. Its frescoed halls are still used occasionally for political meetings and the ground floor houses the municipal registry office. While much of the palazzo is given over to sculpture, including fragments of a huge sculpture of Constantine, the art galleries on the second floor hold works by Veronese, Tintoretto, Caravaggio, Van Dyck and Titian.

VISITORS' CHECKLIST

Practical Information
Musei Capitolini, Piazza del Campidoglio.
Map 3 A5. **Tel** 06 06 08.
🌐 **museicapitolini.org**
Open 9am–8pm Tue–Sun.
Closed 1 Jan, 1 May, 25 Dec.
🎫 Entrance ticket is valid for both museums. 🎫 🏛 ♿ 🖥 📷

Transport
🚌 40, 63, 70, 81, 87 and many other routes through Piazza Venezia.

St John the Baptist
Caravaggio's sensual portrait (1595–6) of the young saint caressing a sheep is a highly unorthodox image of Christ's forerunner.

Medusa
This bust by Bernini of the mythological Medusa is in Room 8.

To temporary exhibition space

Second-floor art gallery

Portico of Marcus Aurelius

First floor

Courtyard

Stairs to first floor

Stairs to ground floor

The Rape of the Sabine Women
Pietro da Cortona glamorized the mass abduction of Sabine women by the Romans in this painting of 1629.

Spinario
This is a charming bronze sculpture from the 1st century BC of a boy trying to remove a thorn from his foot.

Main entrance

❹ Trajan's Forum and Markets

Map 3 B4. Trajan's Forum, Via dei Fori Imperiali. **Closed** to the public. Trajan's Markets, Via IV Novembre. **Tel** 06 06 08. **Open** 9am–7pm Tue–Sun (last adm: 6pm). 🚻 🅿 ♿

Trajan began to build his forum in AD 107 to commemorate his final conquest of Dacia (present day Romania) after successful campaigns in AD 101–2 and 105–6. His new forum was the most ambitious yet, with a vast colonnaded open space centring on an equestrian statue of the emperor, a huge basilica, and two big libraries. Dominating the ruins today is **Trajan's Column**, which originally

Trajan's Column

stood between the two libraries. Spiralling up its 30 m (98 ft) high stem are minutely detailed scenes from the Dacian campaigns, beginning with the Romans preparing for war and ending with the Dacians being ousted from their homeland. The subtly modelled reliefs were designed to be seen from viewing platforms on the libraries, and are consequently difficult to interpret from ground level. If you want to examine the scenes in detail there are casts in the Museo della Civiltà Romana (*see p446*). The **market** complex, which is situated directly behind the forum, was begun slightly earlier. Like the forum it was probably designed by Apollodorus of Damascus, and was the ancient Roman equivalent of the

Via Biberatica, the main street through Trajan's Markets

modern shopping centre. There were around 150 shops selling everything from oriental silks and spices to fruit, fresh fish and flowers. It was also here that the *annone*, or corn dole, was distributed. This was a free ration of corn given to Roman men, a practice which was introduced in the Republic by politicians who wanted to buy votes and prevent unrest during periods of famine.

Reconstruction of Trajan's Markets

Cross vaulting

The Main Hall had 12 shops on two storeys. The corn ration was distributed from the upper floor.

Amphorae, used for storing wine and oil, were discovered on the upper corridor.

The terrace has a good view of Trajan's Forum.

Via Biberatica is named after the drinking inns that once lined it.

Staircase

The shops on the ground floor were cool, and probably sold vegetables, fruit and flowers.

Large hall with semi-domed ceiling

5 Forum of Augustus

Piazza del Grillo 1. **Map** 3 B5. **Tel** 06 06 08. 87, 186. **Open** to research scholars by appt.

The Forum of Augustus, which once stretched from the foot of sleazy Suburra to the edge of Caesar's Forum, was built to celebrate Augustus's victory in 41 BC over Brutus and Cassius, the assassins of Julius Caesar. Consequentially, the temple in its centre was dedicated to Mars the Avenger. The temple, with its cracked steps and four Corinthian columns, is easily identified. Originally it had a statue of Mars that looked very like Augustus, but in case anyone failed to notice the resemblance, a colossal statue of the emperor himself was placed against the wall of the Suburra quarter.

19th-century engraving of the Mamertine Prison

6 Mamertine Prison

Clivo Argentario 1. **Map** 3 A5. **Tel** 06 69 89 61. 80, 85, 87, 175, 186. **Open** 9am–7pm daily (to 5pm in winter). every 20 mins.

Below the 16th-century church of San Giuseppe dei Falegnami is a dank dungeon in which, according to Christian legend, St Peter and St Paul were imprisoned. They are said to have caused a spring to bubble up

Podium of the Temple of Mars the Avenger, Forum of Augustus

into the cell, and to have used the water to baptize two prison guards. The prison was in an old cistern with access to the city's main sewer (the Cloaca Maxima). The lower cell was used for executions, and corpses were thrown into the sewer. However, the inmates, who received no food, often died of starvation.

7 Forum of Caesar

Via del Carcere Tulliano. **Map** 3 A5. **Tel** 06 06 08. 80, 85, 87, 175, 186, 810. **Open** to research scholars by appt only.

The first of Rome's Imperial fora was built by Julius Caesar to relieve congestion in the Roman Forum when Rome's population boomed. He spent a fortune – most of it booty from his recent conquest of Gaul – buying up and demolishing houses on the site. Pride of place went to a temple dedicated in 46 BC to Venus Genetrix (Venus the Ancestor) as Caesar claimed to be descended from the goddess. The temple contained statues of Caesar and Cleopatra as well as of Venus, but all that remains today is a platform and three Corinthian columns. The forum was once enclosed by a double colonnade, under which was sheltered a row of shops. However, this burned down in AD 80 and was rebuilt by Domitian and Trajan. The latter also added the Basilica

Argentaria – which became an important financial exchange – as well as shops and a heated public lavatory.

8 Roman Forum

See pp394–5.

9 Colosseum

See p397.

10 Arch of Constantine

Between Via di San Gregorio and Piazza del Colosseo. **Map** 6 F1. 75, 85, 87, 175, 673, 810. 3. Colosseo.

This triumphal arch is one of Imperial Rome's last monuments, built in AD 315, a few years before Constantine moved the capital of the Empire to Byzantium. It was built to celebrate Constantine's victory in AD 312 over his co-emperor Maxentius at the Battle of the Milvian Bridge. Constantine attributed the victory to a dream in which he was told to mark his men's shields with *chi-rho*, the first two Greek letters of Christ's name. Christian tradition prefers a version in which the emperor has a vision of the Cross, mid-battle. There is nothing Christian about the arch: most of the reliefs were from earlier pagan monuments.

11 Palatine

See pp398–9.

The north side of the Arch of Constantine

❽ Roman Forum

In the early Republic, the Forum was a chaotic place, containing food stalls and brothels as well as temples and the Senate House. By the 2nd century BC it was decided that Rome required a more salubrious centre, and the food stores were replaced by business centres and law courts. The Forum remained the ceremonial centre of the city under the Empire, with emperors renovating old buildings and erecting new temples and monuments.

Arch of Septimius Severus
This triumphal arch was erected in AD 203, the 10th anniversary of Emperor Septimius Severus' accession.

The Temple of Antoninus and Faustina is now incorporated into the church of San Lorenzo in Miranda.

Temple of Saturn

The Rostra was the orator's tribune from which speeches were made.

VIA DELLA CURIA

VIA SACRA

The Curia, or ancient Roman Senate House, has been reconstructed.

Basilica Julia
Named after Julius Caesar, who began its construction in 54 BC, this was the seat of the civil magistrates court.

Basilica Aemilia was a meeting hall for business and money exchange.

Temple of Vesta

Temple of Castor and Pollux
Although there has been a temple here since the 5th century BC, the columns and elaborate cornice date from AD 6, when the temple was rebuilt.

0 metres 500
0 yards 500

★ House of the Vestal Virgins
The priestesses who tended the sacred flame in the Temple of Vesta lived here. The house was a large rectangular building around a central garden.

★ Basilica of Constantine and Maxentius

The basilica's three vast barrel vaults are all that remain of the Forum's largest building. Like other basilicas, it was used for the administration of justice and conducting business.

VISITORS' CHECKLIST

Practical Information
Entrance: Via della Salara Vecchia 5/6.
Map 3 B5. **Tel** 06 39 96 77 00.
Open 8:30am–one hour before sunset. **Closed** 1 Jan, 25 Dec.
Includes entry to the Colosseum and the Palatine.

Transport
85, 87, 117, 175, 186, 810.
Colosseo. 3.

The Temple of Romulus, now part of the church of Santi Cosma e Damiano which stands behind it, retains its original 4th-century bronze doors.

Arch of Titus

This arch was erected by Emperor Domitian in AD 81 to commemorate the sack of Jerusalem by his father Vespasian and brother Titus, 13 years earlier.

Antiquarium Forense

This small museum contains finds from the Forum. Exhibits range from Iron Age burial urns to this frieze of Aeneas from the Basilica Aemilia.

VIA DEI FORI IMPERIALI

VIA SACRA

VIA SACRA

Colosseum

Palatine

The Temple of Venus and Rome

was built in AD 135, and was largely designed by Hadrian.

Santa Francesca Romana

The Romanesque bell tower of Santa Francesca Romana towers over one of a number of churches built among the ruins of the Forum.

The Vestal Virgins

The cult of Vesta, the goddess of fire, dates back to at least the 8th century BC. Romulus and Remus were allegedly born of the Vestal priestess Rhea and the god Mars. Six virgins kept the sacred flame of Vesta burning in her circular temple. The girls, who came from noble families, were selected when they were between 6 and 10 years old, and served for 30 years. They had high status and financial security, but were buried alive if they lost their virginity and whipped by the high priest if the sacred flame died out. Although they were permitted to marry after finishing their service, few did so.

Honorary statue of a Vestal Virgin

Exploring the Roman Forum

To appreciate the layout of the Roman Forum before wandering through its confusing patchwork of ruined temples, triumphal arches and basilicas, it is best to view the whole area from the Capitoline Hill above. From there you can make out the more substantial ruins, and the course of the Via Sacra (Sacred Way), the route followed through the Forum by religious and triumphal processions making their way up to the Capitol to give thanks at the Temple of Jupiter *(see p389)*.

Corinthian columns of the Temple of Castor and Pollux

The Main Sights

The first building you come to on entering the Forum is the **Basilica Aemilia**. A rectangular hall built in 179 BC, it was a meeting place for moneylenders, businessmen and tax collectors. Although little more remains of it than a pastel marble pavement fringed with column stumps, you can still find splashes of verdigrised bronze, reputedly the remains of coins which melted when the Visigoths invaded Rome and burnt down the basilica in the 5th century.

Inside the Curia – the stark brick building next to the basilica – are the **Plutei of Trajan**, relief panels commissioned by either Trajan or Hadrian to decorate the Rostra, the public oratory platform. On one panel are piles of books holding tax records, which Trajan had destroyed in order to free citizens from debts. The **Arch of Septimius Severus** is the best preserved of the Forum's monuments. The marble relief panels depict the military triumphs of the emperor in Parthia (modern-day Iran and Iraq) and Arabia. The **Temple of Saturn** was the

focus of the annual Saturnalia celebrations, when, for up to a week in December, schools closed, slaves dined with their masters, presents were exchanged and a fair and market were held.

Soaring above the remains of the Basilica Julia are three delicately fluted columns and a finely carved slab of entablature taken from the **Temple of Castor and Pollux**. This striking relic is dedicated to the twin brothers of Helen of Troy, who were supposed to have appeared at the battle of Lake Regillus in 499 BC, aiding the Romans in their defeat of the Etruscans.

Restored section of Temple of Vesta

The elegant circular **Temple of Vesta** was one of ancient Rome's most sacred shrines and was dedicated to the goddess of the hearth. The flame, kept alive by the Vestal Virgins, symbolized the perpetuity of the state and its extinction prophesied doom for the city. The building was partly reconstructed in 1930, but the circular form goes back to the

Latin mud huts which originally occupied the site. Just behind is the **House of the Vestal Virgins**, the living quarters of the priestess and the Vestals. This enormous complex of 50 rooms was once annexed to the Temple. Best preserved are the rooms overlooking a pretty courtyard, ornamented with statues of Vestals, ponds of waterlilies and rose trees.

On the other side of the Forum lie the impressive remains of the **Basilica of Constantine**. It was begun in AD 308 by Maxentius, and is therefore also known as the Basilica of Maxentius. Constantine completed it after he defeated his rival at the battle of Milvio in AD 312. The stark remains of the huge arches and ceilings give an indication of the original scale and grandeur of the forum's public buildings. Three enormous coffered vaults remain, which originally measured up to 35 m (115 ft) and were faced with marble. The interior walls, which held niches for statues, were also covered with marble below and stucco above. Remains of a spiral staircase which once led to the roof can be found scattered on the ground.

The basilica's apse and hexagonal arches were often used as models by Renaissance architects striving to recreate a Classical symmetry and nobility in their work. They include Michelangelo, who allegedly studied the basilica's architecture when working on the dome of St Peter's.

Central courtyard of the House of the Vestal Virgins

♥ Colosseum

Rome's greatest amphitheatre was commissioned by Emperor
Vespasian in AD 72. Deadly gladiatorial combats and wild
animal fights were staged by emperors and wealthy citizens,
largely to gain popularity. Slaughter was on a huge scale: at
the inaugural games in AD 80, over 9,000 wild animals were
killed. The Colosseum could hold up to 55,000 people, who
were seated according to rank.

VISITORS' CHECKLIST

Practical Information
Piazza del Colosseo.
Map 7 A1.
Tel 06 39 96 77 00. .
Open 8:30am– one hour
before sunset.
Closed 1 Jan, 25 Dec. 🅿
includes entry to the Forum and
Palatine. 🅰 🄲 🄳 🄴 limited.

Transport
🚌 75, 80, 85, 87, 117, 175, 810.
Ⓜ Colosseo. 🚊 3 to Piazza
del Colosseo.

Internal Corridors
These allowed the large and
often unruly crowd to move
freely and be seated quickly.

The Velarium, a huge
sailcloth awning which
sheltered spectators from the
sun, was supported by poles
on the upper storey.

The Colossus of Nero
This gilt bronze statue
from Nero's palace, over
which the Colosseum was
built, may have given the
amphitheatre its name.

Entry routes
and stairs led
to seats at the
various levels.
The emperor and
consul had their
own, separate
entrances.

Corinthian
columns

Ionic
columns

Doric
columns

The arena floor covered
a network of lifts and
cages for wild animals.

Entrances

Doric, Ionic and Corinthian Tiers
The tiers inspired many Renaissance
architects, who also plundered the
building, using its travertine to build
palaces and part of St Peter's.

Roman Gladiators
These were originally soldiers in training.
Their combat became a sport, and slaves,
prisoners of war or criminals were forced to
fight men or wild animals to the death.

Emperor Vespasian
He ordered the Colosseum
to be built on the site
of Nero's palace, to
dissociate himself from
the hated tyrant.

⓫ Palatine

The Palatine, once the residence of emperors and aristocrats, is the most pleasant of Rome's ancient sites. The ruins range from the simple house in which Augustus is thought to have lived, to the Domus Flavia and Domus Augustana, the public and private wings of a luxurious palace built by Domitian.

Cryptoporticus

★ **House of Augustus**
This building boasts four rooms with magnificent frescoes.

★ **House of Livia**
Many of the wall paintings have survived in the private quarters of the house where Augustus is believed to have lived with his wife Livia.

KEY

① **Domus Augustana** was the private home of the emperors.

② **The Huts of Romulus**, indicated by holes left by the supporting posts, were reputedly founded by Romulus in the 9th century BC.

③ **Temple of Cybele, goddess of fertility**

④ **The courtyard** of the Domus Flavia was lined by Domitian with mirror-like marble, so he could spot would-be assassins.

⑤ **The exedra** of the stadium may have housed a balcony.

★ **Domus Flavia**
The courtyard of the Domus Flavia was lavishly paved with coloured marble. The Roman poets praised this villa as the most splendid.

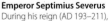

Emperor Septimius Severus
During his reign (AD 193–211), he extended the Domus Augustana and built an impressive bath complex.

Cryptoporticus
This underground gallery, elaborately decorated with stuccoed walls, was built by Emperor Nero.

A History of the Palatine Hill

Romans of the Decadence by Thomas Couture (1815–79)

The Founding of Rome
According to legend the twins Romulus and Remus were brought up on the Palatine by a wolf. Here Romulus, having killed his brother, is said to have founded the village that was destined to become Rome. Traces of mud huts dating back to the 8th century BC have been found on the hill, lending archaeological support to the legend.

The Republic
By the 1st century BC the Palatine was the most desirable address in Rome and home to the leading citizens of the Republic. Its residents, including the erotic poet Catullus and the orator Cicero, were notoriously indulgent, and their villas were magnificent dwellings with doors of ivory, floors of bronze and frescoed walls.

↗ Forum entrance

The Palace of Septimius Severus
This extension of the Domus Augustana projected beyond the hillside, supported on giant arches.

0 metres 75
0 yards 75

Stadium
Part of the Imperial palace, this enclosure may have been used by the emperors as a private garden.

The Empire
Augustus was born on the Palatine in 63 BC, and lived there in a modest house after becoming emperor. The hill was therefore an obvious choice of abode for future emperors. Domitian's ambitious house, the Domus Flavia (1st century AD), and its private quarters, the Domus Augustana, remained the official residence of future emperors (who were referred to as *Augustus*) for more than 300 years.

AROUND PIAZZA NAVONA

The area around Piazza Navona, known as the *centro storico*, has been inhabited for at least 2,000 years. Piazza Navona stands above an ancient stadium; the Pantheon has been a temple since AD 27; and the Theatre of Marcellus in the Ghetto has been converted into exclusive flats. The area's heyday began in the 15th century, when the papacy returned to Rome. Throughout the Renaissance and Baroque eras princes, popes and cardinals settled here, as did the artists and artisans they commissioned to build and adorn lavish palaces, churches and fountains.

Sights at a Glance

Churches and Temples

2 Sant'Ivo alla Sapienza
3 San Luigi dei Francesi
5 Santa Maria della Pace
6 Chiesa Nuova
13 Gesù
15 Santa Maria sopra Minerva
17 Sant'Ignazio di Loyola
20 La Maddalena

Ancient Sites and Buildings

4 Palazzo Altemps
7 Palazzo della Cancelleria
9 Palazzo Farnese
12 Area Sacra di Largo Argentina
16 Pantheon
22 Historic Building

Museums and Galleries

10 Palazzo Spada
14 Palazzo Doria Pamphilj

Historic Piazzas and Areas

1 Piazza Navona
8 Campo de' Fiori
11 Ghetto and Tiber Island
18 Piazza Colonna
19 Piazza di Montecitorio

◀ The starry blue vault of the nave in Santa Maria sopra Minerva, Piazza della Minerva

For keys to symbols *see back flap*

Street-by-Street: Around Piazza Navona

No other piazza in Rome can rival the theatricality of
Piazza Navona. The luxurious cafés are the social centre
of the city, and day and night there is always something
going on in the pedestrian area around the three
flamboyant Baroque fountains. The Baroque is also
represented in many of the area's churches.
To discover an older Rome, walk along
Via del Governo Vecchio to admire
the façades of Renaissance
buildings, browse in the
fascinating antiques shops
and lunch in one of the
many trattorias.

The Torre dell'Orologio by
Borromini (1648) formed part of
the Oratorio dei Filippini.

❻ Chiesa Nuova
This church was rebuilt in
1575 for the order founded
by San Filippo Neri.

The Vatican

VIA DEL CORALLO

VIA DEL GOVERNO VECCHIO

VIA DI PARIONE

VIA DI SANTA

**At the
Oratorio
dei Filippini**
(1637) biblical
stories were
sung and the
congregation
responded with a
chorus: the origin
of the oratorio.

**Via del Governo
Vecchio** preserves a
large number of fine
Renaissance houses.

CORSO VITTORIO EMANUELE II

PIAZZA DI
PASQUINO

❺ Santa Maria della Pace
This Renaissance church has
frescoes of the Four Sibyls by
Raphael and a refined
courtyard by Bramante.
The Baroque
portico is by
Pietro da Cortona.

Pasquino is a 3rd-century BC
Hellenistic statue of Menelaus.
Romans have been hanging
satirical verses at its feet since
the 16th century.

Palazzo
Pamphilj

Fontana del
Moro

Campo de'
Fiori

Palazzo Braschi, a late 18th-century
building designed by Cosimo Morelli, has a
splendid balcony overlooking the piazza.

0 metres	75
0 yards	75

Key

— Suggested route

Sant'Andrea della Valle, begun
in 1591, has a flamboyant
Baroque façade flanked by
angels with outstretched wings
by Ercole Ferrata. The church is
the setting of the first act of
Puccini's *Tosca*.

Sant'Agnese in Agone

by Borromini (1657) is allegedly built on the site where, in AD 304, the young St Agnes was exposed naked to force her to renounce her faith.

Locator Map
See Rome Street Finder map 2

❸ San Luigi dei Francesi

This church, which was completed in 1589, is best known for three paintings by Caravaggio.

Fontana dei Quattro Fiumi

Palazzo Madama, the seat of the Italian Senate, was originally built for the Medici family in the 16th century, on the site of one of their banks.

❷ Sant'Ivo alla Sapienza

This tiny domed church is one of Borromini's most original creations. He worked on it between 1642 and 1650.

❶ ★ Piazza Navona
The piazza is lined with palaces and pavement cafés, and punctuated by flamboyant Baroque fountains.

Largo di Torre Argentina

❶ Piazza Navona

Map 2 E4. 🚌 30, 70, 81, 87, 130, 186, 492, 628.

Rome's most beautiful Baroque piazza follows the shape of a 1st-century AD stadium built by Domitian, which was used for athletic contests *(agones)*, chariot races and other sports. Traces of the stadium are still visible below the church of Sant'Agnese in Agone, which is dedicated to a virgin martyred on the site for refusing to marry a pagan.

The piazza began to take on its present appearance in the 17th century, when Pope Innocent X, whose family palazzo was on the piazza, commissioned a new church, palace and fountain. The fountain, the Fontana dei Quattro Fiumi, is Bernini's most magnificent, with statues of the four great rivers of the world at that time (the Nile, the Plate, the Ganges and the Danube) sitting on rocks below an obelisk. Bernini also designed the muscle-bound Moor in the Fontana del Moro, though the present statue is a copy. Until the 19th century, the piazza was flooded in August by stopping the fountain outlets. The rich would splash around in carriages, while street urchins paddled. Even today the piazza remains the social centre of the city.

Symbolic figure of the River Nile on Bernini's Fontana dei Quattro Fiumi

❷ Sant'Ivo alla Sapienza

Corso del Rinascimento 40. **Map** 2 F4.
Tel 06 361 25 62. ⊞ 30, 70, 81, 87,
116, 186, 492, 628. **Open** 9am–noon
Sun. ♿

Hidden in the courtyard of
Palazzo della Sapienza, seat of
the old University of Rome,
Sant'Ivo's spiral belfry is
nevertheless a distinctive
landmark on Rome's skyline.
Built by Borromini in 1642–60,
the church is astonishingly
complex, an ingenious
combination of concave and
convex surfaces. The work
spanned the reigns of three
popes, and incorporated in the
design are their emblems:
Urban VIII's bee, Innocent X's
dove and olive branch and the
star and hills of Alexander VII.

❸ San Luigi dei Francesi

Piazza di San Luigi de' Francesi 5.
Map 2 F4 & 12 D2. **Tel** 06 68 82 71.
⊞ 70, 81, 87, 116, 186, 492, 628.
Open 10am 12:30pm, 3–7pm daily.
Closed Thu pm. 📷

The French national church
in Rome, San Luigi is a
16th-century building, best
known for three magnificent
canvases by Caravaggio in the
Cerasi chapel. Painted between
1597 and 1602, these were
Caravaggio's first significant
religious works: *The Calling of St
Matthew*, *Martyrdom of St
Matthew* and *St Matthew and the
Angel*. The first version of this
last was initially rejected
because it depicted the saint
as an old man with dirty feet.

Detail from Caravaggio's *The Calling of St Matthew*
(1597–1602) in San Luigi dei Francesi

Side relief of the Ludovisi Throne, on display
in the Palazzo Altemps

❹ Palazzo Altemps

Via di Sant'Apollinare 46. **Map** 2 E3.
Tel 06 39 96 77 00. ⊞ 70, 81, 87, 115,
280, 628. **Open** 9am–7:45pm Tue–
Sun. **Closed** 1 Jan, 25 Dec. 📷 ✓
📷 ♿

An extraordinary collection of
Classical sculpture is housed in
this branch of the Museo
Nazionale Romano (*see p416*).
Restored as a museum during
the 1990s, the palazzo
was originally built
for Girolamo
Riario, nephew of
Pope Sixtus IV in
1480. In the
popular uprising
that followed the
pope's death in
1484, the building
was sacked and
Girolamo fled the
city. In 1568 Cardi-
nal Marco Sittico
Altemps bought
the palazzo, it was
renovated in the
1570s by Martino
Longhi the
Elder, who
added the
obelisk-
crowned belvedere
and marble unicorn.
The Altemps family
were avid collectors; the courtyard
and its staircase are lined with
ancient sculptures,
which complement
the Ludovisi sculp-
tures. One of the
highlights is the
marble statue
Galata's Suicide, a
copy of the original,
in the Salone del
Camino. On the first
floor is the Greek,
5th-century BC
Ludovisi Throne,
a carved relief
shows Aphrodite.

Galata's Suicide in the
Palazzo Altemps

❺ Santa Maria della Pace

Vicolo del Arco della Pace 5. **Map** 2 E3.
Tel 06 686 11 56. ⊞ 70, 81, 87, 116,
492, 628. **Open** 9am–noon Mon, Wed,
Sat. ♿

Named by Pope Sixtus IV to
celebrate the peace he hoped
to bring to Italy, this church
dates from the 1480s and
contains a beautiful fresco
by Raphael. Bramante's
refined cloister was added in
1504, while the façade
was designed in 1656 by Pietro
da Cortona.

❻ Chiesa Nuova

Piazza della Chiesa Nuova.
Map 2 E4. **Tel** 06 687 52 89. ⊞ 46,
64. **Open** 7:30am–noon, 4:30–7:30pm
daily. ♿

San Filippo Neri commissioned
this church in 1575 to replace
the dilapidated one given to his
Order by Pope Gregory XIII.
Neri required his
followers to humble
themselves, and
set aristocratic
young men to
work as labourers on
the church.
Against his wishes,
the nave, apse and
dome were richly
frescoed after his
death by Pietro
da Cortona.
There are three
paintings by
Rubens around the
altar. The first versions
were rejected, so
Rubens repainted them on slate,
placing the originals above his
mother's tomb.

❼ Palazzo della Cancelleria

Piazza della Cancelleria. **Map** 2 E4.
Tel 06 69 88 75 66. ⊞ 46, 62, 64, 116,
916. **Open** 7:30am–2pm, 4pm–8pm.
Closed Sun.

A supreme example of the
confident delicacy of early
Renaissance architecture, this
palazzo was begun in 1485, and
was allegedly financed by the

gambling proceeds of Raffaele Riario, a nephew of Pope Sixtus I. In 1478 Riario was involved in the Pazzi conspiracy against the Medici, and when Giovanni de' Medici became Pope Leo XIII in 1513, he took belated revenge, seizing the palace and turning it into the papal chancellery.

❽ Campo de' Fiori

Map 2 E4. 🚌 116 & routes to Corso Vittorio Emanuele II.

Campo de' Fiori (field of flowers) was one of the liveliest and roughest areas of medieval and Renaissance Rome. Cardinals and nobles mingled with fishmongers and foreigners in the piazza's market; Caravaggio killed his opponent after losing a game of tennis on the square; and the goldsmith Cellini murdered a business rival nearby. Today, the area continues to be a hub of secular activity. The colourful market, trattorias and down-to-earth bars retain the original animated atmosphere.

In the Renaissance the piazza was surrounded by inns, many of which were owned by the 15th-century courtesan Vannozza Catanei, mistress of Pope Alexander VI.

The square was also a place of execution. The statue in its centre is the philosopher Giordano Bruno, burned at the

Tiber Island, with Ponte Cestio, built in 46 BC, linking it to Trastevere

stake for heresy on this spot in 1600 for suggesting the earth moved around the sun.

❾ Palazzo Farnese

Piazza Farnese. **Map** 2 E5. **Tel** 06 68 60 11. 🚌 23, 116, 280 & routes to Corso Vittorio Emanuele II. 📷 only (3pm, 4pm & 5pm on Mon, Wed & Fri. Book in advance). 🌐 www.ambafrance.org

Originally constructed for Cardinal Alessandro Farnese, who became Pope Paul III in 1534, this palazzo was started by Antonio da Sangallo the Younger, and continued after his death by Michelangelo, who created the cornice on the façade and the courtyard's third storey.

The palace, now the French Embassy, is closed to the public, but when the chandeliers are lit at night you may be able to glimpse the ceiling of the Galleria, an illusionistic masterpiece (1597–1603) by Annibale Carracci based on Ovid's *Metamorphoses*.

❿ Palazzo Spada

Piazza Capo di Ferro 13. **Map** 2 E5. **Tel** 06 686 11 58 (Palazzo) and 06 683 24 09 (Galleria). 🚌 23, 116, 280 & routes to Largo di Torre Argentina. **Open** 8:30am–7:30pm Tue–Sun (last adm: 7pm). **Closed** 1 Jan, 25 Dec. 🔲🔲🔲🔲🔲

A stucco extravaganza studded with reliefs of illustrious Romans, this palazzo was built in 1550, but bought in 1637 by Cardinal Bernardino Spada. A keen patron of the arts, he commissioned Borromini to create an illusionistic tunnel that appears four times longer than it is. The cardinal's art collection, in the Galleria Spada, includes works by Guercino, Dürer and Artemisia Gentileschi.

⓫ Ghetto and Tiber Island

Map 2 F5 & 6 D1. 🚌 23, 63, 280, 780 and routes to Largo di Torre Argentina.

The first Jews came to Rome as traders in the 2nd century BC and were greatly appreciated for their financial and medical skills during the Roman Empire. Persecution began in the 16th century, when Pope Paul IV forced all of the Jews to live within a walled enclosure, an area later to form the hub of the present-day Ghetto.

Today Via del Portico d'Ottavia, the district's main street, leads to Rome's central synagogue, passing restaurants and shops selling Roman Jewish food. Ponte Fabricio links the Ghetto with Tiber Island, a centre of healing since 293 BC when a Temple to Aesculapius was founded. The island is now home to a hospital.

Fruit stalls at Campo de' Fiori's lively morning market

Street-by-Street: Around the Pantheon

The maze of narrow streets around the Pantheon is a mixture of lively restaurants and cafés, and some of Rome's finest sights. This is also the city's financial and political district, home to Parliament, government offices and the stock exchange. The Pantheon itself, with its awe-inspiring domed interior, has long been a symbol of the city.

🄱 Sant'Ignazio di Loyola
This church has a superb illusionistic ceiling painted by Andrea Pozzo in 1685.

The Temple of Hadrian now forms the façade of the Stock Exchange.

Piazza della Minerva centres on Bernini's outlandish sculpture of an elephant supporting an Egyptian obelisk.

🄳 ★ Palazzo Doria Pamphilj
Among the masterpieces in the art gallery of this vast family palazzo is this Salomé by Titian painted in 1516 .

Via della Gatta

PIAZZA DI SANT'IGNAZIO

VIA DI SANT'IGNAZIO

PIAZZA DEL COLLEGIO ROMANO

VIA DELLA GATTA

VIA DEL SEMINARIO

PIAZZA DELLA ROTONDA

PIAZZA DELLA MINERVA

VIA DEL PIE DI MARMO

VIA DEL GESÙ

VIA DEL PLEBISC...

The Pie' di Marmo

Santa Maria Sopra Minerva

Palazzo Altieri incorporates the hovel of an old woman who refused to allow her house to be demolished when this palace was built in the 17th century.

🄱 ★ Pantheon
The Pantheon, a temple to "all the gods", is Rome's best-preserved ancient building. It was built in the 1st century AD, probably to a design by Emperor Hadrian.

🄱 Gesù
Built in the late 16th century, this Jesuit church served as a model for the Order's churches throughout the world.

Locator Map
See Rome Street Finder map 3

Via della Gatta is overlooked by this marble statue of a cat *(gatta)* that gives the narrow street its name.

The Pie' di Marmo, an ancient marble foot, is probably part of a giant statue from the temple to the Egyptian goddess Isis.

⑮ Santa Maria sopra Minerva
This is one of Rome's few Gothic churches, with works by Michelangelo, Bernini and Filippino Lippi.

Key

— Suggested route

0 metres   75
0 yards   75

⑫ Area Sacra di Largo Argentina

Largo di Torre Argentina. **Map** 2 F5. 🚌 40, 46, 62, 64, 70, 81, 87, 186, 492. **Closed** to the public.

The remains of four temples were discovered in the 1920s at the centre of Largo Argentina, now a busy bus terminus and traffic junction. They date from the era of the Republic, and are among the oldest found in Rome. For the purpose of identification, they are known as A, B, C and D. The oldest (temple C) dates from the early 3rd century BC. It was placed on a high platform preceded by an altar and is typical of Italic temple plans as opposed to the Greek model. Temple A is from the 3rd century BC, but in medieval times the small church of San Nicola ai Cesarini was built over its podium and the remains of its two apses are still visible. The column stumps to the north belonged to a great portico, known as the Hecatostylum (portico of 100 columns). In Imperial times two marble latrines were built here – the remains of one are visible behind temple A. Behind temples B and C, near Via di Torre Argentina, are the remains of a great platform of tufa blocks. These have been identified as part of the Curia of Pompey, a rectangular building where the Senate met, and where Julius Caesar was assassinated by Brutus, Cassius and their followers on 15 March 44 BC.

Area Sacra, with the ruins of circular temple B

Baroque *Triumph of Faith over Idolatry* by Pierre Legros, Gesù

⑬ Gesù

Piazza del Gesù. **Map** 3 A4. **Tel** 06 69 70 01. 🚌 H, 46, 62, 64, 70, 81, 87, 186, 492, 628 & other routes. **Open** 7am–12:30pm, 4–7:45pm daily.

Built between 1568 and 1584, the Gesù was Rome's first Jesuit church. The Jesuit order was founded in Rome in 1537 by a Basque soldier, Ignatius Loyola, who became a Christian after he was wounded in battle. The order was austere, intellectual and heavily engaged in missionary activity and religious wars.

The much-imitated design of the Gesù typifies Counter-Reformation architecture, with a large nave with side pulpits for preaching to crowds, and a main altar as the centrepiece for the mass. The illusionistic decoration on the nave ceiling and dome was added by Il Baciccia in the 17th century.

The nave depicts the *Triumph of the Name of Jesus* and its message is clear: faithful, Catholic worshippers will be joyfully uplifted to heaven while Protestants and heretics are flung into the fires of hell. The message is reiterated in the Cappella di Sant'Ignazio, a rich display of lapis lazuli, serpentine, silver and gold. The Baroque marble by Legros, *Triumph of Faith over Idolatry*, shows a female "Religion" trampling on the head of the serpent Idolatry, while in Théudon's *Barbarians Adoring the Faith*, an angel aims a kick towards a decrepit old barbarian couple entangled with a snake.

⓮ Palazzo Doria Pamphilj

Via del Corso 305. **Map** 3 A4.
Tel 06 679 73 23. 🚌 64, 81, 119, 492.
Open 9am–7pm daily. **Closed** 1 Jan,
Easter Sun, 1 May, 25 Dec. 🦽 🅱️ 🖵
🎧 📷 by appt for private apartments.

Palazzo Doria Pamphilj is a vast edifice whose oldest parts date from 1435. When the Pamphilj family took over in 1647 they built a new wing, a splendid chapel and a theatre.

The family art collection has over 400 paintings dating from the 15th–18th centuries, including a portrait of Pope Innocent X by Velázquez and works by Titian, Guercino, Caravaggio and Claude Lorrain. The opulent rooms of the private apartments retain many of their original furnishings, including Brussels and Gobelins tapestries, Murano chandeliers and a gilded crib.

Velázquez's *Pope Innocent X* (1650)

⓯ Santa Maria sopra Minerva

Piazza della Minerva 42. **Map** 2 F4.
Tel 06 679 39 26. 🚌 116 & many
other routes. **Open** 7:10am–7pm
Mon–Sat, 8am–noon, 2–7pm Sun.

One of Rome's rare Gothic buildings, this church was built in the 13th century over what were thought to be the ruins of a Temple of Minerva. It was a stronghold of the Dominicans, who produced some of the Church's most infamous inquisitors, and who tried the scientist Galileo in the adjoining monastery.

Inside, the church has a superb collection of art and sculpture, ranging from 13th-century Cosmatesque tombs to a bust

Interior of the Pantheon, burial place for Italian monarchs

by Bernini. Highlights include Antoniazzo Romano's *Annunciation* featuring Cardinal Juan de Torquemada, uncle of the vicious Spanish Inquisitor, and the Carafa Chapel's frescoes by Filippino Lippi.

In the Aldobrandini Chapel are the tombs of the 16th-century Medici popes, Leo X and his cousin Clement VII, and near the steps of the choir is a stocky *Risen Christ*, begun by Michelangelo.

The church also contains the tombs of many famous Italians, such as St Catherine of Siena who died in 1380 and Fra Angelico, the Dominican friar and painter, who died in 1455. Outside, Bernini's spectacular sculpture of an elephant holds an obelisk on its back.

Simple vaulted nave of Santa Maria sopra Minerva

⓰ Pantheon

Piazza della Rotonda. **Map** 2 F4.
Tel 06 68 30 02 30. 🚌 116 & many
routes. **Open** 8:30am–7:30pm daily
(9am–6pm Sun). **Closed** 1 Jan, 1 May,
25 Dec. 🦽

The Pantheon, the Roman "temple of all the gods", is the most extraordinary and best preserved ancient building in Rome. The first temple on the site was a conventional rectangular affair erected by Agrippa between 27 and 25 BC; the present structure was built and possibly designed by Emperor Hadrian in AD 118.

The temple is fronted by a massive pedimented portico screening what appears to be a cylinder fused to a shallow dome. Only from the inside can the true scale and beauty of this building be appreciated: a vast hemispherical dome equal in radius to the height of the cylinder giving perfectly harmonious proportions to the building. A circular opening, the *oculus*, lets in the only light.

In the 7th century Christians claimed to be plagued by demons as they passed by, and permission was given to make the Pantheon a church. Today it is lined with tombs, ranging from a restrained monument to Raphael to huge marble and porphyry sarcophagi holding the bodies of Italian monarchs.

⓱ Sant'Ignazio di Loyola

Piazza di Sant'Ignazio. **Map** 2 F4.
Tel 06 679 44 06. 🚌 117, 119, 492.
Open 7:30am–12:30pm, 3pm–7:20pm
daily (from 9am Sun). 🚻

This church was built by Pope
Gregory XV in 1626 in honour
of St Ignatius of Loyola, founder
of the Society of Jesus (Jesuits)
and the man who most
embodied the zeal of the
Counter-Reformation.

Together with the Gesù (see
p407), Sant'Ignazio forms the
nucleus of the Jesuit area of
Rome. It is one of the most
extravagant Baroque churches
and its vast interior is plated with
precious stones, marble, stucco
and gilt, creating a thrilling
sense of theatre. The church has
a Latin-cross plan, with an apse
and many side chapels. A
cupola was plan–ned but never
built, as the nuns from a nearby
convent objected that it would
obscure the view from their roof
garden. Instead the space was
filled by a perspective painting
of a dome on a flat disc.

Even more striking is the
illusionistic ceiling created by
the Jesuit artist Andrea Pozzo
in 1685, a propagandist extravaganza extolling the success of
Jesuit missionaries throughout
the world. Above four women,
representing Asia, Europe,
America and Africa, lithe angels
and beautiful youths are sucked
into a heaven of fluffy clouds.

Detail from the AD 180 Column of Marcus
Aurelius, Piazza Colonna

⓲ Piazza Colonna

Map 3 A3. 🚌 116, 117, 492.

Home to Palazzo Chigi, official
residence of the prime minister,
Piazza Colonna is dominated by
and named after the majestic
Column of Marcus Aurelius. This
was erected after the death of
Marcus Aurelius in AD 180 to
commemorate his victories over
the barbarian tribes of the
Danube. It is clearly an imitation
of Trajan's Column (see p392)
with scenes from the emperor's
wars spiralling in reliefs up the
column. The 80-year lapse
between the two works
produced a great artistic
change: the wars of Marcus
Aurelius are rendered with
simplified pictures in stronger
relief, sacrificing Classical
proportions for the sake of
clarity and immediacy.

⓳ Piazza di Montecitorio

Map 2 F3. Palazzo di Montecitorio
Tel 06 676 01. 🚌 116. **Open**
10am–3:30pm 1st Sun of month.

The obelisk in the centre of
Piazza di Montecitorio formed
the spine of a giant sundial
brought back from Egypt by
Augustus. It vanished in the 9th
century, and was rediscovered
under medieval houses during
the reign of Julius II (1503–13).

The piazza is dominated by
the rugged façade of Palazzo
di Montecitorio, designed by
Bernini and completed in 1697,
after his death, by Carlo
Fontana. It has been the seat of
Italy's Chamber of Deputies
since the late 19th century.

La Maddalena's stuccoed façade

⓴ La Maddalena

Piazza della Maddalena. **Map** 2 F3.
Tel 06 899 281. 🚌 116 & many other
routes. **Open** 8:30–11:30am,
5–6:30pm daily (Sat am only).

Situated in a small piazza near
the Pantheon, the Maddalena's
Rococo façade, built in 1735,
epitomizes the love of light and
movement of the late Baroque.
The façade has been restored,
despite the protests of Neo-
Classicists who dismissed its
painted stucco as icing sugar.

The diminutive dimensions
of the church did not deter
17th- and 18th-century
decorators from filling the
interior with paintings and
ornaments from the floor to
the top of the elegant cupola.

Baroque illusionistic ceiling by Andrea Pozzo in Sant'Ignazio di Loyola

NORTHEAST ROME

This area stretches from the exclusive shopping streets around Piazza di Spagna to the Esquiline Hill, once bourgeois, but now a poor, often seedy area full of early Christian churches. The Piazza di Spagna and Piazza del Popolo district grew up in the 16th century, when the increase in the influx of pilgrims was such that a road was built to channel them as quickly as possible to the Vatican. About the same time, the Quirinal Hill became the site of a papal palace. When Rome became capital of Italy in 1870, Via Veneto became a lavish residential area, and the Esquiline was covered with apartments for the new civil servants.

Sights at a Glance

Churches
3 Santa Maria del Popolo
7 Sant'Andrea al Quirinale
8 San Carlo alle Quattro Fontane
10 Santa Maria della Concezione
11 Santa Maria della Vittoria
13 Santa Prassede
14 San Pietro in Vincoli
15 Santa Maria Maggiore

Museums and Galleries
9 Galleria Nazionale di Arte Antica: Palazzo Barberini
12 Museo Nazionale Romano Palazzo Massimo

Ancient Sites and Buildings
4 Ara Pacis
5 Mausoleum of Augustus

Historic Buildings
2 Villa Medici

Piazzas and Fountains
1 Piazza di Spagna and the Spanish Steps
6 Trevi Fountain

0 metres 250
0 yards   250

See also Rome Street Finder maps 2, 3, 4, 7

◀ The Spanish Steps leading up to the church of the Santissima Trinità dei Monti

For keys to symbols *see back flap*

Street-by-Street: Piazza di Spagna

The network of narrow streets around Piazza di Spagna forms one of the most exclusive areas in Rome, drawing droves of tourists and Romans to the elegant shops around Via Condotti. The square and its nearby coffee houses have long attracted those who want to see and be seen. In the 18th century the area was full of hotels for frivolous aristocrats doing the Grand Tour, as well as artists, writers and composers, who took the city's history and culture more seriously.

Caffé Greco is an 18th-century café once frequented by writers and musicians such as Keats, Goethe, Byron, Liszt and Wagner.

Trinità dei Monti is a 16th-century church at the top of the Spanish Steps. There are fine views of Rome from the stairway.

Babington's Tea Rooms, founded by two English spinsters in 1896, still serves English teas.

VIALE TRINITA DEI MONTI

Spagna

PIAZZA DI SPAGNA

VIA CONDOTTI

PIAZZA MIGNANELLI

VIA DI PROPAGANDA

The Keats-Shelley Memorial House, where the poet Keats died in 1821, is now a museum honouring English Romantic poets.

1 ★ Piazza di Spagna and the Spanish Steps
These have been at the heart of tourist Rome since the 18th century.

The Colonna dell' Immacolat, erected in 1857, commemorates Pope Pius IX's doctrine of the Immaculate Conception.

The Collegio di Propaganda Fide, built for the Jesuits in 1662, has a superb façade designed by Francesco Borromini.

Locator Map
See Rome Street Finder map 3

Sant'Andrea delle Fratte
contains two angels by Bernini
(1669) made for Ponte
Sant'Angelo, which Pope
Clement X thought too
lovely to expose to
the weather.

0 metres   75

0 yards   75

Key

— Suggested route

The Fontana della Barcaccia at the foot of
the Spanish Steps

❶ Piazza di Spagna and the Spanish Steps

Map 3 A2. 🚌 116, 117. Ⓜ Spagna.

Shaped like a crooked bow tie,
and surrounded by muted,
shuttered façades, Piazza di
Spagna is crowded all day and
(in summer) most of the night.
The most famous square in
Rome, it takes its name from the
Palazzo di Spagna, built in the
17th century to house the
Spanish Embassy to the Holy See.

The piazza has long been the
haunt of foreign visitors and
expatriates. In the 18th and 19th
centuries the square stood at
the heart of the city's main hotel
district. Some of the travellers
came in search of knowledge
and inspiration, although most
were more interested in
collecting statues to adorn
their family homes.

When the Victorian novelist
Charles Dickens visited, he
reported that the Spanish Steps

were crowded with models
dressed as Madonnas, saints
and emperors, hoping to attract
the attention of foreign artists.

The steps were built in the
1720s to link the square with
the French church of Trinità dei
Monti above. The French wanted
to place a statue of Louis XIV at
the top, but the pope objected,
and it was not until the 1720s
that the Italian architect
Francesco de Sanctis produced
the voluptuous Rococo design
which satisfied both camps. The
Fontana Barcaccia, sunk into the
paving at the foot of the steps
due to low water pressure, was
designed by Bernini's less famous
father, Pietro.

❷ Villa Medici

Accademia di Francia a Roma, Viale
Trinità dei Monti 1. **Map** 3 A2.
Tel 06 67 611. 🚌 117. Ⓜ Spagna.
Open garden visits: 11am–noon,
2:30pm–4:30pm Tue–Sun (Cardinal's
apartments: Wed only). 🎨 🖥
🎟 only (at noon in English).

Superbly positioned on the
Pincio Hill, this 16th-century villa
has retained the name that it
assumed when Cardinal
Ferdinando de' Medici bought it
in 1576. It is now home to the
French Academy, founded in
1666 to give artists the chance
to study in Rome. From 1803
musicians were also allowed to
study here: both Berlioz and
Debussy were students.

The villa is only open for
exhibitions, but the formal
gardens, with a gorgeously
frescoed pavilion, and copies
of ancient statues, can be
visited in certain months.

19th-century engraving of the inner façade of the Villa Medici

Pinturicchio's fresco of the *Delphic Sibyl* (1509) in Santa Maria del Popolo

❸ Santa Maria del Popolo

Piazza del Popolo 12. **Map** 2 F1. **Tel** 06 361 08 36. 🚍 117, 119, 490, 495, 926. Ⓜ Flaminio. **Open** 7am–noon, 4–7pm Mon–Sat; 7:30am–1:30pm, 4:30–7:30pm Sun.

Santa Maria del Popolo was one of the first Renaissance churches in Rome, commissioned by Pope Sixtus IV della Rovere in 1472. Lavish endowments by Sixtus's descendants and other powerful families have made it one of Rome's greatest artistic treasures.

Shortly after Sixtus died in 1484, Pinturicchio and his pupils frescoed two chapels (first and third right) for the della Rovere family. On the altar of the first chapel there is a lovely *Nativity* from 1490 that depicts a stable at the foot of a Classical column.

In 1503 Sixtus IV's nephew Giuliano became Pope Julius II and had Bramante build a new apse. Pinturicchio was called in again to paint its vaults with Sibyls and Apostles framed in an intricate tracery of freakish beasts.

In 1513 Raphael created the Chigi chapel (second left) for the wealthy banker Agostino Chigi. The design is an audacious Renaissance fusion of the sacred and profane; there are pyramid-like tombs and a ceiling mosaic of God holding the signs of the zodiac describing Chigi's horoscope. Raphael died before the chapel was finished and it was completed by Bernini who added the dynamic statues of Daniel and Habakkuk. In the Cerasi chapel, left of the altar,

there are two realistic works painted by Caravaggio in 1601: the *Conversion of St Paul* and the *Crucifixion of St Peter*. The artist uses daringly exaggerated lighting effects and foreshortening techniques to intensify the dramatic effect.

Detail of the Ara Pacis frieze

❹ Ara Pacis

Lungotevere in Augusta. **Map** 2 F2. **Tel** 06 06 08. 🚍 70, 81, 117, 119, 186, 628. **Open** 9am–7pm Tue–Sun (last adm: 6pm). **Closed** 1 Jan, 25 Dec. 🖥 **W** arapacis.it

Painstakingly reconstructed over many years from scattered fragments, the exquisitely carved Ara Pacis (Altar of Peace) celebrates the peace created by Emperor Augustus throughout the Mediterranean. Commissioned by the Senate in 13 BC and completed four years later, the altar stands in a square enclosure of Carrara marble, carved with realistic reliefs of such quality that experts think the craftsmen may have been Greek.

The reliefs on the north and south walls depict a procession that took place on 4 July, 13 BC, in which the members of the

emperor's family can be identified, including Augustus's grandson, Lucius, clutching at the skirt of his mother, Antonia. The site is housed in a building by architect Richard Meier.

❺ Mausoleum of Augustus

Piazza Augusto Imperatore. **Map** 2 F2. **Tel** 06 06 08. 🚍 81, 117, 492, 628, 926. **Closed** for restoration. 🖥 🚻

Now just a weedy mound ringed with cypresses and strewn with litter, this was once the most prestigious burial place in Rome. Augustus had the mausoleum built in 28 BC, the year before he became sole ruler, as a tomb for himself and his descendants. The circular building was 87 m (270 ft) in diameter with two obelisks (now in Piazza del Quirinale and Piazza dell'Esquilino) at the entrance. Inside were four concentric passageways linked by corridors where urns holding the ashes of the Imperial family were placed, including those of Augustus who died in AD 14.

❻ Trevi Fountain

Piazza di Trevi. **Map** 3 B3. 🚍 116 & many other routes.

Nicola Salvi's theatrical design for Rome's largest and most famous fountain was completed in 1762. The central figures are Neptune, flanked by two Tritons, one trying to master an unruly sea-horse, the other leading

Rome's largest and most famous fountain, the Trevi

a quieter beast, symbolizing the two contrasting moods of the sea.

The site originally marked the terminal of the Aqua Virgo aqueduct, built by Augustus' right-hand man and son-in-law, Agrippa, in 19 BC to channel water to Rome's new bath complexes. One of the reliefs on the first storey shows a young girl, Trivia, after whom the fountain may have been named. She is said to have first shown the spring, 22 km (14 miles) from the city, to thirsty Roman soldiers.

Interior, Sant'Andrea al Quirinale

❼ Sant'Andrea al Quirinale

Via del Quirinale 29. **Map** 3 B3. **Tel** 06 474 08 07. 🚍 116, 117. **Open** 8:30am–noon, 3:30–7pm Mon–Sat; 9am–noon, 4–7pm Sun. 🚻

Sant'Andrea was designed for the Jesuits by Bernini and executed by his assistants between 1658 and 1670. The site was wide but shallow, so Bernini took the radical step of pointing the long axis of his oval plan towards the sides, and leading the eye round to the altar by means of a strong horizontal cornice. At the altar he combined sculpture and painting to create a theatrical crucifixion of Sant'Andrea (St Andrew); the diagonally crucified saint on the altarpiece looks up at a stucco effigy of himself ascending to the lantern, where the Holy Spirit and cherubs await him in heaven.

The dome of San Carlo alle Quattro Fontane, by Borromini

❽ San Carlo alle Quattro Fontane

Via del Quirinale 23. **Map** 3 B3. **Tel** 06 488 31 09. 🚍 116 & routes to Piazza Barberini. Ⓜ Barberini. **Open** 10am–1pm, 3–6pm daily (only am Sat & Sun).

In 1638, Borromini was commissioned by the Trinitarians to design a church and convent on a tiny cramped site at the Quattro Fontane crossroads. The church, so small that it is said it would fit inside one of the piers of St Peter's, is designed with bold, fluid curves on both the façade and interior to give light and life to the diminutive building. The dome, with its concealed windows, illusionistic coffering and tiny lantern designed to make it look higher than it really is, is a cunning feature.

❾ Galleria Nazionale di Arte Antica Palazzo Barberini

Via delle Quattro Fontane 13. **Map** 3 B3. **Tel** 06 482 41 84. 🚍 52, 53, 61, 62, 63, 80, 116, 175, 492, 590. Ⓜ Barberini. **Open** 8:30am–7pm Tue– Sun (last adm: 6:30pm). **Closed** 1 Jan, 25 Dec. 🚻 📷 🎞 📷 🛗 (lift). 🌐 galleriabarberini.beniculturali.it

When Maffei Barberini became Pope Urban VIII in 1623, he decided to build a grand family

Ceiling fresco detail in Palazzo Barberini (1633)

palazzo. Designed by Carlo Maderno as a typical country villa on the fringes of the city, it now overlooks Piazza Barberini, where traffic hurtles around Bernini's Triton fountain. Maderno died shortly after the foundations had been laid, and Bernini and Borromini took over. The most dazzling room is the Gran Salone, with an illusion-istic ceiling frescoed by Pietro da Cortona in 1633–9. The palazzo also houses part of the Galleria Nazionale d'Arte Antica with works by Titian, Filippo Lippi, Caravaggio and Artemisia Genti-leschi. The most famous is a portrait of a courtesan, reputedly Raphael's lover, *La Fornarina*, although not painted by the artist himself.

❿ Santa Maria della Concezione

Via Veneto 27. **Map** 3 B2. **Tel** 06 487 11 85. 🚍 52, 53, 61, 62, 63, 80, 116, 175. Ⓜ Barberini. Crypt and museum: **Open** 9am–7pm daily. 📷

Below this unassuming church on Via Veneto is a crypt decked with the dismembered skeletons of 4,000 Capuchin monks. They form a macabre reminder of the transience of life, with verte-brae wired together to make sacred hearts and crowns of thorns, and, in one chapel, the poignant skeleton of a tiny Barberini princess.

⓫ Santa Maria della Vittoria

Via XX Settembre 17. **Map** 3 C2.
Tel 06 42 74 05 71. 🚌 61, 62, 175, 910.
Ⓜ Repubblica. **Open** 8:30am–noon,
3:30–7pm daily.

Santa Daria della Vittoria is an intimate Baroque church with a lavish, candlelit interior. Inside the Cornaro chapel is one of Bernini's most ambitious sculptures, the *Ecstasy of St Teresa* (1646). The physical nature of St Teresa's ecstasy is apparent as she appears collapsed on a cloud with her mouth half open and eyes closed, struck by the arrow of a smiling angel. Ecclesiastical members, past and present, of the Venetian Cornaro family, who commissioned the chapel, sit in boxes as if watching and discussing the scene being played out in front of them.

Bernini's *Ecstasy of St Teresa* in Santa Maria della Vittoria

⓬ Museo Nazionale Romano Palazzo Massimo

Palazzo Massimo, Largo di Villa Peretti 1 (1 of 5 sites). **Map** 4 D3. **Tel** 06 39 96 77 00. 🚌 all routes to Termini.
Ⓜ Repubblica. **Open** 9am–7:45pm Tue–Sun. 🎫 ticket valid for all sites.
🔲 ♿ 📷 ✎

Founded in 1899, the Museo Nazionale Romano – one of the world's leading museums of Classical art – houses most of the antiquities found in Rome since 1870, as well as important older collections. During the 1990s it underwent a major reorganization and now has five branches: the Palazzo Altemps *(see p404)*; the Baths of Diocletian; the Aula Ottagona, the Crypta; Balbi, and the Palazzo Massimo. In the latter, exhibits dating from the 2nd century BC to the late 4th century AD are displayed in a series of rooms over three floors. Highlights include the *Quattro Aurighe* mosaics from a villa in northern Rome, the breath-taking series of frescoes from Livia's summer villa, and the famous statue of her husband, the Emperor Augustus.

One of the finely detailed Quattro Aurighe mosaics on display at the Museo Nazionale Romano Palazzo Massimo

⓭ Santa Prassede

Via Santa Prassede 9a. **Map** 4 D4.
Tel 06 488 24 56. 🚌 16, 70, 71, 75, 714. Ⓜ Vittorio Emanuele. **Open** 7:30am–noon, 4–6:30pm daily (from 8am Sun). ♿

The church was founded by Pope Paschal II in the 9th century and decorated by Byzantine artists with the most important, glittering mosaics in Rome. In the apse Christ stands between Santa Prassede and her sister, dressed as Byzantine empresses, among white-robed elders, lambs, feather-mop palms and bright red poppies. The Cappella di San Zeno is even lovelier, a jewel-box

9th-century mosaic, Santa Prassede

of a mausoleum, built by Pope Paschal II for his mother, Theodora. Her square halo shows that she was still alive when the mosaic was created.

⓮ San Pietro in Vincoli

Piazza di San Pietro in Vincoli. **Map** 3 C5. **Tel** 06 97 84 49 50. 🚌 75, 85, 117. Ⓜ Colosseo. **Open** 8am–12:30pm, 3–7pm daily (Oct–Mar: to 6pm). ♿

The church's name means St Peter in Chains, so called because it houses what are said to be the chains with which St Peter was shackled in the Mamertine Prison *(see p393)*. According to tradition, one set of chains was sent to Constantinople by Empress Eudoxia; when it was returned to Rome some years later it miraculously fused with its partner.

San Pietro is now best known for the Tomb of Julius II, commissioned from Michelangelo by the pope in 1505. Much to the artist's chagrin, Julius soon became more interested in the building of a new St Peter's and the tomb project was laid to one side. After the pope died in 1513, Michelangelo resumed work on the tomb, but had only completed the statues of the *Dying Slaves* (now found in Paris and Florence) and *Moses* when he was called away to paint the *Last Judgment* in the Sistine Chapel.

⓯ Santa Maria Maggiore

A confident blend of architectural styles, ranging from Early Christian to late Baroque, Santa Maria is also famous for its superb mosaics. Founded in about AD 420, it retains the original colonnaded triple nave, lined with panels of rare 5th-century mosaics. The Cosmatesque marble floor and bell tower are medieval, as are the spectacular mosaics on the triumphal arch and in the loggia. The lavish coffered ceiling is Renaissance; the façades, domes and chapels Baroque.

VISITORS' CHECKLIST

Practical Information
Piazza di Santa Maria Maggiore.
Map 4 D4.
Tel 06 69 88 68 00.
Open 7am–6:45pm daily. 🕇 &

Transport
🚌 16, 70, 71, 714. 🚃 14.
Ⓜ Termini, Cavour.

Coronation of the Virgin
This is one of the wonderful 13th-century mosaics in the apse by Jacopo Torriti.

Bell tower

5th-century mosaics

Tomb of Cardinal Rodriguez
This Gothic tomb, which dates from 1299, contains magnificent marblework by the Cosmati.

18th-century façade by Ferdinando Fuga

13th-century mosaics

Cappella Paolina
Flaminio Ponzio, architect of the Villa Borghese, designed this sumptuous chapel in 1611 for Pope Paul V who is buried here.

Column in Piazza Santa Maria Maggiore
In 1611 a bronze of the Virgin and Child was added to this ancient marble column which came from the Basilica of Constantine.

Cappella Sistina
This chapel was built for Pope Sixtus V (1584–7) by Domenico Fontana and was opulently covered with ancient marble. It houses the pope's tomb.

THE VATICAN AND TRASTEVERE

Vatican City, the world capital of Catholicism, is the world's smallest state. It occupies 43 ha (106 acres) within high walls watched over by the Vatican guard. It was the site where St Peter was martyred (c.AD 64) and buried, and it became the residence of the popes who succeeded him. The papal palaces, next to the great basilica of St Peter's, are home to the Sistine Chapel and the eclectic collections of the Vatican Museums, as well as being the residence of the pope. Neighbouring Trastevere is quite different, a picturesque old quarter, whose inhabitants consider themselves to be the only true Romans. Sadly, the proletarian identity of the place is in danger of being destroyed by the proliferation of trendy restaurants, clubs and shops.

Sights at a Glance

Churches

2 St Peter's pp422–3
7 Santa Maria in Trastevere
8 Santa Cecilia in Trastevere
9 San Francesco a Ripa
10 San Pietro in Montorio and the Tempietto

Museums and Galleries

3 Vatican Museums pp424–31
5 Palazzo Corsini and Galleria Nazionale d'Arte Antica

Historic Buildings

1 Castel Sant'Angelo
4 Villa Farnesina

Parks and Gardens

6 Botanical Gardens

See Rome Street Finder maps 1, 2, 5, 6, 9

◀ View of St Peter's with the Ponte Sant'Angelo in the foreground

For keys to symbols see back flap

A Tour of the Vatican

The Vatican, a sovereign state since February 1929, is ruled by the pope, Europe's only absolute monarch. About 500 people live here and, as well as accommodation for staff and ecclesiasts, the city has its own post office, banks, currency, judicial system, radio station, shops and a daily newspaper, *L'Osservatore Romano*.

★ **St Peter's**
Most of the great architects of the Renaissance and Baroque had a hand in the design of the Basilica of St Peter's, the most famous church in Christendom *(see pp422–3)*.

★ **Sistine Chapel**
Michelangelo frescoed the ceiling with scenes from Genesis (1508–12), and the altar wall with the *Last Judgment* (1534–41). The chapel is used by cardinals when electing a new pope *(see p428)*.

0 metres   75
0 yards   75

Raphael
Rooms

To Via della Conciliazione

KEY

① **Piazza San Pietro** was laid out by Bernini between 1656 and 1667.

② **Information office**

③ **The Papal Audience Chamber**

④ **Vatican Radio**, broadcasts in 20 languages throughout the world from this tower, part of the 9th-century Leonine Wall.

⑤ **The Vatican Gardens**, open for guided tours, make up a third of the Vatican's territory.

PIAZZA DEL SANT UFFIZIO

PIAZZA
SAN PIETRO

PIAZZA
PIO X

This staircase leading down from the museums, designed in 1932 by Giuseppe Momo, is in the form of a double helix, consisting of two spirals: one to walk up and one to walk down.

Entrance to Vatican Museums

Locator Map
See Rome Street Finder map 1

★ **Vatican Museums**
The marble group of the *Laocoön* (AD 1) is one of many prestigious works of art in the Vatican (*see p426*).

The Cortile della Pigna is named after a bronze pine cone from an ancient fountain.

★ **Raphael Rooms**
Raphael frescoed this suite in the early 16th century. Works like *The School of Athens* established his reputation, to equal that of his contemporary Michelangelo (*see p431*).

❶ Castel Sant'Angelo

Lungotevere Castello. **Map** 2 D3.
Tel 06 681 91 11. 34, 280.
Open 9am–7:30pm Tue–Sun (last entry 6:30pm). **Closed** 1 Jan, 25 Dec.

w castelsantangelo.beniculturali.it

This massive fortress takes its name from the vision of the Archangel Michael by Pope Gregory the Great in the 6th century as he led a procession across the bridge, praying for the end of the plague.

The castle began life in AD 139 as the Emperor Hadrian's mausoleum. Since then it has been a bridgehead in the Emperor Aurelian's city wall, a medieval citadel and prison, and a place of safety for popes during times of political unrest. A corridor links it with the Vatican Palace, providing an escape route for the pope. From dank cells to fine apartments of Renaissance popes, the museums cover all aspects of the castle's history, including the Sala Paolina, with illusionistic frescoes (1546–8) by Pellegrino Tibaldi and Perin del Vaga and the Courtyard of Honour.

Illusionistic frescoes by Pellegrino Tibaldi

View of Castel Sant'Angelo from the Ponte Sant'Angelo

❷ St Peter's

Catholicism's most sacred shrine, the sumptuous, marble-caked basilica of St Peter's draws pilgrims and tourists from all over the world. It holds hundreds of precious works of art, some salvaged from the original 4th-century basilica built by Constantine, others commissioned from Renaissance and Baroque artists. The dominant tone is set by Bernini, who created the baldacchino twisting up below Michelangelo's huge dome. He also created the Cathedra in the apse, with four saints supporting a throne that contains fragments once thought to be relics of the chair from which St Peter delivered his first sermon.

Dome of St Peter's
The 136.5 m (448 ft) high dome, designed by Michelangelo, was not completed in his lifetime.

KEY

① **Entrance to Historical Artistic Museum and Sacristy**

② **The Monument to Pope Alexander VII**, was Bernini's last work in St Peter's. Completed in 1678, it shows the Chigi Pope among figures of Truth, Justice, Charity and Prudence.

③ **A staircase** of 537 steps leads to the summit of the dome.

④ **The Baldacchino** was commissioned by Pope Urban VIII in 1624; Bernini's extravagant Baroque canopy stands above St Peter's tomb.

⑤ **The Papal Altar** stands over the crypt where St Peter is reputedly buried.

⑥ **The church** is 186 m (615 ft) long.

⑦ **The foot of St Peter**, sculpted by Arnolfo di Cambio in the 13th century, has worn thin from the touch of pilgrims over the centuries.

⑧ **Two minor cupolas by Vignola (1507–73)**

⑨ **Markings on** the floor of the nave show how other churches compare in length.

⑩ **Façade by Carlo Maderno (1614)**

⑪ **From this Library window** the Pope blesses the faithful gathered in the piazza below.

⑫ **The Holy Door** is used only in Holy Years.

⑬ **Atrium by Carlo Maderno**

Historical Plan of the Basilica of St Peter's

St Peter was buried in AD 64 in a necropolis near the site of his crucifixion in the Circus of Nero. In AD 324 Constantine constructed a basilica over the tomb. The old church was rebuilt in the 15th century, and throughout the 16th and 17th centuries various architects developed the existing structure. The new church was inaugurated in 1626.

Key

▨ Circus of Nero
▧ Constantinian
▦ Renaissance
▤ Baroque

The Grottoes
A fragment of this 13th-century mosaic by Giotto, salvaged from the old basilica, is now in the Grottoes, where many popes are buried.

Michelangelo's Pietà
Protected by glass since an attack in 1972, the Pietà was created in 1499 when Michelangelo was only 25.

Filarete Doors
These bronze doors from the old basilica were decorated with biblical reliefs by Filarete between 1439 and 1445.

Entrance

Piazza San Pietro
On Sundays, religious festivals and special occasions such as canonizations, the Pope blesses the crowds from a balcony.

❸ Vatican Museums

Home to the Sistine Chapel and Raphael Rooms as well as to one of the world's most important art collections, the Vatican Museums are housed in palaces originally built for Renaissance popes Julius II, Innocent VIII and Sixtus IV. Most of the later additions were made in the 18th century, when priceless works of art accumulated by earlier popes were first put on show.

Etruscan Museum
The Etruscan collection includes a woman's gold clasp *(fibula)* from the 7th-century BC Regolini-Galassi tomb at Cerveteri, north of Rome.

Gallery of Maps
The *Siege of Malta* is one of 40 maps of the Church's territories, frescoed by the 16th-century cartographer Ignazio Danti on the gallery's walls.

Gallery of the Candelabra

Raphael Rooms
This is a detail of the *Expulsion of Heliodorus from the Temple*, one of many frescoes painted by Raphael and his pupils for Julius II's private apartments *(see p431)*.

Gallery of Tapestries

Stairs / down

Upper floor

Sala dei Chiaroscuri

Raphael Loggia

Sistine Chapel *(see p428–30)*

Gallery Guide

The museum complex is vast: the Sistine Chapel is 20–30 minutes' walk from the entrance, so allow plenty of time. There is a strict one-way system, and it is best to be selective or choose one of four colour-coded itineraries, which vary from 90 minutes to a 5-hour marathon.

Borgia Apartment
Pinturicchio and his assistants frescoed these rooms for Alexander VI in 1492–5.

Modern religious art on view here was sent to the popes by artists worldwide, such as Bacon, Ernst and Carrà.

Pio-Clementine Museum
The finest of the Vatican's Classical statues are on display here, like the *Apollo Belvedere*, a Roman copy in marble of a 4th-century BC Greek bronze.

Gregorian Profane Museum

Stairs up to Etruscan Museum

Lower floor

Braccio Nuovo

Chiaramonti Museum

Entrance

Cortile Ottagonale

The Lapidary Gallery
contains inscriptions from pagan and Christian catacombs, but is closed to the public.

Egyptian Museum
The collection of Egyptian artifacts includes this painted bas-relief from a 2400 BC tomb. The museum was organized by Father Ungarelli, a 19th-century Egyptologist.

Pio-Christian Museum
Early Christianity adopted Classical images so that its doctrines could be more easily understood. This 4th-century statue of Christ as the Good Shepherd derives from the pastoral figure of the shepherd.

Pinacoteca
The Vatican's art gallery has 15th- to 19th-century works, and is particularly strong on the Renaissance. This unfinished painting of *St Jerome* by Leonardo da Vinci reveals his mastery of anatomy.

Key to floorplan
- Egyptian and Assyrian art
- Greek and Roman art
- Etruscan art
- Early Christian and medieval art
- 15th- to 19th-century art
- Modern religious art
- Lapidary Gallery
- Non-exhibition space

Exploring the Vatican's Collections

The Vatican's greatest treasures are its superlative Greek and Roman antiquities, together with the magnificent artifacts excavated from Egyptian and Etruscan tombs during the 19th century. Some of Italy's greatest artists, such as Raphael, Michelangelo and Leonardo da Vinci, are represented in the Pinacoteca (art gallery) and parts of the former palaces, where they were employed by popes to decorate sumptuous apartments and galleries.

Head of an athlete in mosaic from the Baths of Caracalla, AD 217

Egyptian and Assyrian Art

The Egyptian collection contains finds from 19th- and 20th-century excavations in Egypt, as well as statues that were brought to Rome in Imperial times. There are also Roman imitations of Egyptian art from Hadrian's Villa (see p472) and from temples in Rome devoted to Egyptian gods and goddesses, such as Isis and Serapis.

The genuine Egyptian works, displayed on the lower floor next to the Pio-Clementine Museum, include statues, mummies, mummy cases and a Book of the Dead. One of the main treasures is a colossal granite 13th-century statue of Queen Mutuy, the mother of Rameses II, which was found on the site of the Horti Sallustiani gardens near Via Veneto. Also noteworthy are the head of a statue of Montuhotep IV (20th century BC), the beautiful mummy case of Queen Hetepheres, and the tomb of Iri, who was the guardian of the Pyramid of Cheops. This dates back to the 22nd century BC.

Roman copy of the Greek *Doryphoros*

Here, the most famous exhibits are the gold jewellery and bronze throne, bed and funeral cart, found in the 650 BC Regolini-Galassi tomb in Cerveteri (see p470).

Prize Greek and Roman pieces form the nucleus of the Pio-Clementine Museum. These include high-quality Roman copies of 4th-century BC Greek statues, such as the *Apoxyomenos* (an athlete wiping his body after a race) and the *Apollo del Belvedere*. The splendid *Laocoön* (1st century AD), originally from Rhodes, was found in 1506 in the ruins of Nero's Golden House. Works such as these inspired Michelangelo and other Renaissance artists.

The much smaller Chiaramonti Museum is lined with ancient busts, and its extension, the Braccio Nuovo, has a 1st-century BC statue of Augustus from the villa of his wife Livia. It is based on the *Doryphoros* (spear-carrier) by

the 5th-century BC Greek sculptor Polyclitus. There is also a Roman copy of this on display opposite. The Gregorian Profane Museum, housed in a separate wing, follows the evolution of Roman art from reliance on Greek models to a recognizably Roman style.

In this museum, original Greek works include large marble fragments from the Parthenon in Athens. Among the Roman pieces are two reliefs, the *Rilievi della Cancelleria*, commissioned by Domitian in AD 81 to glorify the military parades of his father, Emperor Vespasian. There are also fine Roman floor mosaics, two from the Baths of Caracalla (see p441), and one, in the Round Room, dated 3rd century AD, from the Baths of Otricoli in Umbria.

In the Vatican Library is the 1st-century AD *Aldobrandini Wedding*, a beautiful Roman fresco depicting a bride being prepared for her marriage.

Greek, Etruscan and Roman Art

The greater part of the Vatican Museums is dedicated to Greek and Roman art. However, the Etruscan Museum houses a superb collection of Etruscan (see p48) and pre-Roman artifacts from Etruria and the Greek colonies of southern Italy.

Roman mosaic from the Baths of Otricoli, Umbria, in the Round Room

Early Christian and Medieval Art

The main collection of early Christian antiquities is in the Pio-Christian Museum, which contains inscriptions and sculpture from catacombs and early Christian basilicas. The sculpture consists chiefly of reliefs from sarcophagi, though the most striking work is a free-standing 4th-century statue of the *Good Shepherd*. The sculpture's chief interest lies in the way it blends Biblical episodes with pagan mythology. The idealized pastoral figure of the shepherd became Christ himself, while bearded philosophers turned into the Apostles.

The first two rooms of the Pinacoteca are dedicated to late medieval art, mostly wooden altarpieces painted in tempera. The outstanding work is Giotto's *Stefaneschi Triptych* of about 1300 which decorated the main altar of the old St Peter's.

The Vatican Library has a number of medieval treasures including reliquaries, textiles, enamels and icons.

Pietà (c.1471–4) by the Venetian artist Giovanni Bellini in the Pinacoteca

Detail of Giotto's *Stefaneschi Triptych* (1330) in the Pinacoteca

15th- to 19th-century Art

Many Renaissance popes were connoisseurs of the arts who considered it their duty to sponsor the leading painters, sculptors and goldsmiths of the age. The galleries around the Cortile del Belvedere were decorated by great artists between the 16th and the 19th centuries.

The Gallery of Tapestries is hung with tapestries woven in Brussels to designs by students of Raphael. The Apartment of Pope Pius V has beautiful 15th-century Flemish tapestries, and the Gallery of Maps is frescoed with 16th-century maps of ancient and contemporary Italy.

Alongside the Raphael Rooms (*see p431*) are the Room of the Chiaroscuri and Pope Nicholas V's private chapel. This was frescoed between 1447 and 1451 by Fra Angelico. Also worth seeing is the Borgia Apartment, decorated in the 1490s by Pinturicchio and his pupils for the Borgia Pope, Alexander VI. Another set of fascinating frescoes can be found in the Loggia of Raphael, but a visit here requires special permission.

The Pinacoteca has many important Renaissance works. Highlights from the 15th century are a fine *Pietà* by Giovanni Bellini, part of his *Coronation of the Virgin* altarpiece in Pèsaro (*see p372*); and Leonardo da Vinci's unfinished *St Jerome*, discovered, after being long lost, in two halves. One was being used as a coffer lid in an antique shop, the other as the seat of a stool in a shoemaker's.

Exceptional pieces from the 16th century include eight tapestry cartoons, the *Transfiguration* and *Madonna of Foligno* by Raphael, in a room devoted to the artist; a *Deposition* by Caravaggio; an altarpiece by Titian; and *St Helen* by Veronese, which

Pinturicchio's *Adoration of the Magi* (1490), Borgia Apartment

shows the saint as a gorgeously dressed aristocrat.

Sistine Chapel: The Ceiling

Michelangelo frescoed the ceiling for Pope Julius II between 1508 and 1512, working on specially designed scaffolding. The main panels, which chart the Creation of the World and Fall of Man, are surrounded by subjects from the Old and New Testaments – except for the Classical Sibyls who are said to have foreseen the birth of Christ. In the 1980s the ceiling was restored revealing colours of an unsuspected vibrancy.

Libyan Sibyl
The pagan prophetess reaches for the Book of Knowledge. Like most female figures Michelangelo painted, the beautiful Libyan Sibyl was probably modelled on a man.

Creation of the Sun and Moon

KEY

① **Illusionistic architecture**

② **The lunettes** are devoted to frescoes of the ancestors of Christ, like Hezekiah.

③ **The Ignudi** are athletic male nudes whose significance is uncertain.

Key to Ceiling Panels

Genesis: 1 God Dividing Light from Darkness; **2** Creation of the Sun and Moon; **3** Separating Waters from Land; **4** Creation of Adam; **5** Creation of Eve; **6** Original Sin; **7** Sacrifice of Noah; **8** The Deluge; **9** Drunkenness of Noah.

Ancestors of Christ: 10 Solomon with his Mother; **11** Parents of Jesse; **12** Rehoboam with Mother; **13** Asa with Parents; **14** Uzziah with Parents; **15** Hezekiah with Parents; **16** Zerubbabel with Parents; **17** Josiah with Parents.

Prophets: 18 Jonah; **19** Jeremiah; **20** Daniel; **21** Ezekiel; **22** Isaiah; **23** Joel; **24** Zechariah.

Sibyls: 25 Libyan Sibyl; **26** Persian Sibyl; **27** Cumaean Sibyl; **28** Erythrean Sibyl; **29** Delphic Sibyl.

Old testament scenes of salvation: 30 Punishment of Haman; **31** Moses and the Brazen Serpent; **32** David and Goliath; **33** Judith and Holofernes.

Creation of the Sun and Moon
Michelangelo depicts God as a dynamic but terrifying figure commanding the sun to shed light on the earth.

Original Sin
This shows Adam and Eve tasting the forbidden fruit from the Tree of Knowledge, and their expulsion from Paradise. Michelangelo represents Satan as a snake with the body of a woman.

Restoration of the sistine ceiling

The restorers of the Sistine Chapel used computers, photography and spectrum technology to analyse the fresco before cleaning began. They separated Michelangelo's work from that of later restorers and discovered that the restorers had attempted to clean the ceiling with materials ranging from bread to retsina wine. The new restoration revealed the familiarly dusky, eggshell-cracked figures to have creamy skins, lustrous hair and to be dressed in brightly coloured, luscious robes: "a Benetton Michelangelo" mocked one critic, claiming that a layer of varnish that the artist had added to darken the colours had been removed. However, after examining the work, most experts agreed that the new colours probably matched those painted by Michelangelo.

A restorer cleaning the Libyan Sibyl

Sistine Chapel: The Walls

The massive walls of the Sistine Chapel, the main chapel in the Vatican Palace, were frescoed by some of the finest artists of the 15th and 16th centuries. The 12 paintings on the side walls, by artists including Perugino, Ghirlandaio, Botticelli and Signorelli, show parallel episodes from the lives of Moses and Christ. The decoration of the chapel walls was completed between 1534 and 1541 by Michelangelo, who added the great altar wall fresco, the *Last Judgment*.

Key to The Frescoes: Artists and Subjects

The Last Judgment

- ☐ Perugino
- ☐ Botticelli
- ☐ Ghirlandaio
- ☐ Rosselli
- ☐ Signorelli
- ☐ Michelangelo

1 Baptism of Christ in the Jordan
2 Temptations of Christ
3 Calling of St Peter and St Andrew
4 Sermon on the Mount
5 Handing over the Keys to St Peter
6 Last Supper
7 Moses's Journey into Egypt
8 Moses Receiving the Call
9 Crossing of the Red Sea
10 Adoration of the Golden Calf
11 Punishment of the Rebels
12 Last Days of Moses

The Last Judgment by Michelangelo

Revealed in 1993 after a year's restoration, the *Last Judgment* is considered to be the master-piece of Michelangelo's mature years. It was commissioned by Pope Paul III Farnese, and required the removal of some earlier frescoes and two windows over the altar. A new wall was erected which slanted inwards to stop dust settling on it. Michelangelo worked alone on the fresco for seven years, until its completion in 1541.

The painting depicts the souls of the dead rising up to face the wrath of God, a subject that is rarely used for an altar decoration. The pope chose it as a warning to Catholics to adhere to their faith in the turmoil of the Reformation. In fact the work conveys the artist's own tormented attitude to his faith. It offers neither the certainties of Christian orthodoxy, nor the ordered view of Classicism.

In a dynamic, emotional composition, the figures are caught in a vortex of motion. The dead are torn from their graves and hauled up to face Christ the Judge, whose athletic, muscular figure is the focus of all the painting's movement.

Christ shows little sympathy for the agitated saints around him, clutching the instruments of their martyrdom. Neither is any pity shown for the damned, hurled down to the demons in hell. Here Charon, pushing people off his boat into the depths of Hades, and the infernal judge Minos, are taken from Dante's *Inferno*. Minos has ass's ears, and is a portrait of courtier Biagio da Cesena, who had objected to the nude figures in the fresco. Michelangelo's self-portrait is on the skin held by the martyr St Bartholomew.

Souls meeting the wrath of Christ in Michelangelo's *Last Judgment*

Raphael Rooms

Pope Julius II's private apartments were built above those of his hated predecessor, Alexander VI, who died in 1503. Julius was impressed with Raphael's work and chose him to redecorate the four rooms *(stanze)*. Raphael and his pupils began in 1508, replacing works by better-known artists, including Raphael's teacher, Perugino. The new frescoes quickly established the young artist's reputation in Rome, but the project took 16 years to complete and he died before it was finished.

Key to floorplan
① Hall of Constantine
② Room of Heliodorus
③ Room of the Segnatura
④ Room of the Fire in the Borgo

Detail from Raphael's *The Mass of Bolsena* (1512)

Hall of Constantine

The frescoes in this room were started in 1517 and completed in 1525, five years after Raphael's death, and are largely the work of the artist's pupils. The theme of the decoration is the triumph of Christianity over paganism, and the four major frescoes show scenes from the life of Constantine, the first Christian emperor. These include the *Vision of the Cross* and the emperor's victory over his rival, Maxentius, at *The Battle of the Milvian Bridge*, for which Raphael had provided a preparatory sketch.

Room of Heliodorus

Raphael decorated this private antechamber between 1512 and 1514. The main frescoes all contain thinly veiled references to the protective powers of the papacy. The room's name refers to the fresco on the right, *The Expulsion of Heliodorus from the Temple*, showing Heliodorus felled by a horseman as he tries to rob the Temple in Jerusalem. It alludes to Pope Julius II's victory over foreign armies in Italy. *The Mass of Bolsena* on the left wall refers to a miracle that occurred in 1263, in which a priest who doubted the doctrine of the Holy Host was said to have seen blood issue from it at the moment of sacrifice.

Room of the Segnatura

Completed between 1508 and 1511, the frescoes here are the most harmonious in the series. The scheme followed by Raphael, dictated by Pope Julius II, reflected the Humanist belief that there could be perfect harmony between Classical culture and Christianity in the search for truth. The most famous work, *The School of Athens*, centres on the debate about truth between the Greek philosophers Plato and Aristotle. Raphael depicted some of his contemporaries as philosophers, including Leonardo da Vinci, Bramante and Michelangelo.

Room of the Fire in The Borgo

This was originally the dining room, but when the decoration was completed under Pope Leo X, it became a music room. All the frescoes exalt the reigning pope by depicting events in the lives of his 9th-century namesakes, Leo III and IV. The main frescoes were designed by Raphael, but finished by his assistants between 1514 and 1517. The most famous, *The Fire in the Borgo*, shows a miracle of 847, when Pope Leo IV put out a fire by making the sign of the cross. Raphael draws a parallel between this and the legendary flight of Aeneas from Troy, recounted by Virgil. Aeneas appears in the foreground, carrying his father Anchises on his back.

The School of Athens (1511) showing philosophers and scholars

❹ Villa Farnesina

Via della Lungara 230. **Map** 2 E5.
Tel 06 68 02 72 68. 23, 280.
Open 9am–2pm Mon–Sat and every
second Mon of the month.

The fabulously wealthy Sienese
banker Agostino Chigi commissioned this villa in 1508 from his
fellow Sienese Baldassare Peruzzi.
Chigi's main home was across the
Tiber, and the villa was designed
purely for lavish banquets.
Artists, poets, cardinals, princes
and the pope himself were
entertained here in magnificent
style. Chigi also used the villa for
sojourns with the courtesan
Imperia, who allegedly inspired
one of the *Three Graces* painted
by Raphael in the Loggia of
Cupid and Psyche.

The simple, harmonious
design of the Farnesina, with a
central block and projecting
wings, made it one of the first
true villas of the Renaissance.
Peruzzi decorated some of
the interiors himself, such as
the Sala della Prospettiva
upstairs, in which the illusionistic frescoes create the
impression of looking out over
16th-century Rome through a
marble colonnade.

Other frescoes, by Sebastiano
del Piombo and Raphael and his
pupils, illustrate Classical myths,
while the vault of the main hall,
the Sala di Galatea, is adorned
with astrological scenes
showing the position of the
stars at the time of Chigi's
birth. After his death the
business collapsed, and in 1577
the villa was sold off to the
Farnese family.

Raphael's *Three Graces* in the Villa Farnesina

Queen Christina of Sweden's bedroom in
the Palazzo Corsini

❺ Palazzo Corsini and Galleria Nazionale d'Arte Antica

Via della Lungara 10. **Map** 2 D5.
Tel 06 68 80 23 23. 23, 280.
Open 8:30am–7:30pm Tue–Sun.
Closed 1 Jan, 25 Dec, 31 Dec.
**w galleriacorsini.
beniculturali.it**

Built for Cardinal Domenico
Riario in 1510–12, the Palazzo
Corsini has numbered
Bramante, the young Michelangelo, Erasmus and the
mother of Napoleon among
its guests. Queen Christina of
Sweden died here in 1689.
The palazzo was rebuilt by
Ferdinando Fuga, who planned
the façade to be viewed from
an angle, as Via della Lungara is
too narrow for a full frontal view.

When the palazzo was bought
by the state in 1893, the Corsini
family donated their collection of
paintings, which formed the core
of the national art collection, and
was soon augmented. The
collection is now split between
Palazzo Barberini and Palazzo
Corsini. Although the best
works are in the Barberini, there
are paintings by Van Dyck,
Rubens, Murillo, and, notably,
an androgynous *St John the
Baptist* (c.1604) by Caravaggio
and a *Salome* (1638) by Reni.
The strangest work is a portrait
of the rotund Queen Christina
as the goddess Diana by
J Van Egmont.

❻ Botanical Gardens

Largo Cristina di Svezia 24. **Map** 2 D5.
Tel 06 49 91 71 08. 23, 280. **Open**
9:30am–6:30pm (Oct–Mar: 5:30pm)
Mon–Sat. **Closed** public hols.

Sequoias, palm trees, orchids
and bromeliads are among the
7,000 plants from all over the
world represented in the
Botanical Gardens (Orto
Botanico). Indigenous and
exotic species are grouped to
illustrate their botanical families
and their adaptation to different
climates and ecosystems.
There are also some curious
plants like the ginkgo that have
survived almost unchanged
from earlier eras.

Palm trees in the Botanical
Gardens, Trastevere

❼ Santa Maria in Trastevere

Piazza Santa Maria in Trastevere.
Map 5 C1. **Tel** 06 581 94 43. H, 23,
280. **Open** 7:30am–9pm daily.

Santa Maria in Trastevere was
probably the first Christian place
of worship in Rome, founded by
Pope Callixtus I in the
3rd century, when emperors
were still pagan and Christianity
a minority cult. According to
legend, it was built on the site
where a fountain of oil had
miraculously sprung up on the
day that Christ was born. The
basilica became the focus of
devotion to the Madonna, and
although today's church, and its
remarkable mosaics, date
largely from the 12th and 13th
centuries, images of the Virgin
continue to dominate. The
façade mosaics probably date

Apse mosaic of the *Coronation of the Virgin*, Santa Maria in Trastevere

from the 12th century, and show Mary, Christ and ten lamp-bearing women. Inside in the apse is a stylized 12th-century *Coronation of the Virgin*, and below, a series of realistic scenes from the life of the Virgin by the 13th-century artist Pietro Cavallini. The oldest image of the Virgin is a 7th-century icon, the *Madonna di Clemenza*, which depicts her as a Byzantine empress flanked by a guard of angels. It sits above the altar in the Cappella Altemps.

❽ Santa Cecilia in Trastevere

Piazza di Santa Cecilia. **Map** 6 D1. **Tel** 06 589 92 89. 🚌 H, 23, 44, 280. **Open** 9:30am–1pm, 4–6:30pm daily. Cavallini fresco **Open** 10am–12:30pm Mon–Fri.

St Cecilia, aristocrat and patron saint of music, was martyred here in AD 230. After an unsuccessful attempt to suffocate her by locking her in the hot steam bath of her house for three days, she was beheaded. A church was built, possibly in the 4th century, on the site of her house (still to be seen beneath the church, along with the remains of a tannery). Her body was lost, but it turned up again in the Catacombs of San Callisto (*see p446*). In the 9th century it was reburied here by Pope Paschal I, who rebuilt the church. A fine apse mosaic survives from this period. The altar canopy by Arnolfo di

Cambio and the fresco of *The Last Judgment* by Pietro Cavallini can be reached through the adjoining convent; they date from the 13th century, one of the few periods when Rome had a distinctive artistic style.

In front of the altar is a delicate statue of St Cecilia by Stefano Maderno, which is based on sketches made of her perfectly preserved relics when they were briefly disinterred in 1599.

❾ San Francesco a Ripa

Piazza San Francesco d'Assisi 88. **Map** 5 C2. **Tel** 06 581 90 20. 🚌 H, 23, 44, 75, 280. **Open** 7:30am–1pm, 2–7:30pm daily. ♿

St Francis of Assisi lived here in a hospice when he visited Rome in 1219 and his stone pillow and crucifix are preserved in his cell. The church was built by a follower, a local nobleman called Rodolfo Anguillara, who is portrayed on his tombstone wearing the Franciscan habit.

Entirely rebuilt in the 1680s by Cardinal Pallavicini, the church is rich in 17th- and 8th-century sculptures. Not to be missed in the Altieri chapel (fourth left, along the nave) is Bernini's exquisite late work, the *Ecstasy of Beata Ludovica Albertoni* (1674).

Bramante's circular Tempietto at San Pietro in Montorio

❿ San Pietro in Montorio and the Tempietto

P San Pietro in Montorio 2. **Map** 5 B1. **Tel** 06 581 39 40. 🚌 44, 75, 115. **Open** 8:30am–noon daily, 3–4pm Mon–Fri. Tempietto **Open** 9:30am–12:30pm, 2–4:30pm Tue–Sat.

The Tempietto, a diminutive masterpiece of Renaissance architecture completed by Bramante in 1502, stands in the courtyard of San Pietro in Montorio. The name means "little temple" and its circular shape echoes early Christian *martyria*, chapels built on the site of a saint's martyrdom. This was erroneously thought to be the spot in Nero's Circus where St Peter was crucified. Bramante ringed the chapel with Doric columns, a Classical frieze and fine balustrade.

Bernini's *Ecstasy of Beata Ludovica Albertoni*, San Francesco a Ripa

AVENTINE AND LATERAN

This is one of the greenest parts of the city, taking in the Celian and Aventine Hills, as well as the very congested area around San Giovanni in Laterano. The Celian, now scattered with churches, was a fashionable place to live in Imperial Rome. Some of the era's splendour is still apparent in the ruins of the Baths of Caracalla. Behind the Baths rises the Aventine Hill, a peaceful, leafy area, with the superb basilica of Santa Sabina, and lovely views across the river to Trastevere and St Peter's. In the valley below, cars and Vespas skim around the Circus Maximus, following the ancient charioteering track, while to the south lies Testaccio, a lively working-class district.

Sights at a Glance

Churches
❷ Santa Maria in Cosmedin
❸ Santa Maria in Domnica
❹ Santo Stefano Rotondo
❺ Santi Quattro Coronati
❻ *San Clemente see p439*
❼ San Giovanni in Laterano
⓫ Santa Sabina

Ancient Sites and Building
❶ Temples of the Forum Boarium
❽ Baths of Caracalla

Monuments and Tomb
❾ Pyramid of Caius Cestius
❿ Protestant Cemetery

See Rome Street Finder maps 6, 7, 8

0 metres 250
0 yards 250

◀ One of the mosaics in the Baths of Caracalla

For keys to symbols *see back flap*

Street-by-Street: Piazza della Bocca della Verità

The site of Rome's first port and its busy cattle market, this is an odd little corner of the city, stretching from the heavily trafficked road running along the Tiber to the southern spur of the Capitoline Hill, a place of execution from ancient times until the Middle Ages. Although best known for the Bocca della Verità (Mouth of Truth) in Santa Maria in Cosmedin, which is supposed to snap shut on the hands of liars, there are many other sites in the area, notably two temples from the Republican era. In the 6th century the area became home to a Greek community who founded the churches of San Giorgio in Velabro and Santa Maria in Cosmedin.

The Casa dei Crescenzi, studded with ancient fragments, incorporates the ruins of a 10th-century tower built by the powerful Crescenzi family to guard the river Tiber.

Sant'Omobono stands on an archaeological site where finds date back to the 6th century.

❶ ★ Temples of the Forum Boarium
These two buildings are the best preserved of Rome's Republican temples.

Ponte Rotto, as this forlorn ruined arch in the Tiber is called, simply means "broken bridge". Built in the 2nd century BC, its original name was the Pons Aemilius.

The Fontana dei Tritoni, built by Carlo Bizzaccheri in 1715, shows the strong influence of Bernini.

❷ ★ Santa Maria in Cosmedin
The *Bocca della Verità*, a medieval drain cover, is set into the portico.

VIA DI SAN GIOVANNI DECOLLATO

LUNGOTEVERE DEI PIERLEONI

TEVERE

PONTE PALATINO

PIAZZA DELLA BOCCA DELLA VERITà

VIA DELLA GR

Key

— Suggested route

| 0 metres | | 75 |
| 0 yards | | 75 |

San Giovanni Decollato belonged to a confraternity that encouraged condemned prisoners to repent.

Santa Maria della Consolazione was named after an image of the Virgin placed here in 1385 to give consolation to the condemned.

Locator Map
See Rome Street Finder map 6

❶ Temples of the Forum Boarium

Piazza della Bocca della Verità.
Map 6 E1. 🚌 23, 44, 81, 160, 170, 280, 628, 715, 716.

These wonderfully well-preserved Republican-era temples are at their best in moonlight, standing in their grassy enclave beside the Tiber sheltered by umbrella pines. During the day, they look less romantic, stranded in a sea of traffic. They date from the 2nd century BC, and were saved from ruin by being consecrated as Christian churches in the Middle Ages by the Greek community then living in the area. The rectangular temple, formerly known as the Temple of Fortuna Virilis, was probably dedicated to Portunus, the god of rivers and ports. Set on a podium it has four Ionic travertine columns fluted at the front and 12 half-columns embedded in the tufa wall of the *cella* – the room that housed the image of the god. In the 9th century the Temple was converted into the church of Santa Maria Egiziaca, after a 5th-century prostitute who reformed and became a hermit.

The smaller circular Temple, which is made of solid marble and surrounded by 20 fluted columns, was dedicated to Hercules, though it was long believed to be a Temple of Vesta because of its similarity to the one in the Forum.

San Teodoro is a circular church on the edge of the Palatine with exceptional 6th-century apse mosaics.

San Giorgio in Velabro, a 7th-century basilica, was damaged in an explosion in 1994, and has now been restored.

Arco degli Argentari

The 4th-century Arch of Janus, a four-faced marble-plated arch at the edge of the Forum Boarium market, was an ideal place for merchants and customers to do business in the shade.

The Ionic façade of the Republican era Temple of Portunus

Apse mosaic from the 9th century of the Virgin and Child in Santa Maria in Domnica

❷ Santa Maria in Cosmedin

Piazza della Bocca della Verità. **Map** 6 E1. **Tel** 06 678 77 59. 23, 44, 81, 160, 170, 280, 628, 715, 716. **Open** 9:30am–6pm daily (5pm in winter).

This beautiful church was built in the 6th century on the site of the ancient city's food market. The Romanesque bell tower and portico were added during the 12th century. In the 19th century a Baroque façade was removed and the church restored to its original simplicity. It contains many fine examples of Cosmati work, in particular the mosaic pavement, the raised choir, the bishop's throne, and the canopy over the main altar.

Set into the wall of the portico is the Bocca della Verità (Mouth of Truth), a grotesque marble face, thought to have been an ancient drain cover.

The nave of Santa Maria in Cosmedin with its Cosmati floor

Medieval tradition had it that the jaws would snap shut on liars – a useful way of testing the faithfulness of spouses.

❸ Santa Maria in Domnica

Piazza della Navicella 12. **Map** 7 A2. **Tel** 06 772 02 685. 81, 117, 673. Ⓜ Colosseo. **Open** 9am–noon, 3:30–7pm daily (until 6pm in winter).

Santa Maria in Domnica was probably founded in the 7th century, and renovated in the 9th century. By this time the Romans had lost the art of making mosaics, so Pope Paschal I imported mosaicists from Byzantium. They created an ex quisite apse mosaic showing the Virgin, Child and angels in a delicate garden of paradise. Paschal I is kneeling at the Virgin's feet wearing a square halo, indicating that he was alive when it was made.

In 1513 Andrea Sansovino added a portico decorated with lions' heads, a punning homage to Pope Leo X.

❹ Santo Stefano Rotondo

Via di Santo Stefano Rotondo 7. **Map** 7 B2. **Tel** 06 42 11 99. 81, 117, 673. **Open** 9:30am–12:30pm, 3–6pm (2–5pm in winter) Tue–Sun.

Santo Stefano Rotondo was built between 468 and 483 on a circular plan with four chapels in a cruciform shape. Its circular inner area is enclosed by

two concentric corridors. A third, outer corridor was demolished on the orders of Leon Battista Alberti in 1453. In the 1500s Niccolò Pomarancio, Antonio Tempesta and others covered the walls with 34 frescoes detailing the martyrdoms of saints.

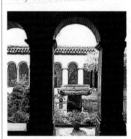

Cloister of Santi Quattro Coronati

❺ Santi Quattro Coronati

Via dei Santi Quattro Coronati 20. **Map** 7 B1. **Tel** 06 70 47 54 27. 85, 117, 810. 3. **Open** 6:30am–12:45pm, 3–7:45pm daily. Cloister & Chapel of St Sylvester **Open** 10–11:45am, 4–5:45pm daily.

This fortified convent was built in the 4th century to house the relics of four Persian stonemasons, martyred after they refused to make a statue of the pagan god Aesculapius. It was rebuilt after invading Normans set fire to it in 1084.

Highlights are a delightful garden cloister and the Chapel of St Sylvester, where 12th-century frescoes recount the legend of Emperor Constantine's conversion to Christianity.

❻ San Clemente

In 1857 Father Mullooly, the Irish Dominican prior of
San Clemente, began excavations beneath the existing
12th-century basilica. Directly underneath he and his
successors discovered a 4th-century church, and below
that a number of ancient Roman buildings. Both basilicas
are dedicated to St Clement, the fourth Pope. On the lowest
level is a temple devoted to the cult of Mithras, a mystical
all-male religion imported from Persia which rivalled
Christianity for popularity.

VISITORS' CHECKLIST

Practical Information
Via di San Giovanni in Laterano.
Map 7 B1. **Tel** 06 774 00 21.
Open 9am–12:30pm, 3–6pm
Mon–Sat (from noon Sun &
public hols). Last adm: 20 mins
before closing. 🚫 to excavations.
🚹 🚻 📷

Transport
🚌 85, 87, 117, 186, 810.
Ⓜ Colosseo. 🚃 3.

Cappella di Santa Caterina
Restored frescoes by the
15th-century artist Masolino
da Panicale show scenes from
the life of St Catherine
of Alexandria.

Entrance

Apse Mosaic
The 12th-century *Triumph
of the Cross* includes
finely detailed animals
and acanthus leaves.

Paschal Candlestick
This splendid 12th-
century spiralling
candlestick, striped
with glittering
multi-
coloured
mosaic, is
the work of
the Cosmati.

12th-century
basilica

18th-century
façade

Piscina

Schola
Cantorum

4th-century basilica

Life of San Clemente
Faded frescoed episodes from
the life of the fourth Pope
decorate the lower church.
This one tells the story of a
boy found alive in his tomb
under the sea.

Temple of
Mithras

Triclinium
An altar to the god
Mithras, showing him
slaying a bull, stands in the
dank triclinium, a room used
for ritual banquets by
cult members.

❼ San Giovanni in Laterano

San Giovanni, the cathedral of Rome, was founded by Emperor Constantine in the early 4th century. It has been rebuilt several times, notably in 1646 when Borromini restyled the interior, but retains its original basilica form. Before the papacy moved to Avignon in 1309, the adjoining Lateran Palace was the official papal residence. The present structure dates from 1589, but older parts survive, like the Scala Santa (Holy Staircase) which Christ is said to have climbed at his trial.

VISITORS' CHECKLIST

Practical Information
Piazza di San Giovanni in Laterano. **Map** 8 D2.
Tel 06 69 88 64 93. Cathedral: **Open** 7am–6:30pm daily.
Cloisters: **Open** 9am–6pm daily.
Museum: **Open** 10am–5:30pm daily. Baptistry: **Open** 7am–12:30pm, 4–6:30pm daily.

Transport
🚌 16, 81, 85, 87, 650. 🚊 3. Ⓜ San Giovanni.

Baptistry
Though much restored, the octagonal baptistry contains some beautiful 5th-century mosaics.

North façade

East Façade
The main entrance, on the east façade (1735), is adorned with statues of Christ and the Apostles.

Museum entrance

Apse

Lateran Palace

Papal Altar
The Gothic baldacchino, which rises over the papal altar, is decorated with 14th-century frescoes.

On Maundy Thursday the Pope, as Bishop of Rome, gives a blessing from the loggia of the city's main cathedral

The Corsini Chapel was built in the 1730s for Pope Clement XII Corsini, who lies buried in a porphyry tomb from the Pantheon.

Main entrance

Boniface VIII Fresco
Possibly by Giotto, this fragment shows the Pope announcing the Holy Year of 1300, which attracted around two million pilgrims.

Cloisters
Built by the Vassalletto family in about 1220, the cloisters are remarkable for their twisted columns and inlaid marble mosaics.

Part of one of the gymnasia in the Baths of Caracalla

❽ Baths of Caracalla

Viale delle Terme di Caracalla 52. **Map** 7 A3. **Tel** 06 39 96 77 00. 🚌 160, 628. 🚋 3. **Open** 9am–1 hr before sunset Tue–Sun, 9am–2pm Mon. **Closed** 1 Jan, 25 Dec. 🔲 🔲 🔲

Rearing up at the foot of the Aventine Hill are the monolithic red-brick ruins of the Baths of Caracalla. Begun by Emperor Septimius Severus in AD 206, and completed by his son Caracalla in AD 217, they remained in use until the 6th century, when the Goths sabotaged the city's aqueducts.

Going for a bath was one of the social events of the day in ancient Rome. Large complexes such as Caracalla, with a capacity for 1,600 bathers, were not simply places to have a natter and get washed, but also areas which offered an impressive array of facilities: art galleries, gymnasia, gardens, libraries, conference rooms, lecture rooms and shops selling food and drink.

A Roman bath was a long and complicated business, beginning with a form of Turkish bath, followed by a spell in the *caldarium*, a large hot room with pools of water to moisten the atmosphere. Then came the lukewarm *tepidarium*, followed by a visit to the large central meeting place known as the *frigidarium*, and finally a plunge into the *natatio*, an open-air swimming pool. For the rich, this was followed by a rub-down with scented woollen cloth.

Most of the rich marble decorations of the baths were scavenged by the Farnese family in the 16th century to adorn the rooms of Palazzo Farnese *(see p405)*. There are, however, statues and mosaics from the Baths in the Museo Nazionale Archeologico in Naples *(see pp494–5)* and in the Vatican's Gregorian Profane Museum *(see p426)*.

So dramatic is the setting that it is the regular venue for the open-air opera season in summer.

❾ Pyramid of Caius Cestius

Piazzale Ostiense. **Map** 6 E4. 🚌 23, 280. 🚋 3. Ⓜ Piramide. 🔲 only.

Caius Cestius was a wealthy but unimportant 1st-century BC *praetor*, or senior magistrate. At the time, inspired by the Cleopatra scandals, there was a craze for all things Egyptian, and Caius decided to commission himself a pyramid as a tomb. Set into the Aurelian Wall near Porta San Paolo, it is built of brick and faced with white marble; according to an inscription, it took just 330 days to build in 12 BC.

The Pyramid of Caius Cestius on Piazzale Ostiense

❿ Protestant Cemetery

Cimitero Acattolico, Via di Caio Cestio. **Map** 6 D4. **Tel** 06 574 19 00. 🚌 23, 280. 🚋 3. **Open** 9am–5pm Mon–Sat, 9am–1pm Sun. Last adm: 30 mins before closing. Donation.

Non-Catholics have been buried in this cemetery behind the Aurelian Wall since 1738. In the oldest part (on the left as you enter) is the grave of the poet John Keats, who died in 1821 in a house on Piazza di Spagna *(see p412)*. He wrote his own epitaph: "Here lies one whose name was writ in water". Close by rest the ashes of Percy Bysshe Shelley, who drowned in 1822.

The interior of Santa Sabina

⓫ Santa Sabina

Piazza Pietro d'Illiria 1. **Map** 6 D2. **Tel** 06 57 94 01. 🚌 23, 44, 170, 781. **Open** 8:15am–12:30pm, 3:30–6pm daily. ♿

High on the Aventine stands an early Christian basilica, founded by Peter of Illyria in AD 425 and later given to the Dominican order. It was restored to its original simplicity in the early 20th century. Light filters through 9th-century windows on to a nave framed by pale Corinthian columns. Above the main door is a blue and gold 5th-century mosaic inscription to Peter. In the side portico outside is a 5th-century panelled door carved with biblical scenes, notably one of the oldest images of the Crucifixion (top left-hand corner).

Further Afield

It is well worth making the effort to see some of Rome's outlying sights. Highlights are the Villa Giulia, home to a magnificent Etruscan museum, and the Museo Borghese on the splendid Villa Borghese estate, with its extraordinary collection of virtuoso statues by Bernini. Other sights range from ancient churches and catacombs to the more modern suburb of EUR, a strange architectural medley begun by Mussolini in the 1930s.

Sights at a Glance

Churches and Temples
- **5** Sant'Agnese fuori le Mura
- **6** Santa Costanza
- **10** San Paolo fuori le Mura

Museums and Galleries
- **2** Museo e Galleria Borghese
- **3** Villa Giulia
- **4** MAXXI

Parks and Gardens
- **1** Villa Borghese

Ancient Roads and Sites
- **7** Via Appia Antica
- **8** Catacombs

City Districts
- **9** EUR

Key

- Central Rome
- Suburbs
- Motorway
- Major road
- Minor road
- City walls

0 kilometres 3
0 miles 3

1 Villa Borghese

Map 3 B1. 52, 53, 88, 116, 490. 3, 19. Park **Open** dawn–sunset daily.

The villa and its park were designed in 1605 for Cardinal Scipione Borghese, the sybaritic nephew of Pope Paul V. An extravagant patron of the arts, he amassed one of Europe's finest collections of paintings, statues and antiquities, many of which are still displayed in the villa which he built especially to house his antique sculptures.

The **park** was one of the first of its kind in Rome, its formal gardens divided by avenues and graced with statues. It contained 400 newly planted trees, garden sculpture by Bernini's father, Pietro, along with many ingenious fountains, "secret" flower gardens, enclosures of exotic animals and birds, and even a grotto with artificial rain. There was also a speaking robot and a trick chair, which trapped anyone who sat in it. At first the grounds were

open to the public, but after a visitor was shocked by the collection of erotic paintings, Paul V decided to keep the park private.

In 1773 work began on redesigning the park in the wilder, Romantic style made fashionable by landscape artists like Claude Lorrain and Poussin. Over the next few years mock-Classical temples, fountains and

Temple of Aesculapius, an 18th-century folly, at the Villa Borghese

casine (summer-houses) were added. In 1901, the park and villa were acquired by the state, and in 1911 the area was chosen as the site for the International Exhibition. Pavilions were built by many of the world's nations, the most impressive of which is the **British School at Rome** by Edwin Lutyens. In the northeastern corner of the park lie the Museo Zoologico and a small redeveloped zoo, known as the Bioparco, where the emphasis is on conservation. Today the estates of the Villa Borghese, Villa Giulia and the Pincio gardens form one vast park, with the **Giardino del Lago**, at its centre, named after an artificial boating lake. Its main entrance is marked by an 18th-century copy of the Arch of Septimius Severus, while on the lake's island is a fake Ionic temple to the Greek god of health, Aesculapius, designed by the 18th-century architect Antonis Aspurucci.

A circular Temple of Diana folly lies between the Porta Pinciana, at the top of Via Veneto, and Piazza di Siena, a grassy amphitheatre which hosts Rome's international horse show in May. Its umbrella pines inspired the composer Ottorino Respighi to write *The Pines of Rome* (1924). The open-air opera season is also held in the park.

To the northwest of the park is the Galleria Nazionale d'Arte Moderna, and the Orangery is now home to the Carlo Bilotti museum.

Sacred and Profane Love by Titian (1514), in the Galleria Borghese

❷ Museo e Galleria Borghese

Villa Borghese, Piazzale Scipione Borghese 5. **Tel** 06 328 10. 🚌 52, 53, 116, 910. 🚃 3, 19. **Open** 8:30am–7pm Tue–Sun (reservations advised; essential on weekends). **Closed** 1 Jan, 25 Dec. 🚫 🚼 📷 💻 📷 ♿ 🌐 **galleriaborghese.it**

Cardinal Scipione Borghese's villa was designed in 1605 as a typical Roman country house, with its wings projecting into the surrounding gardens. It was built by Flaminio Ponzio, Pope Paul V's architect, and was used by Scipione for entertaining guests and for displaying his impressive collection of paintings and sculpture. Between 1801 and 1809 Prince Camillo Borghese, husband of Napoleon's sister Pauline, unfortunately sold many of the family paintings to his brother-in-law, and swapped 200 of Scipione's Classical statues for an estate in Piedmont. These statues are still in the Louvre and, as a consequence, the remaining antique Classical collection is less interesting than it might once have been. However, the hedonistic cardinal was an enthusiastic patron of the arts and the sculptures he commissioned from artists such as the young Bernini now rank among their most famous works.

The eight rooms of the ground floor of the Villa Borghese are set around a central hall, the Salone. The most famous statue is one of Bernini's finest works, *Apollo and Daphne* (1624) in room 3, which shows the nymph Daphne with bay leaves sprouting from her outstretched fingers, roots growing from her toes and rough bark enfolding her smooth body, as she begins to metamorphose into a laurel tree to escape being abducted by the god Apollo. Abduction is also the theme of *The Rape of Proserpina*, again by Bernini, in room 4. Depicting Pluto, the god of the underworld, carrying Proserpina, daughter of Ceres, off to be his bride, the sculpture is a virtuoso piece in which Bernini contrasts the taut musculature of Pluto with the soft yielding flesh of Proserpina, whose thigh dimples in his iron grip.

The third famous Bernini piece, which dates from 1623, is *David* in room 2. The artist captures the tensed, grimacing youth the moment before he releases the stone that slew Goliath. It is said that Pope Urban VIII held a mirror up to Bernini so that the sculptor could model David's face on his own. In the next

Detail of *Rape of Proserpina* by Bernini (1622), Museo Borghese

alcove is the Villa Borghese's most infamous work – a sculpture, executed in 1805 by Canova, of Pauline Borghese as *Venus Victrix* (Venus the Conqueror). The semi-naked Pauline reclining on a chaise-longue shocked those who saw it and Pauline's husband kept the statue locked away, even denying Canova access to it. The next room holds a selection of antiquities, notably a Roman copy of a plump *Bacchus* by the 4th-century BC Greek sculptor Praxiteles, and fragments of a 3rd-century AD mosaic found on one of the Borghese estates in Torrenova, showing gladiators battling with wild animals.

The Galleria Borghese, on the upper floor, houses some magnificent Baroque and Renaissance paintings. Works on display include Raphael's masterpiece, the *Deposition*, various works by Caravaggio, the graceful *Danäe* by the 16th-century artist Correggio, as well as works by Pinturicchio, Barocci, Rubens and Titian.

Bernini's *Apollo and Daphne* (1624)

❸ Villa Giulia

This villa was built in 1550 as a country retreat for Pope Julius III. Designed by Vignola and Ammannati, with contributions by Michelangelo and Vasari, it was intended for entertaining guests of the Vatican, such as Queen Christina of Sweden, rather than as a permanent home. The gardens were planted with 36,000 trees and peppered with pavilions and fountains. Villa Giulia also used to house an outstanding collection of sculptures: 160 boats filled with statues and ornaments were sent to the Vatican after the death of Pope Julius III in 1555.

Since 1889 the villa has been home to the Museo Nazionale Etrusco, animpressive collection of pre-Roman antiquities from central Italy.

VISITORS' CHECKLIST

Practical Information
Piazzale di Villa Giulia 9.
Tel 06 322 65 71.
Open 8:30am–7:30pm Tue–Sun (last adm: 6:30pm).
Closed 1 Jan, 25 Dec. 🎧 with seven days' notice. 📷 🎦 🖥
♿ 📷

Transport
🚌 52. 🚊 3, 19.

Rooms 14–21, the Antiquarium collection, display domestic and votive objects and ceramics, including the Cima-Pesciotti collection.

Ficoroni Cist
Engraved and beautifully illustrated, this 4th-century BC bronze marriage coffer held mirrors and other body care implements.

Rooms 22–24 exhibit finds from the Castellani collection, including early 6th-century ceramics and bronzes.

Rooms 31–36 contain finds from the Ager Faliscus, an area between the Tiber and Lake Bracciano.

Spiralled Faliscan Crater
Painted in the free style of the 4th century BC, this spiral-handled vase was used to hold wines or oil. The Falisci were an Italic tribe influenced by the Etruscans.

Husband and Wife Sarcophagus
This 6th-century BC tomb from Cerveteri shows a deceased couple banqueting in the afterlife. Their tender expression bears witness to the skill of Etruscan artists.

Ninfeo (Nympheum)

Rooms 1–13b are arranged by site, starting with Vulci (most importantly articles from the Warrior's Tomb) and including finds from Cerveteri.

Rooms 37–40 exhibit finds from Veio including the stunning Etruscan statue, Apollo of Veii.

Entrance

Key to Floorplan
▨ Lower ground floor
▨ Ground floor
▨ First floor
☐ Non-exhibition space

MAXXI, the National Museum of 21st Century Arts, designed by Zaha Hadid

❹ MAXXI (National Museum of 21st Century Arts)

Villa Guido Reni 4A. **Tel** 06 399 673 50.
🚌 53, 217, 910. 🚊 2. **Open**
11am–7pm Tue–Sun (11am–10pm Sat).
Closed 1 May, 25 Dec. ♿ 🚫 💻 📷
🅿 (free up to age 14). 🛒
🌐 fondazionemaxxi.it

Along with the nearby Parco della Musica *(see p449)*, MAXXI, the National Museum of 21st Century Arts, has put Rome on the contemporary arts map. Completed in 2009, it is located in a stunning building designed by architect Zaha Hadid. The museum showcases emerging Italian and international artists. An impressive amount of space is also given over to architecture.

❺ Sant'Agnese fuori le Mura

Via Nomentana 349. **Tel** 06 862 054 56.
🚌 60, 82, 90. **Open** 7:30am–noon,
4–7:30pm daily. **Closed** late Oct–late
Nov. 🚫 to catacombs. ♿ 📷

Sant'Agnese fuori le Mura was built in the 4th century above the crypt of the 13-year-old martyr St Agnes, and although much altered it retains the form of the original basilica. According to legend it was founded by Constantine's daughter Constantia, who was cured from leprosy after sleeping beside Agnes's tomb.

In the 7th-century apse mosaic, St Agnes appears as a bejewelled Byzantine empress in a stole of gold and a violet robe. Tradition has it that she appeared like this eight days after her death holding a white lamb. On 21 January two lambs are blessed in the church and a vestment called a *pallium* is woven from their wool, to be given to a new archbishop.

Apse mosaic in Sant'Agnese, showing the saint flanked by popes

❻ Santa Costanza

Via Nomentana 349. **Tel** 06 862 054 56. 🚌 60, 82, 90. **Open** 9am–noon, 4–6pm daily (Sun pm only). **Closed** late Oct–late Nov. 🚫 ♿ 📷

This circular church was built in the early 4th century as a mausoleum for Emperor Constantine's daughters, Constantia and Helena. The dome and its drum are supported by an arcade that rests on 12 magnificent pairs of granite columns. The encircling ambulatory has a barrel-vaulted ceiling decorated with the world's earliest surviving Christian mosaics, which date from the 4th century.

In a niche on the far side of the church is a replica of Constantia's ornate porphyry sarcophagus, carved with cherubs crushing grapes. The

original was moved to the Vatican Museums in 1790. The sanctity of Constantia is somewhat debatable. Described by the historian Marcellinus as a fury incarnate, constantly goading her equally unpleasant husband, Hannibalianus, to violence, her canonization was probably the result of some confusion with a saintly nun of the same name.

❼ Via Appia Antica

🚌 118, 218.

The first part of the Via Appia was built in 312 BC by Appius Claudius Caecus. In 190 BC, when it was extended to the ports of Taranto and Brindisi, the road became Rome's link with its empire in the East. It was the route taken by the funeral processions of the dictator Sulla (78 BC) and Emperor Augustus (AD 14), and it was along this road that St Paul was led as a prisoner to Rome in AD 56. The church of Domine Quo Vadis? marks the spot where St Peter is said to have met Christ when fleeing Rome. The road is lined with ruined family tombs, decaying monuments, and collective burial places *(columbaria)*. Beneath the fields on either side lies a maze of catacombs, including those of San Callisto and San Sebastiano.

Cypresses lining the Roman road, Via Appia

❽ Catacombs

Via Appia Antica 126. 🚌 118, 218. San Callisto **Tel** 06 513 01 580. **Open** 9am–noon, 2–5pm Thu–Tue. **Closed** 1 Jan, late Jan–late Feb, Easter Sun, 25 Dec.

In burying their dead in underground cemeteries outside the city walls, the early Christians were simply obeying the laws of the time. They were not forced to use them because of persecution, as later popular myth has suggested. Many saints were buried here, and the catacombs later became shrines and places of pilgrimage.

Today several catacombs are open to the public. The vast Catacombs of San Callisto, hewn from volcanic tufa, contain niches, or *loculi*, which held two or three bodies, as well as the burial places of several early popes. Close by, walls in the Catacombs of San Sebastiano are covered in graffiti invoking St Peter and St Paul, whose remains may once have been moved here.

Engraving of Christian ceremony in Catacombs of San Callisto (AD 50)

❾ EUR

🚌 170, 671, 714. Ⓜ EUR Fermi, EUR Palasport. Museo della Civiltà Romana Piazza G Agnelli 10. **Tel** 06 06 08. **Open** 9am–2pm Tue–Sun. Last adm 1 hr before closing. **Closed** 1 Jan, 1 May, 25 Dec.

The Esposizione Universale di Roma (EUR), a suburb to the south of the city, was orig-inally built for an international exhibition, a kind of "Work Olympics", that was planned

EUR's Palazzo della Civiltà del Lavoro, the "Square Colosseum"

for 1942, but never took place because of the outbreak of war. The architecture was intended to glorify Fascism, and as a result the bombastic style of the buildings can look overblown and rhetorical to modern eyes. Of all the buildings the best known is probably the Palazzo della Civiltà del Lavoro (the Palace of the Civilization of Work), an unmistakable landmark for people arriving from Fiumicino airport.

The scheme was eventually completed in the 1950s. Despite the area's dubious architecture, EUR has been a planning success, and people are still keen to live here. As well as residential housing, the vast marble halls along the wide boulevards are also home to a number of government offices and museums. Best among the latter is the Museo della Civiltà Romana, famous for its casts of the reliefs from the Column of Trajan, and for a large scale

model depicting 4th-century Rome with all the buildings which then stood within the Aurelian walls. The south of the suburb features a lake and shady park, and the huge domed Palazzo dello Sport, built for the 1960 Olympics.

❿ San Paolo fuori le Mura

Via Ostiense 186. 🚌 23, 128, 170, 670, 761, 766, 769. Ⓜ San Paolo. **Tel** 06 698 80 800. **Open** 7am–6:30pm daily. Cloister: **Open** 9am–6pm daily.

Today's church is a faithful if soulless reconstruction of the great 4th-century basilica destroyed by fire in 1823. Only a few fragments of the earlier church survived, most notably the cloister (1241), with its pairs of colourful in-laid columns, considered one of the most beautiful in Rome.

Elsewhere, the church's triumphal arch is decorated on one side with heavily restored 5th-century mosaics, and on the other with mosaics by Pietro Cavallini originally on the façade. The equally fine mosaics (1220) in the apse represent the figures of Christ with St Peter, St Andrew, St Paul and St Luke.

The single most outstanding work of art is the fine marble canopy over the high altar, the work of Arnolfo di Cambio (1285), with the possible assistance of Pietro Cavallini. Below the altar is the *confessio* where it is alleged St Paul was once buried. To its right is an impressive Paschal candlestick dating from the 12th century by Nicolò di Angelo and Pietro Vassalletto.

19th-century mosaic on façade of San Paolo fuori le Mura

Shopping in Rome

Rome has always been a thriving centre for design and shopping. In ancient times, the finest craftsmen were drawn to the city, and artifacts and products of all kinds, including gold, furs and wine, were imported from far-flung corners of the Empire to satisfy the needs of the wealthy local population. Shopping in Rome today in many ways reflects this diverse tradition. Italian designers have a well-deserved reputation for their luxuriously chic style in fashion, knitwear and leather goods (especially shoes and handbags), as well as in interior design, fabrics, ceramics and glass. The artisan tradition is strong, and the love of good design filters through into the smallest items. Rome is not a city for bargains (although it is often better value than Florence or Milan), but the joys of window shopping here will offer plenty of compensation.

Fashion

Italy is one of the leading lights in high fashion, or *alta moda*. Many famous designers may be based in Milan, but Rome is home to a cluster of sophisticated and internationally distinguished fashion houses. The most notable among them are probably,**Fendi**, **Laura Biagiotti**, **Prada** and **Valentino**, whose studio dominates Piazza Mignanelli.

But even for those unable to splash out on genuine designer gear, much fun can be gained from a stroll down the streets that radiate out from the Piazza di Spagna: some of the window displays here are truly spectacular.

Rome is not a good place to buy everyday wear, since there is a distinct lack of mid-price shops bridging the gap between the dazzlingly priced *alta moda* designer exclusives and the ultra-cheap goods sold in markets. However, at **Discount dell'Alta Moda** you can find end-of-season designer labels at 50 per cent less than the boutique prices.

Books and Gifts

Rome offers huge scope for gift buying, both in the well-established tourist stores in the historic centre and in smaller shops located in less frequented parts of the city that might not feature in your holiday itinerary. The central Via del Pellegrino is a street crammed with small specialist outlets, such as **Le Tre Ghinee**, which sells ceramics and glass objects. If you are more interested in contemporary design, visit the **Palazzo delle Esposizioni**, where a wide range of objects by famous designers is available.

The **Feltrinelli International** bookshop has an excellent range of foreign-language fiction, as well as non-fiction covering various subjects, including Italian art and architecture, cookery, travel and history. It also stocks some superb photographic, art and cinema posters. For cut-price deals on books try the second-hand stalls in Via delle Terme di Diocleziano and in Largo della Fontanella di Borghese.

Near the Pantheon, the Florentine **Il Papiro** sells a great range of illustrious paper-based products, including diaries, notebooks, envelopes and beautiful seal-and-wax sets that make ideal gifts.

Religious artifacts are readily available in bookshops near the main basilicas, such as the **Libreria Belardetti** near St Peter's. Other shops specialize in religious items for both the clergy and the layperson. Facing the Vatican gates, in Via di Porta Angelica, there are several shops, including **Al Pellegrino Cattolico**, that sell mementos to visiting pilgrims.

Food and Drink

If you are tempted to take home some irresistible Italian delicacies, such as pecorino romano cheese, Parma ham, extra virgin olive oil, dried porcini mushrooms, sun-dried tomatoes, olives and grappa, as well as superb wines from Lazio and elsewhere then the traditional food stores, *alimentari*, are a great place to start. Try the well-stocked **Fratelli Fabbi**, near Piazza di Spagna, with its exceptional selection of delicious cold meats and cheeses from every corner of Italy, as well as quality wines and champagnes. A few doors down on the same street is **Focacci**, with its wonderful array of Italian delicacies. The historic but expensive **Volpetti** in Testaccio is synonymous with great service and uncompromising quality. Aside from specializing in unusual cheeses, olive oils, vinegars and a fabulous selection of food hampers, Volpetti also stocks a variety of Italian salt and caviar – you can even try before you buy.

In Pinciano, **Casa dei Latticini Micocci** sells a comprehensive range of cheeses from even the most remote regions of Italy, while in Trastevere, the family-run **Antica Caciara Trasteverina** has a vast assortment of local and regional dairy products, which include sheep's ricotta and the Piedmontese *toma del fen*. More local, reasonably priced cheeses are available at **Cisternino**.

If cakes and chocolate feature on your list, then there is plenty of opportunity to satisfy those cravings too. **Chocolat**, in the historic centre, sells brand-name and home-made chocolate and organizes occasional tastings and dinners for connoisseurs, while **Moriondo e Gariglio** specializes in chocolate delights made to traditional Piedmontese recipes. **La Deliziosa**, near Piazza Navona, offers a great range of Italian desserts and cakes; the ricotta-based variety deserves a special mention.

Bear in mind that customs restrictions can apply to certain foodstuffs.

Markets

Rome's open-air markets are quintessential examples of the bubbling exuberance and earthiness for which Romans are renowned. They are wonderfully vivid experiences too, since Italian stallholders have raised the display of even the humblest vegetable to an art form.

The city is dotted with small local food markets, and there are several fascinating well-established markets near the centre. These include **Campo de' Fiori** for foodstuffs, the **Mercato delle Stampe** for old prints, books and magazines, and the **Nuovo Mercato Esquilino** for international foods.

Trastevere's famous flea market, **Porta Portese**, was established shortly after the end of World War II and is said to have grown out of the thriving black market that operated at

Tor di Nona, opposite Castel Sant'Angelo, during those lean years. Anything and everything seems to be for sale, piled high on stalls in carefully arranged disorder – clothes, shoes, bags, linen, luggage, camping equipment, towels, pots, pans, kitchen utensils, plants, pets, cassettes and CDs, old LPs and 78s.

If you are looking for a traditional food market in the heart of the old city, Rome's most picturesque market is also its most historical. Its name, Campo de' Fiori (see p405), which translates as "field of flowers", sometimes misleads people into expecting a flower market. In fact, the name is said to derive from Campus Florae (Flora's square) – Flora being the lover of the great Roman general Pompey. A market has been held in this beautiful

central piazza for many centuries. Every morning, except Sunday, the piazza is transformed by an array of stalls selling fruit and vegetables, meat, poultry and fish. One or two stalls also specialize in legumes, rice and dried fruits and nuts.

Throughout the year Rome also plays host to many street fairs. If they coincide with your visit, these are fun to go to, because they normally sell a good variety of local produce, handicrafts and clothes. Seasonal fairs also occur, especially around Christmas; among them is **Mercatino di Natale** in Piazza Navona, where you can stock up on toys and crib figures.

Be sure to keep your wits about you at markets: pickpockets work with lightning speed in the bustling crowds.

DIRECTORY

Fashion

Discount dell'Alta Moda
Via di Gesù e Maria 14 & 16A. **Map** 2 F2.
Tel 06 322 37 96.

Fendi
Largo Goldoni 419.
Map 10 E3.
Tel 06 33 45 01.

Laura Biagiotti
Via Mario de' Fiori 26.
Map 10 F1.
Tel 06 679 12 05.

Prada
Via Condotti 92–95.
Map 3 A2.
Tel 06 679 08 97.

Valentino
Via Condotti 15.
Map 3 A2.
Tel 06 673 94 20.

Books and Gifts

Al Pellegrino Cattolico
Via di Porta Angelica 83.
Map 1 C2.
Tel 06 68 80 23 51.

Feltrinelli International
Via VE Orlando 84–86.
Map 3 C3.
Tel 06 487 01 71.

Libreria Belardetti
Via della Conciliazione 4A.
Map 1 C3.
Tel 06 686 55 02.

Palazzo delle Esposizioni
Via Milano 15–17.
Map 3 B4.
Tel 06 48 91 33 61.

Il Papiro
Via del Pantheon 50 (leading to Via degli Orfani).
Map 10 D2.
Tel 06 679 55 97.

Le Tre Ghinee
Via del Pellegrino 90.
Map 2 E4.
Tel 06 687 27 39.

Food and Drink

Antica Caciara Trasteverina
Via San Francesco a Ripa 140A/B.
Map 5 C1.
Tel 06 581 28 15.

Casa dei Latticini Micocci
Via Collina 14. **Map** 4 D2.
Tel 06 474 17 84.

Chocolat
Via del Teatro Valle 54.
Map 10 D3.
Tel 06 68 13 55 45.

Cisternino
Vicolo del Gallo 18–19.
Map 9 C4.
Tel 06 687 28 75.

La Deliziosa
Vicolo Savelli 50.
Map 9 B3.
Tel 06 68 80 31 55.

Focacci
Via della Croce 43.
Map 2 F2.
Tel 06 679 12 28.

Fratelli Fabbi
Via della Croce 28.
Map 2 F2.
Tel 06 679 06 12.

Moriondo e Gariglio
Via del Piè di Marmo 21.
Map 10 E3.
Tel 06 699 08 56.

Volpetti
Via Marmorata 47.
Map 6 D2.
Tel 06 574 23 52.

Markets

Campo de' Fiori
Piazza Campo de' Fiori.
Map 2 E4 & 9 C4.
Open 7am–1:30pm Mon–Sat.

Mercatino di Natale
Piazza Navona.
Map 9 C4.
Open end Nov–early Jan: daily.

Mercato delle Stampe
Largo della Fontanella di Borghese.
Map 2 F3 & 10 D1.
Open 9am–1pm Mon–Sat.

Nuovo Mercato Esquilino
Via Principe Amedeo.
Map 4 E4.
Open 9am–2pm Mon–Fri.

Porta Portese
Via Portuense & Via Ippolito Nievo.
Map 5 C3.
Open 6:30am–2pm Sun.

Entertainment in Rome

There's a particular excitement attached to entertainment in Rome. Football and opera, for example, are worth experiencing for sheer atmosphere alone, whether or not you are a fan. There is also a good jazz scene, with international stars appearing alongside local talent. Unexpectedly, given the general shutdown among shops and restaurants, the summer is Rome's liveliest time in terms of entertainment and cultural events, with the city's Renaissance squares, vast parks, villa gardens, Classical ruins and other open spaces hosting various arts festivals. Concerts and films take on an added dimension when performances take place beneath the stars in the many open-air arenas across the city. Rome also has plenty of nightclubs to choose from.

Practical Information

Good sources of information about what's on are the listings magazine *WHERE Rome* and *Trovaroma*, the weekly Thursday supplement to *La Repubblica* newspaper. Also worth getting hold of is *L'Evento,* available from the Rome Tourist Office (see p617), which gives details in English of cultural events in the city.

Booking Tickets

Among the ticket agencies that will book seats for some performances for you (for a small fee) are **Orbis** and **Box Office**. Many theatres do not accept telephone bookings – you have to visit the box office in person. They will charge you a *prevendita* supplement (about 10 per cent of the normal price) for any tickets sold in advance. The **Teatro dell'Opera** box office handles sales for both summer and winter seasons. Tickets for most big rock and jazz events can be bought at Orbis and at larger record shops, such as **Ricordi Media Store**. Look out for *due per uno* coupons in local bars – these allow two people entrance for the price of one.

Open-Air Entertainment

Open-air opera, cinema, classical music and jazz concerts fill the Roman calendar from late June until the end of September. Both the **Cineporto**, a festival held along the Tiber, at the Ponte Milvio, and the **Festival di Massenzio**, at the Forum, offer films, live music, food and small exhibitions in July and August. The summer months also bring excellent open-air rock, jazz and world-music festivals, while Rome's main autumn performing-arts festival, **RomaEuropa**, has occasional performances in the grounds of the Villa Medici. Theatre also moves outside in the summer months, and some cinemas roll back their ceilings for open-air screenings.

More traditional is Trastevere's community festival, the **Festa de Noantri** (see p71), with music, processions and fireworks. This religious festival begins on the Saturday after 16 July, and celebrations continue until the end of the month.

Classical Music and Dance

Classical concerts take place in a surprising number of venues. Tickets for opera premieres may be hard to find, but soloists, groups or orchestras playing in gardens, churches, villas or ancient ruins are easier to obtain and more reasonably priced.

World-renowned soloists and orchestras make appearances throughout the year in venues such as the stunning Renzo Piano-designed **Parco della Musica** and the **Accademia Filarmonica Romana**. Past visitors have included Luciano Pavarotti and Placido Domingo, the Berlin Philharmonic and prima ballerina Sylvie Guillem. One of the most innovative programmes of classical and contemporary music is provided by the **Aula Magna dell'Università La Sapienza**. The opera season starts late at the **Teatro dell'Opera**, between November and January. The great ballet classics are also staged at this venue. The **Equilibrio Festival** in February brings contemporary dance to the city; performances take place mainly at the Parco della Musica.

Rock, Jazz and World Music

Rome's non-classical music scene is unpredictable and subject to vast seasonal changes. However, there is a huge variety of music at the many clubs and stadiums, such as the **Palalottomatica** and the **Stadio Olimpico**, which attract foreign and home-grown stars. The best jazz musicians play at the splendid **Casa del Jazz**, and **Alexanderplatz**. Trastevere's **Big Mama** is one of the city's legendary addresses for important jazz names, while world music is well served at the aptly named **Villaggio Globale**.

For smaller venues you might need to buy a monthly or annual membership card (between €2 and €11), which often includes the entrance fee for smaller bands.

Cinema and Theatre

Cinema-going is a popular pastime in Rome, with around 40 films on show on an average weekday. Most Roman cinemas are *prima visione* (first run) and show the latest inter-national films in dubbed versions. The best cinemas for decor and comfort are the **Fiamma** (two screens) and the **Barberini** (three screens). Films in their original language are often shown at the excellent **Casa del Cinema** and at the **Nuovo Olimpia**. Smaller art cinemas, such as the **Azzurro Scipioni**, are more likely to show subtitled versions of foreign films.

Theatre productions are performed in Italian whether the plays are national classics or by foreign playwrights. The main theatres – **Teatro Argentina**, **Teatro Quirino** and the **Eliseo** – offer a selection by great Italian playwrights. There are also performances of traditional cabaret, dance and avant-garde theatre at the **Teatro India**. Theatre tickets cost between €8 and €50 and can generally be booked only in advance by visiting the theatre box office in person or through agencies such as Box Office.

Nightlife

Rome's nightlife has never been as vibrant as it is today, with a sharp rise in the number of bars and clubs, all catering for an ever more demanding clientele.

Once the choice was limited to a few well-established bars in the centre and the hugely popular clubs in the Ostiense area and in San Lorenzo, such as the unashamedly commercial **Goa** or the more cutting-edge **Locanda Atlantide**, which hosts a whole range of DJs from funk to reggae. Now, though, the capital offers a wide range of options designed to satisfy all tastes and budgets.

Head first to a stylish pre-clubbing venue such as **'Gusto**, where you can rub shoulders with out-on-the-town locals taking advantage of the range of facilities – on three sites there is a restaurant, a pizzeria, a wine bar and live music. Alternatively, for a more leisurely start to your evening simply relax in a wine bar in one of the historic centre's breathtaking squares.

If you are looking for a gay venue, **Coming Out**, near the Colosseum, attracts both gay and straight drinkers, and **Planet Roma** just off Via Ostiense regularly hosts gay nights.

For an alternative edge to Rome's vivacious nightlife, try out the *centri sociali*, illegally occupied buildings that have been converted into arts and entertainment centres. Top billing goes to **Brancaleone**, which features Italian and international DJs for the best in electronic and house tunes.

A night out in Rome can be expensive – you can be charged as much as €10 for a cocktail in the bars around the central parts of Rome. For a cheaper alternative, visit one of the many bars in the area around San Lorenzo.

DIRECTORY

Booking Tickets

Box Office
Largo Argentina 11 (inside Feltrinelli bookshop). **Map** 10 D4. **Tel** 06 68 30 85 96.

Orbis
Piazza dell'Esquilino 37. **Map** 4 D4.
Tel 06 482 74 03.

Ticketeria
w ticketeria.it

Classical Music and Dance

Accademia Filarmonica Romana
Via Flaminia 118.
Tel 06 320 17 52.
w filarmonicaromana.org

Aula Magna dell'Università La Sapienza
Piazzale Aldo Moro 5.
Map 4 F3.
Tel 06 361 00 51.
w concertiiuc.it

Parco della Musica
Viale de Coubertin 30.
Tel 06 80 24 12 81 (info); 89 29 82 (credit card sales). w auditorium.com

RomaEuropa
Via dei Magazzini Generali 20a.
Tel 06 45 55 30 50.
w romaeuropa.net

Teatro dell'Opera
Piazza Beniamino Gigli 1.
Map 3 C3.
Tel 06 48 16 01.
w operaroma.it

Rock, Jazz and World Music

Alexanderplatz
Via Ostia 9. **Map** 1 B1.
Tel 06 39 74 21 71.

Big Mama
Vicolo San Francesco a Ripa 18. **Map** 5 C2.
Tel 06 581 25 51.

Casa del Jazz
Viale di Porta Ardeatina 55. **Map** 7 A4.
Tel 06 70 47 31.
w casajazz.it

Palalottomatica
Piazzale dello Sport.
Tel 06 54 09 01.

Stadio Olimpico
Viale dei Gladiatori (north-west of city centre, across the Tiber by Monte Mario).

Villaggio Globale
Ex-Mattatoio, Lungotevere Testaccio 1.
Map 6 D4.
Tel 347 413 12 05.

Cinema and Theatre

Azzurro Scipioni
Via degli Scipioni 82.
Map 1 C2.
Tel 06 39 73 71 61.

Barberini
Piazza Barberini 24.
Map 3 B3.
Tel 06 86 39 13 61.

Casa del Cinema
Largo Mastroianni 1.
Map 3 B1. **Tel** 06 06 08.
w casadelcinema.it

Eliseo
Via Nazionale 183. **Map** 3 B4. **Tel** 06 488 21 14.

Fiamma
Via Bissolati 47. **Map** 3 C2.
Tel 06 48 55 26.

Nuovo Olimpia
Via in Lucina 16.
Map 10 E1.
Tel 06 686 10 68.

Teatro Argentina
Largo Argentina 56. **Map** 2 F4. **Tel** 06 684 00 03 11.
w teatrodiroma.net

Teatro India
Via L Pierantoni 6.
Map 5 C5.
Tel 06 684 00 03 11.

Teatro Quirino
Via delle Vergini 7.
Map 3 B3 & 10 F2.
Tel 06 679 45 85.
w teatroquirino.it

Nightlife

Brancaleone
Via Levanna 13 (in Montesacro).
Tel 06 82 00 43 82.

Coming Out
Via San Giovanni in Laterano 8. **Map** 7 B1.
Tel 06 700 98 71.

Goa
Via Libetta 13 (in Ostiense)
Tel 06 574 82 77.

'Gusto
Piazza Augusto Imperatore 9. **Map** 2 F2.
Tel 06 322 62 73.

Locanda Atlantide
Via dei Lucani 22b (San Lorenzo district).
Tel 06 96 04 58 75.

Planet Roma
Via del Commercio 36–8.
Map 8 D5.
Tel 06 574 78 26.

ROME STREET FINDER

Map references given with sights described in the Rome chapters relate to the maps on the following pages. Map references are also given for hotels (see pp562–77) and restaurant listings (see pp580–605) and for useful addresses in the Travellers' Needs and Survival Guide sections at the back of the book. The first figure in the map reference tells you which Street Finder map to turn to, and the letter and number which follow refer to the grid reference on that map. The small map below shows the area of Rome covered by each of the eight maps and the corresponding map number is given in black. All the major sights are sketched out on the maps, and symbols, listed in the key below, are used to indicate the location of other important buildings.

0 kilometres	2
0 miles	1

Key and Scale for Street Finder Pages

Major sight	Synagogue
Place of interest	Railway line
FS Railway station	City walls
M Metro station	Pedestrian street
Tram stop	
Tourist information	
Hospital with casualty unit	
Police station	
Church	

Scale of Maps 1–8

| 0 metres | 250 | |
| 0 yards | 250 | 1:12,000 |

Scale of Maps 9–10

| 0 metres | 150 | |
| 0 yards | 150 | 1:7600 |

LAZIO

Lying between the Apennines and the Tyrrhenian Sea, Lazio is a varied region of volcanic lakes, mountains, ravines, vineyards and olive groves. Before the rise of Rome, it was populated by the Etruscans and various Italic tribes, including the Latins, after whom the region is named. Besides its archaeological sites, Lazio also offers skiing and swimming and water sports in the lakes and sea.

Lazio was inhabited at least 60,000 years ago, although the first signs of a substantial civilization date back to the 10th century BC. By the 7th century BC a flourishing Etruscan and Sabine civilization based on trade and agriculture existed in the north, while the region's southern margins were colonized by the Latins, Volsci and Hernici. History mingles with myth in the writings of Virgil, who describes how Aeneas landed in Lazio where he married the daughter of the king of the Latins. Romulus and Remus (legendary founders of Rome) were descendants of this alliance.

With the rise of Rome as a power, the Etruscan and Latin peoples were, in time, overwhelmed and the focus of the region turned to the city of Rome. Great roads and aqueducts extended out of the city like spokes of a wheel, and wealthy patricians built lavish villas in the surrounding countryside.

The early Middle Ages saw the rise of the Church's temporal power and, with the foundation of monasteries at Subiaco and Montecassino, Lazio became the cradle of western monasticism, and eventually part of the Papal States. In the 16th and 17th centuries, wealthy papal families competed with one another to build luxurious villas and gardens, hiring some of the best architects of the Renaissance and Baroque.

Throughout its history, however, Lazio has been eclipsed and neglected by Rome. The Pontine marshes were a malaria-ridden swamp until the 1920s, when Mussolini had them drained and brought new roads and agricultural improvements to the area.

Looking out over Caprarola during the early evening *passeggiata*

◀ View of Civita di Bagnoregio a small hilltown in Viterbo

Exploring Lazio

Much of Lazio's landscape was formed by the eruption of four volcanoes which showered the area with lava. Lakes formed in the craters, and the soil, rendered fertile by the lava, nourished vines, olives, fruit and nut trees. The volcanic activity also left Lazio with hot springs, notably around Tivoli, Viterbo and Fiuggi. Rome dominates the area, dividing the wooded hills of the north from the reclaimed Pontine marshes in the south. Swimming and sailing are possible in lakes Bracciano, Bolsena and Albano, while Lazio's best beaches lie between Gaeta and Sabaudia in the Parco Nazionale del Circeo.

Sights at a Glance

1 Tuscania
2 Viterbo
3 Montefiascone
4 Bomarzo
5 Caprarola
6 Tarquinia
7 Cerveteri
8 Lake Bracciano
9 Ostia Antica
10 Frascati and the Castelli Romani
11 Tivoli
12 Palestrina
13 Subiaco
14 Montecassino
15 Anagni
16 Sermoneta and Ninfa
17 Terracina
18 Sperlonga
19 Gaeta

ROME pp387–463

The Tolfa hills southwest of Lake Bracciano

Key

═══ Motorway
═══ Major road
= = Road under construction
── Secondary road
⋯⋯ Minor road
── Scenic route
─•─ Main railway
── Minor railway
═══ Regional border
△ Summit

For additional map symbols *see back flap*

The old quarter overlooking the beach at Sperlonga

Getting Around

Rome's two international airports at Fiumicino and Ciampino serve the region. The main motorways are the *Autostrada del Sole* Firenze–Roma (A1) and Roma–Napoli (A1–E45), and the Roma–L'Aquila (A24–E80). The ring road *(raccordo anulare)* around Rome connects the motorways and main roads.

The Lazio bus service, COTRAL, serves all the main towns with changeover points for the smaller locations in Rome and at Latina, Frosinone, Viterbo and Rieti. Train routes into the region from other Italian cities are efficient, although within Lazio the services are slower and less frequent.

Palestrina's terraces climbing up the hill

Carved loggia of the Palazzo Papale, Viterbo

❶ Tuscania

Viterbo. 🄼 8,200. 🚍 🛈 Piazzale
Trieste (0761 43 63 71). 🛒 Fri am.

Tuscania's trim walls and towers
are visible from afar on the
empty low-lying plains between
Viterbo and Tarquinia.
Although shaken by an
earthquake in 1971, its
medieval and
Renaissance
buildings have since
been carefully re-
constructed. Just
outside the city
walls, on the rocky
Colle San Pietro,
two remarkable
churches dating
from the Lombard-
Romanesque period occupy
the site of Tuscana, a major
Etruscan centre conquered by
Rome in 300 BC.

Façade of San Pietro, Tuscania

Santa Maria Maggiore, at the
foot of the hill, has a typically
Lombard-Romanesque
asymmetric façade with blind
arcades and a bold rose
window. Over the central door
lies a simple marble Madonna
and Child, framed by abstract
motifs and biblical scenes.
Inside, a rare 12th-century full-
immersion baptism font stands
in the aisle. The Lombard-
Romanesque church of
San Pietro, on top of the
hill, is a striking building
of ochre-hued tufa
and white marble
details. It stands on a
grassy piazza, along
with two medieval
towers and a
bishop's palace. The
façade features an
intricately inlaid rose
window flanked by
strange reliefs, including three-
headed bearded demons. The
interior is true to its 8th-century
form, with squat columns,
toothed arches, capitals carved
with stylized plants and a
Cosmati floor. Below the church
lies a strange mosque-like crypt.

❷ Viterbo

🄼 63,000. 🚇 🚍 🛈 Via Ascenzi 4
(0761 32 59 92). 🛒 Sat.

Viterbo was an important
Etruscan centre before falling to
the Romans in the 4th century BC.
Its heyday, however, came in the
13th century when it briefly
became the papal seat (1257–81).
During World War II it was
devastated, but the austere grey
stone medieval core, still encircled
by walls, and many of the
town's churches, have been
carefully restored.

In **San Pellegrino**, Viterbo's
oldest and best preserved
quarter, medieval houses with
towers, arches and external
staircases line narrow streets
running between little piazzas
decorated with fountains.

On Piazza San Lorenzo the
12th-century **Duomo** boasts an
elegant black and white striped
bell tower, a solemn 16th-century
façade and a stark Romanesque
interior. The adjacent 13th-century
Palazzo Papale, with a finely
carved loggia, was built for
popes on their visits to the city.

The town's civic buildings
border the main square, Piazza
del Plebiscito. The most
interesting is the 15th-century
Palazzo dei Priori, frescoed
inside by Baldassare Croce with
scenes from the town's history
and mythological past.

Outside the city walls, on Viale
Capocci, the Romanesque
Santa Maria della Verità has
wonderful 15th-century
frescoes by Lorenzo da Viterbo.

Villa Lante's small but splendid Renaissance gardens, considered Vignola's masterpiece

Environs

The **Villa Lante**, northeast of Viterbo, was begun in 1562 by Vignola for Cardinal Gambara. The main attractions are the outstanding Renaissance gardens and fountains. Be careful not to be a victim of a 16th-century practical joke: many of the fountains will sprinkle people without warning.

Palazzo dei Priori

Piazza Plebiscito. **Tel** 0761 30 47 95. **Open** daily.

Villa Lante

Bagnaia. **Tel** 0761 28 80 08. **Open** 8:30am–one hour before sunset Tue–Sun. **Closed** 1 Jan, 1 May, 25 Dec. to gardens.

Carved 11th-century capital in San Flaviano, Montefiascone

❸ Montefiascone

Viterbo. 13,000. Piazza V. Emanuele (0761 83 20 60). Wed.

This pretty town is perched on the edge of a defunct volcanic crater between the shores of Lake Bolsena, over which there are splendid views, and the Via Cassia. It is dominated by the octagonal bulk of its cathedral, **Santa Margherita**, whose dome, created in the 1670s by Carlo Fontana, is second only in size to St Peter's.

On the town's outskirts, along the Via Cassia towards Orvieto, lies **San Flaviano**, a lovely double-decker building with a 12th-century church oriented east over an 11th-century church pointing west. Inside are some fine 14th-century frescoes and freely carved capitals, thought to have been inspired by the traditions of Etruscan art.

The main façade of the pentagonal Palazzo Farnese at Caprarola

Environs

The popular lakeside beach resort of **Bolsena**, 15 km (9 miles) north on Lake Bolsena, has a medieval castle, as well as boats to the islands of Bisentina and Martana.

❹ Bomarzo

Parco dei Mostri, Bomarzo. **Tel** 0761 92 40 29. to Viterbo. from Viterbo (not Sun or public hols). **Open** 8:30am–sunset in winter (8:30am–7pm in summer). **parcodeimostri.com**

The Sacro Bosco beneath the town of Bomarzo was created between 1522 and 1580 by Duke Vicino Orsini as a bizarre memorial to his late wife. Far from a simple monument, Orsini embraced the artificiality and distortion of the Mannerist period by creating lop-sided buildings and sculpting huge boulders of stone into fantastic creatures and vast allegorical monsters.

One of the bizarre stone monsters in Bomarzo's Sacro Bosco

❺ Caprarola

Viterbo. 5,700. Via Filippo Nicolai 2 (0761 64 61 57). Tue.

Perhaps the grandest of the country villas created during the 17th century by the wealthy families of Rome, **Palazzo Farnese** *(see p384)* is the focal point of the medieval village of Caprarola. Designed by Vignola, it was built between 1559 and 1575 and takes its star-shape from the foundations of a large pentagonal fortress designed by Antonio da Sangallo the Younger half a century earlier. On the main floor, reached by an elaborately stuccoed spiral staircase, the rooms were frescoed, largely by the Zuccari brothers in 1560, with scenes depicting heroic episodes from the life of Hercules and the Farnese family.

Environs

Created, according to legend, by the god Hercules ramming his club into the ground, **Lago di Vico**, 4 km (3 miles) west of Caprarola, in fact occupies the remnants of a volcanic crater. An idyllic enclave, the lake is encircled by the wooded slopes of the Cimini Hills (much of which is a nature reserve). A scenic road runs around the lake, and the best place for swimming is on the southeast shore.

Palazzo Farnese

Caprarola. **Tel** 0761 64 60 52. **Open** Tue–Sun. **Closed** 1 Jan, 25 Dec.

Etruscan tumulus tombs from the necropolis at Cerveteri

❻ Tarquinia

Viterbo. 🚗 15,000. 🚉 🚌 ℹ️ Barriera di San Giusto (0766 84 92 82). 🛒 Wed.

Ancient Tarquinia (Tarxuna) was one of Etruria's most important centres. It occupied a strategic position to the northeast of the present town, on a ridge dominating the coastal plain, until the 4th century BC when it fell to Rome.

Tarquinia itself is worth a wander for its crumbling medieval churches and spacious main square, though the main reason to visit is the **Museo Archeologico e Necropoli**, which has one of Italy's better collections of Etruscan finds. Reclining statues of the deceased adorn the sarcophagi on the ground floor, but the star attraction is a group of terracotta winged horses dating from the 4th century BC.

On a hilltop 2 km (1 mile) southeast of town are the frescoed tombs of the **necropolis** dug into the soft volcanic tufa. There are almost 6,000 tombs but only about 15 can be visited at a time. The frescoes that decorate them, designed to remind the dead of life, range from frenetic dancing figures in the Tomba delle Leonesse to the diners reclining in the Tomba dei Leopardi.

🏛️ Museo Archeologico e Necropoli
Piazza Cavour. **Tel** 0766 85 60 36; 85 63 08 (necropolis). **Open** Tue–Sun. **Closed** 1 Jan, 1 May, 25 Dec. 🚫 ♿

❼ Cerveteri

Roma. 🚗 36,000. 🚉 🚌 ℹ️ P.za Risorgimento 19 (06 99 55 19 71). 🛒 Fri.

In the 6th century BC Cerveteri (ancient Kysry) was one of the largest and most culturally rich towns of the Mediterranean, trading with Greece and controlling a large area along the coast. The **necropolis**, a city of the dead 2 km (1 mile) outside town, is a network of streets lined with tombs dating from the 7th to the 1st century BC. Some of the larger tumulus tombs, like the Tomba degli Scudi e delle Sedie, are arranged like houses with rooms, doors and corridors. The Tomba dei Rilievi is decorated with plaster reliefs of tools, pets and mythological figures. Although the best finds from the necropolis are in

Dancers from the 4th-century BC frescoed Tomba del Triclinio in the Museo Archeologico, Tarquinia

museums such as the Vatican Museums, Villa Giulia and the British Museum in London, some can be seen in the small **Museo Nazionale Cerite** in the centre of town.

Environs
There are more traces of the Etruscans to be seen at **Norchia**, where the tombs are carved out of a rock face, and **Sutri**, whose amphitheatre is one of the few relics of the living Etruscans.

🏛️ Necropolis
Via Necropoli. **Tel** 06 994 00 01. **Open** Tue–Sun. **Closed** some pub hols. 🚫

🏛️ Museo Nazionale Cerite
Piazza Santa Maria. **Tel** 06 994 13 54. **Open** Tue–Sun. **Closed** pub hols. 🚫

Medieval Anguillara on Lake Bracciano

❽ Lake Bracciano

Roma. 🚉 🚌 Bracciano. ℹ️ Piazza Mazzini 5, Bracciano (06 99 81 62 62).

Bracciano is a large lake famous for its fish, and popular for water sports and lakeside lunches.

Medieval **Anguillara**, to the south, is the prettiest of the lakeside towns with romantic views over the water. The main town, **Bracciano**, on the east shore, is dominated by the Orsini-Odescalchi fortress, a pentagonal 15th-century structure with frescoes by Antoniazzo Romano and other Tuscan and Umbrian artists.

🏰 Castello Orsini-Odescalchi
P.za Mazzini 14. **Tel** 06 99 80 43 48. **Open** Tue–Sun. **Closed** 1 Jan, 25 Dec. 🚫 📷

⑨ Ostia Antica

Viale dei Romagnoli 717, Ostia. **Tel** 06
56 35 80 03. Ⓜ Piramide, then
🚆 from Porta San Paolo to Ostia
Antica. Excavations & Museum:
Open 8:30am–7:30pm Tue–Sun.
Closed 1 Jan, 1 May, 25 Dec. 📷

For over 600 years Ostia
was Rome's main port
and a busy trading
centre, until the 5th
century AD when a
disastrous combination
of malaria and
commercial
competition brought
the town into decline. Silt
preserved its buildings
and it now lies 5 km
(3 miles) inland.

   The ruins of Ostia give a
vivid idea of life in Classical
times. The main thoroughfare,
the **Decumanus Maximus**, runs
through the Forum, which
houses Ostia's largest temple,
the **Capitol**, and past the
restored **theatre**, still used for
open air concerts in summer.
The road is lined with baths,
shops and multi-storey
buildings. There is even a
Thermopolium, or bar, with a
marble counter and paintings
advertising food and drink.

**The building
material** for the
houses was brick,
left plain or
covered in mural
decoration.

**The internal
courtyard** has
remained a feature
of Italian housing.

Ruins of shops and offices along
the Decumanus Maximus

Balcony

Apartments or
single rooms were
rented out.

Shops
occupied the
ground floor of
the block.

Ostia Apartments

*Much of Ostia's population
lived in blocks of flats, such as this
building, based on the Casa di
Diana (2nd century AD).*

The bar served wine
and snacks.

⑩ Frascati and the Castelli Romani

Roma. 🚆 🚌 Frascati. Villa
Aldobrandini Gardens: **Tel** 06 942 14
34. **Open** Mon–Fri. 📷

The Alban hills have long been
a country retreat for Romans. In
Classical times they were scattered with villas; in the Middle
Ages with fortified castles
(hence the name); and in the
16th and 17th centuries with
luxurious residences and their
spectacular parks. During World
War II German defences were
based in the Alban hills and
many Castelli towns were
damaged by Allied bombs.
Although partly protected by a
nature reserve, the hilltop towns
are popular day-trip
destinations as well as being
famous for their white wine.
Frascati's central piazza is a
belvedere overlooked by the

Villa Aldobrandini, a majestic
17th-century building set in a
splendid park of secret grottoes,
fountains and statues.

   The fortified Abbazia di San
Nilo in **Grottaferrata**, 3 km
(2 miles) south, was founded in
1004 and contains some lovely
17th-century frescoes by
Domenichino in the chapel.
Overlooking Lake Albano, 6 km

(4 miles) south, **Castel Gandolfo**
is the site of the pope's summer
palace. When in residence the
pope addresses the crowd from
the balcony.

   Gathered around a sturdy
9th-century castle, and famed
for its strawberries, **Nemi**, 10 km
(6 miles) southeast, looks down
onto the glassy dark blue waters
of Lake Nemi.

The forested shores around the small, volcanic Lake Nemi

Tivoli, a favourite place to escape the heat of the Roman summer

⓫ Tivoli

Roma. 🏛 57,000. 🚊 🚌 ℹ️ Piazzale Nazioni Unite (0774 31 35 36). 🛍 Wed.

Hill-town Tivoli, a popular excursion from Rome, was once a favoured resort of the ancient Romans, attracted by its fresh water and sulphur springs, and beautiful countryside. The temples that once covered Tivoli's hilltop are still visible in places. Some are half buried in medieval buildings, others, such as the Temples of Sibyl and Vesta, inside the gardens of the Sibilla restaurant (on Via Sibilla), are relatively intact.

The town's most famous sight is the **Villa d'Este**, a sumptuous

Splendours from around the world reproduced in Hadrian's Villa

country residence created in the 16th century by Pirro Ligorio for Cardinal Ippolito d'Este from the shell of a Benedictine monastery. It is known primarily for its gardens, steeply raked on terraces, and studded with spectacular, if somewhat faded and mosshung, fountains. Although suffering from reduced water-pressure and polluted water due to centuries of neglect, the gardens give a vivid impression of the frivolous luxury enjoyed by the papal families. Highlights include the Viale delle Cento Fontane and the Fontana dell'Organo Idraulico, which, thanks to a hydraulic system, can play music. At the other end of town, the **Villa Gregoriana**, now a hotel, is set in a lush wooded valley where paths wind down into a deep ravine.

Environs

About 5 km (3 miles) west of Tivoli are the ruins of **Hadrian's Villa**. Easily seen in conjunction with a visit to the town, this is one of the largest and most spectacular villas ever built in the Roman Empire (it once covered an area greater than the centre of Imperial Rome).

Hadrian was an inveterate traveller and his aim in creating the villa was to reproduce some of the wonders he had seen around the world. The Stoa Poikile, for example, a walkway around a rectangular pool and garden, recalls the painted colonnade of the Stoic philosophers in Athens, while the Canopus evokes the grand sanctuary of Serapis in

Alexandria. There are also ruins of two bath complexes, a Latin and a Greek library, a Greek theatre, and a private study on a little island known as the Teatro Marittimo.

Today the rambling ruins, full of shady nooks and hidden corners, make a lovely place to relax, picnic or explore.

🏛 **Villa d'Este**
Pza Trento 1. **Tel** 0774 31 20 70. **Open** Tue–Sun. **Closed** 1 Jan, 25 Dec. 🅿️

🏛 **Villa Gregoriana**
Largo Sant'Angelo. **Tel** 06 39 96 77 01. **Open** Tue–Sun. **Closed** Dec–Feb.

🏛 **Hadrian's Villa**
Tel 0774 53 02 03. **Closed** pub hols. 🅿️

Mosaic fragment of Nile in flood, Museo Nazionale Prenestino, Palestrina

⓬ Palestrina

Roma. 🏛 18,000. 🚌 ℹ️ Piazza Santa Maria degli Angeli 2 (06 957 31 76). 🛍 Sat.

Medieval Palestrina grew up over the terraces of a huge temple dedicated to the goddess Fortuna Primigenia, the mother of all gods. The temple, founded in the 8th century BC and rebuilt in the 2nd century BC by Sulla, housed one of the most important oracles of ancient times. The terraces of the sanctuary, littered with fragments of columns and porticoes, lead up to the curved **Palazzo Barberini**. Built over the site of a circular temple, it now houses the **Museo Nazionale Prenestino**, best known for a 1st-century BC mosaic of the Nile in flood and a famous sculpture of the Capitoline Triad.

🏛 **Museo Nazionale Prenestino**
Via Barberini. **Tel** 06 953 81 00. **Open** daily. **Closed** 1 Jan, 1 May, 25 Dec. 🅿️

⓭ Subiaco

Roma. 🔼 9,000. 🚌 🚉 Town
Library, Viale della Repubblica 26
(0774 81 64 07). 🗓 Sat.

In the 6th century, weary of the
decadence of Rome, St Benedict
left the city to become a hermit
in a cave above Subiaco. Others
joined him, and eventually there
were 12 monasteries in the area.

Only two now survive: **Santa
Scolastica**, dedicated to
Benedict's sister, is organized
around three cloisters, one
Renaissance, one early Gothic
and the third Cosmatesque.
Higher up, the 12th-century
San Benedetto is a more
rewarding destination.
Overhanging a deep gorge, it
comprises two churches built
on top of each other. The upper
is decorated with 14th-century
Sienese frescoes; the lower,
built over several levels,
incorporates the original cave
where Benedict spent three
years after fleeing Rome.

🏛 **Santa Scolastica**
3 km (2 miles) E of Subiaco.
Tel 0774 824 21. **Open** daily. ♿

🏛 **San Benedetto**
3 km (2 miles) E of Subiaco.
Tel 0774 850 39. **Open** daily. ♿
♿ (upper church only).

⓮ Montecassino

Cassino. **Tel** 0776 31 15 29. 🚆 Cassino
then bus. **Open** 9am–12:30pm,
3:30–6pm daily (Nov–Mar: to 5pm).

The Abbey of Montecassino,
mother church of the Benedictine
order and a centre of medieval
art, was founded in 529 by St
Benedict. By the 8th century it
was an important centre of
learning, and by the 11th
century had become one of the
richest monasteries in Europe.

In 1944 it was a German
stronghold and a target for
Allied bombs. Most of the
complex was devastated,
including the lavish Baroque
church, but the walls remained
intact and the abbey withstood
for three months before falling
to the Allies. The adjoining war
cemeteries commemorate the
30,000 soldiers killed.

The Monasteries of Lazio

St Benedict founded the Abbey of Montecassino
around 529 and there wrote his famous Rule. Based on
the principles of prayer, study and manual labour, this
became the fundamental monastic code of western
Europe. The Cistercian Order, an offshoot of the
Benedictines, came to Italy from Burgundy in the
12th century. The Cistercians were followers of St Bernard,
whose creed was based on austerity and self-sufficiency,
qualities which were reflected in the simple, early Gothic architecture
of their monasteries. Their first

Rose window, Fossanova

abbey was at Fossanova. Other
Cistercian abbeys in Lazio include
Valvisciolo (northeast of
Sermoneta) and San Martino in
Cimino (near Lago di Vico).

The Abbey of Montecassino,
destroyed during World War II,
was rebuilt as a replica of its
17th-century predecessor.

The Abbey of San Benedetto,
Subiaco, was founded in the
11th century over St Benedict's
cave. A staircase carved in the
rock leads to the grotto where
he preached to shepherds.

The Abbey of Casamari, 14 km
(8 miles) east of Frosinone, was
founded by Benedictine monks in
1035 and handed over to the
Cistercians who rebuilt it in 1203.

The abandoned medieval village of Ninfa, now a beautiful garden

⓯ Anagni

Frosinone. 🚠 20,000. FS 🚌
ℹ️ Piazza Innocenzo III (0775 72 78
52). 🗓️ Wed.

According to legend, Saturn
founded five towns in southeast
Lazio, including Anagni, Alatri
and Arpino. This area is now
known as La Ciociaria, from
ciocie, the bark clogs worn in the
area until about 30 years ago.

Before the Romans conquered
this part of Lazio it was
inhabited by several different
tribes: the Volsci, the Sanniti,
and the Hernici. Little is known
of them, apart from the extraordinary walls with which they
protected their settlements. In
later years these were believed
to have been built by the
Cyclops, a mythical giant, which
gave them their present name
of Cyclopean walls.

Anagni was the most sacred
Hernician centre until its
destruction by the Romans in
306 BC. In the Middle Ages it
was the birthplace and family
seat of several popes, an era
from which many buildings
survive, most notably Boniface
VIII's 13th-century mullion-
windowed palace.

The beautiful Romanesque
Duomo, Santa Maria, built over
the ancient Hernician acropolis,
boasts a fine Cosmati mosaic
floor from the 13th century as

well as 14th-century Sienese
frescoes. The crypt of San Magno
is frescoed with one of the most
complete surviving cycles of the
12th and 13th centuries.

Environs
Alatri, perched on an olive-
covered slope 28 km (17 miles)
east of Anagni, was an important
Hernician town. It preserves an
impressive double set of
Cyclopean walls, 2 km (1 mile)
long and 3 m (10 ft) high, from its
7th- century BC acropolis. In the
medieval town below the walls
is the Romanesque church of Santa
Maria Maggiore, greatly restored
in the 13th century.

Arpino, 40 km (25 miles) east
of Alatri, is a bustling town with
a medieval core, and was the
birthplace of the Roman orator,

An unusual pointed arch in the Cyclopean
walls at Arpino

Cicero. About 3 km (2 miles)
above Arpino, at the site of the
ancient town of Civitavecchia, is
a tremendous stretch of Cyclopean walls which includes a rare
gateway with a pointed arch.

⓰ Sermoneta and Ninfa

Latina. FS Latina Scalo. 🚌 from
Latina. ℹ️ Via Duca di Mare 19, Latina
(0773 69 54 04). Ninfa **Tel** 0773 35 42
41(phone for group bookings).
Open Apr–Oct: 1st Sat & Sun of
the month. 🏛️

Sermoneta is a lovely hilltop
town overlooking the Pontine
Plains, with narrow cobbled
streets winding around
medieval houses, palaces and
churches. The **Duomo** has
a fine 15th-century panel by
Benozzo Gozzoli showing the
Virgin cradling Sermoneta
in her hands. At the top
of the town rises the
moated fairy- tale Castello
Caetani, frescoed with
mythological scenes by a
pupil of Pinturicchio.

In the valley below lies the
abandoned medieval village of
Ninfa, converted into lush
gardens by the Caetani family in
1921. Streams and waterfalls
punctuate the picturesque
garden laid out among the
crumbling buildings.

⓱ Terracina

Latina. 🏛 44,000. 🚆 🚌 ℹ️ Viale
Europa 204 (0773 70 77 02). 🛒 Thu.

Roman Terracina was an important
commercial centre on the Via
Appia (the Appian Way). Today it
is a popular seaside resort, with
a fascinating collage of medieval
buildings and Roman ruins in its
historic centre, perched on the
slopes of the Ausonian Hills. The
more modern part of town by
the sea is full of restaurants, bars
and hotels.

Bombing during World War II
uncovered many of the town's
ancient structures, notably a
stretch of the Appian Way and
the original paving of the Roman
Forum in Piazza del Municipio.
The 11th-century **Duomo** was
built in the shell of
a Roman temple,
and is still entered
by the temple's
steps. The medieval
portico is adorned
with a lovely
12th-century
mosaic and the
interior preserves
the 13th-century
mosaic pavement.
Next door, the
modern town hall
houses the **Museo Archeologico**, devoted to local Greek
and Roman finds.

Duomo at Terracina with
original Roman steps

About 3 km (2 miles) above
the town are the podium and
foundations that once supported
the Temple of Jove Anxur, dating
back to the 1st century BC.
This huge arcaded platform is
illuminated at night and offers
vertiginous views of Terracina
and its bay.

🏛 **Museo Archeologico**
P Municipio. **Tel** 0773 70 73 13.
Open daily. **Closed** Mon pm, some
pub hols. 🅿️

⓲ Sperlonga

Latina. 🏛 4,000. 🚌 ℹ️ Corso San
Leone 22 (0771 55 70 00). 🛒 Sat.

Sperlonga is a seaside resort
surrounded by sandy beaches.
The old town sits on a rocky
promontory, a picturesque laby-
rinth of whitewashed buildings,
narrow alleyways, piazzettas and
balconies offering an occasional
glimpse of the sea below. It is
now full of bars, restaurants and
boutiques. The modern part of
town lies down on the seafront.

The area around Sperlonga
was a favourite retreat for
the ancient Romans
during the summer
months. They built
villas along the
coast, and converted
the natural caves
in the nearby cliffs
into places to dine
and relax.

In 1957 archaeologists
excavating the complex of
Tiberius's luxury villa, 1 km (half a
mile) on the southern outskirts of
town, found some marvellous
2nd-century BC Hellenistic
sculptures in a large cave open
to the sea. These sculptures,
representing incidents from

12th-century bell tower at Gaeta

Homer's *Odyssey*, are thought to
be by the same artists from
Rhodes (where the Emperor
Tiberius once lived) who were
responsible for the Laocoön
(*see p421*). They are displayed,
along with other local finds,
in the **Museo Archeologico
Nazionale** which is part of the
archaeological zone.

🏛 **Zona Archeologica**
Via Flacca. **Tel** 0771 54 80 28. **Open**
daily. **Closed** 1 Jan, 25 Dec. 🅿️

⓳ Gaeta

Latina. 🏛 22,000. 🚌 ℹ️ Via Serapide
26 (0771 45 25 18). 🛒 Wed.

According to Virgil, Gaeta was
named after Aeneas's wet nurse
Caieta, who was allegedly
buried here. The town sits on the
southern headland of the gulf
of Gaeta, under Monte Orlando.
The historic centre is dominated
by a mighty Aragonese castle
and the pinnacles of mock-
Gothic San Francesco. To the
north, the modern quarter links
Gaeta to the bay of Serapo,
a picturesque beach resort.

Gaeta's most beautiful feature
is the **Duomo**'s elegant late
Romanesque bell tower, its lofty
summit topped by a roof of
coloured ceramic tiles. On the
seafront lies the tiny
10th-century church of **San
Giovanni a Mare**, with faded
frescoes, a hemispherical dome
and a sloping floor to let the sea
flow out after flooding.

Stretches of sandy beach along the coast between Gaeta and Terracina

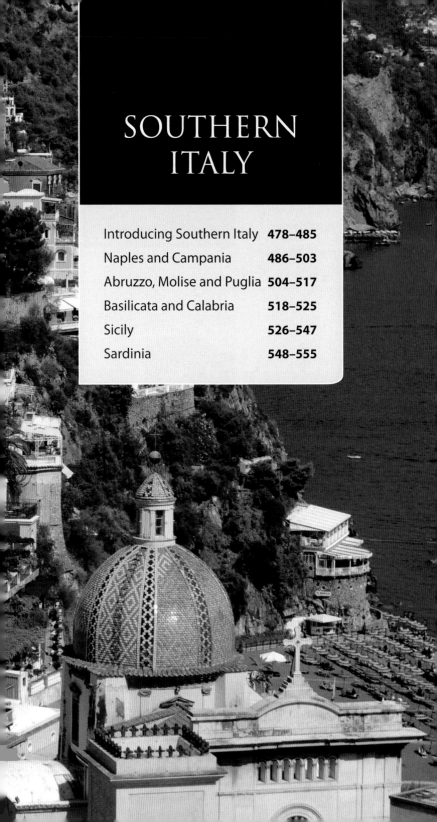

SOUTHERN ITALY

Southern Italy at a Glance

Visitors to southern Italy are rewarded with a rich array of archaeological remains. Although the Roman site at Pompeii is high on everyone's list, there are also Greek ruins in Sicily and on the southern coast, and in Sardinia there are mysterious ancient structures, called *nuraghe*. Puglia, Campania and Sicily are famed for their architecture, while across the south there are magnificent landscapes, abundant wildlife and endless opportunities for outdoor activities. The cuisine alone, with its eclectic heritage and diversity of tastes, provides an excuse to dawdle on the coast or in the mountain villages.

Teramo

L'Ac

Sulm

Porto Torres
Olbia

Alghero

Nuoro

Macomer   SARDINIA
(See pp548–55)

Oristano

Arbatax

Cagliari

The Parco Nazionale d'Abruzzo, a vast unspoilt wilderness, is home to wolves, bears and many species of birds *(see pp506–7)*.

Su Nuraxi at Barumini, built around 1500 BC, is the most celebrated of Sardinia's mysterious stone *nuraghe* sites *(see p549)*.

The cloister decoration at Monreale cathedral is a legacy of Sicily's Arabic past, with elaborate columns adorned with fine mosaics and splendid sculpted capitals *(see pp530–31)*.

Palermo

Trapani

Marsala

SICILY
(See pp526–

Sciacca

Sicily's Valley of the Temples at Agrigento contains some of the best-preserved Greek ruins outside Greece. Mostly Doric in style, they date from the 5th and 6th centuries BC *(see p536)*.

◀ Colourful terraced villas scaling down to the beach in Positano on the Amalfi Coast

The Museo Archeologico Nazionale in Naples is one of Italy's most important museums. It houses the treasures of Pompeii, including sculptures, vases and everyday artifacts which provide a detailed glimpse of Roman life *(see pp490–91)*.

Locator Map

Pompeii's Roman ruins include streets, houses and an amphitheatre *(see pp494–5)*.

Pescara

Chieti

RUZZO
Termoli

MOLISE
pobasso

Foggia

ABRUZZO, MOLISE
AND PUGLIA
(See pp504–17)
Bari

NAPLES AND
CAMPANIA
(See pp486–503)

Naples

PUGLIA
Fasano

Pompeii
Potenza
Matera
Taranto
Brindisi

Lecce

BASILICATA
Otranto

Cassano allo
Ionio

Rossano

BASILICATA
AND CALABRIA
(See pp518–25)

0 kilometres   100

0 miles   50

Crotone

Catanzaro

Tropea   Vibo Valentia

Isole Eolie

CALABRIA

The church of Santa Croce in Lecce is an excellent example of the exuberant Lecce Baroque style, from its elaborate rose window to the intricately carved capitals *(see pp512–13)*.

Messina

Reggio di
Calabria

Mount Etna, one of the world's largest volcanoes, is still active, with lava erupting from fissures that dot its flanks. The nearby city of Catania has suffered repeatedly from volcanic damage *(see p539)*.

Catania

Siracusa

Scicli

The Flavours of Southern Italy

The "land of the midday sun", the *Mezzogiorno* is majestic and fertile, yet in places barren and achingly poor. This is the land of the Mediterranean diet, which relies heavily on bright vegetables, fresh seafood, aromatic herbs and fruity olive oil. Puglia produces more grapes and olives than any other region in Italy, while the fertile volcanic soil around Vesuvius and Etna is ideal for growing plump vegetables, juicy fruits and vines. Naples is the birthplace of the pizza, and the region of Campania also produces the best buffalo mozzarella in the country.

Mixed herbs

Sicilian cheesemaker with a basket of fresh ricotta

Campania

Naples is famous for pizza, but it's also the home of the tomato-based pasta sauce. Especially prized are the distinctive long, tapered tomatoes from San Marzano in Salerno. The tradition of combining mozzarella and tomato originates here. Pasta is generally tubular (in the north it tends to be ribbon-like). Other staple Campanian ingredients are olive oil, garlic, basil, chillies and lemons. Excellent seafood includes octopus and squid, anchovies, mussels and clams, most of which are simply prepared using lemon, garlic and pepper. Lamb, kid and buffalo are the most popular meats. There is also a long tradition of making pastries and ice cream.

Puglia

This region is responsible for producing 80 per cent of Italy's pasta, as well as being the source of most of the country's fish. As in the rest of Southern Italy, meats such as poultry, pork and kid are often roasted over aromatic herbs, such as thyme and rosemary. The distinctive local ear-shaped pasta, *orecchiette*, is popular, and fruits and

Tuna   Lobster   Squid   Sardines
Mussels   Clams
Display of the superb seafood caught along the coastline of the south

Regional Dishes and Specialities

Some of Italy's classic sauces originated in the South, such as the powerful *puttanesca* with tomatoes, anchovies, chilli, capers and olives. Along the Campanian coast, *zuppa di cozze* (mussels in hot pepper sauce) is a speciality. Octopus is particularly good served in dishes such as *polpo alla luciana*, where it is gently cooked in tomatoes and olive oil with parsley and garlic. *Orecchiette con cime di rapa* (ear-shaped pasta with turnip tops) is a signature dish from Puglia, as is *agnello allo squero* – lamb, spit-roasted over a fire scented with thyme and herbs. For those with a sweet tooth, mouthwatering *cassata Siciliana* is a rich sponge cake layered with ricotta cheese, liqueur, candied fruits and pistachio nuts.

Figs

Maccheroncini con le sarde
Sicilian macaroni with sardines, fennel, pine nuts, raisins, breadcrumbs and saffron.

Tresses of vine-ripened tomatoes hanging on a southern market stall

vegetables, especially figs and quinces, are abundant.

A bounty of fish and shellfish is caught along the 400-km (250-mile) coastline. As well as mozzarella, other good cheeses include ricotta, goat's and smoked cheeses.

Sicily

The island's long list of invasions is reflected in its varied cuisine. Greek colonists in the 8th century BC were amazed at the fertility of the volcanic soil. Rice was introduced to the area by the Arabs, while the influence of North African cuisine is shown in *cuscusu* (couscous) and other Arab flavours that appear in sweet and spicy dishes.

The lamb and pork raised in mountain pastures and oak forests is exceptional. Fish is excellent, especially sardines, tuna, anchovies and swordfish. Vegetables are plump and delicious and aubergines (eggplants) are a firm favourite. Sheep's milk ricotta cheese features in many delicious

Newly harvested olives, ready to be pressed into olive oil

pastries and puddings, such as the sinfully rich Sicilian *cassata*.

Other Regions

Mountainous Abruzzo and Molise are good sheep-rearing territory, so lamb is a speciality here, as is guitar-shaped pasta *(maccheroni alla chitarra)*. Food in Calabria and Basilicata is strong on spices, especially chilli peppers, which are considered a cure-all. Sardinia bakes wafer-thin unleavened bread – *carta da musica* (music paper). Honey, wild boar ham and thrushes are popular, as is *torrone*, a delicious almond nougat.

ON THE MENU

Arancini Sicilian rice balls, usually stuffed with a meat, cheese or vegetable filling.

Caciocavallo Spun cow's milk cheese, especially good from Avellino in Campania.

Insalata caprese Salad from Campania with mozzarella, tomato, basil, olives and oregano.

Maccheroni di fuoco Pasta dish from Basilicata with large quantities of garlic and chilli.

Seadas A kind of doughnut from Sardinia, fried and covered with honey.

Soppressata A spicy, dry-cured salami from Calabria.

Pizza Napoletana This thin-crusted pizza is topped simply with tomato, garlic, oregano, basil and anchovies.

Pesce spada In Campania, Puglia, Calabria and Sicily, swordfish steak is grilled with lemon and oregano.

Sfogliatella Paper-thin layers of pastry ooze with butter, sugar, cinnamon, orange peel and ricotta.

Understanding the Architecture of Southern Italy

The Romanesque style of southern Italy owes much to the Normans, who in the 11th century brought from France both form and style in architecture and sculpture. In the southeast, the style has hefty Byzantine overtones; in Sicily it is characterized by strong traditional Islamic motifs and a love of rich colour, pattern and ornamentation. These

Baroque carving on Bagheria's Villa Palagonia

elements surface later in Sicily's Baroque style and are allied to a dynamism that originates in the Baroque of Rome – though in Sicily it is more vivacious. Neapolitan Baroque is more sophisticated and displays a greater interest in the creative use of space.

Byzantine and Romanesque Features

Lateral towers

Interlacing arches

Cefalù, begun in 1131 by Roger II, is one of Sicily's great Norman cathedrals *(see p539)*. Its west front exhibits many northern Romanesque features, such as the massive towers.

Multicoloured marble

Glass and plaster mosaics on gold

Christ Pantocrator, a Byzantine apse mosaic (c.1132), adorns the Cappella Palatina *(see p530)*.

Rich ornamentation

Interlacing arches

The east end of the Norman cathedral of Monreale, founded in 1172 by William II, is built of multicoloured materials with interlacing arches *(see pp534–5)*.

Baroque Features

Massive scale of stairway

Sweeping view down corridor

Bold statue of lion

Lifelike putti

Brilliant realism of drapery

Caserta's Palazzo Reale, a sumptuous royal palace begun by Charles III in 1752, is characterized by its monumental scale *(see p500)*. The richly decorated interior is prefaced by several huge entrances and impressive staircases offering views. The enormous building was designed by Luigi Vanvitelli.

Giacomo Serpotta's stucco reliefs (c.1690) in Palermo's Oratorio di Santa Zita illustrate Sicilians' love of exuberant decoration *(see p533)*.

Where to see the Architecture

The best places to see Romanesque architecture are Puglia and the cathedral cities of northwestern Sicily. Puglia's best churches are those at Trani *(see p513)* and nearby Canosa, Molfetta and Bitonto; Ruvo di Puglia *(p514)*, San Leonardo di Siponto on the Gargano Peninsula and Martina Franca, near Alberobello. The Baroque style of the south is epitomized by the villas, palaces

The Duomo portal in Ruvo di Puglia

and churches of Naples and Sicily, and by the deeply encrusted ornamentation found on church façades in Lecce *(pp516–17)*, in Puglia. In Sicily, the Baroque of Palermo *(pp530–31)*, Bagheria *(p536)*, Noto, Modica and Ragusa *(p547)* and Siracusa *(pp546–7)* is well known. Less so are churches at Piazza Armerina *(p541)*, Trapani *(p536)*, Palazzolo Acreide, close to Siracusa, and Acireale, near Catania.

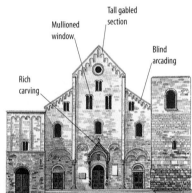

Mullioned window

Tall gabled section

Blind arcading

Rich carving

Bari's Basilica di San Nicola *(founded 1087)* was the model for subsequent churches in Puglia *(see p514)*. Based on Norman architecture, its façade is flanked by towers and divided vertically into three, reflecting the tripartite nature of its plan.

Rose window

Half columns

Blind arcading

The façade of Troia cathedral *(1093 –1125)* owes its design to Pisan architecture and its rich ornamentation to Byzantine and Arab models *(see pp512–13)*.

Carved scroll

Protruding columns

The façade of Siracusa's Duomo, begun in 1728 by Andrea Palma, is animated by broken or curved elements *(see pp546–7)*.

Central bell tower

Three-tiered structure

Curved surface

San Giorgio in Ragusa *(1744)* has a façade by Gagliardi with layers of ornamentation culminating in the tower *(see p547)*.

Stone-carved decoration

Lecce's Chiesa del Rosario *(begun 1691)* was built by Lo Zingarello of soft local sandstone in the Lecce Baroque style of profuse carving *(see pp516–17)*.

SOUTHERN ITALY

The Ancient Greeks in Southern Italy

Some of the best ruins of the ancient Greek world are in Southern Italy. Syracuse, Selinunte, Segesta and Gela are among the better known Sicilian sites while those on the mainland include Crotone, Locri and Paestum. Magna Graecia is the collective name given to these scattered colonies of ancient Greece, the earliest of which were founded in the Naples area between the 8th and 6th centuries BC. Many great figures of the age – including Pythagoras, Archimedes and Aeschylus – lived in these settlements, and it was here that wine-making flourished. Artifacts from this age are exhibited in the excellent archaeological museums of Naples, Syracuse and Taranto.

KYME Cuma

NEAPOLIS Napoli

HERAKLE Ercolano

Ancient Herakleia (Herculaneum) was named after its patron deity, the mighty Hercules. It was buried by the eruption of Mount Vesuvius in AD 79 *(see p499)*.

POSEIDONIA. Paestum

ELE Vel

Poseidonia (today's Paestum), was the city of Poseidon, God of the Sea. Its ruins, dating from the 6th century BC, include the hulks of two of the finest Doric temples in Europe *(see pp502–3)*.

Mount Etna was believed to be the forge of Hephaistos (Vulcan) – God of Fire – and the Cyclops, the one-eyed giant *(see p543)*.

Tyndaris was one of the Greek cities founded on Sicily.

LIPARA Lipari

TYNDAR Tindar

PANORMOS Palermo

SOLUS Solunto

ERYX Erice

EGESTA Segesta

HIMERA Himera

Eryx, founder of the town, was the son of Aphrodite and Poseidon.

Valley of the Temples

SELINUS Selinunte

HENNA Enna

KATA Gatan

MEGARA HYBLAE Megara

The legendary founder of Agrigento was Daedalus, who created wings for himself and his son, Icarus, so they could fly.

AKRAGAS Agrigento

GELA Gela

Gela was prosperous under the rule of Hippocrates in the 5th century BC.

Mus Archeologi Regiona Paolo O

Egesta (built 426–416 BC) was colonized by the Elymians who may have originated at Troy. Among the ruins of this town are a half-completed temple and a theatre *(see p538)*. Ancient Greeks used theatres for plays and cultural entertainment rather than combat.

Aeschylus, the dramatist, died in Gela in 456. Considered the father of Greek tragedy, his plays include Seven Against Thebes, Women of Aetna and Prometheus Bound.

0 kilometres   100

0 miles   50

Metapontion (Metapontum) was home to Pythagoras after his expulsion from Crotone. Its ruins include Doric temples, the Tavole Palatine and a theatre (see p523).

Taras was home to the philosopher and scientist, Archytas, and to Aristoxenes, author of the earliest treatise on music.

Founded by Spartan Greeks (8th century BC), Taras was a rich and powerful city.

Museo Archeologico Nazionale

Museo Nazionale di Metaponto

Greece and its Colonies
7th–5th century BC

TARAS
Taranto

Basento

METAPONTION
Metaponto

SIRIS
Nova Siri

The Sybarites were famed for their luxurious lifestyle, hence the word "sybaritic". The wealth of Sybaris resulted from trade with the Etruscans.

SYBARIS
Sibari

THURII
Thuri

KROTON
Crotone

In about 540 BC Crotone became the chief school of Pythagoras's philosophy. Here the great thinker and mathematician remained for 30 years until the government (which he supported) was overthrown, and he was expelled.

Locri Epizefiri was the first Greek city to have a written code of law.

ZANKLE-MESSENE
Messina

LOKROI
Locri Epizefiri

RHEGION
Reggio di Calabria

OS
dini Naxos

The Straits of Messina vexed Odysseus, the hero of Homer's Odyssey. Here at the meeting of two seas the currents created a "whirlpool" – Charybdis – which posed a threat to safe entry of Messina (see p542). Another threat were the Sirens, who lured voyagers onto rocks with their singing. Odysseus is seen here tied to a mast, so he can hear their song, but resist its call.

Plato the philosopher visited Syracuse and advised the ruler, Dionysius II, how to govern.

KOUSAI
cusa

The mathematician and inventor, Archimedes, was born in Syracuse c.287 BC. His inventions included the famous Archimedean screw, and various weapons to stave off the Romans (see pp546–7).

Demeter and Persephone

The complex web of Greek mythology was part of the daily life of the ancients. Enna was once the seat of the cult of Demeter, the earth goddess, and between 480 and 460 BC a temple was erected there in her honour. According to the legend, Persephone, the daughter of Demeter and Zeus, was abducted in the nearby fields by Hades who carried her off into the Underworld. Demeter then left Olympus and wandered the world searching in vain for her daughter. Discovering that Zeus had allowed the abduction to happen, Demeter put a blight on Sicily: it would remain barren until Persephone returned. Finally Hades allowed her return from the Underworld, but only for a few months of each year – from spring to autumn. Demeter, satisfied with the result, ensured that Sicily became the most fertile place on earth.

Sculpture of Persephone

NAPLES AND CAMPANIA

The capital of Campania, Naples is one of the few European cities of the ancient world that has never been completely extinguished. Founded by Greeks, it was embellished and enlarged by the Romans and in subsequent centuries was the much-prized booty of foreign invaders and Imperialists – most prominently the Normans, Hohenstaufen, French and Spanish.

Naples today is a chaotic yet spectacular metropolis sprawling noisily and dirtily around the edge of the Bay of Naples. To one side is Mount Vesuvius; facing from the sea are the islands of Capri, Ischia and Procida. Pompeii and Herculaneum, lying in the shadow of the volcano that destroyed them, contain the most revealing Roman ruins in Italy.

For centuries Naples dominated the Italian south, or *Mezzogiorno* (land of the midday sun). Unemployment and crime are a problem – the Camorra is as deep-seated here as the Mafia is in Sicily – but there is also an attractive, rude ebullience to the city.

The ancient history of Campania is linked to the Etruscans and the Greeks, whose massive ruins can be seen at Paestum. Next came a time of great prosperity under the Romans; archaeological evidence of this still exists at Benevento, Santa Maria Capua Vetere and Pozzuoli.

The hinterland, with its rich, well-cultivated plains, is eclipsed by the Amalfi coastline with its breath-taking views and the terrific seaboard of the Cilento. The mountainous interior, remote and unvisited, contains small towns that were settled by the Greeks, developed by the Romans and often abandoned in the wake of malaria and Saracen attacks.

A glimpse into the narrow streets of Naples' Quartieri Spagnoli (Spanish Quarter)

◀ Picturesque beach and town of Amalfi, the largest town on the Amalfi Coast

Exploring Naples and Campania

The main centre from which to explore Campania is the city of Naples (Napoli). To the north, verdant plains sweep down to Santa Maria Capua Vetere. To the east, the mountainous province of Benevento overlooks the valley, while earthquake-ravaged Avellino and its province lurk on a plain beyond Vesuvius. The Campi Flegrei area, west of Naples, is famous for the Roman ruins at Cuma. Further south is the splendid, rugged Amalfi Coast. Clean sandy beaches lie beyond the tip of the Sorrentine Peninsula and along the Cilento coast as well as on Capri, Ischia and Procida in the Gulf of Naples.

Sights at a Glance

1. Naples (Napoli) pp490–97
2. Pompeii pp498–9
3. Santa Maria Capua Vetere
4. Caserta
5. Benevento
6. Amalfi Coast
7. Salerno
8. Paestum
9. Capri
10. Ischia and Procida

Typical Naples street viewed from Santa Maria Maggiore

For additional map symbols see back flap

Key

- ▬▬ Motorway
- ▬▬ Major road
- ▬▬ Secondary road
- ▭▭ Minor road
- ▬▬ Scenic route
- ▪▪▪ Main railway
- ▬▬ Minor railway
- ▬▬ Regional border
- △ Summit

0 kilometres 25

0 miles 20

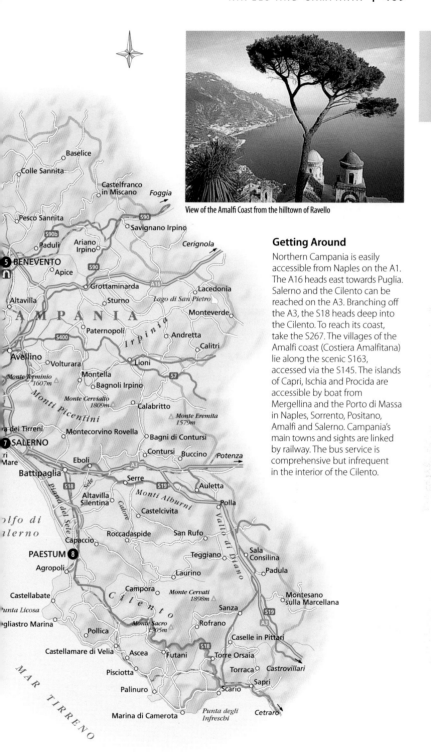

View of the Amalfi Coast from the hilltown of Ravello

Getting Around

Northern Campania is easily accessible from Naples on the A1. The A16 heads east towards Puglia. Salerno and the Cilento can be reached on the A3. Branching off the A3, the S18 heads deep into the Cilento. To reach its coast, take the S267. The villages of the Amalfi coast (Costiera Amalfitana) lie along the scenic S163, accessed via the S145. The islands of Capri, Ischia and Procida are accessible by boat from Mergellina and the Porto di Massa in Naples, Sorrento, Positano, Amalfi and Salerno. Campania's main towns and sights are linked by railway. The bus service is comprehensive but infrequent in the interior of the Cilento.

Baselice
Colle Sannita
Castelfranco in Miscano
Foggia
Pesco Sannita
S90
Savignano Irpino
S90b
Paduli
Ariano Irpino
Cerignola
5 BENEVENTO
Apice
S90
Grottaminarda
A16
Lacedonia
Altavilla
Sturno
Lago di San Pietro
Monteverde
C A M P A N I A
Paternopoli
Irpinia
Andretta
Calitri
Avellino
Volturara
Montella
Lioni
Monte Terminio 1607m
Bagnoli Irpino
S57
Monti Picentini
Monte Cerviallo 1809m
Calabritto
Monte Eremita 1579m
a dei Tirreni
Montecorvino Rovella
Bagni di Contursi
7 SALERNO
Contursi
Buccino
Potenza
ri Mare
Eboli
A3
Battipaglia
Serre
Sele
S18
Altavilla Silentina
Catore
Monti Alburni
S19
Auletta
olfo di lerno
Castelcivita
Polla
Piana del Sele
Capaccio
Roccadaspide
San Rufo
Vallo di Diano
PAESTUM 8
Teggiano
Sala Consilina
Agropoli
Laurino
Padula
Castellabate
Campora
Monte Cervati 1898m
Montesano sulla Marcellana
Cilento
Sanza
S19
unta Licosa
Monte Sacro 1705m
Rofrano
A3
gliastro Marina
Pollica
Caselle in Pittari
Castellamare di Velia
Ascea
Futani
S18
Torre Orsaia
Pisciotta
Torraca
Castrovillari
Palinuro
Sapri
Scario
Marina di Camerota
Punta degli Infreschi
Cetraro
M A R   T I R R E N O

● Naples

The compact centre of Naples, filled
with palaces, churches, convents and
monasteries, revolves around just
a few streets. From the Piazza del
Plebiscito, Via Toledo (also called Via
Roma) proceeds north towards Piazza
Dante. To the east, narrow Via dei
Tribunali and Via San Biagio dei Librai
penetrate the historic and noisy heart
of the city, the *Spaccanapoli* (split
Naples). South of Palazzo Reale is the
Santa Lucia district. To the west is the
port of Mergellina and overlooking the
city is the Vomero district.

View of the Bay of Naples and Mount Vesuvius

Exploring Northeast Naples

Much of the city's most
interesting art and architecture
can be found here, including the
Museo Archeologico Nazionale
and its Roman treasures from
Herculaneum and Pompeii. The
buildings provide a wide range
of architectural styles from the
French-Gothic of the Duomo to
the Florentine-Renaissance style
of the Porta Capuana.

🏛 MADRE

Via Settembrini 79. **Tel** 081 193 13 016.
Open 10am–7pm Mon, Wed–Sun.
🎫 (free Mon). 🚫 📷
W **museomadre.it**

Opened in 2005, the Museo
d'Arte Contemporanea Donna
Regina Napoli (MADRE) is located
in the Palazzo Donnaregina, from
which it gets its name. The
museum houses a remarkable
collection by well-known artists
such as Andy Warhol, Robert
Rauschenberg, Mimmo
Paladino, Claes Oldenburg,

Robert Mapplethorpe and Roy
Lichtenstein among others.
On the first floor is a library and
a children's area, while the third
floor is used for temporary
exhibitions. The museum often
hosts special events such as
cinema screenings, concerts
and theatrical performances.
The church of Santa Maria
Donnaregina, at the back
of the museum, provides
additional exhibition space
in a beautiful setting.

📷 Castel Capuano and Porta Capuana

Piazza Enrico de Nicola.
Begun by Norman King William
I and completed by Frederick II,
Castel Capuano was a royal
palace until 1540, when it
became the Court of Justice.
Today it is a courthouse.
　　Nearby, between the
Aragonese towers of the
Capua Gate and facing
a market, is a rare
sculpture in the
Florentine-Renaissance
manner. Created by
Giuliano da
Maiano (and
finished in
1490 by Luca
Fancelli) as a
defensive gate,
Porta Capuana is
perhaps Italy's
finest Renaissance
gateway.

The beautiful Renaissance gate of
Porta Capuana

| 0 metres | 250 |
| 0 yards | 250 |

For hotels and restaurants in this region see pp562–77 and pp580–605

Sights at a Glance

Interior of the Duomo

🏛 Duomo

Via Duomo 147. **Tel** 081 44 90 97. **Open** 8am–12:30pm, 4:40–7pm Mon–Sat; 8am–1:30pm, 5–7:30pm Sun. **Closed** public hols. ♿

Built between 1294 and 1323, the Cattedrale di Santa Maria Assunta, or Duomo, lies behind a mostly 19th-century façade. The nave is lined with ancient columns, and there is an array of monuments to past rulers, along with paintings by Lanfranco and Domenichino.

The Duomo houses the relics of San Gennaro, Naples' patron saint (martyred AD 305). The Cappella San Gennaro holds phials of his congealed blood, which miraculously liquefies three times a year (the Saturday before the first Sunday in May, 19 Sep and 16 Dec). The Cappella Carafa, a Renaissance masterpiece built from 1497 to 1506, contains the saint's tomb.

Accessible from the Duomo's north aisle is the Cappella di Santa Restituta, founded in the 4th century on the site of a former Temple of Apollo, and rebuilt in the 1300s. It has ceiling paintings by Luca Giordano (1632–1705) and a 5th-century baptistry. The nearby Museo del Tesoro di San Gennaro (Tel: 081 29 49 80) exhibits a range of gold, silverware, jewels, statues and art.

VISITORS' CHECKLIST

Practical Information
🗺 1,300,000. 🛈 P. del Gesù Nuovo (081 551 27 01), Via San Carlo (081 40 23 94). 🗓 daily. 🎉 San Gennaro: 19 Sep. 🌐 inaples.it

Transport
✈ Capodichino 4 km (2.5 miles) NW. 🚆 Centrale, P. Garibaldi. 🚌 P. Garibaldi. ⛴ Stazione Marittima, Molo Beverello & Mergellina.

🏛 Pio Monte della Misericordia

Via dei Tribunali 253. **Tel** 081 44 69 44. Church & gallery **Open** 9am–2:30pm Mon–Tue, Thu–Sun. **Closed** public hols. 📷 Gallery only.

The octagonal church belonging to this charitable foundation houses Caravaggio's *Seven Acts of Mercy* (1607). The art gallery has paintings by Luca Giordano and Mattia Preti.

🏛 Cappella Sansevero

Via F. de Santis 19. **Tel** 081 551 84 70. **Open** 10am–5:40pm Wed–Mon (to 1:10pm Sun & public hols). 📷 🚫 ♿ (church). 🌐 museosansevero.it

This tiny 16th-century chapel is the burial sepulchre of the Princes of Sangro di Sansevero. Featuring both Christian and Masonic symbolism, the chapel has an unusual character.

Remarkable 18th-century sculpture fills the chapel. *The Resurrection of the Prince*, by an unknown artist, is mirrored by that of Christ, above the altar. Giuseppe Sammartino's *Veiled Christ* is an alabaster figure beneath a marble veil, and is a work of technical virtuosity.

Prince Raimondo, an 18th-century alchemist, is associated with the chapel. He performed gruesome experiments on human bodies, for which he was excommunicated. The results of some of his experiments can be seen in the crypt.

Sammartino's Veiled Christ (1753) in the Cappella Sansevero

For keys to symbols *see back flap*

Exploring Central Naples

The part of Santa Lucia bordered by Via Duomo to the east, Via Tribunali to the north, Via Toledo (Roma) to the west and the water to the south, is the old heart of Naples. Especially rich in 14th- and 15th-century churches, the area offers visitors an abundance of sights.

Interior of San Gregorio Armeno

🔼 San Lorenzo Maggiore
Via dei Tribunali 316. **Tel** 081 45 49 48. Church & Excavations: **Open** 9:30am–5:30pm daily (to 1:30pm Sun). 🔲 excavations. 🔲 church.

This mainly 14th-century Franciscan church (with an 18th-century façade) was built during the reign of Robert the Wise of Anjou. The storyteller Giovanni Boccaccio (1313–75) reputedly based the character Fiammetta on King Robert's daughter Maria, whom he saw here on Easter Eve, 1334. For Naples, San Lorenzo Maggiore is a rare Gothic edifice. Its nave and the apse ambulatory have a magnificent period simplicity. The church houses medieval tombs including the Gothic tomb of Catherine of Austria, who died in 1323, by a pupil of Giovanni Pisano. Excavations in the monastic cloister, where the lyric poet and scholar Petrarch (see p163) once stayed, have found the remains of a Roman basilica. There are also important Greek and medieval excavations.

🔼 San Gregorio Armeno
Piazza San Gaetano 1. **Tel** 081 551 70 70. **Open** am daily. 🔲 cloister.

Benedictine nuns still preside over this church. The convent attached to it earned a reputation for luxury since the nuns, traditionally from noble families, were accustomed to lavish living, which continued here.

The sumptuous Baroque interior of the church sports frescoes by Luca Giordano. Via San Gregorio Armeno is lined with the workshops of vendors of Nativity figures (presepi).

🏛 Museo Filangieri
Palazzo Cuomo, Via Duomo 288. **Tel** 081 20 31 75. **Open** 9:30am–2pm, 3:30–7pm Mon–Sat; 9:30am–1:30pm Sun and public hols. 🔲

The 15th-century Renaissance Palazzo Cuomo houses the Museo Filangieri. Founded in 1881, the original museum collections put together by Prince Gaetano Filangieri were destroyed during World War II. The current collection contains interesting and varied objects, including porcelain, embroidery, manuscripts, Italian and Spanish arms, objects from local archaeological excavations and paintings by such artists as Luca Giordano, Ribera and Mattia Preti. There is also an important bust by Antonio Canova.

Renaissance tomb of Cardinal Brancaccio, Sant'Angelo a Nilo

🔼 Sant'Angelo a Nilo
Piazzetta Nilo. **Tel** 081 211 08 60. **Open** 8am–1pm, 4:30–7:30pm daily. 🔲

This 14th-century church contains a fine work of Renaissance sculpture: the Tomb of Cardinal Rinaldo Brancaccio. Designed by Michelozzo, it was sculpted in Pisa, and then shipped to Naples upon completion in 1428. Donatello reputedly carved the right-hand angel drawing back the curtain, the shallow relief Assumption, and the cardinal's head.

The simple Gothic interior of San Lorenzo Maggiore, looking down the nave to the apse

⬆ San Domenico Maggiore

Piazza San Domenico Maggiore.
Tel 081 45 91 88. **Open** 8:30am–1pm,
4–7pm Tue–Sun. ♿ Treasury:
Open same as church. 📷

This Gothic church (1289–1324)
contains some of the finest
Renaissance monuments and
sculpture in Naples. The tomb
slab of John of Durazzo (died
1335), by Tino da Camaino, is in
the south transept. In the sacristy
are the *Apotheosis of Faith*
ceiling frescoes by Solimena
(18th century). The choir
features a paschal candlestick
(1585) supported by
figures by da
Camaino. The
Cappellone del
Crocifisso contains a
medieval painting of
the *Crucifixion*, which
supposedly spoke to
St Thomas Aquinas.
The grand
Brancaccio tomb by
Jacopo della Pila
(1492) is in the Chiesa Antica.

Detail of the embossed
façade of Gesù Nuovo

⬆ Santa Chiara

Via Benedetto Croce. Church: **Tel** 081
797 12 31. **Open** 7am–1pm, 4:30–
8pm daily. ♿ 📷 Cloister: **Tel** 081 797
12 24. **Open** 9:30am–5:30pm Mon–
Sat, 10am–2:30pm Sun & public hols.

This 14th-century church was
bombed in World War II, but a
reconstruction uncovered the
original Provençal-Gothic
structure. The tombs of the
Angevin monarchs are housed
here. The tomb
of Robert the

Wise (died 1343) is by Giovanni
and Pacio Bertini; that of
Robert's son, Charles of Calabria
(died 1328), is by Tino da
Camaino, and the tomb of
Charles' wife, Mary of Valois
(died 1331) is by da Camaino
and his followers. Adjacent is a
convent with a cloister
designed by Vaccaro (1742).
There is also a museum and a
Roman bath house (AD 1).

⬆ Gesù Nuovo

Piazza del Gesù Nuovo 2. **Tel** 081 557
81 11. **Open** daily.

The 16th-century
Jesuit church was
constructed by
Valeriano (and later
Fanzago and Fuga)
from the Severini
palace (15th century),
of which only a
façade survives. The
ebullient decoration
of the interior (1600s)
is fully in accordance
with the needs of the Jesuits, who
used drama and direct appeal to
the emotions to draw the faithful.
It is resplendent with coloured
marble and paintings, including
works by Ribera and Solimena.
In 1688 an earthquake
destroyed the dome – the
present one is 18th-century.

⬆ Sant'Anna e San Bartolomeo dei Lombardi

Via Monteoliveto. **Tel** 081 551 33 33.
Open 9am–noon Tue–Sat.

Mazzoni's *Pietà* (1492) in Sant'Anna e San
Bartolomeo dei Lombardi

Also known as Santa Maria di
Monteoliveto, this church was
built in 1411 and restored after
World War II. It is a repository of
Renaissance art. Entering, past the
tomb (1627) of Domenico Fontana
(who completed the dome of
St Peter's in Rome after
Michelangelo's death), the
richness of the interior unfolds.

The Cappella Mastrogiudice
contains an *Annunciation* panel by
Florentine sculptor Benedetto da
Maiano (1489) and the Cappella
Piccolomini contains Antonio
Rossellino's monument (c.1475)
to Maria d'Aragona (completed by
da Maiano). The Cappella del
Santo Sepolcro houses a *Pietà* by
Guido Mazzoni (1492). Its eight
terracotta figures are considered
life-size portraits of the artist's
contemporaries. The old Sacristy,
frescoed by Vasari (1544), has inlaid
stalls by Giovanni da Verona (1510).

Majolica tiles decorated with scenes of rural life in the cloisters of Santa Chiara

Naples: Museo Archeologico Nazionale

This building, housing one of the world's most important archaeological museums, started life in the late 1500s as the home of the royal cavalry and was rebuilt in the early 17th century as the seat of Naples university. In 1777, when Ferdinand IV transferred the university to the former monastery of Gesù Vecchio, the building was again adapted to house the Real Museo Borbonico and library. In 1860 it became public property. The 1980 earthquake caused much damage to the collections. Major restoration and reorganization of exhibits continue but most areas of the museum are open on Sundays.

Spring Fresco
The fresco removed from the Villa Stabia in the Varano plain is a masterpiece of grace and elegance; the female figure rendered with soft, delicate colours.

Villa of the Papyri

Bust of "Seneca"
Found in the Villa dei Papiri in Herculaneum, this 1st-century BC bronze head was long thought to represent the philosopher Seneca the Elder (c.55 BC–AD 39). Today, however, its identity is less certain.

★ The Battle of Alexander
The splendid mosaic from the House of the Faun in Pompeii *(see p498)* depicts Alexander the Great's victory over Persian emperor Darius III (333 BC).

Key

- Epigraphs
- Egyptian collection
- Engraved gems
- Sculptures
- Mosaics
- Numismatics
- Didactics
- Herculaneum & Pompeii
- Hall of the Sundial
- Prehistoric, Greek and Etruscan collections
- Non-exhibition space

The Secret Cabinet
The erotic works from Pompeii and Herculaneum housed here caused embarrassment at the time of the Bourbons. Today, however, they are available for public viewing (book ahead).

Blue Vase
This wine vessel found in a Pompeii tomb was made with the so-called glass-cameo technique: a layer of opaque white paste was placed over coloured glass and then engraved with decorative motifs.

VISITORS' CHECKLIST

Practical Information
Piazza Museo Nazionale 19.
Tel 081 44 22 149.
Open 9am–7:30pm Wed–Mon.
🔲 ♿ 🖷 🆆 **museo archeologiconazionale. campaniabeniculturali.it**

Transport
Ⓜ Piazza Cavour-Museo. 🚌 C64, C83, E1, R1, R4, 24, 47, 110, 135.

Temple of Isis

Sacrifice of Iphigenia
In this Pompeiian fresco, Iphigenia, daughter of Agamemnon, is about to be sacrificed to Artemis, who saves her by taking a deer instead.

★ Farnese Hercules
Made by Glykon of Athens, this statue is an enlarged copy of a sculpture by the Greek master Lysippus. Napoleon is said to have regretted leaving it behind when he removed his booty from Italy in 1797.

Entrance

Stairs down to Egyptian Collection

★ Farnese Bull
Excavated in the Baths of Caracalla in Rome (see p441), this is the largest sculptural group (c.150 BC) to have survived from antiquity. The best-known piece in the Farnese Collection, it shows the punishment of Dirce who, having ill-treated Antiope, was tied to an enraged bull by the latter's sons.

Exploring Southeast Naples

The area south of Via A. Diaz is home to Naples' castles and royal palace as well as the densely populated Spanish Quarter. On the outskirts of the old town are a number of museums in historic buildings.

🏰 Castel Nuovo

Piazza Municipio. **Tel** 081 795 58 77/ 081 420 13 42. **Open** 9am– 8pm Mon– Sat. Last adm: 7pm. **Closed** some public hols. 🚫 Museo Civico: **Tel** 081 795 58 77. **Open** 9am–6pm Mon–Sat. 🎫

Also known as the Maschio Angioino, this Angevin fortress was built for Charles of Anjou in 1279–82. However, apart from the squat towers and the Cappella Palatina (with Francesco Laurana's *Madonna* of 1474 above the portal), most of the structure is Aragonese.

The castle was the main royal residence. In the Sala dei Baroni, Ferdinand I of Aragon brutally suppressed the ring-leaders of the Baron's revolt of 1486. The Aragonese were capable of violence, but they were also patrons of the arts.

The triumphal arch of the castle's entrance (begun 1454) is theirs. Commemorating Alfonso of Aragon's entry to Naples in 1443, this ingenious application of the ancient triumphal arch design was worked on, in part, by Laurana. The original bronze doors by Guillaume le Moine (1468) are in the Palazzo Reale. Part of the castle houses the **Museo Civico**.

The colourful and compact Quartieri Spagnoli

🚇 Quartieri Spagnoli

Via Toledo (Roma) to Via Chiaia.
The Spanish Quarter – the neighbourhood west of Via Toledo, sloping up to San Martino and Vomero – is one of the city's most densely populated areas. It was named after the Spanish troops who laid out its grid of narrow streets in the 17th century. This is where the archetypal Neapolitan scene comes to life, in which laundry hung above the streets crowds out the sun. This area is lively by day, sinister by night.

🏛 Museo Nazionale di San Martino

Largo di San Martino 5. **Tel** 081 229 45 02/ 081 558 64 08. Museo: **Open** 8:30am–7:30pm Thu–Tue. 🎫 🚫 Castel Sant'Elmo: **Open** 8:30am– 6:30pm Wed–Mon.

High above Santa Lucia, the Baroque Certosa di San Martino, founded in the 1300s as a Carthusian monastery, has great views of the Bay of Naples. It houses a museum featuring a variety of *presepi*, Christmas cribs of Neapolitan tradition. The cloister was completed in 1623–9 by Cosimo Fanzago (the creator of Neapolitan Baroque) to the 16th-century designs of Dosio. The church and choir are other examples of his virtuosity.

Next to the Certosa, **Castel Sant'Elmo**, built from 1329–43 and rebuilt in the 1500s, offers stunning views over the bay.

🏛 Museo Diego di Aragona Pignatelli Cortes

Riviera di Chiaia 200. **Tel** 081 66 96 75. **Open** 9am–1pm, 4–7:30pm Tue–Sun. **Closed** 1 Jan, 1 May, 15 Aug. 🎫

The Neo-Classical Villa Pignatelli, once home to the Rothschilds, houses this museum and its interesting collection of porcelain, period furniture, paintings and sculpture.

The bold Castel Nuovo, with the triumphal arch entrance

For hotels and restaurants in this region see pp562–77 and pp580–605

🔲 Galleria Umberto I
Via Toledo. **Open** daily. Teatro San Carlo: **Tel** 081 797 23 31. **Open** Aug, rehearsals and performances. 🚪 9am–5:30pm daily (081 66 45 45 to book). 🎭 ♿ 🔲 teatrosancarlo.it

Once a focus for fashionable Neapolitans, the handsome ar-cades of the Galleria Umberto I were built in 1887 and rebuilt after World War II. They face Italy's largest and oldest opera house: the **Teatro San Carlo**. Built for Charles of Bourbon in 1737, and later rebuilt, its fine auditorium once aroused envy in the courts of Europe.

Danaë and the Shower of Gold by Titian in the Museo di Capodimonte

Magnificent glass-roofed interior of the Galleria Umberto I

🔲 Palazzo Reale
Piazza Plebiscito. Museo: **Tel** 081 40 05 47. **Open** 9am–8pm Thu–Tue (last adm: 1 hr before closing). **Closed** 1 Jan, 1 May, 25 Dec. 🎭 🚪 Biblioteca: **Tel** 081 781 92 31. **Open** 8:30am–7:30pm Mon–Fri (to 1:30pm Sat). Bring ID.

Begun by Domenico Fontana for the Spanish Viceroys in 1600, and expanded by subsequent residents, Naples' royal palace is a handsome edifice with great halls filled with furniture, tapestries, paintings and porcelain. The small private Teatro di Corte (1768) was built by Ferdinando Fuga. The building houses the riches of the Biblioteca Nazionale (library). The exterior of the palace has been partly restored and the huge Piazza del Plebiscito facing it has been cleaned up. The great colonnades sweep towards 19th-century **San Francesco di Paola**, modelled on Rome's Pantheon.

🔲 Villa Floridiana
Via Aniello Falcone 171. **Tel** 081 578 84 18. **Open** 8:30am–4pm Wed–Mon. 🚪 ♿ Park: **Open** daily. **Closed** 1 Jan, 1 May, 15 Aug, 25 Dec. 🎭 Museum: **Open** 8:30am–2pm Wed–Mon.

Set in handsome gardens, this Neo-Classical villa houses the **Museo Nazionale della Ceramica Duca di Martina**, famous for its ceramics collection, including porcelain and majolica.

🏛 Museo di Capodimonte
Parco di Capodimonte. **Tel** 081 749 91 11. **Open** 8:30am–7:30pm Thu–Tue. 🎭 🔲 museo-capodimonte.it

Begun in 1738 by the Bourbon king Charles III as a hunting lodge, the **Palazzo Reale di Capodimonte** houses this museum and its magnificent collections of Italian paintings. Included are works by Titian, Botticelli, Raphael and Peru-gino, much of it originating in the Farnese family collections. There is also a gallery of 19th-century art, largely from southern Italy.

🔲 Catacombs of San Gennaro
Via di Capodimonte 13. **Tel** 081 744 37 14. **Open** 10am–7pm daily (to 1pm Sun). 🚪 call to book visit. 🎭

These catacombs – the original burial place of San Gennaro – are located near the church of San Gennaro in Moenia. The small church was founded in the 8th century, and is adjoined by a 17th-century workhouse. Two tiers of catacombs dating from the 2nd century penetrate the tufa, and there are mosaics and early Christian frescoes. Further along the street, the Catacombs of San Gaudioso commemorate the 5th-century saint who founded a monastery on the spot. Above is the 17th-century church of Santa Maria della Sanità.

🔲 Castel dell'Ovo
Borgo Marinari. **Tel** 081 795 45 93. **Open** 9am–5:30pm daily (to 2pm Sun & hols). 🎭 for exhibitions.

This castle, begun in 1154, occupies a small island facing, and joining, the Santa Lucia district – once the site of the city's shellfish market. A royal residence under the Normans and Hohenstaufen, today it belongs to the army. Interesting exhibitions are held here.

Beneath its ramparts, tiny Porta Santa Lucia is filled with seafood restaurants, and the Via Partenope running past it is a lovely promenade.

The façade of the Palazzo Reale, Naples' royal palace

❷ Pompeii

An earthquake in AD 62, which shook Pompeii and damaged many buildings, was merely a prelude to the tragic day in AD 79 when Mount Vesuvius erupted, burying the town in 6 m (20 ft) of pumice and ash. Although it was discovered in the 16th century, serious excavation began only in 1748, revealing a city petrified in time. In some buildings paintings and sculpture have survived, and graffiti is still visible on street walls.

Villa of the Mysteries

VICOLO DE' VETTI

VIA DELLA FORTUNA

VIA STABIANA

VICOLO DEL LUP

VIA DEGLI AUGUSTALI

VIA DEL FORO

VIA DELL'ABBONDAN

Forum Baths

★ House of the Vettii
The villa of the wealthy merchants Aulus Vettius Conviva and Aulus Vettius Restitutus contains frescoes (see pp48–9). It is currently closed for renovation.

★ House of the Faun
This famous villa of the wealthy patrician Casii is named after its bronze statuette. Advance booking is necessary to visit this and the other private houses on site.

0 metres 100
0 yards 100

In the bakery
of Modestus, carbonized loaves of bread were found.

Forum

Sacrarium of the Lares
Close to the Temple of Vespasian, this building housed the statues of Pompeii's guardian deities, the Lares Publici.

Macellum
Pompeii's market place was fronted by a portico with two money-changers' kiosks.

Plan of Pompeii

VIA DI NOLA

VIA DELL'ABBONDANZA

WESTERN
POMPEII

Porta Marina
entrance

Piazza
Esedraentrance

Piazza
Anfiteatro entrance

▨ Area illustrated below

Western Pompeii

*This detailed illustration is of the
western area, where the most
impressive and intact Roman
ruins are located. There are
several large patrician villas in
the eastern section, as wealthy
residents built their homes
outside the town centre.
However, much of eastern
Pompeii awaits excavation.*

Amphitheatre and
sports ground

Teatro
Grande

Vesuvius and the Campanian Towns

Nearly 2,000 years after the eruption of Mount Vesuvius, the Roman towns in its shadow are still being released from the petrification that engulfed them. Both Pompeii and Stabiae (Castellammare di Stabia), to the southeast of Naples and the volcano, were smothered by hot ash and pumice-stone blown there by the wind. The roofs of the buildings collapsed under the weight of the volcanic debris. To the west, Herculaneum (Ercolano) vanished under a sea of mud. A large number of its buildings have survived, their roofs intact, and many domestic items were preserved by the mud. In all, about 2,000 Pompeiians perished but few, if any, of the residents of Herculaneum died.

In AD 79 Pliny the Elder, the Roman soldier, writer and naturalist, was the commander of a fleet stationed off Misenum (present-day Miseno, west of Naples) and with his nephew Pliny the Younger observed the impending eruption from afar. Eager to see this natural catastrophe closer to hand, Pliny the Elder proceeded to Stabiae, but was overcome by fumes and died. Based on reports by survivors, Pliny the Younger related the first hours of the eruption and his uncle's death in detail in two letters to the Roman historian Tacitus.

Much of our knowledge of the daily lives of the ancient Romans derives from the excavations of Pompeii and Herculaneum. Most of the artefacts from them as well as Stabiae are now in Naples' Museo Archeologico Nazionale *(see pp494–5)*, creating an outstanding collection.

Mount Vesuvius has not erupted since 1944, but occasional rumbles have caused minor earthquakes. Visitors can reach it by train to Castellammare di Stabia, or by car. A useful website is www.guidevesuvio.it.

Pompeiian vase in Museo
Nazionale Archeologico

Casts of a dying mother and child seen at Pompeii

Via dell'Abbondanza
This was one of the original and
most important roads through
ancient Pompeii. Many inns
lined the route.

➌ Santa Maria Capua Vetere

Caserta. 🅰 34,000. 🚉 🚌 🅸 Palazzo Reale, Caserta (0823 32 22 33). 🛥 Thu & Sun.

This town boasts a 1st-century AD Roman **amphitheatre**, once Italy's largest after the Colosseum, with well-preserved tunnels beneath it. The town occupies the site of ancient Capua, an Etruscan city and then a flourishing centre during the Roman Empire. It was the scene of the revolt of the gladiators, led by Spartacus in 73 BC. The on-site **Gladiator Museum** recreates the history of the gladiators. Nearby is a **Mithraeum** (2nd–3rd century) with well-preserved frescoes. Finds from the sites are shown in the **Museo Archeologico dell'Antica Capua** in Capua.

🅰 Amphitheatre
Pza 1 Ottobre. **Tel** 0823 79 88 64. **Open** 9am–1 hr before sunset Tue–Sun. 🅿 valid for Mithraeum:. **Open** Tue–Sun.

🏛 Museo Archeologico dell'Antica Capua
Via Roberto d'Angio 48, Capua. **Tel** 0823 84 42 06. **Open** 9am–7pm Tue–Sun. 🅿

Tunnels under the amphitheatre in Santa Maria Capua Vetere

➍ Caserta

🅰 79,000. 🚉 🚌 🅸 Palazzo Reale (0823 32 22 33). 🛥 Wed & Sat. 🌐 casertaturismo.it

Magnificently opulent, the vast **Palazzo Reale** dominates Caserta. Built for the Bourbon King Charles III, Italy's largest royal palace boasts over 1,000 rooms, grand staircases and richly adorned

A fountain in the gardens of the Palazzo Reale at Caserta

apartments. It was designed by Luigi Vanvi-telli and construction started in 1752. The surrounding park boasts fountains, ornamental waterworks, statuary and an English Garden. Sound and light shows, in English and Italian, take place in summer.

Environs
The medieval town of **Caserta Vecchia** lies 10 km (6 miles) to the northeast. Its 12th-century cathedral is a fine example of southern Norman architecture. **San Leucio**, 3 km (2 miles) northwest of Caserta, is a model town built by Ferdinand IV, who also founded its silk industry.

🏛 Palazzo Reale
Piazza Carlo III. **Tel** 0823 44 80 84. **Open** 8:30am–7:30pm Wed–Mon. **Closed** public hols. 🅿 🦽 Park: **Open** 8:30am–1 hr before sunset daily.

➎ Benevento

🅰 62,000. 🚉 🚌 🅸 Via Sala 31 (0824 31 99 11/38). 🛥 Mon & Wed–Sat. 🌐 **comune.benevento.it**

Benevento, set in a lonely, mountainous province, is home to one of southern Italy's most interesting ancient Roman monuments: the **Arch of Trajan** on Via Traiano. The Roman city, Beneventum, was

an important centre. It stood at the end of the first extension of the Via Appia from Capua, and the Arch was erected across the old road in honour of Trajan. Built from AD 114–166 of marble, it is extremely well preserved. The relief sculpture adorning it – scenes from the life of Trajan and mythological subjects – is in excellent condition.

Elsewhere, evidence of the Romans is to be found in the ruined **Roman theatre**, built during Hadrian's reign, and in the **Museo del Sannio**, which contains artifacts from the region, from ancient Greek finds to modern art.

During World War II, the city stood directly in the way of the Allied advance from the south. It was heavily bombed, hence its largely modern appearance today. The Duomo, a 13th-century building reconstructed after the war, has a sculpted façade that, though badly damaged, has since been restored. The remains of its Byzantine bronze doors are

The ornate 2nd-century Roman arch in Benevento, built to honour Trajan

within. The town has centuries-old associations with pagan worship, and a liqueur called *Strega* (witch) is made here.

🎭 Roman Theatre
Piazza Caio Ponzio Telesino. **Tel** 0824 47 213. **Open** 9am–1 hr before sunset daily. **Closed** public hols. 🎫 ♿

🏛 Museo del Sannio
Piazza Santa Sofia. **Tel** 0824 218 18. **Open** 9am–7pm Tue–Sun. **Closed** 1 Jan, 25 Dec. 🎫 ♿

❻ The Amalfi Coast

Salerno. 🚃 🚌 Amalfi. 🛈 Corso delle Repubbliche Marinare 27, Amalfi (089 87 11 07). 🌐 **amalfitourist office.it;** 🌐 **ravellotime.it;** 🌐 **aziendaturismopositano.it**

The most enchanting route in Campania is that skirting the southern flank of Sorrento's peninsula: the Amalfi Coast (Costiera Amalfitana). Popular pleasures here include dining on grilled fish and sipping Lacrima Christi from the vineyards on the slopes of Vesuvius, beach-hopping and trips to coastal summits to admire the breathtaking views.

From **Sorrento**, a well developed holiday resort, the road winds down to **Positano**, a village clambering down a

The small town of Atrani on the Amalfi Coast

vertiginous slope to the sea. A top spot for the jet set, it is nonetheless a good place to swim, or to catch the hydrofoil or ferry to Capri. Further on, **Praiano** is just as fashionable.

Amalfi is the coast's largest town and a popular resort. It was a maritime power before being subdued in 1131 by King Roger of Naples. The world's oldest maritime code, the *Tavole Amalfitane*, originated here. The 13th-century Chiostro del Paradiso flanks the Duomo, a magnificent 9th-century structure fronted by a rich 13th-century façade, and facing the town from the top of a long flight of steps. The style is Lombard-Norman, though the

cloisters have a Saracenic-inspired appearance.

Ravello has the best views on this coast, the prime vantage points being the gardens of Villa Cimbrone and Villa Rufolo. Views from the latter provided inspiration for Wagner's *Parsifal*. The 11th-century Duomo has entrance doors by Barisano da Trani (1179) and an ornate 13th-century ambo (pulpit) held aloft by six spiral columns. The chapel of San Pantaleone contains the blood of its 4th-century namesake, which liquefies annually in May and August.

Beyond **Atrani**, the ruins of a Roman villa at **Minori** show that this coastline has always been a popular holiday spot.

A breathtaking view of the steep village of Positano on the Amalfi Coast

❼ Salerno

Salerno. 🚆 🚌 Salerno. 🛈 Piazza Vittorio Veneto 1 (089 23 14 32); Lungomare Trieste (089 22 47 44).

Salerno is a big, busy port. Here the Allies landed in 1943, leaving in their wake a much-bombed city. Once famous for its School of Medicine (12th century), it is visited today for its **Duomo**, an 11th-century structure built on an earlier foundation. Its best feature is the Atrium, whose columns came from nearby Paestum. In the crypt is the Tomb of St Matthew, brought here in 954.

The **Museo Diocesano** is home to most of the cathedral treasures, including an 11th-century ivory altar-front called the Paliotto. Before wandering off down the bustling Corso Vittorio Emanuele, visit the **Museo Provinciale** for local archaeological finds.

Environs

The **Cilento** is a mountainous region south of Salerno with a remote interior and a lovely, quiet coastline that is only slightly more populous. Among the towns along the coast, **Agropoli** is a busy little seaside resort 42 km (25 miles) south of Salerno. Outside Castellammare di Velia, a further 28 km (17 miles) to the southeast, are the ruins of the Greek town of **Elea** (founded 6th century BC). It was much visited by the Romans – Cicero was here and Horace came on his doctor's orders to undergo a treatment of sea bathing. Excavations have revealed a magnificent

The Temple of Hera I (left) and the Temple of Neptune at Paestum

4th-century Roman gateway: the Porta Rosa, Roman baths, the foundations of a temple and the remains of the acropolis.

🏛 Museo Diocesano
Largo Plebiscito. **Tel** 089 23 91 26. **Open** 9am–1pm Mon–Sat, 3–7pm Sun.

🏛 Museo Provinciale
Via San Benedetto. **Tel** 089 23 11 35. **Open** 9am–7pm Tue–Sat,.

❾ Capri

Napoli. 🚢 Capri. 🛈 Piazza Umberto I, Capri (081 837 06 86). Grotta Azzurra 🚢 from Marina Grande; 🚌 from Anacapri. **Open** in calm sea. Certosa: Via Certosa, Capri. **Tel** 081 837 62 18. **Open** 9am–2pm Tue–Sun. ♿ Villa Jovis: Via Tiberio. **Open** daily. 🏞
Ⓦ capritourism.com

Capri's reputation as a sybaritic paradise is nearly eclipsed by its notoriety as a tourist trap. However, the views are unmarred by the throng.

❽ Paestum

Zona Archeologica. 🛈 Via Magna Grecia 887. **Tel** 0828 81 10 16. 🚌 from Salerno. 🚆 Paestum. **Open** 9am–1hr before sunset daily. Museum: **Tel** 0828 81 10 23. **Open** 9am–7pm Tue–Sun. **Closed** 1st & 3rd Mon of month, 1 Jan, 25 Dec. 🏞 ♿

This is the most important ancient Greek site south of Naples in Campania. The Greeks founded this city on the edge of the Piana

The home of emperors, seat of monasteries, place of exile, its fortunes changed during the 19th century when English and German expatriates discovered its charms. Today it barely has a "low season"; farmers run little hotels, and fishermen rent pleasure boats. Capri enjoys its well-deserved reputation as a Garden of Eden.

The Grotta Azzurra, or the Blue Grotto, is a cave bathed in iridescent blue light which can be reached by tour boat from Marina Grande.

Anacapri is Capri's second town.

0 kilometres 1
0 miles 0.5

The busy port of Salerno

For hotels and restaurants in this region see pp562–77 and pp580–605

del Sele in the 6th century BC and called it Poseidonia, the City of Poseidon. The Romans re-named it in 273 BC. It fell into decline and was abandoned in the 9th century due to malaria and a Saracen assault and re-discovered in the 18th century.

Paestum has three massive Doric temples in an excellent state of repair: the **Basilica** or **Temple of Hera I** (mid-6th century BC); the **Temple of Neptune** (5th century BC), the largest and most complete at Paestum; and the **Temple of Ceres**, thought to date between its two neighbours.

Excavations have revealed the remains of the ancient city, its public and religious buildings, roads and protective walls. A **museum** contains the extensive finds from the site, including tomb paintings, tomb treasures, some terracotta votive offerings, architectural fragments and sculpture.

A view from the highest point of Procida, called Terra Murata

⑩ Ischia and Procida

Napoli. 🚗 Ischia & Procida. 🛈 Via Sogliuzzo 72, Ischia (081 507 42 11); Via V. Emanuele 168 (081 810 19 68). La Mortella: **Tel** 081 98 62 20. **Open** Apr–Oct: 9am–7pm Tue, Thu, Sat–Sun. 📱 🌐 infoischiaprocida.it

Ischia is the biggest island in the Bay of Naples and, with its beach resorts, thermal springs and therapeutic mud baths, it is nearly as popular as Capri. Ferries dock at **Ischia Porto**, the harbour and mo-dern part of the main town, **Ischia. Ischia Ponte**, the older part, is a short walk away. The northern and western shores are developed; the southern flank of the island is the quietest. Here, the village of **Sant' Angelo** is dominated by a long-extinct volcano, **Monte Epomeo**, whose summit of 788 m (2,585 ft) offers terrific views across the bay. Also worth a visit are the gardens of **La Mortella** in Forio.

The tiny, picturesque island of Procida is less visited and very tranquil. The swimming is good at **Chiaiolella** and, as at Ischia, there are inexpensive places to stay. The main town, also called **Procida**, is home to the main ferry port – the **Marina Grande**.

There are views towards Vesuvius and the Bay of Naples from the north of the island.

Capri is the main town on the island.

Marina Grande
This is Capri's main port of call for ferries from Naples and other ports on the Tyrrhenian coast. An array of colourful houses overlooks the harbour.

I Faraglioni

Marina Piccola is reached by dramatic Via Krupp.

Villa Jovis
Covering an enormous area, this was the Imperial villa from which Tiberius ruled the Roman Empire during his final years.

Certosa di San Giacomo
Founded in 1371 on the site of one of Tiberius's villas, this Carthusian monastery was suppressed in 1808 and is now in part a school. The distant rocks are I Faraglioni.

ABRUZZO, MOLISE AND PUGLIA

Puglia is the "heel" of the Italian boot, the Gargano Peninsula is its "spur" and Abruzzo and Molise together form the "ankle". Hugging the southeastern seaboard of Italy and looking towards the Balkans, the mountainous regions of Abruzzo and Molise, united until 1963, differ considerably from Puglia, the richest of the three.

Abruzzo and Molise are sparsely populated, quiet places where the wild landscape exerts a strong influence. Settled by various Apennine tribes in the Middle Bronze Age, the areas were later subdued by the Romans, united under the Normans in the 12th century and, thereafter, ruled by a succession of dynasties based in Naples. Abruzzo, dominated by the Apennines, is a brooding, introspective land of shepherds. Vertiginous drops preface the ascent to ramshackle hilltowns clinging to the sides of high mountains, semi-abandoned and poor. Molise's landscape is less dramatic. Legends of witches persist in both regions, as do strange fertility rites and rituals celebrating the changing seasons.

Puglia's advantage over its poverty-stricken neighbours is that it is nearly all flat and highly fertile. It produces the largest amount of olive oil in Italy, and its big cities – Lecce, Bari and Taranto – are lively commercial centres. The region experienced a long- lasting Greek influence, though the golden age of Puglia's past was under the rule of the Normans, followed by Frederick II who, between his return from Germany as emperor in 1220 and his death 30 years later, only spent four years away from here.

Puglia has glorious architecture, particularly in the churches and castles of the north. The curious *trulli* houses in central Puglia, the florid Baroque of Lecce and the Levantine atmosphere of its merchant cities complete the picture of an ancient land subject to more influences from outside the Italian peninsula than from within it.

Traditional dress worn in the town of Scanno in Abruzzo

◀ A row of *trulli* houses in the town of Alberobello, Puglia

Exploring Abruzzo, Molise and Puglia

Dominated by the Apennine mountain range, the hinterland of Abruzzo and Molise forms one of Italy's last wildernesses. At 2,912 m (9,554 ft), the highest peak is the Gran Sasso. Parts of Abruzzo are covered in tracts of forest, while Molise features high plains, gentle valleys and lonely peaks. The coastline of the Gargano Peninsula in Puglia (Apulia) is packed with cliffs, caves and islets. Reaching south is the fertile Tavoliere plain, and further south a series of upland plateaux (the Murge) descends towards the dry Salentine Peninsula and the Adriatic.

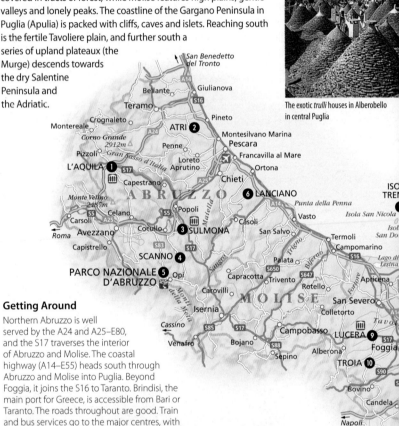

The exotic *trulli* houses in Alberobello in central Puglia

Getting Around

Northern Abruzzo is well served by the A24 and A25–E80, and the S17 traverses the interior of Abruzzo and Molise. The coastal highway (A14–E55) heads south through Abruzzo and Molise into Puglia. Beyond Foggia, it joins the S16 to Taranto. Brindisi, the main port for Greece, is accessible from Bari or Taranto. The roads throughout are good. Train and bus services go to the major centres, with buses only to more remote parts.

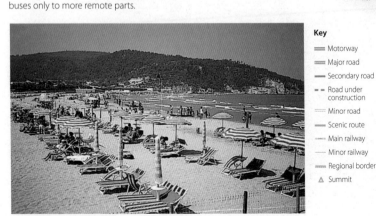

The coast at Vieste on the beautiful Gargano Peninsula in Puglia

Key

- Motorway
- Major road
- Secondary road
- Road under construction
- Minor road
- Scenic route
- Main railway
- Minor railway
- Regional border
- △ Summit

For additional map symbols *see back flap*

Sights at a Glance

The high peaks of the Gran Sasso, north of L'Aquila in Abruzzo

Lecce's exuberant Baroque architecture, epitomized in Santa Croce's rose window

The pink and white stone façade of Santa Maria di Collemaggio in L'Aquila

❶ L'Aquila

🏛 73,000. **FS** 🚌 *i* Via XX Settembre 10 (0862 223 06). 🚪 daily. **W** abruzzoturismo.it

Abruzzo's capital lies at the foot of the **Gran Sasso**, at 2,912 m (9,554 ft) the highest point of the Italian mainland south of the Alps (and good for skiing). Its ancient streets are peppered with churches. In April 2009 an earthquake, measuring 6.3 in magnitude, struck central Italy with the epicentre close to L'Aquila. Many of the historical churches and buildings described below have been seriously damaged by the quake. Restoration work is being carried out on many buildings so do check with the tourist office before visiting.

The domed **Santa Giusta** (1257), off Via Santa Giusta, has a rose window and a *Martyrdom of St Stephen* (1615) by Cavalier d'Arpino. **Santa Maria di Paganica**, off Via Paganica, has a 14th-century façade and a carved portal. The **Duomo** (1257) in Piazza del Duomo was rebuilt in the 18th century. The massive church of **Santa Maria di Collemaggio**, on Piazza di Collemaggio, has a façade of pink and white stone. It was built in the 13th century by Pietro dal Morrone, who later became Pope Celestine V.

Detail of Fontanelle delle Novantanove Cannelle in L'Aquila

San Bernardino, on Via di San Bernardino, houses the tomb (1505) of San Bernardino of Siena. The church (built 1454–1472), has a façade (1527) by Cola dell'Amatrice and an 18th-century carved ceiling by Ferdinando Mosca. The bell tower collapsed in the 2009 earthquake. The second chapel in the south aisle has an altarpiece by Andrea della Robbia, the Renaissance artist.

The medieval **Fontanelle delle Novantanove Cannelle** at the end of Via San Iacopo is a fountain commemorating the 99 villages that Frederick II supposedly united when he founded L'Aquila in 1240.

The **Museo Nazionale d'Abruzzo**, in the 16th-century castle, contains the remains of a prehistoric elephant, Roman artifacts and religious works.

🏛 **Museo Nazionale d'Abruzzo** Castello Cinquecentesco. **Tel** 0862 63 32 29. **Closed** for restoration – call for details. 🅿 ♿

❷ Atri

Teramo. 🏛 12,000. 🚌 *i* 0861 24 42 22. 🚪 Mon. **W** comune.atri.te.it

The prettiest in a series of small hilltowns in Abruzzo, Atri is a warren of stepped streets, alleys and passages bound by mostly brick and stone churches and houses.

The 13th-century **Duomo** occupies the site of a Roman bath; the crypt was once a swimming pool, and fragments of the original mosaic floor are visible in the apse. Also in the apse is Andrea Delitio's beautiful 15th-century fresco cycle, in which he combined landscape and architecture in a variety of religious scenes from the Old and New Testaments. The cloister has views of the 15th-century brick campanile.

Environs
South of Atri is the hilltown of **Penne**, with its homogeneous buildings of reddish brick, which give it a wonderful, warm glow. East of Atri, **Loreto Aprutino** is known for the *Last Judgment* fresco (14th century) in Santa Maria in Piano.

Detail from 15th-century fresco by Andrea Delitio in Atri's Duomo

❸ Sulmona

L'Aquila. 🏛 26,000. **FS** 🚌 *i* Corso Ovidio 208 (0864 532 76). 🚪 Wed & Sat. 🎭 Sep: International Exhibition of Contemporary Art. **W** sulmona.org

This town is famous as the home of both Ovid and *confetti* (sugared almonds). After a wedding celebration, guests are given *confetti* as a good luck token. Sulmona is filled with ancient buildings, especially along medieval **Via dell'Ospedale**. The **Palazzo dell'Annunziata** was founded in 1320 and combines Gothic and Renaissance styles.

The **Museo Civico** holds a collection of local antiquities, costumes, paintings and the work of goldsmiths formerly housed in the palace. The adjacent church of the **Annunziata**, with a Baroque façade, was rebuilt in the 18th century. Behind the church are 1 BC–AD 2 ruins of a Roman house.

At the end of Viale Matteotti is the cathedral of **San Panfilo**, built over a Roman temple. **San Francesco della Scarpa**, in Piazza del Carmine, has a 13th-century portal. Winding past it to the **Fontana del Vecchio** (1474) is an aqueduct that once fuelled local industry.

Environs

East of Sulmona is the Maiella National Park, a massif of 61 peaks and forested valleys offering walking, bird-watching, climbing and skiing. To the west, Cocullo hosts the May Processione dei Serpari (Festival of Snakes) in which a statue of the patron saint, Domenico Abate, is draped with snakes and carried through the town. In the 11th century he is said to have rid the area of venomous snakes.

🏛 Museo Civico
Palazzo dell'Annunziata, Corso Ovidio. **Tel** 0864 21 02 16. **Open** 9am–7pm Mon–Fri, 9am–1pm Sat & Sun.

Ovid, the Latin Poet

Born in 43 BC, Ovid (Publius Ovidius Naso) was Sulmona's most illustrious son. Not much survives here to remind you of his presence, however, apart from a **Corso Ovidio**, a 20th-century statue of him in Piazza XX Settembre and, just outside the town, a ruin traditionally known as **Ovid's Villa**. Known as one of the greatest poets of Classical Rome, his subjects included love (*Ars Amatoria*) and mythology (*Metamorphoses*). In AD 8 he was banished into exile on the Black Sea, the far edge of the Roman Empire, after being implicated in a scandal of adultery with Julia, the granddaughter of Emperor Augustus (*see pp52–3*). Ovid continued to write of his hardships, and died in exile in AD 17.

❹ Scanno

L'Aquila. 🏔 2,400. 🚌 ℹ Piazza Santa Maria della Valle 12 (0864 743 17). 🗓 Tue. 🌐 scanno.org

Wonderfully well-preserved, this medieval hill-town set in beautiful, wild countryside is one of Abruzzo's most popular attractions. There are alleys and narrow flights of steps, oddly-shaped courtyards into which small churches have been pressed, and ancient mansions whose windows women can be seen making lace or embroidering.

Traditional costume still worn in Scanno

In the shadow of Apennine peaks and beside lovely **Lago di Scanno**, the town is also a favoured stop on the way to the Parco Nazionale d'Abruzzo (*see pp510–11*). The summer months are the busiest, with a variety of activities from riding, boating and camping by the lake, to the August classical music festival. During the January Festa di Sant' Antonio Abate, a large lasagna is cooked outside **Santa Maria della Valle**, which is built on the remains of a pagan temple. The food is doled out on a first-come, first-served basis.

High Apennine peaks looming above the medieval hill-town of Scanno in Abruzzo

❺ Parco Nazionale d'Abruzzo, Lazio e Molise

This vast park, inaugurated in 1922, has a rich landscape of high peaks, rivers, lakes and forests, and is one of Europe's most important nature reserves. Part of a royal hunting reserve until 1877, today it provides refuge for 66 species of mammal, 52 types of reptile, amphibian and fish, and 230 species of bird, including the golden eagle and white-backed woodpecker, as well as over 2,000 varieties of flora. The park has an extensive network of paths, and there are opportunities for riding, trekking and climbing.

Golden eagles
may be seen near the Sangro river.

Pescina
Avezzano

Pescasseroli

Opi

Sangro

Cassino

Young Chamois
Dense forests of beech and maple hide the Apennine chamois. There are also red and roe deer in the park.

Forests of Beech
and black pine provide beautiful scenery.

Pescasseroli
This town is a major centre for information on the area. It has good tourist facilities and a small zoological garden with animals living in the region, such as bears and wolves.

Apennine Wolves
The park guarantees protection for the Apennine wolf, and about 60 wolves survive here. The chances of seeing one, however, are fairly remote.

Marsican Brown Bear
Once hunted almost to extinction, between 80 and 100 brown bears now roam in the park.

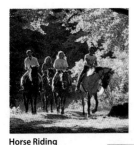

Horse Riding
Trekking is an excellent way to explore more remote areas of the park.

Lake Barrea
Created by the artificial damming of the River Sangro, this lake is surrounded by valleys and forests offering walking and pony trekking.

Dense Forests
Beech and maple forests, dotted with black hornbeam, ash, hawthorn, cherry, wild apple and pear, protect the once persecuted bears and wolves.

The Camosciara is a spectacular area, home to many wild animals.

Key
- Major road
- Minor road
- Walking path

0 kilometres 5
0 miles 5

6 Lanciano

Chieti. 35,000. **FS** **bus** *i* Piazza Plebiscito 50 (0872 71 91 27). Wed & Sat. **w** lanciano.it

Large parts of Lanciano's old nucleus remain from the Middle Ages. In the crumbling Civitanova quarter is the 13th-century church of **Santa Maria Maggiore**, with a magnificent 14th-century portal and a silver processional cross (1422). Also in this area is the now disused **San Biagio** (begun c.1059), near the 11th-century **Porta San Biagio** – a rare surviving town gate. The **Duomo** stands on the remains of a Roman bridge dating from the time of Diocletian. An underground passage links the bridge to the **Sanctuary of the Eucharistic Miracle**, where a host and wine that turned into live Flesh and Blood in the 8th century are kept. The Ripa Sacca (Jewish ghetto) was a busy commercial centre in the Middle Ages – the period of Lanciano's greatest prosperity. The hefty walls of the **Torri Montanara** were built then by the Aragonese as a bulwark against attack.

7 Isole Tremiti

Foggia. 400. San Nicola. *i* Via Perrone 17, Foggia (0881 72 31 41); Via Sant'Antonio Abate 21, Monte Sant'Angelo (0884 56 89 11).
w lecinqueisole.it

Off the Gargano coast, the Tremiti are the Italian islands least visited by foreigners. **San Domino** is the largest, with a sandy beach and coves. Julia, granddaughter of Augustus, was exiled here for adultery from AD 8 until her death in AD 28. The poet Ovid was allegedly involved (see p509).

Santa Maria a Mare, in **San Nicola**, the administrative centre of the islands, is an abbey fortress founded in the 8th century. It was turned into a prison in the late 1700s, a role it maintained until 1945.

Both the islands of San Domino and Santa Maria a Mare are popular with Italians. The swimming is good, though the coastline of San Nicola is rocky.

For additional map symbols see back flap

The coast near Peschici on the Gargano Peninsula

❽ Gargano Peninsula

Foggia. 🚉 🚌 *i* Piazza del Popolo 10, Manfredonia (0884 58 19 98); Via Sant'Antonio Abate 21, Monte Sant'Angelo (0884 56 89 11).
🌐 parcogargano.it

A rocky spur jutting into the Adriatic Sea, the Gargano is dotted with coves and cliffs. Its coastal towns of **Manfredonia**, **Rodi Garganico**, **Peschici** and **Vieste** are popular with holiday-makers. To the east lies the **Foresta Umbra**, a vast woodland of beech, oak, yew and pine, and to the north the salt lakes of

Typical street scene in the town of Vieste on the Gargano Peninsula

Lesina and **Varano**, havens for waterfowl. Plunging through the Gargano is an old pilgrim route (S272) from **San Severo** in the west to the shrine at **Monte Sant'Angelo** in the east. The first stop is **San Marco in Lamis**, dominated by a huge 16th-century convent. Further along, **San Giovanni Rotondo** is a focus for pilgrims visiting the tomb of Padre Pio (1887–1968), a beatified miracle-worker. The last stop is **Monte Sant'Angelo** with its grotto where the Archangel Michael is said to have appeared to the Bishop of Sipontum in 493.

To the south of Manfredonia, beside the ruins of ancient Siponto, is the oriental-inspired 12th-century church of **Santa Maria di Siponto**.

❾ Lucera

Foggia. 🚐 35,000. 🚌 *i* Piazza Nocelli 6 (0881 52 27 62). 🗓 Wed.
🌐 comune.lucera.fg.it

On the northeast edge of town, once a prosperous Roman colony, are the ruins of a Roman **amphitheatre**. Lucera was rebuilt in the 13th century by Frederick II, who peopled it with 20,000 Sicilian Muslims. It became one of the strongest fortresses in southern Italy, and its **castle** is one of Puglia's most magnificent. Built in 1233 by Frederick II, and enlarged after

1269, its fortified wall of 900 m (2,953 ft) is interspersed with 24 towers. Of Frederick's original palace, only the base and some vaulting remains.

In 1300 Charles II, who killed most of Lucera's Muslim population, began the **Duomo** on the site of their main mosque. The high, soaring nave is filled with 15th- and 16th-century frescoes and carvings.

The **Museo Civico Fiorelli** has displays of episodes from throughout Lucera's history.

🏛 **Museo Civico Fiorelli**
Via de Nicastri 44. **Tel** 0881 54 70 41.
Open 10am–1pm Tue–Sun (also 4–7pm Tue, Wed, Sat).

The remains of Lucera castle

❿ Troia

Foggia. 🚐 33,000. 🚌 *i* 0881 97 82 41. 🗓 1st & 3rd Sat of month.
🌐 comune.troia.fg.it

Founded in 1017 as a Byzantine fortress against the Lombards, Troia fell to the Normans in 1066. Until Frederick II destroyed it in 1229, the town had been ruled by a succession of powerful bishops who were responsible for producing many remarkable buildings, including Troia's **Duomo** (see pp482–3).

Begun in 1093 and constructed over the following 30 years, it exhibits an extraordinary diversity of styles. It successfully blends elements of Lombard, Saracenic and Byzantine style with that of the Pisan-Romanesque.

Elegant blind arcading distinguishes the Duomo's lower storey. The upper sections are characterized by powerfully carved sculpture – projecting lions and bulls. The upper façade displays a rose window with Saracenic-style detailing.

The main entrance, with bronze doors by Oderisio da Beneventano (1119), is dominated by carved capitals and an architrave, both Byzantine in style. Within the Duomo is a Romanesque pulpit (1169).

⓫ Trani

Bari. 🅰 55,000. 🚇 🚌 🛈 Piazza Sacra Regia Udienza II (0883 58 88 30). 🛍 Tue. 🖳 traniweb.it

During the Middle Ages this small, lively whitewashed port of Jewish origin bustled with mercantile activity and was filled with merchants and traders from Genoa, Amalfi and Pisa. It reached its peak of prosperity under Frederick II.

Today it is visited for its Norman **Duomo** in Piazza Duomo, built mainly from 1159

The façade of Trani's Duomo

to 1186 over an earlier church whose predecessor, the Ipogei di San Leucio, dates from the 7th century. It is dedicated to St Nicholas the Pilgrim, a little-remembered miracle worker (died 1094) who was canonized as an act of rivalry against the town of Bari, which possessed the bones of another, more memorable St Nicholas. The

Duomo's most notable external features are its sculptures, particularly surrounding the rose window and the arched window below it, and the entrance portal with bronze doors (1175–9) by Barisano da Trani. The vigour of the interior has been revealed following restoration.

Next to the Duomo is the **castle** (1233–49) founded by Frederick II. Rebuilt in the 14th and 15th centuries, it is a well-preserved edifice with one wall dropping sheer into the sea.

The 15th-century Gothic-Renaissance **Palazzo Caccetta**, in Piazza Trieste, is a rare survival. Nearby, on Via Ognissanti, the 12th-century Romanesque church of the **Ognissanti**, the chapel of the Knights Templar erected in the courtyard of their hospital, is notable for its original portico. Other churches worth a visit are Santa Teresa and the monastery of La Colonna.

⓬ Castel del Monte

Località Andria, Bari. 🛈 Beni Culturali (0883 56 99 97). **Open** Mar–Sep: 10:15am–7:45pm daily; Oct–Feb: 9am–6pm daily. **Closed** 1 Jan, 25 Dec. 🅿 🖳 **casteldel monte.beniculturali.it**

Frederick II

Remote in the endless plains near Ruvo di Puglia, Castel del Monte, built in the mid-13th century, out-classes every other castle associated with Frederick II. It is also one of the most sophisticated secular buildings of the Middle Ages. The emperor had broad intellectual interests, and he used his castles as hunting lodges where he could retire from court life with his falcons and books. Inside there are two floors, each with eight rib-vaulted rooms, some still lined with marble. This, and the marble mouldings on the entrance and the upper floor, as well as sophisticated lavatory arrangements, mark the castle as a palace.

Octagonal satellite tower

Graceful, arched windows

Thick and impenetrable walls

Octagonal courtyard

The main entrance portal is in the style of a Roman triumphal arch.

Floor Plan of the Castle

The building is a harmonious geometrical study with two storeys of eight rooms each. The reasons for such precise planning of this giant octagon remain a mystery to this day.

The castle standing alone on the summit of a low hill

⓭ Ruvo di Puglia

Bari. 🚍 24,000. 🚆 🚌 ℹ️ Piazza Matteotti 31 (080 950 71 11). 🚪 Sat. 🌐 ruvodipugliaweb.it

Once celebrated for its vases, Ruvo di Puglia's ceramics industry, producing "Apulian" ware, flourished until the 2nd century BC. The style was inspired by the striking red and black colours of Attic and Corinthian models. The **Museo Archeologico Nazionale Jatta** has a good overview.

The 13th-century **Cattedrale** is a bold example of the Apulian-Romanesque style with a portal that blends Byzantine, Saracenic and Classical motifs.

🏛 Museo Archeologico Nazionale Jatta

Piazza Bovio 35. **Tel** 080 361 28 48. **Open** 8:30am–1:30pm daily (to 7:30pm Thu–Sat). **Closed** 1 Jan, 1 May, 25 Dec. 🅿️ ♿ 🌐 palazzojatta.org

⓮ Bari

🚍 321,000. ✈️ 🚆 🚌 🚢 ℹ️ Piazza Aldo Moro 33a (080 524 23 61). 🚪 daily. 🌐 comune.bari.it

Roman Barium was simply a commercial centre, but the city became the regional capital under the Saracens in 847, and was later the seat of the *catapan*, the Byzantine governor of southern Italy. Under the Normans, to whom it fell in 1071, Bari became a centre of maritime significance. Today it is Puglia's lively capital and an important port with ferries to and from Croatia and Greece.

The **Basilica di San Nicola**, one of Puglia's first great Norman churches (begun 1087), has a plain exterior with a tall gabled section flanked by towers. The Apulian-Romanesque portal has carving on the door jambs and arch in Arabic, Byzantine and Classical styles. Beyond the choir screen is a fine 12th-century altar canopy and an episcopal throne (c.11th century). The relics of St Nicholas – patron saint of the city (and also of Russia) – are buried in the crypt.

Portal detail of Ruvo di Puglia's Duomo

Sculpture at Bari castle

The late 12th-century Apulian-Romanesque **Cattedrale** is based on San Nicola, with a dome and one surviving tower (the other one collapsed in 1613). The Baroque portals on the façade incorporate 12th-century doorways. The interior has been restored to its medieval simplicity. The canopy over the high altar, the pulpit and the episcopal throne are reconstructions from fragments of the originals. The sacristy, built as a baptistry, is known as the *Trulla*. The crypt houses the remains of San Sabino, Bari's original patron saint.

The city's **castle**, founded by Roger II, was adapted by Frederick II in 1233–9. In the vaulted hall is a collection of plaster casts of sculpture and architectural fragments from various Romanesque monuments in the region.

Bari castle, in the old district known as Città Vecchia, where most of the town's sights are clustered

⑮ Alberobello

Bari. 🚇 11,000. 🚈 to Alberobello & Ostuni. 🛈 Piazza Ferdinando IV (080 432 51 71). 🎧 in English, French and German offered by Trulli e Natura (080 432 38 29). 🎪 Oct/Nov: Frantoi Aperti (visits to the major olive-pressing factories). 🌐 alberobello.net

The parched landscape of the **Murge dei Trulli** features olive groves, vineyards and *trulli*. Strange circular buildings with conical roofs and domed within, *trulli* are built from local limestone stacked without using mortar. The walls and openings are generally whitewashed, while the stone roof tiles often have religious, pagan or magical symbols painted on them. The origins of *trulli* are obscure, though the name is traditionally applied to ancient round tombs found in the Roman countryside. Most *trulli* are souvenir shops.

Alberobello is a UNESCO World Heritage site and the *trulli* capital. Here the strange white buildings crowd the narrow streets, and there are *trulli* restaurants, shops and even a *trulli* cathedral.

Whitewashed and sun-baked *trulli* in Alberobello

Environs
The pretty white-washed hilltown of **Locorotondo** is an important wine centre. The elegant streets of **Martina Franca** are enlivened by Rococo balconies. The spectacular **Grotte di Castellana** are caves estimated to be 50 million years old.

Aphrodite in museum in Taranto

⑯ Taranto

🚇 200,000. 🚈 🚌 🛈 Corso Umberto I (099 453 23 92). 🛒 Wed, Fri & Sat. 🌐 comune.taranto.it

Little remains of the old city of Taras, founded by Spartans in 708 BC and at its most prosperous in the mid-4th century BC. The **Museo Archeologico Nazionale**, founded in 1887, has artifacts that shed light on the region's history. The museum has since been expanded to allow for a growing collection of historically significant pieces. Taranto was heavily bombed in World War II and is garlanded by factories. The picturesque **Città Vecchia**, an island dividing the Mare Grande from the Mare Piccolo, was the site of the Roman citadel of Tarentum. A lively fish market offering the shellfish for which the city is famous, is housed in an Art Nouveau building. Here, too, is the **Duomo**. Founded in 1071, it has been the object of subsequent rebuilding. The most interesting features include the catacomb-like crypt, with its sarcophagi and fragmented frescoes, and the antique marble columns of the nave. Behind it is the 11th-century **San Domenico Maggiore**, which later gained a high double-approach Baroque staircase. The huge **castle** built by Frederick of Aragon (15th century) covers the eastern corner of the Città Vecchia. Now a military area, the castle is strictly off limits.

🏛 **Museo Archeologico Nazionale**
Via Cavour 10. **Tel** 0994 53 21 12.
Open 8:30am–7:30pm daily. 🎫

The Tarantella

Italy's lively and graceful folk dance, the Tarantella, grew out of tarantism – the hysteria that appeared in 15th- to 17th-century Italy, and was prevalent in Galatina (*see p517*). Alleged victims of the tarantula spider's bite could supposedly cure themselves through frenzied dancing which sweated out the poison. The dance is characterized by light, quick steps and a "teasing" flirt. The strange, private ritual takes place annually on 29 June at 6am at the celebrations for the Feast of Saints Peter and Paul in Galatina, the only place on the Salentine Peninsula where tarantism has survived.

⓱ Street-by-Street: Lecce

Lecce was the site of the Greek Messapi settlement. It became an important centre of the Roman Empire, and in the Middle Ages developed a strong tradition of scholarship. Much of the architecture is in the highly decorative Lecce Baroque style, which flourished in the 1600s and earned the city the name of Florence of the South. This style was possible due to the *pietra di Lecce*, an easily carved stone. Giuseppe Zimbalo (Lo Zingarello) was its greatest master. Lecce is also famed for its papier-mâché workshops.

★ **Palazzo Vescovile and Duomo**
The bishop's palace (rebuilt in 1632), the adjoining Duomo by Lo Zingarello (after 1659) and a seminary (1709) enclose the Piazza Duomo.

Tourist information

Key

– – – Suggested route

0 metres   100
0 yards   100

Porta Rudiae
This 18th-century city gate leads to the suburbs and to the ruins of Roman Rudiae.

Chiesa del Rosario
Said to be the finest work by Lo Zingarello (begun 1691), the exterior is ornate and idiosyncratic in its detail.

Famous papier mâché (*carta pesta*) workshops

The Seminary once supplied the Vatican with *castrato* singers – eunuchs noted for their high voices.

Chiesa del Carmine

VIA UMBERTO I
PIAZZA CASTROMEDIANO
VIA RUBICHI
PIAZZA SANT'ORONZO
VIA PALADINI
VIA VITTORIO EMANUELE
PIAZZA DUOMO
VICOLO SANTA VENERA
VIA MARCO BASSEO
VIA MORELLI
VIA GIUSEPPE LIBERTINI
VIA G CINO
VIA R CARACCIOLO

B
C

Rer
Ital
rem
imr
thro
ma

Tod
but
alor
Mac
Basi
Cro
The

Af
follc
mer
who
had
relic
of ir
Catt
the

M
but
Ang
occ

★ **Santa Croce**
Built 1549–1679, this church was
begun by Gabriele Riccardi; the
rose window is by Lo Zingarello.
Next door is the ex-convent of
the Celestines.

VIALE XXV LUGLIO

VIA A GRANDI

**Church of
San Matteo**

VIA D'ARAGONA

IA LECCE

ailway
ation

A Roman theatre
was excavated
virtually intact
with its orchestra
and seats.

Roman Amphitheatre
Excavated in 1938, only part
of this 1st-century BC
amphitheatre is visible.

Sparse

◀ Tr

VISITORS' CHECKLIST

Practical Information
105,000. Via Vittorio
Emanuele 23 (0832 33 24 63), Via
Monte San Michele 20 (0832 31
41 17). 24–26 Aug: Sant'
Oronzo; 13– 24 Dec: Fiera dei Pupi
e Pastori. **pugliaturismo.it**

Transport
Viale Oronzo Quarta.
Via Boito & Via Adua.

**The 16th-century
Castello**
lies between ancient city
and modern suburbs.
A 12th-century
construction is enclosed
by a wall built later by
Charles V. Only one floor
is open to the public.

**Colonna di
Sant'Oronzo**
St Oronzo was
appointed Bishop of
Lecce by St Paul in AD
57, and later martyred
by the Roman emperor
Nero. This bronze statue
dates from 1739.

Detail of a 15th-century fresco in Santa
Caterina d'Alessandria

⑱ Galatina

Lecce. 28,000. Sala
dell'Orologio (0836 56 99 84). Thu.
29 Jun: Feast of Saints Peter & Paul.
comune.galatina.le.it

An important Greek colony in
the Middle Ages, this *città d'arte*
(city of art, a status given by the
region) retains its Greek flavour.
It is the centre of one of Puglia's
chief wine-producing regions,
although it is more famous for
the ritual of tarantism *(see p515)*.

The Gothic church of **Santa
Caterina d'Alessandria** (begun
1384) on Piazza Orsini contains
early 15th-century frescoes with
scenes from the Old and New
Testaments that glorify the
Orsini, who were feudal lords.

⑲ Otranto

Lecce. 5,500. Piazza
Castello (0836 84 14 36). Wed.
comune.otranto.le.it

Otranto was one of Republican
Rome's leading ports for trade
with Asia Minor and Greece, and
under the Byzantines was an
important toehold of the
Eastern Empire in Italy. In 1070 it
fell to the Normans.
Turks attacked in 1480
and slaughtered its
inhabitants. The 800
survivors were promised
their lives if they
renounced Christianity:
all refused.

The Norman **Duomo**
(founded 1080) on Via
Duomo houses the
bones of the martyrs.
There is a 12th-century
mosaic floor and a fine
crypt. A **castle** (1485–98)
built by the Aragonese
at the centre of town
adds to Otranto's charm
and there are some fine
beaches close by.

Exploring Basilicata and Calabria

Mostly upland country, Basilicata (or Lucania, as it is also known) is scattered with Greek ruins (like those at Metaponto), medieval abbeys and Norman castles (such as Melfi's). Matera, its most interesting city, stands amid an arid lunar landscape of denuded valleys. Calabria is often described as the land between two seas. The lovely beaches and virgin landscape between Tropea and Maratea attract many visitors. The Ionian coast's chief attractions are its Greek ruins, including Locri Epizephiri, and hill-towns, such as Stilo and Gerace.

Key

=== Motorway

=== Major road

— Secondary road

··· Minor road

— Scenic route

╌╌ Main railway

— Minor railway

=== Regional border

△ Summit

Repairing nets in the town of Pizzo, northeast of Tropea

The picturesque hill-town of Rivello, north of Maratea in Basilicata

Sights at a Glance

1. Melfi
2. Venosa
3. Lagopesole
4. Matera
5. Metaponto
6. Maratea
7. Rossano
8. Tropea
9. Stilo
10. Gerace
11. Reggio di Calabria

For additional map symbols *see back flap*

Foggia

Lavello

MELFI ❶ 🏛

Rionero in Vulture

❷ VENO

🏕 Foren

Acerenz

S93

LAGOPESOLE ❸

S7

Ruoti

Napoli ←

Potenza

BAS

Tito

Anzi

Marsico Nuovo

BA

Corleto Pertica

Grumento Nova

Monte Raparo 1761m

Lagonegro

Monti S 2005m

Rivello

Lauria

Latron

S19

MARATEA ❻

Praia a Mare

Scalea

Monte Caramo 1827

S18

Diamante

Mo 17

Cittadella del Capo

Cetraro

Serra Pantanolat 140

Paola

San Lucido

Longobardi Marina

Amante

Campora S. Giovar

Golfo d Sant'Eufer

MAR TIRRENO

TROPEA ❽ Vi

Valen

Milet

Nicotera

Golfo di Gioia

Rosarno

Gioia Tauro

Palmi

Polist

Bagnara Calabra

S18

Messina

Aspromont

Monti Peloritani

❶❶ REGGIO DI CALABRIA

Pellaro

Staiti

Lazzaro

S106

Stracia

The port of Maratea on the Tyrrhenian coast of Basilicata

Getting Around

Calabria's Tyrrhenian coast is well served by the A3–E45, a spur of which extends to Potenza in Basilicata. To reach the Ionian coast, it is best to skirt the Aspromonte via the S106–E90 from Reggio to Basilicata. Although the mountains can be crossed, namely on the S280–E848 to Catanzaro, the roads are narrow and pass through isolated countryside. Much of Basilicata is even less accessible, and Matera is more easily reached from Puglia. There are airports at Reggio di Calabria, Lamezia Terme (west of Catanzaro), Crotone, Bari and Brindisi (Puglia). Trains connect the bigger centres and country buses serve the small towns.

The countryside near Miglionico, south of Matera

| 0 kilometres | 50 |
| 0 miles | 25 |

The impressive castle at Melfi, showing evidence of both Angevin and later construction

❶ Melfi

Potenza. 🚗 18,000. 🚉 🚌 ℹ️ Piazza Umberto I (0972 23 97 51). 🛒 Wed & Sat. 🌐 aptbasilicata.it

A brooding and now almost deserted medieval town, Melfi is crowned by the **castle** where Pope Nicholas II conducted Robert Guiscard's investiture in 1059, thus legitimizing the Normans in the south. Melfi later became the Norman capital. Here Frederick II proclaimed his *Constitutiones Augustales* (1231), which unified his kingdom as a state. In the castle is the **Museo Nazionale del Melfese**, with its collection of Byzantine jewellery. The **Duomo**, off Via Vittorio Emanuele, was begun in 1155 by William the Bad but rebuilt in the 18th century. Only the campanile survives.

🏛 Museo Archeologico Nazionale del Melfese
Castello di Melfi, Via Castello. **Tel** 0972 23 87 26. **Open** 9am–8pm Tue–Sat (to 2pm Sun). **Closed** Mon am, 1 Jan, 25 Dec. 🅿️ ♿ 📷 (Sat & Sun).

❷ Venosa

Potenza. 🚗 12,200. 🚉 🚌 ℹ️ Piazza Castello 47 (0972 316 09). 🛒 1st & 3rd Thu of month. 🌐 comune.venosa.pz.it

Venosa was one of the most important Roman colonies around 290 BC, and remains of **baths** and an **amphitheatre**

survive in the archaeological zone along Via Vittorio Emanuele. It was also the birthplace of the Latin poet Horace (65–8 BC) and the site where the Roman general Marcellus died at the hands of Hannibal in 208 BC. Marcellus' reputed **tomb** is in Via Melfi. For more treasures, visit the **Museo Archeologico Nazionale**.

The **Duomo**, also on Via Vittorio Emanuele, and the huge **castle** in Piazza Umberto I date from the 16th century.

An abbey complex formed by an older, possibly early Christian (5th–6th century) church, **La Trinità** is backed by an unfinished 11th-century construction, in which Robert Guiscard (died 1085) was buried with his half-brothers and Alberada, his first wife. Only her tomb has survived.

🏛 Museo Archeologico Nazionale
Pza Castello. **Tel** 0972 360 95. **Open** 9am–8pm Wed–Mon. 🏛

❸ Lagopesole

Potenza. **Tel** 0971 860 83. 🚉 to Lagopesole Scalo then bus to town. **Open** 9:30am–1pm, 4–7pm daily (3–5pm in winter). 🌐 aptbasilicata.it

Rising dramatically on a hill, Lagopesole's **castle** (1242–50) was the last castle built by Frederick II. The interesting carved heads above the portal of the keep are said to represent

Frederick Barbarossa (grandfather of Frederick II) and Barbarossa's wife, Beatrice. Inside, the royal apartments and chapel can be visited.

The Sassi district of Matera

❹ Matera

🚗 56,900. 🚉 🚌 ℹ️ Via de Viti de Marco 9 (0835 33 19 83). 📞 0835 31 94 58. 🛒 Sat. 🌐 materaturismo.it

Perched on the edge of a deep ravine, this town consists of the bustling upper district and the silent, lower **Sassi** (caves) district, divided into the Sasso Barisano and the more picturesque Sasso Caveoso. The people of Matera once lived here in dwellings scooped out of the rock. The two parts are odd neighbours, making Matera a truly fascinating city.

For the best overview, walk along the **Strada Panoramica dei Sassi** and look down into the caves. From the 8th to the

13th centuries, such caves probably provided refuge for monks from the Byzantine empire. Many chapels, gouged out of the rock, were taken over in the 15th century by peasants. Later, a cave-dwelling Matera evolved and by the 18th century some buildings fronting the caves had become fairly grand mansions and convents. By the 1950s and '60s the Sassi were overtaken by squalor and poverty, and the inhabitants forcibly rehoused. Carlo Levi (1912–75) drew attention to their living conditions in his book *Christ Stopped at Eboli*, comparing the Sassi to Dante's *Inferno*. The area was made a UNESCO World Heritage site in 1993.

Of the 120 *chiese rupestri* (rock-cut churches; www.parco.murgia. it) in the Sassi and the Agri district outside the town, **Santa Maria di Idris** in the Monte Errone area and **Santa Lucia alle Malve** in the Albanian quarter both contain 13th-century frescoes.

The **Museo della Tortura** (torture), in Via San Biagio, has exhibits dating back to the time of the Inquisition, while the **Museo Nazionale Ridola** provides a background to Matera and the Sassi. The artifacts from many Neolithic trench villages, necropolises and other ancient sites are displayed here.

The Apulian-Romanesque **Duomo** (13th century) in Piazza Duomo has a 12th-century painting of the *Madonna della Bruna*, the patroness of Matera. Via Duomo leads toward **San Francesco d'Assisi** (13th century with Baroque overlay). Other churches to visit are **San Domenico** and **San Giovanni Battista** on Via San Biagio (both 13th century), and the **Purgatorio** (1770) on Via Ridola.

Matera is where Mel Gibson's *The Passion of the Christ* (2004) was largely filmed.

🏛 **Museo Nazionale Ridola**
Via Ridola 24. **Tel** 0835 31 00 58. **Open** 9am–8pm daily (from 2pm Mon). **Closed** 1 Jan, 25 Dec. 🛇

The Tavole Palatine in Metaponto

❺ Metaponto

Metaponto Borgo. 🚌 🚈 to Metaponto. ℹ Via Apollo Licio (0835 74 52 20). **Open** 9am–1 hr before sunset daily. **Closed** Mon am, 1 Jan, Easter, 25 Dec. 🛇 ♿ 🅿 aptbasilicata.it

Founded in the 7th century BC, ancient Metapontum was once the centre of a wealthy city-state with a philosophical tradition expounded by Pythagoras, who settled here after his expulsion from Croton. Its ruins include the **Tavole Palatine** (6th century BC) at the Bradano River bridge, 15 columns that are part of a Doric temple, probably dedicated to Hera. The **Museo Nazionale di Metaponto** displays artifacts from the site. The ruins of a theatre and the Doric **Temple of Apollo Lycius** (6th century BC)

Church of San Francesco in Matera

are in the **Archaeological Zone**. Further south, modern **Policoro** occupies the site of ancient Heracleia (founded 7th– 5th century BC). Its **Museo Nazionale della Siritide** has finds from this and other sites.

🏛 **Museo Nazionale di Metaponto**
Via Aristea 21. **Tel** 0835 74 53 27. **Open** 9am–8pm daily. **Closed** Mon am, pub hols. 🏛 includes Archaeological Zone.

🏛 **Museo Nazionale della Siritide**
Via Colombo 8, Policoro. **Tel** 0835 97 21 54. **Open** 9am–7pm daily. **Closed** Tue am, 1 Jan, 1 May, 25 Dec. 🛇

❻ Maratea

Potenza. 🚗 5,200. 🚈 🚌 ℹ Piazza del Gesù 32 (0973 87 69 08). 🛍 1st & 3rd Sat of month.

A tiny stretch of Basilicata meets the Tyrrhenian Sea in the Gulf of Policastro. This unblemished coast is home to Maratea. Its small port (Maratea Inferiore) is beneath the old centre (Maratea Superiore), which straddles the flank of a hill. From here the road climbs Monte Biagio to a summit with breathtaking views where a huge statue of the **Redeemer** stands.

Environs
Dramatically sited **Rivello**, 23 km (14 miles) to the north, once had a largely Greek population. Byzantine influences can be seen in the churches of **Santa Maria del Poggio** and **Santa Barbara**.

The small port of Marina di Maratea with fishing boats

A page from the precious *Codex Purpureus Rossanensis*

❼ Rossano

Cosenza. 🚉 39,000. 🚆 🚌 **ℹ** Piazza Matteotti (0983 52 09 08). 🛒 2nd & 4th Fri of month.

This pretty hill-town was one of the main centres of Byzantine civilization in Calabria. It assumed power when Reggio di Calabria fell to the Saracens (9th–11th centuries). The **Museo Diocesano** houses the *Codex Purpureus Rossanensis*, a rare 6th-century Greek Gospel with silver lettering and splendidly detailed miniatures.

The Baroque **cathedral** contains the *Madonna Acheropita* fresco, a much venerated Byzantine relic of the 8th or 9th century.

Environs

On a hilltop to the southeast is the five-domed Greek church of **San Marco** (10th century). The 12th-century **Panaghia**, another Greek church, lies off Via Archivescovado. Both contain fragments of early frescoes.

Santa Maria del Patirion, on a hilltop 18 km (11 miles) to the west, is magnificently adorned with coloured brick-work, tile and stone. It offers great views over the Piana di Sibari (Plain of Sibari), the alleged location of the fabled city of Sybaris, destroyed in 510 BC.

🏛 **Museo Diocesano**
Palazzo Arcivescovile, Via Arcivescovado 5. **Tel** 0983 52 52 63. **Open** 9:30am–noon, 3–5pm Tue–Sun; 10am–noon, 4–6pm public hols.

❽ Tropea

Vibo Valentia. 🚉 6,700. 🚆 🚌 **ℹ** Piazza Ercole (0963 614 75). 🛒 Sat. 🇼 tropea.biz

One of the most picturesque towns on Calabria's largely built-up Tyrrhenian coast, Tropea offers superb views of the sea and beaches. The old town hangs on to a cliffside facing a large rock, formerly an island. The rock is topped by **Santa Maria dell'Isola**, a former medieval Benedictine sanctuary. The **cathedral** at the end of Via Roma is of Norman origin, although it has been rebuilt several times. Inside is a 14th-century painting, the *Madonna di Romania*, by an unknown artist.

Casa Trampo (14th century) and **Palazzo Cesareo** (early 20th century) in Vicolo Manco are the most interesting of the small palaces in Tropea. The latter has a splendid balcony adorned with carvings.

Below the town are pretty beaches and a good choice of places to eat. Other seaside towns to visit are **Scilla** to the south and **Pizzo** to the north.

❾ Stilo

Reggio di Calabria. 🚉 3,000. 🚌 **ℹ** Town hall (0964 77 60 06). 🛒 Tue.

A short distance from the coast, Stilo is an earthquake-damaged town clamped to the side of Monte Consolino. Standing on a ledge looking out over the olive trees is the **Cattolica**, which has made Stilo a focus of pilgrimage for lovers of Byzantine architec-ture. Built in the 10th-century by Basilian monks, the brick building with its terracotta-tiled roof is based on a Greek cross-in-a-square plan. Four antique, mismatched marble columns divide the interior into nine quadrants. The capitals are placed at the base of the columns, instead of on top, to indicate the triumph of Christianity over paganism. The frescoes within, discovered and restored in 1927, date from the 11th century.

The Cattolica dominates the town, but on Via Tommaso Campanella there is a medieval **Duomo** as well as the 17th-century ruins of the **Convent of San Domenico**, where the philosopher and Dominican friar Tommaso Campanella (1568–1639) lived. The church of **San Francesco**, built around 1400, has an ornate carved wooden altar and a lovely 16th-century painting of the *Madonna del Borgo* (unknown origin). Bivongi, northwest of Stilo, has two churches dedicated to St John: the Byzantine-Norman **San Giovanni Theresti**, and the Norman **San Giovanni Vecchio**.

🏛 **Cattolica**
2 km (1 mile) above Stilo on Via Cattolica. **Tel** 0965 81 22 56.

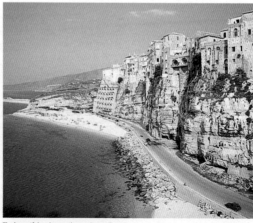

The beautiful and unspoilt coastline at Tropea

The distinctive five-domed Cattolica in Stilo

⑩ Gerace

Reggio di Calabria. 🚹 3,000. 🚌
ℹ️ Pro Loco, Via Regina Margherita
77, Locri (0964 23 27 60). 🌐 comune.
gerace.rc.it

Occupying a crag on the north-eastern flank of the Aspromonte, Gerace was founded by refugees from **Locri Epizephiri** who fled in the 9th century to escape Saracen attack. Its defensive character is reinforced by the medieval town walls and the remains of the castle.

Apart from the slow pace of life here – where you are as likely to meet a flock of sheep in an alley as a Fiat 500 – the main attraction is Calabria's grandest **Duomo**. This large structure indicates the significance of Gerace at least up to the time of the Normans. Constructed around the early 12th century, rebuilt in the 13th century and restored in the 18th century, the crypt is its chief treasure. Both crypt and church are simple, adorned by a series of antique coloured marble and granite columns probably stolen from the site of ancient Locri

Epizephiri. At the end of Via Cavour is 12th-century **San Giovanello**, part Byzantine and part Norman. Nearby is the Gothic church of **San Francesco d'Assisi** which contains a Baroque marble altar (1615) and the Pisan-style tomb of Niccolò Ruffo (died 1372), a member of a prominent Calabrian family.

Environs

The vast site of **Locri Epizephiri**, the first Greek city to have a written code of law (660 BC), was a famous centre of the cult of Persephone. There are remains of **temples**, a **theatre** and Greek and Roman **tombs**. The **Museo Nazionale** displays a ground plan of the site, as well as Greek and Roman votive statues, coins and sculptural fragments.

🏛 **Locri Epizephiri**
Southwest of Locri on the SS 106, Contrada Marasà. **Open** 9am–7pm Tue–Sun. 🌐 locriantica.it

🏛 **Museo Nazionale**
Contrada Marasà, SS 106.
Tel 0964 39 00 23. **Open** Tue–Sun.
Closed 1 May, 25 Dec.

⑪ Reggio di Calabria

🚹 183,000. ✈️ 🚆 🚌 ⛴
ℹ️ Station. 🛍 Fri.
🌐 turismo.reggiocal.it

One reason to visit Reggio di Calabria, which was heavily rebuilt after a major earth-quake in 1908, is the **Museo Nazionale della Magna Grecia**. It houses a fine collection of artifacts from ancient Rhegion – a Greek city on the site of the present town – and from other Greek sites.

Chief among its treasures are the Greek bronzes, larger-than-life statues of warriors dredged from the sea off Riace Marina in 1972. Statue A (460 BC) is thought to be by Phidias, the Athenian sculptor and chief exponent of the idealizing, Classical style. If true, it is a rare survivor because his works were hitherto only known to us from Roman copies. Statue B (430 BC) has been attributed to Polyclitus. It is possible that the statues originated from an Athenian shrine at Delphi built to cele brate the victory of Marathon.

🏛 **Museo Nazionale della Magna Grecia**
Piazza de Nava 26. **Tel** 0965 81 22 55.
Closed closed for renovations; call 800 98 51 64 to visit Riace bronzes at the Palazzo della Regione. 🚫 📷 ♿
🌐 museonazionalerc.it

Riace Bronzes (6th and 5th century BC) in Reggio's Museo Nazionale

SICILY

On a crossroads in the Mediterranean, part of Europe and Africa, yet belonging to neither, Sicily was tramped across by half the ancient civilized world. As conquerors came and went, they left behind elements of their culture, resulting in the rich and varied mixture that typifies every aspect of Sicilian life from language, customs and cooking to art and, most notably, the architecture of the island.

During the 6th and 5th centuries BC, there cannot have been much difference between Athens and the Greek cities of Sicily. Their ruins are among the most spectacular of the ancient Greek world. The Romans took over in the 3rd century BC, followed by the Vandals, Ostrogoths and Byzantines. Not much that is tangible has survived from the days of the Arabs, who ruled from the 9th to 11th centuries, though Palermo's Vucciria is more souk than market. The Norman era, beginning in 1061, spawned brilliant artistic achievements, such as the cathedrals of Monreale and Cefalù, while the eclecticism of that period's architecture is best seen at Santi Pietro e Paolo outside Taormina.

The Sicilian Baroque of the 17th and 18th centuries is just as individual. The palaces and churches of Palermo, reflecting the elaborate ritual of the Spanish Viceregal court, tend towards extravagant display. At Noto, Ragusa, Modica, Siracusa and Catania the buildings are a useful vehicle for the Sicilians' love of ornamentation, itself a remnant from the island's early fling with the Arab world. The style is an expression of the nature of Sicilians, whose sense of pomp and pageantry is both magnificent and extreme.

Sicily is a curiosity, and the legacy of the past is redolent everywhere. The fact that it is an island has intensified the cultural impact of each successive occupier. They say that today there's less Italian blood in Sicilian veins than there is Phoenician, Greek, Arabic, Norman, Spanish or French. The resulting mixture – exotic, spicy and highly inflammable – has created a separate nation at the foot of Italy.

Detail of a 12th-century mosaic from the Palazzo dei Normanni in Palermo

◄ The fishing harbour in the town of Cefalù on a clear summer evening

Exploring Sicily

The vast coastline of Sicily (Sicilia) provides hundreds of long, sandy beaches, particularly at Taormina and the Golfo di Castellammare by San Vito Lo Capo – part of a large nature reserve. Sicily's varied interior is characterized by remote hill towns and plains punctuated by mountain ranges known for spring flowers and wildlife. Among the most famous sights is Mount Etna, an active volcano whose lava flows over the centuries have fertilized the land, which supports an abundance of walnut trees, citrus groves and vineyards.

Fishermen at work in their boats at Siracusa

Sights at a Glance

- ① Palermo pp530–33
- ② Monreale pp534–5
- ③ Bagheria
- ④ Trapani
- ⑤ Erice
- ⑥ Marsala
- ⑦ Segesta
- ⑧ Selinunte
- ⑨ Cefalù
- ⑩ Agrigento
- ⑪ Piazza Armerina
- ⑫ Enna
- ⑬ Tindari
- ⑭ Messina
- ⑮ Taormina
- ⑯ Mount Etna
- ⑰ Catania
- ⑱ Pantalica
- ⑲ Siracusa
- ⑳ Noto

Getting Around

The A19–E932 links Palermo and Catania, the A18–E45 Catania and Messina, and the A20–E90 Palermo and Messina. The west is accessible from Palermo on the A29–E90. Ferry routes run from Messina to Reggio di Calabria, and from Palermo to Genoa or Naples. Between the larger towns, train services are efficient, but for smaller towns the buses are better. Catania, Palermo and Trapani have international airports.

The magnificent temple at Segesta

For additional map symbols see back flap

The Norman Duomo in Palermo

Key

━━ Motorway
= = Road under construction
▬▬ Major road
▬ Minor road
═ Other road

━ Scenic route
─ Main railway
─ Minor railway
△ Summit

0 kilometres   50
0 miles   25

❶ Palermo

Nestling on the protective flank of Monte Pellegrino with Monte Alfano to the east, Palermo lies in a natural amphitheatre called the Conca d'Oro (Golden Shell). The city is an eclectic mix of Oriental and old European influences, and it features architectural styles that range from Arabic to Norman, Baroque and Art Nouveau. This cultural infusion is unmatched in Italy, making this exotic city an exciting place to explore.

Ruined cloister with the red domes of San Giovanni degli Eremiti behind

🏛 San Giovanni degli Eremiti

Via dei Benedettini. **Tel** 091 651 50 19.
Open 9am–7pm Tue–Sun.

Reflecting Islamic architectural tradition with bulbous domes, corner arches and filigreed windows, this deconsecrated Norman church (1132–48) was built in the grounds of a mosque. Beyond church and mosque, a ruined cloister from a 13th-century monastery encloses a pretty garden.

🏛 Palazzo dei Normanni

Piazza Indipendenza. **Tel** 091 626 28 33. **Open** 8:30am–5pm daily (to 12:30pm Sun & hols). Last adm: 45 mins before closing. Cappella Palatina: **Open** 8:30am–noon, 2:30–5pm Mon–Sat; 8:30am–2pm Sun. **Closed** for Mass; Easter, 25 Apr, 1 May, 26 Dec. Sun.

This site has been the focus of power since the days of Byzantine rule and is now home to Sicily's regional government. The nucleus of the present building was constructed by

❹ Gesù

Piazza Casa Professa 21. **Tel** 091 607 62 23. **Open** 7–11:30am, 5–6:30pm daily (to 12:30pm Sun; Aug: 7–10am only). **Closed** for Mass.

This Baroque church (1564–1633) is also known as the church of the Casa Professa. The interior is an example of the skill of Sicilian craftsmen in the treatment of marble carving and inlay. The oldest Jesuit church in Sicily, it was restored after World War II.

the Arabs, but after the Norman conquest of the city in 1072, it was enlarged for the Norman court. See the luxurious royal apartments, especially the Sala di Ruggero, and the splendid Cappella Palatina. Built by Roger II (1132–40), this dazzling chapel blends Byzantine, Islamic and Norman styles. It is lavishly adorned with fine mosaics and marble inlaid with gold. Next to the palace is the eccentrically decorated Porta Nuova (1535).

Sumptuous interior of the Cappella Palatina, Palazzo dei Normanni

Duomo's exterior displaying a mixture of styles

Sights at a Glance

① San Giovanni degli Eremiti
② Palazzo dei Normanni
③ Gesù
④ Duomo
⑤ Santa Caterina
⑥ La Martorana
⑦ Vucciria
⑧ Oratorio del Rosario di San
   Domenico
⑨ San Domenico
⑩ Museo Archeologico Regionale
⑪ Oratorio di Santa Zita
⑫ Oratorio di San Lorenzo
⑬ Palazzo Abatellis and Galleria
   Regionale di Sicilia
⑭ La Magione
⑮ Villa Giulia

🏛 Santa Caterina
Piazza Bellini. **Tel** 091 616 24 88.
Open 9:30am–1pm daily (summer:
also 5–7pm Mon–Sat).

Although begun in 1580, most
of the internal decoration of this
unique church dates from the
17th and 18th centuries.
A powerful example of the
Palermitan Baroque, it boasts
sculpture, marble inlay and
illusionistic ceiling frescoes (18th
century) – by Filippo Randazzo
in the nave and by Vito d'Anna
in the dome.
   The church is flanked by Piazza
Pretorio, which is dominated by
the huge Mannerist Fontana
Pretoria (1544).

🏛 Duomo
Corso Vittorio Emanuele. **Tel** 091 33 43
73. **Open** 7am–7pm Mon–Sat,
9am–5:30pm Sun & hols. **Closed**
during Mass. ☐ Treasury: **Open**
9:30am–1:30pm, 2:30–5:30pm daily.
w cattedrale.palermo.it

Founded in 1184, the Duomo
displays many architectural
styles. The exterior shows the
development of the Gothic style
from the 13th–14th centuries.
The south porch (1453) is a
masterpiece of the Catalan style,
and at the apse end, sturdy
Norman work can be seen
through an Islamic-inspired
overlay. The dome is 18th
century. Within the much-altered
interior are the tombs of Sicily's
kings. Squeezed into an
enclosure by the south porch
are the remains of Emperor
Frederick II; his wife, Constance
of Aragon; his mother, Constance,
daughter of Roger II (also
entombed here); and his father,
Henry VI. The Treasury houses
the 12th-century Imperial
Diadem of Constance of Aragon,
which was removed from her
tomb in the 18th century.

Fontana Pretoria with Santa Caterina
in the background

For keys to symbols *see back flap*

Exploring Palermo

East of the Quattro Canti, where Via Maqueda and Corso Vittorio Emanuele meet, the city is sprinkled with ornate palaces and more churches. Squeezed behind them are labyrinthine medieval quarters where ancient, crumbling buildings still stand.

🏛 La Martorana

Piazza Bellini. **Tel** 345 828 82 31.
Open 8:30am–1pm, 3:30–5:30pm Mon–Sat; 8:30am–1pm Sun & hols (to 7pm in summer).

Also called Santa Maria dell' Ammiraglio, this church was built around 1140 by George of Antioch, Roger II's admiral. The design derives from Norman and Islamic traditions with mosaics possibly by Greek artisans. In the right aisle, King Roger receives the Imperial Diadem from Christ; in the left aisle, George of Antioch is portrayed.

A nearby convent, founded by Eloisa Martorana in 1193, was the site where the Sicilian Parliament met in 1295 and decided to hand the crown of Sicily to Frederick of Aragon. The church was presented to the convent in 1433.

Mosaic of Christ with Four Angels in the dome of La Martorana

🏛 Vucciria

Via Roma. **Open** daily.
Nowhere is Palermo's Arabic past more apparent than in this medieval casbah-style market which burrows through the ruinous Loggia district below Via Roma. Merchants, hawkers, shoppers and pick-pockets crowd an area once the haunt of artisans. The alleys all around are named after their professions, such as silversmiths, dyers and keymakers. This busy market, the largest in Palermo, offers the usual market ware from daily objects to junk, as well as a wide selection of fresh fruit, vegetables, fish and meat.

Stuccoed interior of the Oratorio del Rosario di San Domenico

🏛 Oratorio del Rosario di San Domenico

Via dei Bambinai 2. **Open** 9am–1pm daily. 🅿 ♿
The interior of this tiny 16th-century chapel displays elegant Baroque decoration by the master of stucco, Giacomo Serpotta. Created around 1720–30, this was possibly his finest work. Serpotta's technical virtuosity, not to mention the sensory indulgence and whimsical fantasy in evidence here, is remarkable. The altarpiece is the famous *Madonna of the Rosary* (1624–8)

by Anthony Van Dyck, and there are wall paintings by Luca Giordano and Pietro Novelli.

🏛 San Domenico

P.za San Domenico. **Tel** 091 32 95 88.
Open 9–11:30am Tue–Sat (also 5–7pm Sat & Sun). Cloister: **Open** call to check. Museo del Risorgimento:
Tel 091 58 27 74. **Open** 9am–1pm Mon, Wed & Fri. **Closed** Aug.
🌐 storiapatria.it

Although the present building was begun in 1640, there has been a Dominican church on the site since the 14th century. Tommaso Maria Napoli, one of the masters of Sicilian Baroque, created the exuberant church façade (1726) and square in front (1724).

Within, the most interesting feature is Antonello Gagini's bas-relief of *Santa Caterina* (1528) in the third chapel on the left. Next to the church is a 14th-century cloister that gives access to the Museo del Risorgimento.

🏛 Museo Archeologico Regionale

P.za Olivella 24. **Tel** 091 68 06 07.
Closed closed for repairs. End date not known; call ahead before visiting. 🅿

Housed in a former monastery of the Filippini, Sicily's most important museum contains sculpture, architectural fragments and ceramics, bronzes, glassware, jewellery, weapons and terracottas. The collection is taken from the island's Phoenician, Greek and Roman sites of antiquity – Tindari, Termini Imerese, Agrigento, Siracusa, Selinunte and Mozia. The highlights are sculptures from the friezes of the ancient Greek temples at Selinunte.

Palermo's noisy, bustling Vucciria market east of Via Roma

🏛 Oratorio del Rosario di Santa Cita

Via Valverde 3. **Tel** 091 843 16 05 or 091 609 03 08 (to book). **Open** Apr–Oct: 9am–6pm Mon–Fri, 9am–3pm Sat; Nov–Mar: 9am–3pm Mon–Sat. 🔊

This small chapel is dedicated to the Virgin of the Rosary after her miraculous intervention at the Battle of Lepanto (see pp62–3). The stucco relief decoration is the work of Giacomo Serpotta (after 1688): the panel on the rear wall depicts the battle, and other reliefs show scenes from the New Testament. The neighbouring 16th-century church of Santa Zita, from which the oratory takes its name, is filled with sculptures (1517–27) by Antonello Gagini.

Ornate interior of the Oratorio di Santa Cita

🏛 Oratorio di San Lorenzo

Via Immacolatella 5. **Tel** 091 611 81 68. **Open** 10am–6pm daily. 🔊

Lining the walls of this tiny oratory are incredible stucco scenes from the lives of St Francis and St Lawrence, and allegorical figures and putti by Giacomo Serpotta (1699–1706). These remarkable works exhibit the virtuosity of their creator in the handling of his medium. Caravaggio's *Nativity with St Francis and St Lawrence* (1609) was stolen from above the altar in 1969. The oratory lies hidden next to the 13th-century church of San Francesco d'Assisi, which brims with great sculpture. The highlight of the church is the triumphal arch (1468) by Pietro da Bonitate and Francesco Laurana in the Cappella Mastrantonio.

The Palazzina Cinese (c.1799) set in the Parco della Favorita

🏛 Palazzo Abatellis and Galleria Regionale di Sicilia

Via Alloro 4. **Tel** 091 623 00 11. **Open** 9am–6pm Tue–Fri, 9am–1pm Sat. 🔊

Matteo Carnelivari built this palace combining Spanish late-Gothic and Italian Renaissance styles in the 15th century. It is home to the Galleria Regionale di Sicilia, which houses Antonello da Messina's *Vergine Annunziata* (1476) and Francesco Laurana's marble head of Eleanor of Aragon (15th century). Nearby, the 15th-century church of Santa Maria degli Angeli (or La Gancia) contains works by Antonello Gagini and Giacomo Serpotta.

Vergine Annunziata (1476) by da Messina in the Galleria Regionale

🏛 La Magione

Via Magione 44. **Tel** 091 617 05 96 or 339 377 41 37 (mobile). **Open** 8:45–11:45am, 3–6pm Mon–Sat; 8:45am–12:30pm Sun. 🔊 🏛 🔊

🌐 basilicalamagione.diocesipia.it

Restorations have revealed the ancient structure of this church

founded in 1191 by Roger II's chancellor, Matteo d'Aiello. A highlight of Norman architecture, it has a simple nave flanked by fine Gothic columns.

🔵 Villa Giulia

Via Abramo Lincoln. **Open** 9am–5pm daily. 🔊 Orto Botanico: **Tel** 091 740 40 28. **Open** Nov–Mar: 8am–5pm daily (to 2pm Sun); longer opening hours in the summer. **Closed** pub hols. 🔊 🔊

The villa's formal gardens were established in the 1700s. Once, with their statues and fountains, they evoked the antique world. Nowadays, their tropical flora and faded grandeur make them delightful for walks. There are splendid tropical plants in the adjacent Orto Botanico (botanical gardens), and plant specimens can be examined in Léon Dufourny's Neo-Classical Gymnasium (1789). Palermo's only central park, Villa Giulia has good children's facilities.

🔵 Parco della Favorita

Entrance on Piazza Leoni & Piazza Generale Cascino. **Open** daily. 🔊 Museo Etnografico Siciliano Pitré: Via Duca degli Abruzzi 1. **Tel** 091 740 48 90. **Open** 8:30am–7:30pm Sat–Thu. **Closed** pub hols. 🔊

This park, laid out as a hunting ground in 1799 by the Bourbon Ferdinand IV, was surrounded by the nobles' summer villas. One of these, the Palazzina Cinese (c.1799), was built in a Chinese style for Ferdinand III and Maria Carolina, the sister of Marie Antoinette. The Museo Etnografico Siciliano Pitré, in the stables of the Palazzina Cinese, has a fine collection of Sicilian objects.

❷ Monreale

Magnificently adorned, and with a splendid view of the Conca d'Oro, the Duomo at Monreale is one of the great sights of Norman Sicily. Founded in 1172 by the Norman King William II, it flanks a monastery of the Benedictine Order. The interior of the cathedral glitters with mosaics carried out by Sicilian and Byzantine artists – the inspiration of a king who wanted to rival the power of the Archbishop of Palermo. Like Cefalù, and later Palermo, it was to serve as a royal sepulchre.

★ **Christ Pantocrator**
The cathedral's Latin-cross plan focuses on the imposing mosaic of the all-powerful Christ (12th–13th century).

Apse Exterior
With their rich multi-coloured ornamentation in tufa and marble, the three apses represent the apogee of Norman decoration.

KEY

① **Barisano da Trani's bronze door** (1179) on the north side is shielded by a portico designed by Gian Domenico and Fazio Gagini (1547–69).

② **Original Cosmati floor in choir**

③ **Nave and aisles separated by Roman columns**

④ **The royal tomb** of William II, in white marble, flanks the porphyry tomb of William I in the corner of the transept.

⑤ **Magnificent gilded wood ceiling**

⑥ **The south wall and cloisters** survive as elements from the Benedictine monastery.

⑦ **Small Oriental-inspired fountain**

⑧ **The 18th-century porch** is surrounded by two squat towers.

Entrance to Cappella del Crocifisso and Treasury

★ **Mosaic Cycle**
Completed in 1182, the rich mosaics show scenes from the Old Testament (nave), Teachings of Christ (aisles, choir and transepts), and the Gospels (side apses). The story of Noah's Ark is depicted here.

★ Cloisters
A masterpiece of Norman artistic expression from the time of William II, the columns – plain, carved or inlaid with richly lustred tiles – support elaborate capitals from which spring Saracenic-style arches.

VISITORS' CHECKLIST

Practical Information
Piazza Duomo.
W duomo monreale.it
Church: **Tel** 091 640 44 13.
Open Mar–Oct: 8:30am–12:45pm, 2:30–5pm daily; Nov–Feb: 8am–12:30pm, 3:30–6pm daily. Cloister: **Tel** 091 640 44 03. **Open** 9am–1pm Mon–Sat. Treasury: **Open** same as the church.

Transport
389, 809, 8/9 and many others going west.

Column Detail
Craftsmen from Campania, Puglia, Lombardy and Sicily worked on the cloister columns. The detail here shows Adam and Eve.

Bronze Door Panel
Bonanno da Pisa's fine bronze door (1185), signed by him, depicts 42 scenes from the Bible set within elaborate borders. The lion and griffin are symbols of the Norman kingdom.

❸ Bagheria

Palermo. 🚗 50,000. 🚉 🚌 ℹ️ Corso Umberto I (091 90 90 20). 🏪 Wed.
🌐 comune.bagheria.pa.it

Today Bagheria is almost a suburb of Palermo, though open countryside with olive and orange groves once separated them. In the 17th century Giuseppe Branciforte, Prince of Butera, built a summer retreat here, starting a fashion that was quickly followed by other Palermitan aristocrats. The town's core is sprinkled with their Baroque and Neo-Classical villas.

The **Villa Palagonia** was designed in 1705 by the architect Tommaso Maria Napoli for Ferdinando Gravina, the Prince of Palagonia. It has remarkable architectural qualities: a complex open-air staircase leads to the first floor, and the principal rooms, all with unusual shapes, are arranged around a curved axis. A later prince adorned the perimeter wall with the grotesque stone monsters which amused the 18th-century traveller Patrick Brydone, and

Stone figure on Villa Palagonia

horrified Goethe, who also travelled here and called this the "Palagonian madhouse". Across the piazza are **Villa Valguarnera** (begun in 1713 by Napoli), set in its own park, and **Villa Trabia** (mid-18th century), but neither is open to the public. **Museo Guttuso** (18th century) houses a modern art gallery.

🏛 **Villa Palagonia**
Piazza Garibaldi 3.
Tel 091 93 20 88.
Open daily (except during functions). 🗓

🏛 **Museo Guttuso**
Via Rammacca 9. **Tel** 091 94 39 02.
Open daily. 🗓

Fishing and pleasure boats moored in the harbour of Trapani

❹ Trapani

🚗 70,000. 🚉 🚌 🚢 ℹ️ Piazza Scarlatti 1 (0923 290 00). 🏪 daily.
🌐 apt.trapani.it

Old Trapani occupies a narrow peninsula. The best buildings in this lively quarter are the churches, such as the **Cathedral of San Lorenzo** (1635) and the **Chiesa del Collegio dei Gesuiti** (c.1614–40). The façades of both, and that of the **Palazzo d'Alì** (17th century) on Via Garibaldi, display magnificently the ebullience of west Sicilian Baroque architecture.

The 17th-century **Purgatorio** on Via San Francesco d'Assisi contains 18th-century *Misteri* – realistic, life-sized wooden statues used annually in the Good Friday procession. **Santa Maria del Gesù** on Via Sant' Agostino should be visited for the *Madonna degli Angeli* by Andrea della Robbia (1435–1525) and Antonello Gagini's canopy (1521). In the Jewish quarter, west of Via XXX Gennaio, the **Palazzo della Giudecca** (16th century) has a strangely textured façade.

The **Museo Pepoli** has a collection of local antiquities. Of interest are the coral objects and the Christmas crib figures (*presepi*), modern versions of which are made here. Next to the museum, the **Santuario di Maria Santissima Annunziata** contains the *Madonna di Trapani*, a statue revered by fishermen and sailors for its legendary miraculous powers.

🏛 **Museo Pepoli**
Via Conte Agostino Pepoli. **Tel** 0923 55 32 69. **Open** 9am–1:30pm Mon–Sat, 9am–12:30pm Sun & hols (also 3–5:30pm Tue & Thu). 🗓

Open-air staircase of the eccentric Villa Palagonia in Bagheria

⑤ Erice

Trapani. 🏛 29,000. 🚌 *i* Via Conte a
Repoli 11 (0923 50 21 11). 🚗 Mon.

Poised on a crag overlooking
Trapani, the medieval town of
Erice was once the seat of the
cult of the fertility goddess Venus
Erycina. Her temple stood on
the present site of the Norman
castle (**Castello di Venere**),
beyond the **Villa Balio** public
gardens. On a clear day, you can
see all the way to Tunisia from
the castle. The ancient town of
Eryx was renamed Gebel-
Hamed by the Arabs, Monte San
Giuliano by the Normans and
finally Erice in 1934 by Mussolini.

The **Duomo** (14th century)
has a battlemented campanile
and a 15th-century porch.
Inside is a *Madonna and Child*
(c.1469), attributed to either
Francesco Laurana or Domenico
Gagini. The deconsecrated
13th-century **San Giovanni
Battista** on Viale Nunzio Nasi
(now a hotel) contains
Antonello Gagini's *St John the
Evangelist* (1531) and Antonino
Gagini's *St John the Baptist*
(1539). **San Cataldo**, a plain
14th-century building on Via
San Cataldo, houses a holy
water stoup (c.1474) from
Domenico Gagini's workshop.
In the **Museo Cordici** are
Antonello Gagini's *Annunciation*
(1525), a variety of Classical
remains and an old library.

🏛 **Museo Cordici**
Piazza Umberto I. **Open** 8:30am–
1:30pm, 2:30–5:30pm Mon & Thu;
8am–1:30pm Tue, Wed & Fri.

A typical medieval street in the small
hill-town of Erice

Sicilian Islands

Surrounding Sicily are several island groups. The Isole Eolie (Aeolian
Islands), to which Panarea, Lipari, Vulcano and Stromboli belong, are
a mass of volcanoes (most of them nearly extinct) poking out of the
sea off the coast of Milazzo. The Isole Egadi (Egadi Islands), off the coast
of Trapani, have a distinctly Arabic flavour. They include Favignana,
Levanzo (which has Palaeolithic and Neolithic paintings and drawings),
and Marettimo – the smallest and most unspoilt. Ustica, renowned
for its marine life and popular among divers, lies north of Palermo. To
the south are the remarkably tourist-free Isole Pelagie (Pelagic Islands)
– Lampedusa and Linosa, which are North African in character.
Remote Pantelleria lies closer to Tunisia than to Sicily.

**The biggest and most
popular** of the Isole Eolie is
Lipari, which has a pretty
port and a good range of
bars, restaurants and hotels.
Nearby sulphur-smelling
Vulcano offers hot mudbaths
and black beaches.

Favignana, the largest and most
populous of the Isole Egadi, is the
scene of the traditional tuna
slaughter – *la mattanza*. This
takes place, as it has for centuries,
in May. These fishermen are
bringing in the nets following
the slaughter.

Part of the Isole Pelagie,
Lampedusa was once owned
by the family of Giuseppe
Tomasi di Lampedusa, author
of *The Leopard*, Sicily's most
famous novel. The island is
nearer to Malta than Sicily
and has limpid water and
white beaches.

Ustica

Isole Eolie
(Lipari)

Isole
Egadi

Palermo

Sicily

Pantelleria

Isole Pelagie

0 kilometres   100
0 miles   50

❻ Marsala

Trapani. 🚗 83,000. 🚆 🚌 🚢 **ℹ** Via XI Maggio 100 (0923 71 40 97). 🚢 Tue. 🌐 **consorziovinomarsala.it**

The port of Marsala is the home of a thick, strong, sweet wine that has been in production here since the 18th century. In 1798 Admiral Nelson ordered vast quantities of it following the Battle of the Nile. Its early manufacture was presided over by three British families living in Sicily. One of the old warehouses where the wine was produced is now the **Museo Archeologico di Baglio Anselmi**, housing important Phoenician artifacts.

The ruins of **Lily-baeum** are another attraction. Founded in 397 BC, this outpost of the Phoenician Empire was peopled by the survivors of the massacre by Dionysius I of Siracusa at Mozia (ancient Motya) – the island used by the Phoenicians as a commercial centre. Best of all are the reconstructed remains of a Punic ship thought to have been active in the First Punic War (263–241 BC). The **Museo di Mozia** in the Whitaker villa contains a remarkable early 5th-century BC statue of a Greek youth.

The excavations here are important; what we know of the Phoenicians today comes mostly from the Bible, and from

Mozia. The **Duomo**, begun in the 17th century, was built on the site of an earlier church; both were dedicated to Marsala's patron saint, Thomas Becket of Canterbury. Its interior is full of sculptural works by members of the Gagini family. The small **Museo degli Arazzi**, behind the Duomo, contains several magnificent 16th-century Brussels tapestries.

Statue of a Greek youth in Museo di Mozia

🏛 Museo Archeologico di Baglio Anselmi
Via Lungomare. **Tel** 0923 95 25 35. **Open** 9am–6pm daily. 🚫 ♿

🏛 Museo degli Arazzi
Via Garaffa 57. **Tel** 0923 71 13 27. **Open** 9:30am–1pm daily (and 4:30–6pm Tue–Sat). 🚫

🏛 Museo di Mozia
Isola di Mozia. **Tel** 0923 71 25 98. **Open** 9am–1pm, 3–6pm daily. 🚫 ♿

❼ Segesta

Trapani. 🚗 7,500. 🚌 from Trapani & Palermo. **Tel** 0924 95 58 41. **Open** 9:30am–6pm daily (to 4pm in winter).

According to legend, the ancient town of Segesta – still largely unexcavated – was founded by Trojan followers of Aeneas. It presents one of the most spectacular sights on the island: a massive unfinished **temple** stranded on a remote hillside. Its construction was started between 426 and 416 BC, and it was left incomplete following the devastation of Selinunte by

the Carthaginians in 409 BC. Archaeologists regard the temple as a good example of "work in progress". Nearby, close to the summit of Monte Barbaro, the ruins of an ancient theatre (3rd century BC) can be visited. Summer concerts are now held here.

❽ Selinunte

Trapani. **Tel** 0924 462 77. 🚆 Castelvetrano then bus. **Open** 9am–6pm daily (to 4pm in winter). **Closed** Sun pm. 🚫

Founded in 651 BC, Selinunte became one of the great cities of Magna Graecia – the part of southern Italy that was colonized by ancient Greece – and its toppled ruins are among Sicily's most important historic sites. Its ancient name, Selinus, derives from the wild celery that still grows here. The city was an important port, and its wall defences can still be seen around the Acropolis. The Carthaginians, under Hannibal, completely destroyed the city in 409 BC in a battle famous for its epic and savagely savage proportions.

While the city itself has virtually disappeared, eight of its temples are distinguishable, particularly the so-called **Eastern Temples** (E, F and G). Of these, the columns of huge Doric **Temple E** (490 – 480 BC) have been partially re-erected. **Temple F** (c.560–540 BC) is in ruins. **Temple G** (late 6th century BC), which had 17 massive side columns, was one of the greatest Greek temples ever built.

Higher on the Acropolis lie the remains of **Temples A, B, C, D and O**. Metope sculpture from **Temple C** (early 6th century), originally located on the frieze between the triglyphs, can be seen in the Museo Archeologico Regionale in Palermo (see p532), along with ceramics, jewellery and other artifacts excavated here. A small **museum** on site houses less important finds, as does one in Castelvetrano, 14 km (8.5 miles) north of Selinunte. The ancient city is still being excavated; its **North Gate** entrance is well preserved and further north there is also a **necropolis**.

The spectacularly situated, unfinished Doric temple at Segesta

9 Cefalù

Palermo. 🚠 14,000. 🚉 🚌 ℹ️ Corso Ruggero 77 (0921 42 10 50). 🗓️ Sat. 🌐 cefalu.it

This pretty seaside town, with sandy beaches, restaurants and hotels, is dominated by a huge rock known as **La Rocca** – once the site of a Temple of Diana – and by one of the finest Norman cathedrals in Sicily. Begun in 1131 by Roger II, the **Duomo** was intended as the main religious seat in Sicily. Though it failed to fulfil this function, the building's magnificence has never been eclipsed. Its splendid mosaics (1148), which feature an image of Christ Pantocrator in the apse, are remarkable and often celebrated as purely Byzantine works of art on Sicilian soil.

The **Museo Mandralisca** houses a fine *Portrait of a Man* (c.1465) by Antonello da Messina and a collection of coins, ceramics, vases and minerals.

🏛️ **Museo Mandralisca**
Via Mandralisca. **Tel** 0921 42 15 47. **Open** 9am–1pm, 3–7pm daily (later in summer).

The twin-towered façade of the Norman Duomo in Cefalù

The lavish apse of Cefalù's Duomo

10 Agrigento

🚠 59,000. 🚉 🚌 ⛴️ ℹ️ Via Empedocle 73 (0922 203 91); Piazzale Aldo Moro (0922 204 54). 🗓️ Fri.
🌐 comune.agrigento.it

Modern Agrigento occupies the site of Akragas, an important city of the ancient Greek world. Founded by Daedalus, according to legend, it was famed for the luxurious lifestyle of its inhabitants, and was a great power and rival to Siracusa. In 406 BC it fell to the Carthaginians, who sacked and burned it.

The historic core of the city, with its medieval streets, focuses on the Via Atenea. **Santo Spirito** (13th century) houses stuccoes by Giacomo Serpotta (1695). **Santa Maria dei Greci** was built on the remains of a 5th-century BC temple – see the flattened columns in the nave. The **Duomo**, founded in the 14th century and altered in the 16th and 17th centuries, exhibits a unique mixture of Arab, Norman and Catalan detailing.

Environs
The chief reason to visit Agrigento is to see the archaeological zone known as the Valley of the Temples (see p540). The **Museo Regionale Archeologico** houses an interesting display of artifacts from the temples and the city, including a collection of vases, coins and Greek and Roman sculpture.

🏛️ **Museo Regionale Archeologico**
Contrada San Nicola, Viale Panoramica. **Tel** 0922 40 15 65. **Open** 9am–7:30pm daily (to 1:30pm Mon, Sun).

The Mafia

An international organization founded in Sicily, the Mafia developed as a result of the cruel State and severe poverty. By the late 19th century it had become a criminal organization thriving on property speculation and drug trafficking. Since the "singing" of Tommaso Buscetta and the capture of Toto Riina, the Mafia has been on the defensive against a State that has doubled its efforts against it. The "Boss of Bosses", Bernardo Provenzano, was arrested in 2006 after 43 years on the run. Violence is common in Sicily, but it is not directed at tourists.

Mafia assassination depicted in this scene from the film *The Godfather Part III* (1990)

Valley of the Temples

Straddling a low ridge to the south of Agrigento, the Valley of the Temples (Valle dei Templi) is one of the most impressive complexes of ancient Greek buildings outside Greece. Its Doric temples, dating from the 5th century BC, were destroyed in part by the Carthaginians in 406 BC, and in part by Christians, who believed the temples to be pagan, in the 6th century. Earthquakes wreaked further havoc. Nine of the original ten temples are still visible, and the whole area can be covered in a day. To avoid crowds, visit early in the morning (some temples open as early as 8:30am) or late afternoon.

① Temple of Hephaistos
Apart from a couple of incomplete columns still standing, very little remains of this temple, built c.430 BC. It is also called the Temple of Vulcan.

② Sanctuary of the Chthonic Divinities
At this group of shrines, the forces of nature were worshipped.

Telamone from the Temple of Olympian Zeus

San Biagio

Rock Sanctuary of Demeter →

(see p539)
Museo Regionale Archeologico

San Nicola

Via dei Templi

• **Hellenistic and Roman Quarter**

Strada Panoramica

• **Catacombs**

P

S115

Via Sacra

Temple of Asklepios

S115

④ Temple of Olympian Zeus
Begun c.480 BC, this was the biggest Doric temple ever built. Unfinished at the time of the Carthaginian attack, it is now a toppled ruin. Giant figures known as telamones were used in its construction.

⑥ Temple of Herakles
This is the oldest temple in the valley (late 6th century BC).

⑧ Temple of Juno
Built around 450 BC, this temple still has many intact columns.

⑤ Tomb of Theron
Here are the ruins of a Roman tomb (1st century AD).

③ Temple of Castor and Pollux
This is a controversial assemblage of pieces from other buildings, erected in the 19th century. Modern Agrigento (see p539) is in the background.

Key
— Suggested route
— Ancient walls

0 metres   500
0 yards   500

⑦ Temple of Concord
This beautifully preserved temple (c.430 BC) was converted into a Christian church in the 4th century AD, thus saved from destruction.

⓫ Piazza Armerina

Enna. 🏛 21,000. 🚌 *i* Via Generale
Muscara (0935 68 02 01). 🛥 Thu.
w piazzaarmerina.org

This active town is half medieval
and half Baroque. The 17th-
century **Duomo**, at its highest
point, is the most interesting of
the Baroque buildings.

In August, the lively *Palio dei
Normanni* festival attracts many
visitors, but the real draw are
the mosaics in the UNESCO-
listed **Villa Romana del Casale**,
5 km (3 miles) southwest of the
town. The mosaics were only
excavated in the 20th century.

It is thought that this huge,
once sumptuous villa with its
public halls, private quarters,
baths and courtyards, belonged
to Maximianus Herculeus,
Diocletian's co-emperor, from
AD 286 to 305. His son and
successor, Maxentius, probably
continued its decoration, with
Constantine taking over on
Maxentius's death in 312.

Although little remains of the
building fabric, the floors have
some of the finest surviving
mosaics from Roman antiquity.
The hunting, mythological and
domestic scenes, and exotic
landscapes, all exhibit realistic
attention to detail.

🏛 **Villa Romana del Casale**
Contrada Casale. **Tel** 0935 68 00 36.
Open 9am–4:30pm Fri–Sun. 🚫

Roman *Girls in Bikinis* mosaic from the Villa Romana del Casale

⓬ Enna

🏛 28,000. 🚆 🚌 *i* Piazza
Colaianni 6 (0935 50 08 75). 🛥 Tue.
w apt-enna.com

Impregnable on a crag above
a fertile landscape where
Persephone, mythological
daughter of Demeter, once
played, Sicily's highest town
(942 m/3,090 ft) has been
coveted by successive invaders
since its earliest days. The
venerated seat of the Cult of
Demeter (goddess of fertility)
was at Enna. Her temple stood
on the **Rocca Cerere**, not far from
the huge **Castello di Lombardia**
(13th century) built by Frederick II.

Most of Enna's sights are
clustered in the old town, among
the ancient streets that open out
of the Via Roma. The church of

San Francesco has a 16th-century
tower. **Piazza Crispi**, with its
fine views to nearby Calas-
cibetta, is dominated by a copy
of Bernini's *Rape of Persephone*.
The 14th-century **Duomo**, altered
in later centuries, contains parts
of Demeter's temple.

The **Museo Alessi** houses
the Cathedral Treasury and an
interesting coin collection. The
Museo Varisano has exhibits
on the area's history, from
Neolithic to Roman. Away from
the centre, the octagonal **Torre
di Federico II** (13th century) is a
former watchtower.

Environs
The ancient hill-town of **Nicosia**,
northeast of Enna, was damaged
in the 1967 earthquake, but still
contains a smattering of
churches. San Nicola, built in the
14th century, has a magnificent,
carved entrance portal. Inside
there is a much venerated
wooden crucifix (17th century)
by Fra Umile di Petralia. Santa
Maria Maggiore houses a 16th-
century marble poly-ptych by
Antonello Gagini and a throne
reputedly used by Charles V in
1535. Further east is **Troina**. It
was captured in 1062 by the
Normans, whose work survives
in the Chiesa Matrice. Southeast
of Enna, **Vizzini** commands fine
views of the countryside.

🏛 **Museo Alessi**
Via Roma 475. **Open** 8am–8pm daily.
🚫

🏛 **Museo Varisano**
Piazza Mazzini. **Tel** 0935 52 81 00.
Open 9am–6:30pm daily.

A view from the hills overlooking Vizzini, southeast of Enna

For hotels and restaurants in this region see pp562–77 and pp580–605

Taormina's magnificently situated Greek theatre, with Mount Etna in the distance

⑬ Tindari

Messina. **i** **Tel** 0941 24 11 36. **FS** Patti or Oliveri, then bus. **Open** 9am–7pm daily (to 4pm in winter). ♿ ♾

Poised on the edge of a cliff overlooking the Golfo di Patti are the ruins of **Tyndaris**, one of the last Greek cities to have been founded in Sicily (395 BC). Apart from the city walls, the ruins are mostly Roman, including the **basilica** and **theatre**. An **antiquarium** houses artifacts from the site. A combined ticket allows entry at the massive 2nd-century **Villa Romana** in Patti Marina.

Tindari is also known for its shrine to a Byzantine icon, the **Black Madonna** on Piazzale Belvedere.

⑭ Messina

🚹 250,000. **FS** 🚌 ⛴ **i** Piazza Cairoli 45 (090 293 52 92). ⛴ daily. **w** azienturismomessina.it

Messina has been the victim of earthquakes and World War II bombing. The **Museo Regionale** houses treasures that include works by Antonello da Messina and Caravaggio. **Santissima Annunziata dei Catalani** in Piazza Catalani displays the eclecticism of 12th-century

Norman architecture, with rich decoration. To visit the church, ask at the tourist office.

Outside, GA Montorsoli's **Fontana d'Orione** (1547) is the finest fountain of its kind from 16th-century Sicily. His **Fontana di Nettuno** (1557) celebrates Messina's foundation and position in the world as a principal commercial port.

🏛 Museo Regionale

Via Libertà 465. **Tel** 090 36 12 92. **Open** 9am–7pm Tue–Sat, 9am–1pm Sun. ♾ ♿

Antonello da Messina's *Madonna and Child* (1473), Museo Regionale

⑮ Taormina

Messina. 🚹 10,000. **FS** 🚌 **i** Palazzo Corvaja, Piazza Santa Caterina (0942 232 43). ⛴ Wed.

Splendidly situated, Taormina is Sicily's best-known resort. It retains an air of exclusivity while being on the tourist trail, with sandy beaches and a wide range of restaurants and hotels.

The most illustrious relic of the past is the **theatre**. Begun in the 3rd century BC by the Greeks, it was subsequently rebuilt by the Romans. Among other Classical remains are the ruins of the **odeon** (for musical performances) and the **naumachia** (an artificial lake for mock-battles). On Piazza Vittorio Emanuele (site of the Roman Forum), **Palazzo Corvaia** (14th century) was built using stone from a temple that once stood here. The 13th-century **Duomo** (renovated in 1636) is a fortress-like building.

Environs

Taormina's main beach, **Mazzarò**, boasts clear waters and is easily reached from the town. South of Taormina at **Capo Schisò** are the ruins of ancient **Naxos**. To the west is **Gole dell'Alcantara**, a 20-m (66-ft) deep gorge of basalt rock, a river and waterfalls.

⑯ Mount Etna

Catania. **FS** Linguaglossa or Randazzo; Circumetnea railway from Catania to Riposto. **BUS** to Nicolosi. **i** Via G. Garibaldi 63, Nicolosi (095 91 15 05). To hire a guide: 095 791 47 55. **W** http://turismo.provincia.ct.it

Europe's highest (3,370 m/ 11,050 ft) and most active volcano, Mount Etna was thought by the Romans to have been the forge of Vulcan (god of fire). The climb to the summit should be made only with an experienced guide. The Circumetnea railway runs around the base, offering a good alternative to hiking and good views.

⑰ Catania

🏙 315,000. **✈** **FS** **BUS** **i** Via Cimarosa 10 (095 73 06 211). **🛒** Mon–Sat (general); Sun (antique & bric-a-brac). **W** apt.catania.it

Having been decimated by the earthquake of 1693, Catania was comprehensively rebuilt. While it is not immediately beautiful, it

The façade of Catania's Duomo

contains some of the most imaginative lava-built Baroque buildings in Sicily. **Piazza del Duomo**, featuring a lava elephant (Catania's symbol) carrying an Egyptian obelisk, offers a dramatic vista to Mount Etna. In 1736 the Norman **Duomo** was given a new façade by Vaccarini, who also worked on the **Municipio** (finished 1741), on the façade of **Sant'Agata** (1748), on the designs of **Collegio Cutelli**, built

around 1779, and on **Palazzo Valle** (c.1740–50).

Carrying on the Vaccarini tradition is Stefano Ittar's **San Placido** (around 1768). The frenzied stone carving on the **Palazzo Biscari** (early 18th century) is exceeded by Antonino Amato's unrestrained decoration of the vast Benedictine **convent** (1704) and the adjacent huge church of **San Niccolò** (1730)

On Via Vittorio Emanuele is the **Museo Belliniano**, birthplace of composer Vincenzo Bellini (1801–35). The lava ruins of the **Teatro Romano** (21 BC) are at Piazza Stesicono. **Verga's House**, home of the great Sicilian novelist Giovanni Verga (1840–1922), is on Via Sant' Anna. Via Crociferi is home to 18th-century churches **San Francesco Borgia, San Benedetto** and **San Giuliano**, whose interior is Vaccarini's masterpiece (1760). Further along Via Crociferi, the church of **Santo Carcere** contains the prison of St Agatha, who was martyred in AD 253.

Influences on Traditional Sicilian Cuisine

Sicily has one of Italy's most varied cuisines. The island's unique location – marooned between North Africa, Europe and the eastern Mediterranean – and the invaders it attracted are responsible for this culinary diversity. The earliest Western cookbook, the now lost *Art of Cooking* (5th century BC), was written by Mithaecus, a Siracusan Greek. Sicily's fertility attracted Greek colonists, who exported oil, wheat, honey, cheese, fruit and vegetables to their homeland. The Arabs introduced oranges, lemons, aubergines and sugar cane. Their love of sweet confections inspired *granita*, a form of flavoured ice, and *cassata*, an elaborate sponge cake with ricotta and candied

A colourful selection of vegetables at a Sicilian market stall

fruit. The Sicilians love to claim an Arabic origin for their ice cream, but the Greeks and Romans had created an earlier version by chilling their wine with snow from Mount Etna. Traditionally, the peasants existed on a subsistence diet while the aristocracy enjoyed extravagant fare, and one

of the peculiarities of Sicilian food today is that it can be both frugal and handsomely ornate. All of the usual Italian dishes are available, but the more interesting meals are those that use local ingredients like swordfish, sardines, ricotta cheese, red chillies, aubergines, capers, olives and almond paste to create unusual taste combinations.

Marzipan fruits made from almond paste

A picturesque beach at Capo Tindari, Sicily ▶

Shorefront in Siracusa, one of the most beautiful cities of the ancient Greek world

⑱ Pantalica

Siracusa. 🚌 from Siracusa to Sortino then 5-km (3-mile) walk to entrance (partial access), or bus from Siracusa to Ferla then 10-km (6-mile) walk to entrance. Necropolis 🛈 Pro Loco, Ferla. **Tel** 0931 79 06 81.

Remote in the desolate Monti Iblei and overlooking the River Anapo is the prehistoric **necropolis** of Pantalica – a pleasant place to walk and picnic. The dead of a large, unexcavated village (occupied from 13th–8th century BC) were buried here in cave-like tombs cut into the rock. More than 5,000 of these tombs were arranged in tiers with a single flat stone sealing each opening.

The inhabitants of Pantalica are thought to have come from coastal **Thapsos**, which was abandoned after raids by warlike tribes from mainland Italy. The site was re-inhabited in the Byzantine period when some tombs were made into cave dwellings and chapels.

Rock-cut tombs in the prehistoric necropolis of Pantalica

Artifacts from the necropolis are displayed in Siracusa's Museo Archeologico Regionale.

Interior of Duomo in Siracusa

⑲ Siracusa

🏙 125,000. 🚊 🚌 ⛴ 🛈 Via Maestranza (0931 46 42 55). 🛍 Wed.

Siracusa (Syracuse) was the most important and powerful Greek city from the 5th to the 3rd centuries BC, and, according to the Roman consul Cicero, the most beautiful. The peninsula **Ortigia** is the hub of the old city. On the mainland, **Achradina, Tyche** and **Neapolis** have been occupied almost without a break since the expansion of the city in 480 BC. These were the years of Gelon, tyrant of Gela, when Siracusa was enriched with new temples, theatres and dockyards. The city was a powerful force until 211 BC, when it fell to the Romans in a battle that also killed the

mathematician Archimedes, its most famous inhabitant.

The highlight of Ortigia is the extraordinary **Duomo**, begun in 1728 by architect Andrea Palma. Its Baroque façade masks the **Temple of Athena** (5th century BC), which has been absorbed into the Duomo. Facing the Ponte Nuovo are the ruins of Sicily's earliest Doric temple, the **Temple of Apollo**, which had monolithic columns.

Across from the Duomo is the **Palazzo Beneventano del Bosco** (1778–88), a bold example of Siracusan Baroque, as is **Santa Lucia alla Badia** (1695–1703). In the Municipio a small museum records the history of Ionic temples, and the coin collection of the Galleria Numismatica records Siracusa's past wealth. The delightful **Fonte Aretusa** is frequently referred to by Classical writers as the point where Aretusa emerged from the ground, having been changed into a spring by Artemis to help her escape her lover Alpheus.

At Ortigia's furthest point is the **Castello Maniace**, built by Frederick II around 1239. Here too is the **Gallerie Regionale di Palazzo Bellomo**, with sculpture and paintings including the *Burial of St Lucy* (1608) by Caravaggio.

The painting comes from the church of **Santa Lucia** in the Achradina quarter. This area was flattened during World War II, but the church survived. It is mostly 17th century with a

Norman campanile, and occupies the site where St Lucy, patron saint of Siracusa, was martyred in AD 304. Achradina is now the centre of modern Siracusa.

To the north, in Tyche, is the **Museo Archeologico Regionale Paolo Orsi**, with its important collection of artifacts from the Palaeolithic to the Byzantine era, taken from southeastern sites in Sicily. Included are vases, coins, bronzes, sculpture and fragments from Siracusan temples.

The Neapolis quarter and its **Parco Archeologico** feature the Teatro Romano, the Altar of Hieron II and the spectacular Teatro Greco, carved from the hillside. Beyond the Nymphaeum is the 2nd-century AD Roman amphitheatre and the stone quarries – the Latomia del Paradiso featuring the **Ear of Dionysius**. It is thought that 7,000 Athenians were incarcerated here and left to die after their calamitous defeat in 413 BC, in a battle described by Thucydides as "the greatest action in Hellenic history".

Environs
At **Epipolae**, 8 km (5 miles) north of Neapolis is the **Castle of Euryalus** – the most important ancient Greek fortification to have survived.

🏛 **Gallerie Regionale di Palazzo Bellomo**
Palazzo Bellomo, Via Capodieci 14. **Tel** 0931 695 11. **Open** 9am–6:30pm Tue–Sun (to 1pm public hols). 🚫 ♿

🏛 **Museo Archeologico Regionale Paolo Orsi**
Viale Teocrito 66. **Tel** 0931 46 40 22. **Open** 9am–6:30pm Tue–Sun (to 1pm Sun). Last adm: 1 hr before closing. 🚫 ♿

⑳ Noto

Siracusa. 🚗 24,000. 🚆 🚌 ℹ Piazza XVI Maggio (0931 83 67 44). 🛒 Mon & 1st & 3rd Tue of the month. 🖥 comune.noto.sr.it

Noto was built from scratch in the early 18th century to replace Noto Antica, which was devastated by an earthquake in 1693. The town was comprehensively designed in Baroque style, using

The façade of the Duomo in Noto rises above a huge staircase

the local white tufa, a limestone that has turned a honey-brown colour from the sun. Noto is a UNESCO World Heritage site, but unfortunately much of its beauty is behind scaffolding due to ongoing restoration.

The twin-towered **Duomo** (completed 1770s) that dominates Noto is by architect Rosario Gagliardi, who also designed the eccentric tower façade of the seminary of **San Salvatore** (18th century) in Piazza Municipio, the convex façade of **San Domenico** (1730s) in Piazza XVI Maggio, and the oval interior of **Santa Chiara** (1730) on Corso Vittorio

Emanuele. The magnificent **Palazzo Trigona** (1781) stands on Via Cavour behind the Duomo. On Via Nicolaci, the **Palazzo Villadorata** (1730s) features a splendid façade adorned with elaborate stone carvings. At the north end of Via Nicolaci, the **Monastery of Montevergine** has a striking curved façade. In mid-May, Via Nicolaci is the site of the Infiorata flower festival. Gagliardi's church of the **Crocifisso** (1728) stands on the town's summit. It contains a sculpture of the Madonna by Francesco Laurana (1471). The **Municipio** (1740s), facing the Duomo, has a fine "billowing" ground floor design.

Environs
The earthquake of 1693 also devastated the towns of **Modica**, around 30 km (19 miles) to the west, and **Ragusa**, a short distance further. Like Noto, they were rebuilt in the region's rich Baroque style. Gagliardi worked on Modica's **San Giorgio** (early 18th century), on Ragusa's **San Giorgio** (begun around 1746, and one of his masterpieces) and **San Giuseppe** (mid-18th century).

Boisterous carving on the façade of the Palazzo Villadorata in Noto

Relax
◀ T

The extravagantly beautiful, macchia-scented Costa Smeralda

❶ Costa Smeralda

Sassari. **FS** 🚢 Olbia. 🚌 Porto Cervo.
i AAST La Maddalena, Cava Civetta
(0789 73 63 21); AAST Palau, Via
Nazionale 94 (0789 70 95 70).
w quicostasmeralda.it

Stretching from the Golfo di
Cugnana to the Golfo di
Arzachena, the Costa Smeralda
was developed by a consortium of magnates in the 1950s.
One of the world's most opulent
holiday resorts, it is kept
immaculate by strict controls.

In **Porto Cervo**, the main
town, boutiques jostle with
nightclubs, fine restaurants and
luxury hotels. It caters for the
seriously rich – billionaires,
crowned heads and pop stars.

Environs
Head north to rural **Baia
Sardinia** and **Cannigione**. From
Palau ferries leave for **La
Maddalena** and **Isola Caprera**,
the home of Garibaldi and the
Museo Nazionale Garibaldino.

🏛 **Museo Nazionale Garibaldino**
Frazione Caprera, La Maddalena.
Tel 0789 72 71 62. **Open**
9am–1:30pm, 2–7:15pm Tue–Sun.
Closed 1 Jan, 1 May, 25 Dec. 🅿 ♿

❷ Cassari

🏔 130,000. ✈ **FS** 🚌 **i** Viale
Caprera 36 (079 27 99 54). 🗓 Mon.
w comune.sassari.it

Founded by Genoese and Pisan
merchants early in the 13th
century, Sassari is known for its
spectacular *Cavalcata Sarda*
festival on Ascension Day, and
for being the site of Sardinia's
first university. There is a
raucous, tight, church-filled
medieval quarter around
the **Duomo** (11th
century, with later,
mostly Baroque,
additions), and to
the north is the
huge **Fonte Rosello**,
a late-Renaissance
fountain. The **Museo
Archeologico
Nazionale "GA
Sanna"** is a good
starting point for
an investigation into
the region's
nuraghic history.
Environs: To the
southeast along
the S131 is the
Pisan-Romanesque
church of **Santissima Trinità
di Saccargia** (1116), with the
only extant 13th-century
fresco cycle in Sardinia. Further
on is the 12th-century
church of **San Michele
di Salvenero**,
and at **Ardara**
the basalt-built
Romanesque
**Santa Maria
del Regno**, or
"Black
Cathedral".

Façade of Santissima
Trinità di Saccargia

🏛 **Museo
Archeologico
Nazionale "GA
Sanna"**
Via Roma 64.
Tel 079 27 22 03.
Open 9am–7:30pm
Tue–Sun (to 7pm
Sun). 🅿 ♿

❸ Alghero

Sassari. 🏔 41,000. ✈ **FS** 🚌 🚢 **i**
Lungomare Dante 1 (079 97 59 96).
🗓 Wed. **w** comune.alghero.ss.it

Founded on a peninsula facing
the Bay of Alghero early in the
12th century, and taken from the
Genoese Dorias by the
Aragonese in 1353, Alghero was
peopled by settlers from
Barcelona and Valencia. Its
original occupants – Ligurians
and Sardinians – were expelled
with such thoroughness that
today the Catalan language and
culture is enjoying a revival and
the look of old Alghero is
consistently Spanish.

Filled with labyrinthine alleys
and cobbled streets, the lively
port of old Alghero is flanked by
battlemented walls and
defensive towers on all but the
landward section. Facing the
Giardino Pubblico is the massive
16th-century **Torre di Porta
Terra**, also known as the Jewish
Tower after its
builders. Around the
periphery of the old
town are more
towers, including
**Torre dell'Espero
Reial** and **Torre San
Giacomo** on
Lungomare Colombo,
and **Torre della
Maddalena** on Piazza
Porta Terra.

The 16th-century **Duomo** at the
bottom of Via Umberto is
predominantly Catalan-Gothic
with an Aragonese portal. Off
Via Carlo Alberto, **San Francesco**
(14th century) has a pretty

A typical house in Alghero

The waterfront at Bosa

cloister and octagonal campanile towering over Alghero, and Baroque **San Michele** has a bright tiled dome. In Via Principe Umberto is the **Casa Doria**, the house where the pre-Hispanic rulers of Alghero lived. It has a beautiful Renaissance portal and Gothic-arched window.

Environs
Take a boat or car trip (the latter involves much climbing down) to the spectacular **Grotta di Nettuno**, a deep natural cave round the point of Capo Caccia, or the nearby **Grotta Verde**.

❹ Bosa

Nuoro. 🚗 8,500. 🚉 🚌 🚹 Pro Loco, Via Azuni 5 (0785 37 61 07). 🚻 Tue. 🌐 comune.bosa.nu.it

Bosa is a small, picturesque seaside town at the mouth of Sardinia's only navigable river, the Temo. The historic **Sa Costa** district struggles up the side of a low hill capped by the **Castello di Serravalle**, built in 1122 by the Malaspina family. The narrow passages and alleys here have changed little since the Middle Ages. By the Temo are **Sas Conzas** – the former dyers' houses and workshops.

Languishing on the riverside, the cosmopolitan **Sa Piatta** district houses the Aragonese-Gothic **Duomo** (15th century) and Romanesque **San Pietro Extramuros** (11th century), with a Gothic façade added by Cistercian monks in the 13th century.

Nuraghe in Sardinia
The dominant feature of Sardinia is the 7,000 or so *nuraghe* dotted around the island. Dating from 1800 to 300 BC, these strange, truncated cone structures were built without any bonding from huge basalt blocks taken from extinct volcanoes. To this day, little is known about the identity of the nuraghic people. They must have been well organized and possessed remarkable engineering skills, judging by their buildings, but appear to have left no written word. The mystery of these enigmatic people has intrigued Sardinians for years.

The individual *nuraghe* are fairly small. A few of these structures were fortresses, equipped with wells and other defensive features.

Su Nuraxi at Barumini (*above*), Serra Orrios, near Dorgali, and Santu Antine at Torralba are among the most important *nuraghe* complexes. Houses, temples, tombs, and even a theatre have been identified.

This bronze figure of a hero with four eyes and four arms is among the many objects and statues discovered on nuraghic sites and associated with the nuraghic people.

• Sassari

Nuoro

SARDINIA

• Oristano

Cagliari

Key

• Nuraghic sites

0 kilometres 100
0 miles 50

Nobel Prize-winning novelist Grazia Deledda from Nuoro

❺ Nuoro

🏔 38,000. **FS** 🚌 **ℹ** Piazza d'Italia 19 (0784 300 83). 🛒 Fri & Sat. 🎭 29 Aug: Sagra del Redentore. **W comune.nuoro.it**

This town, in a spectacular setting beneath Monte Ortobene and the dramatic Supramonte, was the home of Grazia Deledda, who won the Nobel Prize for Literature in 1926 for her portrayal of the power and passions in the primitive communities around her. A comprehensive collection of ethnic items, such as traditional Sardinian costumes and jewellery, can be seen in the excellent **Museo Etnografico Sardo**. Attending the *Sagra del Redentore* festival is the best way to witness the region's dancing and dialects.

Environs
Nuoro is on the edge of the Barbagia region, which has isolated villages of shepherds who have never experienced the hand of any overlord, so impenetrable are the **Gennargentu** mountains. This region was known to the Romans as Barbaria, an area they were never able to subdue. Traces of the traditional lawlessness of the Barbagia can be seen in **Orgosolo**, with its wall murals calling for Sardinia's independence. Rival clans were locked in bloody vendetta for almost 50 years, and the deeds of native bandits form part of local folklore.

In **Mamoiada**'s *Feast of the Mamuthones*, men in sinister masks and traditional costume perform a ritual dance ending with a symbolic "killing" of a scapegoat. The fervour of the event is indicative of the fierce folkloric tradition and deep resistance to change.

🏛 **Museo Etnografico Sardo**
Via Mereu 56. **Tel** 0784 25 70 35.
Open 9am–1pm Tue–Sun (to 8pm Jun–Sep). 🅿 ♿ **W isresardegna.it**

❻ Cala Gonone

Nuoro. 🏔 800. 🚌 **ℹ** Pro Loco, via Lamormara 108, Dorgali (0784 962 43). 🛒 daily. 🚤 from Dorgali to grottoes (Apr– mid-Oct). **Tel** 0784 933 05.

East of Nuoro, between the sea and the mountains, is the hamlet of Cala Gonone – a bustling seaside resort and fishing port, with magnificent beaches. Along the unspoilt coast are the isolated coves of **Cala Luna**, linked with Cala Gonone by a well-marked two-hour trail, and

Cala Sisine. The famous **Grotta del Bue Marino**, adorned with weird rock formations, can only be reached by boat.

Environs
To the south, the villages of **Urzulei, Baunei** and **Santa Maria Navarrese**, along the spectacular SS125 road to Tortolì, feature breathtaking landscapes.

Ruins of Tharros near Oristano

❼ Oristano

Cagliari. 🏔 32,000. **FS** 🚌 **ℹ** EPT, Piazza Eleonora 1 (0783 79 13 06); Pro Loco, Via Vittorio Emanuele 8 (0783 706 21). 🛒 Tue & Fri.

The province of Oristano corresponds roughly with historical Arborea, over which Eleonora ruled *(see opposite)*. She is commemorated by an 18th-century statue in **Piazza Eleonora**. On Corso Vittorio Emanuele is the 16th-century **Casa di Eleonora**, and nearby the **Antiquarium Arborense**, which has Neolithic, nuraghic, Punic and Roman artifacts. The **Torre di San Cristoforo** (1291) in Piazza Roma once formed part of Oristano's fortifications. The **Duomo** (13th century) was later rebuilt in the Baroque style. More interesting are the churches of **Santa Chiara** (1343) on Via Garibaldi and 14th-century **San Martino** on Via Cagliari.

Environs
The 12th-century Pisan-Romanesque **Cathedral** at Santa Giusta has columns probably taken from Tharros, an 8th-century BC Punic

Entrance to the Grotta del Bue Marino, south of Cala Gonone

The tiny resort of Carloforte, the capital of Isola di San Pietro

settlement, 20 km (12 miles) west of Oristano on the Sinis peninsula.

🏛 **Antiquarium Arborense**
Palazzo Parpaglia. **Tel** 0783 79 12 62.
Open 9am–2pm, 5–8pm Tue, Thu, Sun. 🅿 🅲 ♿

❽ Sant'Antioco

Cagliari. 🚈 🚌 **i** Pro Loco, Piazza Repubblica 31a (0781 84 05 92).

The main town on this unspoilt island off Sardinia's southern coast is **Sant'Antioco**, once a Phoenician port and an important Roman base. Proof of almost continuous occupation is clear from the **catacombs**, a Phoenician burial place later used by Christians, under the 12th-century basilica of **Sant'Antioco Martire**. The **Museo Archeologico** contains Phoenician artifacts. The Punic **Tophet** (sanctuary of the goddess Tanit) and the **necropolis** are nearby. The small **Isola di San Pietro** can be reached by ferry from Calasetta.

🏰 **Catacombs**
Piazza Parrocchia.
Tel 0781 830 44. **Open** 9am–noon, 3:30–6pm daily.
🅲 only. 🅿 ♿

🏛 **Museo Archeologico**
Via Regina Margherita 113.
Tel 0783 744 33.
Open 9am–2pm, 3–8pm daily. **Closed** 1 Jan, Easter, 8, 25, 26 Dec. 🅲 🅿 (& Tophet & necropolis). ♿

❾ Cagliari

🏙 165,000. ✈ 🚈 🚌 🚢 **i** Piazza Matteotti 🏰 (070 66 92 55). 🚢 daily; also Sun (flea) and 2nd Sun of month (antiques). 🌐 **visit-cagliari.it**

The capital of Sardinia, this site was occupied by the Phoenicians, Carthaginians and Romans, and extensive ruins of the Phoenician city of Nora lie to the southwest of Cagliari. A 2nd-century **amphitheatre** survives from the Roman era, cut from rock. Discover the town's earlier history in the **Cittadella dei Musei**, the former royal arsenal. It houses several museums, including the **Museo Archeologico Nazionale**. The nuraghic items are the most interesting in the collection, especially the bronze votive statuettes. Also in the Cittadella dei Musei is the **Pinacoteca**, an art gallery.

The old core of Cagliari has an appealing North African character. In the high **Castello** district, the Romans and, later, Pisans built defences. The gracious **Bastione San Remy** on Piazza Costituzione offers magnificent views over the city and surrounding countryside. The **Duomo** is a 20th-century rehash of a Romanesque building. Flanking the entrance are two 12th-century pulpits originally destined for the cathedral in Pisa.

Nearby is the Pisan tower **Torre San Pancrazio** (14th century). From the partially ruined **Torre dell'Elefante** on Via dell'Università to the port lies the **Marina** quarter, which expanded from the old town in the 16th to 17th centuries. In Piazza San Cosimo, the 6th-century church of **San Saturnino** is a rare monument to Byzantine occupation.

🏰 **Amphitheatre**
Viale Sant'Ignazio. **Tel** 070 677 64 70.
Open 9am–5pm Tue–Sun (summer: 9am–1pm, 3:30–7:30pm). 🅿 ♿

🏛 **Cittadella dei Musei**
Piazza Arsenale. **Tel** 070 675 76 27.
Museo Archeologico Nazionale
Open 9am–8pm Tue–Sun. 🅿 ♿
Pinacoteca **Tel** 070 66 24 96.
Open 9am–8pm Tue–Sun. **Closed** 1 Jan, 1 May, 25 Dec. 🅿 ♿

Eleonora of Arborea

A champion against rule from abroad, Eleonora was governing *giudicessa* (judge) of Arborea, one of four administrative divisions of Sardinia, from 1383–1404.

Her marriage to Brancaleone Doria consolidated Genoese interests in Sardinia. She rallied the island to keep out Spanish invaders who tried to claim land that had been given to the Aragonese King James II. Her greatest legacy was the completion of the codifying of laws begun by her father. Written in Sardinian, they called for community of property in marriage and the right of women to seek redress from rape.

The 6th-century church of San Saturnino in Cagliari, built on a Greek-cross plan

TRAVELLERS' NEEDS

WHERE TO STAY

People come from all over the world to visit Italy and most Italians spend their holidays here as well, particularly in the mountains or by the sea. This means that there is a dazzling range of accommodation options, from splendid hotels in old palazzi and historic residences, to simple family-run *pensioni* and hostels and most major cities also offer up-market B&Bs. Those who want self-catering accommodation are well served too, with everything from stately villas in Tuscany to purpose-built holiday flats in, or near, seaside resorts. Italian hotels can have a reputation for being expensive and short on services, but this is not always the case and you can find excellent value in all price ranges. The hotels listed on pages 562–77 have been selected from every price category as among the best value in each area for style, comfort or location.

The Gritti Palace, one of Venice's historic palazzi *(see p562)*

Gradings

Hotels in Italy are classified with a rating system of one to five stars. The grading depends on the facilities offered and each region awards stars according to slightly different criteria.

Sometimes a hotel has a lower rating than it deserves. This may be because the local tourist office has not upgraded it yet or the hotel itself has opted to stay in a lower category to avoid higher taxes.

Alberghi

Albergo is Italian for hotel, but the term tends to refer to establishments classified as three-star or above. Room sizes vary considerably: in city centres even expensive hotels can have small rooms, especially if the hotel is located in a historic building, whereas you get far more space for your money in rural areas. *Alberghi* will have private baths or showers in all rooms. Many top-range and boutique hotels also offer spa and fitness facilities.

Pensioni

Although the term *pensione* is no longer in official use, one- and two-star hotels still use the term to describe their status. On the whole you will find immaculate standards of cleanliness and friendly, helpful service with basic, although perfectly functional rooms. Be aware that while your *pensioni* may be in an old building full of historic charm, this can also mean noisy, erratic plumbing and dark rooms. Many *pensioni* do not have public rooms other

Street sign showing the direction and location of hotels

than a sparsely furnished breakfast room. Most will offer at least some bedrooms with a private shower although rarely a bath. If you intend to be out late, check that you'll be able to get back into the *pensione*. Not all of them have night porters after midnight or 1am, but most will at least be able to provide a key to the main door.

A *locanda* was traditionally an inn, offering cheap food and a place to sleep for the traveller. The word is still in use, particularly in central and northern Italy, but is now synonymous with *pensione* and may be more of an affectation for the benefit of the tourist.

Chain Hotels

There are various Italian chain hotels, including **Atahotels** and **Una Hotels and Resorts**, as well as the usual big internationals. **NH Hoteles** hotels appeal to the business traveller and there are one or two in most large cities; **Marriott**, **Hyatt** and **Best Western** are international luxury chains, while **Italia Lodging** caters for the more modest budget. **Relais et Châteaux** run charming hotels in historic castles, villas and monasteries with facilities to match.

Meals and Facilities

There has been a general improvement in the facilities offered by Italian hotels, especially in the more modern four- and five-star hotels. However, in some older establishments there may not

Romantic Hotel Villa Pagoda in Nervi, Genoa *(see p568)*

In larger hotels there is often a considerable difference in quality and price between standard and more luxurious, deluxe rooms. If you would like a view or a terrace this is also likely to be more expensive, though for those who prefer peaceful nights, it is generally best to avoid rooms facing the street in busy cities.

Also, beware of extra charges: the mini-bar can be very expensive as can the cost of parking, laundry or for making telephone calls directly from your hotel bedroom.

always be air-conditioning or 24-hour room service so it's best to check before you book..

Some hotels may insist on full board *(pensione completa)* or half board *(mezza pensione)* in peak season. Most hotel rates include breakfast, which in many establishments will consist of a large buffet, although smaller hotels and *pensioni* may offer a simple continental breakfast.

For a double room, state if you want twin beds *(letti singoli)* or a double bed *(matrimoniale)*. Bathrooms in most hotels will have showers rather than baths.

Most hotels offer Internet access, but it is not always free, and charges will vary. If a city centre hotel does not have its own parking spaces, it may have an arrangement with a nearby garage. Check the availability and cost of parking with the hotel prior to booking.

Children

Italians love children, and although most hotels may not offer special facilities for families, kids are always welcome.

Some of the cheaper hotels may not be able to provide cots. However, virtually all hotels will be happy to put a small bed into a double room for families travelling together. The price of this is usually an extra 30–40 per cent of the double room rate per bed. Many large hotels also offer babysitting services.

Prices

As a rule hotels in Italy are not cheap, although prices vary considerably between regions. Hotels in major cities and resorts are likely to be more expensive. Booking online is one way to secure a better rate, as hotel websites may offer special deals. Or you can save money by booking your hotel and flight together on most travel websites.

Prices, which include tax and service and are quoted per room, start from around €60 for a double room without a bathroom, and can rise to at least €80 with a bath, even for a very basic hotel. A single room will cost about two thirds of a double. Outside the big cities, €100 should get you something comfortable and often picturesque, although not particularly luxurious. For €210 and upwards you can expect a good range of facilities, a pleasant or central location and often a hotel with local or historic charm. In Rome, all campsites, B&Bs and hotels must add a city tax *(contributo di soggiorno)* to the bill. At present, these rates are fixed at €1 per day per person for campsites, €2 for establishments up to and including three-star hotels, and €3 for four- and five-star hotels.

Booking

Book as soon as possible, particularly if you have special requests such as a room with a view, off the street or with a bath. August tends to be very busy at beach resorts and February is high season at mountain resorts. Peak times for cities and towns depend on their particular cultural calendars *(see pp70–73)*.

You will be asked for a deposit when you book; this can usually be paid for by credit card (even in hotels that do not accept credit cards for final payment); otherwise you can use PayPal for online transactions, or tranfer the money via BACS from your bank account.

Under Italian law the hotel must issue you with a receipt *(ricevuta fiscale)* for final payment, which you must keep until you leave Italy.

The Italian State Tourist Office (**ENIT**) has accommodation lists for every region, although this might not be the most up-to-date resource. Rooms can also be booked via the **APT** (Azienda Provinciale per il Turismo).

A traditional Florentine hotel interior

The multi-level terrace of the Raphael in Rome *(see p573)*

Checking In and Out

Italian hotels are legally obliged to register you with the police, which is why you'll always be asked for your passport when checking in. This is a mere formality, and your passport should be returned to you within an hour or two.

Checking-out time is usually before noon, although some larger hotels may extend your checking-out time upon request, but only if your room is not already reserved for another guest. All rooms must be vacated on time, but, most hotels will allow you to leave your luggage in a safe place to be collected later in the day.

Al Sole, Venice *(see p563)*

Self-Catering and Agriturismo

Across rural Italy, there are more than 2,000 farms, villas and mountain chalets offering reasonably priced self-catering or hotel-style accommodation as part of the **Agriturismo** scheme. Options range from beautifully kept villas or ancient castles with first-class facilities, to simple rooms in the family home on a working farm. Some places have excellent restaurants, which serve farm and local produce, while others can arrange riding, fishing or other

sporting activities *(see p610)*. Note that there may be a minimum stay requirement at some of these establishments, especially during peak season. The annual *Agriturist* publication can be found in the central tourist office in Rome, in regional offices and in bookshops. Other self-catering options can be arranged through specialized agencies such as **Villas4you** and **Simply Travel** before you leave for Italy, but again, make sure you do this well in advance, as accommodation can be booked up months ahead.

There are also so-called *residenze*, found in the ENIT accommodation lists. These are halfway between hotels and self-catering flats and normally offer cooking facilities and some sort of restaurant service.

For stays of several months or more, accommodation agencies for apartments in the city centre, as well as the nearby countryside, can be found under *Immobiliari* in the *Pagine Gialle* (Yellow Pages).

Budget Accomodation

As well as the International Youth Hostels Association (**AIG** in Italy), tourist offices in the major cities have lists of hostels. Prices start at around €12 per person per night (€15 during peak season), and are much lower than even the cheapest *pensione*. Accom-

modation may be in single- or mixed-sex dormitories, though many hostels also have small private rooms. A room in a private house is another cheap option, often offering small but clean rooms. Bed-and-breakfast accommodation is available but is of variable quality.

The **Centro Turistico Studentesco** can help students find rooms in university accommodation across Italy. This is not limited to students, however, particularly in the summer when resident students are on holiday.

A peaceful alternative is to stay in a convent or monastery with guest accommodation. The rooms are clean, if a little spartan, and they are usually in a secluded area. Note that strict rules may be the price for a cheap room: most have early curfews and many will not admit members of the opposite sex even when with their spouses. There is no central agency dealing with these but they are included in the ENIT accommodation lists for each region.

Mountain Refuges and Campsites

Basic accommodation in huts and refuges is available in mountainous areas where there are hiking trails. Most of these huts are owned and run by the **Club Alpino Italiano** whose headquarters are in Milan. Campsites abound in the

A boat carrying visitors' luggage to a hotel in Venice

mountains and around the coastal regions. Many of them offer basic accommodation in family-sized cabins *(bungalow)* as well as spaces for tents, caravans and trailers, along with facilities such as water, electricity and washing. There is usually a restaurant and, especially in campsites by the sea, there may also be sports facilities such as swimming pools, boat and water sports equipment hire and tennis courts. The **Touring Club Italiano** publishes a good list

A Park Spa Suite bedroom in the Park Hyatt Milano *(see p566)*

A high-altitude refuge in the Valsesia Alps

of campsites with details of facilities for each one, as does **Federcampeggio**.

Disabled Travellers

In general, only newer hotels in Italy have special facilities for disabled travellers, although in many cases, older hotels will do all they can to accommodate people in wheelchairs by giving them downstairs rooms (when available) and help with lifts or stairs. It is best to contact the hotel of your choice directly before booking, to check whether they are wheelchair accessible and what facilities they have *(for more information see pp616–17).*

Recommended Hotels

The hotels listed in this guide-book have been chosen because they represent the best Italy has to offer in hospitality, service, value or location. A huge variety of accommodation options are covered, from simple farmhouses and alpine chalets to family-run B&Bs and luxury palaces.

Entries labelled DK Choice are outstanding in some way. They may be set in beautiful surroundings or in a historically important building, offer excellent service, have a romantic atmosphere, be particularly charming, environ-mentally friendly or have a great spa. Whatever the reason it is a guarantee of a memorable stay.

DIRECTORY

Chain Hotels

Atahotels
Tel 066 964 69 64.
W atahotels.com

Best Western Hotels
Tel 800 820 080.
W bestwestern.it

Hyatt
Tel 02 88 21 12 34.
W hyatt.com

Marriott
Tel 800 22 89 29 00.
W marriott.com

NH Hoteles
Tel 848 390 227.
W nh-hotels.com

Relais & Châteaux
Tel 02 62 69 00 64.
W relaischateaux.com

Una Hotels and Resorts
Tel 800 60 61 62.
W unahotels.it

Booking

ENIT
Via Marghera 2–6, 00185 Rome. Tel 06 497 11.
W enit.it

Italian State Tourist Board
1 Princes Street, London W1B 2AY. Tel 020 7408 1254. W italiantourist board.co.uk

Self-Catering and Agriturismo

Agriturismo
Corso Vittorio Emanuele II 101, 00186 Rome.

Tel 06 685 23 37.
W agriturist.it

Simply Travel
Tel 0871 231 40 50.
W simplytravel.co.uk

Villas4you
PO Box 1310, Maidstone ME14 9QH.
Tel 0800 096 3439.
W villas4you.co.uk

Budget Accommodation

AIG (Associazione Italiana Alberghi per la Gioventù)
Via Cavour 44, 00184 Rome. Tel 06 487 11 52.
W aighostels.com

Bed and Breakfast
W bed-and-breakfast.it

Centro Turistico Studentesco
Tel 06 462 04 31.
W cts.it

Italia Lodging
Tel 06 77 25 05 43.
W italialodging.com

Mountain Refuges and Campsites

Club Alpino Italiano
Via E Petrella 19, Milan.
Tel 02 205 72 31. W cai.it

Federcampeggio
Via Vittorio Emanuele 11, 50041 Calenzano, Firenze.
Tel 055 88 23 91.
W federcampeggio.it

Touring Club Italiano
Corso Italia 10, 20122 Milano. Tel 02 852 61.
W touringclub.it

Where to Stay

Venice

CANNAREGIO: Al Saor €
B&B **Map** 3 A4
Calle Zotti 3904/A, 30121
Tel 041 296 06 54
W alsaor.com
Simple and elegant, this guest-house offers cosy rooms and a friendly atmosphere.

CANNAREGGIO: Hotel Giorgione €€
Luxury **Map** 3 B5
Calle dei Proverbi 4587, 30121
Tel 041 522 58 10
W hotelgiorgione.com
Lovely old building, completely and charmingly refurbished.

CANNAREGIO: Palazzo Abadessa €€
Historic **Map** 3 A4
Calle Priuli 4011, 30131
Tel 041 24 137 84
W abadessa.com
Charming 16th-century palace furnished with antiques and rich colours. Spacious rooms.

CANNAREGIO: Ca' Sagredo €€€
Historic **Map** 3 A5
Campo Santa Sofia 4198, 30121
Tel 041 241 31 11
W casagredohotel.com
Just across from Rialto market, this modernized 13th-century palazzo offers superb views.

CASTELLO: Locanda La Corte €€
Historic **Map** 3 C5
Calle Bressana 6317, 30122
Tel 041 241 13 00
W locandalacorte.it
Inviting rooms in a converted 16th-century palace with a charming courtyard.

CASTELLO: Metropole €€
Luxury **Map** 8 D2
Riva degli Schiavoni 4149, 30122
Tel 041 520 50 44
W hotelmetropole.com
The somewhat nondescript exterior belies the comforts within.

CASTELLO: Pensione Wildner €€
Pensione **Map** 8 D2
Riva degli Schiavoni 4161, 30122
Tel 041 522 74 63
W hotelwildner.com
Family-run establishment with wonderful views from the terrace.

CASTELLO: Londra Palace €€€
Boutique **Map** 8 D2
Riva degli Schiavoni 4171, 30122
Tel 041 520 05 33
W londrapalace.com

Excellent service and spacious, luxurious rooms. Splendid views of the lagoon and city.

DORSODURO: Locanda Ca' Zose €
B&B **Map** 6 F4
Calle del Bastion 193/B, 30123
Tel 041 522 66 35
W hotelcazose.com
Charming guesthouse run by two sisters with an eye for quality.

DORSODURO: Agli Alboretti €€
Pensione **Map** 6 E4
Rio Terrà Foscarini 884, 30123
Tel 041 523 00 58
W aglialboretti.com
Simple, comfortable rooms equipped with free minibar.

DORSODURO: Hotel Pausania €€
Historic **Map** 6 D3
Fondamenta Gerardini 2824, 30123
Tel 041 522 20 83
W hotelpausania.it
Elegant light-filled rooms and a lovely veranda for breakfast.

DORSODURO: Instituto Artigianelli €€
Historic **Map** 6 E4
Rio Terrà Foscarini 909/A, 30123
Tel 041 522 40 77
W donorione-venezia.it
Religious institution offering simple, modern rooms with en suite bathrooms. Nice, quiet courtyard.

DORSODURO: Locanda San Barnaba €€
Rooms with a view **Map** 6 D3
Calle del Traghetto 2785-2786, 30123
Tel 041 241 12 33
W locanda-sanbarnaba.com
The perfect place to return to after a hard day's sightseeing. Spacious

Elegant interiors and great views at the Cipriani hotel, Giudecca

foyer and spotless rooms, most overlooking the canal.

GIUDECCA: Cipriani €€€
Luxury **Map** 7 C5
Giudecca 10, 30133
Tel 041 520 77 44
W hotelcipriani.com
Exquisite rooms in this Venice institution. There's a private launch to and from Piazza San Marco.

LIDO: Villa Mabapa €€
Rooms with a view
Riviera San Nicolò 16, 30126
Tel 041 526 05 90
W villamabapa.com
Attractive period villas over-looking the Venice lagoon.

DK Choice

MAZZORBO: Venissa €€
Pensione **Map** 3 B4
Fondamenta Santa Caterina 3, 30170
Tel 041 527 22 81
W venissa.it
A stylish option on a little known island for those who want a more exclusive Venetian experience. Rooms are modern and spacious. Delicious meals are served in the restaurant.

SAN MARCO: Saturnia and International €€
Luxury **Map** 7 A3
Via XXII Marzo 2398, 30124
Tel 041 520 83 77
W hotelsaturnia.it
Opulence wrapped in a homely setting. Antique furnishings and a pretty courtyard.

SAN MARCO: Splendid Venice €€
Luxury **Map** 7 B7
Mercerie 760, 30124
Tel 041 520 07 55
W splendidvenice.starhotels.com
This hotel is comfortable and quiet, with a well stocked library and peaceful reading areas.

SAN MARCO: Bauer €€€
Luxury **Map** 7 A3
Campo San Moisè 1459, 30124
Tel 041 520 70 22
W bauerhotels.com

Beautifully decorated rooms and stunning views of the Grand Canal.

SAN MARCO: Europa & Regina   €€€
Luxury   **Map** 7 A3
Calle Larga XXII Marzo 2159, 30124
Tel *041 240 00 01*
w westineuropareginavenice.com
Panoramic terraces with magnificent views. Impeccable service.

SAN MARCO: Gritti Palace   €€€
Luxury   **Map** 7 A3
Santa Maria del Giglio 2467, 30124
Tel *041 79 46 11*
w thegrittipalace.com
Iconic palazzo, dating back to 1475, with modern comforts.

SAN MARCO: Luna Hotel Baglioni   €€€
Luxury   **Map** 7 B3
Calle Large dell'Ascension 1243, 30124
Tel *041 528 98 40*
w baglionihotels.com
Spacious rooms in a historic palazzo. Arrive by water taxi at the private jetty.

SAN POLO: Al Campaniel   €
B&B   **Map** 6 E2
Calle del Campaniel 2889, 30125
Tel *041 275 07 49*
w alcampaniel.com
Clean and cosy guesthouse in a quiet street. The small apartment is great for families.

DK Choice

SANTA CROCE: Al Sole   €€
Historic   **Map** 5 C1
Fondamenta Minotto 136, 30135
Tel *041 244 03 28*
w alsolehotels.com
Housed in Palazzo Marcello, a 15th-century palace with a beautiful façade and marble-floored reception area, this hotel offers well-appointed rooms. Enjoy the rich breakfast spread served in a patio garden.

SANTA CROCE: Hotel Falier   €€
Charming   **Map** 5 C1
Salizzada San Pantalon 130, 30135
Tel *041 71 08 82*
w hotelfalier.com
This hotel is full of light, airy rooms and has a pretty wisteria-filled garden and helpful staff.

TORCELLO: Locanda Cipriani   €€
Rooms with a view
Piazza Santa Fosca 29, 30012
Tel *041 73 01 50*
w locandacipriani.com
Comfortable old-world inn located far from the madding crowd. Famed for its discerning guests and quiet elegance.

Romantic natural setting of Hotel Cappella in Colfosco

The Veneto and Friuli

ASOLO: Albergo al Sole   €€
Rooms with a view
Via Collegio 33, 31011
Tel *0423 95 13 32*
w albergoalsoleasolo.com
Pleasant spacious rooms looking out over the town square.

ASOLO: Villa Cipriani   €€
Historic
Via Canova 298, 31011
Tel *0423 52 34 11*
w villaciprianiasolo.com
Comfortable hotel in a 16th-century villa once home to poet Robert Browning.

CASTELROTTO: Cavallino d'Oro €
Spa hotel
Piazza Kraus 2, 39040
Tel *0471 70 63 37*
w cavallino.it
Charming hotel in a pretty setting with a cosy atmosphere.

CIVIDALE DEL FRIULI: La Cjase dai Toscans   €
B&B
Corso Mazzini 15/1, 33043
Tel *349 076 52 88*
w lacjasedaitoscans.it
Friendly, well-positioned B&B with a terrace for summer breakfasts.

CIVIDALE DEL FRIULI: Locanda al Pomo D'Oro   €
Historic
Piazzetta San Giovanni 20, 33043
Tel *0432 73 14 89*
w alpomodoro.it
Traditional family inn set in a quiet square in the historic centre.

COLFOSCO: Hotel Cappella   €€
Rooms with a view
Strada Pecei 17, 39033
Tel *0471 83 61 83*
w hotelcappella.com

A chalet in the Dolomites opened by the present owner's grandfather. Various styles of suite to choose from.

CONEGLIANO: Il Faè   €
Rooms with a view
Via Faè 1, San Pietro di Feletto, 31020
Tel *0438 78 71 17*
w ilfae.com
Pleasant guesthouse surrounded by vineyards. Good views over the foothills of the Alps.

CORNO DI ROSAZZO: Villa Butussi   €
Rooms with a view
Via San Martino 29, Visinale dello Judrio, 33040
Tel *0432 75 99 22*
w butussi.it
A 17th-century villa tastefully converted into a guesthouse that offers both rooms and apartments.

CORTINA D'AMPEZZO: Cristallo Hotel   €€€
Luxury
Via R. Menardi 42, 32043
Tel *0436 88 11 11*
w cristallo.it
Beautifully presented rooms, some with balconies that have views of the Alps. Excellent facilities include a spa and a nine-hole golf course.

CORTINA D'AMPEZZO: Montana   €€€
Pensione
Corso Italia 94, 32043
Tel *0436 86 21 26*
w cortina-hotel.com
Quiet hotel with neat rooms and a hearty breakfast.

FOLLINA: Villa Abbazia   €€
Historic
Piazza IV Novembre 3, 31051
Tel *0438 97 12 77*
w hotelabbazia.it
Delightful 17th-century villa with spacious rooms decorated in English country-house style.

For more information on types of hotels *see p561*

GARDA: Locanda San Vigilio €€
Rooms with a view
Località San Vigilio 17, 37016
Tel *045 725 66 88*
w locanda-sanvigilio.it
Exuding old-world charm, this
is one of the loveliest, most
exclusive hotels on Lake Garda.

**MALCESINE: Sailing Center
Hotel** €€
Rooms with a view
Via Gardesana 187, 37018
Tel *045 740 00 55*
w hotelsailing.com
Located on the shores of Lake
Garda, this hotel has comfortable
rooms and its own private beach.

PADUA: Augustus Terme €€
Spa Hotel
Viale Stazione 150, 35036
Tel *049 79 32 00*
w hotelaugustus.com
Comfortable hotel with opulent
rooms, thermal swimming pools
and a reputable restaurant.

PADUA: Belludi 37 €€
Boutique
Via L. Beato Belludi 37, 35124
Tel *049 66 56 33*
w belludi37.it
Steps from the Basilica del Santo,
this hotel is decorated with a flair
of contemporary design.

**PESCHIERA DEL GARDA:
Active Hotel Paradiso & Golf** €
Boutique
Via Coppo 2/b, 37014
Tel *045 640 58 11*
w golfhotelparadiso.it
A stylish hotel with pleasant, airy
rooms. Amenities include an
18-hole golf course.

POVOLETTO: La Faula €€
Agriturismo
Via Faula 5, 33040
Tel *334 399 67 34*
w faula.com
Lovingly restored farmhouse
surrounded by vineyards and
farmland. The rooms are spacious.

Comfortable furnishings at Hotel Laurin
in Bolzano

Key to prices *see p562*

**TORRI DEL BENACO: Hotel
Gardesana** €€
Historic
Piazza Calderini 5, 37010
Tel *045 722 54 11*
w gardesana.eu
A 15th-century former harbour
master's house converted into
a friendly, comfortable hotel.

TREVISO: Locanda da Renzo €
B&B
Via Terraglio 108, 31100
Tel *0422 40 20 68*
w locandadarenzo.it
A small family-run guesthouse
with a home-cooked evening
meal available on request.

TRIESTE: Le Corderie €€
Boutique
Via di Calvola 43, 34143
Tel *040 322 92 77*
w lecorderiehotel.it
You're assured a warm welcome
at this comfortable, modern
hotel. Great breakfast spread.

**UDINE: Hotel Clocchiatti &
Next** €€
Boutique
Via Cividale 29, 33100
Tel *0432 50 50 47*
w hotelclocchiatti.it
Choose between rooms with
traditional period decor or
modern fittings.

DK Choice

**VALDOBBIADENE: Villa
Barberina** €€
Historic
Via Roma 2, 31049
Tel *0423 97 24 79*
w villabarberina.it
In past centuries wealthy
Venetians would live part of the
year in their country estates. This
hotel gives guests an idea of the
opulence of such residences.
This handsome 18th-century
villa has elegantly decorated
rooms, magnificent grounds
and a well-stocked library.

VERONA: Giulietta e Romeo €€
Charming
Vicolo Tre Marchetti 3, 37121
Tel *045 800 35 54*
w giuliettaeromeo.com
The rooms are comfortable and
bright. The breakfast is hearty.

VERONA: Il Torcolo €€
Charming
Vicolo Listone 3, 37121
Tel *045 800 75 12*
w hoteltorcolo.it
Small, family-run hotel with
simple rooms and a pleasant
terrace where breakfast is served.

**VICENZA: Glam Boutique
Hotel** €€
Boutique
Via A. Giuriolo 10, 36100
Tel *0444 32 64 58*
w gboutiquehotel.com
Stylish hotel with a perfect blend
of traditional and modern decor.

Trentino-Alto Adige

BOLZANO: Hotel Laurin €€
Historic
Via Laurin 4, 39100
Tel *0471 31 10 00*
w laurin.it
Marvel at the original Art Nouveau
features in this charming hotel.

BOLZANO: Luna-Mondschein €€
Spa hotel
Via Piave 15, 39100
Tel *0471 97 56 42*
w hotel-luna.it
This stylish hotel in the city
centre has fabulous grounds.

BRESSANONE: Hotel Dominik €
Rooms with a view
Via Terzo di Sotto 13, 39042
Tel *0472 83 01 44*
w hoteldominik.com
Furnished with antiques, most
rooms boast views of the river.

**FIE ALLO SCILIAR: Edelansitz
Zimmerlehen** €
Agriturismo
Via Kühbach 15, Obervöls, 39050
Tel *0471 72 50 53*
w zimmerlehen.it
A 13th-century manor farm
with four tower-like buildings
converted into homely flats.
Enjoy a breakfast of farm-produce.

**MERANO: Hotel Castel
Fragsburg** €€
Rooms with a view
Via Fragsburg 3, 39012
Tel *0473 24 40 71*
w fragsburg.com
This hotel boasts fine views of the
mountains and the town below.

DK Choice

MERANO: Ottmanngut €€
Boutique
Via Verdi 18, 39012
Tel *0473 44 96 56*
w ottmanngut.it
Surrounded by lush greenery,
this family-run guesthouse is
within walking distance of the
spa town. The suites are
elegantly decorated with
period furnishings and modern
conveniences. There is also a
lovely garden to relax in.

**ORTISEI: Adler Dolomiti Spa
& Sport Resort** €€
Spa hotel
Via Rezia 7, 39046
Tel *0471 77 50 01*
w adler-dolomiti.com
A good choice for all seasons.
Excellent service and facilities
including vast gardens.

**REDAGNO: Berghotel
Zirmerhof** €€
Agriturismo
Oberradein 59, 39040
Tel *0471 88 72 15*
w zirmerhof.com
Homely accommodation in a
beautiful mountain setting.

TRENTO: Accademia €€
Historic
Vicolo Colico 4-6, 38122
Tel *0461 23 36 00*
w accademiahotel.eu
Restored medieval building with
a pleasant courtyard.

Lombardy

APRICA: Relais Volla Brioschi €€
Boutique
Via Valeriana 187, 25040
Tel *0342 74 56 81*
w relaisvillabrioschi.com
A luxury Art Nouveau-style
country house with a garden,
parking and its own restaurant.

BELLAGIO: Hotel Florence €€
Spa hotel
Piazza Mazzini 46, 22021
Tel *031 95 03 42*
w hotelflorencebellagio.it
This lakeside hotel offers stylish
decor, canopy beds, roll-top baths
and a gourmet restaurant.

BELLAGIO: Hotel Suisse €€
Historic
Piazza Mazzini 8/10, 22021
Tel *031 95 17 55*
w hotelsuissebellagio.com
This lakeside hotel has an
excellent restaurant.

**BELLAGIO: Grand Hotel
Villa Serbelloni** €€€
Luxury
Via Roma 1, 22021
Tel *031 95 02 16*
w villaserbelloni.com
The hotel boasts frescoed ceilings
and views of Lake Como.

BERGAMO: Hotel Gombit €€€
Design
Via Mario Lupo 6, 24129
Tel *035 24 70 09*
w gombithotel.it
A concept hotel with distinctive
architecture and interior design.

The stately Grand Hotel Villa Serbelloni in Bellagio

BORMIO: Hotel Cristallo €€
Spa hotel
Via Milano 44, 23032
Tel *0342 90 27 00*
w cristallohotelresidence.it
A short stroll from ski-lifts and
thermal baths, this hotel offers
a large garden, a ski room and
a games room.

BRATTO: Hotel Milano €€
Spa hotel
Via Silvio Pellico 3, 24020
Tel *0346 31 211*
w hotelmilano.com
Large Alpine resort hotel and spa.
Plenty of comfort and style.

BRESCIA: Park Hotel Cà Noa €
Rooms with a view
Via Triumplina 66, 25123
Tel *030 39 87 62*
w hotelcanoa.it
Situated in a quiet park, this hotel
has an outdoor pool.

BRESCIA: AC Hotel Brescia €€
Design
Via Giulio Quinto Stefana 3, 25126
Tel *030 24 05 511*
w hotelacbrescia.com
This minimalist design hotel with
modern facilities has a fitness
centre and a gourmet restaurant.

CERNOBBIO: Villa d'Este €€€
Luxury
Via Regina 40, 22012
Tel *031 34 81*
w villadeste.it
An elegant and sumptuous
hotel set in 25 acres (10 ha)
of lush parkland.

**CERVESINA: Hotel Castello
di San Gaudenzio** €€
Historic
Via Mulino 1, 27050
Tel *0383 33 31*
w castellosangaudenzio.com
A 15th-century castle boasting
romantic rooms, a gym, a pool
plus a top-class restaurant.

COLOGNE: Cappuccini €€
Historic
Via Cappuccini 54, 25033
Tel *030 715 72 54*
w cappuccini.it
This former monastery has a
wellness centre, an outdoor pool
and a restaurant.

COMO: Hotel Firenze €
Rooms with a view
Piazza Volta 16, 22100
Tel *031 30 03 33*
w albergofirenze.it
A renovated Neo-Classical hotel
situated in a pedestrianized
square in the town centre.

COMO: In Riva al Lago €
B&B
Via Crespi 4, 22100
Tel *031 30 23 33*
w inrivaallago.com
Basic, spotless hotel that also
offers self-contained apartments.

**CREMONA: Dellearti Design
Hotel** €€
Boutique
Via Bonomelli 8, 26100
Tel *0372 231 31*
w dellearti.com
Accommodation with arty
touches. Close to the cathedral
and the medieval bell tower.

**DESENZANO DEL GARDA: Park
Hotel** €€
Luxury
Lungolago Cesare Battisti 17, 25015
Tel *030 914 34 95*
w parkhotelonline.it
Elegant hotel with well-furnished
rooms, some with lake views.

**GARDONE RIVIERA: Villa
del Sogno** €€€
Historic
Via Zanardelli 107, 25083
Tel *0365 29 01 81*
w villadelsogno.it
A Neo-Classical villa with tennis
courts and an outdoor pool.

For more information on types of hotels *see p561*

Stylish minimalist decor at Nhow Milano in Milan

GARDONE RIVIERA: Villa Fiordaliso €€€
Luxury
Corso Zanardelli 132, 25083
Tel 0365 201 58
W villafiordaliso.it
Beautiful three-storey villa overlooking Lake Garda. Furnished with eclectic decor with a floral theme.

GARGNANO: Villa Sostaga €€€
Boutique
Via Sostaga 19, 25084
Tel 0365 79 12 18
W villasostaga.it
This family-run hotel offers large rooms with modern facilities and an Art Nouveau dining room.

ISEO: Iseolago €€
Spa hotel
Via Colombera 2, 25049
Tel 030 98 891
W iseolagohotel.it
Extensive gardens with swimming pools, a tennis court and a children's playground.

DK Choice

LIMONE SUL GARDA: Hotel Capo Reamol €
Budget
Via IV Novembre 92, 25010
Tel 0365 95 40 40
W hotelcaporeamol.it
This hotel's idyllic location offers breathtaking views of Lake Garda. Rooms are compact but clean and the staff are friendly. A fitness room and spa services are available to guests, along with a private beach and a swimming pool. Excellent value for money.

LIVIGNO: Hotel Capriolo €
Pensione
Via Borch 96, 23030
Tel 0342 99 67 23
W capriololivigno.com
Family-run hotel located close to ski lifts and hiking paths. Offers traditional Valtellina cuisine.

MANTUA: Casa Poli €€
Boutique
Corso Giuseppe Garibaldi 32, 46100
Tel 0376 28 81 70
W hotelcasapoli.it
Near the harbour, this hotel has cosy rooms and minimalist decor.

MANTUA: Hotel La Favorita €€
Business
Via S. Cognetti De Martiis 1, 46100
Tel 0376 25 47 11
W hotellafavorita.it
A modern and elegant hotel with an excellent restaurant.

DK Choice

MILAN: Antica Locanda Leonardo €€
Boutique
Corso Magenta 78, 20123
Tel 02 48 01 41 97
W anticalocandaleonardo.com
Peacefully located in an elegant 19th-century palazzo, this family-run hotel has well decorated rooms overlooking a charming and picturesque inner garden. The staff are helpful and friendly.

MILAN: Antica Locanda Solferino €€
Boutique
Via Castelfidardo 2, 20121
Tel 02 65 70 12 9
W anticalocandasolferino.it
A welcoming guesthouse with eclectic old-world charm.

MILAN: Ata Hotel Executive €€
Business
Viale Sturzo 45, 20154
Tel 02 62 941
W atahotels.it/executive
Rooms are spacious and facilities include a gym and sun terrace.

MILAN: Nhow Milano €€
Design
Via Tortona 35, 20144
Tel 02 48 98 861

W nh-hotels.it
This hotel boasts an interesting collection of contemporary art.

MILAN: Una Hotel Century €€
Business
Via Fabio Filzi 25/B, 20124
Tel 02 67 50 41
W unahotels.it
Modern facilities are available in this contemporary hotel.

MILAN: Hotel Manzoni €€€
Luxury
Via Santo Spirito 20, 20121
Tel 02 76 00 57 00
W hotelmanzoni.com
Beautiful hotel set in a quiet, yet central location.

MILAN: Park Hyatt Milano €€€
Luxury
Via Tommaso Grossi 1, 20121
Tel 02 88 21 12 34
W milan.park.hyatt.com
Housed in a former bank, this elegant hotel has a spa and gym.

PAVIA: Hotel Italia €
Pensione
Corso Partigiani 48, 27012
Tel 0382 92 56 56
W italiacertosa.pavia.it
Family-run hotel in an 18th-century farmhouse. Rooms are simply but tastefully decorated with antique pieces.

RANCO: Il Sole di Ranco €€
Rooms with a view
Piazza Venezia 5, 21020
Tel 0331 97 65 07
W ilsolediranco.it
Overlooking Lake Maggiore, this hotel boasts a private garden and an infinity pool.

RIVA DI SOLTO: Albergo Ristorante Miranda €
Pensione
Via Cornello 8, 24060
Tel 035 98 60 21
W albergomiranda.it
This family-run guesthouse has views over Lake Iseo and comfortable rooms with balconies.

RODIGO: Hotel Villa dei Tigli €€
Historic
Via Cantarana 20/I, 46040
Tel 0376 65 06 91
W hotelvilladeitigli.it
A 20th-century former aristocratic villa with an outdoor pool and a high-class terrace restaurant.

SALÒ: Hotel Laurin €€
Boutique
Viale Landi 9, 25087
Tel 0365 22 022
W laurinhotelsalo.com
A romantic lakeside villa with a restaurant and an outdoor pool.

SIRMIONE: Hotel Catullo €€
Historic
Piazza Flaminia 7, 25019
Tel *030 990 58 11*
W hotelcatullo.it
This hotel offers rooms with
balconies and a rooftop terrace.

TREMEZZO: Hotel la Darsena €€
Rooms with a view
Via Regina 3, 22019
Tel *0344 431 66*
W hotelladarsena.it
A lakeside hotel-cum-restaurant
in a great location for visiting
nearby villas and other sights.

**TREMEZZO: Grand Hotel
Tremezzo** €€€
Historic
Via Regina 8, 22019
Tel *0344 424 91*
W grandhoteltremezzo.com
A prestigious lakeside hotel, in Art
Nouveau style; great facilities.

VARENNA: Hotel Du Lac €€
Rooms with a view
Via del Prestino 11, 23829
Tel *0341 83 02 38*
W albergodulac.com
A peaceful hotel at the water's
edge with enchanting views.

Valle d'Aosta and Piedmont

ACQUI TERME: Hotel Rondò €
Spa hotel
Viale Acquedotto Romano 44, 15011
Tel *0144 32 28 89*
W albergorondo.it
Rooms are bright and basic, and
the staff friendly and helpful.

**ACQUI TERME: Hotel Talice
Radicati** €€
Historic
Piazza Conciliazione 12, 15011
Tel *0144 32 86 11*
W taliceradicati.com
The rooms in this 15th-century
palazzo are elegant and refined.

DK Choice

**ALBA: Villa La Meridiana
Cascina Reinè** €
Agriturismo
Località Altavilla 9, 12051
Tel *0173 44 01 12*
W villalameridianaalba.it
This 18th-century villa benefits
from enchanting views over the
surrounding vineyards. Rooms
are furnished with antiques and
there are three cosy apartments.
Guests can join in harvesting the
crop from the estate's vineyards
and hunt for truffles.

**ALESSANDRIA: Hotel Alli
Due Buoi Rossi** €€
Historic
Via Cavour 32, 15121
Tel *0131 51 71 71*
W hotelalliduebuoirossi.com
A welcoming and friendly hotel
with a renowned *trattoria*.

AOSTA: Hotel Village Aosta €€
Resort
Località Torrent de Maillod 1, 11020
Tel *0165 77 49 11*
W hotelvillageaosta.it
This small but charming hotel
offers both rooms and chalets.

ARONA: Hotel Giardino €
Pensione
Corso Repubblica 1, 28041
Tel *0322 459 94*
W giardinoarona.com
A comfortable hotel with splendid
views across Lake Maggiore from
the large terrace and grounds.

**BARDONECCHIA: Hotel
Jafferau** €€
Resort
Località Fregiusia, 10052
Tel *0122 998 99*
W hoteljafferau.it
High-altitude hotel with a pool, a
sauna and hydromassage.

DK Choice

BAVENO: Hotel Splendid €€
Resort
Via Sempione 12, 28831
Tel *0323 92 45 83*
W zaccherahotels.com
This luxurious and elegant hotel
has its own private beach
(which has sun beds and a
private jetty), and an outdoor
pool. The rooms are
comfortable and well
appointed – most have
balconies with lakeside views.
Helpful and attentive staff
provide excellent service.

Stone steps leading to the charming Villa
La Meridiana Cascina Reinè in Alba

**CANNOBIO: Residenza
Patrizia** €
Pensione
Viale Vittorio Veneto 9, 28822
Tel *0323 73 97 13*
W residenzapatrizia.com
Inviting rooms and self-
contained flats are on offer here,
plus amenities such as a sauna
and a pool.

**ORTO SAN GIULIO: Hotel
San Rocco** €€
Historic
Via Gippini 11, 28016
Tel *0322 91 19 77*
W hotelsanrocco.it
Unwind at the lakeside pool or
enjoy the excellent restaurant,
and views of San Giulio Island.
The town centre is a pleasant
walk away and offers additional
dining choices.

STRESA: Hotel La Palma €€
Resort
Lungolago Umberto I 33, 28838
Tel *0323 324 01*
W hlapalma.it
This hotel offers a private beach,
an outdoor pool, spa facilities
and a terrace bar. There is also
a well-regarded restaurant.

TORTONA: Villa Giulia €
Boutique
Corso Alessandria 7/A, 15057
Tel *0131 86 23 96*
W villagiulia-hotel.com
Former private villa, with elegant
decor. Homely atmosphere and
an ample breakfast.

TURIN: Albergo Serenella €
Pensione
Via Tarino 4, 10124
Tel *011 83 70 31*
W albergoserenella.com
This family-run establishment
has clean and basic rooms at
unbeatable prices for the city
centre. Prices do not change
during the high season and
include all charges.

**TURIN: Hotel Conte
Biancamano** €
Pensione
Corso Vittorio Emanuele 73, 10128
Tel *011 562 32 81*
W hotelcontebiancamano.com
An intimate hotel with elegant
decor located on the third floor
of a 19th-century palazzo.

TURIN: Grand Hotel Sitea €€
Luxury
Via Carlo Alberto 35, 10123
Tel *011 517 01 71*
W grandhotelsitea.it
Set in a Neo-Classical palazzo,
this place offers elegant suites
and a top-class restaurant.

For more information on types of hotels see p561

TURIN: Nh Lingotto Tech €€
Design
Via Nizza 230, 10126
Tel *011 664 20 00*
ⓦ nh-hotels.com
A contemporary hotel located
in the Lingotto Building, once
a huge Fiat factory.

TURIN: Turin Golden Palace €€€
Luxury
Via dell'Arcivescovado 18, 10121
Tel *011 551 21 11*
ⓦ goldenpalace.it
This hotel, set in a 19th-century
palazzo, offers a spa with a pool,
sauna and fitness centre.

**VARALLO SESIA: Vecchio
Albergo Sacro Monte** €
Pensione
Località Sacro Monte 14, 13019
Tel *0163 542 54*
ⓦ sacromontealbergo.it
A comfortable hotel with simple
rooms and a small private garden.

Liguria

DK Choice

**CAMOGLI: Locanda I Tre
Merli** €€
Rooms with a view
Via Scalo 5, 6032
Tel *0185 77 67 52*
ⓦ locandaitremerli.com
Located right on the enchanting
fishing port of Camogli, this
cosy hotel offers wonderful
views and personalized service.
Room amenities include basic
cooking facilities. A small spa
area offers a Jacuzzi and a steam
bath. Ferries to Portofino and the
Cinque Terre are nearby. Parking
is available upon request.

CAMOGLI: Villa Rosmarino €€
Rooms with a view
Via Figari 38, 16032
Tel *0185 77 15 80*
ⓦ villarosmarino.com
At the foot of Monte di Portofino,
this villa has an outdoor pool.

CAMOGLI: Cenobio dei Dogi €€€
Luxury
Via Nicolò Cuneo 34, 16032
Tel *0185 72 41*
ⓦ cenobio.it
Built for the Doges of Genoa, this
17th-century villa houses a vast
hotel with a private beach.

FINALE LIGURE: Punta Est €€€
Luxury
Via Aurelia 1, 17024
Tel *019 60 06 11*
ⓦ puntaest.com

An 18th-century villa with superb
views over the Ligurian bay.

GARLENDA: La Meridiana €€
Resort
Via ai Castelli, 17033
Tel *0182 58 02 71*
ⓦ lameridianaresort.com
This relaxing country house-style
hotel is perfect for walking
holidays and outdoor activities.

GENOA: Hotel Villa Pagoda €€
Rooms with a view
Via Capolungo 15, 16167
Tel *010 372 61 61*
ⓦ villapagoda.it
This luxurious 19th-century villa
is only steps from the coast.

GENOA: NH Marina €€
Rooms with a view
Molo Ponte Calvi 5, 16124
Tel *0848 39 02 27*
ⓦ nh-hotels.com
An international hotel overlooking
the harbour and close to the
Aquarium, old town and markets.

**ISOLA PALMARIA: Locanda
Lorena** €€
Rooms with a view
Via Cavour 4, 19025
Tel *0187 79 23 70*
ⓦ locandalorena.com
A small beach hotel accessible
by stylish Venetian motorboats.

LEVANTO: Hotel Stella Maris €€
Boutique
Via Marconi 4, 19015
Tel *0187 80 82 58*
ⓦ hotelstellamaris.it
Close to the beach, this place
is exquisitely decorated.

MANAROLA: Ca' d'Andrean €
Pensione
Via Discovolo 101, 19017

Charming views from the vibrant Locanda I
Tre Merli, Camogli

Tel *0187 92 00 40*
ⓦ cadandrean.it
This family-run guesthouse serves
breakfast alfresco in summer.

MONTEROSSO: Hotel Marina €
Pensione
Via Buranco 40, 19016
Tel *0187 81 76 13*
ⓦ hotelmarina5terre.com
Cooking lessons are available on
request from this quiet hotel.

OSPEDALETTI: Hotel Firenze €
Rooms with a view
Corso Regina Margherita 97, 18014
Tel *0184 68 92 21*
ⓦ firenze.azurline.com
A small hillside hotel with basic
but cheerful rooms, most of
which have balconies.

**PORTO VENERE: Hotel della
Baia** €
Rooms with a view
Via Lungomare 111, 19025
Tel *0187 79 07 97*
ⓦ baiahotel.com
All rooms have balconies and
views over the bay. There's an
outdoor pool and a restaurant.

PORTOFINO: Splendido €€€
Luxury
Salita Baratta 16, 16034
Tel *0185 26 78 01*
ⓦ hotelsplendido.com
Housed in a former monastery,
this hotel has elegantly furnished
rooms, many with private terraces.

RAPALLO: Hotel Stella €
Rooms with a view
Via Aurelia Ponente 6, 16035
Tel *0185 503 67*
ⓦ hotelstella-riviera.com
This small hotel lies in the centre
of Rapallo, close to the beach
and seafront promenade.

RAPALLO: Hotel Italia E Lido €€
Rooms with a view
Lungomare Castello 1, 16035
Tel *0185 504 94*
ⓦ italiaelido.com
Overlooking the Gulf of Tigullio,
this hotel has bright, airy rooms.

SAN REMO: Hotel Nazionale €€
Rooms with a view
Corso Matteotti 3, 18038
Tel *0184 57 75 77*
ⓦ hotelnazionalesanremo.com
A high level of service and
classically furnished rooms.

SAN REMO: Royal Hotel €€€
Luxury
Corso Imperatrice 80, 18038
Tel *0184 53 91*
ⓦ royalhotelsanremo.com
Located on the seafront, this place
is renowned for its restaurants.

SESTRI LEVANTE: Hotel Helvetia €€
Boutique
Via Cappuccini 43, 16039
Tel *0185 411 75*
w hotelhelvetia.it/
This hotel boasts its own private beach, garden and solarium.

VENTIMIGLIA: La Riserva di Castel d'Appio €€
Rooms with a view
Via Peidaigo 71, 18039
Tel *0184 22 95 33*
w lariserva.it
Enjoy panoramic views over the Italian Riviera and the Côte d'Azur at this hotel. Excellent service.

Emilia-Romagna

BOLOGNA: Delle Drapperie €
Pensione
Via Drapperie 5, 40124
Tel *051 223 955*
w albergodrapperie.com
Decoratively painted ceilings and luxurious bathrooms characterize this well-priced option.

BOLOGNA: Il Guercino €
Boutique
Via Luigi Serra 7, 40129
Tel *051 369 893*
w guercino.it
An Indian flavour prevails at this charming hotel, which has two solariums and a relaxation area.

BOLOGNA: Indipendenza Suite €
Pensione
Via dell'Indipendenza 30, 40121
Tel *331 4575 920*
Four independent apartments decorated in simple, classic style.

BOLOGNA: Panorama Hotel €
Budget
Via Giovanni Livraghi 1, 40121
Tel *051 221 802*
w hotelpanoramabologna.it
A clean and central option; some rooms have a private bath.

BOLOGNA: Commercianti €€
Historic
Via De' Pignattari 11, 40124
Tel *051 745 75 11*
w commercianti.hotelsbologna.it
Located next to the Bologna Cathedral, this 13-century building is bursting with romantic details.

BOLOGNA: Corona d'Oro €€
Romantic
Via Guglielmo Oberdan 12, 40126
Tel *051 7457 611*
w hco.it
Historic hotel with an eclectic style: from medieval to Art Deco.

Outdoor swimming pool at La Riserva di Castel d'Appio in Ventimiglia

BOLOGNA: Il Convento dei Fiori di Seta €€
Historic
Via Orfeo 34, 40124
Tel *051 272 039*
w silkflowersnunnery.com
Ten well-appointed rooms in this converted medieval convent.

BOLOGNA: Roma €€
Pensione
Via Massimo D'Azeglio 9, 40123
Tel *051 226 322*
w hotelroma.biz
Quaint rooms, ask for one of the few with balconies.

DK Choice

BOLOGNA: Grand Hotel Majestic €€€
Luxury
Via Indipendenza, 8 40121
Tel *051 225 445*
w grandhotelmajestic.
hotelsbologna.com
This legendary hotel expertly combines opulent old-world elegance with modern comfort and hospitality. Each room is individually decorated with lush fabrics and antique furniture. Breakfast is served on the romantic rooftop terrace with sweeping views of the city. The dining room boasts beautiful frescoes.

BOLOGNA: Royal Hotel Carlton €€€
Luxury
Via Montebello 8, 40121
Tel *051 249 361*
w monrifhotels.it/RoyalCarltonHotel
Elegant, grand hotel with a fully-equipped wellness centre.

FERRARA: Principessa Leonora €€
Boutique
Via Mascheraio 39, 44121
Tel *0532 20 60 20*
w principessaleonora.it

A 16th-century residence exquisitely decorated with antique French tapestries and traditional furniture.

FERRARA: Duchessa Isabella €€€
Historic
Via Palestro 70, 44121
Tel *0532 20 21 21*
w duchessaisabella.it
Minute attention to detail in both decor and service. Rooms are sumptuously furnished.

MODENA: Daunia €
Pensione
Via del Pozzo 158, 41125
Tel *059 37 11 82*
w hoteldaunia.it
A simple, modern building with restaurant. Breakfast is served in the garden, weather permitting.

MODENA: Canalgrande €€€
Historic
Corso Canal Grande 6, 41100
Tel *059 21 71 60*
w canalgrandehotel.it
Housed in a former convent and with fresh, Neo-Classical decor.

PARMA: Button €
Budget
Borgo della Salina 7, 43121
Tel *0521 20 80 39*
w hotelbutton.it
Courteous service makes up for the basic accommodation.

PARMA: Stendhal €€
Romantic
Via Giambattista Bodoni 3, 43121
Tel *0521 20 80 57*
w hotelstendhal.it
Eclectically decorated rooms in a centrally located old palazzo.

PIACENZA: San Francesco €
Pensione
Galleria San Francesco 2, 29121
Tel *0523 32 66 88*
Excellent location and prices for spotlessly clean accommodation.

PIACENZA GENEPRETO:
La Pobiella   €€
Agriturismo
Località Pobiella 16, 29010
Tel *0523 99 75 14*
This rustic stone villa is ideal for
a relaxed hillside holiday.

RAVENNA: Sant'Andrea   €
Boutique
Via Carlo Cattaneo 33, 48121
Tel *0544 21 55 64*
W santandreahotel.com
A converted convent with a
tranquil cloister-garden.

RAVENNA: Cappello   €€
Romantic
Via IV Novembre 41, 48121
Tel *0544 21 98 13*
W albergocappello.it
The rooms in this exquisite hotel
have coffered ceilings.

RIMINI: Acasamia   €
Budget
Viale Renato Parisano 34, 47921
Tel *0541 39 13 70*
W hotelacasamia.com
Colourful rooms and located
a short stroll from the beach.

RIMINI: Grand Hotel Rimini €€€
Luxury
Parco Federico Fellini 1, 47900
Tel *0541 560 00*
W grandhotelrimini.com
Deluxe seaside establishment
made famous by Federico Fellini.

Florence

Antica Dimora Firenze   €
B&B   **Map** 2 D3/4
Via San Gallo 72/r, 50129
Tel *055 462 72 96*
W johanna.it

Pleasantly bright, large rooms at the Relais
Uffizi in Florence

Canopy beds and antique
furniture set this B&B apart.

Palazzo Guadagni   €
Historic   **Map** 5 B5
Piazza di Santo Spirito 9, 50125
Tel *055 265 83 76*
W palazzoguadagni.com
Fantastic service, a great location
and reasonable prices.

Relais Il Campanile   €
B&B   **Map** 6 E1
Via Ricasoli 10, 50125
Tel *055 21 16 88*
W relaiscampanile.it
Quaint rooms with wrought-iron
accents in a 17th-century palazzo.

Residenza Johanna   €
Pensione   **Map** 2 D3
Via Bonifacio Lupo 14, 50129
Tel *055 48 18 96*
W johanna.it
This tiny and charming hotel is
fantastic value. Free parking.

Brunelleschi   €€
Historic   **Map** 6 D2
Piazza Sant'Elisabetta 3, 50122
Tel *055 273 70*
W hotelbrunelleschi.it
Located in a Byzantine tower, this
place offers classy, opulent rooms.

David   €€
Pensione   **Map** 4 E3
Viale Michelangiolo 1, 50125
Tel *055 681 16 95*
W davidhotel.com
Some rooms have balconies that
look out over leafy Oltrarno in
this family-owned guesthouse.

Grifone   €€
Business
Via Gaetano Pilati 20, 50136
Tel *055 62 33 00*
W hotelgrifonefirenze.com
Comfortable and spacious rooms,
some with a kitchenette.

Hotel Home   €€
Boutique   **Map** 4 F2
Piazza Piave 3, 50122
Tel *055 24 36 68*
W hhflorence.it
All white and extremely elegant
decor in this stylish hotel.

DK Choice

Relais Uffizi   €€
Romantic   **Map** 6 D4
Chiasso del Buco 16, 50122
Tel *055 267 62 39*
W relaisuffizi.it
Located behind the Piazza della
Sugnoria, this hotel is fantastic
value. All rooms are charmingly
decorated, and the breakfast
room looks out onto the Piazza.

Four Seasons Hotel Firenze €€€
Luxury   **Map** 2 E4
Borgo Pinti 99, 50121
Tel *055 262 61*
W fourseasons.com/florence
The epitome of elegance, with
silk wall hangings, frescoes and
bas-reliefs. Service is impeccable,
and the restaurant worth visiting
even if you are not staying here.
The hotel runs a frequent shuttle
bus into the centre of Florence.

Grand Hotel Minerva   €€€
Historic   **Map** 5 B2
*Piazza di Santa Maria Novella 16,
50123*
Tel *055 272 30*
W grandhotelminerva.com
A panoramic terrace with a pool
gives a modern touch to one of
the city's oldest hotels. Its
convenient location near the
train station means many sights
are in walking distance.

The Westin Excelsior   €€€
Luxury   **Map** 5 A2
Piazza d'Ognissanti 3, 50123
Tel *055 271 51*
W westinflorence.com
Opulent rooms, some with
balconies that have views of
the Arno. The roof terrace is
exquisitely presented.

Tuscany

DK Choice

AREZZO: Badia di Pomaio €€
Boutique
Loc. Pomaio 4, 52100
Tel *0575 37 14 07*
W badiadipomaio.it
This superbly converted
17th-century abbey is situated
in a picturesque spot amidst
lush gardens with a swimming
pool and panoramic views
of the medieval town below.
Comfortable and quiet rooms
with elegant furnishings. The
staff are warm and hospitable.

AREZZO: Graziella Patio Hotel €€
Boutique
Via Cavour 23, 52100
Tel *0575 40 19 62*
W hotelpatio.it
Charming hotel with rooms in
African and Far Eastern styles.

CORTONA: Italia   €
Budget
Via Ghibellina 5/7, 52044
Tel *0575 63 02 54*
W hotelitaliacortona.com
Excellent value at this lovely
central spot full of character.

CORTONA: San Michele €€
Historic
Via Guelfa 15, 52044
Tel *0575 60 43 48*
🅆 hotelsanmichele.net
Modern comfort in Renaissance
setting. Very classy decor.

DK Choice

**ELBA MARCIANA: Cernia
Isola Botanica** €€
Rooms with a view
Via San Gaetano 23, 57030
Tel *0565 90 82 10*
🅆 hotelcernia.it
A lush flower-filled park and
botanical garden surround this
charming hotel. Rooms are
spacious and minimalist, with
interesting design elements.
There is a freshwater swimming
pool and wellness centre.
Situated a short walk from Capo
Sant'Andra, the location is hard
to beat.

ELBA SPARTAIA: Desiree €€
Rooms with a view
Spartaia, Procchio, 57030
Tel *0565 90 73 11*
🅆 htdesiree.it
Clean rooms and private beach
access at this comfortable hotel.

LUCCA: Piccolo Hotel Puccini €
Pensione
Via di Poggio 9, 55100
Tel *0583 554 21*
🅆 hotelpuccini.com
The prices may be low but you get
warm service and charming rooms.

**LUCCA: Alla Corte degli
Angeli** €€
Boutique
Via degli Angeli 23, 55100
Tel *0583 46 92 04*
🅆 allacortedegliangeli.it
A jewel of a hotel with distinc-
tively personalized rooms.

MONTEPULCIANO: San Biagio €
Budget
Via San Bartolomeo 2, 53045
Tel *0578 71 72 33*
🅆 albergosanbiagio.it
Located just outside of the town
with glorious views, this hotel has
comfortable and neat rooms and
a heated swimming pool.

**MONTERIGGIONI: Borgo
Gallinaio** €€
Agriturismo
Strada del Gallinaio 5, 53035
Tel *0577 30 47 51*
🅆 gallinaio.it
This converted 15th-century
stone-built farmhouse is
surrounded by cyprus and olive
trees. There is an outdoor pool.

Dining area with medieval details in the
Antica Residenza Cicogna, Siena

PISA: Guerrazzi €
B&B
Via Francesco da Buti 4, 56125
Tel *3389 328169*
🅆 bbguerrazzi.hostel.com
Simple but quaint, with
comfortable and clean rooms.

PISA: Royal Victoria Hotel €€
Historic
Lungarno Antonio Pacinotti 12, 56126
Tel *050 94 01 11*
🅆 royalvictoria.it
Housed in a 10th-century tower,
Pisa's very first hotel has stately
decor and spacious rooms.

PISA: Relais dell'Orologio €€€
Historic
Via della Faggiola 12, 56126
Tel *050 83 03 61*
🅆 hotelrelaisorologio.com
Built into a 14th-century tower,
this hotel has elegant rooms and
a delightful reading room. Enjoy
breakfast on the veranda.

**SAN GIMIGNANO:
Bel Soggiorno** €
Budget
Via San Giovanni 91, 53037
Tel *0577 94 03 75*
🅆 hotelbelsoggiorno.it
Comfortable and well-priced
hotel run by the same family since
1886. Excellent restaurant.

**SAN GIMIGNANO:
Leon Bianco** €€
Rooms with a view
Piazza Cisterna 13, 53037
Tel *0577 94 12 94*
🅆 leonbianco.com
Elegant rooms with spectacular
views of the hillside piazza.

**SIENA: Antica Residenza
Cicogna** €
Pensione
Via Termini 67, 53100
Tel *0577 28 56 13*
🅆 anticaresidenzacicogna.it

Romantic location set in a
medieval building full of
charming details.

SIENA: Palazzo Ravizza €€
Romantic
Piano dei Mantellini 34, 53100
Tel *0577 28 04 62*
🅆 palazzoravizza.it
Lovely rooms with original period
furniture. Some rooms overlook
a picturesque garden.

**SIENA: Grand Hotel
Continental** €€€
Luxury
Via Banchi di Sopra 85, 53100
Tel *0577 560 11*
🅆 grandhotelcontinentalsiena.com
The most prestigious address in
Siena. This 17th-century building
has impressive frescoes and
luxurious rooms.

VIAREGGIO: London €€
Rooms with a view
Viale Daniele Manin 16, 55049
Tel *0584 498 41*
🅆 hotellondon.it
Simple, comfortable rooms and
an elegant lobby. Located a short
walk from the sea.

VOLTERRA: Villa Rioddi €
Historic
*Strada Provinciale del Monte
Volterrano 71, 56048*
Tel *0588 880 53*
🅆 hotelvillarioddi.it
Experience ultimate relaxation in
this medieval 15th-century villa.

VOLTERRA: Marcampo €€
Agriturismo
*Località San Cipriano, Podere
Marcampo 30, 56048*
Tel *0588 853 93*
🅆 agriturismo-marcampo.com
There are just six rooms in this
tranquil slice of Tuscan paradise.
Enjoy the pool with views of the
surrounding vineyards.

Umbria

ASSISI: Sole €
Budget
Corso Giuseppe Mazzini 35, 06081
Tel *075 81 23 73*
🅆 assisihotelsole.com
Basic but spacious rooms in a
15th-century medieval building.

ASSISI: Subasio €€
Romantic
Via Elia Frate 2c, 06081
Tel *075 81 22 06*
🅆 hotelsubasio.com
Located beside the famous
basilica: atmospheric and spacious
rooms, some with a terrace.

For more information on types of hotels *see p561*

GUBBIO: La Cinciallegre €
Agriturismo
Fraz. Pisciano, 06024
Tel *075 925 59 57*
🆆 lecinciallegre.it
This is a jewel hidden in the countryside. Small but cosy rooms.

GUBBIO: Relais Ducale €€
Romantic
Via Galeotti 19, 06024
Tel *075 922 01 57*
🆆 mencarelligroup.com
Beautiful rooms in a converted manor house. Panoramic views.

NORCIA: Casale nel Parco dei Monti Sibillini €
Agriturismo
Vocabolo Fontevena 8, 06046
Tel *0743 81 64 81*
🆆 casalenelparco.com
Canopy beds and wood-beamed ceilings; some rooms also have kitchenettes. Great service.

ORVIETO: Filippeschi €
Budget
Via Filippeschi 19, 05018
Tel *0763 34 32 75*
🆆 albergofilippeschi.it
Basic but comfortable rooms in the historic centre. Spacious lobby.

ORVIETO: La Badia €€
Historic
Località La Badia 8, 05018
Tel *0763 30 19 59*
🆆 labadiahotel.it
Breathtaking hotel built into the ruins of an 8th-century monastery.

ORVIETO: Locanda Pallazzone €€
Agriturismo
Località Rocca Ripesena 66, 05018
Tel *0763 39 36 14*
🆆 locandapalazzone.it
Elegant accommodation in a former cardinal's residence; surrounded by vineyards.

PERUGIA: Fortuna €
Historic
Via Luigi Bonazzi 19, 06121
Tel *075 572 28 45*
🆆 hotelfortunaperugia.com
Restoration work revealed over 300-year-old frescoes at this hotel.

PERUGIA: Castello di Monterone €€
Historic
Strada Montevile 3, 06126
Tel *075 572 42 14*
🆆 castellomonterone.com
Luxurious rooms and two stellar restaurants are on offer here.

PERUGIA: La Rosetta €€
Boutique
Piazza Italia 19, 06121
Tel *075 572 08 41*
🆆 larosetta.eu

Fantastic rooms, either decorated in 1920s or Baroque style.

PERUGIA: Brufani Palace €€€
Luxury
Piazza Italia 12, 06121
Tel *075 573 25 41*
🆆 brufanipalace.com
Sumptuous accommodation plus a roof garden with views of the town and countryside.

SPOLETO: Hotel Aurora €
Budget
Via dell'Apollinare 3, 06049
Tel *0743 22 03 15*
🆆 hotelauroraspoleto.it
Great value at this central but quiet family-run hotel.

SPOLETO: San Luca €€
Boutique
Via Interna delle Mura 21, 06049
Tel *0743 22 33 99*
🆆 hotelsanluca.com
Sophisticated elegance in one of the loveliest palaces in Spoleto.

TODI CANONICA: Tenuta di Canonica €€
Agriturismo
Vocabolo Casalzetta 75, 06059
Tel *075 894 75 45*
🆆 tenutadicanonica.com
Sublime country residence on the site of a 9th-century farm. Superb location.

Le Marche

ANCONA: Grand Hotel Palace €€
Historic
Lungomare Luigi Vanvitelli 24, 60121
Tel *071 20 18 13*
🆆 hotelancona.it
Old-world elegance at this grand 17th-century portside palazzo.

Luxuriously decorated room in the Locanda Pallazzone in Orvieto

ANCONA: NH Ancona €€
Rooms with a view
Via XXIX Settembre 14, 60122
Tel *071 20 11 71*
🆆 nh-hotels.it
Stylish, contemporary hilltop hotel with simple rooms.

ASCOLI PICENO: Pennile €
Budget
Via Gaetano Spalvieri 1, 63100
Tel *0736 416 45*
🆆 hotelpennile.it
Reasonable prices for simple and well-kept rooms.

DK Choice

ASCOLI PICENO: Villa Cicchi €€
Agriturismo
Via Salaria Superiore 137, 63100
Tel *0736 25 22 72*
🆆 villacicchi.it
An exquisite meticulously presented villa is at the heart of this agriturismo that combines luxury accommodation with rustic hospitality. There are magnificent grounds, a large pool, period furniture and frescoed ceilings. Activities on offer include trekking, wine tasting, cooking and photography courses and yoga.

PESARO: Bellevue €
Resort
Viale Trieste 88, 61121
Tel *0721 690 18*
🆆 bellevuehotel.net
Great value for this simple but accommodating beach resort.

DK Choice

PESARO: Alexander Museum Palace Hotel €€
Historic
Viale Trieste 20, 61121
Tel *0721 344 41*
🆆 alexandermuseum.it
As the name implies this unique accommodation is part museum, part hotel. Both established and emerging Italian artists have collaborated to transform this elegant hotel into a literal work of art. Each room is different and every single design element from the colours, to the chairs and floors is one of a kind. The sea views are a bonus.

SAN MARINO: Villa Giardi €
B&B
Via Palamede Ferri 22, 47890
Tel *0549 99 10 74*
Warm atmosphere and a handful of simple rooms.

Key to prices *see p562*

SAN MARINO: Cesare €€
Boutique
Salita alla Rocca 7, 47890
Tel *0549 99 23 55*
🅦 hotelcesare.com
This hotel blends convenience with refined elegance. Rooms are clean and bright. The staff is very attentive.

URBINO: Cà Andreana €
Agriturismo
Via Gadana 119, 61029
Tel *0722 32 78 45*
🅦 caandreana.it
This farmstay is located in a magnificent country setting with stunning views. Rooms are quaint and well-presented.

URBINO: Raffaello €
Rooms with a view
Via Santa Margherita 38, 61029
Tel *0722 47 84*
🅦 albergoraffaello.com
Situated near the famous artist's childhood home. Rooms are simple but inviting.

Rome

The Ancient Centre

Nicolas Inn €€
B&B **Map** 3 B5
Via Cavour 295, 00184
Tel *06 97 61 84 83*
🅦 nicolasinn.com
Basic service, but the rooms are pleasant and cosy, and all have en-suite bathrooms. The hosts are warm and friendly.

Fortyseven €€€
Rooms with a view **Map** 6 E1
Via Luigi Petroselli 47, 00186
Tel *06 678 78 16*
🅦 fortysevenhotel.com
Stellar views of the ancient city from this retro-styled hotel. Elegant rooms; there are two suites, both with private terraces.

Hotel Forum €€€
Rooms with a view **Map** 3 B5
Via Tor de' Conti 25, 00184
Tel *06 679 24 46*
🅦 hotelforum.com
Enjoy magnificent views of ancient Rome from a charming terrace. Graceful interiors and plenty of old-world charm.

Palazzo Manfredi €€€
Rooms with a view **Map** 7 A1
Via Labicana 125, 00184
Tel *06 77 59 13 80*
🅦 palazzomanfredi.com
The Colosseum seems close enough to touch at this hotel. Elegantly decorated rooms and excellent service.

Glass walls of the Alexander Museum Palace Hotel in Pesaro

Around Piazza Navona

Albergo Santa Chiara €€
Boutique **Map** 10 D3
Via di Santa Chiara 21, 00186
Tel *06 687 29 79*
🅦 albergosantachiara.com
The lobby is the most impressive part of this hotel, the rooms are pleasant but don't compare. Enjoy a drink in the alfresco bar.

Sole al Biscione €
Historic **Map** 9 C4
Via del Biscione 76, 00186
Tel *06 68 80 68 73*
🅦 solealbiscione.it
This basic but charming hotel claims to be the oldest in Rome.

Campo de'Fiori Hotel €€
Rooms with a view **Map** 9 C4
Via del Biscione 6, 00186
Tel *06 68 80 68 65*
🅦 hotelcampodefiori.com
Romantically decorated rooms with refined furnishings, and views of rooftops and domes.

Casa di Santa Brigida €€
Religious institution **Map** 9 B4
Via Monserato 54, 00186
Tel *06 68 89 25 96*
🅦 brigidine.org
Not the cheapest convent in town, but the location is worth the price. Clean and spacious rooms.

Due Torri €€
Historic **Map** 9 C1
Vicolo del Leonetto 23, 00186
Tel *06 68 80 69 56*
🅦 hotelduetorriroma.com
Small but lovely rooms in a converted Renaissance palace.

Portoghesi €€
Charming **Map** 10 D2
Via dei Portoghesi 1, 00186
Tel *06 686 42 31*
🅦 hotelportoghesiroma.it
Nestled in a quiet cobbled alley, this hotel has a charming breakfast terrace.

Teatro di Pompeo €€
Historic **Map** 9 C4
Largo del Pallaro 8, 00186
Tel *06 68 30 01 70*
🅦 hotelteatrodipompeo.it
Built on the ruins of Pompey's ancient theatre, this hotel has simple rooms and friendly staff.

Teatropace33 €€
Rooms with a view **Map** 9 C3
Via del Teatro Pace 33, 00186
Tel *06 687 90 75*
🅦 hotelteatropace.com
Excellent price-quality ratio at this charming Baroque-style hotel with elegant decor.

Albergo del Sole al Pantheon €€€
Rooms with a view **Map** 9 C4
Piazza della Rotonda 63, 00186
Tel *06 678 04 41*
🅦 solealpantheonrome.com
Unparalleled views of the bustling Piazza Navona, if you don't mind the noise.

Grand Hotel de La Minerve €€€
Luxury **Map** 10 D3
Piazza della Minerva 69, 00186
Tel *06 69 52 01*
🅦 grandhoteldelaminerve.com
Excellent views from nearly every room. The decor is luxurious and the service is excellent.

Locanda Cairoli €€€
Boutique **Map** 10 D4
Piazza Benedetto Cairoli 2, 00186
Tel *06 68 80 92 78*
🅦 hotelcairoliroma.com
Centrally located hotel with comfortable rooms. Spacious family-style breakfast room.

Raphael €€€
Romantic **Map** 9 C2
Largo Febo 2, 00186
Tel *06 68 28 31*
🅦 raphaelhotel.com
World-class service, gorgeous decor and a terrace with views.

For more information on types of hotels *see p561*

Charming outdoor garden area at Beehive, Northeast Rome

St George Hotel €€€
Luxury **Map** 9 A3
Via Giulia 62, 00186
Tel 06 68 66 11
W stgeorgehotel.it
This elegant five-star hotel offers rooms with contemporary design.

Northeast Rome

DK Choice

Beehive €
Budget **Map** 4 E3
Via Marghera 8, 00185
Tel 06 44 70 45 53
W the-beehive.com
A gem of a hotel with both private rooms and small dormitories available. Some rooms are en suite. Extras include yoga lessons, massage and a café serving organic food and drink.

Blue Hostel €
Budget **Map** 4 D4
Via Carlo Alberto 13, 00185
Tel 34 09 25 85 03
W bluehostel.it
A charming hotel with clean and spacious rooms.

Hostel des Artistes €
Budget **Map** 4 E2
Via Villafranca 20, 00185
Tel 06 445 43 65
W hostelrome.com
Friendly and clean, with private rooms and dorm accommodation.

DK Choice

Casa Howard €€
B&B **Map** 3 A3
Via di Capo le Case 18, 00187 & Via Sistina 149, 00187
Tel 06 69 92 45 55
W casahoward.com
This funky B&B, inspired by E. M. Forster's novel *Howard's End* comprises 10 uniquely decorated rooms in 2 adjacent locations.

Daphne Inn €€
B&B **Map** 3 B2
Via di San Basilio 55, 00187
Tel 06 87 45 00 86
W daphne-rome.com
Top-notch B&B with personal service and a modern look.

Deko Rome €€
Pensione **Map** 3 C1
Via Toscana 1, 00187
Tel 06 42 02 00 32
W dekorome.com
Small rooms in minimalist style; surprisingly luxurious bathrooms.

Hotel Suisse €€
Pensione **Map** 3 A2
Via Gregoriana 54, 00187
Tel 06 678 36 49
W hotelsuisserome.com
Great value at this elegantly appointed hotel.

Locarno €€
Historic **Map** 2 F1
Via della Penna 22, 00186
Tel 06 361 08 41
W hotellocarno.com
A masterpiece of Art Deco and the location for many classic films.

Piranesi €€
Boutique **Map** 2 F1
Via del Babuino 196, 00187
Tel 06 32 80 41
W hotelpiranesi.com
Quiet elegance in an ideal location. There's a roof garden, sauna and a solarium. It also has a small gym.

Residenza Cellini €€
Pensione **Map** 3 C3
Via Modena 5, 00184
Tel 06 47 82 52 04
W residenzacellini.it
Large, simply furnished rooms; some bathrooms have Jacuzzi tubs.

Aldrovandi Palace €€€
Luxury
Via Ulisse Aldrovandi 15, 00197
Tel 06 322 39 93
W aldrovandi.com

A spectacular five-star hotel with airy rooms, a swimming pool and views of the park.

Aleph €€€
Luxury **Map** 3 B2
Via di San Basilio 15, 00185
Tel 06 42 29 01
W aleph-roma.boscolohotels.com
Experience modern opulence at this relaxing, luxurious spa.

Babuino181 €€€
Boutique **Map** 2 F1
Via del Babuino 181, 00187
Tel 06 32 29 52 95
W romeluxurysuites.com
Splendid modern hotel with luxurious details. Set in a Renaissance palace with a leafy roof terrace.

Eden €€€
Luxury **Map** 3 B2
Via Ludovisi 49, 00187
Tel 06 47 81 21
W edenroma.com
A grand hotel with elegantly furnished rooms and a rooftop dining area. Service is exceptional.

es hotel €€€
Rooms with a view **Map** 4 E4
Via Filippo Turati 171, 00185
Tel 06 44 48 41
W radissonblu.com/eshotel-rome
Splendid five-star hotel with sleek modern design and all white rooms.

Exedra €€€
Luxury **Map** 3 C3
Piazza della Repubblica 47, 00185
Tel 06 48 93 81
W exedra-roma.boscolohotels.com
Lavish five-star hotel with plush rooms, a rooftop pool and an award-winning spa.

DK Choice

Hassler €€€
Luxury **Map** 3 A2
Piazza Trinità Dei Monti 6, 00187
Tel 06 69 93 40
W hotelhasslerroma.com
The discrete service, plush furnishings and stunning bedrooms make this a firm favourite with celebrities. Guests can also take advantage of the Michelin-stared Imàgora restaurant or enjoy a signature Venschuas cocktail in the Hassler Bar.

Hotel d'Inghilterra €€€
Romantic **Map** 3 A2
Via Bocca di Leone 14, 00187
Tel 06 69 98 11
W hoteldinghilterrarome.com

Spacious accommodation in an enviable location near the Spanish Steps. All the rooms and suites are individually styled..

Portrait Suites €€€
Boutique **Map** 3 A2
Via Bocca di Leone 23, 00187
Tel *06 69 38 07 42*
W lungarnocollection.com
Accommodation with style; owned by famed shoe designer Salvatore Ferragamo's family, and it shows.

Westin Excelsior €€€
Romantic **Map** 3 B2
Via Veneto 125, 00187
Tel *06 470 81*
W westinrome.com
This favourite with honeymooners is the perfect place to enact *la dolce vita*.

The Vatican and Trastevere

Arco del Lauro €
B&B **Map** 6 D1
Via dell'Arco de' Tolomei 27, 00153
Tel *06 97 84 03 50*
W arcodellauro.it
Tiny hotel in a picturesque medieval location with simple but lovely rooms.

Casa Internazionale delle Donne €
Budget **Map** 2 D5
Vicolo di San Francesco di Sales 47, 00165
Tel *06 68 89 24 65*
W casainternazionaledelledonne.org
Basic accommodation in a quiet but central area; women only.

Centro Diffusione Spiritualità €
Religious institution **Map** 2 D5
Via dei Riari 44, 00153
Tel *06 68 80 61 22*
Budget accommodation including breakfast and dinner. There is an 11pm curfew.

Domus Tiberina €
Budget **Map** 6 D1
Via in Piscinula 37, 00153
Tel *06 581 36 48*
W hoteldomustiberina.it
This tiny, quaint hotel is just steps from the Tiber. Offers simple rooms and continental breakfast.

Hotel Ottaviano €
Budget **Map** 1 C2
Via Ottaviano 6, 00192
Tel *06 39 73 81 38*
W pensioneottaviano.com
A few steps from the Vatican Museums, this hotel is a backpacker's paradise. Great views of St Peter's square.

Hotel Trastevere €
Budget **Map** 5 C1
Via Luciano Manara 24, 00153
Tel *06 581 47 13*
W hoteltrastevere.net
Simple, clean and large rooms at this hotel which offers good value for money. Good breakfast spread.

Bramante €€
Historic **Map** 1 C3
Vicolo delle Palline 24, 00193
Tel *06 68 80 64 26*
W hotelbramante.com
In the shadow of St Peter's, this family-run accommodation has quiet and tasteful rooms.

Relais Casa della Fornarina €€
Historic **Map** 2 D5
Via di Porta Settimiana 7, 00153
Tel *06 64 56 22 68*
W casadellafornarina.com
Guesthouse where Raphael's muse once lived. Spacious rooms and good service.

Sant'Anna €€
Boutique **Map** 1 C3
Borgo Pio 134, 00193
Tel *06 68 80 16 02*
W santannahotel.net
Modern convenience with an old-world feel. Rooms are spacious, and there is an exquisite courtyard.

DK Choice

Donna Camilla Savelli €€€
Romantic **Map** 5 B1
Via Garibaldi 27, 00153
Tel *06 58 88 61*
W hoteldonnacamillasavelli.com
Designed by Baroque genius Borromini, this meticulously restored monastery still belongs to the nuns of the original order, but is now a four-star hotel. The cloister is an oasis in the heart of the bustling city.

Chic and comfortable sitting area at Portrait Suites, Northeast Rome

Aventine and Lateran

Domus Aventina €€
Budget **Map** 5 E2
Via di Santa Prisca 11b, 00153
Tel *06 574 61 35*
W hoteldomusaventina.com
Simple but elegant rooms opening onto a lush courtyard. Rooms are quiet, and a number of attractions are in easy walking distance. Staff are welcoming and helpful.

Sant'Anselmo €€
Romantic **Map** 6 E3
Via Santa Melania 19, 00153
Tel *06 57 00 57*
W aventinohotels.com
Four-poster beds and clawfoot tubs are available at this simple and graceful hotel, on a residential street and close to many restaurants and sights. There is a lovely courtyard. Parking is free.

Villa San Pio €€
Romantic **Map** 6 E3
Via Santa Melania 19, 00153
Tel *06 57 00 57*
W aventinohotels.com
Quiet and secluded, but located conveniently in the city centre. Good breakfasts and drinks are taken in the lovely garden.

Lazio

BRACCIANO: Villa Clementina Spa & Resort €€
Spa hotel
Traversa Quarto del Lago 12, 00062
Tel *06 998 62 68*
W hotelvillaclementina.it
Beautifully frescoed rooms in lush surroundings with a large pool.

CERVETERI L'Isola di Rosa €€
Spa hotel
Via del Grano 20, 00052
Tel *06 99552819*
W isoladirosa.com
Old manor house with well appointed rooms.

FRASCATI: Poggio Regillo €
Agriturismo
Via Pietra Porzia 30, 00044
Tel *06 941 78 00*
W poggioregillo.it
An environmentally friendly hotel which offers excellent value for money. Pets welcome.

SPERLONGA: Grotta di Tiberio €€
Rooms with a view
Via Flacca km 15, 700, 04029
Tel *0771 54 81 37/0771 54 89 44*
W hotelgrottaditiberio.it
Charming beachside hotel with a large pool. Rooms are spacious.

For more information on types of hotels *see p561*

TARQUINIA: Casale Poggio Nebbia €
Agriturismo
S.S. Aurelia km 84, 100, Loc. Farnesiana, 01016
Tel *0766 84 12 68*
Ⓦ poggionebbia.it
Relaxing farm stay nestled in a valley and popular with Italians. Ideal for families.

TARQUINIA: Hotel all'Olivo €
Budget
Via Palmiro Togliatti 15, 01016
Tel *0766 85 73 18*
Ⓦ allolivo.it
Old-fashioned hotel in the countryside with an excellent traditional restaurant.

TIVOLI: Palazzo Maggiore €
B&B
Via Domenico Giuliani 89, 00019
Tel *393 104 49 37*
Ⓦ palazzomaggiore.com
This sweet hotel provides the perfect base to explore Tivoli.

TIVOLI: Grand Hotel Duca d'Este €€
Business
Via Tiburtina Valeria 330, 00019
Tel *0774 38 83*
Ⓦ ducadeste.com
Large, comfortable hotel with fully equipped wellness centre.

VITERBO: Hotel Viterbo Best Western €
Budget
Via San Camillo de Lellis 6, 01100
Tel *0761 27 01 00*
Ⓦ hotelviterbo.com
Comfortable hotel with good service and an abundant breakfast.

VITERBO: Niccolò V €€
Spa hotel
Strada Bagni 12, 01100
Tel *0761 35 01*
Ⓦ termedeipapi.it
Historic thermal baths and wellness centre in an elegant four-star hotel.

Outdoor pool beside the beach at Grotta di Tiberio hotel in Lazio

Naples and Campania

AMALFI COAST: Hotel Desirée €
Rooms with a view
Via Capo 31, 80067
Tel *081 878 15 63*
Ⓦ desireehotelsorrento.com
This simple, cliff-side hotel offers excellent value. There's an elevator to a small private beach.

AMALFI COAST: Antica Repubblica €€
Boutique
Vico dei Pastai 2, 84011
Tel *089 873 63 10*
Ⓦ anticarepubblica.it
A charming hotel with elegantly furnished rooms and a terrace.

AMALFI COAST: Miramare €€
Rooms with a view
Via Trara Genoino, 84017
Tel *089 87 50 02*
Ⓦ miramarepositano.it
Rooms are brightly decorated and have views looking out over Positano and the ocean beyond.

AMALFI COAST: Bellevue Syrene €€€
Luxury
Piazza della Vittoria 5, 80067
Tel *081 878 10 24*
Ⓦ bellevue.it
A dreamy 18th-century villa with a flowering terrace and private beach access.

AMALFI COAST: La Sirenuse €€€
Luxury
Via Cristoforo Colombo 30, 84017
Tel *089 87 50 66*
Ⓦ sirenuse.it
World-class hotel with spectacular views of Sorrento and the coast.

CAPRI: Bellavista €€
Boutique
Via Giuseppe Orlandi 10, 80071
Tel *081 837 14 63/081 837 18 21*
Ⓦ bellavistacapri.com

Enjoy the spectacular views from this sweet 1960s-style hotel.

CAPRI: Grand Hotel Quisisana €€€
Luxury
Via Camerelle 2, 80073
Tel *081 837 07 88*
Ⓦ quisisana.com
Deluxe accommodation in an extraordinary setting.

CASERTA: Amadeus €
Boutique
Via Giuseppe Verdi 72/76, 81100
Tel *0823 35 26 63*
Ⓦ hotelamadeuscaserta.it
A centrally located, comfortable hotel with spacious rooms.

DK Choice

ISCHIA AND PROCIDA: Miramare €€
Spa hotel
Via Maddalena Comandante 29, Sant'Angelo, 80070
Tel *081 99 92 19*
Ⓦ hotelmiramare.it
This gorgeous old-world hotel is perched on the rocks right over the Tyrrhenian Sea. The lovely rooms, most with canopy beds and balconies, all face the sea. A short walk leads to the spa complex with thermal pools and a private beach. The ample breakfast is served on a flowering terrace with spectacular views.

NAPLES: Decumani €€
Historic
Piazzetta Giustino Fortunato 8, 80100
Tel *081 420 13 79/081 410 91 44*
Ⓦ palazzodecumani.com
Tasteful furnishings and elegant bathrooms in a Baroque palace.

NAPLES: Grand Hotel Vesuvio €€€
Rooms with a view
Via Partenope 45, 80121
Tel *081 764 00 44*
Ⓦ vesuvio.it
Sumptuous lodgings with views of the gulf and Castel dell'Ovo.

SALERNO: Hotel dei Templi €€
B&B
Via Tavernelle 64, 84063
Tel *082 881 17 47*
Ⓦ www.hoteldeitempli.it
Stylish hotel located minutes from the ruined temples at Paestum.

SALERNO: Lloyd's Baia €€
Rooms with a view
Via Enrico de Marinis 2, 84013
Tel *089 763 31 11*
Ⓦ lloydsbaiahotel.it
Lovely hotel hanging over a cliff offering remarkable views.

Abruzzo, Molise and Puglia

DK Choice

ALBEROBELLO: B&B Fascino Antico €
Historic
Strada Statale 172, 74015
Tel *080 432 50 89*
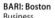 fascinoantico.eu
At this charming B&B, you can lodge a 19th-century huts without losing the comforts of a modern holiday. Surrounded by centuries-old olive trees, the stone-built apartments face a large courtyard, and there is an outdoor pool.

BARI: Boston €
Business
Via Niccolò Piccinni 155, 70122
Tel *080 521 66 33*
w bostonbari.it
Functional and comfortable rooms in a convenient location.

ISOLE TREMITI: Baely Resort €€
Resort
Via Matteotti, 71040
Tel *0882 46 37 67*
w baely.it
Intimate hotel with comfortable, distinctively decorated rooms.

L'AQUILA: Magione Papale €€
Boutique
Via Porta Napoli 67, 67100
Tel *0862 41 49 83/0862 42 21 94*
w magionepapale.it
Set in a restored mill, this is quaint country inn has plenty of character.

Basilicata and Calabria

MARATEA: La Locanda delle Donne Monache €€
Romantic
Via Carlo Mazzei 4, 85046
Tel *0973 87 61 39*
w locandamonache.com
Spacious, bright rooms at this lovely former convent.

DK Choice

MATERA: Sassi Hotel €
Historic
Via San Giovanni Vecchio 89, 75100
Tel *0835 33 10 09*
w hotelsassi.it
Matera's famous rock dwellings make an evocative setting for this one-of-a-kind hotel. Each

Ultra-modern lounge area of Riva del Sole in Cefalù

room is carved into the mountain, with distinctive vaulted stone ceilings and panoramic views of the medieval town below. Furnishings are simple and classic, letting the natural elements of the 18th-century building shine.

MELFI: Relais la Fattoria €
Agriturismo
Località la Cavallerizza, 85025
Tel *0972 247 76*
w relaislafattoria.it
A country inn set amid olive trees and vineyards. Charming rooms.

TROPEA: Cala di Volpe €€
Resort
Località Torre Marino, 89865
Tel *0963 66 92 22/0963 66 96 99*
w caladivolpe.it
A beautiful seaside resort surrounded by a lush tropical garden. A short walk to the beach.

Sicily

AGRIGENTO: Camere del Sud €
B&B
Via Ficani, 92100
Tel *349 638 44 24*
w camereasud.it
Warm, simple rooms in this sunny B&B. Friendly, helpful owners.

CEFALÙ: Riva del Sole €€
Rooms with a view
Lungomare Giardina 25, 90015
Tel *0921 42 12 30*
w rivadelsole.com
A modern hotel ideally located between the sea and city centre.

ERICE: Elimo €€
Rooms with a view
Via Vittorio Emanuele 73, 91016
Tel *0923 86 93 77*
w hotelelimo.it
Small but lovely rooms with panoramic views of the countryside.

PALERMO: Principe di Villafranca €€€
Luxury
Via Giuseppina Turrisi Colonna 4, 90141
Tel *091 611 85 23*
w principedivillafranca.it
Elegant hotel full of intricate details, antique art and furnishings.

Sardinia

ALGHERO: Villa Las Tronas €€€
Spa hotel
Lungomare Valencia 1, 07041
Tel *079 98 18 18*
w hotelvillalastronas.it
Scenic views at this elegant hotel, with indoor and outdoor pools.

CAGLIARI: T Hotel €€
Design
Via dei Giudicati 66, 09131
Tel *070 474 00*
w thotel.it
Modern design hotel with large rooms and a fitness centre.

COSTA SMERALDA: Nibaru €€
Resort
Località Cala di Volpe
Tel *0789 960 38*
w hotelnibaru.it
A tranquil oasis a short walk from the sea. Comfortable and clean rooms, and a lovely pool.

COSTA SMERALDA: Pitrizza €€€
Luxury
Via Nazionale 35, 07020
Tel *0789 93 01 11*
w pitrizzahotel.com
A grand hotel with fabulous amenities and breathtaking views.

SASSARI: Grazie Deledda €
Business
Viale Dante 47, 07100
Tel *079 27 12 35*
w hotelgraziadeledda.it
Remarkable low prices for this large and comfortable hotel.

For more information on types of hotels *see p561*

WHERE TO EAT AND DRINK

Food is a serious subject in Italy. The Italians are justly proud of their fine cuisine and wines and many sociable hours are spent around the table. One of the great pleasures of travelling in Italy is sampling regional variations in pasta, breads and cheeses. You don't have to head to the most expensive places for good food; a simple *trattoria*, which serves the local clientele, will often produce a better meal than the nearby international restaurant. However, whether it is a crowded *osteria*, a local *pizzeria* or a terrace with sea views, this introduction gives plenty of practical tips on types of restaurants, ordering and service to help you enjoy eating out in Italy.

Places to Eat

Traditionally a *trattoria* and an *osteria* are cheaper and more casual alternatives to the smarter *ristorante*.

A *pizzeria* is usually a cheap place to eat (as little as €18 with beer) and many serve pasta, meat and fish dishes as well as pizzas. *Pizzerie* are often open in the evening only, especially those with wood-fired ovens (*forno a legna*).

A *birreria* is another cheap option, serving pasta and snacks such as sausages and burgers. An *enoteca*, or *vineria*, will offer a selection of wines to try, along with a range of light dishes. Prices vary and tend to be relatively expensive for the quantities served.

At lunch time and in the early evening, *rosticcerie* sell roast chicken, slices of pizza (*pizza al taglio*) and other snacks to take away. *Pizza al taglio* can also be bought straight from the baker. Many bars offer filled rolls (*panini*) and sandwiches (*tramezzini*), and some also

A restaurant in Chioggia offering a cosy environment in a vaulted room

serve simple hot dishes from the *tavola calda* counter for around €8.

Stop at a *gelateria* for ice cream, with a sometimes bewildering choice of different flavours, or a *pasticceria* for one of a dazzling variety of sweet and savoury pastries, cakes and biscuits.

Opening Times

Lunch is generally served between 12:30pm and 2:30pm and, particularly in the south, all other activity stops between these hours. Dinner is at about 7:30pm and goes on until 11pm or later (in the south eating hours tend to be later). It is not unusual to see tables still full from lunch at 4pm or diners sipping *digestivi* well after midnight.

Reservations

Good restaurants in Italy are likely to be popular, so book a table in advance if you can (*prenotazione*). Otherwise, get there early to avoid having to queue. Many restaurants close one day a week and for a few weeks in either winter or the

Villa Crespi in Piedmont, inspired by the Arabian Nights (*see p588*)

summer holiday season; this information will be included in the list of restaurants on the pages that follow, but phone first if in doubt.

The Menu

Italian meals consist of three or four courses, and restaurants generally expect patrons to order at least two, though you should not feel obliged to do so. The *antipasto* (starter), is followed by the *primo*, of pasta, rice or soup. The *secondo* is the main meat or fish course, for which you will need to order vegetables (*contorni*) separately. Fruit (*frutta*), cheese (*formaggi*) or dessert (*dolce*) follow, with coffee and the preferred *digestivo* of the region to finish the meal.

Menus usually change with the season to make use of the freshest local produce, and the day's specials may be recited to you by the waiter rather than written down. Persevere, if you don't immediately understand, using the menu information at the beginning of each section. Try to avoid restaurants that do not state prices on their menus.

Vegetarians

Italian restaurants offer plenty of choices for vegetarians as the menu will always feature a selection of seasonal vegetables and pulses. Many pasta and *antipasto* dishes use no meat at all and for a main course you can ask for an omelette *(frittata)* with a side dish of vegetables from the *contorni*. Most menus are adaptable because dishes are prepared to order – tell your waiter that you are *vegetariano* (female – *vegetariana*) and they will advise you accordingly.

Wine and Drinks

Many regions have their own *aperitivo* served before the meal and a *digestivo* for afterwards. Universal alternatives are *prosecco* (dry, fizzy white wine) or an *analcolico* (non-alcoholic) aperitif, and *grappa* as a digestive. House wine (red or white) will be a simple local wine served by the litre or by the glass and will generally be perfectly palatable. In addition, all but the cheapest eateries have a range of other local and regional wines specially selected to accompany the food on the menu, with smarter establishments also offering foreign vintages.

Tap water *(acqua del rubinetto)* is always drinkable and often very good, but Italy has a large range of mineral waters. Fizzy ones *(frizzante)* may contain carbon dioxide, while *naturale* can mean still or naturally sparkling. If you particularly want a still water, ask for *non gassata*. Espresso bars usually charge more for table service.

Paying

Tax and service are usually included in the menu prices, but it is normal to leave a tip of around 10 per cent. Note that many restaurants include a cover charge *(coperto)*, on the bill *(il conto)*, which covers bread (whether you eat it or not) and is charged per person.

Credit cards are not always accepted in Italy, particularly in smaller towns, so it is wise to check before you order.

Diners enjoying a meal *al fresco* in Chianti, Tuscany

Dress

Italians generally tend to look smart but don't necessarily expect visitors to do the same. However, very scruffy or dirty clothes are unlikely to get you good, efficient or particularly friendly service.

Children

Children are welcome in all but the smartest establishments and restaurants are likely to be filled with extensive Italian families for Sunday lunch. Facilities such as high-chairs or special menus are rare, but most places will provide a small or half portion *(mezza porzione)*.

Smoking

Smoking is still popular in Italy. However, smoking laws now mean that all restaurants in the country are non-smoking establishments. Unless a smokers' room is provided, you should step outside if you want to light up.

Outdoor tables at the seafood restaurant Il Riccio on Capri *(see p600)*

Wheelchair Access

Few restaurants have special facilities for people in wheelchairs, but if you book in advance, the establishment can reserve a suitable table and be ready to help if necessary when you arrive.

The charming interior of U'Giancu in Rapallo, Liguria *(see p590)*

Recommended Restaurants

The restaurants listed in this guidebook cover a wide range of eateries, from the simple *pizzeria* and *tavola calda* (cafeteria) to family-run *trattoria* and elegant *ristorante*. Each restaurant has a cuisine type listed beneath the name of the establishment. Most of these descriptions are self explanatory but the *Places to Eat* section will provide more information on what you can expect from the menu.

The DK Choice label means the restaurant has outstanding qualities and is highly recommended. It may serve delicious local dishes, offer excellent value for money, be in a beautiful location, have a romantic atmosphere or be particularly charming. Whatever the reason it is a guarantee of a great meal.

Where to Eat and Drink

Venice

BURANO: Da Romano €€
Seafood
Via Piazza Galuppi 221, 30012
Tel *041 73 00 30* **Closed** *Sun dinner, mid-Dec–Jan: Tue*
A wide range of fish dishes served in the traditional Venetian fashion. Advance booking advised.

DK Choice

BURANO-MAZZORBO:
Venissa €€€
Modern Italian
Fondamenta Santa Caterina 3, 30170
Tel *041 527 22 81* **Closed** *Mon; Nov: Mon, Tue, Wed; Dec–Mar*
Dine at the elegant Venissa restaurant for an extra special gastronomic experience. The menu features a wide selection of seafood, meat and vegetarian options using fresh, seasonal ingredients grown in the restaurant's own garden. The menu changes daily.

CANNAREGIO: Osteria al Timon €
Regional Italian **Map** 2 E3
Fondamenta Ormesini 2754, 30121
Tel *041 524 60 66* **Closed** *Wed, 2 wks Oct*
Fantastic range of *cicchetti* (finger food) to accompany a glass of wine, but also good meat dishes.

CANNAREGIO:
Trattoria da Gigio €
Regional Italian **Map** 2 D3
Rio Terrà San Leonardo 1594, 30121
Tel *041 71 75 74* **Closed** *Sun, Mon dinner*
Seafood is a popular option here, as are the generous hors d'oeuvres.

DK Choice

CANNAREGIO: Osteria da Rioba €€
Seafood
Fondamenta della Misericordia 2553, 30121
Tel *041 524 43 79* **Closed** *Mon*
Charming canal-side restaurant specializing in fish. Friendly and knowledgeable staff. Try the seafood mosaic. Reservations are recommended.

CANNAREGIO:
Osteria l'Orto dei Mori €€
Regional Italian **Map** 2 F3
Campo dei Mori 3386, 30121
Tel *041 524 36 77* **Closed** *Tue*

This off-the-beaten-track *osteria* has a refined take on local cuisine. Elegant Modernist interiors.

CANNAREGIO: Vini da Gigio €€
Regional Italian **Map** 3 A4
Fondamenta San Felice 3628A, 30121
Tel *041 528 51 40* **Closed** *Mon, Tue; mid-Jan–first wk Feb, 2 wks Aug*
The menu largely depends on what Rialto market has to offer that morning. Booking is advised.

CANNAREGIO:
Fiaschetteria Toscana €€€
Seafood **Map** 3 B5
Salizzada San Giovanni Grisostomo 5719, 30121
Tel *041 528 52 81* **Closed** *Tue, Wed lunch; end Jul–mid-Aug, 1 wk Dec*
Try the delectable warm octopus salad and the turbot in caper sauce. Book ahead.

CASTELLO:
Enoteca La Mascareta €
Enoteca **Map** 7 C1
Calle Santa Maria Formosa 5183, 30122
Tel *041 523 07 44* **Closed** *lunch*
Wine expert Mauro Lorenzon provides some delicious food to accompany the excellent drinks.

CASTELLO: Al Covo €€
Seafood **Map** 8 E2
Campiello della Pescaria 3968, 30122
Tel *041 522 38 12* **Closed** *Wed, Thu; 2 wks Jan, 1 wk Aug*
Tucked away behind the Arsenale boat strip, Al Cova has interesting tasting menus.

CASTELLO: Da Remigio €€
Seafood **Map** 8 D2
Salizzada dei Greci 3416, 30122
Tel *041 523 00 89* **Closed** *Mon dinner, Tue; 2 wks Jan–Aug; 3 wks Dec–Jan*
Book early as space is limited. Specials include the fish and shellfish risotto.

CASTELLO:
Ristorante Giorgione €€
Regional Italian **Map** 8 F3
Via Garibaldi 1533, 30122
Tel *041 522 87 27* **Closed** *Wed; 2 wks Nov*
Great neighbourhood *trattoria* serving flavoursome fish dishes, including lasagne and risotto.

CASTELLO: Ristorante Wildner €€
Regional Italian **Map** 8 D2
Riva degli Schiavoni 4161, 30122
Tel *041 522 74 63* **Closed** *Tue; 3 wks Jan*
Fresh fish, locally grown organic vegetables and an interesting wine list at this restaurant.

CASTELLO:
Osteria di Santa Marina €€€
Regional Italian **Map** 3 B5
Campo Santa Marina 5911, 30122
Tel *041 528 52 39* **Closed** *Sun, Mon lunch; 2 wks Jan, 2 wks Aug*
A restaurant with a reputation for its creative take on local cuisine.

DORSODURO: La Rivista €
Vegetarian **Map** 6 E4
Rio Terrà Foscarini 979/A, 30123
Tel *041 240 14 25* **Closed** *Mon; 2 wks Jan*
A welcoming restaurant offering salads and cold platters for lunch.

DORSODURO: Ai Gondolieri €€
Regional Italian **Map** 6 F4
San Vio 366, 30123
Tel *041 528 63 96* **Closed** *Tue; 1 wk Aug: lunch; 25 Dec.*
Here, regional meat and vegetable dishes are served with flair.

GIUDECCA: Trattoria Altanella €€
Regional Italian
Rio del Ponte Lungo 268, 33035
Tel *041 522 7780* **Closed** *Mon, Tue.*
A charming canalside restaurant run by the same family for four generations.

GIUDECCA: Cipriani €€€
Fine dining
Giudecca 10, 30133
Tel *041 520 77 44* **Closed** *Nov–Mar*
Guests are ferried from the San Marco waterfront to these exclusive island hotel restaurants.

Spectacular setting of one of the waterfront restaurants at Cipriani, Giudecca

SAN MARCO: Acqua Pazza €€
Seafood **Map** 7 A2
Campo Sant'Angelo 3808, 30124
Tel *041 277 06 88* **Closed** *Mon;*
Jan–Feb
This is where the Amalfi Coast
meets Venice. A different take on
fish, with wines to match.

**SAN MARCO: Gran Caffè
e Ristorante Quadri** €€€
Fine dining **Map** 7 B2
Piazza San Marco 121, 30124
Tel *041 522 21 05* **Closed** *Mon*
Fantastic historic site now in the
capable, creative hands of star
chef Massimiliano Alajmo.

**SAN MARCO:
Trattoria Do Forni** €€€
Fine dining **Map** 7 B2
Calle dei Specchieri 468, 30124
Tel *041 523 21 48*
Two dining areas with different
decors serve careful interpreta-
tions of classic Venetian cuisine.

SAN POLO: Muro €
Pizzeria **Map** 6 E1
Rio Terà dei Frari 2604, 30125
Tel *041 524 53 10* **Closed** *Thu*
A branch of the Muro pizza
restaurants, popular with young
locals. Mega salads also available,
along with a wide selection of
beer on tap.

SAN POLO: Osteria da Fiore €€€
Fine dining **Map** 6 D1
Calle del Scaleter 2202, 30125
Tel *041 72 13 08* **Closed** *Sun, Mon;*
8–22 Jan; 3 wks Aug
Many deem this as the city's best
restaurant. Seasonal produce is
the rule. Leave room for dessert.

**SANTA CROCE:
Enoteca al Prosecco** €
Enoteca **Map** 2 E3
*Campo San Giacomo dell'Orio
1503, 30135*
Tel *041 524 02 22* **Closed** *Sun;*
Jan, Aug
Enjoy light meals indoors or
outside in the square, with a
glass of excellent wine.

SANTA CROCE: Il Rèfolo €
Pizzeria **Map** 2 E5
Campo del Piovan 1459, 30135
Tel *041 524 00 16* **Closed** *Mon,*
Tue lunch; Jan
Set in a picturesque square, this
modern establishment serves
innovative gourmet pizzas.

**SANTA CROCE:
Osteria La Zucca** €
Regional Italian **Map** 2 E5
Ponte del Megio 1762, 30135
Tel *041 524 15 70* **Closed** *Sun*
Pretty canalside restaurant popular
with Venetians as well as visitors.

Tasteful interiors and charming garden at Villa Cipriani, Asolo

**SANTA CROCE:
Antiche Carampane** €€€
Seafood **Map** 2 F5
Rio Terà Carampane 1911, 30125
Tel *041 524 01 65* **Closed** *Sun, Mon;*
10 days Jan, 3 wks Aug
Seek out this local favourite, for
great fish and pasta dishes.

TORCELLO: Locanda Cipriani €€€
Fine dining
Piazza Santa Fosca 29, 30012
Tel *041 73 01 50* **Closed** *Tue; Jan–Feb*
Charming and exclusive island
restaurant with a shady courtyard.

The Veneto and Friuli

ARCO: Alla Lega €
Regional Italian
Via Vergolano 8, 38062
Tel *046 451 62 05* **Closed** *Nov: Wed*
Lively restaurant serving traditional
regional fare. Housed in a rustic
18th-century building with a
lovely courtyard.

ASOLO: Locanda Baggio €€
Regional Italian
*Via Bassane 1, Località Casonetto,
31011*
Tel *0423 52 96 48* **Closed** *Mon*
Changing seasonal menu with
innovative interpretations of
traditional fare. Cooking classes
are also available.

ASOLO: Villa Cipriani €€€
Fine dining
Via Canova 298, 31011
Tel *0423 52 34 11*
A hotel restaurant offering
creative cuisine, and overlooking
a glorious garden with breath-
taking views of the hills below.

**BASSANO DEL GRAPPA:
Osteria Trinità** €
Regional Italian
Contrà San Giorgio 17, 36061
Tel *0424 50 37 00* **Closed** *Wed,*
Sat lunch

Traditional eatery serving Venetian
classics such as *pasta e fagioli*
(bean and pasta soup) and
baccalà (cod) in various forms.

**BASSANO DEL GRAPPA:
Pulierin Enotavola** €
Enoteca
*Strada Soarda 26, San Michele,
36061*
Tel *042 450 55 62* **Closed** *Sat
lunch, Sun*
A wine-tasting facility in a lovely
rural setting serving food based
on local products.

**BELLUNO:
Ristorante Terracotta** €
Regional Italian
Borgo Garibaldi 61, 32100
Tel *043 729 16 92* **Closed** *Tue, Wed
lunch; Aug*
Friendly family-run restaurant
specializing in regional seasonal
dishes. Delicious selection of
desserts and extensive wine list.

CASTELFRANCO: Barbesin €€
Regional Italian
*Via Montebelluna di Salva Rosa 41,
31033*
Tel *042 349 04 46* **Closed** *Sun dinner,
2 wks Jan, 2 wks Aug*
Dishes based on local radicchio
predominate, but there are also
mixed grills and salted cod in the
Vicenza tradition.

CHIOGGIA: Osteria Penzo €
Seafood
Calle Larga Bersaglio 525, 30015
Tel *041 400992* **Closed** *Mon dinner,
Tue*
The place for traditional fare such
as squid with peas or gnocchi with
onions, mussels and red chicory.

CHIOGGIA: La Taverna €€
Seafood
Via Felice Cavallotti 348, 30015
Tel *041 40 18 06* **Closed** *Wed; mid-
Jan–mid-Feb*
Classic seafood dishes in an
elegant setting. The outdoor
tables look over the main square.

CIVIDALE DEL FRIULI:
Al Castello   €
Regional Italian
Via del Castello 12, 33043
Tel *043 273 32 42*   **Closed** *Wed;*
2 weeks Aug
Set in a magnificent castle, the
menu boasts traditional dishes
and fine local wines.

CONEGLIANO: Al Salisa   €€
Regional Italian
Via XX Settembre 2–4, 31015
Tel *0438 242 88*   **Closed** *Tue dinner,*
Wed; last 2 wks Jun
An elegant restaurant housed in
a medieval building. Serving
fresh fish, game and even sushi.

CORMONS: Ristorante al
Cacciatore – La Subida   €€€
Regional Italian
Via Subida 52, 34071
Tel *048 16 05 31*   **Closed** *lunch: Mon,*
Thu, Fri; Tue, Wed; 2 wks Feb
Inventive Friulian and Slovenian
menu that changes with the
seasons. Beautiful country setting.

CORTINA D'AMPEZZO:
Baita Fraina   €
Regional Italian
Località Fraina 1, 32043
Tel *0436 36 34*   **Closed** *low season:*
Mon; after Easter–Jun, Oct–Nov
Attractive wood-panelled B&B
with an on-site restaurant,
panoramic terrace and a
spacious play area for kids.

CORTINA D'AMPEZZO:
Ristorante El Zoco   €€
Regional Italian
Località Cademai 18, 32043
Tel *043 686 00 41*   **Closed** *Mon;*
May, Nov
Small but cosy restaurant on the
outskirts of trendy Cortina. Good
grilled meats and fresh vegetables.

FUMANE: Ristorante Scamperle
alla Rosa   €
Regional Italian
Via Incisa 8, 37022
Tel *045 770 10 06* **Closed** *low season:*
Mon, 1st wk Jul, 2nd wk Jan

One of the oldest restaurants in
the Valpolicella. All pasta, bread
and pastries are made on site.

GARDA:
Locanda San Vigilio   €€
Traditional Italian
Punta San Vigilio, 37016
Tel *045 725 66 88*   **Closed** *mid-Nov–*
end Mar
Five centuries of experience in
delighting guests with excellent
food, wine and gorgeous views.

GRADO: Trattoria de Toni   €€
Seafood
Piazza Duca d'Aosta 37, 34073
Tel *043 18 01 04*   **Closed** *Wed,*
Dec–Feb
The house speciality here is
boreto alla gradese, a delicious
fish stew cooked in vinegar.

GRANCONA: Isetta   €
Regional Italian
Via Pederiva 96, 36040
Tel *044 488 99 92* **Closed** *Tue dinner,*
Wed; 1 wk Jan
Pretty restaurant in a hilly area
outside Vicenza. Regional food,
with emphasis on grilled meats.

LONIGO: La Peca   €€€
Fine dining
Via Giovanelli 2, 36045
Tel *044 483 02 14*   **Closed** *Sun, Mon;*
1 wk mid-Aug
Traditional ingredients revisited
with inventive flair. Similar mixture
of classic and creative in the decor.

MESTRE: La Vivanderia   €
Regional Italian
Via Pasqualigo 59/H, 30175
Tel *041 61 07 42*   **Closed** *Sat lunch;*
Jun–Aug: Sun; Sep–May: Thu
Dishes based on seasonal
ingredient are the focus at this
osteria. Limited but excellent
wine selection.

MIANE: Da Gigetto   €
Regional Italian
Via De Gasperi 5, 31050
Tel *043 896 00 20*   **Closed** *Mon*
dinner, Tue; 2 wks Jan, 3 wks Aug

An elegant take on traditional
dishes made with seasonal
ingredients, including pumpkin
and mushrooms in autumn.

MONTECCHIA DI CROSARA:
Ristorante Cassandra   €€
Regional Italian
Via Cabalao 11, 37030
Tel *045 745 02 22*   **Closed** *Sun*
dinner, Mon
A refined country restaurant with
a modern, interesting menu and
an oustanding wine list.

NOVENTA PADOVANA:
Boccadoro   €€
Regional Italian
Via della Resistenza 49, 35027
Tel *049 62 50 29*   **Closed** *Wed; 3 wks*
Aug, 27 Dec–6 Jan
Quietly elegant family-run
restaurant offering well-balanced
fish and meat dishes.

PADUA: Da Giovanni   €
Regional Italian
Via Pietro Maroncelli 22, 35129
Tel *049 77 26 20*   **Closed** *Sat lunch,*
Sun; Aug, 1 week Christmas
Time-honoured *trattoria* offering
classics such as home-made
pasta, risotto and meat stews.

PADUA: Trattoria San Pietro   €
Regional Italian
Via San Pietro 95, 35139
Tel *049 876 03 30*   **Closed** *Sun, Jul*
The perfect place for regional
dishes cooked with fresh local
ingredients. Informal atmosphere.

RUBANO: Le Calandre   €€€
Fine dining
Via Liguria 1, 35030
Tel *049 630303*   **Closed** *Sun, Mon;*
2 wks Jan, 2 wks Aug
The cuisine at this three-Michelin-
starred restaurant will enchant
the senses.

DK Choice

SAN GIORGIO DI
VALPOLICELLA: Trattoria
Dalla Rosa Alda   €
Regional Italian
Strada Garibaldi 4, 37015
Tel *045 770 10 18*   **Closed** *Sun*
dinner, Mon; Jan–Feb
Nestled in a charming village
surrounded by vineyards, this
family-run *trattoria* has been
serving excellent traditional fare
for several generations. The
ingredients are carefully sourced
from local producers. The cellars
are full of carefully chosen wines,
from the Valpolicella region, to
accompany your meal. Guests
can eat alfresco on a beautiful
terrace, weather permitting.

Guests relaxing under the shade of umbrellas at Locanda San Vigilio in Garda

SANTA MARIA DI SALA:
Trattoria Barison €
Regional Italian
Via Ronchi 14, Borgoricco, 35010
Tel *049 579 80 63* **Closed** *Mon dinner, Tue; 2 wks Jan, 3 wks Aug*
Serves not only the traditional *baccalà*, but also grilled meats, cooked vegetables and wild salads.

SOLIGHETTO:
Locanda da Lino €
Regional Italian
Via Roma 19, 31053
Tel *043 88 21 50* **Closed** *Mon; last 2 wks Jul*
This restaurant is part of an inn overlooking the Prosecco hillsides. Home-made pasta and good grilled meats on offer.

TREVISO:
Antico Ristorante Beccherie €€
Regional Italian
Piazza Ancilotto 11, 31100
Tel *0422 54 08 71* **Closed** *Sun dinner, Mon; last 2 wks Jul*
The name is derived from a word in the local dialect that means "butcher's", so not surprisingly, meat is the speciality here.

TRIESTE: Antica Ghiacceretta €€
Regional Italian
Via dei Fornellli 2, 34121
Tel *040 322 03 07* **Closed** *Sun; 1 wk Feb, 1 wk Aug*
Enjoy fish dishes revisited with an inventive, light touch in a modern setting. Wines to match.

UDINE: Da Raffaele €
Pizzeria
Via Leonardo da Vinci 56, 33100
Tel *043 229 58 31* **Closed** *Wed lunch; 3 wks Jul-Aug*
More than just a classic pizzeria, this place boasts a traditional wood-fired oven and beer on tap.

DK Choice

UDINE: Agli Amici €€€
Fine dining
Via Liguria 252, 33100
Tel *043 256 54 11*
Closed *summer: Sun, Mon, Tue lunch, first 3 wks Aug; winter: Sun dinner, Tue lunch;*
Agli Amici whips up a cuisine that draws on local influences, traditions and ingredients and served with elegance. Sample one of the tasting menus for chance to taste a few dishes.

VALEGGIO SUL MINCIO:
Antica Locanda Mincio €
Traditional Italian
Via Michelangelo Buonarroti 12, 37067
Tel *045 795 00 59* **Closed** *Wed, Thu; 2 wks Feb, 2 wks Nov*

Frescoed walls, open fireplaces and an outdoor terrace. Specials include trout from Lake Garda.

VERONA: Al Bersagliere €
Regional Italian
Via Dietro Pallone 1, 37121
Tel *045 820 48 24* **Closed** *Sun, Mon*
This pleasantly informal, yet chic restaurant offers great risotto with Amarone and pasta dishes.

VERONA: Arche €€
Regional Italian
Via Arche Scaligere 6, 37121
Tel *045 800 74 15* **Closed** *Sun, Mon lunch; 2 wks Jan*
Established in 1879, this seafood restaurant serves unmatched marinated rock lobster.

VERONA: Il Desco €€€
Fine Dining
Via Dietro San Sebastiano 5-7, 37121
Tel *045 59 53 58* **Closed** *Sun, Mon; 2 wks Jun & Dec; Jul–Aug & Dec: Mon lunch*
This elegant Michelin-starred restaurant offers a creative take on traditional dishes.

VICENZA:
Antica Casa della Malvasia €
Regional Italian
Contrà delle Morette 5, 36100
Tel *044 454 37 04* **Closed** *Mon; 2 wks Jul*
Osteria serving pumpkin pancakes, local cheeses and cold cuts, and pork fillet with truffles.

VICENZA: Locanda Veneta €
Regional Italian
Via Battaglione Valtellina 138, 36100
Tel *044 456 80 07* **Closed** *Mon dinner, Sat lunch*
A wide range of fish and meat dishes is served at this family restaurant with a kids' play area.

Trentino-Alto Adige

DK Choice

BOLZANO: Cavallino Bianco €
Regional Italian
Via dei Bottai 6, 39100
Tel *0471 97 32 67* **Closed** *Sat dinner, Sun*
Also known by its German name, Weisses Rössl, this busy family restaurant serves traditional South Tyrol fare. A large-buffet breakfast is followed by good lunch options and a waiter-service dinner at this hotel restaurant. The gastronomic theme evenings are popular with the locals. Good value and speedy service.

Wood-beamed ceilings and soft lighting at the informal Al Bersagliere, Verona

BOLZANO: Forst €
Birreria
Goethestrasse 6, 39042
Tel *0471 97 72 43* **Closed** *Sun*
Popular restaurant serving not only the hallmark beer, but also good wines and excellent food.

BOLZANO: Hopfen & Co €
Birreria
Obstplatz 17, 39100
Tel *0471 30 07 88*
A sought-after brewery serving cold cuts, sausages and desserts.

BRESSANONE: Fink €
Regional Italian
Via Portici Minori 4, 39042
Tel *0472 83 48 83* **Closed** *Tue dinner, Wed; 3 wks May*
Dining areas comprise elegant seating upstairs, and more casual rooms on the ground floor. Classic local cuisine revisited with flair.

BRUNICO: Oberraut €
Regional Italian
Via Ameto 1, Località Amaten, 39031
Tel *0474 55 99 77* **Closed** *Thu; 2 wks Jan*
Nestled in the countryside, this Tyrolean-style guesthouse specializes in game and seasonal dishes.

CALDARO: Ristorante Ritterhof €
Regional Italian
Weinstrasse 1A, 39052
Tel *0471 96 33 30* **Closed** *Sun dinner; Mon*
Set in a charming chalet with views over the lake. Fine fare and seasonally changing menu.

CERMES: Restaurant Miil €€
Fine dining
Gampenstrasse 1, 39010
Tel *0473 56 37 33* **Closed** *Sun, Mon; 2 wks Jan*
Head to the Kränzelhof wine estate for a modern take on classic fare.

GUDON: Unterwirt   €€
Regional Italian
Chiusa (Klausen), 39043
Tel *0472 84 40 00*   **Closed** *Sun, Mon;*
2 wks mid-Jun
Chef Thomas Haselwanter's home-made breads are a tasty intro-duction to the seasonal menu.

LEVICO TERME: Boivin   €
Regional Italian
Via Garibaldi 9, 38056
Tel *0461 70 16 70*   **Closed** *lunch*
(except Sun, Jul, Aug), Mon; 2 wks Jan
Cosy *trattoria* serving classic dishes such as potato dumplings stuffed with cheese and walnuts.

ROVERETO: Novecento   €
Regional Italian
Corso Rosmini 82d, 38068
Tel *0464 43 54 54*   **Closed** *Sun*
Run by the Zani family, this restaurant is renowned for its home-made pasta and pizzas.

TRENTO: Happy Hour   €
Seafood
Via Perini 57, 38122
Tel *0461 39 23 94*   **Closed** *Sun dinner, Mon*
Pleasantly informal, with a menu that changes daily, according to the top picks from the fish market.

TRENTO:
Osteria Alle Due Spade   €€
Regional Italian
Via Don Rizzi 11, 38122
Tel *0461 23 43 43*   **Closed** *Sun, Mon lunch; last 2 wks Jun*
Welcoming cellar restaurant serving traditional fare including game and freshwater fish.

VAL SENALES:
Zur Goldenen Rose   €€
Regional Italian
Kartaus 29, 39020
Tel *0473 67 91 30*   **Closed** *20 Apr–25 May; 10 Nov–5 Dec*
Explore the surrounding countryside and then unwind at this excellent hotel restaurant.

Lombardy

BELLAGIO:
Albergo Ristorante Silvio   €
Regional Italian
Via Carcano 12, 22021
Tel *031 95 03 22*   **Closed** *Nov–mid-Mar*
Enjoy freshwater fish on a vine-clad terrace. Offers fishing trips.

BELLAGIO: Barchetta   €€
Regional Italian
Salita Mella 13, 22021
Tel *031 95 13 89*   **Closed** *Tue; Nov–Easter*

A creative Mediterranean menu, including fresh fish and home-made desserts.

BERGAMO:
Colleoni Dell'angelo   €€
Modern Italian
Piazza Vecchia 7, 24129
Tel *035 23 25 96*   **Closed** *Mon*
Offers excellent service and imaginative cuisine.

BERGAMO: Vineria Cozzi   €€
Enoteca
Via Colleoni 22, 24129
Tel *035 23 88 36*   **Closed** *1 wk end Jan, 1 wk Jun*
A century-old Bergamo favourite serving local dishes.

BERGAMO: Roof Garden   €€€
Mediterranean
Piazzale della Repubblica 6, 24122
Tel *035 36 61 59*   **Closed** *Sat lunch, Sun*
This rooftop restaurant offers great views, a fusion of world flavours and Mediterranean dishes.

BORMIO: Al Filò   €
Regional Italian
Via Dante 6, 23032
Tel *0342 90 17 32*   **Closed** *Mon & Tue lunch; 3 wks Jun, 3 wks Nov*
Dishes based on game, cured meats and mushrooms are served in a converted barn.

BRESCIA: Osteria Delle Streghe   €
International
Via Sorbana 72, 25125
Tel *030 32 12 15*   **Closed** *Sat lunch, Sun; 2 wks Aug, 2 wks Dec*
Serves grilled meats, including kangaroo. Reservation mandatory.

BRESCIA: Trattoria Mezzeria   €
Regional Italian
Via Trieste 66, 25121
Tel *030 40 306*   **Closed** *Sun, Aug*

The welcoming entrance to Barchetta, in Bellagio, which specializes in local cuisine

Try the home-made *gnocchi di zucca* (pumpkin dumplings) in this busy little *trattoria*.

CANTÙ: Le Querce   €
Modern Italian
Via Marche 27, 22063
Tel *031 73 13 36*   **Closed** *Mon, Tue; 3 wks Aug; 27 Dec–6 Jan*
Set amid oak and rhododendron, Le Querce serves local dishes and offers a rich selection of wines.

CASTELVECCANA:
Sant'Antonio   €
Traditional Italian
Località Sant'Antonio, 21010
Tel *334 276 65 85*   **Closed** *Sep–May (except weekends & hols)*
Trattoria set in an old farm house overlooking Lake Maggiore. Try the local cheeses and cured meats.

COMO: Al Giardino   €
Regional Italian
Via Monte Grappa 52, 22100
Tel *031 26 50 16*   **Closed** *Sun dinner, Mon; 2 wks Aug*
Child-friendly restaurant serving local and regional specialities.

DK Choice

COMO: L'Angolo Del Silenzio €
Regional Italian
Viale Lecco 25, 22100
Tel *031 377 21 57*   **Closed** *Mon & Tue lunch, 2 wks August*
This reasonably priced *osteria*, just a few steps from the cathedral and lake, offers home-made pasta, meat, game and fish dishes in a friendly atmos-phere. Try the wild boar with redcurrant sauce and Roquefort. An inexpensive one-dish lunch is available on weekdays and gluten-free dishes are available upon request. Book ahead.

COMO: Sant'anna 1907   €
Regional Italian
Via Turati 3, 22100
Tel *031 50 52 66* **Closed** *Sat lunch, Sun*
Creative local cuisine, including seafood and vegeatrian options.

CREMONA: Il Violino   €€
Traditional Italian
Via Sicardo 3, 26100
Tel *0372 46 10 10*   **Closed** *Tue*
Traditional local cuisine is served in this elegant restaurant.

GARGNANO DEL GARDA:
La Tortuga   €€
Modern Italian
Via XXIV Maggio 5, 25084
Tel *0365 712 51*   **Closed** *Tue; Mar–Oct: lunch*
Light imaginative cuisine in this renowned lakeside restaurant.

ISEO: Trattoria Al Castello €€
Modern Italian
Via Mirolte 53, 25049
Tel *030 98 12 85* **Closed** *Mon–Fri lunch, Wed; 2 wks Jan; 10 days Nov*
Classic and creative dishes in a restored 17th-century wine cellar in the historic centre of Iseo.

LAKE COMO:
Locanda dell'Isola Comacina €€
Seafood
Isola Comacina, 22010
Tel *034 455 083* **Closed** *Tue; Nov–Mar*
A unique experience on this wonderful island, deserted except for this spot serving fresh fish.

LECCO: Osteria del Filet €
Regional Italian
Corso Matteotti 71, 23900
Tel *0341 28 30 17* **Closed** *Jun–Sep: Sun; Oct–May: Thu*
Offers grilled meat, fish, and local salami. A fixed-price two-course lunch is offered on weekdays.

LECCO:
Antica Osteria Casa di Lucia €€
Fine dining
Via Lucia 27, Località Acquate, 23900
Tel *0341 49 45 94* **Closed** *Sat lunch, Sun; 2 wks Aug*
A superb gourmet restaurant set in a 17th-century house.

LEGNANO: Al Vintun Osteria €
Modern Italian
Via Bramante 95, 20025
Tel *0331 45 49 59* **Closed** *lunch, Sun*
Serves Italian fish and meat dishes. A fixed-price menu is offered every Thursday evening.

MANERBA DEL GARDA:
Capriccio €€€
Regional Italian
Piazza San Bernardo 6, Località Montinelle, 25080
Tel *0365 55 11 24* **Closed** *Tue; Jan–Feb*
Refined dining in an elegant setting with a breathtaking view from all tables of Lake Garda.

MANTUA:
Antica Osteria Ai Ranari €
Regional Italian
Via Trieste 11, 46100
Tel *0376 32 84 31* **Closed** *Mon*
Traditional Mantuan dishes, including the famous *tortelli di zucca* (pumpkin-filled pasta).

MANTUA: L'ochina Bianca €
Regional Italian
Via Finzi 2, 46100
Tel *0376 32 37 00* **Closed** *Mon–Thu lunch; Jul–Aug: Fri–Sun lunch*
Regional dishes with a modern touch; try the local *torta sbrisolona*, a classic Mantuan sweet cake.

Casual dining at Pasta Madre, near Porta Romana, Milan

MANTUA: Il Cigno Trattoria dei Martini €€
Modern Italian
Piazza Carlo D'Arco 1, 46100
Tel *0376 32 71 01* **Closed** *Mon, Tue; Aug*
Fine fare complemented by an impeccable wine list.

MILAN: Be Bop Ristorante €
Pizzeria
Viale Col di Lana 4, 20136
Tel *02 83 76 972* **Closed** *Aug*
This restaurant offers gluten-free and vegetarian pizzas.

MILAN: Bianco Latte €
Mediterranean
Via Turati 30, 20121
Tel *02 60 08 61 77* **Closed** *Mon dinner; 2 wks Aug*
Stop here for a hearty brunch or light dinner. Great bread selection and excellent coffee.

MILAN: Erba Brusca €
Mediterranean
Alzaia Naviglio Pavese 286, 20144
Tel *02 87 38 07 11* **Closed** *Mon, Tue*
This small restaurant has its own kitchen garden, where the creative cuisine can be enjoyed alfresco.

MILAN: Omelette E Baguette €
Bistro
Via Pollaiuolo 9, 20159
Tel *02 688 46 87* **Closed** *Mon; Aug*
Burgers, sandwiches, quiches and salads to have here or takeaway.

MILAN: Osteria Brunello €
Regional Italian
Corso Garibaldi 117, 20121
Tel *02 659 29 73* **Closed** *lunch; 2 wks Aug*
Dishes based on Tuscan traditions; try the *pappardelle* (broad, flat pasta) with wild boar.

MILAN: Pasta Madre €
Modern Italian
Via Bernardo Corio 8, 20135
Tel *02 55 19 00 20* **Closed** *Sun; Aug*

Contemporary decor with an relaxed atmosphere and creative Italian cuisine. Gluten-free desserts available.

MILAN: Premiata Pizzeria €
Pizzeria
Via Alzaia Naviglio Grande 2, 20144
Tel *02 89 40 06 48*
A great pizzeria with delicious toppings like salami, gorgonzola cheese and truffle oil. Casual dining on shared tables.

MILAN: Trattoria Aurora €
Traditional Italian
Via Savona 23, 20144
Tel *02 89 40 49 78* **Closed** *Mon*
This upmarket brasserie near the Navigli district offers hearty Piedmontese food. Finish your meal with a slice of *tiramisu*.

MILAN: U Barba €
Regional Italian
Via Decembrio 33, 20137
Tel *02 45 48 70 32* **Closed** *Mon, Tue–Fri lunch*
Friendly traditional Genoese *osteria* with a bocce ball court. Great fish and game dishes. Try the freshly made gnocchi.

MILAN:
Alla Cucina delle Langhe €€
Traditional Italian
Corso Como 6, 20144
Tel *02 65 54 279* **Closed** *Sun, last 3 wks Aug*
Delectable interpretations of classic Piedmontese fare, just a few steps from the outlet store 10 Corso Como.

MILAN: Da Giacomo €€
Regional Italian
Via Sottocorno 6, corner of Via B. Cellini, 20129
Tel *02 76 02 33 13* **Closed** *2 wks Aug, 2 wks Dec*
An insider Milanese address offering simply cooked fish and seafood in a friendly atmosphere.

For more information on types of restaurants *see p579*

Exquisite grounds of the lovely Locanda del Pilone di Alba, Alba

MILAN: Giglio Rosso €€
Fine dining
Piazza Luigi di Savoia 2, 20124
Tel *02 669 41 74* **Closed** *Sat & Sun lunch; Aug, 23 Dec–6 Jan*
This elegant restaurant offers innovative Tuscan dishes, staples such as variations of risotto, gnocchi and ravioli.

DK Choice

MILAN:
Nobile Bistrò de Milan €€
Regional Italian
Corso Venezia 45, 20121
Tel *02 49 52 65 92* **Closed** *2 wks Aug*
This reasonably priced restaurant is a short walk from the Montenapoleone shopping area. Well-known Milanese chef Claudio Sadler offers traditional regional meat and fish dishes with a modern twist. Continental breakfast, lunch, afternoon tea, *aperitivo* and dinner are all served in an informal atmosphere, with tables both indoors and in a private courtyard.

MILAN: Victoria €€
Pizzeria
Via Clerici 1, 20121
Tel *02 869 07 92*
A few steps behind La Scala, Victoria offers traditional fare and pizza in an Art Nouveau setting.

MILAN:
Il Ristorante Bulgari Hotel €€€
Fine dining
Via Privata Fratelli Gabba 7/B, 20122
Tel *02 80 50 52 33*
A luxury dining experience a few steps from Via Montenapoleone.

MONTE ISOLA: La Foresta €€
Regional Italian
Via Peschiera 174, Maraglio, 25050
Tel *030 988 62 10* **Closed** *Wed; 10 days Dec*

Family-run lakeside restaurant serving fresh Lake Iseo fish; sun-dried salted fish is a speciality.

PAVIA: Le Tre Torri €
Pizzeria
Via Lazzaro Spallanzani 6, 27100
Tel *0382 30 28 20* **Closed** *Sun, Mon, Sat lunch; Aug*
This restaurant offers a varied selection of pizza and pasta dishes.

PAVIA: La Locanda
Vecchia Pavia Al Mulino €€
Regional Italian
Via Al Monumento 5, Località Certosa, 27012
Tel *0382 92 58 94* **Closed** *Mon; Apr–Oct: Tue lunch; Nov–Mar: Sun dinner*
Located in the grounds of the Certosa di Pavia, with local specialities on offer.

SALÒ: Osteria dell'Orologio €
Traditional Italian
Via Butturini 26, 25087
Tel *0365 29 01 58* **Closed** *Wed, 1 wk end Jan; 1 wk end Nov*
This bistro offers great-value, traditional local cuisine and a reasonably priced wine list.

SALÒ:
Antica Trattoria alle Rose €€
Regional Italian
Via Gasparo da Salò 33, 25087
Tel *0365 432 20* **Closed** *Wed; Nov*
A traditional *trattoria* offering lake fish, local dishes and home-made pasta. There is a delicious selection of desserts.

SALÒ: La Campagnola €€
Modern Italian
Via Brunati 11, 25087
Tel *0365 22 153* **Closed** *Mon, Tue lunch*
One of the oldest establishments around Lake Garda, La Campagnola has a extensive selection of dishes, with a separate steak menu and an extensive wine list. Book ahead.

Valle d'Aosta and Piedmont

ACQUI TERME: La Schiavia €
Regional Italian
Vicolo della Schiavia, Acqui Terme, 15011
Tel *0144 559 39* **Closed** *Sun; 3 wks Aug*
Piedmontese and Ligurian cuisine in a renovated ancient palace. Extensive wine list. Booking compulsory.

ALBA:
Ristorante Madonna di Como €
Regional Italian
Frazione Madonna di Como 31, 12051
Tel *017 336 33 21* **Closed** *Tue*
Set in the hills above Alba and with panoramic views, this restaurant offers regional dishes.

DK Choice

ALBA:
Locanda del Pilone di Alba €€
Regional Italian
Strada della Cicchetta Frazione Madonna di Como 34, 12051
Tel *0173 36 66 16* **Closed** *Tue, Wed (Oct–Nov: Tue, Wed lunch); Jan–Feb*
Set in a stunning location, this converted *cascina* (barn) has views over the Alps. The menu features classic Piedmontese cuisine with touches of Neapolitan cooking. Each dish is served with a carefully selected wine. The wide range of desserts are delicious. Cookery classes and wine tasting is also provided.

ALBA: Piazza Duomo €€€
Regional Italian
Piazza Risorgimento 4, 12050
Tel *0173 36 61 67* **Closed** *Sun dinner, Mon; 2 wks Aug, 3 wks Dec–Jan*
Gourmet fare and impeccable service on offer near the main square of Alba.

ALESSANDRIA: Il Grappolo €€
Regional Italian
Via Casale 28, 15121
Tel *0131 25 32 17* **Closed** *Mon dinner, Tue*
Located in a 17th-century palace. Offers Piedmontese food with a modern twist; there's also a very good wine list.

AOSTA: Grotta Azzurra €
Pizzeria
Via Croce di Citta' 97, 11100
Tel *0165 26 24 74* **Closed** *Wed; Jul*
Reasonably priced pizzeria in the town centre. Varied menu features a delicious fish soup.

AOSTA:
Trattoria Degli Artisti €€
Regional Italian
Via Maillet 5-7, 11100
Tel *0165 40 96 04* **Closed** *Sun, Mon;*
15 days Jan, 15 days Nov
On a cobbled street in the town
centre, this *trattoria* offers a
regional menu and great home-
made cakes and desserts.

AOSTA: Il Vecchio Ristoro €€€
Regional Italian
Via Tourneuve 4, 11100
Tel *0165 332 38* **Closed** *Wed*
This restaurant in an old water mill,
uses local ingredients to make
creative dishes.

ARONA: Il Calicanto €€
Mediterranean
Piazza Nazario Sauro 6, 28041
Tel *0322 24 33 50* **Closed** *Mon*
A well-chosen wine list
accompanies fish and meat
dishes of high quality.

DK Choice

ARONA:
La Taverna del Pittore €€
Fine dining
Piazza del Popolo 39, 28041
Tel *0322 24 33 66* **Closed** *Mon*
With a verandah offering
stunning views of the Rocca di
Angera, this restaurant whips
up creative Italian cuisine using
seafood, fish, and meat. Dishes
include ravioli with truffles,
tagliolini with lobster sauce, and
grilled beef fillet with porcini
mushrooms. The menu is
presented on an artist's palette,
owing to the restaurant's past as
a meeting place for painters.

ASTI: L'Angolo del Beato €
Regional Italian
Vicolo Cavalleri 2, 14100
Tel *0141 53 16 68* **Closed** *Sun*
Family-run spot in a medieval
setting offering Piedmontese
dishes; try the varied antipasti.

ASTI: Gener Neuv €€
Traditional Italian
Lungo Tanaro dei Pescatori 4, 14100
Tel *0141 55 72 70* **Closed** *Sun,*
Mon dinner
Family-run restaurant near the
river with excellent local cuisine;
booking compulsory.

ASTI: Osteria da Marisa
al Castello €€
Regional Italian
Piazza Castello 1, 14100
Tel *0141 20 41 15* **Closed** *Mon, Tue*
Set in an 18th-century castle
overlooking the Monferrato hills.
Excellent Piedmontese cuisine.

BRA: Battaglino €
Regional Italian
Piazza Roma 18, 12042
Tel *0172 41 25 09* **Closed** *Sun*
dinner, Mon; 2 wks Jan, 3 wks Aug
Traditional Piedmontese meat
dishes offered in this convivial
restaurant in the heart of Bra.

BRA: Guido Ristorante €€
Regional Italian
Via Fossano 19, 12042
Tel *0172 45 84 22* **Closed** *Mon; Tue–*
Fri: lunch; 2 wks Jan, 1st wk Aug
Located inside the castle of
Pollenzo. Refined regional meat
and fish dishes a la carte, or a
high-price tasting menu.

BREUIL-CERVINIA:
Al Solito Posto €
Regional Italian
Via Meynet 10 11021
Tel *0166 94 91 26*
Charming, rustic restaurant with
a good fixed-price menu.

BREUIL-CERVINIA:
Les Neiges D'Antan €€
French
Cretes Perreres
Tel *0166 94 87 75* **Closed** *May–*
mid-Jun, mid-Sep–end Oct
This restaurant-cum-hotel serves
refined rustic and rich mountain
fare accompanied by great wines.

CANNOBIO: Del Lago €
Traditional Italian
Via Nazionale 2, Località Carmine
Inferiore, 28822
Tel *0323 705 95* **Closed** *Tue, Wed*
lunch; Nov
Simple yet imaginative dishes
and views of Lake Maggiore.

CANNOBIO: Osteria Vino
Divino €
Modern Italian
Strada Valle Cannobina 1, 28822
Tel *0323 719 19* **Closed** *Wed;*
Jan–Feb

Stunning views of the Rocca di Angera from
La Taverna del Pittore, Arona

Traditional dishes reinvented
with a twist in a converted 19th-
century stable block. Good wine.

CANNOBIO: Lo Scalo €€
Seafood
Piazza Vittorio Emanuele 32, 28822
Tel *0323 714 80* **Closed** *Apr & Oct:*
Wed; Nov–Easter
Daily catch of lake fish baked in
foil, plus an array of shellfish and
local produce.

CASALE MONFERRATO:
La Torre €€
Modern Italian
Via Candiani d'Olivola 36, 15033
Tel *0142 702 95* **Closed** *Tue, Wed*
lunch; 3 wks Aug
La Torre offers creative regional
cuisine and has a good wine list.

CHIUSA SAN MICHELE:
Ristorante Della Sacra €
Mediterranean
Piazzale della Sacra di San Michele,
10057
Tel *011 93 98 43* **Closed** *Apr–mid-*
Oct: Mon; mid-Oct–end Mar: Mon,
Tue, Wed
Good-quality café , hotel and
restaurant next to the famous
Sacra San Michele monastery.

COGNE: Lou Rossignon €
Traditional Italian
Rue Mines De Cogne 22, 11012
Tel *0165 740 34* **Closed** *Mon dinner,*
Tue (except Aug, Dec–Feb); May, Nov
Traditional Alpine and local fare
in a cosy mountain taverna.

COSSANO BELBO: Trattoria
Della Posta Da Camulin €
Regional Italian
Corsi Fratelli Negro 3, 12054
Tel *0141 881 26* **Closed** *Sun dinner,*
Mon; mid-Jul–mid-Aug
Friendly century-old *trattoria*
serving regional dishes and
home-made pasta.

COSTIGLIOLE D'ASTI:
Caffè Roma €
Traditional Italian
Piazza Umberto I 14, 14037
Tel *0141 96 65 44* **Closed** *Mon;*
1 wk end Feb, 1 wk Jun
A wine bar at the foot of the
castle with light dishes in a
cosy atmosphere.

COSTIGLIOLE D'ASTI:
Cascina Collavini €
Traditional Italian
Strada Traniera 24, 14037
Tel *0141 96 64 40* **Closed** *Tue dinner,*
Wed; 2 wks Jan, 2 wks Aug
Simple, elegant restaurant
located in an old farmhouse.
The menu features traditional
regional fare . Wines come
from the local vineyard.

For more information on types of restaurants *see p579*

COURMAYEUR: Du Tunnel €
Pizzeria
Via Circonvallazione 80, 11013
Tel *0165 84 17 05* **Closed** *winter:
Wed lunch*
A simple snack bar-pizzeria
offering wood-fired pizzas and
a convivial atmosphere.

**COURMAYEUR:
Cadran Solaire** €€
Traditional Italian
Via Roma 122,11013
Tel *0166 84 46 09* **Closed** *Tue; May,
2 wks Nov*
Local dishes including *risotto alla
Valdostana* (made with Fontina
cheese) served in a cosy setting.

**CUNEO:
Osteria Della Chiocciola** €
Regional Italian
Via Fossano 1, 12100
Tel *0171 662 77* **Closed** *Sun*
Top-quality regional cuisine.
Home-made classics such as
gnocchi, ravioli and risotto are
served with excellent wine.

**CUNEO:
La Ciau del Tornavento** €€
Regional Italian
Piazza Baracco 7, 12050
Tel *0173 63 83 33* **Closed** *Wed, Thu
lunch; Feb*
Piedmontese dishes are served in
a dining room with wonderful
views of rolling vineyards.

**DOMODOSSOLA: Antica
Ristorante Piemonte Da Sciolla** €
Regional Italian
Piazza della Convenzione 4, 28845
Tel *0324 24 26 33* **Closed** *Sun dinner,
Wed; 10 days Jan, 1 wk Aug, 1 wk Sep*
Known for its local mountain fare
of hearty meat and game dishes.

IVREA: Trattoria Boccon Divino €
Regional Italian
Via Aosta 47,10015
Tel *0125 489 98* **Closed** *Thu*
A small *trattoria* in the historic
centre of Ivrea serving traditional
regional cuisine.

NOVARA: I Due Ladroni €
Traditional Italian
Corso Cavallotti 15, 28100
Tel *0321 62 45 81* **Closed** *Sun*
Classic cuisine in a 16th-century
palazzo in the heart of town.
Excellent food with great flavours.

**NOVARA:
Osteria Del Laghetto** €€
Regional Italian
Via Case Sparse 11, 28100
Tel *0321 47 29 62* **Closed** *Sun;
10 days Aug; 24 Dec–7 Jan*
Truffles, mushrooms and fish are
on offer at this restaurant set in
its own grounds. Book ahead.

Rustic and charming entrance of
the popular Al Soriso, Soriso

**ORTA SAN GIULIO:
Ristoro Olina** €
Traditional Italian
Via Olina 40, 28016
Tel *0322 90 56 56* **Closed** *Wed;
mid-Nov–mid-Dec*
Serves home-made pasta. Local
mushrooms and truffles feature
on the menu as do fish dishes.

**ORTA SAN GIULIO:
Villa Crespi** €€€
Modern Italian
Via Fava 18, 28016
Tel *0322 91 19 02* **Closed** *Mar–Dec:
Mon, Tue (except Apr–Oct: Tue dinner)*
Set in a 19th-century folly, this
restaurant offers high-level
gastronomy and a vast wine list.

RIVOLI: Combal.Zero €€€
Modern Italian
*Il Castello, Piazza Mafalda di Savoia
62, 10098*
Tel *010 956 52 25* **Closed** *Sun, Mon,
Sat lunch; Aug*
Located in the grounds of the
Castello di Rivoli, this restaurant
offers a creative Italian menu.

DK Choice

SAINT VINCENT: Le Grenier €€
Modern Italian
Piazza Monte Zerbion 1, 11010
Tel *0166 51 01 38* **Closed** *Mon–
Fri lunch, Wed; Jul*
Housed in an old barn with soft
lighting and a copper fireplace
create a warm ambience. Try the
carpaccio di filetto (thin slices of
raw beef) with curry sauce, the
venison or the *ravioli di carciofi e
robiola con gamberi rossi* (pasta
filled with artichokes, robiola
cheese and shrimp). There is
an ample choice of Italian and
French wines and a good
cheese selection.

**SESTRIERE:
La Vineria del Colle** €€
Enoteca
Via Assietta 1, 10058
Tel *0122 764 76* **Closed** *Mon;
May, Oct*
Housed in an old wine cellar next
to the ski slopes, this *enoteca*
combines traditional flavours
with contemporary tastes.

SORISO: Al Soriso €€€
Regional Italian
Via Roma 18, 28016
Tel *0322 98 32 28* **Closed** *Mon, Tue;
1 wk Jan, 10 days Aug*
Renowned for its good, creative
cuisine with a range of seasonal
specialities. Book ahead.

STRESA: Il Vicoletto €€
Modern Italian
Vicolo del Poncivo 3, 28838
Tel *0323 93 21 02* **Closed** *Nov–
Mar: Thu*
Piedmontese cuisine including
classic dishes with a touch of
creativity. Good wine cellar.

STRESA: Piemontese €€
Regional Italian
Via Mazzini 25, 28838
Tel *0323 30 235* **Closed** *Mon;
Dec–Jan*
Intimate family-run restaurant with
interesting versions of local fare.
There is also a pretty alfresco
terrace for summer dining.

TORTONA: Aurora Girarrosto €
Regional Italian
Strada Statale per Genova 13, 15057
Tel *0131 86 30 33* **Closed** *2 wks Aug*
The speciality here is barbecued
meats, with all produce coming
from local organic farmers.

TURIN: Birilli €€
Modern Italian
Strada Val San Martino 6, 10131
Tel *011 819 05 67* **Closed** *1st wk Jan;
Oct–May: Sun*
Hearty home cooking offering a
good variety of pasta, grilled fish
and meat dishes.

TURIN: Dai Saletta €€
Regional Italian
Via Belfiore 37, 10126
Tel *011 668 78 67* **Closed** *Sun;
first week Jan, Aug*
Typical *trattoria* ambience. Has a
classic Piedmontese menu and a
good wine list. Good selection of
home-made desserts.

TURIN: La Porta Rossa €€
Seafood
Via Passalacqua 3/B, 10122
Tel *011 53 08 16* **Closed** *Sat lunch,
Sun; 7 Aug; 25 Dec–6 Jan*
Serving fresh fish accompanied
by fine wines.

TURIN: Neuv Caval' D Brons €€€
Fine dining
Piazza San Carlo 155, 10123
Tel *011 53 90 30*
Set in a beautiful square, this
restaurant offers Piedmontese
dishes with an international twist.

VENARIA REALE:
Il Convito della Venaria €
Regional Italian
Via Andrea Mensa 37G, 10078
Tel *011 459 83 92* **Closed** *Sun
dinner, Mon*
A menu of meat and fish dishes,
pizza cooked in a wood-fired
oven and home-made desserts.

VERBANIA PALLANZA:
Osteria del Castello €
Enoteca
Piazza Castello 9, 28921
Tel *0323 51 65 79* **Closed** *Sun;
1 wk Dec*
A local favourite serving pasta and
Piedmontese beef. Good wine list.

VERBANIA PALLANZA:
Osteria dell 'Angolo €
Regional Italian
Piazza Garibaldi 35, 28048
Tel *0323 55 63 62* **Closed** *Mon; Nov*
Typical regional taverna offering
fish dishes, Piedmontese and
Lombardy cuisine. Book ahead.

VERBANIA PALLANZA:
Milano €€
Regional Italian
Corso Zanitello 2, 28922
Tel *0323 55 68 16* **Closed** *Tue;
Nov–Easter*
Choose from a selection of fish
served with organic vegetables.

VERCELLI: Acqua Pazza €
Pizzeria
Corso Gastaldi 25, 13100
Tel *0161 21 74 20* **Closed** *Wed*
In addition to a range of pizzas,
this centrally located restaurant
also offers Vercellese dishes.

VERCELLI: Il Giardinetto €
Regional Italian
Via Sereno 3, 13100
Tel *0161 25 72 30* **Closed** *Mon;
1 wk Jan, 3 wks Aug*
Housed in a 19th-century villa,
this restaurant serves delicious
fare using Piedmontese delicacies.

VERCELLI: Il Paiolo €
Regional Italian
Viale Garibaldi 72, 13100
Tel *0161 25 05 77* **Closed** *Thu;
mid-Jul–mid-Aug*
A *trattoria* set in the rice-growing
country. Serves excellent risotto.

Liguria

DK Choice
CAMOGLI:
La Cucina di Nonna Nina €€
Regional Italian
Via Molfino 126, 16032
Tel *0185 77 38 35* **Closed** *Wed;
10 days Jan; Nov*
This restaurant is nestled on a
picturesque hill and is encircled
by citrus and olive trees. The
chef produces excellent dishes,
using top-quality local products
including olive oil from the
Ligurian coast, fish bought from
local fishermen, and organic
vegetables grown in its own
garden. The focaccia amongst
other breads, cakes and Ligurian
pasta are all home-made on the
day of serving.

CAMOGLI: Rosa €€
Seafood
Via Jacopo Ruffini 13, 16032
Tel *0185 77 34 11* **Closed** *Tue, Wed
lunch; Jun–Aug: Tue lunch*
Try the seafood and pasta in this
Art Nouveau-style restaurant.

Spacious terrace with spectacular views, perfect for alfresco dining at Rosa in Camogli

CERVO: San Giorgio €€
Seafood
Via Volta 19, 18010
Tel *0183 40 01 75* **Closed** *Sep–Jun:
Tue lunch; Oct–Easter: Mon dinner*
Popular, charming restaurant
offering simple dishes. Book ahead.

GENOA: Da Genio €
Regional Italian
Salita San Leonardo 61r, 16128
Tel *010 58 84 63* **Closed** *Sun; Aug*
Sample the classic *trenette al
pesto* (local pasta with pesto
sauce) and fish dishes.

GENOA: Da O' Colla €
Regional Italian
Via alla Chiesa di Murta 10, 16162
Tel *010 740 85 79* **Closed** *Mon,
Sun dinner*
Excellent home-cooked Ligurian
cuisine. Located away from the
city centre, but worth the taxi fare.

GENOA: Cantine Squarciafico €€
Regional Italian
Piazza Invrea 3r, 16123
Tel *010 24 70 82 3* **Closed** *1 wk Jan,
2 wks Aug*
Ligurian wine bar offering local
specialities including *stracci*
(a type of lasagne).

LEVANTO: Cavour €€
Regional Italian
Piazza Cavour 1, 19015
Tel *0187 80 77 86* **Closed** *Mon;
Dec–Jan*
Traditional *trattoria* specializing
in local seafood dishes.

MANAROLA: La Scogliera €€
Regional Italian
Via Birolli 103, 19017
Tel *0187 92 07 47* **Closed** *Thu*
A pretty, family-run restaurant
renowned for seafood specialities.

NERVI: Astor €
Regional Italian
Viale delle Palme 16, 16167
Tel *010 32 90 11*
Steps away from the seashore,
Astor offers local cuisine in a
simple and elegant setting.

PORTOFINO: Da U Batti €€
Seafood
Vico Nuovo 18, 16034
Tel *0185 26 93 79* **Closed** *Mon;
Nov–mid-Jan*
A chic, intimate restaurant, in
Liguria's most elegant towns,
offers exceptional fish cuisine.

PORTOVENERE: Da Iseo €€
Regional Italian
Calata Doria 9, 19025
Tel *0187 79 06 10* **Closed** *Wed;
20 days Nov*
This *trattoria* on the waterfront
serves typical fish dishes.

For more information on types of restaurants *see p579*

PORTOVENERE: Le Bocche €€
Regional Italian
Calata Doria 102, 19025
Tel *0187 79 06 22* **Closed** *Jan;*
Sep–Apr: Tue
Delicate Ligurian fish dishes served
alfresco overlooking Portovenere.

RAPALLO: U'Giancu €
Regional Italian
Via San Massimo 78, 16035
Tel *0185 26 05 05* **Closed** *lunch, Thu;*
last 2 wks Dec
Ligurian specialities are served
here, and the walls are full of
drawings by comic masters.

RAPALLO:
Hostaria Vecchia Rapallo €€
Seafood
Via Cairoli 10, 16035
Tel *0185 500 53* **Closed** *Mon;*
Dec–first wk Feb
This elegant restaurant offers
creative seafood dishes and
a good selection of wine.

RAPALLO: La Nave €€
Seafood
Via Pomaro 15, 16035
Tel *0185 66 95 02* **Closed** *Wed*
Excellent location on the beach.
Sample the *frittura di pesce* (fried
fish) and home-made pesto.

DK Choice

SANREMO:
Da Paolo e Barbara €€
Seafood
Via Roma 47, 18038
Tel *0184 53 16 53* **Closed** *Mon–*
Fri: lunch, Wed, Thu; 1 wk Jan;
2 wks mid-Jun; 17–28 Dec
This small family-run restaurant
serves local fresh fish, meat
sourced from the nearby Langhe
region, vegetables from its own
farm and home-made focaccia.
Try the pasta with *gambero rosso
di Sanremo* (local red prawn) or
trofie al Marò (pasta with bean
and mint sauce). A special
"Saturday shopping" menu is
offered to shoppers.

SANREMO: Da Vittorio €€
Seafood
Piazza Bresca 16, 18038
Tel *0184 50 19 24* **Closed** *2 wks Nov*
A traditional favourite close to
the shore. Daily caught fish and
seafood are the main draw.

SANTA MARGHERITA:
Cinzia e Mario €
Seafood
Via Palestro 6, 16038
Tel *0185 28 75 05* **Closed** *Thu*
Good choice of four different
tasting menus, together with à la
carte dishes and a range of pizzas.

SANTA MARGHERITA:
L'insolita Zuppa €
Traditional Italian
Via Romana 7, 16038
Tel *0185 28 95 94* **Closed** *Wed; 2 wks*
Feb, Nov
A cosy place offering traditional
meat and fish dishes.

SESTRI LEVANTE:
Ristorante Olimpo €€
Mediterranean
Via Della Chiusa 28, 16039
Tel *0185 426 61* **Closed** *7 Jan–22*
Mar; 4 Nov–26 Dec
Overlooking the Baia del Silenzio,
this restaurant serves fine cuisine
with an emphasis on fish.

VERNAZZA: Gambero Rosso €€
Seafood
Piazza Marconi 7, 19018
Tel *0187 81 22 65* **Closed** *Thu;*
mid-Jan–Feb
Inventive modern interpretations
of Ligurian seafood dishes.

Emilia-Romagna

BOLOGNA:
Antica Trattoria della Gigina €
Regional Italian
Via Stendhal 1, 40128
Tel *051 32 23 00*
Delivers a modern take on
regional cuisine without
compromising the flavours.

BOLOGNA: Battibecco €
Regional Italian
Via Battibecco 4, 40123
Tel *051 22 32 98*
Classic Bolognese cuisine and
seafood dishes in this centrally
located, elegant restaurant.

BOLOGNA: Pepperoni €
Pizzeria
Via di Barbiano 7, 40136
Tel *051 33 36 58*
Minimalist decor in this trendy
spot serving high-quality pizzas.

BOLOGNA: Pino €
Pizzeria
Via Goito 2, 40126
Tel *051 22 72 91*
Boisterous spot in the heart of
town offering first-rate pizzas
topped with quality ingredients.

BOLOGNA: Posta €
Regional Italian
Via della Grada 21, 41022
Tel *051 649 21 06* **Closed** *Mon, Sat
lunch, last 2 wks Aug*
Enjoy Tuscan cuisine at this rustic
spot with wood-beamed ceilings
and terracotta-tiled floors.

BOLOGNA: Cesarina €€
Regional Italian
Via Santo Stefano 19, 40125
Tel *051 23 20 37* **Closed** *Mon, Tue
lunch*
This over 100-year-old restaurant,
situated beside an exquisite
church, offers regional dishes.

BOLOGNA: Il Cantuccio €€
Seafood
Via Volturno 4, 40121
Tel *051 23 34 24* **Closed** *Mon, Tue;
Sun lunch, Aug*
Fresh Mediterranean cuisine in
an intimate setting. Family-run,
with courteous service.

BOLOGNA: Marco Fadiga €€
Bistro
Via Rialto 23/C, 40124
Tel *051 22 01 18* **Closed** *Mon, Sun,
1 wk Aug*
Part bistro, part *osteria* offering
local cuisine with a creative
spin; classic French dishes are
available too.

BOLOGNA: Pappagallo €€
Fine Dining
Piazza della Mercanzia 3, 40125
Tel *051 23 28 07*
Excellent traditional cuisine
is served here, under dramatically
high ceilings. The desserts on
offer are delicious and the cellar
is well stocked.

Elegant seating at Sanremo's noted Da Paolo e Barbara restaurant

BOLOGNA: Bitone €€€
Fine Dining
Via Emilia Levante 111, 40134
Tel *051 54 61 10*   **Closed** *Mon, Tue, Aug*
Just outside the city centre, this find is more than worth the trek. Fantastic Bolognese dishes and attentive service.

BOLOGNA: I Portici €€€
Fine Dining
Via dell'Indipendenza 69, 40121
Tel *051 421 85*   **Closed** *Mon, Sun*
The Michelin-starred chef here creates traditional Bolognese and modern Italian cuisine. Romantic setting in a former theatre.

CASTELL'ARQUATO:
Da Faccini €€
Regional Italian
Località S. Antonio, 29014
Tel *0523 89 63 40*   **Closed** *Wed, Jun, Jul*
In-season local ingredients decide the daily changing menu at this warm, family-run eatery.

FAENZA: La Pavona €
Regional Italian
Via Santa Lucia 45, 48018
Tel *0546 310 75*   **Closed** *Tue, Sat lunch, 3 wks Jul*
Just outside the historic centre, this rustic and cosy spot serves the favourites of Emilian cooking.

FERRARA: Ca d'Frara €
Regional Italian
Via del Gambero 4, 44121
Tel *0532 20 50 57*   **Closed** *Tue, Wed*
A slightly sterile atmosphere does not detract from the quality of the Emilian cuisine; low prices.

FERRARA:
Big Night-da Giovanni €€
Regional Italian
Largo Castello 38, 44121
Tel *0532 24 23 67*   **Closed** *winter*
Large windows afford castle views at this restaurant serving traditional dishes from land and sea.

FIDENZA FORNIO:
Osteria di Fornio €
Regional Italian
Via Fornio 78, 43036
Tel *0524 601 18*   **Closed** *Mon dinner, Tue*
Tucked away in the countryside, this restaurant has a changing menu of regional delicacies.

MODENA:
Al Boschetto da Loris €
Regional Italian
Via Due Canali Nord 218, 41122
Tel *059 25 17 59*
Housed in a 16th-century hunting lodge, this place serves home-cooked style meals.

DK Choice

MODENA: Osteria
Francescana €€€
Fine Dining
Via Stella 22, 41121
Tel *059 21 01 18*   **Closed** *Jan & Aug: Sat lunch, Sun*
This two-Michelin-starred restaurant is avant-garde and experimental. The regional speciality – Parmigiano Reggiano is available in five different stages of ageing and the most notable dishes include ravioli with veal offal, chloro-phyll and black truffles. Sample the marinaded suckling pig with cream of fennel, and the famous Modena balsamic vinegar.

PARMA: I Tri Siochètt €
Regional Italian
Strada Farnese-Vigheffio 74/A, 43125
Tel *0521 96 88 70*   **Closed** *2 weeks in Dec*
Named for the three "mad" siblings who opened this *trattoria* years ago. Hearty local cuisine.

PARMA: Parizzi €€
Fine Dining
Strada della Repubblica 71, 43100
Tel *0521 28 59 52*   **Closed** *Mon, last 3 wks Aug*
Modern decor with spotlights and gold floors and a menu of contemporary and classic dishes.

PARMA: Le Viole €
Modern Italian
Strada Nuova di Castelnuovo, 60
Tel *0521 60 10 00*   **Closed** *15 Jan; Jul & Aug: Mon, Sun (15–30 Aug); Dec–Feb: Wed, Thu (10 Feb)*
Seasonal produce inspires gastronomic inventions by the two sisters who run this friendly spot.

PIACENZA: Vecchia Piacenza €€
Modern Italian
Via Taverna/C.ne S. Bernardo 1, 29100
Tel *0523 30 54 62*   **Closed** *Sun*
A husband-and-wife team combine innovative cuisine with original interior artwork.

PIACENZA:
Antica Osteria del Teatro €€€
Fine Dining
Via Giuseppe Verdi 16, 29121
Tel *0523 32 37 77*
French-inspired choices include *foie gras* marinated in port and Armagnac.

RAVENNA:
Antica Trattoria al Gallo 1909 €
Regional Italian
Via Maggiore 87, 48123
Tel *0544 21 37 75*   **Closed** *Sun dinner, Mon, Tue*

Sophisticated at the Michelin-starred Osteria Francescana, Modena

The rustic exterior of this historic *trattoria* hides an Art Deco interior. Ample Emilian specialities.

RAVENNA: Ca de Ven €
Regional Italian
Via Corrado Ricci 24, 48121
Tel *0544 301 63*   **Closed** *Mon*
Authentic eatery popular with locals. Shared tables available for a more casual dining experience.

RAVENNA: Bella Venezia €€
Regional Italian
Via 4 Novembre 16, 48121
Tel *0544 21 27 46*   **Closed** *Sun; 3 wks Jan, 1 wk Jun*
Excellent pasta and fresh fish in a romantic, intimate setting. Great service and a central location.

RIMINI: Osteria de Borg €
Regional Italian
Via Forzieri 12, 47921
Tel *0541 560 74*
A rustic setting in which to sample meat specialities, local cheeses and cured meats.

RIMINI: Dallo Zio €€
Seafood
Via Santa Chiara 16, 47921
Tel *0541 78 67 47*
The cuisine at this fresh, modern spot is inspired from the classic flavours of the Adriatic.

RIMINI: Europa €€
Seafood
Via Roma 51, 47922
Tel *0541 287 61*
Traditional yet inventive restaurant serving fresh fish and meat dishes.

RIMINI: Guido €€
Seafood
Lungomare Guido Spadazzi 12, 47924
Tel *0541 37 46 12*   **Closed** *Mon; 1 wk Dec*
Cuttlefish, oysters and calamari are just a few of the specialities served at this spot on the beach.

For more information on types of restaurants *see p579*

Florence

Bar 53 Bottega €
Enoteca **Map** 2 D3
*Via di Santa Caterina d'Alesssandria
3, 50129*
Tel *055 463 38 95* **Closed** *Sat*
There's a chilled vibe at this wine
bar that's also a popular spot for
breakfast and lunch. Free Wi-Fi.

Il Pizzaiuolo €
Pizzeria **Map** 4 E1
Via de' Macci 113, 50122
Tel *055 24 11 71* **Closed** *3 wks Aug;
1 wk Dec*
Treat yourself to a thick-crusted
Neapolitan-style pizza.

Il Vegetariano €
Vegetarian **Map** 2 D3
Via delle Ruote 30, 50129
Tel *055 47 50 30* **Closed** *Mon, Sat &
Sun lunch; 3 wks Aug, Christmas*
There's excellent value to be
had at this long-established
restaurant. Service is meagre,
but portions are not.

La Bussola €
Pizzeria **Map** 5 C3
Via Porta Rossa, 58 50123
Tel *055 293376*
Charming, low-key pizzeria
with a wood-burning oven.
The service is excellent, and the
wine list surprisingly ample.

Ruth's €
Kosher/Vegetarian **Map** 2 E5
Via Luigi Carlo Farini 2, 50121
Tel *055 248 08 88* **Closed** *Fri dinner,
Sat lunch, Jewish festivities*
Located beside the synagogue,
this kosher restaurant serves
Jewish-inspired recipes; many
vegetarian and seafood options.

Tarocchi €
Pizzeria **Map** 6 E5
Via dei Renai 12, 50125
Tel *055 234 39 12* **Closed** *Mon*
Great prices at this off-the-beaten-
path pizzeria. Pasta dishes are
available, too.

Trattoria Zàzà €
Regional Italian **Map** 1 C4
Piazza del Mercato Centrale 26, 50123
Tel *055 21 54 11*
Traditional Florentine favourites
from land and sea, as well as,
vegetarian and gluten-free fare.

Da Kou €€
Japanese **Map** 5 C1
Via del Melarancio 19/r, 50123
Tel *055 28 29 22* **Closed** *Tue*
Fresh and authentic sushi
prepared with skill; portions are
generous. The decor is modern
and informal.

Key to prices *see p580*

DK Choice

Alle Murate €€
Regional Italian **Map** 6 E2
Via del Proconsolo 16/r, 50122
Tel *055 24 06 18* **Closed** *Sun
lunch, Mon*
This unique restaurant offers a
one-of-a-kind opportunity to
combine Florentine art and
food. Housed in a 14th-century
palace, it boasts original frescoes
on the walls and vaulted ceilings,
hidden for centuries and
uncovered in a painstaking
restoration process. The excellent,
understated local cuisine is a
perfect companion to the
stunning early-Renaissance art.

Dei Frescobaldi €€
Enoteca **Map** 6 D3
Via dei Magazzini 2, 50122
Tel *055 28 47 24* **Closed** *Mon
lunch; 1 wk Jan, 3 wks Aug*
Sample top fine wines and
meticulously matched dishes in
a setting of frescoed walls and
exposed stonework.

Ora d'Aria €€
Modern Italian **Map** 6 D4
Via dei Georgofili 11/r, 50100
Tel *055 200 16 99* **Closed** *Sun, Mon
lunch; 2 wks Jan, 2 wks Aug*
Tucked away in an alley, this
place is well worth the hunt for
its authentic speciality dishes.

Osteria Santo Spirito €€
Regional Italian **Map** 5 A5
Piazza Santo Spirito 16, 50125
Tel *055 238 23 83* **Closed** *Mon,
public holidays*
Tuscan specialities with a twist
at this cosy eatery.

Pane e Vino €€
Modern Italian **Map** 3 A1
Piazza di Cestello 37/r, 50124
Tel *055 247 69 56*
Cosy and familial restaurant
offering traditional Florentine
dishes and more modern ones.

Bistrò Del Mare €€€
Fine Dining **Map** 5 C3
Lungarno Corsini 4/r, 50123
Tel *055 239 92 24* **Closed** *Mon;
1 wk Aug*
Steps away from Ponte Vecchio,
this refined restaurant serves
dishes inspired by old Tuscan
recipes but brought up to date.

Cibrèo €€€
Modern Italian **Map** 4 E1
Via Andrea del Verrocchio 8/r, 50122
Tel *055 234 11 00* **Closed** *Mon;
3 wks Aug*
This trendy place delights diners
with its take on local cuisine.

Interiors of Pane e Vino, popular for
traditional Florentine dishes, Florence

DK Choice

Enoteca Pinchiorri €€€
Fine Dining **Map** 4 E1
Via Ghibellina 87, 50122
Tel *055 24 27 57* **Closed** *Sun,
Mon; Aug; public holidays*
This triple Michelin-starred
restaurant is considered by
some to be the finest in Italy.
Its modern, understated interior
and soft lighting provide the
ideal setting to indulge in any
of the exquisite gastronomic
creations. Specials include the
ravioli with taggiasche olives
and burrata cheese and the
roast pigeon with honey, spices
and breaded aubergine. The
wine cellar is legendary. A
private dining room is available.

Tuscany

AREZZO:
La Lancia d'Oro €€
Regional Italian
Piazza Grande 18, 52100
Tel *0575 210 33* **Closed** *Mon;
2 wks Feb; 2 wks Nov*
Hearty Tuscan meals on offer in
a stunning setting with outdoor
seating under *Vasari's Loggias*
(Vasari's Corridor).

AREZZO:
Le Chiavi d'Oro €€
Modern Italian
Piazza San Francesco 7, 52100
Tel *0575 403 313* **Closed** *Mon;
1 wk Feb; 1 wk Aug*
This stylish Danish-designed
restaurant is elegantly decorated
with 1960s swivel stools and
blond wood floors. The kitchen
specializes in contemporary
regionally inspired cuisine.

ARTIMINO: Da Delfina €€
Regional Italian
Via della Chiesa 1, 59015
Tel *055 871 80 74* **Closed** *Mon, Tue;
1 wk Jan, 1 wk Feb*
The chef's creations are inspired
by his mother's cooking. Hidden
away in a delightful walled town.

CORTONA:
Hostaria la Bucaccia €
Regional Italian
Via Ghibellina 17, 52044
Tel *0575 606 039* **Closed** *15–30 Jan;
Dec–Feb: Mon*
This restaurant has original
features, built over an Roman
road. Home cooking is served.

CORTONA: Il Falconiere €€€
Fine Dining
Località San Martino 370, 52044
Tel *0575 612 679* **Closed** *7–30 Jan*
Nestled among olive and cypress
trees, this restaurant is out of a
fantasy. Great place to sample
exalted Tuscan cuisine.

ELBA: La Lucciola €€
Seafood
Lungomare Pino Nomellini 64, 57034
Tel *0565 976 395* **Closed** *Nov–Apr*
The catch of the day is served
directly on the beach at this
romantic and intimate spot.

ELBA: Publius €
Regional Italian
Piazza del Castagneto 11, 57030
Tel *0565 992 08* **Closed** *Mon;
Nov–Mar*
A wide variety of dishes and an
impressive wine cellar at this
charming restaurant boasting
fantastic sea views.

ELBA: Stella Marina €€
Seafood
Via Vittorio Emanuele II 1, 57037
Tel *0565 915 983* **Closed** *Mon*
Fish doesn't get much fresher
than at this tiny restaurant on
the edge of the port; excellent
wine list.

LUCCA: Da Giulio in Pelleria €
Regional Italian
Via delle Conce 47, 55100
Tel *0583 559 48* **Closed** *3 wks Jan*
Prices are reasonable at this
popular *trattoria* serving Tuscan
fare such as polenta and *zuppa
di farro* (bean and spelt soup).

LUCCA: La Tana dell'Orco €
Pizzeria
Viale Regina Margherita 225, 55100
Tel *0583 023 32 34* **Closed** *Tue*
The concept is simple at this
pizzeria just outside the city walls
– minimal service and low prices.

LUCCA: Buca di Sant'Antonio €€
Regional Italian
Via della Cervia 3, 55100
Tel *0583 558 81* **Closed** *Sun dinner,
Mon; 1 wk Jan; 1 wk Jun*
Ancient local recipes are lovingly
prepared at this historic eatery
in a medieval stable.

MONTALCINO:
Il Boccon Divino €€
Regional Italian
*Strada Provinciale Traversa dei
Monti 201, 53024*
Tel *0577 848 233* **Closed** *Tue*
Enjoy classic Tuscan dishes and
admire the sweeping views of
the countryside. Fantastic wines.

MONTE ARGENTARIO:
Osteria dei Nobili Santi €€
Seafood
Le Piane, 58019
Tel *0564 833 015* **Closed** *Mon*
Good prices at this intimate
restaurant serving plenty of
delectable fish dishes.

MONTEPULCIANO:
Osteria Acquacheta €
Regional Italian
Via del Teatro 22, 53045
Tel *0578 717 086* **Closed** *Tue*
This tiny, popular restaurant is
always packed. The Tuscan meat
dishes are a speciality.

MONTEPULCIANO: La Grotta €€
Regional Italian
Via di San Biagio 15, 53045
Tel *0578 757 479* **Closed** *Wed;
Jan; Feb*
A restaurant set in a 16th-century
building. The menu features
expertly revisited Tuscan classics.

MONTERIGGIONI: Il Pozzo €€
Regional Italian
Piazza Roma 20, 53035
Tel *0577 304 127* **Closed** *Sun
dinner, Mon; 2 wks Jan; 2 wks Feb*
Well located in the centre of the
walled town, this rustic *osteria*
serves traditional fare.

PIENZA: Latte di Luna €
Regional Italian
Via San Carlo 2, 53026
Tel *0578 748 606* **Closed** *Tue*
Classic Tuscan dishes at this
quaint, family-friendly eatery.
Dont forget to try the locally
produced Pecorino cheese.

PISA: La Taverna di Emma €
Modern Italian
Carlo Salomone Cammeo 50, 56122
Tel *050 555 003* **Closed** *Sun;
1 wk Feb; last wk Aug*
Simple local eatery with a
talented chef who whips up
imaginative yet tradition-inspired
recipes. Gorgeous desserts.

PISA: Osteria del Porton Rosso €
Regional Italian
Via Porton Rosso 11, 56126
Tel *050 580 566* **Closed** *Mon*
The menu of classic Tuscan meat
and seafood are scrawled on a
blackboard at this eatery hidden
in the backstreets.

PISA: V. Beni €€
Seafood
Piazza Chiara Gambacorti 22, 56125
Tel *050 250 67* **Closed** *Sun;
2 wks Aug*
Slightly off the tourist track, this
favourite with the locals is housed
in a rustic 600-year-old building.

PISA: A Casa Mia €
Regional Italian
Via Provinciale Calcesana 10, 56010
Tel *050 879 265* **Closed** *Sun;
1 wk Jan; Aug*
Traditional recipes are served
with familial warmth in the
one-time home of the owners.

PISTOIA: La Bottegaia €
Enoteca
Via Del Lastrone 17, 51100
Tel *0573 365 602* **Closed** *Mon;
2 wks Aug*
Cheeses, cured meats, tempting
desserts and, of course, plenty of
fantastic bottles at this friendly,
unpretentious wine bar.

The well-stocked wine cellar at Da Delfina in Artimino

For more information on types of restaurants *see p579*

The traditionally decorated dining area of Osterie le Logge in Siena

PRATO: Osteria Cibbè €
Regional Italian
Piazza Mercatale 49, 59100
Tel *0574 607 509*   **Closed** *Sun;*
3 wks Aug
Try the traditional Tuscan recipes
and comforting home-made
desserts at this charming eatery.

SAN GIMIGNANO:
Antica Macelleria €
Regional Italian
Via Dei Marsili 1/3, 53037
Tel *0577 942 228*
Pick your meat from the old-style
butcher's counter and the chef
will prepare it to your liking.

SAN GIMIGNANO: Dorandò €€
Regional Italian
Vicolo dell'Oro 2, 53037
Tel *0577 941 862*   **Closed** *Dec–Feb*
Enjoy the Slow Food dining
experience at Dorandò.

SAN SEPOLCRO:
Ristorante da Ventura €
Regional Italian
Via Aggiunti Niccolò 30, 52037
Tel *0575 742 560* **Closed** *Sun dinner,*
Mon; 2 wks Aug
Enjoy home-made delights at this
family-run eatery. Try the slow-
cooked veal, or truffle-filled ravioli.

DK Choice

SIENA: 53 Cento €
Enoteca
Viale Pietro Toselli 19, 53100
Tel *0577 050 169*   **Closed** *Sun;*
2 wks Aug
This eclectic wine bar open
from breakfast to the early
hours. The well-stocked cellar
and the capable staff are happy
to make suggestions. The
cuisine is pan-Mediterranean
with imaginative takes on
Italian staples, including many
vegetarian options. There is also
an oyster bar.

SIENA: Enoteca i Terzi €
Enoteca
Via dei Termini 7, 53100
Tel *0577 443 29*   **Closed** *Sun*
Airy, spacious wine bar with
copious varieties of cheeses and
smoked and cured meats.

SIENA: Grotta Santa Caterina
da Bagoga €
Regional Italian
Via della Galluzza 26, 53100
Tel *0577 282 208* **Closed** *Sun dinner,*
Mon; 2 wks Jan; 1 wk Jul
Tucked in a narrow back street
this authentic restaurant offers
good food and great service.

SIENA:
La Taverna di San Giuseppe €
Regional Italian
Via Giovanni Duprè 132, 53100
Tel *0577 422 86*   **Closed** *Sun;*
2 wks Jul; 2 wks Dec
Rustic eatery with local flavours.
Check out the wine cellar, carved
from an ancient Etruscan dwelling.

SIENA: Trattoria Papei €
Regional Italian
Piazza del Mercato 6, 53100
Tel *0577 280 894*
This informal spot is run by an
entire family, with mamma
preparing Tuscan specialities.

SIENA: Osteria le Logge €€
Modern Italian
Via del Porrione 33, 53100
Tel *0577 480 13*   **Closed** *Sun;*
1 wk Jan
This lovely restaurant with
traditional furnishings presents
a novel interpretation of classic
cuisine and has a fine wine list.

SIENA: Il Canto €€€
Modern Italian
Strada di Certosa 82, 53100
Tel *0577 288 180*   **Closed** *Nov–Feb*
Siena's most experimental and
creative restaurant offers a
gastronomic adventure.

VIAREGGIO: Cabreo €€
Seafood
Via Firenze 14, 55049
Tel *0584 546 43*   **Closed** *Sun; Nov*
Whatever is caught on any given
day ends up on the plate at this
authentic fish eatery. Meat dishes
are available.

VIAREGGIO: Piccolo Principe €€€
Fine Dining
Piazza Giacomo Puccini 1, 55049
Tel *0584 40 11*   **Closed** *Nov–May*
Creative and sophisticated cuisine
served in a rooftop garden with
magnificent sea views. Its
Michelin star is well earned.

VOLTERRA: Enoteca del Duca €
Enoteca
Via di Castello 2, 56048
Tel *0588 815 10* **Closed** *Tue; Jan; Feb*
Cosy wine bar serving rustic
snacks. There's also an elegant
restaurant for full meals in the
typical Tuscan tradition.

VOLTERRA: Il Sacco Fiorentino €
Regional Italian
Via Turazza 13, 56048
Tel *0588 885 37*   **Closed** *Tue;*
1 wk Jan
An intriguing tasting menu, as well
as numerous à la carte options,
offering traditional Tuscan with
international touches.

Umbria

ASSISI: I Monaci €
Pizzeria
Via Scalette 10, 06081
Tel *075 81 25 12*
A warm and rustic pizzeria in the
heart of the medieval centre.

ASSISI: La Fortezza €
Regional Italian
Vicolo della Fortezza 2b, 06081
Tel *075 81 29 93*   **Closed** *Thu; Jul*
Mostly traditional cuisine, with
some creative touches. Friendly
but professional service and
good price-quality ratio.

GUBBIO: Grotta dell'Angelo €€
Enoteca
Via Gioia 47, 06024
Tel *075 9271 747* **Closed** *Tue; 7 Jan,*
7 Feb
This rustic wine bar is carved into
a 13th-century cave. Enjoy dining
in the garden in summer.

GUBBIO: Taverna del Lupo €€
Regional Italian
Via Ansidei 6, 06024
Tel *075 92743 68*   **Closed** *Mon*
Succulent local cuisine at this
centrally located spot run by
a husband and wife team.

MONTEFALCO: Coccorone €
Regional Italian
Largo Tempestivi 11, 06036
Tel *074 2379 535* **Closed** *Wed*
Traditional seasonal ingredients, including truffles and porcini mushrooms, make for a fresh and authentic dining experience.

NORCIA: Beccofino €
Regional Italian
Piazza San Benedetto 12, 06046
Tel *0743 81 60 86* **Closed** *Wed; 25 Dec*
Traditional Umbrian cuisine served in a simple setting. Ample wine cellar with over 250 labels.

NORCIA:
Taverna de' Massari €€
Regional Italian
Via Roma 13, 06046
Tel *0743 81 62 18* **Closed** *Tue; 2 wk Jan, 1 wk Jul*
Intimate spot offering the time-honoured cured meats and dishes that make this tiny town famous.

ORVIETO: Del Moro-Aronne €
Regional Italian
Via San Leonardo 7, 05018
Tel *0763 34 27 63* **Closed** *Tue*
Simple, home-style cooking is served up enthusiastically at this restaurant with low prices.

ORVIETO: La Volpe e l'Uva €
Regional Italian
Via Ripa Corsica 2, 05018
Tel *0763 34 16 12*
A wide variety of tempting options – even for vegetarians – at this bustling restaurant in town.

ORVIETO: Duca di Orvieto €€
Regional Italian
Via della Pace 5, 05018
Tel *0763 34 46 63* **Closed** *Wed*
A family-run restaurant using centuries-old local recipes. Patient servers will explain the day's specials in detail.

Traditional rustic charm at the cosy Duca di Orvieto, Orvieto

ORVIETO: I Sette Consoli €€
Modern Italian
Piazza Sant'Angelo 1A, 05018
Tel *0763 343 911* **Closed** *Sun dinner, Wed*
Original and imaginative cuisine in a rustic yet dignified setting. Dine in the garden in summer, weather permitting.

PASSIGNANO SUL TRASIMENO: Cacciatori da Luciano €€€
Seafood
Lungolago Aganor Pompilj 3, 06061
Tel *075 827 210* **Closed** *Wed; 6–30 Jan*
Fresh fish from the adjacent lake and delicacies from the sea are cooked using authentic recipes. Extensive wine list.

PERUGIA: Il Falchetto €
Modern Italian
Via Bartolo 20, 06123
Tel *075 5731 775* **Closed** *Mon*
Gorgeous little restaurant inside a medieval building, with seating on the piazza in summer. Classic Umbrian dishes fill the menu.

PERUGIA: La Botte €
Pizzeria
Via Volte della Pace 31, 06122
Tel *075 5722 679* **Closed** *Sun*
Simple, no-frills pizzeria serving time-honoured family recipes.

PERUGIA:
Antica Trattoria San Lorenzo €€
Modern Italian
Piazza Danti 19/a, 06122
Tel *075 5721 956*
Creative Umbrian-inspired cuisine is on offer at this cosy spot just behind the Duomo.

PERUGIA: Il Gradale €€
Modern Italian
Strada Montevile, 06126
Tel *075 5717 402*
A branch of Castello di Monterone's restaurant delights diners with a choice of light and sophisticated dishes.

PERUGIA: Il Postale €€€
Fine Dining
Strada Montevile 3, 06126
Tel *075 5724 214* **Closed** *Sun dinner, Mon, Tue; 15 Jan–15 Feb*
Set within a wonderful castle location, this award-winning restaurant serves meals rich with local ingredients.

SPOLETO: Il Tempio del Gusto €
Modern Italian
Via Arco di Druso 11, 06049
Tel *0743 471 21* **Closed** *Thu*
Stone floors and small tables create an intimate atmosphere in this restaurant serving creative and top-notch cuisine.

DK Choice

SPOLETO: Il Tartufo €
Regional Italian
Piazza Giuseppe Garibaldi 24, 06049
Tel *0743 40 236* **Closed** *Sun dinner, Mon*
The decor may be simple and old-fashioned, but the local truffles that this restaurant is proudly named for make it worth a special trip. The owners, members of the family who opened the restaurant in 1927, are dedicated to creating dishes based on traditional local recipes. Look out for the ancient Roman paving tiles in one of the dining rooms. In good weather, it's possible to eat outside on the bustling piazza.

TODI:
Antica Hostaria della Valle €
Modern Italian
Via Augusto Ciuffelli 19, 06059
Tel *075 894 48 48* **Closed** *Mon*
Imaginative gastronomic delights at this cosy and welcoming *osteria*. The home-made pasta is the star of the show.

TODI: Umbria €€
Regional Italian
Via San Bonaventura 13, 06059
Tel *075 894 27 37* **Closed** *Tue*
Traditional cuisine is carefully prepared at this legendary restaurant. There is a dining terrace with picturesque views.

Le Marche

ANCONA: Boccon Divino €
Regional Italian
Via Giacomo Matteotti 13, 60121
Tel *071 572 69* **Closed** *Sun; Aug*
Classic Marchegiana cuisine is served up by a young but capable staff here.

ANCONA: La Moretta €
Regional Italian
Piazza Plebiscito 52, 60121
Tel *071 20 23 17* **Closed** *Sun; 1–6 Jan*
This traditional restaurant has been in the same family for over 100 years. Sample the excellent *stoccafisso* (dried cod) in broth.

ANCONA: Sale Grosso €€
Modern Italian
Via Guglielmo Marconi 3, 60125
Tel *071 207 52 79*
Imaginative reinvention of Italian cuisine using local ingredients from land and sea. The decor is fresh and minimalist.

For more information on types of restaurants *see p579*

ASCOLI PICENO: Gallo d'Oro €
Regional Italian
Corso Vittorio Emanuele 54, 63100
Tel *0736 25 35 20*   **Closed** *Sun dinner, Mon*
Despite the sophisticated interior, prices are reasonable at this spot serving regional fare.

ASCOLI PICENO: Del Corso €€
Seafood
Corso Giuseppe Mazzini 277, 63100
Tel *0736 25 67 60*   **Closed** *3 wks Jan, 2 Dec*
Tiny stone-walled restaurant located in a historic palazzo. Most dishes on the changing menu are fish-based.

LORETO: Andreina €
Regional Italian
Via Buffolareccia 14, 60025
Tel *071 97 01 24*   **Closed** *Tue, Wed*
Rustic with a few modern touches. Tuscan specialities reign, with tempting options from the grill.

LORETO: Vecchia Fattoria €
Regional Italian
Via Manzoni 19, 60025
Tel *071 97 89 76*
This converted farmhouse offers classic regional dishes in a welcoming family atmosphere.

PESARO: Da Gennaro €
Seafood
Via Santa Marina Alta 30/1, 61100
Tel *0721 273 21*   **Closed** *Sun dinner, Mon; 1–20 Sep*
Perched in the mountains 7 km (4 miles) west of the sea, this is one of the most authentic eateries in town.

PESARO: Il Commodoro €€
Enoteca
Viale Trieste 269, 61121
Tel *0721 326 80*   **Closed** *Mon*
This inviting modern spot serves up fresh fish and much more. Cosy wine bar attached.

PESARO: Da Alceo €€€
Seafood
Strada Panoramica Ardizio 101, 61100
Tel *0721 513 60*
A panoramic seaside terrace provides an exquisite setting in which to sample some of the best seafood in the area.

SAN MARINO:
Righi la Taverna €€€
Fine Dining
Piazzale della Libertà 10, 47825
Tel *0549 99 11 96* **Closed** *Sun dinner, Mon; Jan, Feb*
The most famous restaurant in this republic serves a mix of age-old and modern Italian cuisine.

URBANIA: Big Ben €
Regional Italian
Corso V. Emanuele 61, 61049
Tel *0722 31 97 95*
Marchegiana specialities such as truffles, snails and wild fennel are offered at this restaurant.

URBINO: Guanábana €
Modern Italian
Via Giuseppe Mazzini 65, 61029
Tel *366 726 55 51*
This quirky little restaurant offers an interesting fusion of local and Venezuelan cuisines. The flavours are surprisingly complementary.

URBINO: Taverna degli Artisti €
Regional Italian
Via Donato Bramante 52, 61029
Tel *0722 26 76*
Opulent frescoed ceilings make a dramatic contrast to the simple home-style cooking.

URBINO:
Antica Osteria da la Stella €€
Regional Italian
Via Santa Margherita 1, 61029
Tel *0722 320228*
This historic restaurant counts famous painters Raphael and Piero della Francesca among its one-time clientele. Elegant interior with a cosy fireplace.

Rome

The Ancient Centre
Enoteca Provincia Romana €€
Enoteca   **Map** 3 A4
Largo di Foro Traiano 82-84, 00187
Tel *06 69 94 02 73*   **Closed** *Sun & Mon dinner*
Both the wine list and the menu ingredients are refreshingly local at this *enoteca*.

Aroma €€€
Fine Dining   **Map** 7 1A
Via Labicana 125, 00184
Tel *06 77 59 13 80*
A sleek interior and unequalled views of the Colosseum. Seasonal menu of regional favourites.

Around Piazza Navona
Acchiappafantasmi €
Pizzeria   **Map** 9 B3
Via dei Cappellari 66, 00186
Tel *06 687 34 62*   **Closed** *Mon*
Its name means "Ghostbusters" and the ghost-shaped pizzas are as tasty as they are amusing.

Angolo Divino €
Enoteca   **Map** 9 C4
Via dei Balestrari 12, 00186
Tel *06 686 44 13* **Closed** *Sun & Mon lunch; 10–20 Aug*

Intimate and romantic spot. The warm chocolate cake is almost as divine as the wine list.

Baffetto €
Pizzeria   **Map** 9 B3
Via del Governo Vecchio 114, 00186
Tel *06 686 16 17*   **Closed** *Tue*
The crunchy Roman-style pizza is considered by those in the know to be the best in Rome, but be prepared for a long wait and to share a table when you do get served.

Capricci Siciliani €
Regional Italian   **Map** 9 B2
Via di Panico 83, 00186
Tel *06 45 43 38 23*   **Closed** *Aug*
Elegant Sicilian dining in the heart of the historic centre; specialities include swordfish medallions and anchovy rolls.

Cul de Sac €
Enoteca   **Map** 9 C3
Piazza di Pasquino 73, 00186
Tel *06 68 80 10 94*   **Closed** *24, 25 & 31 Dec*
This narrow wine bar boasts hundreds of labels as well as a wide variety of tasty eats.

Nonna Betta €
Regional Italian   **Map** 10 D5
Via del Portico d'Ottavia 16, 00186
Tel *06 68 80 62 63*   **Closed** *Tue*
An authentic Jewish eatery. Don't expect an English translation on the handwritten menu, but the food is glorious.

Old Bear €
Regional Italian   **Map** 9 C2
Via dei Gigli d'Oro 3, 00186
Tel *06 68 21 00 09*   **Closed** *Apr; Nov: Mon, Tue*
Dark wood beams and low ceilings create a warm and inviting ambience. Don't miss the Tuscan soup with truffle oil.

Diners at the well-known Jewish-Roman eatery Nonna Betta

Open Baldin €
Birreria **Map** 10 D5
Via degli Specchi 6, 00186
Tel *06 683 89 89* **Closed** *2 wks Aug,
24, 25 & 31 Dec*
Over 120 labels of craft beers on
offer, as well as original, all-natural
sodas. Staple snack food is served.

Camponeschi €€
Fine Dining **Map** 9 C4
Piazza Farnese, 50/50a, 00186
Tel *06 687 49 27*
World-class dining in the heart of
town. Try tagliolini with lobster
and black truffles; wild game is
the house speciality.

Da Giggetto €€
Regional Italian **Map** 10 E5
*Via del Portico d'Ottavia 21/22,
00186*
Tel *06 686 11 05* **Closed** *Mon; last
2 wks Aug, 24 & 31 Dec*
Dine in the shadow of ancient
ruins at this famous Jewish-
Roman eatery. Don't miss the
deep fried artichokes.

Il Bacaro €€
Modern Italian **Map** 10 D2
Via degli Spagnoli 27, 00186
Tel *06 687 25 54*
Romantic with specialities such
as trofie with asparagus and beef
carpaccio with chicory and truffles.

Il Pagliaccio €€
Fine Dining **Map** 9 B2
Via dei Banchi Vecchi 129, 00186
Tel *06 68 80 95 95* **Closed** *Tue lunch;
Aug*
Surprising blend of pan-Asian and
Mediterranean fare on offer. Try
one of the tasting menus, some
of which have up to 12 courses.

Roscioli €€
Enoteca **Map** 9 C4
Via dei Giubbonari 21, 00186
Tel *06 687 52 87* **Closed** *Sun*
Part wine bar, part salumeria with
drool-worthy meats and cheese
and a dizzying selection of labels.

Terra di Siena €€
Regional Italian **Map** 9 C3
Piazza di Pasquino 77, 00186
Tel *06 68 30 77 04* **Closed** *Sun in
summer*
Hearty Tuscan dishes such as
Florentine steak and ribollita
soup; seating in a cheerful dining
room or on the buzzing piazza.

Al Bric €€€
Enoteca **Map** 9 C4
Via del Pellegrino 51, 00186
Tel *06 687 95 33* **Closed** *Mon,
2 wks Aug*
The impeccable wine list at cosy
Al Bric is matched with tempting
creations from the kitchen.

Bright and inviting interior of Al Bric, around Piazza Navona

Hostaria dell'Orso €€€
Fine Dining **Map** 9 C2
Via dei Soldati 25c, 00186
Tel *06 68 30 11 92* **Closed** *Aug*
This legendary restaurant and
nightclub, located in a beautiful
old house, has been welcoming
guests since the start of the
16th century.

Northeast Rome

Ai Tre Scalini €
Enoteca **Map** 3 C4
Via Panisperna 251, 00184
Tel *06 48 90 74 95*
One of the hippest wine bars in
town, with excellent wines, beers
and savoury delicacies.

Antica Birreria Peroni €
Birreria **Map** 10 F3
Via di San Marcello 19, 00187
Tel *06 679 53 10* **Closed** *Sun; 2 & 5
Aug; 24, 25 & 31 Dec*
Casual spot that's been serving
beer for over 100 years (wine is
also available). All-Italian grilled
beef and pork is on the menu.

Cavour 313 €
Enoteca **Map** 3 C5
Via Cavour 313, 00184
Tel *06 678 54 96* **Closed** *Sun in Aug*
Highly trained staff help guests
select a memorable vintage in
this wood-lined wine bar.

'Gusto €
Pizzeria **Map** 2 E2
Piazza Augusto Imperatore 9, 00186
Tel *06 322 62 73* **Closed** *1 Jan; 24 Dec*
Factory-like setting with exposed
brick and iron. The Neapolitan-
style pizzas are thick-crusted.

Hang Zhou €
Chinese **Map** 9 E5
Via Principe Eugenio 82, 00184
Tel *06 487 27 32* **Closed** *Aug*
Unanimously touted the best
Chinese food in town. The all-
you-can eat buffet is a steal; other
meals are higher than average.

La Carbonara €
Regional Italian **Map** 3 C4
Via Panisperna 214, 00184
Tel *06 482 51 76* **Closed** *Sun; Aug*
This busy, inexpensive *osteria*
serves hearty local fare and of
course a delicious Carbonara. The
pistachio pasta is also popular.

San Marco €
Pizzeria **Map** 3 C1
Via Sardegna 38, 00187
Tel *06 42 01 26 20* **Closed** *1 wk Aug;
24 Dec*
A wine bar and grill noted for
its pizzas and warm service.
Blackboard covered walls list
the day's specials.

Trattoria Monti €
Regional Italian **Map** 4 D4
Via di San Vito 13, 00185
Tel *06 446 65 73* **Closed** *Sun dinner,
Mon; Aug 24 Dec – 3 Jan*
The day's specials, featuring
local seasonal ingredients, are
explained by the brothers who
own this heavenly spot.

Trimani il Wine Bar €
Enoteca **Map** 4 D2
Via Cernaia 37b, 00185
Tel *06 446 96 30* **Closed** *Sun; 1 Jan;
2 wks Aug; 25 & 26 Dec*
Modern wine bar with labels that
pair perfectly with cold and hot
dishes, as well as Italian cheeses.

Urbana 47 €
Modern Italian **Map** 3 C4
Via Urbana 47, 00184
Tel *06 47 88 40 06* **Closed** *2 wks Aug*
Eclectic place offering creative and
delicious dining. Great range of
desserts and exceptional value.

Ambasciata d'Abruzzo €€
Regional Italian
Via Pietro Tacchini, 26
Tel *06 807 82 56* **Closed** *2–4 Aug*
Traditional Abruzzese dishes,
such as maccheroni with lamb
ragu mingle with Roman
favourites in a convivial setting.

Cuoco e Camicia €€
Modern Italian Map 3 C5
Via Monte Polacco 2/4, 00184
Tel *06 88 92 29 87* **Closed** *Sun, Sat lunch; 2 wks Aug; 24 & 25 Dec*
Cheerful eatery that prides itself on using only the freshest local ingredients. Good tasting menu.

Hamasei €€
Japanese Map 10 F1
Via della Mercede 35/36, 00187
Tel *06 679 21 34* **Closed** *Mon; Aug*
Inventive sushi and sashimi dishes are served in a minimalist setting, with low tables for authentic Nipponese dining.

La Campana €€
Regional Italian Map 10 D1
Vicolo della Campana 18, 00186
Tel *06 687 52 73* **Closed** *Mon; Aug*
Packed any night of the week, this is the oldest restaurant in Rome dating back to 1518. Traditional favourites are served.

Doozo €€€
Japanese Map 3 C4
Via Palermo 51, 00184
Tel *06 481 56 55* **Closed** *Sun lunch, Mon; 1 wk Aug; 22 Dec–15 Jan*
Excellent sushi and origami courses, at this restaurant and Japanese cultural centre.

Imàgo €€€
Fine Dining Map 3 A2
Piazza Trinità dei Monti 6, 00187
Tel *06 69 93 47 26* **Closed** *lunch*
Creative Italian cuisine and exceptional views from the top of the Spanish Steps. The desserts are divine and the wine list is expertly chosen.

L'Olimpo €€€
Fine Dining Map 3 B2
Piazza Barberini 23, 00187
Tel *06 48 89 31*
Dine with sweeping views of the entire city. Considerable savings at lunchtime; a more expensive menu in the evenings.

Oliver Glowig €€€
Fine Dining
Via Ulisse Aldrovandi, 15 00197
Tel *06 321 61 26* **Closed** *Sun & Mon in winter*
Try Mediterranean delicacies such as scampi with artichoke heart and burrata cheese at this exquisite poolside restaurant.

Osteria Margutta €€€
Modern Italian Map 3 A2
Via Margutta 82b, 00187
Tel *06 323 10 25* **Closed** *Sun dinner, Mon lunch; 1 wk Aug*
Historic restaurant on a vine-covered street.serving classic Roman fare with a modern twist.

Sleek interiors at the Japanese restaurant Doozo, Northeast Rome

The Vatican and Trastevere

Arian €
Persian Map 2 D2
Via Tacito 54a, 00193
Tel *06 45 44 11 22* **Closed** *Sun & Mon lunch; 1 wk Aug*
Iranian cuisine in a vibrant atmosphere. Live belly dancing on Friday and Saturday nights.

Arlù €
Regional Italian Map 1 C3
Borgo Pio 135, 00193
Tel *06 686 89 36* **Closed** *Sun; 1 Jan; 2 wks Aug; 25 & 26 Dec*
The most authentic restaurant in the area. A husband and wife team serve up delectable cuisine. Great choice of beverages.

Bir and Fud €
Birreria Map 2 E5
Via Benedetta 23, 00153
Tel *06 589 40 16* **Closed** *25, 31 Dec*
Boutique beers and microbrews accompany crusty pizzas and gourmet chips.

BRASSERIE 4:20 €
Birreria Map 5 C3
Via Portuense 82, 00153
Tel *06 58 31 07 37*
Craft beers from around the world are paired with snacks such as burgers, fries and hotdogs as well as a selection of desserts.

Da Gildo €
Regional Italian Map 2 D5
Via della Scala 31/A, 00153
Tel *06 580 07 33* **Closed** *Thu*
Quirky decoration and a cosy outdoor seating area. Try the divine *gnocchi alla romana* (baked *gnocchi* with cheese on top).

Da Lucia €
Regional Italian Map 5 B1
Vicolo del Mattonato 2b, 00153
Tel *06 580 36 01* **Closed** *Mon; 2 wks Aug; 24, 25 & 31 Dec*

Simple pasta dishes as well as more hearty meals and delicious home-made desserts are served on a beautifully-lit street.

Dar Poeta €
Pizzeria Map 2 E5
Vicolo del Bologna 45, 00153
Tel *06 588 05 16* **Closed** *24, 31 Dec*
Perfect balance between thick- and thin-crusted pizza; the buffalo mozzarella topping is unmatched.

Fish Market €
Seafood Map 5 C2
Vicolo della Luce 2/3, 00153
Tel *06 914 41 57*
This restaurant has no frills; choose your fish, state how you would like it cooked, and pick it up from the counter when it's ready.

In Vino Veritas €
Enoteca Map 2 D5
Via Garibaldi 2a, 00153
Tel *06 583 320 12*
Cosy and informal wine bar with over 200 varieties of wine. Food is simple and made for sharing.

Ivo a Trastevere €
Pizzeria Map 5 C1
Via di San Francesco a Ripa 158, 00153
Tel *06 581 70 82*
Snacks and thin-crusted pizza has this eatery bustling with locals.

Panattoni L'Obitorio €
Pizzeria Map 5 C1
Viale di Trastevere 53, 00153
Tel *06 580 09 19* **Closed** *Wed; 10, 28 Aug*
Nicknamed "the morgue" for its long marble-top tables. Try the *supplì al telefono* (fried rice balls).

Rajdhani €
Indian Map 6 D1
Via di Santa Cecilia 8, 00153
Tel *06 581 85 08* **Closed** *Mon*
Tandoori chicken is the speciality at this friendly spot.

DK Choice

Isole di Sicilia €€
Regional Italian **Map** 5 B1
Via Garibaldi 68, 00153
Tel *06 58 33 42 12* **Closed** *Wed*
This cheerful restaurant dishes
up some of the best Sicilian
food in town. The elaborate
dishes are inspired by the native
cuisine of the tiny islands
around Sicily. A vast antipasto
spread kicks off a memorable
meal. In good weather, dine on
the tree-lined street.

Spirito Divino €€
Modern Italian **Map** 6 D1
Via dei Genovesi 31, 00153
Tel *06 589 66 89* **Closed** *Sun*
Fine dishes served in a converted
medieval synagogue; take a peek
in the 2,000-year-old wine cellar.

Taverna Trilussa €€
Regional Italian **Map** 2 E5
Via del Politeama 23, 00153
Tel *06 581 89 18* **Closed** *Sun, lunch
daily, Sun; 3 days mid-Aug; 24, 25 &
31 Dec*
A bustling yet elegant spot.
Some pasta dishes are served in
the pan it was cooked in.

Antico Arco €€€
Fine Dining **Map** 5 A1
Piazzale Aurelio 7, 00152
Tel *06 581 52 74* **Closed** *1 Jan*
Truffles, wild strawberries and
other such delights are on offer.
The vast wine list is as tantalizing.

Antica Pesa €€€
Fine Dining **Map** 5 B1
Via Garibaldi 18, 00153
Tel *06 580 92 36* **Closed** *Sun; 1 Jan;
26 Dec*
Eat exquisite cuisine in a beautifully
decorated restaurants with murals
covering the walls. Dine alfresco
in warm weather.

Settembrini €€€
Modern Italian
Via Luigi Settembrini 25, 00195
Tel *06 323 26 17* **Closed** *Sun, Sat
lunch; 2 wks Aug*
Renowned Chef Gigi Nastri
serves creative Italian cuisine
that is as beautiful as it is tasty.

Aventine and Lateran

Angelina a Testaccio €
Regional Italian **Map** 6 D3
Via Galvani 24, 00153
Tel *06 57 28 38 40* **Closed** *Sat lunch,
Sun*
The gem of Testaccio, this shabby
chic bistro offers a tempting
Sunday brunch. The desserts are
scrumptious.

Oasi della Birra €
Birreria **Map** 6 D3
Piazza Testaccio 39, 00153
Tel *06 574 61 22* **Closed** *1 wk Aug;
24 & 25 Dec*
This oasis of beer starts serving
in the early afternoon and no
one leaves thirsty.

Checchino dal 1887 €€
Regional Italian **Map** 6 D4
Via di Monte Testaccio 30, 00153
Tel *06 574 38 16* **Closed** *Sun,
Mon; Aug*
Lovingly prepared hearty Roman
dishes make this restaurant a
favourite with discerning diners.

Further Afield

La Gatta Mangiona €
Pizzeria
*Via Federico Ozanam 30, Monteverde
Nuovo, 00152*
Tel *06 534 67 02* **Closed** *Mon;
10–25 Aug; 24–26 & 31 Dec*
Creative toppings and daily
specials make it popular with
locals and in-the-know visitors.

DK Choice

Momò Republic €€
Pizzeria
*Piazza Forlanini 10, Monteverde
Nuovo, 00151*
Tel *06 537 30 87*
A 19th-century mansion in a
garden is the setting for this
trendy pizzeria. Huge
chandeliers and parquet floors
add to the ambience. In
summer, start with *aperitivo* on
the lawn. Pasta, meat and fish
are also available.

Osteria Flaminio €€
Modern Italian
Via Flaminia 297, 00196
Tel *06 323 69 00* **Closed** *lunch daily*
Trek north of the centre to try the
innovative and original Italian
cuisine on offer here.

Bastianelli al Molo €€€
Fine Dining
Via Torre Clementina 312, 00054
Tel *06 650 53 58*
A terrace overlooking the
Tyrrhenian Sea is the setting for a
meal of ultra-fresh seafood.

DK Choice

La Pergola €€€
Fine Dining
Via Alberto Cadlolo 101, 00136
Tel *06 350 91* **Closed** *Sun, Mon*
Rome's finest restaurant, La
Pergola is also the only one to
earn the coveted three Michelin

stars. Chef Heinz Beck dazzles
with exquisite Mediterranean
creations. Perched atop Monte
Mario hill, it offers great views of
St Peter's Basilica. The award-
winning wine cellar boasts over
53,000 bottles, the oldest 1888.

Lazio

**BRACCIANO: Quattro
Castagni** €
Regional Italian
Via Olmata Tre Cancelli, 7
Tel *06 99 84 91 55* **Closed** *Tue*
Traditional cuisine, specializing in
wild game, served in a rustic
setting with exposed stonework.

**BRACCIANO: Trattoria La
Tavernetta** €
Modern Italian
Via Giuseppe Garibaldi 73, 00062
Tel *06 999 90 26*
Welcoming atmosphere and
regional cuisine. The patio offers
spectacular views of the lake.

**CASTELLI ROMANI FRASCATI:
Pezzafina** €
Modern Italian
Vicolo Manara 2, 00044
Tel *06 60 65 17 80* **Closed** *lunch
daily, Sun*
The menu features daring
ingredient combinations, whilst
keeping traditional flavours.

CERVETERI: Trattoria Zi Maria €
Regional Italian
Via Sasso Manziana 2, 00050
Tel *06 99 07 90 29* **Closed** *Tue*
Typical regional cuisine at good
prices. Hearty specialities include
venison with wild berries.

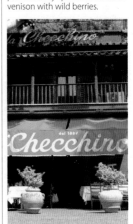

Exterior of the friendly Checchino dal 1887,
known for its filling Roman dishes

For more information on types of restaurants *see p579*

CERVETERI: Rendez-vous Bistrot €€
Regional Italian
Pizza Risorgimento16, 00052
Tel *06 90 20 97 50*
A romantic getaway on a pedestrian piazza. Creative cuisine, modern decor and attentive service.

GAETA: Narì €
Seafood
Via Duomo 15, 04024
Tel *0771 46 30 94* **Closed** *Mon*
Excellent fish and pasta dishes in the medieval centre of Gaeta.

OSTIA: La Bussola €€
Seafood
Lungomare A. Vespucci 72, 00122
Tel *06 56 47 08 67* **Closed** *Mon*
Inspired by the recipes of the owners' great aunt. Try the gnocchi with octopus and the fish stew.

SERMONETA: Il Giardino del Simposio €
Modern Italian
Corso Garibaldi 33, 04010
Tel *339 284 69 05* **Closed** *Mon; Jan–Feb: Sat & Sun*
Innovative dishes such as pasta with fresh ricotta and wild fennel.

SPERLONGA: Gli Archi €€
Traditional Italian
Via Ottaviano 17, 04029
Tel *0771 54 83 00* **Closed** *Wed; Jan*
Simple traditional cuisine in the heart of this seaside village. Outdoor seating in warm weather.

TARQUINIA: La Cantinetta €
Regional Italian
Via XX Settembre 27, 01016
Tel *0766 85 68 10* **Closed** *Tue; summer*
Simple spot offering staples from land and sea. Try the spaghetti with octopus and clams.

TIVOLI: Avec 55 €€
Modern Italian
Via Domenico Giuliani 55, 00019
Tel *0774 31 72 43* **Closed** *Mon*

Gastronomic feats paired with excellent wine. Divine desserts.

TIVOLI: La Sibilla €€
Regional Italian
Via della Sibilla 42, 00019
Tel *0774 33 52 81* **Closed** *Mon*
Fine views of the Roman ruins provide a great setting to indulge in high-quality regional cuisine.

DK Choice

VITERBO: Il Labirinto €
Pizzeria
Via di San Lorenzo 46, 00100
Tel *0761 30 70 26* **Closed** *Mon*
This charming restaurant prepares a variety of bruschetta, pizza, pasta and main courses in traditional style. The outdoor seating area is next to a quaint fountain and a medieval church.

VITERBO: Ristorantino La Torre €€
Fine Dining
Via della Torre 5, 01100
Tel *0761 22 64 67* **Closed** *Sun dinner, Mon lunch; 3 wks Aug*
The chef and sommelier create an unforgettable dining experience at this vibrant spot.

VITERBO: Villa San Michele €€€
Fine Dining
Via Pian di Quercia, 01030
Tel *338 501 03 87* **Closed** *Mon, Tue*
Icelandic *baccalà* (salt cod) in coconut milk, cinnamon and orange zest is a menu highlight.

Naples and Campania

AMALFI: Da Ciccio Cielo Mare Terra €€
Regional Italian
Via Nazionale per Sorrento, 84011
Tel *089 83 12 65* **Closed** *Tue; Jan, Nov*

Great views of the coastline are matched by the delicious food.

AMALFI: La Caravella €€€
Fine Dining
Via Matteo Camera 12, 84011
Tel *089 87 10 29* **Closed** *Tue; Jan, Nov*
The award-winning chef here uses local flavours to exalt the regional cuisine.

BENEVENTO: Pascalucci €€
Regional Italian
Via Appia 1, 82010
Tel *0824 77 84 00* **Closed** *winter*
Simple recipes prepared with fresh local ingredients.

CAPRI: Da Gelsomina €€
Regional Italian
Via Migliara 72, 80071
Tel *081 837 14 99* **Closed** *Tue; Jan–Feb*
Much of the produce is grown on site at this delightful restaurant.

CAPRI: Da Paolino €€
Regional Italian
Via Palazzo a Mare 11, 80073
Tel *081 837 61 02* **Closed** *Oct–Apr*
Rustic country restaurant with rich regional cuisine.

CAPRI: L'Olivo €€
Fine Dining
Via Capodimonte 14, 80071
Tel *081 978 01 11* **Closed** *mid-Oct–mid-Apr*
Uses saffron, bergamot, fava beans and asparagus to make gorgeous flavour combinations.

CAPRI: Il Riccio €€€
Seafood
Via Grotta Azzurra 11, 80071
Tel *081 837 13 80* **Closed** *Nov–Mar*
Pleasant atmosphere in which to enjoy exceptional seafood dishes.

CASERTA: Antica Locanda €
Regional Italian
Piazza della Seta 7, 81100
Tel *0823 30 54 44* **Closed** *Sun dinner, Mon; Aug; 24 & 31 Dec*
Simple, characterful *osteria* with rustic details. Southern Italian cooking and excellent risotto.

CASERTA: Leucio €
Seafood
Via Giardini Reali 86, 81100
Tel *0823 30 12 41* **Closed** *Sun dinner, Mon; 1 wk Aug*
Exceptional prices at this simple fish restaurant run by a father and son. Also serves great pasta.

CASERTA: Le Colonne €€
Fine Dining
Viale Giulio Douhet 7, 81100
Tel *0823 46 74 94* **Closed** *Tue*
Indulge in superbly reinterpreted local cuisine in a luxurious setting.

Romantic dining amid lemon trees at Da Paolino, Capri

Sunny patio of the Neapolitan gem, Il Comandante, Naples

ISCHIA AND PROCIDA:
La Stadera €
Enoteca
Via C. Maddalena 15, Sant'Angelo, 80070
Tel *081 99 98 93*
Narrow alleys lead to this *enoteca* where the owners delight with unusual wines and liqueurs. The food here is also delicious.

ISCHIA AND PROCIDA:
La Tinaia €
Pizzeria
Via Matteo Verde 39, Forio, 80075
Tel *081 99 84 48* **Closed** *24 Dec*
Fantastic thick-crusted pizza, as well as pasta and seafood. Basic but friendly service.

ISCHIA AND PROCIDA:
Lo Scoglio €
Seafood
Via Cava Ruffano 58, Sant'Angelo, 80077
Tel *081 999529*
Stunningly located on a rock jutting over the sea, this simple restaurant serves quality fish. There is also a good selection of wine.

ISCHIA AND PROCIDA:
Alberto €€
Modern Italian
Via Cristoforo Colombo 8, Ischia, 80077
Tel *081 98 12 59* **Closed** *Nov–Mar*
Sample traditional Italian seafood specialities with creative reinterpretation at this lovely beachfront restaurant.

ISCHIA AND PROCIDA:
Gorgonia €€
Seafood
Via Marina di Corricella 50, Procida, 80079
Tel *081 810 10 60*
Set high above a picturesque bay, Gorgonia serves the catch of the day.

ISCHIA AND PROCIDA:
Il Mosaico €€€
Fine Dining
Piazza Bagni, Casamicciola Terme, 80074
Tel *081 99 47 22* **Closed** *Tue; mid-Oct–Mar*
Rich Neapolitan cuisine inspires this multi-talented chef's innovative and exquisite menu. The wine list is excellent and the desserts are divine.

DK Choice

ISCHIA AND PROCIDA:
Umberto a Mare €€€
Fine Dining
Via del Soccorso 2, Forio, 80075
Tel *081 99 71 71* **Closed** *Nov–Mar*
Time seems to stand still as you take a seat on the tiny terrace that juts out over the sea in the shadow of the evocative Santa Maria del Sorrorso church. The tasting menus feature the gastronomic delights of the Mediterranean. The wine selection is outstanding, and the staff attends to every need.

DK Choice

NAPLES: Da Michele €
Pizzeria
Via Cesare Sersale 1, 80139
Tel *081 553 92 04* **Closed** *Sun*
A trip to Naples wouldn't be complete without tasting a Margherita at this institution, probably the most famous pizzeria in the world. Only Margherita and Marinara pizzas are served here.

NAPLES: Di Matteo €
Pizzeria
Via dei Tribunali 94, 80138
Tel *081 455 262* **Closed** *Sun*
A Naples institution serving classic chewy pizza and tasty *fritti* (fried food). Popular with locals and celebrities.

NAPLES: La Notizia €
Pizzeria
Via Michelangelo da Caravaggio 53, 80126
Tel *081 714 21 55* **Closed** *Mon; Aug; 25 Dec*
Tiny pizzas with intense flavours at this popular spot, considered one of the world's best pizzerias.

NAPLES: La Piazzetta €
Regional Italian
Via Nazario Sauro 21, 80132
Tel *081 764 61 95* **Closed** *Mon*
Traditional local fare and pizzeria at this quaint restaurant designed to look like a small-town piazza.

NAPLES: Sorbillo €
Pizzeria
Via dei Tribunali 38, 80138
Tel *081 033 10 09* **Closed** *Sun; 1 wk Feb*
A comfortable setting, good pizza and attentive service for a great price.

NAPLES: Kukai Nibu €€
Japanese
Via Carlo de Cesare 52, 80132
Tel *081 42 58 88*
Generous portions of sushi and sashimi; a glass kitchen allows diners a great view of the action.

NAPLES: La Cantinella €€
Fine Dining
Via Cuma 42, 80132
Tel *081 764 86 84* **Closed** *Sun dinner*
A bamboo forest is re-created in this award-winning restaurant with an imaginative chef.

NAPLES: La Scialuppa €€
Seafood
Piazzetta Marinari 4, 80132
Tel *081 764 53 33* **Closed** *Mon; Jan*
Right on the gulf, this traditional restaurant serves fresh fish, as well as pasta and pizza.

NAPLES: Palazzo Petrucci €€
Modern Italian
Piazza San Domenico Maggiore 4, 80134
Tel *081 552 40 68* **Closed** *Sun dinner, Mon lunch; 2–4 Aug; 25 Dec*
This Michelin-starred restaurant in an ancient setting serves modern fare made with local ingredients.

NAPLES: Il Comandante €€€
Fine Dining
Via Cristoforo Colombo, 80133
Tel *081 01 75* **Closed** *Tue*
The chef creates exquisite dishes from a few basic ingredients.

POSITANO: Chez Black €€
Seafood
Via del Brigantino, 84017
Tel *089 87 57 96* **Closed** *mid-Jan–mid-Feb*
Idyllic beachfront location. Serves traditional fish recipes.

POSITANO: Le Terrazze €€
Regional
Via Grotte Dell'Incanto 51, 84017
Tel *089 87 58 74* **Closed** *Oct–Apr*
Wine bar with panoramic sea views. The wine cellar is carved right into the hillside rock.

POSITANO: Zass €€€
Fine Dining
Via Laurito 2, 84017
Tel *089 87 54 55*
Mouth-wateringly delicious elevation of regional cuisine. Desserts to die for.

For more information on types of restaurants see p579

SALERNO: Addor I Pizza €
Pizzeria
Piazza San Francesco d'Assisi, 84122
Tel *089 24 18 76* **Closed** *Mon, Sun*
Courteous service in this tiny
pizzeria that also serves pasta.

SALERNO: Il Timone €€
Seafood
Via Generale Allende 29/35, 84122
Tel *089 33 51 11* **Closed** *Mon;*
15–31 Aug
Friendly, bright fish restaurant
with fast, courteous service.

SALERNO: Osteria Dedicato
a mio Padre €€
Seafood
Vicolo Giudaica 8, 84100
Tel *089 23 15 55* **Closed** *Sun*
Numerous varieties of fresh fish,
served up in a cosy setting in the
heart of the historic centre.

SORRENTO: La Basilica €
Regional Italian
Via Sant'Antonino 28, 80067
Tel *081 877 47 90* **Closed** *Mon*
It's possible to dine until 1am at
this restaurant. Fish, meat and
vegeatrian options in classic
regional style.

SORRENTO: Zi'ntonio €
Regional Italian
Via Luigi De Maio 11, 80067
Tel *081 878 16 23*
Local favourites served in a room
with exposed tufa blocks and
wood-beamed ceilings.

SORRENTO: Il Buco €€
Modern Italian
Il Rampa Marina Piccola 5, 80067
Tel *081 878 23 54* **Closed** *Wed; Jan*
Elegant yet informal restaurant
housed in the cellar of an ancient
monastery. A perfect blend of
tradition and more daring cuisine.

Abruzzo, Molise and Puglia

ALBEROBELLO: Trullo d'Oro €
Regional Italian
Via Felice Cavallotti 27, 70011
Tel *080 432 18 20* **Closed** *Mon*
Local cuisine in the characterful
setting of an *authentic trullo*.
Great antipasto spread.

ALBEROBELLO: Il Poeta
Contadino €€
Fine Dining
Via Indipendenza 21, 70011
Tel *080 432 19 17* **Closed** *Mon;*
Jan (except for group bookings)
Awarded a Michelin star for its
delectable regional cuisine and
a stunning location. The desserts
are heavenly.

Homely setting for regional cuisine at Il Cortiletto, Lucera

BARI:
Osteria delle Travi "Il Buco" €
Regional Italian
Largo Ignazio Chiurlia 12, 70122
Tel *339 157 88 48* **Closed** *Sun*
dinner, Mon
Authentic home-style cooking in
the old Pugliese style *osteria*.

BARI: Bacco €€
Modern Italian
Corso Vittorio Emanuele II 126, 70122
Tel *080 527 58 71* **Closed** *Sun*
dinner, Mon; Aug
Both meat and fish are on the
menu at this award-winning
restaurant. Ample wine list.

GARGANO PENINSULA:
Medioevo €
Regional Italian
Via Castello 21, 71037
Tel *0884 56 53 56* **Closed** *Nov: dinner;*
Dec–Feb: Mon
This simple *osteria* uses the best
seasonal produce available. Meat
and soup specialities.

GARGANO PENINSULA:
Porta di Basso €€
Seafood
Via Cristoforo Colombo 38, 71010
Tel *0884 91 53 64* **Closed** *Thu*
Creative reinterpretations of
Pugliese fish recipes. Located
on a cliff above the sea.

GARGANO PENINSULA:
Al Dragone €€
Regional Italian
Via Duomo 8, 71019
Tel *0884 70 12 12* **Closed** *Apr–Nov:*
Tue; Dec–Mar
Dining in this restaurant built into
a natural cave is an experience in
itself. Delicious regional dishes
and a good wine list.

ISOLE TREMITI: La Nassa €
Seafood
Via Aldo Moro 24, 71040
Tel *0882 46 33 45* **Closed** *Easter;*
Apr–Oct
Nestled in a lush garden, this
restaurant offers fresh fish served
in the simple but rich tradition.

L'AQUILA: Le Rocce dell'Aquila €
Regional Italian
Viale della Croce Rossa 40, 67100
Tel *0862 41 90 12*
Creativity meets local produce at
this small restaurant.

L'AQUILA: Elodia €€
Fine Dining
Via Valle Perchiana 22, 67100
Tel *0862 60 68 30* **Closed** *Mon, Tue*
Gourmet interpretations of great
local recipes; delicious desserts.

LECCE: Osteria degli Spiriti €
Regional Italian
Via Cesare Battisti 4, 73100
Tel *0832 24 62 74*
Local cuisine served in a high-
ceilinged *trattoria* that was once
a warehouse.

LUCERA: Il Cortiletto €
Regional Italian
Via Famiglia de Nicastri 26, 71036
Tel *0881 54 25 54* **Closed** *Sun dinner*
The short weekly menu is
described by the staff. Regional
favourites with original touches.

DK Choice

LUCERA: Osteria Utz €
Modern Italian
Corso Garibaldi 103, 71036
Tel *0881 61 82 34* **Closed** *Sun*
This warm, cosy restaurant
selects only the freshest local
ingredients – from cured meats
and cheeses to native herbs –
and uses them to craft innovative dishes inspired by the area's
cuisine. The atmosphere is
informal but romantic. Their
speciality is numerous varieties
of fresh home-made bread.

OSTUNI: Osteria Piazzetta
Cattedrale €
Modern Italian
Largo Arcidiacono T. Trinchera 7,
72017
Tel *0831 33 50 26* **Closed** *Tue*
This elegant restaurant serves local
cuisine with a modern touch.

OSTUNI:
Osteria del Tempo Perso €€
Modern Italian
Via Gaetano Tanzarella Vitale 47, 72017
Tel *0831 30 48 19*   **Closed** *Mon; 15–20 Jan*
Set in an antique mill, the dishes are reinventions of classic recipes.

OSTUNI: Porta Nova €€
Seafood
Via Gaspare Petrarolo 28, 72017
Tel *0831 33 89 83*
This fish restaurant boasts fine food and views of the surrounding area from its large terrace.

OTRANTO: Peccato di Vino €€
Modern Italian
Via Rondachi 7, 73028
Tel *0836 80 14 88*   **Closed** *Tue*
One of the finest restaurants in town, serving creative Pugliese cuisine in a jovial atmosphere.

SULMONA: Rigoletto €
Regional Italian
Via Stazione Introdacqua 46, 67039
Tel *086 45 55 29*
Home-made dishes with local ingredients such as rabbit, truffles and scamorza cheese.

TARANTO: Al Canale €€
Seafood
Scesa Vasto, 74100
Tel *099 476 42 01*   **Closed** *Sun dinner; 1–15 Nov*
Seafood specialities are prepared at this luminous restaurant.

TARANTO:
Trattoria al Gatto Rosso €€
Regional Italian
Via Cavour 2, 74123
Tel *099 452 98 75*   **Closed** *Sun lunch, Mon*
Innovative contemporary cuisine based on local recipes.

TRANI: Torrente Antico €€€
Fine Dining
Via Edoardo Fusco 3, 70059
Tel *0883 48 79 11*   **Closed** *Mon*
Light and modern versions of Puglia's traditional recipes at the finest restaurant in the area.

Basilicata and Calabria

MARATEA:
Il Giardino di Epicuro €
Regional Italian
Contrada Massa Piano, 85046
Tel *0973 87 01 30*   **Closed** *Jan, Feb, Nov*
The owner's mother creates heavenly traditional meals.

MARATEA: Zà Mariuccia €€
Seafood
Via Grotte 2, 85040
Tel *0973 87 61 63*   **Closed** *Mon; mid-Oct–Mar*
Book ahead to secure one of the few terrace tables with splendid sea views. Top-notch local seafood with an excellent wine list.

MARATEA: Taverna Rovita €€€
Regional Italian
Via Rovita 12, 85046
Tel *0973 87 65 88*
Serves tempting meat and fish dishes and home-made pasta with in-season ingredients.

MATERA: Alle Fornaci €
Seafood
Piazza Cesare Firrao 5/7, 75100
Tel *0835 33 50 37*   **Closed** *Mon*
Fresh fish from the Ionian and Tyrrhenian seas is brought in daily for the no-fuss dishes.

MATERA: Don Matteo €€
Modern Italian
Via San Potito 12, 75100
Tel *0835 34 41 45*   **Closed** *lunch*
Dine inside a *sassi* (characteristic stone dwelling). A modern take on traditional local recipes.

DK Choice

MELFI: La Villa €
Regional Italian
Contrada Cavallerizza, 85025
Tel *0972 23 60 08*   **Closed** *Sun dinner, Fri; 2 wks mid-Jul*
Set in the heart of the countryside, this rustic restaurant mills its own flour and grows its own grapes. Every ingredient used is local, and the traditional recipes are executed with attention to detail. The family who run the estate treat guests like family members.

The warmly-lit entrance to seafood restaurant Porta Nova in Ostuni

MELFI: Novecento €
Regional Italian
Contrada Incoronata, 85025
Tel *0972 23 74 70*
Authentic local cuisine served in a welcoming restaurant. Worth the trek outside town.

MELFI: La Grotta Azzurra €€
Regional Italian
Via Carmine 13, 85025
Tel *0972 23 81 34*
Bring a big appetite to this excellent restaurant with hearty Lucano specialities. Heavenly desserts and a good wine list.

REGGIO DI CALABRIA:
Il Fiore del Cappero €
Seafood
Via Zaleuco 7, 89125
Tel *0965 209 55*   **Closed** *Sun, first wk Jan*
Sicilian cuisine, based mostly on fish, in this welcoming restaurant with ample Calabrian wines.

REGGIO DI CALABRIA:
Bistrot 15 €€
Bistro
Via Nazionale Pellaro 15, 89134
Tel *0965 35 03 41*   **Closed** *May–Sep; Dec–Feb: Mon*
Innovative and artistic seafood served in a modern setting. Worth the small journey out of the centre.

ROSSANO: Bella Napoli €
Pizzeria
Via Capri 5, 87067
Tel *0983 51 01 53*
Authentic Neapolitan-style pizzas are served in generous portions. Pasta and meat dishes also on the menu.

ROSSANO: Paridò €
Modern Italian
Via dei Normanni, 87067
Tel *0983 29 07 31*
Regional staple ingredients such as cuttlefish, swordfish, citrus fruits and aubergines are reinterpreted in modern Mediterranean style.

TROPEA: Al Pinturicchio €
Pizzeria
Via Dardano, 89861
Tel *0963 60 34 52*
Come early to this popular pizzeria with tables that spill out onto the narrow street.

TROPEA: La Lamia €
Modern Italian
Largo Vulcano, 89861
Tel *0963 612 74*
Both meat and fish dishes feature heavily on the menu at this characteristic and popular neighbourhood *osteria*.

For more information on types of restaurants *see p579*

TROPEA: Pimm's €€
Seafood
Largo Migliarese 10, 89861
Tel *0963 66 61 05* **Closed** *Mon*
Elegant and quiet restaurant in
the heart of town.

**VENOSA: Locanda Accademia
dei Piacevoli** €€
Modern Italian
Via Discesa Capovalle 1, 85029
Tel *0972 360 82* **Closed** *Mon;
first 2 wks Nov*
Small gourmet restaurant built
into a tiny stone house.

Sicily

**AGRIGENTO:
Trattoria dei Templi** €
Seafood
*Via Panoramica Valle dei Templi 15,
92100*
Tel *0922 40 31 10*
This inviting restaurant overlook-
ing the temples offers expertly
prepared seafood specialities.

AGRIGENTO: Kokalos €€
Regional Italian
Via Cavaleri Magazzeni 3
Tel *0922 60 64 27*
Traditional Sicilian cuisine using
local ingredients such as oranges,
almonds and sun-dried
tomatoes.

CATANIA: La Siciliana €
Regional Italian
Viale Marco Polo 52, 95126
Tel *095 37 64 00* **Closed** *Sun dinner*
Classic Sicilian recipes, including
dishes specific to the town. One
of Catania's best restaurants.

CATANIA: Il Cuciniere €€
Modern Italian
Via Finocchiaro Aprile 110, 95129
Tel *095 747 07 02* **Closed** *Sun*

Erice's Monte San Giuliano restaurant,
serving local dishes

The chef uses traditional Sicilian
ingredients in unique ways, such
as fish with Modica chocolate.

CEFALÙ: La Brace €
Bistro
Via 25 Novembre 10, 90015
Tel *0921 42 35 70* **Closed** *Mon, Tue;
15 Dec–15 Jan*
Hints of the Orient mingle with
local flavours at this bistro hidden
away in the historic centre.

ENNA: Ariston €
Regional Italian
Piazza Napoleone Colajanni 6, 94100
Tel *0935 260 38*
Fresh local ingredients from land
and sea served with enthusiasm
at this friendly spot.

ERICE: Monte San Giuliano €
Regional Italian
Vicolo San Rocco 7, 91016
Tel *0923 86 95 95* **Closed** *Mon;
15 Nov*
The remarkable terrace-garden
here is an ideal setting to enjoy
some authentic local cuisine.

ERICE: Osteria di Venere €€
Regional Italian
Via Roma 6, 91016
Tel *0923 86 93 62*
Sample diverse Mediterranean
cuisine including home-made
pasta and grilled catch of the day.

MARSALA: Garibaldi €
Regional Italian
Piazza dell'Addolorata 1, 91025
Tel *0923 95 30 06* **Closed** *Sat lunch,
Sun dinner*
Dizzying selection of regional
favourites, as well as fish cooked
any way you please.

MESSINA: La Durlindana €
Regional Italian
Via Nicola Fabrizi 143, 98123
Tel *090 641 31 56*
This modern restaurant with an
open kitchen offers regional
dishes and wines

MESSINA: Piero €€
Regional Italian
Via Ghibellina 119, 98123
Tel *090 640 93 54* **Closed** *Aug*
This restaurant has been serving
large plates of fish, big salads
and hearty meat dishes since its
opening in 1962.

**MONREALE:
Taverna del Pavone** €
Regional Italian
Vicolo Pensato 18, 90046
Tel *091 640 62 09* **Closed** *Mon;
2 wks Jan, 2 wks Jul*
Sample authentic, no-frills Sicilian
specialities served in a cosy and
friendly setting.

**PALERMO:
Antico Caffè Spinnato** €
Enoteca
Via Principe di Belmonte 111, 90139
Tel *091 749 51 04* **Closed** *Christmas*
Come for the wines, liqueurs and
espresso, but stay for the *cassata*
(traditional Sicilian dessert),
cannoli (fried pastry with a
creamy filling) and gelato.

PALERMO: Santandrea €
Regional Italian
Piazza Sant'Andrea 4, 90133
Tel *091 33 49 99*
In a tranquil oasis of exposed
wood and stone this eatery
dishes up time-honoured
regional fare.

PALERMO: Bye Bye Blues €€
Fine Dining
Via del Garofalo 23, 90149
Tel *091 684 14 15* **Closed** *Mon;
2 wks Jan*
Fantastic prices for a Michelin-
starred restaurant. Diners can
watch their dishes being
prepared at this restaurant.

PALERMO: Lo Scudiero €€
Seafood
Via Filippo Turati 7, 90139
Tel *091 58 16 28* **Closed** *Sun;
2 wks Aug*
The impeccable and attentive
service is almost as refreshing as
the delectable fish.

PALERMO: Sapori Perduti €€
Modern Italian
Via Principe di Belmonte 32, 90139
Tel *091 32 73 87* **Closed** *Mon; Aug*
Modern design goes hand-in-
hand with expertly prepared
modern Italian cuisine.

SIRACUSA: Enoteca Solaria €
Enoteca
Via Roma 86, 96100
Tel *0931 46 30 07*
The oldest wine bar in the city,
with labels from Italy and France.

SIRACUSA: Oinos €€
Modern Italian
Via della Giudecca 69/75, 96100
Tel *0931 46 49 00*
Intimate and informal setting
for a variety of modern dishes
based on recipes from across
Italy. There is also a good range
of beverages to accompany meals.

SIRACUSA: Porta Marina €€
Regional Italian
Via dei Candelai 35, 96100
Tel *0931 225 53* **Closed** *Mon;
2 wks Feb*
A lovely restaurant set in a
crumbling early Renaissance
palazzo. It offers good vaule for
the quality of food it serves.

DK Choice

TAORMINA: Al Duomo €€
Seafood
Vico Ebrei (Piazza Duomo), 98039
Tel *0942 62 56 56*   **Closed** *Mon*
The picturesque location for
this restaurant is set on a terrace
in Taormina's most beautiful
piazza, with the backdrop of
a 12th-century cathedral.
Classic and modern fish dishes
are whipped up by the chefs
with enthusiasm. The kitchen is
open well past midnight.

TAORMINA: Principe Cerami €€€
Fine Dining
Piazza San Domenico 5, 98039
Tel *0942 61 31 11* **Closed** *lunch, Mon*
Heavenly terrace overlooking
crystal waters offering uber-
refined Sicilian fare. Book early.

TRAPANI: Taverna Paradiso €€
Seafood
Lungomare Dante Alighieri 22, 91100
Tel *0923 223 03*
Ask the friendly staff for their
recommendations at this lovely
eatery with super-fresh fish.

Sardinia

ALGHERO: Al Tuguri €€
Seafood
Via Maiorca 113, 07041
Tel *079 97 67 72*   **Closed** *Sun;
mid-Dec–Mar*
Just a few tables are available in
this cosy seafood restaurant.

ALGHERO: Andreini €€€
Modern Italian
Via Ardoino 45, 07041
Tel *079 98 20 98*   **Closed** *Dec–Apr*
A romantic, family-run place
offering Mediterranean cuisine.

**BOSA:
Mannu da Giancarlo e Rita** €€
Seafood
Viale Alghero 14, 08013
Tel *0785 37 53 07*   **Closed** *winter*
A modern restaurant where
Lobster dominates the menu.

**CAGLIARI:
La Stella Marina di Montecristo** €
Seafood
Via Sardegna 140, 09124
Tel *347 578 89 64*   **Closed** *Sun*
This simple *osteria* with cordial
service. Wild game on Thursdays.

CAGLIARI: Dal Corsaro €€
Modern Italian
Viale Regina Margherita 28, 09124
Tel *070 66 43 18*   **Closed** *Sun;
3 wks Jan*

Buzzing atmosphere at Hivaoa, Costa Smeralda

Sardinian classics are recreated
with a contemporary twist.

CALA GONONE: Il Pescatore €€
Seafood
Lungomare Acqua Dolce 1, 08022
Tel *0784 931 74*
A seaside spot serving classic
Sardinian fish dishes.

**COSTA SMERALDA:
Corbezzolo** €€
Seafood
*Piazzetta della Fontana, Baia
Sardinia, 07021*
Tel *0789 998 93*   **Closed** *Dec–May*
Tasty classic seafood dishes
served on a sea-view terrace.

COSTA SMERALDA: Hivaoa €€
Pizzeria
Via della Marina, Porto Cervo, 07021
Tel *0789 914 51*
Dine on a breezy terrace. Pizza,
pasta and excellent seafood.

**COSTA SMERALDA:
Spinnaker** €€€
Seafood
Res. Alba Ruja, Porto Cervo, 07020
Tel *0789 912 26*   **Closed** *winter*
One of the Emerald Coast's best-
known restaurants. Excellent fish.

DK Choice

**COSTA SMERALDA:
Pedristellas** €€
Regional Italian
*Via Monte Ladu, Porto Rotondo,
07026*
Tel *377 236 92 01* **Closed** *winter*
Literally "rocks and stars" in the
Sardinian dialect, this restaurant
is set in a rock garden dotted
with centuries-old pine trees.
The tables, lighting and
meandering paths complement
the natural setting. It offers an
abundant menu of seafood and
meat in the Sardinian tradition.

**COSTA SMERALDA:
Stella di Gallura** €€
Regional Italian
*Loc. Monte Ladu, Porto Rotondo,
07026*
Tel *0789 344 02*   **Closed** *winter*
Dine by the poolside and sample
typical Sardinian dishes from
both land and sea.

**COSTA SMERALDA:
Da Giovannino** €€€
Fine Dining
*Piazza Quadra 10, Porto Rotondo,
07026*
Tel *0789 352 80*   **Closed** *winter*
High-profile restaurant with a
pretty garden. Excellent
Mediterranean cuisine.

NUORO: Il Rifugio €€
Regional Italian
Via Antonio Mereu 28, 08100
Tel *0784 23 23 55*   **Closed** *winter*
An ample variety of classic
Sardinian dishes. Excellent pizza.

ORISTANO: Craf da Banana €€
Regional Italian
Via De Castro S. A. 34, 09170
Tel *0783 42 01 82*   **Closed** *winter*
Wild game is the house speciality.
Try the mixed grill for a range.

**SANT'ANTIOCO:
Moderno da Achille** €€
Regional Italian
Via Nazionale 82, 09017
Tel *0781 831 05*   **Closed** *winter*
Tasty Sardinian fare expertly
prepared by a talented chef who
makes each dish his own, served
in an elegant setting.

SASSARI: Liberty €€
Seafood
Piazza Nazario Sauro, 07100
Tel *079 23 63 61*   **Closed** *winter*
The look is distinctly Art Deco at
this sophisticated spot serving
super-fresh fish. Long list of
Sardinian wines.

For more information on types of restaurants *see p579*

SHOPPING IN ITALY

Italy is known for its quality designer goods, ranging from chic clothing and sleek cars to stylish household items. There is a strong tradition of craftsmanship, often from family-run businesses, and there are numerous markets selling regional specialities. Apart from the town markets, it is not a country for bargains, but the joys of window shopping will offer plenty of compensation. If you come from outside the European Union, you may be able to claim back the 21 per cent IVA tax (VAT). Make sure you leave time at your departure airport to fulfil all administrative requirements.

Fresh vegetables on display at a Venetian market stall

Opening Hours

Opening times for shops are usually 9:30am–1pm and around 3:30–8pm, Tuesday to Saturday and Monday afternoons. However, shopkeepers are increasingly using more flexible hours. There are few department stores, but most large towns will have a Standa, Upim, Coin or Rinascente. These stores are often open non-stop (*orario continuato*) from 9am–8pm, Monday to Saturday. Music and bookshops sometimes stay open after 8pm and on Sundays.

Food Shops

Even though there are super-markets throughout Italy, the specialist shops, although more expensive, are still the most interesting way to shop. A *forno* has the best bread and a *macellaio* has the finest meat (go to a *norcineria* for pork products). Vegetables are freshest from market stalls or the *fruttivendolo*. You can buy cakes at the *pasticceria*, milk at the *latteria*, and pasta, ham, cheese and general foods at the often impressively stocked *alimentari*. Here you can also buy wine, but for a wider choice, head for the *enoteca*, *vineria* or *vinaio*, where you can sometimes taste the wine before purchasing.

Markets

All towns have regional weekly markets. Large towns will have several small daily markets followed by a weekly flea market, usually on Sunday. In this guide the main market days are listed under each town. Traders set up at 5am and start to clear away at about 1:30pm. Food is sold by the *etto* (100 grams) and the *chilo* (kilo) (see p665), or in numbers (two onions, etc). Food stalls selling seasonal products generally have fresher and cheaper produce than the shops. Bargaining is not usual when buying food, but it is worth asking for a discount (*sconto*) for clothes.

Seasonal Produce

To make the most of Italian food, try to buy and eat what is in season. Grapes and mushrooms are best in autumn, whereas spring is the season for asparagus and strawberries. In winter, vegetables such as Roman artichokes, cauliflower and broccoli are at their best, as are lemons from Amalfi and Sicilian blood oranges. Summer is the time for plums, pears and cherries, as well as courgettes, aubergines, tomatoes and melon.

Clothes and Designer Shops

Italy is renowned worldwide for its fashion industry. Milan is the fashion capital and Via Monte Napoleone, in the city centre, is lined with designer boutiques. All large towns will have a selection of designer shops, usually situated near each other. Less expensive clothes are

Souvenir shop in Ostuni, near Brindisi, Puglia

available in markets and many high-street shops, where the styles tend to be more conventional. Italy is also famous for leather shoes and bags, the prices of which tend to be reasonable.

Sales (saldi) are held in summer and winter. Second-hand shops can be expensive, but the quality and condition of the clothes are usually very good. Larger markets have stalls piled high with used clothes. Rummage through and you will often find bargains.

An elegant designer clothes boutique in Treviso

country. Italian kitchenware is particularly striking, with its stainless steel and copper pots, pans and utensils. For the lowest prices, avoid the tourist shops and, if possible, buy directly from the manufacturer. Less expensive items include the characteristic brown espresso and cappuccino cups sold in all markets.

Regional Specialities

Many of Italy's regional specialities are world famous: Parma ham, Chianti wine, olive oil and grappa. Regional sweets, including the Sienese panforte and Sicilian marzipan, are also well-known, as are cheeses such as Gorgonzola from Lombardy and Parmesan from Emilia-Romagna. Traditional crafts are

still practised in Italy and range from delicate lacework and glassware in the Veneto to leatherwork, jewellery and marbled paper in Florence. Italian ceramics include elaborate Tuscan pottery, hand-painted dishes around Amalfi and De Simone's stylized designer plates from Sicily.

Display of decorative glazed pottery from Tuscany

Colourful shop display of leather handbags in Florence

Jewellery and Antique Shops

Glitzy gold jewellery is very popular in Italy and every gioielleria (jewellery shop) will have a wide selection. For more unusual items, try the bigiotteria or artisan shops (oreficeria). Antique stores like Antichità and Antiquariato sell furniture and ornaments of varying quality and prices. You will rarely find bargains in Italy, except perhaps at the Fiere dell'Antiquariato (antique fairs), held throughout the year all over the country.

Interior Design and Household Wares

Interior design is another Italian sector where top names demand extravagant prices, with many shops concentrating on modern, high-tech styles. There are household shops in cities and towns throughout the

Size Chart

For Australian sizes follow the British and American conversions.

Women's dresses, coats and skirts

Italian	38	40	42	44	46	48	50
British	8	10	12	14	16	18	20
American	6	8	10	12	14	16	18

Women's shoes

Italian	36	37	38	39	40	41
British	3	4	5	6	7	8
American	5	6	7	8	9	10

Men's suits

Italian	44	46	48	50	52	54	56	58 (size)
British	34	36	38	40	42	44	46	48 (inches)
American	34	36	38	40	42	44	46	48 (inches)

Men's shirts (collar size)

Italian	36	38	39	41	42	43	44	45 (cm)
British	14	15	15½	16	16½	17	17½	18 (inches)
American	14	15	15½	16	16½	17	17½	18 (inches)

Men's shoes

Italian	39	40	41	42	43	44	45	46
British	6	7	7½	8	9	10	11	12
American	7	7½	8	8½	9½	10½	11	11½

ENTERTAINMENT IN ITALY

Italians exude strong national pride and passion about every aspect of their cultural heritage. One of Europe's key centres of culture since Roman times, Italy was the cradle of the Renaissance, and it is known today as the home of opera and a mixed bag of regional styles of folk music. The country holds one of the most acclaimed international film festivals and every town boasts a *teatro*, an elaborate classical venue with mixed programmes incorporating every aspect of classic and traditional culture. Add to this the many street festivals and fairs, often in celebration of food, wine and the *dolce vita*, and you will never have a dull moment.

Practical Information

Most venues have booking facilities online or a booking line to call. However, major events and most opera performances tend to sell out well in advance, so it is wise to book through specialist ticket companies such as **Liaisons Abroad** that may still have availability when the venue itself has sold out.

If you wish to find out what's on in Italy during your stay, check the Italian tourism website (www.italiantourism.com) or pick up a copy of *Dove*, a monthly publication about culture, travel and gastronomy that also highlights the month's events in Rome and Milan. *Il Corriere della Sera*, Italy's oldest daily, contains sections on events and culture; its Vivimilano website (www.corriere.it/vivimilano) is a mine of information on events taking place in the fashion capital. Another website (www.romaturismo.it) offers an excellent service for Rome.

Tourist information offices *(see p617)* will also provide information on programmes, events and venues, as will the **Italian State Tourist Board**. Few Italian venues provide easy access for people with restricted mobility. The situation improves a little in the summer, when many events are held outside.

Opera and Classical Music

Italy has some of the world's most beautiful and historic opera houses. Venice's **La Fenice**, destroyed by fire in 1996, has been restored to its former splendour, and **Teatro alla Scala** *(see p197)* in Milan also underwent a major renovation. In addition to the original building, there is also an extra theatre, **Teatro degli Arcimboldi**, allowing the Scala to host more performances.

Verona hosts a summer season of opera and classical music in the outdoor **Arena di Verona** *(see p151)*, while Rome's venues include the open-air **Baths of Caracalla** *(see p441)*, the breathtaking Renzo Piano-designed auditorium **Parco della Musica** and the **Teatro dell'Opera**.

In May and June, Florence's **Maggio Musicale** *(see p70)* is packed with opera, ballet and classical performances.

Poster advertising the Venice Film Festival

Rock, Jazz and Contemporary Music

Large concerts tend to be held in classic theatres or in sports stadiums. The **Arena di Verona** hosts big names in summer, as does the **Stadio Olimpico** in Rome. In Milan, the **Forum di Assago** sports stadium is a popular venue. Tickets for concerts are sometimes sold in record shops.

World-class jazz performers gather annually in Perugia for the **Umbria Jazz** festival in July. The website provides booking details and information.

Theatre and Ballet

Italy has the highest concentration of traditional theatres in Europe, offering a mixture of theatre, ballet and classical music all under one roof. All theatres also hold ballet performances, mainly by international touring troupes. The **Scala**'s ballet company has gained international renown. Both tradition and innovation can be seen at the international festival of ballet that takes place at Genoa's **Teatro Carlo Felice** in July.

The opera festival in Verona attracts huge crowds to the Roman arena

Cinema

One of the highlights of the cinema year is the **Venice Film Festival** *(see p71)*, which takes place from August to September. The Rome International Festival of Cinema *(see p72)* also draws major film stars. A smaller International Film Festival *(see p71)* is held in Taormina, Sicily, while Florence has the Festa dei Popoli *(see p72)* in winter.

A thrilling moment in the Sienese Palio race held in Piazza del Campo

Regional Festivals, Music and Dance

Seasonal festivals are either religious, relating to patron saints, or food-orientated. The best known is *Carnevale* (literally "farewell to meat") *(see p73)*, which celebrates the end of winter and introduces Lent. Venice holds the most opulent and the oldest masquerade party, while Viareggio, in Tuscany, is famous for its lively themed floats.

Another festival highlight is the Palio of Siena *(see pp71 and 345)*, a bareback horse race that takes place twice a year in one of Italy's most beautiful squares. For further details on festivals throughout Italy, see pp70–73.

Every region in Italy has its own ancient music and dance, but the best known is the *tarantella*, a lively dance and rhythmic song from Puglia *(see p515)*. Legends trace the origins of the name to the tarantula spider, since victims of a tarantula bite would perform a frenzied dance in order to sweat out the poison.

An elaborate Carnival mask

Culture

Spectating, whether at sporting events, rural festivals or even grand events, is what entertainment is all about. And part of this, of course, involves that very Italian pastime – seeing and being seen. You can witness this in daily life in the café culture – visit any of the large cities' popular squares, such as Piazza di Spagna or Piazza Navona in Rome, Piazza del Duomo in Milan or Piazza San Marco in Venice, and you will see people of all ages parading around in their best clothes. This is referred to as *la passeggiata*, a walk around that becomes a ritual at weekends, along the seafront and lakeside promenades in summer and in city and town centres.

Another aspect of daily life is *l'aperitivo*. This ritual of joining friends for an early evening drink after work or before going on to dinner or to a nightclub is back in fashion. Bars provide abundant finger-food buffets to accompany the drinks, which are generally priced higher than at other times of day. This trend has spawned lounge clubs in the major cities.

DIRECTORY

Practical Information

Italian State Tourist Board
1 Princes Street, London W1B 2AY.
Tel 020 7408 1254.
Ⓦ italiantouristboard. co.uk

Liaisons Abroad
Tel 020 7808 7330.
Ⓦ liaisonsabroad.com

Opera and Classical Music

Arena di Verona
Piazza Brà, Verona.
Tel 045 800 51 51.
Ⓦ arena.it

Baths of Caracalla
Via delle Terme di Caracalla 52, Rome.
Map 7 A3.

La Fenice
Campo San Fantin, Venice.
Map 7 A2. **Tel** 041 786 511. Ⓦ teatrolafenice.it

Maggio Musicale
Florence. **Tel** 055 277 93 50.
Ⓦ maggiofiorentino.it

Parco della Musica
Viale de Coubertin 30, Rome. **Tel** 06 80 24 12 81.
Ⓦ auditorium.com

Teatro alla Scala
Via Filodrammatici 2, Milan. **Tel** 02 72 00 37 44.
Ⓦ teatroallascala.org

Teatro degli Arcimboldi
Viale dell'Innovazione 20, Milan.
Tel 02 641 142 212.
Ⓦ teatroarcimboldi.it

Teatro dell'Opera
Piazza B Gigli 7, Rome.
Map 3 C3.
Tel 06 48 16 01.
Ⓦ operaroma.it

Rock, Jazz and Contemporary Music

Forum di Assago
Via G Di Vittorio 6, Assago, Milan.
Tel 02 48 85 71.
Ⓦ mediolanumforum.it

Stadio Olimpico
Viale dei Gladiatori, Rome.

Umbria Jazz
Tel 075 573 24 32.
Ⓦ umbriajazz.com

Theatre and Ballet

Teatro Carlo Felice
Passo E Montale 4, Genova.
Tel 010 58 93 29.
Ⓦ carlofelicegenova.it

Cinema

Venice Film Festival
Tel 041 521 87 11.
Ⓦ labiennale.org

Specialist Holidays and Outdoor Activities

Italy offers an amazing variety of cultural, sporting and leisure activities. However, many schools and groups require annual membership and short-term activities are often expensive and difficult to find. Information on current leisure and sporting events in a specific region is available from the tourist office listed for each town in this guide. For details on annual festivals, see *Italy Through the Year* on pages 70–73. The following suggestions include some of the most popular as well as some more unusual pursuits.

Cycling on the tree-lined flatlands of the Po Delta

Walking, Cycling and Horse Riding

Some Italian branches of the **World Wide Fund for Nature (WWF)** organize walks and treks. **Club Alpino Italiano (CAI)** runs trekking and climbing excursions and the **Italian Birds Protection League (LIPU)** arranges nature walks and bird-watching trips. The military *IGM*

maps are the most detailed but unfortunately are only available from specialist map shops.

Cycling is popular despite Italy's mountainous landscape. Travel bookshops stock publications with suggested routes, such as the Po Delta, which has miles of scenic flatlands.

Many riding schools organize trips and outings, which are also advertised in the local press. For general information, contact the **Federazione Italiana Sport Equestri**.

Mountain Sports

The most well-equipped and famous ski resorts are in the Dolomites, in the Italian Alps and around Turin, the city chosen to host the 2006 Winter Olympics. There are also smaller and less expensive resorts in the Apennines and in Sicily. Package ski holidays, arranged from outside Italy, offer the best deals.

The **Federazione Arrampicata Sportiva Italiana** has a list of mountain climbing schools that arrange climbs for all levels.

Ski lift near the desolate Falzarego Pass, in the heart of the Dolomites

Archaeological Digs

The British monthly magazine *Archaeology Abroad*, available in the UK, gives a comprehensive list of archaeology groups and digs worldwide. In Italy, the **Gruppo Archeologico Romano** runs two-week digs in various regions. There are summer and winter digs, for both adults and children. The group has contacts with local archaeological organizations as well.

Italian Language and Culture

For a wide selection of material on courses and schools in Italy, contact the Italian consulate in your home country. The **Società Dante Alighieri** provides courses in the Italian language, history of art, literature and culture. There are both full- and part-time courses available, for every level. Language schools abound in Italy's main cities and are advertised in the Yellow Pages (*Pagine Gialle*) or foreign language bookshops and newspapers. For young students, **Intercultura** will organize weekly, monthly and year-long exchanges including language courses, accommodation with Italian families and enrolment in Italian schools. Cooking holidays run by

Group hiking tour in the Dolomites of Trentino-Alto Adige *(see p82)*

A lesson in Italian cookery in Sicily

English-speaking experts in Italian cooking have become very popular. **Tasting Places**, for example, does wine tours and week-long courses in Italian cuisine, and provides beautiful accommodation. The course locations include the Veneto, Sicily, Tuscany and Umbria. Wine-tasting tours are organized by local tourist boards. The Università per Stranieri in Perugia runs courses in Italian, art history and literature (www. unistrapg.it).

Water Sports

Most lakes and many seaside resorts rent out sailing boats, canoes and windsurfing equipment. Lessons and courses are organized by clubs, which usually require membership. For a list of authorized associations contact the **Federazione Italiana Canoa Kayak** and the **Federazione Italiana Vela**. Weekend and weekly sailing holidays and courses are featured in the magazine *Avventure nel Mondo* and most travel agents have a selection of sailing holidays.

Swimming pools are expensive in Italy and many do not accept people on a daily basis. You often have to pay a membership fee and a monthly tariff. Some of the luxurious hotels open their pools to the public in summer, but at pricey rates. Water parks are popular and provide pools, slides, wave machines and games. Before diving into any lakes or rivers (and even the sea near main towns) it is best to check that the water is not polluted. The **Federazione Italiana di Attività**

Subacquee runs underwater diving courses, and can give information on all local centres.

Air Sports

There are schools nationwide that offer hang-gliding and flying courses, but the minimum duration of each course is one month. For information and a list of schools contact the **AeroClub Italia**. You must be licensed before you can fly and all crafts must be registered with AeroClub.

Other Sports

Golf is a popular sport in Italy and there are plenty of courses to choose from. Home membership and handicap are often required for daily access to a club. Italian tennis clubs usually operate on a membership basis, unless you are invited as a member's guest. The national **Federazione Italiana di Tennis** has a list of all the tennis clubs in Italy. The opportunity to watch a professional football game should not be missed. Seats can be scarce, so book tickets in advance from the stadium. Most Serie A matches are played on Sundays, with international games taking place on Tuesdays and Wednesdays.

Playing golf

Sailing in Italy, a popular leisure activity and competitive sport

DIRECTORY

AeroClub Italia
Via Cesare Beccaria 35a, 00196 Rome. **Tel** 06 36 08 46 00.
W aeci.it

Club Alpino Italiano
Via E Petrella 19, Milan.
Tel 02 205 72 31. W cai.it

Federazione Arrampicata Sportiva Italiana
Via del Terrapieno 27, 40127 Bologna. **Tel** 051 601 48 90.
W federclimb.it

Federazione Italiana Attività Subacquee
Via A Doria 8, Milan.
Tel 02 670 50 05. W fias.it

Federazione Italiana Canoa Kayak
Viale Tiziano 70, 00196 Rome.
Tel 06 36 85 81 88.
W federcanoa.it

Federazione Italiana Sport Equestri
Viale Tiziano 74, 00196 Rome.
Tel 06 836 68 41. W fise.it

Federazione Italiana di Tennis
Stadio Olimpico, Rome.
Tel 06 36 85 82 18.
W federtennis.it

Federazione Italiana Vela
Piazza Borgo Pila 40, Genova.
Tel 010 54 45 41. W federvela.it

Gruppo Archeologico Romano
Via Baldi degli Ubaldi 168, 00167 Rome. **Tel** 06 638 52 56.
W gruppoarcheologico.it

Intercultura
Via Venezia 25, 00184 Rome.
Tel 06 48 88 24 01.
W intercultura.it

Italian Birds Protection League (LIPU)
Via Udine 3A, 43122 Parma.
Tel 0521 27 30 43. W lipu.it

Società Dante Alighieri
Piazza Firenze 27, 00186 Rome.
Tel 06 687 36 94. W ladante.it

Tasting Places Cookery and Wine Tours
PO Box 38174, London W10 5ZP.
Tel 020 8964 5333.
W tastingplaces.com

World Wide Fund for Nature
Via Po 25c, 00198 Rome.
Tel 06 84 49 71. W wwf.it

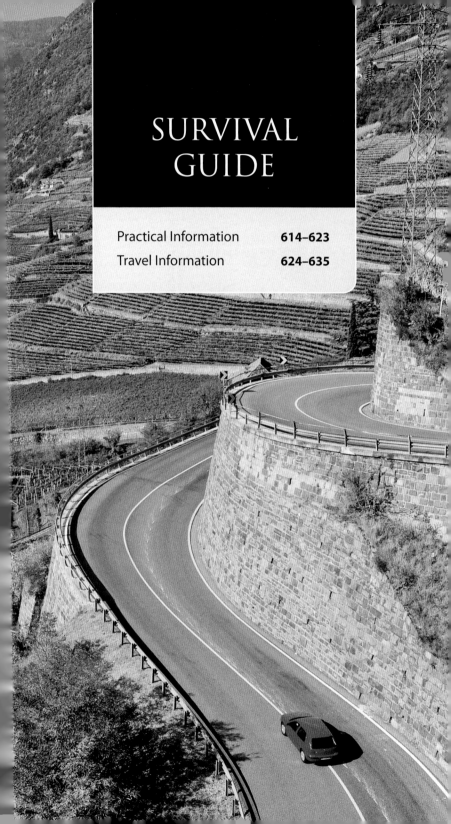

SURVIVAL GUIDE

PRACTICAL INFORMATION

Ask any Italian and they will almost certainly tell you that Italy is the most beautiful country in the world. They may not be far wrong. However, the charm and allure of Italy may help to veil some of her numerous practical problems. Getting any kind of information is rarely straightforward; public offices and banks are nearly always crippled by long queues and bureaucracy; and the postal service is renowned for its inefficiency. This section, together with some forward planning and a little patience, should help you cope with some of Italy's idiosyncrasies.

Tourists crossing the Ponte della Paglia in Venice *(see p113)*

When to Visit

The northern part of Italy is generally more temperate than the south, which has a Mediterranean climate. From June to September the weather is hot throughout the country and, in peak summer, also humid. Seaside resorts tend to get very busy. Spring and autumn are ideal for visiting cities as temperatures are milder, making sightseeing much more comfortable, although you should be prepared for the odd downpour.

Italy's towns and historic sites are extremely popular attractions and it is worth considering this when planning your trip. Most sights are open all year, except on some public holidays *(see p73)*, and most close one day a week. Rome, Florence and Venice are all crowded from spring to October and it is advisable to book a hotel well in advance. In August the cities are generally slightly less busy, abandoned by their inhabitants for the summer holidays.

In February, Venice triples its population during Carnevale *(see p73)* and at Easter, Rome is overrun by pilgrims and tourists. Winter can be bitterly cold, especially in the north, and December to March is the time of year for skiing in the high altitude resorts of the Italian Alps. *The Climate of Italy* on pages 76–7 takes a detailed look at the country's regional weather.

Visas and Permesso di Soggiorno

European Union nationals and citizens of the US, Canada, Australia and New Zealand do not need visas for stays of up to three months. Most European Union (EU) visitors need only a valid passport including a photograph.

All visitors should check requirements with the Italian embassy before travelling and, officially, declare themselves to the Italian police within eight days of arrival. If you are staying in a hotel or campsite, this will be done for you by the staff, otherwise you will need to contact the local *Questura* (police station) yourself.

Anyone wishing to stay in Italy for more than three months will have to obtain a *permesso di soggiorno* (permit to stay or residence permit). Non-EU citizens must apply for one within eight days of arrival. You can apply for a residence permit at any main police station, (*Questura*). In some cases you can obtain a kit containing the necessary application form from main post offices. You must apply for the correct permit, either a permit to work *(lavoro)* or a permit to study *(studio)*. The necessary documentation is listed on the *Questura* website *(see p617)*.

To apply for a study permit, it is necessary to get a letter from the relevant school or university at which you intend to study, giving details of your course. This then has to be sent to the Italian consulate in your own country of origin to obtain an official covering letter, or declaration.

You will also need some form of guarantee that your medical bills will be paid if you become ill or have an accident where you require medical treatment. A comprehensive insurance policy for the length of your stay *(see p619)* will usually be sufficient.

Rome's renowned Tazza d'Oro café, an ideal rest stop after sightseeing

◀ The wonderful view from the A22 road that carves through the mountains and vineyards that surround Bolzano

Customs

On 30 June 1999, the intra-EU Duty and Tax Free Allowances, better known as Duty-free and mainly affecting such high-tax items as alcohol, perfumes and tobacco, were abolished. However, for EU residents the amount of these goods that can be imported for personal use has increased.

Consulates can generally provide up-to-date information on particular customs regulations. To find out what you can take back from Italy to non-EU countries, contact that particular country's customs department, which will be able to advise you.

Sign for tourist information

Tax Exemption

Value Added Tax (IVA in Italy) ranges from about 21 per cent, with a reduced rate of 4–10 per cent on some items. Non-European Union citizens making purchases in Italy can claim an IVA rebate, provided the total expenditure in the one shop is over €155. It is a long process, and it is easier to get a refund if you shop where you see the "Euro Free Tax" sign, rather than from a market stall. In this instance, show your passport to the shop assistant, complete a form, and the IVA will be deducted from your bill. Alternatively, present a customs officer with your purchases and their receipts on your departure from Italy. He or she will stamp the receipts, which you then send to the vendor. A refund should eventually be sent to you.

Tourist Information

The national tourist board, **ENIT**, has a good website as well as branches in capital cities worldwide, and offers general information on Italy. For specific requests, contact the local tourist offices. The addresses and telephone numbers are listed under each town or city, directly under the title, and they are plotted on the town and city

maps. An EPT *(Ente Provinciale di Turismo)* has information on its town and surrounding province, whereas an APT *(Azienda di Promozione Turistica)* deals exclusively with individual towns. Both offices help with practical information such as hotel bookings and tours. They also provide free maps and guidebooks in various languages. The EPT and APT can refer you to local tour guides and advise on trips and excursions.

Small towns will have a *Pro Loco*, a tourist office run by the local administration, which is sometimes open only during the tourist season. It is usually located in the town hall.

Tours

Many tour companies organize coach trips, with English-speaking guides, that include all the main tourist attractions in Italy. Companies such as the UK-based **Leger Holidays** offer coach tours that go all over the country. If you are looking for something a little more personal and off the beaten track, check the local pages of national newspapers for tour groups or organizations. Local tourist boards will also be able to advise you. Always employ official guides and be sure to establish the fee in advance. For information on specialist holidays, such as sporting or cultural activities, turn to pages 610–11.

A guided group tour through the streets of Florence

Daytime sightseeing on a tranquil canal in Venice

Sightseeing Opening Hours

Italian museums are gradually conforming to regulations, particularly in the northern and central regions of the country, opening from 9am–7pm daily, except for Mondays. In winter, however, many musuems revert to slightly earlier closing times, particularly on Sundays, but it is best to check.

Privately run and smaller museums set their own opening times, so it is advisable to phone in advance to avoid disappointment. Archaeological sites are generally open from 9am to one hour before sunset, Tuesday to Sunday. Churches are usually open from about 7am–12:30pm and 4–7pm. However, they often prefer not to let tourists in during services, so Sunday is not the best day to visit.

Admission Charges

Sightseeing fees range from €2 to €12. Churches are usually free, but some expect a donation, and you will need coins to illuminate some works of art. Reductions for students are not always offered but many state-run museums and archaeological sites allow free entry for EU residents under 18 and over 60 or 65 years of age. Large groups are often entitled to a discount as well. If reductions are available, you will need to show a valid form of identification.

Etiquette and Tipping

People in Italy are friendly towards foreign visitors. On entering a shop or bar it is customary to greet people with a general *buon giorno* (good morning) or *buona sera* (good evening), and the same applies when leaving. They will also try to be helpful when asked directions in the street. If your Italian is slight, simply saying *scusi*, followed by the name of the place you wish to go to, will often suffice. *Grazie* (thank you) is replied to with *prego* (you're welcome).

Tipping in restaurants is expected when the 10–15 per cent service is not included. However, as much as 10 per cent would be considered generous and a tip is often not expected at all in more basic restaurants. Taxi drivers and hotel porters expect a few euros if they have been helpful. You could simply round the bill up to the nearest €2.

Italians are very dress-conscious and unusual clothes do get noticed. Be aware that in places of worship you should cover your torso and upper arms; shorts and skirts must reach below the knee.

Smoking is forbidden in all buildings open to the public (including offices, shops, bars and restaurants). However, it is tolerated in outdoor public places, whereas drunkenness is definitely frowned upon.

A student relaxing in the sun in Gaiole in Chianti

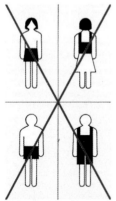

Unacceptable dress in church: both sexes are required to cover torsos and upper arms

Religious Services

Around 35 per cent of the population is practising Catholic. Sunday mass is celebrated throughout the country, while in the principal churches, services are also held during the week. In major cities some churches, such as the church of Santa Susanna (Via XX Settembre 14) in Rome, offer services and confession in English. For some visitors, a trip to Rome will include an audience with the pope *(see p423)*.

With increasing numbers of foreigners making their home in Italy, all the main religious beliefs are also represented. For details contact the main centres in Rome.

Student Information

The national student travel organization, **CTS** (Centro Turistico Studentesco), has branches throughout Italy and Europe. They issue the International Student Identity Card (ISIC) and the Youth International Educational Exchange Card (YIEE). Both can be used, along with a passport, for discounts at museums and other tourist attractions. The ISIC card also gives holders access to a free 24-hour telephone helpline in cases of emergency. As well as issuing youth cards, CTS offers cut-price car hire and will organize holidays and courses. For details about youth hostels,

ISIC card

contact the **Associazione Italiana Alberghi per la Gioventù** (the Italian YHA), providing that you are a current member.

Travelling with Children

On the whole, Italians love children, to an extent that sometimes seems over-indulgent. Most trattorias and pizzerias welcome them and there are no rules excluding children from bars; however, high chairs are unusual. Hotels also welcome children, but smaller establishments may have limited facilities. Some of the more up-market hotels will arrange a babysitting service. Very few museums, on the other hand, provide special child-orientated activities. It is common to see children playing outside fairly late at night, especially in summer. Most towns have city parks with playgrounds and many have summer funfairs. Regular stops for *gelato* are guaranteed to go down well with youngsters. For young swimmers, the calm Mediterranean is ideal, though care should always be taken.

Disabled Travellers

Awareness of the needs of the disabled is improving in Italy, especially in major cities, with ramps being added to museums and some churches. Trains and buses are also becoming more disabled-friendly. In Milan **AIAS**

(Associazione Italiana Assistenza Spastici) and in Rome **CO.IN. Sociale** and **Roma per Tutti** provide information and general assistance. Train travellers with **Trenitalia** on both international and domestic routes receive help with special reservations and assistance at stations.

Public Toilets

Gabinetto means public toilet, though signs often say WC. Tourist cities have well-signed public conveniences that charge around €1. Some have cleaning staff on hand and a tip may be left. Italian cafés usually have a toilet for their customers, though it is worth checking. Old-style "crouch" toilets are still common.

Electrical Adaptors

The voltage in Italy is 220 volts, with two-pin round-pronged plugs, so it is advisable to bring a universal adaptor with you or buy one in the country. Most hotels with three or more stars have hair-driers and shaving points in all bedrooms, but check the voltage first, to be safe.

Italian Time

Italy is one hour ahead of Greenwich Mean Time (GMT). The clocks are put forward one hour in March and back in October. For example: London is one hour behind Italy; Sydney is nine hours ahead; while Ottawa is six hours behind.

Responsible Travel

Local attitudes towards environmental issues are developing rather slowly in Italy, despite the efforts of many concerned groups such as the Verdi political party. However, there are opportunities for low impact travel and alternative green options available.

Staying at family run guest-houses instead of international hotel chains helps support local economies. National and regional parks award eco labels to hotels and guesthouses that adhere to EU rules governing sustainable tourism, which cover issues such as energy and water saving, waste disposal and use of local products. The **National Association for Agritourism** *(see p560)* offers countrywide

farm stays. These are a great way of enjoying the countryside and experiencing local traditions, as well as helping supplement the income of small farm owners. Facilities vary and some farms offer visitors the opportunity to help out.

Farmers' markets and growers who sell their produce direct to the public are now more common, guaranteeing fresh, seasonal produce. Look for the label *biologico* when searching for organic produce.

Conversion Chart

Imperial to Metric
1 inch = 2.54 centimetres
1 foot = 30 centimetres
1 mile = 1.6 kilometres
1 ounce = 28 grams
1 pound = 454 grams
1 pint = 0.57 litre
1 gallon = 4.6 litres

Metric to Imperial
1 centimetre = 0.4 inch
1 metre = 3 feet 3 inches
1 kilometre = 0.6 mile
1 gram = 0.04 ounce
1 kilogram = 2.2 pounds
1 litre = 1.8 pints

DIRECTORY

Questura and Permits

w poliziadistato.it

w portale immigrazione.it

w esteri.it/visti

Italian Customs and Tax

w agenziadogane.it

Tourist Information and Tours

APT Florence
Via Cavour 1r. **Map** 2 D4.
Tel 055 29 08 32.
w firenzeturismo.it

APT Siena
Piazza del Campo 56.
Tel 0577 28 05 51.
w terresiena.it

APT Venice
Piazza San Marco 71f.
Map 7 B2.
Tel 041 529 87 11.
w turismovenezia.it

ENIT
w italia.it

IAT Milan
Piazza Castello 1.
Tel 02 77 40 43 43.
w visitamilano.it

Leger Holidays
Tel 0844 846 08 08.
w leger.co.uk

Rome Tourist Office
Termini Station, Platform 24. **Map** 4 D3. **Tel** 06 06 08. **w** 060608.it

Religious Organizations

Catholic
Ufficio Informazioni Vaticano, Piazza San

Pietro, Vaticano, Rome.
Map 1 B3. **Tel** 06 69 88 16 62. **w** vatican.va

Jewish
Unione delle Comunità Ebraiche Italiane, Lungotevere Sanzio 9, Rome. **Map** 6 D1.
Tel 06 45 54 22 00.
w ucei.it

Muslim
Centro Islamico Culturale d'Italia, Viale della Moschea 85, Rome.
Tel 06 808 22 58.

Student Information

Associazione Italiana Alberghi per la Gioventù
Via Cavour 44 (3rd floor), Rome. **Map** 3 C5.
Tel 06 487 11 52.
w aighostels.com

CTS
Via Solferino 6A, Rome.
Map 4 D3.
Tel 06 462 04 31.
w cts.it

Disabled Tours

AIAS
Via P Mantegazza 10, Milan. **Tel** 02 330 20 21.
w aiasmilano.it

CO.IN.Sociale
Via E Giglioli 54A, Rome.
w coinsociale.it

Roma per Tutti
Tel 06 57 17 70 94.
w romapertutti.it

Responsible Travel

National Association for Agritourism
w agriturist.it

Personal Security and Health

Although Italy is generally a safe place for visitors, it is wise to keep a watchful eye on your personal belongings, especially in the larger towns and cities. There is a conspicuous police presence throughout the country, and in the event of an emergency or crime, any of the police officers described in this section will be able to assist you and tell you where to go to report an incident. If you fall ill, pharmacies are a good first stop where medically trained staff can give advice or tell you where to find further help. In an emergency, the Casualty Department (*Pronto Soccorso*) of any hospital will treat you and it is likely that you will encounter English-speaking staff, especially in large towns.

Commissariato di Polizia – a police station

Police car

Green Cross ambulance in Venice

Roman fire engine

Personal Property

Petty theft such as pickpocketing, bag snatching and car theft is common in Italian cities. In the event of a theft you must report it within 24 hours to the nearest questura or commissariato di polizia (police station). If possible, show them some ID.

Avoid leaving anything visible in an unattended car, including a car radio. If you have to leave luggage in a car, find a hotel that has private parking. When making a purchase, always check your change and do not keep wallets in back pockets, especially on buses or in other crowded places. "Bum bags" and money belts are a favourite target for pickpockets, so try to keep them hidden. When

walking, hold bags and cameras in front of you and on the inside of the pavement so as not to tempt motorized snatchers, and do not show expensive cameras and video equipment in areas off tourist routes.

If attacked, never attempt to hang on to your things as you could be seriously injured and dragged along the street.

Avoid carrying large sums of money – take out only what you need for the day. It is advisable to get comprehensive travel insurance that covers theft of personal possessions in addition to covering cancellation/delay of flights, loss/damage of luggage, money and other valuables, as well as personal liability and accidents. It should include cover for legal assistance and advice.

If you do need to make an insurance claim for stolen or lost property, you must get a copy of the report (denuncia) from the police station when you report the incident. In case of lost passports, go to your embassy or consulate; for lost credit cards or travellers' cheques, contact the issuing company's nearest office.

If you do not have insurance cover, contact your embassy as soon as possible after an incident, such as an accident,

occurs. The embassy can offer advice and should provide you with a list of English- and Italian-speaking lawyers who are knowledgeable about both the Italian and English legal systems.

Personal Security

Although petty crime in cities is frequent, violent crime in Italy is rare. However, it is common for people to raise their voices aggressively during an argument. Usually, remaining calm and being polite will help to defuse the situation.

Always be wary of unofficial tour guides, taxi drivers or strangers who wish to assist you or advise you on accommodation, restaurants or shops as they may expect something in return. Decline their offers politely but firmly.

A team of *carabinieri* in their usual police uniform

Women Travellers

Women travelling on their own in Italy are likely to meet with a lot of attention. This is often more of an irritation than a danger, but it is best to keep away from lonely, unlit streets and areas near railway stations at night, and to carry an alarm or whistle and be equipped with the telephone numbers of your hotel and a local taxi service. Walking quickly and purposefully is a good way to avoid any unwanted attention. The staff at hotels and restaurants generally treat their single female guests and customers with extra care and attention.

The Police

There are several different police forces in Italy and each one fulfils a particular role. The state police, *la polizia*, wear blue uniforms and drive blue cars. They deal with most crimes.

The carabinieri are militarily trained and wear dark blue and black uniforms with red striped trousers. These officers deal with a variety of offences from organized crime to speeding and can also conduct random security checks.

The *guardia di finanza* are the financial police force (the fraud squad), and wear grey uniforms with yellow striped trousers. The *vigili urbani*, or the municipal traffic police, wear blue and white uniforms in winter and white during the summer.

Even though they are not official police officers, the *vigili urbani* can issue heavy fines for traffic and parking offences. They can usually be spotted patrolling the streets, enforcing laws or directing traffic. Officers from any of the forces will be able to help in an emergency.

Outside a Florentine pharmacy with a green cross sign

Medical Treatment

Emergency medical care in Italy is free for all EU and Australian citizens, thanks to reciprocal agreements. The EHIC European Health Insurance Card, which is available from the UK Department of Health offices, website or from a main post office, covers emergencies only; private medical insurance is needed for all other types of treatment. The card comes with a booklet that contains general health advice and information about how to claim free medical treatment when travelling abroad. You may find you have to pay and reclaim the money later. Australians need to apply to Medicare.

Non-EU citizens should try to arrive in Italy with comprehensive private medical insurance to cover all eventualities. If you do need emergency treatment, go to the Pronto Soccorso (Casualty Department) of the nearest hospital. If necessary, you will be referred to the appropriate specialist or department within the same structure. As an alternative, ask your hotel to call the night doctor – guardia medica – who can be consulted on the phone.

No inoculations are needed for Italy, but mosquito repellent is advisable in summer. Repellent creams and sprays are found in pharmacies, as are electrical repellers which burn pellets to deter the bugs.

Municipal policeman

Pharmacies

Various medical products, including homeopathic medicines, are available in any pharmacy (*farmacia*), but a prescription is often required. Qualified staff will offer advice for minor ailments and common illnesses and provide appropriate medicines. Thanks to a night rota (*servizio notturno*), there is always a pharmacy open in all cities and most towns. Those that are open at night are listed in the local pages of daily newspapers and on all pharmacy doors.

Pharmacies also sell toiletries and beauty items. Common non-prescription pharmaceutical products such as aspirin are also sold at lower prices in many large supermarkets.

DIRECTORY

Embassies and Consulates

Australia
Via A. Bosio 5, Rome. **Tel** 06 85 27 21. W **italy.embassy.gov.au**

Canada
Via Zara 30, Rome. **Tel** 06 8544 429 11. W **canada.it**

United Kingdom
Via XX Settembre 80a, Rome. **Map** 4 D2. **Tel** 06 42 20 00 01. W **ukinitaly.fco.gov.uk**

United States
Via Veneto 119a, Rome. **Map** 3 C1. **Tel** 06 467 41. W **italy.usembassy.gov**

Emergency Numbers

General Emergency
Tel 113.

Fire Service
Tel 115.

Medical Emergencies
Tel 118.

Police (Carabinieri)
Tel 112.

Medical Treatment

Medicare Australia
Information for Individuals and Families
W **medicareaustralia.gov.au**

UK Department of Health
Information for Travellers
W **dh.gov.uk**

Banking and Local Currency

Virtually all Italian hotels, many shops, large restaurants and petrol stations accept major credit cards. Only in the more off-the-beaten-track locations will you have difficulties without euros, and some establishments will offer a discount for payments made in cash, especially in low season. When you pay with a credit card, you might be asked to show identification, such as your passport. Foreign currency can be changed in banks, although these are often crowded and service tends to be slow. All banks will cash travellers' cheques, and cashpoint machines *(bancomat)* will accept cards with a PIN number. Most machines also accept MasterCard, VISA and American Express cards. Although banks often have the best exchange rates, bureaux de change and foreign exchange machines can be more convenient.

Cash dispenser, which also accepts VISA and MasterCard (Access)

Changing Money

Banking hours are somewhat restrictive and can also be slightly erratic so it is safest to acquire a small amount of local currency before you arrive in Italy. Exchange rates will vary from place to place.

Travellers' cheques are still a safe way to carry money, though commission charges can be hefty. Choose a well known name such as Thomas Cook or American Express. Once you arrive, the most convenient way to change money is to use the electronic exchange machines, which are located at all major airports, train stations and some banks. The machines have multi-lingual instructions and the exchange rate is clearly displayed on the screen. Simply feed in notes of the same foreign currency and you will receive euros in return.

Bureaux de change can be found in all main towns. Although they are easier to use,

they usually have worse exchange rates and charge more commission than banks.

Regional Differences in Cost of Living

The north is generally more expensive than the south, but there are many exceptions. Restaurants and hotels off the beaten track are usually better value, and buying locally made produce is cost effective if you avoid obvious tourist traps.

Banking Hours

Banks are usually open between 8:30am and 1:30pm, Monday to Friday. Most also open for an hour in the afternoon, from about 2:15pm to 3pm or 2:30pm until 3:30pm, depending on the bank. All banks close at weekends and for public holidays, and they also close early the day before a major

Metal-detecting security doors found at most banks

holiday. Bureaux de change, however, are often open all day, and in some places they also stay open until late at night.

Using Banks

For security purposes, most banks have electronic double doors with metal detectors, allowing one person in at a time. Metal objects and bags should first be deposited in lockers situated in the foyer. Press the button to open the outer door, then wait for it to close behind you. The inner door then opens automatically. Do not be alarmed by the heavily armed guards that patrol most banks in Italy.

Changing money at a bank can be a frustrating process involving endless form-filling and queuing. First you have to go to the window that displays the *cambio* sign and then to the *cassa* to obtain your money. If in doubt, ask someone in order to avoid waiting in the wrong queue.

If you need to have money sent to you in Italy, banks at home can transfer money to an Italian bank, but it can take up to a week. American Express, Thomas Cook and Western Union all provide swifter money transfer services, with a charge to the sender.

Cash Machines

Withdrawing cash from an ATM (automatic teller machine) with a credit card is a straightforward process. Choose your language on the screen and follow the instructions. You will need to type in your PIN number, so have it handy. Should your card be swallowed up by a cash machine for some reason (for example if you used an incorrect PIN number), it may be sent back to the issuing bank. However, if the bank is open do ask inside. Costs for cash withdrawals are set by your bank so check before you travel. It may be advisable to take out a largish amount of money in one go, but bear in mind that ATMs may run out of notes during weekends.

The Euro

The euro (€) is the common currency of the European Union. It came into general circulation on 1 January 2002, initially for twelve participating countries. Italy was one of those twelve countries taking the euro and the lire was phased out by March 2002.

EU members using the Euro as sole official currency are known as the Eurozone. Several EU members have opted out of joining this common currency. Euro notes are identical throughout the Eurozone countries, each one including designs of fictional architectural structures. The coins, however, have one side identical (the value side) and one side with an image unique to each country. Notes and coins are exchangeable in each participating country.

Bank Notes

Euro bank notes have seven denominations. The €5 note (grey in colour) is the smallest, followed by the €10 note (pink), €20 note (blue), €50 note (orange), €100 note (green), €200 note (yellow) and €500 note (purple). All notes show the 12 stars of the European Union.

€5 note

€10 note

€20 note

€50 note

€100 note

€200 note

€500 note

€2 coin

€1 coin

50 cents

20 cents

10 cents

Coins

The euro has eight coin denominations: €1 and €2; 50 cents, 20 cents, 10 cents, 5 cents, 2 cents and 1 cent. The €2 and €1 coins are both silver and gold in colour. The 50-, 20- and 10-cent coins are gold. The 5-, 2- and 1-cent coins are bronze.

5 cents

2 cents

1 cent

Communications and Media

Although the Italian postal service is known for being very slow, Italy's other forms of communication, at least in the cities, are more efficient. Fax machines, courier services and telephones are all widespread, and Internet points are available throughout Italy. Foreign-language newspapers and magazines are on sale in all cities and most large towns. Both state-run and privately owned television stations exist, but only satellite television and radio stations broadcast foreign-language programmes.

Telephone company logo

Public Telephones

The Italian national telephone company is Telecom Italia. Coin-operated telephones have been phased out and replaced by card-operated machines. Most public telephones have instructions in five languages (Italian, English, French, Spanish and German). To select a language, push the top right-hand button. To use a public telephone you will need a Telecom Italia phone card. Phone cards (carta or scheda telefonica) can be purchased from bars, newspaper kiosks, post offices and tabacchi displaying the black-and-white T sign.

International phone cards, on sale at tabacchi and newsstands, are still a very cheap way to call abroad. Some cards offer as many as 3 hours of calls for about €10, depending on the country being called. Dial the toll-free number on the card and then enter the secret code found by scratching off the silver strip on the back of the card. You will be told the amount of credit available and

Telephone sign

then asked to dial the number you wish to call. Rates are slightly higher when calling from a mobile or public phone. Check with your hotel before using a card from your room as extra charges may be applied.

Email and Internet

Internet and email services are widely available throughout Italy, particularly in urban areas, so it should not be difficult to access email accounts or connect to the web. Telecom Italia, the Italian national phone company, has set up Internet services in the country's major train stations and public phone centres. Internet time can be purchased using a regular phone card.

Some major chains of Internet points sell magnetic cards with credit that can be used in any of their stores throughout Italy. **Internet Train**, with branches in over 40 towns, is the most visible. Visit its website for a full list of stores. In addition, small Internet points are very common. These are usually

clustered around train stations, cheap hotels and university areas and can range from the back room of a café or bar to the corner of a laundrette. Users can buy computer time in blocks as short as 15 minutes. There are usually student discounts available, and cost per minute decreases as the amount of time purchased increases.

Many hotels have Wi-Fi so travellers with their own laptop can have easy access. You'll probably need a plug adaptor too. Remember that with **Skype** or **Voip Stunt** installed it's possible to make phone calls over the Internet with the help of a small microphone. Calls are free between Skype users.

Mobile Phones

There are four main GSM frequencies (Global System for Mobile Communications) in use around the world, so to guarantee that your phone will work, make sure you have a quad-band phone. Tri-band phones from outside the US are also usually compatible but, because the US uses two frequency bands itself, a US tri-band phone may only have limited global coverage. Contact your service provider for clarification.

To use your mobile phone abroad you may need to get "permission" from your network operator, as often they need to enable "roaming" for your phone. At the moment, you are charged for the calls you receive as well as the calls you make, and you have to pay a substantial premium for the international leg of the call.

Another option is to purchase a local SIM card – the electronic chip that links your phone to a particular network – that can be

Using a public Telecom Italia telephone

topped up with credit and uses the local mobile phone networks. You can only do this if your handset is "unlocked" – some operators lock their phones to specific networks.

It is worth checking your insurance policy in case your phone gets stolen. You should also keep your network operator's helpline number handy for emergencies.

TV and Radio

Television channels in Italy include the state-owned RAI (Uno, Due and Tre) and Mediaset (Retequattro, Canale Cinque and Italia Uno). There are also many local channels. Most foreign programmes are dubbed into Italian, although satellite channels, such as BBC World News, Sky and CNN, show news and sports programmes in English. There are three national radio stations and hundreds of local stations.

A selection of newspapers available at a newsstand

Newspapers

There are several national daily newspapers, including *La Stampa*, Il Corriere della Sera and La Repubblica. Papers with the most detailed news of Italy's major cities include Il Mattino for Naples, Il Messaggero for Rome, La Nazione for Florence and Il Giornale for Milan.

All newspapers will have local pages and listings for cinemas, theatres, main concerts and other cultural events. In Rome and Milan, *La Repubblica* also publishes regular "what's on and where to go" supplements called TrovaRoma and ViviMilano respectively.

Florence's *Firenze Spettacolo* has weekly entertainment listings magazines. The latter also has a useful restaurant section and a summary of listings in English at the back.

British and American papers, such as the *International Herald Tribune*, *The Guardian*, and *USA Today*, are readily available and tend to arrive in the main cities at around midday on the day of publication.

Post Office

Local post offices open from 8:25am–1:50pm weekdays, and from 8:25am–noon on Saturday. Main city post offices are open from 8:25am–7pm non-stop. Many tobacconists also sell stamps.

The Vatican City and the state of San Marino have their own postal systems and stamps. Bear in mind that letters bearing San Marino or Vatican stamps can only be posted in San Marino and Vatican post boxes.

The red post boxes (blue in the Vatican) usually have two slots labelled *per la città* (for the city only) and *tutte le altre destinazioni* (for all other destinations).

Italian post is notorious for its unreliability and letters can take between four days and two weeks to arrive.

For a faster service it is best to send letters by express post services such as Postacelere (for letters) and Paccocelere (for larger packages). Both are based at all main post offices and guarantee delivery within 24–72 hours. They are far cheaper than private couriers. Another reliable option is recorded delivery (*raccomandata*). Anything of value should be sent by insured post (*assicurata*).

City letters   Other destinations

Italian post box

DIRECTORY

Remember to always use the full area code (including the first zero), even when phoning within a city.

Useful Numbers

Directory Enquiries
Tel 1254 (Option 1).

Multilingual Directory Enquiries
Tel 1254 (Option 2).

Operator Services
Tel 170 (also for reverse charge and calling card calls).

American Operators
Tel 800 17 24 44 (AT&T).
Tel 800 17 24 01 (Verizon).
Tel 800 17 24 05 (Sprint).

Australian Operators
Tel 800 17 26 10 (Telstra).
Tel 800 17 26 11 (Optus).

Country Codes

To call Italy from these countries dial the code and then the full area code (including the 0) and the number.

Tel 00 39 – UK
Tel 0 1139 – US & Canada
Tel 00 39 – Ireland
Tel 00 1139 – Australia

Email and Internet

Internet Train
🌐 internettrain.it

Skype
🌐 skype.com

Voip Stunt
🌐 voipstunt.com

Post and Couriers

Italian Post Office
🌐 poste.it

Private Couriers

DHL
Tel 199 199 345.
🌐 dhl.it

Fedex
Tel 199 151 119.
🌐 fedex.com

UPS
Tel 02 30 30 30 39.
🌐 ups.com

TRAVEL INFORMATION

Italy has transport systems of varying efficiency, from the modern road, bus and rail networks of the north to the slower systems of the south. Numerous airlines operate flights to several of the country's major airports, while within Italy itself the national carrier Alitalia, and several smaller companies, provide an extensive network of internal flights. Connections by road to the rest of Europe are good, though Alpine roads can be adversely affected by the weather in winter. Motorways and other roads within the country are generally good, but can be busy at weekends and peak periods. Italy also has an efficient system of ferries connecting Sicily, Sardinia and many of the smaller off-shore islands. Many of these are car ferries, and are busy in summer.

Green Travel

Travelling in Italy without using high-impact flights or long car drives is straight-forward, thanks to the excellent public transport network. Rail and bus systems both offer regular and reliable services and are reasonably priced. Connections with major European cities are good and travellers can often choose between day services on the Eurocity trains and overnight services on the EuroNight trains. There are also high speed trains, known as the *Alta Velocità* (*see pp628–9*).

Where only a few people use a service (such as to outlying hamlets in the Alps and Apennines), some authorities have set up a *servizio a chiamata* (demand-responsive service), whereby passengers phone a toll-free number to book a vehicle. This results in cost savings for the council and a reduction in carbon emissions, plus passengers get a personalized taxi for the price of a single bus ticket. Within cities, less polluting vehicles such as battery- or methane-powered buses and *vaporetti* have been introduced.

Bicycle tracks and cycle hire points are increasing in number, and many cities such as Milan and Rome have plenty of hire points and marked safe tracks. The Trentino-Alto Adige regions are especially well organized with long-distance cycle routes. For a small charge bicycles can be trans-ported on many regional and international trains.

Arriving by Air

Rome's Leonardo da Vinci (Fiumicino) and Milan's Malpensa are the key airports for long-haul flights into Italy. Milan's Linate airport handles some European flights, and most European airlines also fly to Venice, Turin, Naples and Pisa (for Florence). Many airlines are now flying regularly to smaller cities such as Florence, Genoa, Bologna, Verona and Bergamo, while charter flights serve summer destinations in peak season such as Catania, Olbia and Rimini.

Part of the extension to Fiumicino airport, Rome

Long-Haul Flights

If you are flying from the United States, **Delta** and **United Airlines** operate regular direct scheduled flights to Rome and Milan, with services from New York, Philadelphia, Los Angeles, Boston and Chicago. **Air Canada** flies from Montreal and Toronto, and **Qantas** flies from Sydney and Melbourne.

A regular service between Rome and Milan and New York, Boston, Chicago, Miami and Toronto is also offered by the Italian state airline, **Alitalia**.

It may, however, be more convenient and cheaper for long-haul passengers to take a budget flight to London, Frankfurt, Paris, Athens or Amsterdam and then continue to Italy from there.

European Low-Cost Flights

It has never been so easy to get to Italy by air. British Airways and Alitalia and its partners fly to major destinations in Italy from large European cities. However, low-cost, "no-frills" airlines offer many more destinations.

Ryanair flies to more than 20 airports (including Genoa, Rome-Ciampino, Turin and Venice-Treviso) from Stansted; while easyJet, from Gatwick or Stansted, serves Rome-Ciampino, Milan, Venice, Pisa, Palermo and Naples, and also Rome, Olbia and Pisa from Bristol. Meridiana flies to Florence and Olbia from Gatwick and, like Blu-Express, also offers a number of domestic flights.

The entrance hall at Pisa airport

Tickets and Fares

Fares vary enormously according to season and supply and demand. You can usually get the best deals by booking online well in advance.

Consult a good travel agent or check availability on the Internet. If you are based in the UK, it may be worthwhile to scour the small ads of newspapers for charter and discounted scheduled flights on major routes. Most charters leave from Gatwick or Luton, and may land at a city's second (and often less convenient) airport. Fares tend to vary greatly during the year, but the most expensive periods are during the summer months and over the Christmas and Easter holidays. Where possible, ask for available student discounts.

Package Holidays

Package holidays to Italy are usually cheaper than travelling independently, unless you are travelling on a tight budget and are prepared to make use of youth hostels and campsites. Rome, Florence and Venice are often offered as separate or linked package deals, and many operators have packages to the Tuscan and Umbrian countryside, Sicily, the Italian Lakes, the Italian Riviera, Naples and the Amalfi coast. In winter, ski packages are available to many Alpine resorts. Specialist packages, such as cooking, walking and art tours are common.

In cities, different tour operators may use different hotels, so it is worth researching the most pleasant (and centrally located) accommodation options. Many operators include transfers from the airport to your hotel. Some include tour guides.

DIRECTORY

Green Travel

Cycling in Trentino
W visittrentino.it

Airlines

Air Canada
W aircanada.com

Alitalia
Tel 89 20 10. W alitalia.com

Blu-Express
W blu-express.com

British Airways
Tel 02 69 63 36 02.
W britishairways.com

Delta
W delta.com

easyJet
W easyjet.com

Meridiana
W meridiana.it

Qantas
W qantas.com

Ryanair
W ryanair.com

United Airlines
W united.com

Airport	Information	Distance to city centre	Taxi fare to city centre	Public transport to city centre
Rome (Fiumicino)	06 659 51 W adr.it	35 km (22 miles)	€48	FS 30 mins
Rome (Ciampino)	06 659 51 W adr.it	15 km (9 miles)	€35	M 45 mins
Milan (Linate)	02 23 23 23 W seamilano.eu	8 km (5 miles)	€20	15 mins
Milan (Malpensa)	02 23 23 23 W seamilano.eu	50 km (31 miles)	€90	FS M 60 mins
Pisa (Galileo Galilei)	050 84 91 11 W pisa-airport.com	2 km (1 mile)	€10	FS to Pisa: 10 mins FS to Florence: 80 mins
Venice (Marco Polo)	041 260 111 W veniceairport.it	13 km (8 miles)	€35 (€100 water taxi)	60 mins 20 mins
Venice (Treviso)	0422 31 51 11 W trevisoairport.it	25 km (15 miles)	€70 to Venice	to Treviso: 20 mins to Venice: 70 mins
Verona	045 809 56 66 W aeroportoverona.it	12 km (7 miles)	€25	15 mins
Bergamo	035 32 63 23 W orioaeroporto.it	5 km (3 miles)	€18	25 mins
Turin	011 567 63 61 W turin-airport.com	15 km (9 miles)	€30	20 mins
Naples	081 789 61 11 W portal.gesac.it	7 km (4 miles)	€20	30 mins
Palermo	091 702 02 73 W gesap.it	35 km (21 miles)	€40–€45	50 mins 1 hr

Arriving by Sea, Rail and Road

Italy is served by an extensive network of roads, railways and international ferry lines. Road and rail links cross into the country from France, Switzerland, Austria and Slovenia, and there are through train services from as far afield as Budapest, London and Barcelona. Road connections into the country are generally of motorway standard, though delays can occur at some of the many Alpine passes and tunnels during bad weather or peak summer holiday periods.

Do-it-yourself help points with train information on screens

Ticket windows at Florence's Santa Maria Novella station

Arriving by Car

Most roads into Italy from the rest of Europe involve Alpine crossings by tunnel or mountain passes. The notable exceptions are the approach from Slovenia in the northeast (on the A4 motorway) and the route along the French Riviera that enters Italy as the A10 motorway at Ventimiglia.

The most popular route from Geneva and southeast France is via the Mont Blanc tunnel and A5 motorway, entering Italy close to Aosta and Turin. Another busy approach (from Switzerland) uses the St Bernard Pass and tunnel.

Further east, the main route from Austria and southern Germany crosses the Brenner Pass and goes down to Verona on the A22 motorway via Trento and the Adige valley. Weather conditions rarely close the passes, but snow and fog can make progress slow on the winding roads through the mountains. Most motorways are toll-roads; you pay as you exit the motorway.

Arriving by Train

After air travel, arriving by train is the least painful way to reach Italy. Countless through services (including many sleepers) link Italian towns and cities with places as far afield as Brussels, Budapest and Barcelona. Connections from Paris (and London, via Eurostar) run to Turin, Milan, Venice, Bologna, Florence or along Italy's west coast, via Genoa and Pisa, to Rome and Naples. Services also operate from German, Swiss and other northern European cities to

BINARIO 17

Platform sign

← uscita

Exit sign

The sleeping car on an international Eurocity train

Milan, Turin, Venice and Verona. There are also direct services from Vienna, Spain and the south of France. Motorail connections exist from several centres in northern Europe and the Channel ports.

The popularity of low-cost airlines has forced international train travel to be a little more competitive – if booked online. Special discount fares, however, are often available for senior travellers and for people under 26.

Trains can be extremely busy during peak periods, particularly on Friday and Sunday evenings, and during the Christmas and Easter holiday periods. July and August can also be frantically busy, especially on routes from Germany and ports connecting with Greek ferries in the south. Reservations on most services are advisable.

Arriving by Boat

Most people arriving in Italy by boat do so from Greece, using services from Corfu and Patras to Brindisi and other south-eastern ports. Boats are crowded in summer, as are connecting train services from Brindisi to the rest of Italy.

Other international connections include ferries from Malta and North African ports to Palermo, Naples and various southern Italian ports. Boats also run from towns in the south of France to Genoa, Livorno and ports on the Italian Riviera, and from the Croatian coast across the Adriatic to Venice.

Arriving by Bus

Bus travel to Italy is relatively cheap, but long travel times make it one of the least comfortable ways to travel. The travel time from London to Milan is about 24 hours, and it is about 33 hours from London to Rome. A night on the road is thus unavoidable. **Eurolines** runs buses from London's Victoria Coach Station to most of Italy's major cities as far as Rome and Naples (a change at Milan or Paris is often necessary). Buses travel via Dover, Calais, Paris, and Dijon and it is useful to have some euros with you for stops en route. Travel around Italy by long-distance bus is feasible with SITA.

SITA bus arriving at the station in Florence

Traveling Around by Ferry

Italy's large number of off-shore islands mean that it has a large and well-developed network of ferries, as well as services to the rest of Europe and North Africa.

One of the Moby Lines car ferries that sail the Mediterranean

Ferries

Car ferries are a convenient link with the beautiful islands scattered off the Italian mainland. Boats for Sardinia leave from Civitavecchia (north of Rome), Livorno, and Genoa, and depart for Sicily from Naples and Reggio di Calabria. Ferries run from the major Sicilian ports to the Egadi and the Aeolian archipelagoes, as well as to countless other small islands around Sicily (although be aware that ferries to the smaller islands do not always carry cars).

Boats also ply between Elba and Piombino, as well as the smaller islands of the Tuscan archipelago such as Capraia. Ferries run from ports close to Rome to Ponza and its surrounding islands, and from Naples to Capri and Ischia. On the east coast the Tremiti islands are linked to ports on the Gargano peninsula.

Hydrofoils are increasingly complementing conventional ferries, particularly on busy routes to Capri and Ischia. Hydrofoils, and ferries, also run on some of Italy's lakes, such as Como and Garda.

Lines for ferries are common in summer, so make reservations well in advance if you wish to travel in July or August, especially if taking a vehicle. Ferry services are more frequent and reliable in summer than in winter.

Reservations can be made online, through travel agents, or at a ferry line's agents in your own country. Ticket prices can vary according to the time of year but are generally reasonable. To check schedules and fares, visit the relevant website.

DIRECTORY

Arriving by Train

Ferrovie dello Stato
Tel 89 20 21 (in Italy).
🔲 trenitalia.com

Arriving by Bus

Eurolines
Tel 0861 199 19 00.
🔲 eurolines.co.uk

SITA
🔲 sitabus.it

Ferries

Corsica Sardinia Ferries
Tel 199 400 500.
🔲 corsicaferries.com
Civitavecchia/Livorno – Golfo Aranci

Grandi Navi Veloci
Tel 010 209 45 91.
🔲 gnv.it Genoa/Civitavecchia – Palermo
Genoa – Porto Torres/Olbia

Moby Lines
Tel 199 303 040; 02 76 02 81 32.
🔲 moby.it
Piombino – Elba
Genoa/Livorno – Olbia

SNAV
Tel 081 428 55 55.
🔲 snav.it
Ancona – Split
Naples/Sorrento – Capri/Ischia
Naples – Aeolian Islands

Tirrenia
Tel 892 123; 02 26 30 28 03. 🔲 tirrenia.it
Bari – Durazzo
Genoa – Porto Torres
Civitavecchia – Olbia
Naples – Palermo/Cagliari
Cagliari – Palermo

Venezia Lines
Tel 041 882 11 01.
🔲 venezialines.com
Venice – Rabac
Venice – Porec/Rovinj/Pula
Bari – Durazzo

Travelling Around by Train

Train travel is one of the best ways to explore Italy. Tickets are inexpensive, services frequent, and rolling stock some of the most modern in Europe. Services can be busy, but the days of rampant overcrowding are mostly over. Lines often run through lovely countryside, from mountain lakes to rolling plateaux, and they provide more convenient links between cities than roads or air travel. Only in the south, or deeply rural areas, are services slow and infrequent.

A Eurostar – one of Italy's fastest trains

The Network

The bulk of Italy's rail network is an integrated state-run system operated by Trenitalia of the Ferrovie dello Stato (FS), which has introduced super-fast services reducing travel times between major cities. In this, it competes with the NTV consortium, whose trains are known as Italo by most people. Smaller privately run lines also fill crucial gaps left by the FS, but through-tickets are generally available where travel involves both networks. State and private lines often share the same main station (*stazione*), and also charge similar fares.

Trains

Trenitalia and NTV (Italo) take advantage of the *Alta Velocità* (AV) network between major cities in the north and southwards as far as Naples. These, the fast Eurostar (ES) and a handful of other special high-speed trains always require pre-booking of seats. Intercity (IC) trains and Eurocity (EC) trains only stop at major stations and require the payment of a supplement (*un supplemento*) on top of the standard ticket (supplements can be bought on the train, but are more expensive). *Regionali* and *Interregionali* trains make more stops and require no supplement.

All AV, ES, EC and Intercity trains are usually air-conditioned. Branch line carriages can still be ancient.

Facilities for the disabled, including assistance at stations, exist on all fast trains and international services. For assistance ask at the special *Sale Blu* (Blue Halls) in mainline stations.

Tickets and Fares

Tickets (*biglietti*) are available as single (*andata*) or return (*andata e ritorno*) in first (*prima*) or second class (*seconda classe*). They can be bought at some travel agents or at any station ticket office (*biglietteria*).

Major stations have automatic ticket machines and you can also buy tickets for journeys of up to 250 km (155 miles) from newsstands or station tobacconists (such a ticket is called *biglietto a fascia chilometrica*). Be sure to validate all tickets on both outbound and return journeys, or you will be fined. A ticket's validity usually starts on the day of purchase, so be sure to specify the day of travel when buying tickets. Fares are calculated on a kilometric basis and are among the cheapest in western Europe. Many discounted fares are offered, including special family tickets. Some online ticket purchases also carry discounts.

Refunds involve a complicated process – enquire at the *Assistenza* counter at major stations. It is important, therefore, to buy the correct ticket before travelling.

Passes

The most useful pass for visitors is the **Interrail Pass**, which gives unlimited travel for consecutive or non-consecutive days over varying periods, with special rates for those under 26. It can be purchased online or at most mainline stations and various agencies outside Italy. An Interrail One Country Pass allows travel on any five or ten days within a specific period.

Timetables

If you plan to use trains often, it is a good idea to pick up an official Trenitalia timetable (*un orario*) at the railway station or newsstands. It is updated yearly. Alternatively, visit www.trenitalia.com for the online timetable.

Validity and Reservations

Single or return tickets are valid for up to two months from the date of purchase. If a seat reservation is made with the ticket, however, the date you wish to travel will be stamped automatically on the ticket. Reservations are automatic on AV and Eurostar services, and they are a good idea on all trains on and around public holidays. Reservations can be made at most main stations or online.

The concourse at Stazione Termini, Rome

Reductions

The Smart Price deal offers discounts on international trains between Italy and various European countries. Single prices range from €19 to €70, though there are additions for couchettes and wagon-lits. Tickets can be bought at mainline stations or on the Trenitalia website, though only a fixed number are available so book ahead.

Left Luggage

Main city stations usually have left luggage facilities. Most are manned (but the smaller stations have self-service lockers), and you may need to present identification when depositing or collecting bags. Fees are calculated per bag and by the number of hours bags are left.

Scenic Rail Routes

Italy's varied geography makes for some memorable train trips across the length and breadth of the country. The glacially shaped Adige valley between Bolzano and Verona in the north is thick with apple orchards and surrounded by soaring alpine peaks, with the pretty Trento-Male line branching off it. The Tuscan countryside south of Florence boasts views of hill towns and rolling wheat fields, while close by in Lazio the Roma Nord-Viterbo line winds its way through beautiful rural scenery.

DIRECTORY

Trains

Erail Travel Ltd
Tel 020 7619 1083 (UK).
ⓦ **erail.co.uk**

FTI (Ferrovie Turistiche Italiane)
ⓦ **ferrovieturistiche.it**

Interrail Pass
ⓦ **interrail.eu**

NTV
ⓦ **ntvspa.it**

Trenitalia
Information for travel all over Italy. **Tel** 89 20 21.
ⓦ **trenitalia.com**

Further south, trains cross the Straits of Messina to Sicily on a special ferry, while a narrow gauge line circles Mount Etna. For steam train enthusiasts there are trips run by the **FTI (Ferrovie Turistiche Italiane)** groups in the north through alpine foothills and past picturesque lakes, as well as in the countryside outside Siena.

Machines for Trenitalia Rail Tickets

These machines are easy to use, and most have instructions on screen in a choice of six languages. They accept coins, notes and credit cards.

1 Touch screen: choose destination, train and ticket type, make seat reservations and choose payment method.

2 Insert coins here.

3 Insert banknotes here.

4 Payment with credit card: touchpad with slot for card below.

5 Receive train tickets, seat reservations and change here.

Italy's Principal FS Network

The Italian state rail network operates various types of service. Check what is on offer before buying your ticket.

Key

● Main stations
○ Other stations
— Principal rail route
-- Route over water

Travelling Around by Car

A motoring tour is a practical way of exploring the country, though you should take into account high petrol prices, parking difficulties, driving restrictions in cities and the Italians' occasionally erratic approach to driving. A car is invaluable in the countryside and for extensive touring, but less useful in major towns and cities, due to congestion and the fact that most city centres are off-limits to non-residents' cars.

One-way street

Automatic tollbooths on the motorway outside Florence

Blue signs showing main roads and green signs showing motorways

tollbooths (*Alt Stazione*) at busy periods. Payment is made at the end of the journey in cash, credit card or pre-paid magnetic VIA cards, available from tobacconists and the **ACI**. There is a congestion charge in Milan (7:30am–7:30pm Mon–Fri); phone 800 437 437 or visit www.comunemilano.it/ecopass before entering the city.

Secondary roads are known as *Nazionali* (N) or as *Strade Statali* (SS), and vary enormously in quality. Mountain roads are usually good, but distances can be deceptive. In winter, snow chains are obligatory on many higher routes. Some back roads (known as *strade bianche*, or "white roads") have only a gravel surface. These are slow, but usually passable to cars.

What to Take

Drivers from outside Italy bringing their own foreign-registered cars into the country must carry a Green Card (for insurance purposes), all the vehicle's registration documents, and a full, valid driving licence (*patente* in Italian). Any EU nationals who do not have the standard EU "pink" licence and are planning to stay for more than six months will need an Italian translation of their licence, obtainable from most motoring organizations or from the Italian state tourist office in your home country. A red warning triangle and fluorescent vests must also be carried at all times, for use in the event of a breakdown.

Petrol

Petrol (*benzina*) in Italy is some of the most expensive in Europe (diesel, or *gasolio*, is a little cheaper). Although many petrol stations are now self-service, it is still common to be served by an attendant. Most petrol stations follow normal shop hours so make sure you have a full tank before lunchtime or public holidays. On motorways petrol stations tend to be open 24 hours a day. Credit cards are usually accepted.

Roads

Italy has a good network of motorways, though many have a total of only four lanes, often leading to congestion. Busy routes include the A1 from Bologna to Florence and between Bologna, Parma and Milan. Tolls are payable on most motorways (*autostrade*), again leading to congestion at

Rules and Regulations

Drive on the right and give way to traffic from the right. Seat belts are compulsory for all passengers. Heavy fines are levied for using a mobile phone while driving. Headlights must be turned on even during the day on motorways and outside built-up areas. The speed limit in urban areas is 50 km/h (30 mph); outside urban areas it is 110 km/h (70 mph) on dual carriageways and 90 km/h on other secondary roads. On motorways the limit is 130 km/h (80 mph) for vehicles over 1100cc, 110 km/h (70 mph) for those under 1100cc.

No stopping

End of speed restriction

Pedestrianized street – no traffic

Give way to oncoming traffic

No parking

Danger (often with description)

Logo for international car hire company

Car Hire

Car hire *(autonoleggio)* is expensive in Italy, and should be organized beforehand through fly-drive deals or pre-booked with firms who have branches in Italy. For on the spot hire Italian firms may be cheaper than big international names. Agencies are listed in Yellow Pages *(Pagine Gialle)* under Autonoleggio. Most airports conveniently have car hire offices on site.

To rent a car in Italy you must generally be over 21 (and sometimes older) and have held a valid driver's licence for at least a year. Visitors from outside the EU require an international licence, though in practice not all hire firms insist on this. Check the small print of the agreement for insurance cover.

Accidents and Breakdowns

If you have an accident or a breakdown, switch on your hazard warning lights and place a warning triangle 50 m (164 ft) behind your car. Then (for breakdowns) call the **ACI** emergency number (803 116) or the emergency services (112 or 113). The ACI will tow any foreign-registered car free to the nearest ACI-affiliated garage. They also do free repairs for members of affiliated associations, such as the AA and RAC in Britain.

If you have an accident keep calm, and do not admit liability or make any statements that might incriminate you later. Simply swap car and insurance details, names and addresses.

Parking

Parking in most Italian cities and large towns is a problem. Many historic centres have restricted daytime access and baffling one-way systems. Other areas

may be reserved for residents' parking (marked *riservato ai residenti*). Most towns have metered parking areas that charge an hourly fee paid with coins, cards or coupons bought from *tabacchi*. Cars can be towed away or clamped, especially in areas marked *zona rimozione*, particularly on street-cleaning days. Call the Municipal Police *(Vigili)* to retrieve your car.

Official parking area patrolled by attendant

Safety

Car theft is rife in Italy. Never leave anything in your car, and (if possible) always remove radio-CD players and sat-nav

devices. Leave your car in a guarded car park whenever you can. Be especially careful driving at night, when Italian driving is more cavalier than usual, and when many traffic lights switch to flashing amber. Hitching *(autostop)* is not a good idea (and is not common), certainly never for women on their own.

DIRECTORY

Car Hire

Avis
Tel 06 452 10 83 91.
W avisautonoleggio.it

Europcar
Tel 199 307 030.
W europcar.it

Hertz
Tel 06 65 01 15 53 (Rome airport).
W hertz.it

Maggiore
Tel 199 151 120.
W maggiore.it

Sixt
Tel 06 65 21 11 (Rome).
W sixt.it

Emergencies

ACI emergency
Tel 803 116. W aci.it

Police
Tel 112 or 113.

Ambulance
Tel 118.

Distance Chart

Rome									**10 Distance in kilometres**		
									10 Distance in miles		
286	Ancona										
178											
748	**617**	Aosta									
465	383										
383	**219**	**401**	Bologna								
238	136	249									
645	**494**	**449**	**280**	Bolzano							
401	307	279	174								
278	**262**	**470**	**106**	**367**	Florence						
173	163	292	66	228							
510	**506**	**245**	**291**	**422**	**225**	Genoa					
317	315	152	181	262	140						
601	**614**	**1220**	**822**	**1097**	**871**	**1103**	Lecce				
373	382	758	511	682	541	685					
575	**426**	**181**	**210**	**295**	**299**	**145**	**1029**	Milan			
357	265	113	130	183	186	90	639				
219	**409**	**959**	**594**	**856**	**489**	**714**	**393**	**786**	Naples		
136	254	596	369	532	304	444	244	488			
673	**547**	**110**	**332**	**410**	**395**	**170**	**1150**	**138**	**884**	Turin	
418	340	68	206	255	245	106	715	86	549		
530	**364**	**442**	**154**	**214**	**255**	**397**	**967**	**273**	**741**	**402**	Venice
329	226	275	96	133	158	247	601	170	460	250	

Travelling within Cities

The best ways of getting around Italian cities differ from place to place. In Rome buses are most useful, in Milan the metro is more efficient, and in Venice you will need to take a boat to get about. Trams still run in some cities, such as Milan and Rome. Cars are a liability almost everywhere, unlike walking, which in many cases is the easiest way to negotiate the tight historic cores of Italian towns and cities. Florence and Rome have a large limited-traffic zone, and most towns now have a pedestrian area in the centre.

Bus stop displaying the route

A Roman bus in the red and grey livery of ATAC

One of the distinctive orange city buses, central Verona

Buses and Trams

Virtually every Italian city and large town has a bus system. Most are cheap, comprehensive and as efficient as traffic and narrow streets will allow and vary only slightly from city to city. Bus stops are known as *fermate*, and increasingly (notably in Rome) list full details of the routes they serve. Buses (*autobus*) usually run from about 6am to midnight, and there are night buses (*servizio notturno*) in larger cities. If you arrive in a town by train, stations are invariably linked to the centre by shuttle buses from the station forecourt (tickets are usually available from the station bar or tobacconist).

Tickets

Tickets (*biglietti*) must be bought before boarding the bus from kiosks belonging to the bus company (ATAF in Florence, ATAC in Rome), bars, newsstands or tobacconists displaying the bus company's sticker. A few cities also have on-street vending machines around the main transport hubs. It is worth buying more than one ticket at a time, as outlets often close in the afternoon or early evening. Discounted tickets (*un blocchetto*), or day- or week-long visitors' tickets and passes (*una tessera* or *tesserino*) are also available. In some cities tickets are valid for any number of journeys within a given time. The ATAC website has more details on buses in Rome.

ATAC
W atac.roma.it

Using Buses and Trams

Board buses via the front and rear doors, and exit via the central doors. Buses usually only have a driver and no conductor (though night buses may have a conductor from whom tickets can be bought). Tickets must be validated by punching them in machines at the front or rear of the bus. There are large on-the-spot fines if you are caught without a properly validated ticket. The front, low seats on buses are for people with children, the elderly and the disabled.

Most larger cities have transport information offices at the main train station or piazza which provide free maps, timetables and tickets.

The majority of city buses are painted bright orange and display the final destination (*capolinea*) on the front.

Metropolitana

Underground systems, known as *metropolitana* (*la metro* for short), are found in Rome and Milan. Rome's network amounts to just two lines, A and B, which converge at Stazione Termini, the city's central railway station. Several stations are useful for key sights, and at peak times the lines provide the best way of crossing the city quickly. Stations are fairly dingy – though rarely dangerous – and train carriages can be stiflingly hot in summer. In Milan the network is more extensive, with three principal lines – MM1 (the red line), MM2 (green) and MM3 (yellow) – that meet at the hub stations of Stazione Centrale, Duomo, Cadorna and Loreto. These three

Metro sign

Termini Metro station, Rome

An official taxi waiting at a pedestrian crossing

lines give easy access to the majority of the city's main sights.

Metro tickets in both cities are available from the same sources as bus and tram tickets, and from machines and ticket offices in underground stations. Tickets in Rome are valid for 75 minutes for one metro journey only, but can be used on any number of bus and tram journeys. One-day, three-day and seven-day tickets are also available and offer unlimited metro, bus and tram travel. In Milan, by contrast, ordinary metro tickets are valid for 90 minutes for one metro journey and can also be used on the buses and trams.

Walking

Walking can be a wonderful way to explore Italy's historic towns and cities, most of whose historic centres are smaller than you might expect. Traffic can be a curse, however, especially in narrow streets (Rome is worst in this respect), but many cities are introducing pedestrianized areas or cutting down on car access around key tourist sights. On certain Sundays (Domenica a Piedi), entire town centres may be designated traffic-free zones.

Italian towns have plenty of shady squares and cafés to escape the heat of the summer sun, and churches and cathedrals also provide cool retreats from the rigours of sightseeing. Most sights are well signposted

Stay on the pavement at all costs

Marginally less dangerous to cross

(churches, museums and other places of interest are often indicated by yellow signs). Always carry your valuables well out of sight. The best times to walk are in the cool of the morning, or in the early evening, when you can join in the pre-dinner stroll known as the *passeggiata*.

Taxis

Only accept rides in official taxis. Most drivers are honest but there are many supplements that can be legitimately levied. Generally an extra charge is made for each piece of luggage placed in the

boot, for rides between 10pm and 7am, on Sundays and public holidays, and for journeys to and from airports.

In theory, taxis cannot be hailed. Take one at an official taxi stand (usually found at the station, main piazza or close to key tourist sights) or reserve one by phone. When you order a taxi by phone, take the driver's code name, eg Napoli 18. If you call a cab, the meter will run from your call.

Cycle Hire

Many towns and cities, especially those popular with visitors, have stands and shops offering bikes and scooters for rent. You can usually rent hourly or by the day, and you may have to leave your passport with the shop as a deposit. Be very careful, however, if riding a bike in the busy traffic of the larger towns and cities.

BikeMi in Milan gives access to bikes at various places in the city. The initial fee is €2.50 a day (€6 a week), which covers the first 30 minutes of hire. Rates are then €0.50 for 30 minutes, rising to €2 per hour after the first two hours. You can register by phone (800 80 81 81) or via the website (www.bikemi.it).

Inter-City Transport: Coaches

Long-haul buses (*pullman* or *corriere*) between towns operate in a similar way to local buses, though you can usually buy tickets on board, and services are often run by different companies in different-coloured buses (blue is the most common colour for *pullman*, orange for city buses). Coaches in some

Rome – Gubbio bus

areas may be run by several companies (notably around Florence and in Tuscany), and not all operate from the same termini. Services often depart from outside railway stations, or from a town's main piazza. If in doubt, ask at local tourist offices. A reduced service may operate at weekends, when offices are shut.

Rome
COTRAL
Tel 800 174 471 or 06 72 05 72 05.
W cotralspa.it
Appian
Tel 06 48 78 66 01.
W appianline.it

Tuscany
Lazzi **Tel** 0573 193 79 00. W lazzi.it
Sita **Tel** 800 37 37 60. W sitabus.it
Tra-In **Tel** 0577 20 41 11. W trainspa.it

National & International
Eurolines
Tel 0861 199 19 00.
W eurolines.it

Travelling Around Venice

For visitors to Venice, the *vaporetti* or waterbuses *(see pp140–41)* provide an entertaining form of public transport, although most journeys within the city can usually be covered more quickly on foot. The main route through the city for the *vaporetti* is the Grand Canal. Waterbuses also supply a useful service connecting outlying points on the periphery of Venice, and linking the city to the islands in the lagoon. The most important service from a visitor's point of view is the No. 1. This operates from one end of the Grand Canal to the other and travels slowly enough for you to admire the parade of palaces at the waterside *(see pp92–95)*.

Vaporetto stop at the Giardini Pubblici, Venice

A *vaporetto* or waterbus

The smaller, sleeker *motoscafo*

The Boats

The original *vaporetti* were steam-powered (*vaporetto* means little steamer); today they are mostly diesel-run motor boats, with a handful of electric, battery-powered prototypes. Although all the boats tend to be called *vaporetti*, the word only really applies to the large wide boats used on slow routes, such as No. 1. These boats provide the best views. *Motoscafi* are the slimmer, smaller boats that look old but go at a fair pace, while *motonavi* are two-tier boats that run to the islands. To visit the islands of Murano, Burano or Torcello, take the LN Line, which departs from San Zaccaria and Fondamenta Nuove.

Types of Ticket

If booths at landing stages are closed, single tickets can be purchased on board at no extra charge – the tickets are valid for 1 hour from purchase. A good way to save money, however, is

by buying a travel card, available for 12, 24, 36, 48 or 72 hours. Such a card entitles the holder to unlimited travel on most lines. Discounts on advance tickets are also available, especially if booked seven days in advance. A single or return journey supplement to/from Marco Polo airport can also be added to the price of the card (see www.veniceconnected.com).

If you are staying more than a few days, it is worth buying a weekly season ticket (*abbonamento*), available from ticket offices, though non-residents are charged €50 for the privilege. Holders of Rolling Venice cards (with information packs and discounts for 14–29-year-olds) can buy a three-day youth pass. Tickets include transport for one piece of luggage, so be prepared to buy another ticket for extra items.

Hours of Service

The main routes run every 10 to 20 minutes until the early evening. Services are reduced after midnight, but they run all night. From June to September the services are more frequent and certain routes are extended. Timetables are available at main landing stages. Be warned: from May to September the main routes and island boats are very crowded.

Vaporetto Information

ACTV (Hello Venezia Office) Piazzale Roma, Venice. **Map** 5 B1. **Tel** 041 2424. 🕸 actv.it

Traghetti

Traghetti are gondola ferries that cross the Grand Canal at seven different points, providing a useful service for pedestrians. Few tourists make use of this cheap (about 50 cents per trip), constant service. Points where *traghetti* cross the Grand Canal are marked on the Street Finder maps *(see pp130–39)*. A gondola on yellow street signs points to *traghetti* stops.

A two-tier *motonave* boat

Gondolas

Gondolas are a luxury form of transport used only by visitors and Venetians at weddings. Before boarding, check the official tariffs and agree a price with the gondolier. Official costs are around €80 for 40 minutes, rising to €100 after 7pm. During the low season, you may also be able to negotiate a lower fee, and a journey shorter than the usual 40 minutes.

Water Taxis

For those with little time and sufficient funds, the fastest and most practical means of getting from A to B in Venice is by water taxi. The craft are sleek, white or polished wood motorboats, and all are equipped with a cabin.

They zip efficiently to and from the airport in only 20 minutes. There are 16 water taxi ranks, including one at the airport and one at the Lido.

A water taxi

Beware of extra charges for transporting luggage, waiting, night service and for calling out a taxi. When the *vaporetti* go on strike, taxis are scarce.

Water Taxi Stands

Radio Taxi (all of Venice)
Tel 041 522 23 03.

Piazzale Roma
Map 5 B1. **Tel** 041 71 69 22.

Crossing the Grand Canal by *traghetto*

The Main Routes

① This is the slow boat down the Grand Canal, stopping at every landing stage. The route starts at Piazzale Roma, travels the length of the Grand Canal, then from San Marco it heads east to the Lido.

② The 2 is the faster route down the Grand Canal. With an extension to the Lido during the summer months, the route serves San Zaccaria, continuing westwards along the Giudecca Canal to Tronchetto and Piazzale Roma, then down the Grand Canal back to San Zaccaria.

④ ④ ⑤ ⑤ ⑥ These lines all sail around the central islands. The circular *Giracittà* routes 4.1-4.2 provide a scenic tour of Venice and Murano, while lines 5.1-5.2 and 6 also extend to the Lido.

⑫ ⑭ The 12 departs from the Fondamenta Nuove and runs to the main islands in the northern lagoon – Murano, Mazzorbo and Burano (with a connection to Torcello) – then calls at Punta Sabbioni. The 14 takes you to the Lido, before concluding at San Zaccaria.

Using the Vaporetti

1 Tickets are available at most landing stages, some bars, shops and tobacconists displaying the ACTV sign. It is also possible to buy them on board. The price of a ticket remains the same whether you are going one stop or travelling the whole line.

2 Signs on the landing stage tell you the direction of the boats stopping there.

3 Imob electronic chip tickets are in use and should be validated before each journey at the electronic machines on the landing stages. Inspectors rarely board the boats and this makes it surprisingly easy to hop on and off the boats without a validated ticket. However, there are steep fines for any passengers caught without tickets.

4 An indicator board at the front of each boat gives the line number and main stops. (Ignore the black numbers on the boat's side.)

5 Each landing stage has its name clearly marked on a board. Most stops have two landing stages and it is quite easy, particularly if it is crowded and you can't see which way the boat is facing, to board a boat travelling in the wrong direction. It is helpful to watch which direction the boat is approaching from; if in doubt, check with the boatman.

General Index

Acknowledgments

Dorling Kindersley would like to thank the following people whose contributions and assistance have made the preparation of this book possible.

Contributors

Paul Duncan is an expert on art and architectural history and has published a guide to Sicily as well as one on Italy's hill-towns.

Tim Jepson, formerly Rome correspondent for the *Sunday Telegraph*, has written guides to Tuscany, Umbria, Rome and Venice, a complete guide to Italy, *Italy by Train* and *Wild Italy*, a guide to Italy's nature reserves.

Andrew Gumbel, former Reuters correspondent in Rome, has written a number of guide books and is the correspondent for the *Independent* in Rome.

Christopher Catling has written guides to Florence and Tuscany, the Veneto and the Italian Lakes and is particularly interested in archaeology.

Sam Cole works for Reuters in Rome, where he has lived for some years, and contributes regularly to guidebooks on Rome and the Lazio region.

Additional Contributors

Dominic Robertson, Mick Hamer, Richard Langham Smith, Gillian Price.

Additional Photography

Francesco Allegretto, Giuseppe Carfagna & Associati, Peter Chadwick, Andy Crawford, Philip Dowell, Mike Dunning, Philip Enticknap, Steve Gorton, Dave King, Rough Guides/James McConnachie, Neil Mersh, Anna Mockford, Roger Moss, Poppy, Rough Guides/Martin Richardson; Kim Sayer, Helena Smith, James Stevenson, Clive Streeter, Jo-Ann Titmarsh, David Ward, Matthew Ward, Christine Webb.

Additional Illustrations

Andrea Corbella, Richard Draper, Kevin Jones Associates, Chris Orr and Associates, Robbie Polley, Simon Roulstone, Martin Woodward.

Cartographic Research

Jane Hugill, Samantha James, Jennifer Skelley.

Revisions Team

Tora Agarwala, Beverley Ager, Gillian Allan, Gaye Allen, Douglas Amrine, Emma Anacootee, Emily Anderson, Claire Baranowski, Peter Bently, Marta Bescos Sanchez, Sonal Bhatt, Uma Bhattacharya, Tessa Bindloss, Hilary Bird, Sally-Ann Bloomfield, Samantha Borland, Isabel Boucher, Hugo Bowles, Reid Bramblett, Caroline Brooke, Nick Bruno, Paola Cacucciola, Stefano Cavedoni, Margaret Chang, Susi Cheshire, Elspeth Collier, Sherry Collins, Lucinda Cooke, Cooling Brown, Imogen Corke, Michelle Crane, Gary Cross, Felicity Crowe, Cristina Dainotto, Peter Douglas, Mandy Dredge, Stephanie Driver, Julia Dunn, Michael Ellis, Adele Evans, Mariana Evmolpidou, Danny Farnham, Emer FitzGerald, Karen Fitzpatrick, Sarah Fraser, Kyra Freestar, Anna Freiberger, Camilla Gersh, Jackie Gordon, Angela-Marie Graham, Caroline Greene, Vanessa Hamilton, Amy Harrison, Sally-Ann Hibbard, Elinor Hodgson, Tim Hollis, Paul Jackson, Gail Jones, Bharti Karakoti, Roberta Kedzierski, Amy Knauff, Steve Knowlden, Shikha Kulkarni, Suresh Kumar, Jude Ledger, Leonie Loudon, Siri Lowe, Carly Madden, Hayley Maher, Nicola Malone, Sarah Martin, Georgina Matthews, Alison McGill, Ferdie McDonald, Sam Merrell, Ian Midson, Rebecca Milner, Adam Moore, Cherrye Moore, John Murphy, Cristina Murroni, Jennifer Mussett, Claire Naylor, Catherine Palmi, Tiffany Parks, Helen Partington, Alok Pathak, Julia Paynton, Susie Peachey, Alice Peebles, Tamsin Pender, Marianne Petrou, Gillian Price, David Pugh, Alessandra Pugliese, Rada Radojicic, Jake Reimann, Catherine Richards, David Roberts, Evelyn Robertson, Ellen Root, Carolyn Ryden, Simon Ryder, Giuseppina Russo, Collette Sadler, Sands Publishing Solutions, Baishakhee Sengupta, Marcella Simoni, Kunal Singh, Kate Singleton, Ellie Smith, Susana Smith, Alison Stace, Solveig Steinhardt, Donald Strachan, Hugh Thompson, Jo-Ann Titmarsh, Conrad Van Dyk, Elaine Verweymeren, Ingrid Vienings, Karen Villabona, Stewart J Wild, Rebecca Winke, Debra Wolter, Veronica Wood.

Dorling Kindersley would also like to thank the following for their assistance: Azienda Autonoma di Soggiorno Cura e Turismo, Napoli; Azienda Promozione Turistica del Trentino, Trento; Osservatorio Geofisico dell'Università di Modena; Bell'Italia; Enotria Winecellars.

Photography Permission

Dorling Kindersley would like to thank the following for their assistance and kind permission to photograph at their establishments: Assessorato Beni Culturali Comune di Padova. Le Soprinten-denze Archeologiche di Agrigento, di Enna, di Etruria Meridionale, per il Lazio, di Napoli, di Pompei, di Reggio Calabria e di Roma. Le Soprintendenze per i Beni Ambientali e Architettonici di Bolzano, di Napoli, di Potenza, della Provincia di Firenze e Pistoia, di Ravenna, di Roma, di Siena e di Urbino. Le Soprintendenze per i Beni Ambientali, Architettonici, Artistici e Storici di Caserta, di Cosenza, di Palermo, di Pisa, di Salerno e di Venezia. Le Soprintendenze per i Beni Artistici e Storici della Provincia di Firenze e Pistoia, di Milano e di Roma. Also all the other churches, museums, hotels, shops, restaurants, galleries and sights too numerous to thank individually.

Picture Credits

a-above; b-below; c-centre; f-far; l-left; r-right; t-top.

Works of art have been reproduced with the permission of the following copyright holders: © ADAGP, Paris and DACS, London 2006 *Bird in Space* by Constantin Brancusi 109cl; © DACS, 2006 *Mother and Son* by Carlo Carrà 203tl.

Dorling Kindersley would like to thank the following for their assistance: **Eric Crighton:** 87cra, **FIAT:** 224c, **Gucci Ltd:** 43cr, **Prada, Milan:** 43c, **National Archaeological Museum, Naples:** 499br, **National Maritime Museum:**

44cla, **Royal Botanic Gardens, Kew:** 87ca, **Science Museum, Telecom Italia:** 622tr.

The publisher would like to thank the following individuals, companies and picture libraries for permission to reproduce their photographs: **Accademia Italiana:** Sue Bond 499c; **Actv S.p.A:** 634br, 635crb; **AFE, Rome:** 42cb, 43tl; Giuseppe Carfagna 198br, 206br, 222tl, 222br, 225bl, 226cla, 229tl, 239tr, Claudio Cerquetti 72tc, 73bl, 73tr; Enrico Martino 62clb, 70tr; Roberto Merlo 240bl, 243tl, 243br; Piero Servo 271t, 273bl, Gustavo Tomsich 231tl; **APT Turin:** 228bl, 228tr; **Archivio APT Monregalese:** 233tr; **Action Plus:** Mike Hewitt 74cla; Glyn Kirk 75tr; **Alamy Images:** Peter Adams Photography 16bl; Arco Images GmbH 17cr; Krys Bailey 618cl, Adriano Bacchella 185tl, Bluered 329tl; Enrico Caracciolo 253c; Caro 582bl; Cristina Fumi 28br; funkyfood London - Paul Williams 96-7; gkphotography 83cl; INTERFOTO 225cr; Jon Arnold Images Ltd. 8-9, 434; Brian Johnson 629c, Norma Joseph 352, 368; Jtb Media Creation, inc. 13br; Theodore Liasi 618cla, LOOK Die Bildangentur der Fotografen GmbH 142; David Lyons 13tl, 24, 212-3; Marka 17tr; Steven May 634cla; David Noton Photography 258, 318; Chuck Pefley 26tr; Prisma Bildagentur AG 410; Robert Harding Picture Library Ltd. 173cr; Robert Harding World Imagery 170; tbkmedia.de 603bc; Travel Pictures 15tr; vario images GmbH & Co.KG/Ulrich Baumgarten 620cl, 622bl; Steve Vidler 398cla; Woodstock 548; **Alexander Museum Palace Hotel:** 573 tr; **Allsport:** Mark Thompson: 75ca; **Ancient Art and Architecture:** 485br; **Antica Residenza Cicogna:** 571tc; **Archiv für Kunst und Geschichte, London:** 32bl, 38b, *Rossini (1820)*, Camuccini, Museo Teatrale alla Scala, Milan 40br, 41bl, 45br, *Pope Sixtus IV Naming Platina Prefect of the Library*, Melozzo da Forlì (1477), Pinacoteca Vaticana, Rome 48cla, *Statue of Augustus from Prima Porta* (1st century AD) 53tl, *The Gift of Constantine* (1246), Oratorio di San Silvestro, Rome 54cl, *Frederick I Barbarossa as a Crusader* (1188), Biblioteca Apostolica Vaticana, Rome 57bl, *Giving the Keys to St Peter*, Perugino (1482), Sistine Chapel, Vatican, Rome 60cla, 60bl, *Machiavelli*, Santi di Tito, Palazzo Vecchio, Florence 61br, Andrea Palladio, Meyer 62cb, *Goethe in the Campagna*, Tischbein (1787), Stadelsches Kunstinstitut, Frankfurt 64cl, *Venetian Carnival in the Eighteenth Century*, Anon (19th century) 64clb, *Bonaparte Crossing the Alps*, David, Schloss Charlottenburg, Berlin 65cr, 65bl, 110tr, 110bl, 203bc, 470bl, *Archimedes*, Museo Capitolino, Rome 485tla, 509tc, 513cl; Stefan Diller *St Francis Appearing to the Brothers at Arles* (1295–1300), San Francesco, Assisi 57tl; Erich Lessing Margrave *Gualtieri of Saluzzo Chooses the Poor Farmer's Daughter, Griseldis, for his Wife, di Stefano*, Galleria dell'Accademia Carrara, Bergamo 38crb, *The Vision of St Augustine* (1502), Carpaccio, Chiesa di San Giorgio degli Schiavoni, Venice 61cr, 226bl, 272b, 495cr; **Archivio IGDA, Milan:** 208cl, 208br, 209bc, 525br; **Emporio Armani:** 43tc; **Artemide, GB Ltd:** 43clb.

Badio & Coltibuono: 579; **Beehive, Rome:** 574; **Al Bersagliere:** 583tr; **Mario Bettella:** 539clb, 546c; **La Biennale di Venezia:** 608cra; **Frank Blackburn:** 271c; **Osvaldo Böhm, Venice:** 93tc, 98c, 115tc; **Bridgeman Art Library, London/ New York:** 50c, Ambrosiana, Milan 199tl; Bargello, Florence

283bc, 287c; **Bibliothèque Nationale, Paris:** *Marco Polo with Elephants and Camels Arriving at Hormuz, Gulf of Persia, from India*, Livre des Merveilles Fr 2810 f.18v 45tr; British Museum, London *Etruscan Vase Showing Boxers Fighting* 49tl, *Flask Decorated with Christian Symbols* 54tl, *Greek Attic Red-Figure Vase depicting Odysseus with the Sirens*, Stamnos 485cb; Galleria dell'Accademia Carrara, Bergamo 205tc; Galleria Borghese, Rome 443cl; Galleria degli Uffizi, Florence 30tc, 30tr, 33tl, 33cb, *Self-Portrait*, Raphael Sanzio of Urbino 61bl, 291br, 293bc; K & B News Photo, Florence 280tl; Santa Maria Novella, Florence 301bl; Museo Civico, Prato 332bl; Ravenna 272tr; Louvre, Paris *Statuette of Herakles Brandishing his Club*, Classical Greek, Argive period 484tc; Mausoleo di Galla Placidia, Ravenna 272tr; Museo di San Marco, Florence 301bl; Musée d'Orsay, Paris - Giraudon *les Romains de la Decadence*, Thomas Couture 399tr; Museo delle Sinopie, Camposanto, Pisa 31clb; Palazzo dei Normanni, Palermo *Scene with Centaurs from the Room of King Ruggero* 527b; Pinacoteca di Brera, Milan 202cla, 202bl, 203ca, Private Collection *Theodoric I* (455–526 AD) *Ostrogothic King of Italy* 54br; San Francesco, Arezzo 31tr; San Francesco, Assisi 359cb; San Sebastiano, Venice 33crb; San Zaccaria, Venice 37c, 37tr, 103cr; Santa Croce, Florence 288bl, 289cl; Santa Maria Gloriosa dei Frari, Venice 32tr; Santa Maria Novella, Florence 31cla; Scrovegni (Arena) Chapel, Padua 31tr; Scuola di San Giorgio degli Schiavoni, Venice 124b; Staatliche Museen, Berlin *Septimius Severus and Family* 53b; Vatican Museums and Galleries, Rome 425bl; Walker Art Gallery, Liverpool *Aeschylus and Hygieia* 484bc; **Al Bric, Rome:** 597tr; **British Museum, London:** 50cl; **Brufani Palace:** 572bc.

Capitoline Museum, Rome: 391cr; **Hotel Cappella Romantik:** 563tr; **Demetrio Carrasco:** 106br, 634tr; **Cephas Picture Library** Mick Rock: 28tl, 186tr, 187bl, 187tr, 255tl, 255tr; JL Charmet, Paris: 357br; **Ciga Hotels:** 95cl; **Foto Elio e Stefano Ciol:** 81cra, 168bc, 168br, 169bl, 169bc, 169br; **Hotel Cipriani, Guidecca:** 562bc; Fortuny Restaurant 580br; **Villa Cipriani:** 581tr; **Stephani Colasanti:** 80bl; **Il Comandante:** 601tr; **Comune di Asti:** 72cl; **Consorzio Motoscafi Venezia:** 634clb; **Corbis:** Assignments Photographers/Bryn Colton 184cla; Dave Bartruff 480cla; Owen Franken 252cla, 253tl, 481c; Michelle Garrett 481tl; In Pictures/Michael Aitchison 16tr; John Heseltine 382cla; Robert Harding World Imagery/ Jeremy Bright 112cla; Robert Holmes 83tl; Hemis/ Stefano Torrione 556-7; Frank Krahmer 2-3; Jose Fuste Raga 180-1; Reuters/Tony Gentile 383tl; Sylvain Sonnet 378-9, 400; Hubert Stadler 543crb; **Joe Cornish:** 86tr, 164tl, 337br, 465b, 541bl; **Il Cortiletto:** 602tr; **Giancarlo Costa:** 39cr, 39cra, 39tl, 79c.

Il Dagherrotipo: 549b, 628bl; Archivio Arte 211tl; Archivio Storico 39br, 210br, 265bc; Alberto Berni 229cl; Riccardo Catani 505b; Marco Cerruti 182cla, 217crb, 219br, 220cl; Antonio Cittadini 193tr, 196bl, 206tl; Gianni Dolfini 554bl; Riccardo d'Errico 74tr, 251tl, 272cl; Maurizio Fraschetti 500br; Diane Haines 177br, 611bc; Maurizio Leoni 71c; Marco Melodia 510clb, 510bl, 511cb, 551tr, 610cl; Stefano Occhibelli 73c, 405bl; 256t, 517tr; Donato Fierro Perez 537cb; Marco Ravasini 174tl, 553cr; Giovanni Rinaldi 29t, 70bl, 71tl, 183bl, 235b, 402c, 371tr, 377tl, 470cr, 503tc, 511c, 537cr, 555tl,

555crb; Lorenzo Scaramella 472cr; Stefania Servili 176tl; **Da Delfina:** 593bl; **CM Dixon:** 425cb; **Chris Donaghue The Oxford Photo Library:** 121cla; **Doozo, Rome:** 598tr; **Dreamstime:** Abey79 12br; Ange84 476-7; Cipriansalceanu 12tl; Gmv 214; Mcristale 157tr; Mirohasch 11br; Pavlinec 544-5; Rundywong 234; Sborisov 386; **Duca di Orvieto:** 596bc.

Electa: 160c, 161c, 161tc; **Empics:** 74clb; **ET Archive:** 40bc, 49c, 53cr, 56–7c, 61tl, 63tl, 67bc, 416tr, 485cra, 535br; **Mary Evans Picture Library:** 38bl, 45ca, 66b, 66crb, 67cr, 68cb, 84tr, 324cla, 330tc, 395ca, 397bl, 413br, 446clb, 515cr, 515brb, 554tl.

Ferrari: 42b; **Archivio Storico Fiat, Turin:** 68tr; **Fiat Press Office:** 224ca; **APT Folignate e Nocera Umbra:** 365tr; by kind permission of **Fondazione Arena di Verona:** Gianfranco Fainello 608bl; **Werner Forman Archive:** 49br, 55tr, 439br; **Fotolia:** LianeM 14tr; **Consorzio Frasassi:** 376br.

Studio Gavirati, Gubbio: 356c; **APT Genova:** Roberto Merlo 242bl; **Getty Images:** Peter Adams 504, AFP/Valery Hache 75bl; Daryl Benson 91tr; Mel Curtis 464; Garrett Ellwood 74ca; Robert Everts 190; Julian Finney 74bc; Godong 46; Robert Harding 10cla; The Image Bank/Andrea Pistolesi 82cla; Image Source 340-1; Jean-Pierre Lescourret 14bl; Adam Jones 248-9; Michal Krakowiak 486; David Lyons 526; Maremagnum 623cl; Clive Mason 75cb; Sergio Pitamitz 78-9; Roy Rainford 15cb; Stefano Scata 518; SOPA RF/SOPA/ Franco Cogoli 88; Stone/Simone Huber 609tr; Steve Sucsy 246-7; Guy Vanderelst 418; **Giraudon, Paris:** *Aphrodite Persuading Helen to Follow Paris to Troy*, Museo Nazionale di Villa Giulia, Rome 49clb, *Pharmacy*, Museo della Civiltà Romana 52cb, *Grandes Chroniques de France*; *Coronation of Charlemagne in St Peter's by Leon III*, Musée Goya, Castres 55tl, *Taking of Constantinople*, Basilica of St John the Evangelist, Ravenna 57cr, *Dante's Hell with Commentary of Guiniforte delli Bargigi* (Ms2017 fol 245), Bibliothèque Nationale, Paris 58crb, *Portrait of St Ignatius of Loyola*, Rubens, Musée Brukenthal, Sibiu 63ca, *Charles III's Fleet at Naples 6th October 1759*, Joli de Dipi, Museo del Prado, Madrid 64tr, *Inauguration of the Naples-Portici Railway*, Fergola (1839), Museo Nazionale di San Martino, Naples 66clb, *Piedmontese and French at the Battle of San Martino in 1859* Anon, Museo Centrale del Risorgimento, Rome 67tl, 110crb, 111tl, 203cr; **Alinari-Giraudon:** *St Mark Appearing to the Venetians Looking for His Body*, Tintoretto (1568), Brera Art Gallery, Milan 33tr, *Shrine*, House of the Vettii, Pompeii 53cb, *St Gregory in his Study* (Inv 285), Pinacoteca Nazionale, Bologna 55bl, *Portrait of Victor Emmanuel II*, Dugoni (1866), Galleria d'Arte Moderna, Palazzo Pitti, Florence 111br, 203tl, *Louis II of Gonzaga and his Court*, Andrea Mantegna (1466–74), Museo di Palazzo Ducale, Mantova 8-9, 291tl-tc, *History of Pope Alexander III: Building of the City of Alexandria*, Aretino Spinello (1407), Palazzo Pubblico, Siena 59cr; **Alinari-Seat-Giraudon:** 231c; **Flammarion-Giraudon:** *Poem by Donizo in Honour of Queen Matilda*, Biblioteca Apostolica, Vatican 56ca; **Lauros-Giraudon:** *Portrait of Francis Petrarch* 58bc, *Liber notabilium Philippi Septimi, francorum regis a libris Galieni extractus* (Ms 334 569 fig17), Guy of Pavia (1345), Musée Condé, Chantilly 59bl, *Gallery of Views of Ancient Rome*, Pannini (1758),

Musée du Louvre, Paris 64–5c, *Four Angels and Symbols of the Evangelists*, 36tr, 37t; **Orsi-Battaglini-Giraudon:** *Madonna of the Shadow*, Museum of San Marco, Florence 36c, *Supplice de Savonarola* Anon 60clb; **Grand Hotel Villa Serbelloni:** 565tr; **The Ronald Grant Archive:** 69bc; Paramount *The God-father Part III* (1990) 539br; Riama *La Dolce Vita* (1960) 68cra; TCF *Boccaccio '70 The Name of the Rose* (1986) 38cla; **Grotta di Tiberio:** 576bl; **Palazzo Venier dei Leoni, Peggy Guggenheim Collection, Venice:** 95cla.

Photo Halupka: 124tr; **Robert Harding Picture Library:** 41br, 195br, 394cl, 423br, 610bl; Dumrath 273crb; Gavin Hellier 12crb; 610tr; Roy Rainford 503cr; **John Heseltine:** 471tr; **Hivaoa:** 605tr; **Michael Holford:** 51ca; **Hotel Raphaël - Relais & Châteaux:** 560tl; **Hotel Villa Pagoda:** 559tl; **HSL:** 631tl; **The Hulton Deutsch Collection:** 68br, 93cla, 94cla, 94br, 161br; Keystone 68ca.

Icona Roma: 4cla; **The Image Bank, London:** 51cb, 338br; Marcella Pedone 191b; Andrea Pistolesi 259b; **The Image Bank, Milan:** 199br; **Impact:** 319b; **Index, Florence:** 286c, 331tr, 331cr; **Istituto e Museo di Storia della Scienza di Firenze:** Franca Principe 44br, 289c.

Tim Jepson: 355tr.

Frank Lane Picture Agency: 220tr, 221tl, 221ca, 221cr; M Melodia/Panda 510cla; **La Riserva di Castel D'appio:** 569tr; **Hotel Laurin, Bolzano:** 564bl; **Locanda del Pilone di Alba:** 586tl; **Locanda I Tre Merli:** 568bc.

Magnum, London: Abbas 68crb; **The Mansell Collection:** 56clb; **Marconi Ltd:** 44cl; **Marka:** L Barbazza 101tr; E Cerretelli 125br; M Motta 619tc; **Masterstudio, Pescara:** 508cr; su concessione del **MAXXI:** Roberto Galasso 445tl; **Ministero per i Beni Culturali e Ambientali:** *The Last Supper*, da Vinci, Leonardo 204b; **Mirror Syndication International:** 44c; **Moby Lines:** 627cl; **Foto Modena:** 270tl, 375c; **Monte san Giuliano:** 604bl; **Tony Mott:** 474t; **Museo Diocesano di Rossano:** 524tl.

NHPA: Laurie Campbell 87crb; Gerard Lacz 87br; Silvestris Fotoservice 87cr; **Grazia Neri:** Marco Bruzzo 72br; Cameraphoto 112bl; Marcello Mencarini 92br; **Newimage s.r.l:** Rolando Fabriani 606cla; **Nhow Milano:** 566tl; **Nippon Television Network:** 428–9 all pics, 430bl; **Peter Noble:** 322tr, 345br, 618br; **Nonna Betta:** 596br.

L'Occhio di Cristallo/Studio Fotografico di Giorgio Olivero: 233bl; **APT Orvieto:** Massimo Roncella 362tr; **Osteria Francescana:** 591tr; **Osteria Le Logge:** 594tl; **Oxford Scientific Films:** Stan Osolinski 351cr.

Padova - Musei Civici - Cappella Scrovegni: 81cr, 160 all pics, 161cra, 161crb, 161bl; **Padova - Musei Civici Agli Eremitani:** 162tr, 162c; **Palazzo Grassi S.p.A:** Thomas Mayer 109br; **Pane e Vino:** 592tc; **Pasta Madre:** 591tr; **Da Paolo e Barbara:** Toni Meneguzzo 590br; **Da Paolino:** 600bl; **Luciano Pedicini - Archivio dell'Arte:** 366bl, 408tr, 479tc, 494tr, 494cl, 494clb, 495tl, 495ca, 495br, 497tr, 534b; **APT Pesaro - Le Marche:** 372br; **Pictures Colour Library:** 50clb,

552tl; **Andrea Pistolesi:** 25; **PNALM Archive:** in association with www.abruzzonatura.com 510bc; **Polis Photo Library;** **Popperfoto:** 68tl, 69tl, 69clb; **Portrait Suites, Rome:** 575bc.

Sarah Quill, Venice: 94t, 98bc, 104tl.

Relais Uffizi, Florence: 570bl; **Retrograph Archive:** 41c; **Rex Features:** 41tl; Steve Wood 43tr; **Reuters:** Toru Hanai 74crb; Ferran Paredes 75tl; **Il Riccio Restaurant:** 579bc; **Hotel Riva Del Sole:** 577tr; **Ristorante Rosa:** 589bl.

Sauraya & Moroni Milton: 42cr; **Scala Group S.p.A:** 30bl, 31br, 32br, 33ca, 33bl, 92cla, 56bl, 402cla, *Portrait of Claudio Monteverdi*, Domenico Feti, Accademia, Venice 40bl, *Portolan of Italy* (16th century), Loggia dei Lanzi, Firenze 295bl, Museo Correr, Venice 47b, *Etruscan Bronze Liver*, Musco Civico, Piacenza 48clb, *Earrings*, Museo Etrusco Guarnacci, Volterra 48br, 48r–9c, *Crater from Pescia Romana*, Museo Archeologico, Grosseto 49bc, *Terracotta Vase in the Shape of an Elephant*, Museo Nazionale, Naples 50cr, *Cicero denounces Catiline*, Palazzo Madama, Rome 51tl, 51bl, *Circus Scene Mosaic - Gladiator Fight*, Galleria Borghese, Rome 52ca, 52br, *Theodolinda Melts the Gold for the New Church* (15th century), Famiglia Zavattari, Duomo, Monza 54clb, 54–5, 55br, *Tomb Relief depicting a School*, Matteo Gandoni, Museo Civico, Bologna 56bc, *Detail from an Ambo of Frederick II* (13th century), Cattedrale, Bitonto 57cb, *Guidoriccio da Fogliano at the Siege of Note Massi*, Simone Martini, Palazzo Pubblico, Siena 58clb, 59tl, *Return of Gregory XI from Avignon* Giorgio Vasari, Sala Regia, Vatican 59crb, 60br, 60r–61c, 61crb, *Clement VII in Conversation with Charles V*, Giorgio Vasari, Palazzo Vecchio, Florence 62cla, *Portrait of Pierluigi da Palestrina*, Istituto dei Padri dell'Oratorio, Rome 62br, *Revolt at Masaniello*, Domenico Gargiulo, Museo di San Martino, Naples 63crb, 64br, 65tl, 65crb, 66cla, 66–7c, 67crb, 99cla, 104c, 122br, 150cla, 226tr, 230br, 264tl, 267tl, 269tr, 273tl, 278cla, 278bl, 279tr, 280c, 280bl, 281tl, 281b, 284cl, 286tc, 287tr, 287br, 290cl, 290cb, 290br, 291ca, 291cb, 292tr, 292b, 293tr, 293cl, 295bl, 296cl, 296bc, 297tr, 297clb, 298tr, 298cl, 299tc, 300cl, 302–3 all, 305clb, 306tr, 306cla, 306c, 307tl, 307cl, 307bl, 329c, 329br, 334–5 all, 336tl, 336br, 342bl, 344tl, 345cl, 348cla, 349br, 358cla, 358br, 359bl, 362bl, 363cl, 374tr, 375tl, 375bc, 381br, 388cl, 404bl, 406tr, 408cl, 415c, 420cla, 421bl, 421tl, 423tl, 424tr, 424c, 425cr, 427tr, 427clb, 427br, 431cla, 431br, 494bc, 515clb, 517tl, 533b, 534tr, 540tc, 541tr, 542bc, 553bc; **Science Photo Library:** Argonne National Laboratory 45cr; **John**

Ferro Sims: 369b, 546bl; **Agenzia Sintesi, Rome:** Antonella Girolamo 618clb; **Al Sorriso:** 588tc; **Mario Soster di Alagna:** 561cl; **Frank Spooner Pictures:** Diffidenti 552br; Gamma 69tr; **Sporting Pictures:** 75cra; **STA Travel Group:** 616crb; **Tony Stone Images:** 87cla; Stephen Studd 35tr, 189cr; **Agenzia Fotografica Stradella, Milan:** Bersanetti 195tl; Francesco Gavazzini 221br; F Giaccone 530cla; Mozzati 263bc, 374bc; Massimo Pacifico 511tl; Ettore Re 503crb; Ghigo Roli 503bl; Giulio Vegi 537ca; Amedeo Vergani 218br, 238tl, 261tr; **SuperStock:** age fotostock 383c; **Sygma:** 71tr.

Tasting Italy: Martin Brigdale 611tl; **Tate Gallery Publications:** 68bl; **Taverna del Pittore:** 587bc; **Tipsimages:** Mario Verin 612-3; **Touring Club of Italy:** 208cb, Cresci 538ca; **Archivio Città di Torino Settore Turismo:** 225tl; Davide Bogliacino 217tr; **Travel Library:** 279cb, Fototeca APT del Trentino: Foto di Banal 178tl; Foto di Faganello 177tr, 179cr.

U'Giancu Restaurant: 579cr.

Vela SpA: 635cr, 635br; **Villa Crespi:** 578bl; **Villa Meridiana Cascina Reine:** 567.

Edizione White Star: Giulio Veggi 79; **Peter Wilson:** 5t..

Front Endpaper
Alamy Images: David Noton Photography Rftl, Lcra, Norma Joseph Rcla, Rcra, LOOK Die Bildagentur der Fotografen GmbH Rtr, Robert Harding World Imagery Rtl, Woodstock Lfclb; **Corbis:** SOPA RF/SOPA/Franco Cogoli Rftr, Sylvain Sonnet Lfbr; **Dreamstime:** Gmv Ltc, Rudywong Lca; **Getty Images:** Peter Adams Rfcra, Mel Curtis Lbr, Robert Everts Lcla, Michal Krakowiak Lfcrb, David Lyons Rfbr, Stefano Scata Rfcrb.

Back Endpaper: Alamy Images: Jon Arnold Images Ltd Rcrb, Prisma Bildagentur AG Rtr; **Corbis:** Sylvain Sonnet Lca; **Dreamstime.com:** Rbl; **Getty Images:** Guy Vanderelst Ltl.

Front jacket and spine top: **Alamy Images:** Rod Edwards.

Map Cover
Corbis: Atlantide Phototravel.

All other images © **Dorling Kindersley.** For further information: www.dkimages.com

Special Editions of DK Travel Guides

DK Travel Guides can be purchased in bulk quantities at discounted prices for use in promotions or as premiums. We are also able to offer special editions and personalized jackets, corporate imprints, and excerpts from all of our books, tailored specifically to meet your own needs.

To find out more, please contact:
in the United States **SpecialSales@dk.com**
in the UK **travelspecialsales@uk.dk.com**
in Canada DK Special Sales at **general@tourmaline.ca**
in Australia **business.development@pearson.com.au**

Phrase Book

In an Emergency

Help!	**Aiuto!**	*eye-yoo-toh*
Stop!	**Fermate!**	*fair-mah-teh*
Call a	**Chiama un**	*kee-ah-mah oon*
doctor.	**medico**	*meh-dee-koh*
Call an	**Chiama un'**	*kee-ah-mah oon*
ambulance.	**ambulanza**	*am-boo-lan-tsa*
Call the	**Chiama la**	*kee-ah-mah lah*
police.	**polizia**	*pol-ee-tsee-ah*
Call the fire	**Chiama i**	*kee-ah-mah ee*
brigade.	**pompieri**	*pom-pee-air-ee*
Where is the	**Dov'è il telefono?**	*dov-eh eel teh-leh-*
telephone?		*foh-noh?*
The nearest	**L'ospedale**	*loss-peh-dah-leh-pee*
hospital?	**più vicino?**	*oo vee-chee-noh?*

Communication Essentials

Yes/No	**Sì/No**	*see/noh*
Please	**Per favore**	*pair fah-vor-eh*
Thank you	**Grazie**	*grah-tsee-eh*
Excuse me	**Mi scusi**	*mee skoo-zee*
Hello	**Buon giorno**	*bwon jor-noh*
Goodbye	**Arrivederci**	*ah-ree-veh-dair-chee*
Good evening	**Buona sera**	*bwon-ah sair-ah*
morning	**la mattina**	*lah mah-tee-nah*
afternoon	**il pomeriggio**	*eel poh-meh-ree-joh*
Evening	**la sera**	*lah sair-ah*
yesterday	**ieri**	*ee-air-ee*
today	**oggi**	*oh-jee*
tomorrow	**domani**	*doh-mah-nee*
here	**qui**	*kwee*
there	**là**	*lah*
What?	**Quale?**	*kwah-leh?*
When?	**Quando?**	*kwan-doh?*
Why?	**Perchè?**	*pair-keh?*
Where?	**Dove?**	*doh-veh?*

Useful Phrases

How are you?	**Come sta?**	*koh-meh stah?*
Very well,	**Molto bene,**	*moll-toh beh-neh*
thank you.	**grazie.**	*grah-tsee-eh*
Pleased to	**Piacere di**	*pee-ah-chair-eh dee*
meet you.	**conoscerla.**	*coh-noh-shair-lah*
See you later.	**A più tardi.**	*ah pee-oo tar-dee*
That's fine.	**Va bene.**	*va beh-neh*
Where is/are ...?	**Dov'è/Dove sono ...?**	*dov-eh/doveh soh -noh?*
How long does	**Quanto tempo ci**	*kwan-toh tem-poh*
it take to get to ...?	**vuole per**	*chee voo-oh-leh pair*
	andare a ...?	*an-dar-eh ah ...?*
How do I	**Come faccio per**	*koh-meh fah-choh*
get to ...?	**arrivare a ...?**	*pair arri-var-eh ah..?*
Do you speak	**Parla inglese?**	*par-lah een-gleh -zeh?*
English?		
I don't understand.	**Non capisco.**	*non ka-pee-skoh*
Could you speak	**Può parlare**	*pwoh par-lah-reh*
more slowly,	**più lentamente,**	*pee-oo len-ta-men-teh*
please?	**per favore?**	*pair fah-vor-eh?*
I'm sorry.	**Mi dispiace.**	*mee dee-spee-ah-heh*

Useful Words

big	**grande**	*gran-deh*
small	**piccolo**	*pee-koh-loh*
hot	**caldo**	*kal-doh*
cold	**freddo**	*fred-doh*
good	**buono**	*bwoh-noh*
bad	**cattivo**	*kat-tee-voh*
enough	**basta**	*bas-tah*
well	**bene**	*beh-neh*
open	**aperto**	*ah-pair-toh*
closed	**chiuso**	*kee-oo-zoh*
left	**a sinistra**	*ah see-nee-strah*
right	**a destra**	*ah dess-trah*
straight on	**sempre dritto**	*sem-preh dree-toh*
near	**vicino**	*vee-chee-noh*
far	**lontano**	*lon-tah-noh*
up	**su**	*soo*
down	**giù**	*joo*
early	**presto**	*press-toh*
late	**tardi**	*tar-dee*
entrance	**entrata**	*en-trah-tah*
exit	**uscita**	*oo-shee-ta*
toilet	**il gabinetto**	*eel gah-bee-net-toh*
free, unoccupied	**libero**	*lee-bair-oh*
free, no charge	**gratuito**	*grah-too-ee-toh*

Making a Telephone Call

I'd like to place a	**Vorrei fare**	*vor-ray far-eh oona*
long-distance call.	**una interurbana.**	*in-tair-oor-bah-nah*
I'd like to make	**Vorrei fare una**	*vor-ray far-eh oona*
a reverse-charge	**telefonata a carico**	*teh-leh-fon-ah-tah ah*
call.	**del destinatario.**	*kar-ee-koh dell dess-*
		tee-nah-tar-ree-oh
I'll try again later.	**Ritelefono più**	*ree-teh-leh-foh-noh*
	tardi.	*pee-oo tar-dee*
Can I leave a	**Posso lasciare**	*poss-oh lash-ah-reh*
message?	**un messaggio?**	*oon mess-sah-joh?*
Hold on.	**Un attimo,**	*oon ah-tee-moh,*
	per favore	*pair fah-vor-eh*
Could you speak	**Può parlare più**	*pwoh par-lah-reh*
up a little please?	**forte, per favore?**	*pee-oo for-teh, pair*
		fah-vor-eh?
local call	**telefonata locale**	*te-leh-fon-ah-tah*
		loh-cah-leh

Shopping

How much	**Quant'è,**	*kwan-teh*
does this cost?	**per favore?**	*pair fah-vor-eh?*
I would like ...	**Vorrei ...**	*vor-ray*
Do you have ...?	**Avete ...?**	*ah-veh-teh.. ?*
I'm just looking.	**Sto soltanto**	*stoh sol-tan-toh*
	guardando.	*gwar-dan-doh*
Do you take	**Accettate**	*ah-chet-tah -teh kar-teh*
credit cards?	**carte di credito?**	*dee creh-dee-toh?*
What time do	**A che ora apre/**	*ah keh or-ah*
you open/close?	**chiude?**	*ah-preh/kee-oo-deh?*
this one	**questo**	*kweh-stoh*
that one	**quello**	*kwell-oh*
expensive	**caro**	*kar-oh*
cheap	**a buon prezzo**	*ah bwon pret-soh*
size, clothes	**la taglia**	*lah tah-lee-ah*
size, shoes	**il numero**	*eel noo-mair-oh*
white	**bianco**	*bee-ang-koh*
black	**nero**	*neh-roh*
red	**rosso**	*ross-oh*
yellow	**giallo**	*jal-loh*
green	**verde**	*vair-deh*
blue	**blu**	*bloo*

Types of Shop

antique dealer	**l'antiquario**	*lan-tee-kwah-ree-oh*
bakery	**il forno**	*eel forn-oh*
	/il panificio	*/eel pan-ee-fee-choh*
bank	**la banca**	*lah bang-kah*
bookshop	**la libreria**	*lah lee-breh-ree-ah*
butcher	**la macelleria**	*lah mah-chell-eh-ree-ah*
cake shop	**la pasticceria**	*lah pas-tee-chair-ee-ah*
chemist	**la farmacia**	*lah far-mah-chee-ah*
delicatessen	**la salumeria**	*lah sah-loo-meh-ree-ah*
department store	**il grande**	*eel gran-deh*
	magazzino	*mag-gad-zee-noh*
fishmonger	**il pescivendolo**	*eel pesh-ee-ven-doh-loh*
florist	**il fioraio**	*eel fee-or-eye-oh*
greengrocer	**il fruttivendolo**	*eel froo-tee-ven-doh-loh*
grocery	**alimentari**	*ah-lee-men-tah-ree*
hairdresser	**il parrucchiere**	*eel par-oo-kee-air-eh*
ice cream parlour	**la gelateria**	*lah jel-lah-tair-ee-ah*
market	**il mercato**	*eel mair-kah-toh*
newsstand	**l'edicola**	*leh-dee-koh-lah*
post office	**l'ufficio postale**	*loo-fee-choh pos-tah-leh*
shoe shop	**il negozio di**	*eel neh-goh-tsioh dee*
	scarpe	*skar-peh*
supermarket	**il supermercato**	*eel su-pair-mair-kah-toh*
tobacconist	**il tabaccaio**	*eel tah-bak-eye-oh*
travel agency	**l'agenzia di viaggi**	*lah-jen-tsee-ah dee*
		vee-ad-jee

Sightseeing

art gallery	**la pinacoteca**	*lah peena-koh-teh-kah*
bus stop	**la fermata**	*lah fair-mah-tah*
	dell'autobus	*dell ow-toh-booss*
church	**la chiesa**	*lah kee-eh-zah*
	la basilica	*lah bah-seel-i-kah*
closed for	**chiuso per le**	*kee-oo-zoh pair leh*
holidays	**ferie**	*fair-ee-eh*
garden	**il giardino**	*eel jar-dee-no*
library	**la biblioteca**	*lah beeb-lee-oh-teh-kah*
museum	**il museo**	*eel moo-zeh-oh*
railway station	**la stazione**	*lah stah-tsee-oh-neh*
tourist	**l'ufficio**	*loo-fee-choh*
information	**di turismo**	*dee too-ree-smoh*

Central Rome

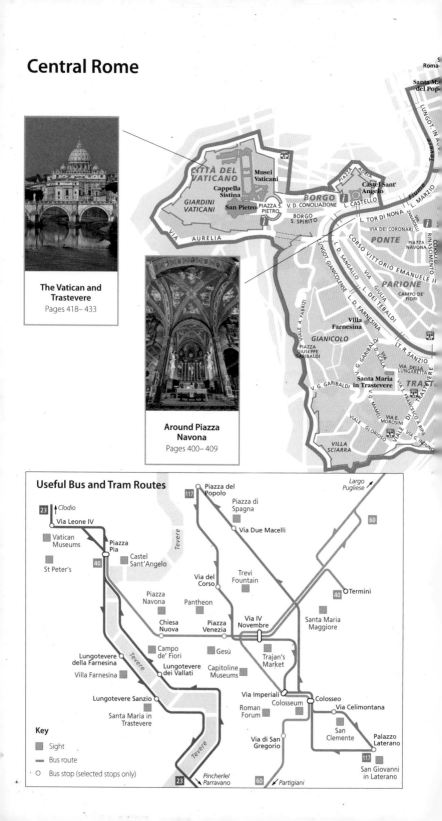

The Vatican and Trastevere
Pages 418–433

Around Piazza Navona
Pages 400–409

Santa Maria del Popolo

CITTÀ DEL VATICANO

Musei Vaticani

Cappella Sistina

GIARDINI VATICANI

San Pietro

PIAZZA S. PIETRO

BORGO

V. D. CONCILIAZIONE

BORGO S. SPIRITO

VIA AURELIA

Castel Sant' Angelo

PIAZZA ADRIANA

L. CASTELLO

Fiume

L. MARZIO

VIA DEI CORONARI

L. TOR DI NONA

PONTE

PIAZZA NAVONA

PARIONE

CORSO VITTORIO EMANUELE II

CAMPO DE' FIORI

VIA GIULIA

L. DEI TEBALDI

L. DI SANGALLO

LUNGOT. GIANICOLENSE

L. D. FARNESINA

VIALE F. FABRIZI

Villa Farnesina

GIANICOLO

PIAZZA GIUSEPPE GARIBALDI

VIA G. GARIBALDI

V. G. GARIBALDI

VIA DELLA LUNGARETTA

Santa Maria in Trastevere

VIALE GLORIOSO

VILLA SCIARRA

VIA E. MOROSINI

VIA S. FRANCESCO A RIPA

TRAST

LT. R. SANZIO

Useful Bus and Tram Routes

23 ↑ Clodio

117 Piazza del Popolo

Largo Pugliese

Piazza di Spagna

Via Leone IV

Vatican Museums

St Peter's

Piazza Pia

40

Castel Sant'Angelo

Tevere

Via Due Macelli

60

Via del Corso

Trevi Fountain

Piazza Navona

Pantheon

Chiesa Nuova

Piazza Venezia

Via IV Novembre

40 ○ Termini

Santa Maria Maggiore

Lungotevere della Farnesina

Villa Farnesina

Campo de' Fiori

Gesù

Lungotevere dei Vallati

Capitoline Museums

Trajan's Market

Lungotevere Sanzio

Santa Maria in Trastevere

Tevere

Via Imperiali

Roman Forum

Colosseum

Colosseo

Via Celimontana

San Clemente

Palazzo Laterano

Via di San Gregorio

117

San Giovanni in Laterano

Tevere

23 ↗ Pincherle/ Parravano

60 ↗ Partigiani

Key

■ Sight

— Bus route

○ Bus stop (selected stops only)